Guillaume de Machaut

GUILLAUME DE MACHAUT

Secretary, Poet, Musician

ELIZABETH EVA LEACH

CORNELL UNIVERSITY PRESS

Ithaca and London

This project was funded by

 Arts & Humanities
Research Council

First published 2011 by Cornell University Press

Printed in the United States of America

Library of Congress Cataloging-in-Publication Data
Leach, Elizabeth Eva.
  Guillaume de Machaut : secretary, poet, musician / Elizabeth Eva Leach.
    p. cm.
  Includes bibliographical references and index.
  ISBN 978-0-8014-4933-8 (cloth : alk. paper)
  1. Guillaume, de Machaut, ca. 1300–1377. I. Title.
  ML410.G966L23 2011
  841'.1—dc22
  [B]   2011000393

Cloth printing   10 9 8 7 6 5 4 3 2 1

Contents

Illustrations

Music Examples

Acknowledgments

As this book is the result of many years of studying, teaching, and writing about Machaut, my debts to the generosity of other scholars are several and large. First among these are Margaret Bent and Kevin Brownlee, who set me on nonparallel interdisciplinary tracks in 1995. During my years of initial study, Alison Bullock, Hannah Vlček, and their supervisor Daniel Leech-Wilkinson generously shared ideas and unpublished materials, which were formative to my thinking. Several larger groups of people were very helpful, and I apologize for not naming here all the many individuals who participated in the interdisciplinary conference that Margaret Bent and I organized in Oxford in 2001. Of those at the Dozza *seminario* on Machaut in 2004, I thank my co-tutors Margaret Bent, Kevin Brownlee (on whose handout synopses of *Remede* and *Voir dit* mine here are based), Roger Bowers, and Domenic Leo for many stimulating conversations, as well as the graduate students who participated. Special thanks go to Giuliano di Bacco for inviting me and for arranging such delicious food.

As I have worked on the material covered in the book for many years, various passages draw on my own publications since 2000, although these have mostly been completely rewritten and rethought. The exception to this is the material on *De triste cuer / Quant vrai amans / Certes, je di* (B29), now in chapter 3, which was a paper given at the Plainsong and Medieval Music Society conference in 2007, and at the Renaissance Society of America meeting in Chicago in 2008, and appears here in a form very similar to "Music and Verbal Meaning: Machaut's Polytextual Songs," *Speculum* 85 (2010): 561–97. I am grateful to the conference audiences and to *Speculum*'s anonymous readers for their input.

For answering specific queries as I was writing, I especially thank Roger Bowers, who very generously revisited his own notes on the composer to answer a plethora of email queries, and also Benjamin Albritton and Henry Hope. Wulf Arlt very generously went through much of the manuscript: as he repeatedly noted, I am too much myself to make all the changes that he suggested, but I hope the finished product nevertheless meets with his approval. My return to the idea of writing a book on Machaut—something I considered a decade ago but was then unable to pitch successfully to a publisher—was encouraged by my former colleague and cispontine neighbor J. P. E. Harper-Scott, who has read and discussed with me various parts of the book over his fine South Indian cooking; the prose that follows is informed by his rather singular style.

Relief from duties of teaching and administration was sponsored by Royal Holloway, University of London, and a grant of Matching Leave from the Arts and Humanities Research Council, UK. I am grateful to RHUL and the AHRC, and in particular to those individuals who positively peer-reviewed my book proposal en route to getting it funded. The costs of obtaining images and permissions were met by a kind grant from the Music & Letters Trust, to whose trustees I am very thankful.

I also thank Lawrence Earp, Winthrop Wetherbee III, and an anonymous reader who reviewed the entire manuscript and suggested many improvements, as well as the editorial team at Cornell University Press. Nonetheless, I take personal responsibility for all views and errors in this book, not as a traditional sign-off to the acknowledgments but because to do so is only right.

Abbreviations

MS sigla are printed in boldface throughout.

A	Paris, Bibliothèque nationale de France, MS français 1584
Alerion	*Le dit de l'alerion* (The Story of the Alerion), cited here from the edition of Hoepffner
Ars	Paris, Bibliothèque de l'Arsenal, MS 683
B	Paris, Bibliothèque nationale de France, MS français 1585
B–	balade set to music, numbered according to editions of Ludwig and Schrade; music examples here newly edited by Leach
Behaingne	*Le jugement dou roy de Behaingne*, cited here from the edition of Wimsatt and Kibler
Bk	Berlin, Staatliche Museen Preussischer Kulturbesitz, Kupferstichkabinett, MS 78
C	Paris, Bibliothèque nationale de France, MS français 1586
Ca	cantus (voice) part
CaB	Cambrai, Bibliothèque municipale, MS B 1328
Cerf Blanc	*Le dit du cerf blanc* (opus dubium)
Ch	Chantilly, Musée Condé, MS 564 (*olim* 1047); "the Chantilly Codex"
Ch–	number of item in the order of **Ch**
CMM	Corpus Mensurabilis Musicae (series)
Confort	*Le confort d'ami* (Comfort for a Friend), cited here in the edition of Palmer with translations based on Palmer
Cp–	Complaint, numbered according to the edition of Chichmaref
D	Paris, Bibliothèque nationale de France, MS français 1587
Des–	lyric by Eustache Deschamps, numbered according to the edition of the Marquis de Queux de Saint-Hilaire
E	Paris, Bibliothèque nationale de France, MS français 9221
Fauvel	*Le roman de Fauvel*, specifically here the version contained in Paris, Bibliothèque nationale de France, MS français 146
F-G	Paris, Bibliothèque nationale de France, MS français 22545–46
Fonteinne	*Le dit de la fonteinne amoureuse* (The Story of the Fountain of Love), cited here in the edition of Palmer; translations based on those in Palmer
F-Pn	Paris, Bibliothèque nationale de France

G	see F-G
Gr 3360	Ghent, Rijksarchief, Varia D. 3360
Grove	*New Grove Dictionary of Music and Musicians*, cited here from the online edition at www.oxfordmusiconline.com
Harpe	*Le dit de la harpe* (The Story of the Harp), cited here from the edition of Young
I	Paris, Bibliothèque nationale de France, MS nouvelles acquisitions françaises 6221
Iv	Ivrea, Biblioteca capitolare, MS 115
J	Paris, Bibliothèque de l'Arsenal, MS 5203
Jp	*Le jardin de plaisance et fleur de rethoricque* (Paris: Ant. Vérard, [1501])
K	Bern, Burgerbibliothek, MS 218
L–	lay numbered according to editions of Ludwig and Schrade with Ludwig number given before the slash where these differ; music examples newly edited by Leach
Lis et marguerite	*Le dit de la fleur de lis et de la marguerite*
Lo–	*Loange* item numbered according to the edition of Chichmaref
Loange	*La loange des dames*, cited from the edition of Chichmaref
Lyon	*Le dit dou lyon* (The Story of the Lion), cited from the edition of Hoepffner
M	Paris, Bibliothèque nationale de France, MS français 843
M–	motet numbered according to the editions of Ludwig and Schrade and the listing in Earp
m./mm.	measure/measures
Mo	motetus (voice) part
ModA	Modena, Biblioteca Estense, MS α. M. 5. 24 (lat. 568); "the Modena codex"
Navarre	*Le jugement dou roy de Navarre* (The Judgment of the King of Navarre), cited here from the edition of Palmer; translations based on those of Palmer
OED	*Oxford English Dictionary*, cited from the online edition at www.oed.com
Pa	Philadelphia University of Pennsylvania Libraries, MS Codex 902, available online at http://dla.library.upenn.edu/dla/medren/record.html?id=MEDREN_3559163&
Pa–	lyric numbered according to the order in **Pa**
PadA	Oxford, Bodleian Library, MS Canonici Pat. lat. 229
Pe	Cambridge, Magdalene College, Pepysian Library, MS 1594
Pm	New York, Morgan Library, MS M. 396
PMFC	Polyphonic Music of the Fourteenth Century (series)
PR	Paris, Bibliothèque nationale de France, MS nouvelles acquisitions françaises 6771
Prise	*Le prise d'Alexandre* (The Taking of Alexandria), cited from the edition of Palmer
Prologue	*Le prologue* (The Prologue), cited from the edition of Hoepffner

R–   Rondeau set to music (or in the music section of the manuscripts),
              numbered according to the musical edition of Ludwig and Schrade; mu-
              sic examples here newly edited by Leach

Remede   *Le remede de Fortune* (Fortune's Remedy, or, A Cure for Ill Luck), cited
              from the edition of Wimsatt and Kibler

RF–   number of lyric item in *Remede* according to the edition of Ludwig

St   Stockholm, Kungliga Biblioteket, MS V.u.22

Str   Strasbourg, Bibliothèque municipale, MS M 222 C 22 (destroyed in 1870)

T   tenor (voice) part

Ta   Turin, Archivio di Stato, MS J.b.IX.10

Tr   triplum (voice) part.

Trém   Paris, Bibliothèque nationale de France, nouvelles acquisitions
              françaises 23190

Tu   Turin, Biblioteca Nazionale J.II.9, "the Cyprus Codex"

V–   virelay in the music section of the Machaut MSS, numbered according
              to the editions of Ludwig and Schrade, with Ludwig's number preced-
              ing a slash where these differ

VD–   lyric item in *Voir dit* numbered as listed in Earp

Vergier   *Le dit dou vergier* (The Story of the Orchard), cited from the edition of
              Palmer

Vg   Ferrell-Vogüé MS, on loan to the Parker Library, Corpus Christi, Cam-
              bridge (*olim* New York, Wildenstein Collection, MS without shelfmark)

Vi   London, British Library, additional 15224, "the Visconti Chansonnier"

Voir dit   *Le livre dou voir dit* (The Book of the True Story), cited from the edi-
              tion of Leech-Wilkinson and Palmer

W   Aberystwyth, National Library of Wales, MS 5010 C

Introduction

Guillaume de Machaut (ca. 1300–1377) is central chronologically within the literary "long fourteenth century." His artistic output is weighty in terms of its sheer size, and his projection of a self-conscious poetic creativity prompted his contemporaries to call him a "poète," a term that had earlier been reserved for classical authors.[1] He is marked out from his contemporaries, however, by the importance he ascribed both to music *within* his poetry, and to the musical performance *of* his works. Machaut's ability to make his own musical settings of his lyrics, and his knowledge of the latest ways of writing them down in musical notation, makes him the most important poet and composer of fourteenth-century France. The goal of this book is to reflect the centrality of music within Machaut's poetry and poetics by integrating discussion of his songs into the overall thematic treatment of his works.

Machaut's early career as a court servant to the king of Bohemia, John of Luxembourg, gave way after John's death in 1346 to a period in which Machaut was a widely famed poet, patronized by various members of the French royal house. Machaut's clerical training and role as an administrative court functionary mean that in many ways he typifies the makers of vernacular poetry in his day. For example, his interest in bookmaking and attention to the preservation of his own works in large manuscripts that contained nothing else occur near the beginning of this particular authorial trend, influencing his successors, but are a logical extension of the clerkly cast of literature in this

---

1. See Sarah Kay, *The Place of Thought: The Complexity of One in Late Medieval French Didactic Poetry* (Philadelphia, 2007), 1–2. Also see chapter 3 in this volume.

I

period. His didacticism, modeled particularly on Boethius but responding also to the *Roman de la Rose,* is similarly of a piece with that discernible in the literature of his contemporaries.

Despite his contemporaries' perception of the high quality of Machaut's poetry, one would be pressed to argue for any particular originality in terms of the thematization of desire, love, and mourning, treated by means of re-working the Boethian model. Sarah Kay easily integrates Machaut within her discussion of a number of poets in the long fourteenth century who re-vitalized and updated the lyric quality of the model to bring "knowledge, emotion, and poetry" into more intimate mutual association.[2] What does dif-ferentiate Machaut from his contemporaries, however, is the central role of *music* within his literary output. The present book departs from the tendency outside musicology to regard Machaut as incidentally "also a composer," as if music were but a meaningless ornament to lyric rather than—as the im-portance of Orpheus to narratives of desire, love, loss, and mourning in this period shows—transformative of it.[3] Music's performative reading of poetry, its links to human emotion, and its place as a very specific kind of knowledge in medieval society allowed Machaut to go beyond his contemporaries in re-sponding to the needs of his readers for entertaining edification and effective consolation in the central matters of life, love, and death. It is thus critically important that an overview of Machaut's work integrate the specific features offered by his music into the wider consideration of his literary works.

The complete output of Guillaume de Machaut thus presents a problem to modern scholarship. As a man who was at once a secretary, poet, and musi-cian, Machaut is important in historical, literary, and musical terms. But these kinds of importance represent three discrete faculties in the modern university, so the modern divisions of scholarship serve Machaut's highly integrated out-put badly. This book attempts to reintegrate the various strands of scholarly treatment, thereby to present a more complete picture of Machaut as a creative artist. In particular it is designed to bring the discussion of the musical works more centrally into a consideration of Machaut's poetic themes, to show that music functions variously to enshrine and transform them.

Chapter 1 reviews the—surprisingly meager—documentary evidence about Machaut's life, giving attention to the historical record and its interpretation in the modern period. What emerges is that knowledge about Guillaume de Machaut's life is largely illusory, much of it based in his own fiction, as if the works themselves are best able to reflect the life and preoccupations of Machaut and his contemporary readers. Many of the "facts" reported about Machaut's life in modern scholarship thus actually provide a window on the

2. Kay, *Place of Thought,* 179.

3. Kay, for example, does not refer to music, despite discussion of Orpheus in the *Ovide moralisé* (ibid., 64–69). She does not mention Machaut as a composer, nor does her discussion of *Navarre* consider the power of its musical "resolution." On the latter, see chapter 5.

reading of his fiction by various contemporary scholars and on the assumptions that they have brought to bear at different times and from within different modern scholarly disciplines.

As any attempt to synthesize the various approaches of modern scholarship
to Machaut's work must also be attentive to the different agendas pursued by
those modern scholarly disciplines in their rediscovery and use of specific parts
of it, chapter 2 reviews the historiography of Machaut studies. In so doing,
it presents an introduction to the core themes of his work, combining meth-
odologies from literary studies and musicology, and recognizing Machaut's
centrality to the history of the manuscript book—which he is instrumental in
transforming into a visual "performance space" involving text, illuminations,
musical notation, and paratextual rubrics and marginalia.

Some of the blame for the too easy mapping of fictional truth onto historical reality can be attributed to the mischievous manipulation of personal
truth by Machaut himself. Machaut's presentation of his authorial persona is
considered in chapter 3's opening examination of the *Prologue* to his works.
This poem outlines a poetics within which Machaut's status as a poet and—
perhaps more surprisingly, given the *Prologue*'s lack of musical notation—a
musician are central. In addition, the *Prologue*'s paired images emphasize the
wholeness of Machaut's book and the importance of making connections between its parts, leading the reader to appreciate a poetics that is as scribal
as it is musical. This chapter goes on to explore the way in which Machaut
linked his art, life, and truth through his own particular take on the necessity
of composing in line with one's own *sentement*. Chapter 4 examines a related
central plank in his doctrine of courtly love: Hope. Together, chapters 3 and 4
outline a way of experiencing joy in the world, in spite of actual events, which
are in the sway of the character treated in chapter 5, Fortune. Understanding
the workings of Fortune as a persona increasingly associated with real ladies
and their skittishness is, for Machaut, a means of possessing Hope. Taken
together, chapters 3 through 5 concentrate on the emotional functionality of
Machaut's art, that is, the way in which it relates to his particular social situation, being both formed by it and in turn seeking to form its audience for
it. Machaut's collected works have their own existence as an emotional and
social world every bit as complex and human as the one that forms their mirror, that of the late medieval court. Moreover, chapters 3 through 5 integrate
discussion of the aspect of Machaut's multimedia art that differentiates his
work from his contemporaries' treatment of similar thematic issues: music.
The musical discussion is designed to be comprehensible to the general scholarly reader without disguising the fact that the articulation of music's ways of
meaning requires some technical knowledge. To further this end, a glossary is
appended to the book, which gives short definitions of key terms used in these
central chapters.

Chapter 6 looks at the ultimate fortune of all humanity—death—and
places Machaut's ostensibly secular works within the sacred, devotional,

and moral-religious contexts that both he and his audiences inhabited. Once more the role of music is integrated within the discussion of commemoration, including the commemoration of Machaut's own death, for which Eustache Deschamps wrote two balades, which were set to music by the contemporary composer F. Andrieu. The chapter ends with an examination of Machaut's immediate afterlife, reception, and ultimate neglect, bringing the narrative chronologically full circle to the point of his scholarly resurrection outlined in the second chapter.

The current project is fundamentally interdisciplinary and designed not only to interest musicologists but also to be read by literary scholars (in medieval French and English particularly), historians of the book, and social and cultural historians of the later Middle Ages. It profits greatly from the multiplicity of excellent specialist scholarship that already exists on the composer, but in bringing together different disciplines it illuminates Machaut's work in a distinctively interdisciplinary light. In placing musical pieces centrally within this illumination, it argues that musico-literary performance occupied a special place in the courts of fourteenth-century France, providing another means of both meditating on human temporality and consoling loss. Like Orpheus, whom he invokes repeatedly, Machaut was eventually dismembered. This attempted "re-membering" of Machaut seeks to deepen contemporary understanding of his significance for the history of the book, European literature, and European music.

Reference to poems by their incipit texts follows the orthography found in Lawrence Earp's *Guillaume de Machaut: A Guide to Research* (1995). This book is also the reference point for the manuscript sigla associated with the Machaut sources, which are given, as there, in boldface. Text from narrative poems follows the presentation in the published edition specified in the list of abbreviations. Texts of lyrics given as figures in the main text use the orthography of a specified manuscript source (usually the earliest), although on advice from specialist readers I have followed the standard practice of differentiating *i/j* and *u/v*, marking elisions, adding punctuation and diacritical markings, and silently expanding abbreviations.

Literary studies often focus on the narrative poems (William Calin's *Poet at the Fountain* [1974]), or consider Machaut's lyrics as a model for later *forme fixe* lyrics (Daniel Poirion's *Poète et le prince* [1965]; Leonard W. Johnson's *Poets as Players* [1990]). Sylvia Huot's chapters on the Machaut manuscripts in *From Song to Book* (1987) offer exemplary analysis of their interaction of bibliographic, iconographic, and literary aspects, but less detail on the music. Yet in the Middle Ages music was more central to literate culture in general than it is today. The only book at this writing that considers all of Machaut's music is Gilbert Reaney's short (seventy-six-page) monograph *Guillaume de Machaut* (1971). Both Machaut studies and musicology have undergone such enormous changes since its publication that this volume can no longer serve as a reliable and informative resource. More recent studies focus on single musical genres (Daniel Leech-Wilkinson's *Machaut's Mass* [1990] on the Mass; Anne Walters Robertson's *Guillaume de Machaut and Reims* [2002], on the motets; there is to date no book on the songs).

Earp's indispensable *Guillaume de Machaut: A Guide to Research* magisterially covers all works, genres, and scholarly disciplines, but its purpose is to provide a thoroughly annotated guide to the extant specialist literature on the composer, not a synthetic interdisciplinary study of Guillaume de Machaut as a complete artist. But any recent book on Machaut that is not heavily reliant on Earp's *Guide* is a bad book, and what follows here will at times read like a lyricization of Earp's ever-useful narrative. Earp's book, however, is now obsolescing, slowly to be sure, but at an ever-increasing rate as more work on Machaut appears. And while it is a far more enjoyable read than most texts of the "Research Guide" kind, it is not designed in itself to serve as a core text for advanced students.

Earp's *Guide* was partly a result of, but then further fueled an increased interest in, studying Machaut in the late twentieth century. It certainly gave the sense that "expertise is now within the grasp of all."[4] Long-awaited editions of the *Voir dit* appeared in 1998 and 1999 with translations into English and modern French, and this poem became a core text in public examinations in France. The *Prise* was edited with parallel translation into English in 2002, and the same year saw the publication of the hefty prizewinning tome by Anne Walters Robertson mentioned earlier. A specifically music-analytical collection of essays appeared in 2003, and the first art-historical dissertation focusing exclusively on Machaut was completed in 2005.

Meanwhile, sound recordings continued to appear, several of which will be referenced in the pages that follow in an attempt to direct the reader to the issues that the performance of music raises.[5] Non-musicologists (and musicologists who work on later periods) often express their disappointment with, or even dislike of, medieval music that they have heard on recordings. This helps them to imagine that they are missing little by excluding it from their purview. Two responses can be made to this. First, what a listener today does not like is a modern performance of medieval music, not medieval music itself, to which

---

4. Peter Meredith, review of *Guillaume de Machaut: A Guide to Research* by Lawrence Earp, and *The Tale of the Alerion* by Guillaume de Machaut, ed. Minnette Gaudet and Constance B. Hieatt, *Modern Language Review* 92 (1997): 968.

5. The reader is directed particularly to *Guillaume de Machaut (1300?–1377): Intégrale des motets*, Ensemble Musica Nova, Harmonia Mundi, HM 76 x 2, 2002; *Guillaume de Machaut: Ay mi! Lais et virelais*, Emmanuel Bonnardot, Opus 111, OPS 30–171, 1997; *Guillaume de Machaut: Chansons*, Orlando Consort, Deutsche Grammophon (Archiv), 457 618–2, 1998; *Guillaume de Machaut: Motets*, Hilliard Ensemble, ECM New Series, ECM 1823, 2004; *Guillaume de Machaut: Unrequited*, Liber Unusualis, LU 1001, 2003; Jeremy Summerly, Oxford Camerata, *Guillaume de Machaut: La Messe de Nostre Dame / Songs from Le Voir Dit*, Naxos, 8.553833, 1996; Crawford Young, Ferrara Ensemble, *Guillaume de Machaut: Mercy ou Mort*, Arcana: A305, 1998.

we ultimately have no access. Second, why should one imagine that pleasure in medieval music is less mediated for a modern reader or listener than pleasure in medieval French texts? In both cases one has to learn the language, its conventions, and something about what its audience knew and expected before one can really "enjoy" it at all. And those medieval expectations involve unlearning both the post-Kantian idea that aesthetic pleasure is all that art is good for and the suspicion of those who find it instead fascinating and/or ethically salutary. Studying, reading, and listening to Machaut is not for the sake of instant, unmediated amusement, but for the deeper satisfaction that comes from stretching imagination and understanding to their limits in an attempt to project the parameters of other lives and possibilities.

1

Life

Guillaume de Machaut's Living

Guillaume de Machaut was the foremost poet and composer of four-teenth-century France. He was an extraordinary creative artist, who by the middle decades of the fourteenth century had already composed a substantial body of literary and musical works, to which he added until his death in 1377. His contemporaries recognized him as one of the greatest writers of his day, and his reputation as a poet lasted for some time after his death, which was commemorated in music and poetry. He was patronized by royalty, and his works were performed and read throughout Europe. His narrative poems marry clerkly didacticism with the most fashionable traditions in love poetry, and they develop a first-person narrative persona that greatly influenced Chaucer, Froissart, Christine de Pizan, and other vernacular authors. Unlike those poets, however, he set more than a hundred of his own lyrics to music, helping to establish the lyrico-musical forms of balade, rondeau, and virelay, which, by the end of the century, came to be called the *formes fixes*. He also wrote expansive polytextual motets in a fashion pioneered by his contemporary Philippe de Vitry, which modern musicology calls *ars nova*. Machaut's is also the first surviving polyphonic setting of the cycle of the Mass ordinary that is known to be by a single composer. In terms of number of lines, his narrative verse places him among the most prolific poets of his age. More musical pieces by him survive than are known to be by any other French composer of this period. His training for being a court secretary may have been formative in his practice of a distinctly scribal authorial poetics, which led him to oversee the copying of his own works: his complete works survive in several large manuscripts dating from his lifetime, some of which seem to have been prepared to Machaut's own specifications. These sources advance the artistic use of the book for vernacular poetry, making play with *mise-en-page,* internal cross-referencing, and paratextual features such as indexes and rubrics. Machaut's works can be seen as the logical conclusion of the troubadour and trouvère tradition in which scribal reverence for a body of works has been exercised not by later collectors but by the author himself.[1] If he didn't invent it, Machaut certainly bolstered and enshrined the idea of the vernacular author figure, complete with a problematic and ironic relationship to his own poetry's truth-value. For Machaut, written authorship directs both of the oral arts, poetry and music. At no other point in time was such centrality to the histories of both European literature and European music combined in one person; even if Schubert and Goethe had been one man, his *Lieder* would still need to occupy the cultural places given respectively to the symphony and the novel for him to signify as much to the nineteenth century as Machaut did to the fourteenth (and he'd probably also have needed to be one of Napoleon's closest counselors).

But what do we really know about Guillaume de Machaut? Despite his reputation and the sizable body of works that he has left, the more workaday details that pertain to the man behind the artist are hard to extract. To write a narrative biography of Guillaume de Machaut is to perform a lot of gap-filling. Scholars have had to work by inference and supposition to assemble a fuller life for this centrally important cultural figure.

The paper trail—actually primarily a "skin trail," since most of it is on parchment—comprises two main groups of sources. The first group includes more discursive, literary writings, principally deluxe manuscripts of Machaut's own works, but also poetic treatises and literature by his contemporaries.[2] The second encompasses various kinds of archival evidence, most pertaining to monetary aspects of Machaut's life such as employment, patronage, taxation, and the receipt of gifts. Both groups of documents require a degree of interpretation, albeit of rather differing kinds, before they can be made to speak frankly about Machaut's life. The balder information of the documentary items has often been bolstered by using supposed facts extracted from his fictional texts: adding two and two together has frequently made five.

---

1. The usual more direct precedents cited for Machaut's scribal authorial poetics are vernacular poets and musicians such as Adam de la Halle and Rutebeuf; see Sylvia Huot, *From Song to Book: The Poetics of Writing in Old French Lyric and Lyrical Narrative Poetry* (Ithaca, 1987). Anne Walters Robertson, *Guillaume de Machaut and Reims: Context and Meaning in His Musical Works* (Cambridge, 2002), 140–44, finds a Reims-based precedent in the collected works of Dreux de Hautvilliers, whose poetry seems to have influenced that in *Fons / O livoris* (M9).

2. Although medieval culture arguably lacked a category called literature, the category is clear enough for the purposes of this chapter. As Peter Haidu comments, aspects of the process of the elaboration of a disciplined civilization can be seen above all in literature, which does ideological work, explores and constitutes subjectivity, and provides "performative models of human comportment." See Peter Haidu, *The Subject Medieval/Modern: Text and Governance in the Middle Ages* (Stanford, 2004), 5.

The power of overinterpretation—together with specific latter-day disciplinary agendas and scholarly fashions—forms the subject of chapter 2, which looks at Machaut's modern rediscovery. The present chapter merely strives to satisfy two more basic questions: What survives, and what does it tell us? It begins by describing both kinds of surviving material traces, starting, albeit briefly, with the manuscripts of Machaut's work. Then a description of the more factual documents outlines the current state of documented knowledge about Machaut's life while acknowledging that even factual documentation requires a degree of contextual interpretation. It focuses principally on the archival record and only secondarily on the more problematic evidence from Machaut's fiction. As will be seen, this introductory chapter proposes that we know far less about Machaut as a historical figure than most other studies have claimed.[3]

What Survives?

The manuscript holdings of the National Library of France in Paris include six large manuscripts that contain works exclusively by Machaut—the so-called Machaut manuscripts—complete with musical notation where appropriate. Not only do these books contain nothing *except* Machaut's works, but also they have the appearance of being more or less complete reflections of the total number of his works at the specific points in his career when they were compiled. Today they are referred to by using sigla standardized in the early twentieth century by Ernest Hoepffner, the editor of the narrative poems for the Société des anciens textes français.[4] There is a good sextet, represented by sigla from the start of the alphabet, comprising manuscripts A, B, C, E, F, and G (although F and G are really two halves of a single book, now bound as two separate sources, F-G), to which can be joined manuscripts D and M, also in the Parisian Bibliothèque nationale de France, but not containing musical notation, although manuscripts D and M contain all the texts of the musical pieces in the relevant section of the manuscript, with the exception of the motets.[5] Outside Paris, a fragment of what was once a large notated Machaut manuscript is held at the National Library of

3. The best summary is in Lawrence Earp, *Guillaume de Machaut: A Guide to Research* (New York, 1995), chap. 1; a more fully fleshed-out biography is in Robertson, *Guillaume de Machaut and Reims,* which accepts the standard idea of Machaut's basic residency in Reims from soon after his acquisition of a canonicate there (that is, from about 1340). A trenchant corrective to this view, which places Machaut in Reims only from around 1360, can be found in Roger Bowers, "Guillaume de Machaut and His Canonry of Reims, 1338–1377," *Early Music History* 23 (2004): 1–48. See further discussion in this chapter.

4. Ernest Hoepffner, *Oeuvres de Guillaume de Machaut,* 3 vols. (Paris, 1908–1922), 1:xliv.

5. See the list of manuscripts in the abbreviations, and see also Earp, *Guillaume de Machaut,* 73–128 (chap. 3).

Wales, now designated **W**. A valuable complete notated source, known as **Vg** because it once belonged to the Marquis Melchior de Vogüé (d. 1916), was inaccessible to scholars for much of the twentieth century while it was owned by the Wildenstein family; thanks to the beneficence of its new owners, it is now on loan to Corpus Christi library in Cambridge as part of the James E. and Elizabeth J. Ferrell Collection.[6] A number of other similar "Machaut manuscripts" once existed but are now lost and can be traced only through early library catalogues.[7] Nearly all other traces of Machaut's work duplicate works known from these collected single-author codices. A couple of the narrative dits are copied solo into manuscripts (*Lyon* in **Bk** and *Remede* in **Pe**), and a fragment survives of what may have been a manuscript solely of Machaut's lays (**Ars**). But aside from these, Machaut's works survive in books containing his works among those of others.[8]

An account of manuscript **A** is a practical place to begin an assessment of Machaut's total output, since this fat book contains nearly everything that can be ascribed to him with certainty, and its musical items are fully notated. Of Machaut's unanimously accepted canon, manuscript **A** omits only one short dit (*Lis et marguerite*), six unnotated *forme-fixe* lyrics, two complaints, one notated rondeau, one notated balade, and two untexted triplum parts (of *Se quanque amours* [B21] and *Dous viaire* [R1]).[9] **A** was copied in the early 1370s, during Machaut's final years, and has an index that was drawn up before the copying of the volume and which by means of a seemingly authorial rubric prescribes an order that is very nearly followed in the codex as it

6. At this writing the Parker Library Web page says "recently acquired, on loan for five years," without giving any dates. See www.corpus.cam.ac.uk/parker/.

7. See Earp, *Guillaume de Machaut*, 94–95, nos. [8] and [9], unless these rather vague descriptions should be matched to members of the group of surviving sources. To these should be added [39] (ibid., 109), whose explicit remained unidentified by Earp, but which is the last line of *Se quanque Diex (Le lay du mirouer amoureux)* (L11). It should read "mon bien ma pais ma souffisance" not "mon bien ma pars ma souffisance," although without an examination of the inventory, it is difficult to assess whether the misreading of *i* as *r* (easily confused in many hands) is the scribe's or Pellegrin's; see Elisabeth Pellegrin, *La bibliothèque des Visconti et des Sforza, ducs de Milan, au XVe siècle* (Paris, 1955), 271, item A. 889.

8. Full details can be found in Earp, *Guillaume de Machaut*, 73–128 (chap. 3).

9. A few items are found only in the posthumous manuscripts F-G and/or E; the items found only in J and/or K are considered at best *opera dubia*. See ibid., 234–35 (for *Lis et marguerite* and *Cerf blanc*), 254–55 (for *Loange* items), 269 (for *Je me plein* [Cp9] and *J'ay, passét* [Cp10]), 318 (on *En demantant* [L24/18]), 343 (on *Mes esperis* [B39]), 357 (on *Pour ce que plus [Un lay de consolation]* [L23/17]), and 361 (on *Quant je ne voy* [R21]). Of these, the authenticity of the two lays and *Cerf blanc* has been questioned. The musical parts that are added to a few of the songs in manuscript E may not be by Machaut, although they could represent performative or alternative traditions which could conceivably stem from the composer or his circle; they certainly represent valuable indications of musical practice of the period; see Earp, *Guillaume de Machaut*, 295 (on *Biauté qui* [B4]), 309 (on *De Fortune* [B23]), 311 (on *De toutes flours* [B31]), 334 (on *Je suis aussi* [B20]), 351 (on *On ne porroit* [B3]), 378 (on *Se vous n'estes* [R7]), and 385 (on *Une vipere* [B27]). Manuscript A omits the triplums of R1 (see ibid., 317n51) and of B21 (see ibid., 377).

stands.[10] Like most of the later sources it follows the broad pattern of opening with the narrative poems, followed by the lyrics without music, and then lyrics with musical notation. It opens with a pair of author portraits (see figures 3.1 and 3.2), which head a short, late poem, usually called the *Prologue* after its designation in manuscript **E**.[11] This is linked by means of its explicit, which functions as an incipit to the following poem, *Le dit dou vergier* (The Story of the Orchard), to a series of narrative poems.[12] All of these longer narrative poems have illuminations. After *Vergier* come two debate poems that decide the same question in opposite ways: *Le jugement dou roy de Behaingne,* which concludes that a man whose beloved is unfaithful has more sorrow than a woman whose lover has died, and *Le jugement dou roy de Navarre,* which reverses the judgment. One of Machaut's most important works, the didactic *Remede de Fortune* (*The Remedy for Fortune,* or *A Cure for Ill Luck*) follows the debate poems. As well as an important program of illuminations, it has lyrics with musical notation set into the course of its narrative, thereby creating parallel Arts of Music and Poetry to mirror the ostensible Art of Love that the narrative presents. Four further long narrative poems follow: *Le dit dou lyon* (The Story of the Lion), *Le dit de l'alerion* (The Story of the Alerion), *Le confort d'ami* (Comfort for a Friend), and *La fonteinne amoureuse* (The Fountain of Love). A short dit about a harp (*Le dit de la harpe*) then fittingly leads into a large number of unnotated lyric poems (268 texts), usually referred to as the *Loange des dames* after a title in manuscript **G**.[13] The short poem *Marguerite* then precedes a number of complaints, and two late dits: the late hybridized masterwork *Le livre dou voir dit* (The Book of the True Story), with its mixture of lyrics, letters, and narrative; and the historical chronicle *La prise d'Alexandre* (The Taking of Alexandria). Next come two short items—the poems, *Le dit de la rose* (108 lines) and *Vesci les biens*—which were possibly composed during the copying of manuscript **A** in order to effect a transition into the music section of the manuscript, which follows them. This final section of the manuscript contains twenty-two lays (six without music), twenty-three motets, a Mass, a hocket, thirty-seven balades, nineteen rondeaux (one copied twice), and thirty-eight virelays (six without music).

It seems likely that manuscript **A** represents Machaut's final thoughts on the ordering of his collection, and the *Prologue* seems to have been created specifically for this book, where it appears in its fullest version in terms of text

10. Differences and their copying rationale are detailed in Lawrence Earp, "Scribal Practice, Manuscript Production, and the Transmission of Music in Late Medieval France: The Manuscripts of Guillaume de Machaut" (Ph.D. diss., Princeton University, 1983); on this and the authorial rubric, see Earp, "Machaut's Role," and chapter 3.

11. See Earp, *Guillaume de Machaut,* 203–5.

12. On the narrative poems, see ibid., 189–235 (chap. 5).

13. See the list of designations for this section, ibid., 237–38 and notes 237–71 (chap. 6) in general.

and illuminations (see chapter 3). Earlier sources simply open with the narrative poems, although some (which seem to be further removed from Machaut's purview) reverse the order of the first two large sections of the manuscript and start instead with the unnotated lyrics, followed by the narrative poems.[14] The music is always in the final part of any given codex, even when notation is not provided (as in **M**), and in notated sources the musical notation permeates parts of the manuscript outside the music section proper: the notated *Lai de plour, Qui bien aimme* (L22/16), is copied amid the narrative poems immediately after *Navarre* in **Vg**, **B**, and **E**, and the seven notated items of the *Remede* are copied in situ within the dit in all notated sources. (They are never copied in any music section, and all are indexed separately at the end of the prescriptive index in **A**.)[15] Manuscript **E** similarly includes the notated items of the *Voir dit* in situ, although earlier copies merely cue them using rubrics and include the notated songs in the music section (see chapter 3).

Obtaining information about Machaut's life from these sources is problematic. Earlier studies of the poet-composer certainly pulled a great deal of information from his texts, but Machaut's works are fiction, however much they feint at verisimilitude. And what might conceivably have been deduced from knowledge concerning the original owners or patrons of the manuscripts is hampered by how little we know about who commissioned or originally owned them.[16] It therefore seems sensible, now that I have outlined the extent of the work, to start with the other kinds of documentation and turn back to Machaut's poetry only when that is exhausted in the hope that the factual record, such as it is, will enable a better evaluation of what can (and cannot) be gleaned from the fiction.

What It Tells Us: Funding a Career

Most of the hard evidence for Machaut's life concerns the granting of clerical benefices. Recipients of these grants were paid money by a particular ecclesiastical institution at which the benefice was held, although the benefice was not granted by that institution. Instead a higher authority, often the pope, would receive a supplication from someone powerful asking him to make such a grant to a particular individual.[17] Usually the individual for whom the grant

14. **Vg**, **W**, **D**, **J**, and **K** start with the *Loange*. See ibid., 190, table 5.1, showing the order in the Machaut sources.

15. The incipit of the lay in *Remede, Qui n'aroit* (RF1), is also given seventh in **A**'s index listing of lays, though without any page number. See figure 3.1.

16. Original owners are unknown or only insecurely assumed for most of the principal manuscripts. See details in Earp, *Guillaume de Machaut*, chap. 3. Putative and known patrons of individual dits are discussed here as appropriate.

17. A fuller description of the process with reference to further specialist reading can be found ibid., 14–16.

was sought was a cleric in the employ of the noble or royal person supplicating, typically in an administrative capacity as part of a noble or royal household or entourage. The patron-client relation between the two parties would be buttressed by securing the cleric a source of a reliable independent income. The beneficiary did not necessarily have to do anything for the ecclesiastical institution in return, nor did he have to reside there to receive the benefice's income. This means that benefices alone cannot tell us where Machaut was or what he was doing, although this has often been assumed by biographers.[18] Benefices are not in themselves indicative of employment, but as they were usually collated by the pope at the request of a member of the nobility or higher clergy, they often give information about the relation of that supplicant to the beneficiary. That is, Machaut was not employed as a full-time resident canon of Reims, but rather held the canonicate because he was employed by the man who had petitioned for it on his behalf, King John of Luxembourg.

The earliest surviving documentation of a benefice for Guillaume de Machaut so far discovered is a bull of Pope John XXII dated Avignon, 30 July 1330, which grants an expectative canonicate and prebend at Verdun cathedral. The sense of a grant "in expectation" means that Machaut was effectively receiving official confirmation of being first in line for such a benefice when one became available. This would require one of the current incumbents to cause a vacancy (usually by dying, but sometimes by resigning in favor of a more lucrative benefice elsewhere).[19] The bull provides some additional information: the request is made by the king of Bohemia, John of Luxembourg, and Machaut is cited as John's "clerico, elemosinario et familiari suo domestico" (clerk, almoner, and member of his household). These terms imply that Machaut was working in John's household administration as part of the king's immediate retinue. As almoner he would have been responsible for a wide range of duties, including gift-giving, counsel, and perhaps also

18. Ibid., 16, comments that for his canonicate "Machaut presumably did not obtain...a dispensation of residence, since he is found at Reims in 1340, and regularly thereafter." Armand Machabey, *Guillaume de Machault 130?–1377: La vie et l'oeuvre musical*, 2 vols. (Paris, 1955), 36–40, recounts the quiet life of the resident canon as a change of life for the forty-year-old Machaut. Robertson, *Guillaume de Machaut and Reims*, who bases her book on the link between Machaut and Reims, thinks "there is little reason to suspect that he actually lived anywhere but Reims during the last four decades of his life" (69). Strong disagreement with this view is expressed by Bowers ("Guillaume de Machaut"), who denies that his canonicate in any sense represented a full-time residential job for Machaut, at least for a couple of decades after its grant. My view, like Bowers's, is that he had strong ties to the town, and may have visited intermittently until his retirement, but that he was essentially an itinerant court functionary until at least 1360. On this issue, see the discussion later in this chapter.

19. The holding of multiple benefices was commonplace, but successive popes after Benedict XII tried to reduce duplication, especially of those held in expectation. See my later discussion and Earp, *Guillaume de Machaut*, 19, item 1.6.1f. For example, from 1339 until his death in 1342, Benedict froze the granting of expectative benefices to Parisian masters. See William J. Courtenay, "The Early Career of Nicole Oresme," *Isis* 91 (2000): 547.

the organization of religious services.[20] Nor would he be the first almoner from this period known to have written vernacular poetry with interpolated lyrics.[21] The bull also allows Machaut to retain a benefice that by this time he already held: a perpetual chaplaincy at the Hospital Sainte-Marie-de-Houdain (diocese of Arras, *département* of Pas-de-Calais).[22] The date of the grant of this benefice, which was at the collation of the abbot of St.-Rémi in Reims, has not been discovered.[23]

Grants of two further expectative cathedral canonicates followed: at Arras (17 April 1332) and Reims (4 January 1333). Each new grant mentions all previously held benefices: that for Arras mentions the expectative at Verdun; that for Reims cites those at Arras and Verdun. In both cases Machaut was allowed to retain the earlier benefices, as well as the perpetual chaplaincy at the Hospital of Sainte-Marie-de-Houdain. The grant of the Arras canonicate in expectation confirms that the chaplaincy is *sine cura* (a sinecure—literally "without care [of souls]"), that is, Machaut was required to do nothing in return. As with the Verdun grant, the two further canonicates and prebends in expectation were granted at Avignon by Pope John XXII, and the requester was King John of Bohemia. In each case Machaut is given slightly modified descriptors of his relation to his employer: by 1332 he is "domestico, familiari, notario," and by 1333 he is "familiari et domestico ac notario secretario." This appears to show Machaut progressing to positions of increasing trust and responsibility, being promoted from almoner (1330), to notary (1332), to secretary (1333).[24] The role of secretary included signing the private correspondence of

20. Earp, *Guillaume de Machaut,* 17, item 1.6.1b. For a study of the function of French royal almoners, see Xavier de la Selle, *Le service des âmes à la cour: Confesseurs et aumôniers des rois de France du XIIIe au XVe siècle* (Paris, 1995). Malcolm Vale, *The Princely Court: Medieval Courts and Culture in North-West Europe, 1270–1380* (Oxford, 2001), 258–59, points out that the diversity of court culture in this period means that it "has as much to do with the use and function of textiles, plate, and jewellery, the role of ritual and ceremony, and the distribution of alms and oblations, as with books, panel and wall paintings, music, and the other arts. 'High' art was so often an integral part of these activities that it makes little sense to consider it apart from them." See also Elizabeth Eva Leach, "Guillaume de Machaut, Royal Almoner: *Honte, paour* (B25) and *Donnez, signeurs* (B26) in Context," *Early Music* 36 (2010): 21–42.

21. Vale, *The Princely Court,* 236, notes precedents for almoners' being involved in the court's literary life; see also Janet F. van der Meulen, "De panter en de aalmoezenier: Dichtkunst rond het Hollands-Henegouwse hof," in *Een zoet akkoord: Middeleeuwse lyriek in de Lage Landen,* ed. Frank Willaert (Amsterdam, 1992), 93–108, 343–48, which reattributes the *Dit de la panthere* to Nicole de Gavrelle, chaplain and almoner to the court of Hainaut-Holland in the first third of the fourteenth century (see my discussion in chapter 2).

22. Almoners typically exercised jurisdiction over hospitals; see La Selle, *Le service des âmes,* chap. 4.

23. See Earp, *Guillaume de Machaut,* 17, item 1.6.1a and n. 57. On this grant's possible connection with Machaut's education, see Robertson, *Guillaume de Machaut and Reims,* 35–37.

24. At the date of the grant of the Arras benefice, John is known to have been already in Paris in preparation for the wedding of his seventeen-year-old daughter Jutta Přemyslovna (known in France after her marriage as Bonne, Duchess of Normandy) to John, Duke of Normandy, Count

the king, little of which survives, as well as authorizing other kinds of more official documents: a letter patent from 1 May 1334, which detailed a ceremony
of feudal homage between King John and Count William I of Hainaut, from
whom the king held lands in fief, including his castle at Durbuy, was signed
at Noyon, "par le roy, Guillaume de Machaut."[25] The letter survives in at
least three near-contemporary copies in cartularies now in Brussels and Lille;
the original, which would have been in Machaut's own hand, has not been
identified.[26]

A bull dating from the same day as the grant of Guillaume de Machaut's
Reims benefice granted his brother Jean de Machaut an expectative benefice
at the Abbey of Our Lady in Montebourg (diocese of Coutances, *département*
of Manche).[27] Like his brother's, Jean's benefice was requested by the king
of Bohemia; Jean de Machaut is described as John's "familiari et domestico
eleemosynario," that is, in much the same terms as Guillaume had been three
years earlier. Unlike Guillaume, however, Jean seems not to have been holding
any preexisting benefices; he is simply designated as a clerk of Reims.

From soon after his election on 20 December 1334, the new pope, Benedict XII, began to adjust the roster of benefices that he inherited from his
predecessor, John XXII, in order to prevent single individuals from holding
several at once. This practice, which many—Pope Benedict among them—
saw as an abuse, particularly affected those held in expectation, which were
very often held multiply (for the understandable reason that these were not
yet generating income, and the point at which they might become "live" was
unknown; holding several at once was a way of hedging one's bets). In an
Avignon bull of 17 April 1335, Benedict XII suppressed Machaut's expecta-
tives at the cathedrals of Verdun and Arras, allowing him to retain the chaplaincy at Houdain only until such time as the next vacant prebend at Reims
became available to him.[28] This document also makes mention of Guillaume
de Machaut's holding of a prebend at St.-Quentin in Vermandois, a benefice
not mentioned in the 1333 document, and thus perhaps one obtained without

---

of Anjou and Maine (from 1350 John II of France), at Notre-Dame de Melun (Seine-et-Marne)
on 28 July 1332.

25. Earp, *Guillaume de Machaut,* 14, item 1.5.4a; Nigel Wilkins, "A Pattern of Patronage:
Machaut, Froissart and the Houses of Luxembourg and Bohemia in the Fourteenth Century,"
French Studies 37 (1983): 257–84; and Bowers, "Guillaume de Machaut," 9n22.

26. See Wilkins, "A Pattern of Patronage," 259 and 282–84, which gives a facsimile of the
two copies in Brussels, Algemeen Rijksarchief, manuscrits divers, no. 20, 82r–v and 84r.

27. Earp, *Guillaume de Machaut,* 30, item 1.1.11a.

28. Earp cites Dricot's diagnosis that "Benedict XII usually left canons with their appoint-
ments at the metropolitan churches in their home provinces" (ibid., 19, citing Michel Dricot,
"Note sur la formation de Guillaume de Machaut," in *Guillaume de Machaut: Poète et Compositeur* [Reims, 1982], 144). Although from what we know of Machaut his retention of the Reims
expectative seems to fit that pattern, it could equally be that he opted to retain the benefice in
expectation at the most prestigious of his three cathedrals.

papal intervention between 1333 and 1335; in 1364 Machaut was taxed on the income from this benefice, so he seems to have been able to retain it even after taking up his prebend at Reims.[29]

On 28 January 1338 Machaut's expectation of a canonicate at the cathedral church of Notre-Dame of Reims was finally realized: in his absence he was collated by proxy to prebend number forty.[30] His absence is typical: this benefice was designed by its petitioner as a way of rewarding a secretary whom he wished to retain in his service; it was not designed as an alternative career. Nonresident canons could, and certainly did, turn up at important cathedral events, such as the installation of Jean de Vienne as archbishop on 13 April 1340, at which Machaut was the most recently appointed of the thirty canons in attendance; but the atypical appearance of his name seems to have convinced most scholars that Machaut was in fact largely resident after taking up the prebend.[31] The position of secretary in a noble household, however, was one that involved close ongoing personal contact with the lord, and there is evidence that Machaut retained such a post and visited Reims periodically, probably in the retinue of his employer, who had reason enough to be there from time to time.[32] For example, Machaut's presence in the city of Reims on 30 May 1344 was clearly on business relating to King John of Luxembourg, rather than on account of anything to do with his canonicate at the cathedral. He and his brother Jean were two of eight witnesses to a feudal ceremony on Trinity Sunday at the abbey of St.-Rémi between King John of Luxembourg and the abbot of St.-Rémi. This solemn marking of the renewal "of the homage and fealty due from him to the abbot in respect of all the estates that he held in fee of the abbey" was a ceremony similar in kind to the one that Machaut's signature had witnessed between King John and Count William of Hainaut in the letter patent from 1334. At St.-Rémi a decade later, Guillaume de Machaut is listed as "chenoine de Reins" (canon of Reims) and Jean as "frere dou dit Guillaume chenoine de Verdun" (brother of the said Guillaume, [and] canon of Verdun).[33] Although they are listed by their canonicates, there

29. After disagreements with Archbishop Guillaume de Trie, from 1330 the canons of Reims met each year in St.-Quentin; for Machaut's motet in honor of Saint Quintinus (M19), see Robertson, *Guillaume de Machaut and Reims*, 68–75.

30. Earp, *Guillaume de Machaut*, 19, item 1.6.1g, gives the date as 1337. This is corrected to 1338 NS in Bowers, "Guillaume de Machaut," 7–8 (see especially nn. 16–17). The start of the year was reckoned differently in the city of Reims than at its cathedral.

31. See note 18.

32. See L. B. Dibben, "Secretaries in the Thirteenth and Fourteenth Centuries," *English Historical Review* 25 (1910): 433, 439, 444. For Machaut's particular case, see Bowers, "Guillaume de Machaut."

33. Bowers, "Guillaume de Machaut," 22n22: "Roye de boheme [*margin*]. L'an mil CCC xliiij le iour de la trinitet. Reprist de monsigneur de S[aint] Remy de Reins nobles princes et puissans messires Johans roye de bohe[me] tout ce qu'il tenoit en foy et hommaige de l'eglise S[aint] Remy de Reins et en entra en la foy [et] en l'omage dou dit monsigneur l'abbe, present monsigneur Ernoul d'augimont, monsigneur Jeh[an] de Trugny, Guill[aum]e de machaut chenoine de Reins,

was no reason for the two cathedrals of Reims and Verdun to offer witnesses for a ceremony between John of Luxembourg and the abbot of St.-Rémi. Since neither brother was employed at the abbey itself, it seems likely that they were both still in the entourage of King John. When Jean de Machaut was granted the benefice at Verdun in 1342, he had been listed as *secretarius* to King John. By 1344 Jean de Machaut was also expecting a rémois canonicate and prebend that the king had requested for him the previous year, although he had to wait over a decade for it to materialize.[34]

It seems that the parallel careers of the two brothers, Jean slightly behind Guillaume, reflect their joint employment as secretaries to the king of Luxembourg. Increasingly visually impaired since 1337, the king had special need of close and expert secretarial servants.[35] Other evidence supports this reading: a letter of Pope Clement VI dated 4 December 1345 names Guillaume de Machaut as one of three guarantors for the request of an expectative for Johannes Arbalistarius (or Arbalestrarius) at Saint Mary Magdalene in Verdun. Johannes was a clerk to one of the other secretaries in the service of King John of Bohemia, and Machaut's guarantee was a means of confirming his physical identity. For such a guarantee to be credible, Machaut must still have been intimately in the king's service as a secretary.[36] Objections that see him being replaced in the 1340s by other named secretaries of the king (whether by his brother Jean or Pierre de Waben) fail to take account of the usual practice by French royalty of having many secretaries (as opposed to the English royal practice of having only one).[37] It seems likely that Machaut remained as King

---

Jeh[an] frere dou dit Guill[aum]e chenoine de Verdun, Gilequin de Rodem[ac], Jeh[an] dit des pres de landres, Pensart lauribi de montois, Pierre de saumaise": RsADM, MS 56 H 74, pièce A, fol. 30r."

34. On the canonicate at Verdun, see Earp, *Guillaume de Machaut*, 31, item 1.11.1b. Ibid., 31, item 1.11.1c, lists a bull of Clement VI from 18 April 1343 in which Jean is cited only as "clerico et familiari domestico" rather than secretary. Unless he had been demoted since the Verdun request, this suggests that job titles were not always listed in full, although given the fact that a secretary is a special type of clerk and would be a household familiar, this does not suggest that he had another post, nor does it put in question the career trajectory (from almoner, to notary, to secretary) outlined earlier for Guillaume de Machaut. The request for a Reims canonicate was unnecessarily renewed in 1350 by Yolande of Flanders, who cites Jean as her familiar (ibid., 31, item 1.11.1e). During the papacy of Innocent VI the same request was lodged by Charles of Navarre, who cites Jean as "dilecto suus"—his favorite (ibid., 31, item 1.11.1f). By this date of the last of these, Jean had canonicates and prebends at Leuze, Verdun, Bar-le-Duc, and Toul. He was finally collated to prebend number forty-four at the cathedral in Reims on 13 September 1355; see ibid., 32, item 1.11.1g.

35. See Bowers, "Guillaume de Machaut," 10.

36. Strongly argued ibid., 9.

37. Replacement of Guillaume de Machaut by Pierre de Waben, secretary by 1341, is claimed by Wilkins, "A Pattern of Patronage," 259. Guillaume Pichnon, who was an executor of Machaut's benefices in 1332 and 1335 (see Earp, *Guillaume de Machaut*, 18, item 1.6.1c and n. 62, and 19, item 1.6.1f) was also a secretary of King John's at the time that Machaut was serving in this capacity. It seems likely that Jean de Machaut joined rather than replaced his brother as John's

John's secretary until John's death at the battle of Crécy the following year (26 August 1346).

Machaut's employment is even more sparsely documented after John of Luxembourg's chivalric demise. Chapter records from the cathedral of Reims attest to Machaut's presence at the installation of two archbishops there in the 1350s—Jean de Vienne's successor, Hugues d'Arcy, in January 1352, and Jean de Craon in 1355—although he was absent from that of the intervening incumbent, Humbert II de la Tour du Pin, in 1353, and from the installations of two of Jean de Craon's successors.[38] Tax records show him paying dues on his benefices: that at Reims in 1346, and that at St.-Quentin in 1362.[39] Another document reveals the location of Machaut's house in Reims in 1372.[40] Although it is no longer standing, its site, thought to be at what is now 4–10 rue d'Anjou (formerly rue de la Pourcelette) and 25–37 rue des Fuseliers, suggests that toward the end of his life Machaut was living in a large house with courtyard and garden located outside the cathedral close.[41]

Sometime before 9 November 1377, when prebend number forty passed to Johannes de Gibourty, Machaut died.

Remaining Questions

A large number of fairly basic questions remain. The dates of Machaut's birth and death are unknown. His birthplace, early schooling, training, and route into King John's service also remain obscure, as does the employment in

secretary; he is named as secretary in his supplication for a canonicate and prebend at Verdun cathedral from 23 September 1342; see ibid., 31, item 1.11.1b (and see note 34 in this chapter). On the somewhat different roles of French secretaries, see Dibben, "Secretaries," 437–39.

38. Earp, *Guillaume de Machaut*, 23, item 1.7.1e, and 24, item 1.7.1h, respectively. Bowers, "Guillaume de Machaut," 6n13, notes that Reims, Archives départementales de la Marne, MS 2 G 323, *pièce* 15, "is plainly dated 1 January 1352 (= 1353 modern style); however, local specialist authority...dates d'Arcy's enthronement to 1 January 1352 (modern style)," and modern scholarship "states that d'Arcy received papal provision to the see on 24 October 1351 and died on 18 February 1352 (modern style)." Archbishop Jean III de Craon served from 31 July 1355 to 26 March 1374 and was installed on 4 November 1355. The other two installations during Machaut's lifetime were of Louis Thésard (14 April 1374–12 October 1375) and Richard Picque dit de Besançon (12 November 1375–7 December 1389). See Pierre Desportes, *Diocèse de Reims* (Turnhout, 1998), 174–76, 178–85.

39. Earp, *Guillaume de Machaut*, 23, item 1.7.1d, and 44–45, item 1.15.1b.

40. Bowers argues persuasively that the Guillemete de Machaut who is granted tax relief in 1364 on a house in the parish of St.-Timothée in Reims (information contained in a document found independently by Robertson and Leech-Wilkinson according to ibid., 46, item 1.15.1d) is not the poet but the citizen of Reims who appears elsewhere in the town records from the 1340s; see Bowers, "Guillaume de Machaut," 17n47.

41. Earp, *Guillaume de Machaut*, 50, item 1.18.1a; and M.-É. Brejon de Lavergnée, "Note sur la maison de Guillaume de Machaut à Reims," in *Guillaume de Machaut, poète et compositeur* (Paris, 1982), 149–52, with two plates following 152.

which he engaged after John's death. As I have indicated, most scholars accept that the final availability of the canonicate and prebend at Reims prompted Machaut to leave the king's service to live out the rest of his long life in Reims, positing it as the city of his early education if not his birth.[42] Some of the problems with this theory and the assumptions on which it rests have already been hinted at; they have been more fully discussed by Roger Bowers, whose conclusions are worth summarizing here.[43]

As noted briefly in the factual summary given earlier, canonicates were usually granted as a reward for administrative service. They were a means of ensuring the administrator income and, should he become unable to serve through old age or infirmity, a residence and (effectively) a pension. Most important, an employer would not usually reward an employee by promoting him out of his service: benefices were designed to *retain* trusted servants. Canons certainly could be resident at the cathedral to whose chapter they belonged, but this was the exception: such benefices were usually held in absentia. Reims cathedral in this period had its seventy-two prebends held by seventy-four canons (holding seventy full prebends and four semi-prebends).[44] But even at an event as prominent as an archbishop's enthronement—when residents were required, and nonresidents encouraged, to attend—the total proportion of canons present was always less than half: the number of thirty mentioned as having attended Jean de Vienne's enthronement in 1340 is typical. The cathedral chapter was deemed quorate for business with only twelve members in attendance.[45]

Although residency allowed canons to generate income above the basic level of their prebend, it required many duties in return. A number of modern studies, including that of Anne Walters Robertson, report that resident canons were allowed five months of leave during any given year while still retaining their status as resident. Bowers argues that this "fact" rests on a series of misunderstandings, starting with Pierre Desportes's misreading of the chapter statues in his 1976 thesis.[46] Having reexamined the published statues, Bowers

42. See in particular the arguments in Robertson, *Guillaume de Machaut and Reims*, 35–37.

43. The cut and thrust of the duel between Roger Bowers and Anne Walters Robertson, who had seen an earlier draft of Bowers's essay and makes a number of footnote references to it, is an entertaining "footnotes quarrel" of medieval musicology. See especially Bowers, "Guillaume de Machaut," 29n78, refuting Robertson, *Guillaume de Machaut and Reims*, 399–400.

44. The number of prebends was seventy-two, but two were divided in half at the innovation of Pope Clement V in 1313; see Desportes, *Diocèse de Reims*, 18.

45. Statute 14 cited in Bowers, "Guillaume de Machaut," 5n11.

46. Bowers refers to the published version of the thesis: Pierre Desportes, *Reims et les Rémois aux XIIIe et XIVe siècles* (Paris, 1979), 296–97. The statement appears in Pierre Desportes, "Reims et les Rémois aux XIIIème et XIVème siècles" (doctoral thesis, University of Paris I, 1976), 413, without a footnote reference. Robertson, *Guillaume de Machaut and Reims*, 33, indirectly justifies her statement that "a person who obtained a canonicate at Reims had to be in residence twenty-eight weeks out of each year" by pointing out its similarity to other cathedrals. Her footnote references Millet's study of Laon (Hélène Millet, *Les chanoines du chapitre*

is unable to support the idea that Machaut based himself at Reims but traveled freely for nearly half the year, which is the scenario envisaged by most scholars.[47] He proposes that this conclusion might have arisen from Statute 61 of the cathedral statutes of 1327, which governed the point in a given year at which a residentiary could draw as emoluments specified amounts of wood and wax: residence of twenty-eight weeks and attendance at a minimum of forty obits was needed between 29 August and 24 June in a given year to qualify. By implication, residentiaries *were* permitted time away from Reims, but a complementary maximum of five months is not what this stipulation of seven months' residence implies; this statute is merely about entitlement to free light and heat.[48] Bowers proposes instead that the ninety days' absence permitted in the eighteenth century might reflect medieval practice, although as with so much about the late medieval period, the proper conclusion is that the facts of the matter have been lost.

Being a resident canon at Reims could not have been combined with Machaut's basic career as a court administrator. A domestic familiar would be required to have a primary domicile in the household of his master; even if this were in Reims, the duties of a secretary, who would have had daily and often lengthy personal contact with his lord, would not permit the managerial duties of the canons resident. For such high-level court service the servant would be one who had taken a level of holy orders that forbade him to marry; celibates were unencumbered with their own family and thus formed an intimate part of the *familia* of their master, traveling with him, advising him, performing various private tasks, and relaying confidential messages. Resident canons, by contrast, were usually priests, since their managerial duties were to a large degree sacerdotal (that is, they had to be carried out by those fully ordained as priests). Machaut was a subdeacon (that is, still in orders and celibate, but two ranks below priest).[49] It was simply not the place of a court servant, however famed as a writer, to offer his services only intermittently or sporadically on account of his personal wish to enjoy a semi-settled home life in his native city and a bit of extra money from the mundane tasks of servicing the liturgy in its cathedral.[50]

---

cathédral de Laon, 1272–1412 [Rome, 1982], 236). Millet notes only that an initial *stagium* of twenty-eight weeks was required at Laon in order that canons might thereafter get the fruits of their prebend, much the same kind of evidence that Bowers points out is designed to give criteria not for residency per se but only for emoluments.

47. Robertson, *Guillaume de Machaut and Reims*, 33–34, believes there is "no reason to believe that he resided anywhere else, although it is likely that he took advantage of the liberal absence policy to spend brief periods of time in royal service or elsewhere." See also note 18 in this chapter.

48. Bowers, "Guillaume de Machaut," 7n16.

49. Ibid., 6; and Desportes, *Diocèse de Reims*, 524, no. 309.

50. See all these arguments at greater length and with supporting detail in Bowers, "Guillaume de Machaut."

Bowers argues that the written record suggests that Machaut was not resident in Reims before about 1360.[51] As we have seen, this would not pre-
clude Machaut's occasional presence both at the cathedral and in Reims more
broadly, or his celebration of Reims-related saints and figures in his motets;
after all, Reims was hardly unrelated to the royal circles in which Machaut
moved, being the place where French kings were crowned and anointed.[52]
Notification of intent to reside would have been offered at a chapter meeting
held on the Feast of the Assumption (15 August). This and the listing of those
present at each successive chapter meeting in a given year would have been
recorded in the formal volume of chapter acts, made and kept by the chapter
clerk to record resolutions taken at, and notifications made to, the (usually
weekly) chapter meetings.[53] Unfortunately, no volumes of chapter acts from
this period survive from Reims, so the only evidence of the participation of
resident canons in chapter business has to be gleaned from chance surviv-
als of other pieces of cathedral paperwork or parchment. Leases of chapter
estates, for example, might generate bi- or multipartite indentures, and most
other forms of business would produce the chapter's letters patent. In all cases,
office copies would have been made and kept on file by the chapter clerk for
potential future consultation. In many institutions these individual items were
also recopied into great ledgers, complete with indexes to facilitate consultation. At Reims, however, only the individual discrete copies were made, a large
number of which were bound ad hoc in the sixteenth century into a collection now called "Le Livre Rouge" (MS 2 G 1650), while many also remained

51. Interpretation of the same record varies widely. For Robertson, *Guillaume de Machaut
and Reims*, 33, "the documents from Reims that record [Machaut's] activities relating to the
church after this time [the late 1330s] do so steadily," citing the listing in Earp, *Guillaume de
Machaut*, 20–50, in support of this. Those thirty pages, however, contain documents as well
as deductions from literary evidence that link Machaut to places other than Reims and persons
based elsewhere than Reims. The record seems to me rather thin.

52. The importance of the Virgin Mary in his works, along with their royal and archiepis-
copal aspects, is cited as a rémois aspect of his works in Robertson, *Guillaume de Machaut and
Reims*, 52, together with the influence of books in the "nascent chapter library." Machaut, however, moved in royal circles in relation to his administrative posts, whose personnel also had well-
stocked libraries, and Marian devotion was extremely widespread. The importance of Reims and
its cathedral to certain items in Machaut's compositional output nevertheless remains, since this
locale was of interest to royalty. The combination of being a royal apparatchik and a local man
probably worked to make Reims a central place for Machaut, but the former may have been more
of a driving factor than the latter. The idea of a man not quite in his forties becoming semi-retired,
returning to his roots, and dedicating the rest of his life to art should be resisted.

53. Bowers, "Guillaume de Machaut," 5n8. Chapter act books are lacking from Reims in this
period, which is why no such trace is found of Machaut either before or after the period when he
is assumed by Bowers to have been resident. In a personal communication Bowers clarifies that
"had any of the Chapter Act volumes of this period survived, they would have preserved both
the record of the protestations of intent to reside, and—at the head of the record of each weekly
meeting—the names of those canons actually in attendance. Machaut's name appears in no register of residents, and in no Chapter Act book, because no examples of either have survived."

as individual pieces of parchment or paper. It is these items that were transcribed in the nineteenth century by Pierre Varin and from which we know of those instances when, for example, Machaut was present at the installation of a new archbishop. Machaut, however, could have witnessed enthronements as a nonresident; only one of Varin's documents mentions Machaut as having taken part in something that would have necessitated his having residentiary status: the business concerning Hugues de Chastillon.

The date of the unique document attesting to Machaut's residency (18 August 1352) locates the business it reports at the principal chapter meeting held at the Assumption, which suggests that this date represents either the beginning or the end of a year of residence for Machaut. But given that Machaut was absent from the enthronement of a new archbishop on 2 May 1353, Bowers concludes that this record must note the end of a year in residence, which therefore lasted from August 1351 to August 1352.[54] Bowers suggests that Machaut chose to reside for this year on account of a crisis in the staffing of the choir, decimated probably as a direct and indirect result of the Black Death; by 1 February 1352, papal approval for an endowment to increase the amount paid to vicars in twelve of the cathedral's chaplaincies had been given, and the musical foundation of the cathedral was shored up.[55] There is no direct evidence of Machaut's role in the negotiations that must have taken place in regard to the choir, but at the annual chapter meeting—as attested by the document from 18 August 1352—Machaut was one of three canons who proposed that a fourth canon, Hugues de Chastillon, be granted remuneration and the wearing of a vestment to which he was not properly entitled, licenses that he had apparently enjoyed on an earlier occasion. Wearing the almuce—a marten or gray squirrel fur bonnet that covers the head and shoulders—was a privilege reserved for those in one of the major orders (subdeacon, deacon, or priest). Machaut, a subdeacon, is shown with an almuce thrown over his left arm—the correct carriage of this vestment for French canons—in the author portrait at the head of the *Prologue* in manuscript A.[56] Hugues de

54. Personal communication. He also notes that the original document that details this event is now missing. Varin gives the reference as MS 2 G 323, no. 415, but no document now in the Reims archive corresponds to this, so only Varin's transcription remains.

55. Bowers, "Guillaume de Machaut," 18.

56. Earp, *Guillaume de Machaut*, 23n86; and see figure 3.2. In the Western Church, the subdiaconate constituted a major order from 1207. Percy Dearmer, *The Parson's Handbook*, 8th ed. (London, 1913), appears to differentiate the almuce (or "amess") from the amice, although the two are conflated in *OED*, which lists them both under the latter (with no entry for "almuce"); the fur-lined almuce is *OED amice*². Dearmer, *The Parson's Handbook*, 148, describes the almuce as a "shaped fur scarf, worn in ordinary weather, and carried, according to old custom, on the arm when the weather is hot" but does not give a source; the same carriage is suggested as proper to French canons for "Amice, Aumusse, Amusse" by Marc Carlson at www.personal.utulsa.edu/~marc-carlson/cloth/glossary.html. Domenic Leo, "Authorial Presence in the Illuminated Machaut Manuscripts" (Ph.D. diss., New York University, 2005), 108n234, corrects Earp, *Guillaume de Machaut*, 23n86, saying that "the almice [*sic*] is not the hooded capelet that Machaut

Chastillon was neither officially resident nor in major orders, yet Machaut and his co-proposers wanted him not only to be allowed to sport this fancy furry headgear but also to enjoy the full sum of his prebend and to take part in the deliberations of the chapter as if he were officially resident. Machaut and his companions held up proceedings in the chapter by refusing to vote. The situation was resolved after a few days of deadlock by the provost's persuading his chapter that such a serious contravention of custom would require a two-thirds majority vote.[57] The supporters of Hugues of Chastillon, including Machaut, were defeated.

Bowers explains this curious incident by looking at the patronage network that might have been in play for Machaut to have taken such an unpopular stand during a period when he was, unusually, resident. He suggests that the answer may lie in Machaut's relation to Hugues de Chastillon. In 1352 Hugues was, like Machaut, a canon of the cathedral, but was nonresident.[58] Like Machaut, Hugues had tight administrative connections with a royal household, though in his case with the king of France. He had trained as a lawyer, was Conseilleur du Roy, and succeeded Philippe de Vitry in the senior judicial office of Maistre des Requestes de l'Hostel du Roi.[59] Unlike Machaut he was a nobleman, a "prince" according to the chapter document.[60] His father was Jean de Chastillon, who until 1327 owned—among a number of other lordships—that of a village suggestively called Cauroy de les Machaut. This village, now simply named Cauroy (*département* of Ardennes) is 2.4 kilometers (just over a mile) west (in the direction of Reims) on what is now the D980 of the very Machault (*département* of Ardennes) that Guillaume has been thought by most scholars to be toponymically "de."[61]

---

wears in the *Prologue* image in **A**," giving as evidence only the picture in Carra Ferguson O'Meara, *Monarchy and Consent: The Coronation Book of Charles V of France, British Library MS Cotton Tiberius B. VIII* (London, 2001), plate 2 (f. 43r of *The Coronation Book of Charles V*), in which one of the clergy in the archbishop of Reims's procession sports a square-cut black head covering with dangly tassels on the lower trim. This item looks to me more like an appareled black tippet. This figure carries a book with double clasps in two hands; a similar depiction on f. 44v even leads O'Meara to speculate that it might represent Machaut.

57. Bowers, "Guillaume de Machaut," 20n56, citing Pierre Varin, *Archives administratives a la ville de Riems: Collection de pièces inédites pouvant servir à la histoire des institutions dans l'intérieur de la cité*, vol. 3 (Paris, 1843–1848), 31–32, n. 1.

58. He was collated and received in 1348. He later took up residency after his appointment on royal recommendation as precentor of the cathedral. From 1359 or 1360 until his death in 1387 he was *chantre* of the cathedral; in 1372 he was a near neighbor to Machaut in a canonical residence; see Bowers, "Guillaume de Machaut," 22n58; and Desportes, *Diocèse de Reims*, 328, no. 349.

59. See Bowers, "Guillaume de Machaut," 22, citing André du Chesne, *Histoire de la Maison de Chastillon sur Marne* (Paris, 1621), 409–11, 418–21, 430, 439.

60. Bowers, "Guillaume de Machaut," 19.

61. The other Machaut that Guillaume has been associated with is in the Île-de-France. Some scholars have argued that he could be from Reims itself because individuals surnamed "de Machaut" are found there and in other towns in the environs, so the surname does not necessarily

Bowers has suggested that this link between Cauroy de les Machaut and the father of Machaut's fellow canon Hugues de Chastillon might point to Machaut's actual birthplace, thereby creating a neat link with the Porcien branch of the Chastillon family for whose son Hugues Machaut stood up so resolutely in the chapter meeting of August 1352. As villages typically adopted further titles from geographical features or local churches, Bowers hypothesizes that the nominal reference to "les Machaut" in the full medieval title of Cauroy indicates that the de Machaut family was of some local importance.[62] He therefore disagrees with Robertson's idea that Machaut was a "simple, perhaps penniless, youth," claiming instead that Machaut most likely sprang from a landowning gentry family.[63] This seems likely, given that Guillaume's brother Jean was also able to gain enough education to move in the circles of European royalty, something that would be difficult for two impoverished brothers to achieve. The wish to see Machaut as a prototype of the professional artist, making good on wit and merit alone, is one that, as I discuss further in chapter 2, was of particular attractiveness in late-twentieth-century scholarship, espousing values of egalitarianism and meritocracy—but it may be a distortion of the truth. Machaut did not turn into the highly erudite and literary writer that he was without routes to education in the Church. Perhaps his family was able to see to his basic education (at a church, or at the cathedral school in Reims, as Robertson suggests), but he was then able to find employment in the household of Hugues of Chastillon's father.[64] Perhaps Machaut even tutored Hugues or his elder brother Gaucher (d. 1377) before gaining entry into the service of John of Luxembourg.[65] Another branch of the Chastillon family had direct connections to the house of Luxembourg, and

---

denote birth in a place called Machaut. Some of these other figures have been conflated; see note 40; Machabey, *Guillaume de Machault*, 1:14–19; and Earp, *Guillaume de Machaut*, 4.

62. Bowers, "Guillaume de Machaut," 23n60.

63. Robertson, *Guillaume de Machaut and Reims*, 36. Cf. Bowers, "Guillaume de Machaut," 23: "An explanation for Guillaume de Machaut's ostensibly irrational willingness in 1352 to court the displeasure of his fellow residentiaries at Reims may well be sought in the probability that Cauroy de les Machaut was the place of his birth and his youth, and the historic home of his family, so that the canon whose extra-legal privileges he was so keen to support was no less than an influential son of his own sometime manorial lord Jean de Chastillon. This latter individual thus emerges as very likely to have been his earliest supporter and patron." Robertson's hypothesis that Machaut was schooled in Reims could still be compatible with Bowers's statement.

64. See Robertson, *Guillaume de Machaut and Reims*, 35–37; and Dricot, "Note sur la formation," 143–44.

65. Gaucher de Chastillon was captain of the city of Reims during its siege by the English from 1359 to 1360. Following the building of walls in the grounds of the archbishop's palace as part of the siege defenses, he was involved in a dispute with the archbishop, Jean de Craon. This dispute was mediated by Charles the Dauphin (who supported Jean de Craon, while the king his father supported Gaucher). This mediation, according to a document from the seventeenth century, took place at Machaut's house in Reims in 1361. See Earp, *Guillaume de Machaut*, 44, item 1.15.1a.

although Bowers has been unable to link the Porcien branch to them directly, the prominence of the family as a whole makes overarching networks of patronage highly likely. For example, Hugues's father was constable of France (commander-in-chief of the French military forces) and Grand Master of the Household to Kings Philippe VI and Jean II. The latter, before he ascended to the throne, had been married to the daughter of John of Luxembourg, Bonne, who was related to the St.-Pol Chastillons by marriage.[66]

This chapter has now gone the way of all Machaut biographies in its descent into guesswork and speculation. However toothsome they smell, these suggestions about Machaut's birthplace, early life, and route into King John's service could well be pie in the sky. But before we turn—in desperation—to his fictional works, it is worth considering other kinds of nonfictional documentation that mention Guillaume de Machaut aside from the records of benefices and employment examined so far.

General Patronage

Machaut's links to other historical figures can be noted but not fully assessed: a distinction between general networks of patronage or acquaintance on the one hand, and actual employment on the other, is worth maintaining. The knowledge we have nearly all relates to one period of employment, but a number of brief documentary references, especially those granting Machaut gifts or payment for manuscripts, are suggestive of more general patronage. Machaut also features in certain other kinds of accounting documents. An account of 14 July 1341 at Binche records the spending of twenty scuta for a gift of a gilded goblet to "Willelmo de Machaut" from William IV of Avesnes, Count of Holland and Zeeland. What this was for is unspecified; Machaut was then in King John's service.[67] Other gifts are clearly in exchange for items associated with Machaut's poetic production. In 1368 Machaut was given three hundred gold francs, plus a favor of ten francs, by Amadeus VI of Savoy (the "Green Count") as payment for a *roman* that Amadeus seems to have received from him while he was at Parisian festivities for Lionel, Duke of Clarence, who was en route to Milan for his marriage to Violante Visconti.[68]

66. See Bowers, "Guillaume de Machaut," 20–23 and n. 62.

67. This man was the future brother-in-law of the English king Edward III; he was also the son of the man commemorated in Jehan de le Mote's *Li Regret Guillaume* (1339), a work whose lyric insertions Machaut cites and which influenced a number of his works, including the *Prologue* (see chapter 3). He was also the first husband of the woman who would later marry Wenceslas of Brabant, John of Luxembourg's son by his second marriage. The deep familial interconnections among the noble dynasties of Europe in this period make it difficult to assess the resonance of gifts between particular persons.

68. The document is dated at Paris 5 May 1368; see Earp, *Guillaume de Machaut*, 46, item I.15.2c.

A warrant of issue from Gavray (between Coutances and Avranches in Normandy), now in the archives of Pamplona and dated 16 October 1361, records King Charles of Navarre asking the tellers of his treasury to pay money to "our well-beloved esquire Juan Testador" so as to reimburse him fifty écus "in respect of a trusty hackney appropriated from him by our officers and given, upon our command, to Guillaume de Machau."[69] This later reimbursement for an out-of-pocket payment might well record an event that actually took place some time—possibly years—earlier, and could support the idea of Machaut's employment by King Charles of Navarre for a period after John of Luxembourg's death.[70] All other links between Machaut and Charles, however, relate to Machaut's poetic works and will be considered later in this chapter.

Fiction as True History

To restate the case: nothing certain is known of Machaut's date or place of birth, his family, his education, his means of entry into John of Luxembourg's service, or whose employ he entered after King John's death in 1346. Even the start of his service to King John is difficult to date from the documentation that survives, which in turn makes his education and date of birth uncertain too. Most commentators have understandably looked to Machaut's literary works to amplify or supplement the documentary record. The problems of obtaining factual information from fictional works should not rule out such an approach, but its place at the tail end of this chapter serves to separate fact from fiction and further underscore how little is really known about Machaut as a historical figure.

Biographers have resorted to Machaut's fiction as a source in part because it is by far the largest section of the "skin trail" that he has left us. It also satisfies a desire to see the life and works of an artist as inextricably connected. While it might be thought that this desire is either an anachronistically romantic one, or one primarily predicated on a postmodern crisis of epistemology that insists on grounding everything in the only true authenticity (that of personal experience), there is ample evidence that it replicates medieval understandings of the correct relation between a first-person narrator and his

---

69. Translation in Bowers, "Guillaume de Machaut," 13n35, from the text in Jacques Chailley, "Du cheval de Guillaume de Machaut à Charles II of Navarre," *Romania* 94 (1973): 253.

70. Chailley, "Du cheval de Guillaume de Machaut," 257, finds an ingenious solution to the apparent late date of this warrant, given Machaut's closeness to Charles's enemies in the early 1360s. But see Bowers, "Guillaume de Machaut," 13; and Earp, *Guillaume de Machaut*, 38. Andrew Wathey, "Musicology, Archives, and Historiography," in *Musicology and Archival Research / Musicologie et Recherches en Archives / Musicologie en Archiefonderzoek,* ed. Barbara Haggh, Frank Daelemans, and André Vanrie (Brussels, 1994), 15–16, points out that "even privileged creditors could sometimes wait for long periods (in extreme cases up to four or five years) before a warrant was issued to settle their dues."

or her text. Chaucer's Wife of Bath opens the prologue to her tale by declaring that "Experience, though noon auctoritee / Were in this world, is right ynogh for me." A reliance on *sentement*—a term that is difficult to translate but can denote not just emotional but more knowledge-based sensory aspects of personal experience—will be explored for Machaut's works more fully in chapter 3. Constructing a poet's life from his works is a practice seen most clearly in the *vidas* and *razos* of the troubadours and trouvères, which preface retrospective author-centered collections of the thirteenth century.[71] As evidence of reception and reading practices, such "lives" are highly valuable; as sources of historical information, however, they are problematic. These vernacular collections represent the immediate precedents both for Machaut's poetic and courtly doctrine and for his interest in using techniques of scribal compilation in their presentation.

Machaut's self-presentation—self-projection—in his works is extremely strong. His narrative dits in particular, in which the first-person narrator is a courtier-poet called Guillaume, seem to provide various pieces of evidence about his character, personality, and biography. That Machaut plays with autobiographical modes and creates a "metafictional" self should encourage extreme caution and point to the fact that historical truth and poetic sincerity are central fictional topoi (see chapter 3 for further discussion).[72] One of Machaut's latest, and arguably greatest, works is his fantastic multimedia confection called *Le livre dou voir dit*. The title of this work is indicative of the problem of seeing Machaut's voluminous first-person dits as any kind of factual source. The word *dit* comes simply for the verb *dire*, whose most literal meaning is "to say" or "to speak," but which can be used to describe oral performance anywhere along the spectrum from spoken recitation to singing.[73] In Machaut's highly textualized self-presentation, it can also mean, by extension, the visual image of such oral performance provided by the written "dit" on the page. Machaut's dits include such clearly fictional contents as a tale of a man meeting the blind god Love in an orchard (*Vergier*), a story about a voyage to an enchanted island involving a magic lion (*Lyon*), and a story about training four birds, which is expounded allegorically (*Alerion*, sometimes titled *Le dit des quatre oiseaus*).[74] The rubricated titles of these literary works therefore

71. For an introduction, see Elizabeth W. Poe, "The *Vidas* and *Razos*," in *A Handbook of the Troubadours*, ed. F. R. P. Akehurst and Judith M. Davis (Berkeley, 1995), 185–97.

72. See especially Laurence de Looze, *Pseudo-autobiography in the Fourteenth Century: Juan Ruiz, Guillaume de Machaut, Jean Froissart, and Geoffrey Chaucer* (Gainesville, 1997), 66–101 (chap. 3); and Helen J. Swift, "The Poetic I," in *A Companion to Guillaume de Machaut: An Interdisciplinary Approach to the Master*, ed. Deborah McGrady and Jennifer Bain (Leiden, forthcoming).

73. See Sylvia Huot, "Voices and Instruments in Medieval French Secular Music: On the Use of Literary Evidence for Performance Practice," *Musica Disciplina* 43 (1989): 69–70.

74. For the other dits, see the discussion earlier in this chapter and Earp, *Guillaume de Machaut*, 189–235 (chap. 5).

suggest that the word *dit* was a generic term for a narrative poem presenting a fictional story or tale. *Voir dit* is thus a deliberate paradox—a verisimilitudinous telling, a true fiction. It explores and plays with the fraught relation between personal and literary truths, which is central to the sincerity topos that Machaut frequently invokes and critiques elsewhere in his lyrics and narratives (see chapter 3). Like the *Lyon* or *Navarre*, *Voir dit* contains deliberate markers of historical "truth" in the form of dates, events, and people, which seem to locate its events in a particular period of time. Literary verisimilitude, however, is a dangerous ground for biography.

Nevertheless, certain claims by the first-person narrator of particular dits seem to support facts already known from the petition rolls. In *Behaingne* the narrator describes the castle of Durbuy, where King John held court when he was in western Europe, and notes a clerk reading to the king.[75] In the later *Confort,* written for Charles of Navarre, the narrator holds up John of Luxembourg as an exemplum. Passages detailing King John's generosity reflect the knowledge of gift-giving that would have been part of the role of almoner; and mention of places to which the king journeyed on military campaigns suggests that Machaut might have traveled with him.[76]

Machaut's works contain a number of topical references, both overt and oblique, but whether any of these proves his personal experience of the event in question is hard to assess, although scholars frequently assume it does. For example, the three motets that appear only in the later sources, *Christe / Veni* (M21), *Tu qui gregem / Plange* (M22), and *Felix virgo / Inviolata* (M23), have been fairly securely associated with the siege of Reims by the English in 1359–60 and thus used as evidence that Machaut was in Reims at this time.[77] On the one hand, however, the more famous an event, the less need for Machaut to have been there in person for him to be able to represent it realistically in his poetry; on the other hand, there is no contrary evidence to suggest that Machaut was anywhere *other* than Reims at this time, and his presence in Reims can be attested for dates either side of the siege.

When the event supposedly being referenced is even less clear, additional problems result. The upper-voice texts of *Bone pastor / Bone pastor* (M18) refer to a "Guillaume," who has been chosen by the French king to be shepherd of the rémois; all modern commentators have assumed that this refers to the only archbishop of Reims of that name during Machaut's lifetime, Guillaume de Trie, archbishop of Reims from 28 March 1324 to 26 September 1334. The early date of Guillaume de Trie's tenure—before Machaut

---

75. Ibid., 7, item 1.2.7a, 9, and *Behaingne*, ll. 1468–85.

76. On gift-giving, see Earp, *Guillaume de Machaut*, 20, item 1.6.2; and *Confort*, ll. 2930–46. On geographical detail of campaign-related travels, see Earp, *Guillaume de Machaut*, 12–13, item 1.5.3, and especially *Confort*, ll. 2923–3086.

77. Earp, *Guillaume de Machaut*, 38–40; Robertson, *Guillaume de Machaut and Reims*, 189–223 (chap. 7).

was a canon—have given some writers pause, however. Robertson's neat solution is to view the motet as admonitory rather than celebratory, although she continues to consider it as dating from 1324 or 1325.[78] One might easily, however, build on the former idea while abandoning the latter. The most significant musical admonition of the early fourteenth century is the interpolated version of the *Roman de Fauvel* found in Paris, Bibliothèque nationale de France, MS français 146. The "topical" motets in this manuscript refer to their events in reverse chronological order, and none was written during the lifetime of their subject, Enguerrand de Marigny. Margaret Bent points out that such motets, while topical, are not a medieval "newspaper"; motets planned to exemplify a point of admonishment would retain their currency.[79] According to this reasoning, even if it indeed refers to Guillaume de Trie, M18 could have been written years after his death as an admonition to a later rémois pastor.[80]

Rather than fitting historical events to textual references, scholars have sometimes been tempted to operate the other way round. The warrant of issue relating to the "trusty hackney" mentioned earlier was considered by Jacques Chailley to have prompted the composition of *Donnez, signeurs* (B26), a balade on the theme of generosity.[81] The balade's general tone, however, has meant that this thesis has not been accepted by later scholars and remains rather speculative.[82]

Reference to actual historical figures is particularly noteworthy when the figure is the dedicatee of the poem. The addressee of *Confort* implies at least the patronage of Charles of Navarre, whose "reply" is appended to its conclusion.[83] Nor is it the only poem that Machaut wrote for Charles: *Navarre,* which overturns the decision in *Behaingne,* is implicitly adjusted by Charles of Navarre, although some scholars have argued that this represents a hasty revision after the death of its proposed originally intended dedicatee, Bonne of Luxembourg.[84] In the prologue to *Navarre* the narrator describes holing up in his house from 9 November 1349 to the spring of 1350 in order to escape the Black Death. Wishing to argue that Machaut was actually employed as King Charles's secretary at this time, Roger Bowers has shown that these very deliberately given dates are far too late to correspond to the approach of

78. Robertson, *Guillaume de Machaut and Reims,* 53–68.

79. Margaret Bent, "Fauvel and Marigny: Which Came First?," in *Fauvel Studies: Allegory, Chronicle, Music, and Image in Paris, Bibliothèque Nationale de France, MS français 146,* ed. Margaret Bent and Andrew Wathey (Oxford, 1998), 35–38.

80. I intend to treat the arguments relating to chronology at length elsewhere.

81. Chailley, "Du cheval de Guillaume de Machaut," 256–58.

82. See the summary in Earp, *Guillaume de Machaut,* 38, item 1.12.2.

83. *Confort,* ll. 3979–4004.

84. In this reading, Lady Bonneürté is seen as a personification meant to be recognized as Bonne, who prompts the palinode by asking the narrator to reconsider the outcome of her father's judgment in *Behaingne.* See Earp, *Guillaume de Machaut,* 24–26 and 209.

the plague in Reims, where it was already on the wane at that time.[85] Instead this period represents the onset and peak of plague mortality in Pamplona, whither, Bowers argues, as secretary or almoner, Machaut would have been sent on ahead to make preparations for Charles's forthcoming coronation.[86] In a supplication to Pope Innocent VI dated 14 October 1354, Charles of Navarre renews the request for an expectative canonicate and prebend at Reims for Machaut's brother Jean, which had already been made to the previous pope, Clement VI, by John of Luxembourg in 1343 and again (redundantly) by Yolande of Flanders in 1350. Jean de Machaut is listed as a favorite of Charles ("dilectus suus"), the vagueness of the relationship implying that he was not directly in Charles's employ. Perhaps the petition reflects the influence of Jean's brother Guillaume, signifying that Machaut was indeed an intimate servant of Charles of Navarre in the early 1350s.[87]

Bowers and other scholars have pointed to the 1361 warrant of issue (mentioned earlier) and linked it to a complaint, *Sire, a vous fais ceste clamour* (Cp7), in which the narrator asks an unspecified king, who has made him his secretary, for a trusty hackney or mule. Other scholars, pointing out that support for Charles of Navarre had dissipated by that date, link this poem to other kings. As noted by Andrew Wathey, however, the warrant could have been issued several years after the event it describes.[88] If Machaut did leave Charles's service in the late 1350s, as seems likely, the complaint would have to date from slightly earlier than scholars have stated. So if Cp7 does relate to the warrant, and does therefore show ongoing service to Charles of Navarre, it could date from the mid-1350s. A later dating for the poem, however, has been favored on the strength of its manuscript transmission, which "separates Cp7 from the earlier group Cp1–6," all of which appear in **Vg**.[89] The assumption is that Cp7 was written after the latest datable content of **Vg**, which is presumed to have included everything Machaut had written to that date.[90] This might give cause for some reflection: arguments about the chronology of Machaut's works based on manuscript inclusion can only strictly function as dates before which something included was certainly written; exclusion from an earlier source is not proof, but only suggestive, of the work's being written in between the dates of the two sources, if the assumption of completeness

---

85. Michel Zink, "The Time of the Plague and the Order of Writing: Jean le Bel, Froissart, Machaut," *Yale French Studies* 80 (1991): 269–80, notes the historical inaccuracy but considers this to represent Machaut working instead to poetic imperatives.

86. Bowers, "Guillaume de Machaut," 10–13.

87. Suggested ibid., 16n42.

88. See note 70.

89. See Earp, *Guillaume de Machaut*, 271.

90. The dating of **Vg** is tricky; see ibid., 84. The decoration is thought to date from around 1370. With the exception of *Prise*, which seems to have been a later addition, the corpus of poems—excluding, to avoid circularity, those dated solely on the basis of manuscript transmission—dates no later than 1360–61 (*Fonteinne*).

at the stage each manuscript is produced is accepted (something that can be shown to be not wholly the case, or else **Vg** would include *Voir dit*). On balance, the idea that Machaut was employed by Charles, Count of Evreux and king of Navarre, after King John's death is highly plausible, although it is difficult to say exactly when that employment ended.[91]

The marriage of documentary and literary testimony is not always harmonious. The bull of 17 April 1335, cited earlier, in which the new pope, Benedict XII, made adjustments to Machaut's funding by reducing the number of his expectative benefices confirms what the surviving bulls of John XXII state: that the requests for the canonicates and prebends at Arras and Verdun had been made by the king of Bohemia. The archival evidence thus points unequivocally to Machaut's employment in the household of the king of Bohemia, John of Luxembourg, in the period 1330–1335. But Pope Benedict's bull makes a further statement from which an approximate date for Machaut's entry into John's service has been deduced. It affirms that Machaut has been "hitherto [John's] clerk, secretary, and household familiar, whom he maintains served him for twelve years or thereabouts."[92] Employing a level of deduction that seems uncontroversial would give Machaut a start date of around 1323, but the "vel circa" that follows "duodecim annis" (twelve years or thereabouts) nags, particularly as this figure is apparently contradicted in Machaut's last major narrative poem, the chronicle *La prise d'Alexandre* (probably written between 1370 and 1372), in which he claims that he served John for over thirty years.[93] Given that John died in 1346, this would place Machaut's entry into John's service earlier than 1316. But how old would Machaut have been then? When he received his first expectative benefice in 1330, he must have been at least twenty-five, the minimum age for a canon, but could have been as old as thirty, the age at which a canonicate might have been thought appropriate as a reward for good service.[94] Whether Machaut was only eleven or around sixteen, 1316 would have been a very early date for entry into the service of King John.

Some scholars have entertained this possibility as indicating that King John sponsored Machaut's university education, so that although he technically entered John's service, he didn't show up as serving in his court until some

91. See ibid., 33–38.

92. Ibid., 19, item 1.6.1g: "adhuc clerico suo secretario et familiari domestico, quem asserit duodecim annis vel circa suis obsequiis institisse." I have adapted the translation, since "obsequia" are not necessarily divine services but could be any other kind of obedience or deferential service.

93. *Prise*, ll. 785–86: "je fu ses clers ans plus de.xxx. / si congnui ses meurs et sentente" (I was his clerk for more than thirty years / And knew well his manner and his beliefs). It should be noted that this figure could easily be construed as hyperbole constrained by rhyme. Discussions of the relative truth-value of poetry and prose in this period often drew attention to the regretful tendency of poetry to distort the truth in favor of rhyme.

94. Earp, *Guillaume de Machaut*, 4.

time later, after completing his education.[95] Two problems beset this idea. First, there is the perennial problem of obtaining factual information from fictional works. Second, there is no proof that Machaut ever received a university education. The title *magister* is used of him in three documents, three manuscript rubrics, four literary references, three library inventories, and one music theory treatise, but never by Machaut himself nor in the official papal documents that relate to his benefices.[96] Earp notes that comparable studies of canons at Laon suggest that although university education was usual for canons who were not familiars of the pope or king, it was optional if they were. With Machaut's extensive royal and noble connections, he could certainly have obtained the benefices he received without having a university degree.[97] Later writers who might not have known Machaut except by reputation could simply have assumed that Machaut had a degree, or applied it as a general honorific for a non-noble clerical type. And when Machaut is listed among other canons in the chapter documents, the title seems to be applied en masse and is never directly before Machaut's name.[98]

The probable size of Machaut's house as identified in the document from 1372 (mentioned earlier) would have made it ideal for lodging and entertaining nobles and their retinues. This function is suggested by comments in *Voir dit*, when Guillaume complains to Toute Belle that he has been prevented from working on her poem (the *Voir dit* itself) because of the comings and goings, late nights, and early mornings caused by the presence of the Duke of Bar and several other lords who are staying in his house.[99] Guillaume's vaguer mention in an earlier letter of some "gens du roi" lodging with him has been linked to a known visit of King John II of France between 30 September and 23 October 1364.[100] The house that we know Machaut to have inhabited in 1372 was certainly large enough to cope with such eminent guests, but whether he was living there a decade earlier is unknown, although this too seems plausible. It has even been suggested that Jean de Machaut, who finally took up a canonicate at the cathedral of Reims in 1355 and served as an officer in its chapter

---

95. Ibid., 12. Cf. Robertson, *Guillaume de Machaut and Reims*, 35–37.

96. See Earp, *Guillaume de Machaut*, 7–8, item 1.2.8. Bowers, "Guillaume de Machaut," 23n61, assesses that the use of the title "master" is honorific rather than academic in Machaut's case.

97. Earp, *Guillaume de Machaut*, 8n19, citing Millet, *Les chanoines*, 142–43.

98. Joyce Coleman, "Doctors of Love: The Medieval French Love-Poet Depicted as Magister," paper given at at conference entitled Poetry, Knowledge, and Community in Late Medieval France, Princeton University, 1–4 November 2006, discusses the illumination on folio 75v of F, "which shows Guillaume de Machaut reading aloud to a group of listeners seated on a grassy hill...wearing the robe of a university magister, sitting on a raised chair, and reading from a lectern." This is a posthumous manuscript whose artist, Perrin Remiet, has a keen "interest in transferring the authority and prestige of the magister to the vernacular poet." See abstract at www.mml.cam.ac.uk/french/poeticknowledge/abs.html.

99. *Voir dit*, letter 35.

100. Earp, *Guillaume de Machaut*, 28, item 1.10.2d.

from 1356 to 1358, lived with his brother there until his own death sometime before 3 May 1372, when his prebend was reallocated.[101]

Direct documentation is lacking for many patrons for whom there is reasonable circumstantial evidence, such as that linking Machaut to King John II of France (even before he became king); to his first wife, Bonne of Luxembourg (d. 1349); to their son the Dauphin, regent, and future Charles V of France (whose coronation in Reims Machaut probably attended); to Charles's brothers, John, Duke of Berry, and Philip the Bold, Duke of Burgundy; as well as to the king of Cyprus, Pierre de Lusignan, and to Robert I, Duke of Bar.[102] Other named persons in Machaut's poetry include the Count of Tancarville, Jean II de Melun (in Cp7), Raoul de Vienne, Sire de Louppy (in *Mes dames qu'onques ne vi* [Lo250]), and Thomas Paien, who can be identified as one of Machaut's fellow canons between 1359 and 1364, and a secretary in the household of John, Duke of Berry.[103]

Much that lies beyond the very scanty facts of Machaut's ecclesiastical benefices relies on a web of inference and a series of assumptions about motives of individuals in the workings of French noble courts in this period to be stacked one upon another into a historical house of cards. As Daniel Leech-Wilkinson said in 1990, "Guillaume de Machaut exists mainly in our imagination, a fate which would probably have delighted him."[104] In the central chapters of this book, explicit and factual issues of biography will rarely impinge, as the exploration of Machaut's works takes center stage. The next chapter, however, presents a historiographical sketch of Machaut's rediscovery by the modern university disciplines that have a share in this multitalented, multimedia artist, and shows how the agendas of specific readers have led to certain kinds of assumptions, interests, and conclusions—all of them historically contingent, some deeply damaging, many patently false.

---

101. See ibid., 32, items 1.11.1i and 1.11.2; and Desportes, *Diocèse de Reims*, 393, no. 568.

102. See Earp, *Guillaume de Machaut*, 24–28, 40–48.

103. See ibid., 30 and 46, item 1.15.2b. On the identity of Thomas Paien, see Elizabeth Eva Leach, "Machaut's Peer, Thomas Paien," *Plainsong and Medieval Music* 18 (2009): 1–22.

104. Daniel Leech-Wilkinson, *Machaut's Mass: An Introduction* (Oxford, 1990), 1.

2

Resurrection

Dismembering Machaut

The modern scholarly picture of Guillaume de Machaut is multifaceted and multidisciplinary. As an artist who wrote both poetry and music *and* oversaw the collection of his works into luxuriously illuminated manuscripts, carefully ordering and cross-referencing them so as to create a whole world of meanings, he is represented by at least three different Machauts in the writings of the contemporary academy: Machaut the poet, Machaut the musician, and Machaut the bookmaker. While most scholars understand that Machaut's works range among the disciplinary divisions of the modern academy, their willingness and ability to combine approaches is usually affected by thoroughly modern concerns and capabilities. As the most technically specialized discipline, whose materials are least linguistic in type, music is the least well integrated into the picture of the composer that exists outside musicology. When music is considered, its integration into the picture sometimes overlooks the historical contingency of "music" as both an ontological category and a social practice. Art-historical approaches can be similarly affected by popular conceptualization from outside the discipline. Unlike music, however, visual art is a pictorial and representational medium in this period, so that description in ordinary language—and thus easier extradisciplinary comprehensions of specialist studies—is at least feasible. In each of the different disciplines that have a stake in Machaut studies, dismembered parts of the poet's corpus are studied as if they were wholes. Ironically for someone who figured himself as Orpheus, Machaut, like Orpheus, has been rent limb from limb by modern scholarly bacchantes, yet his dead tongue still sings and his lyre still sounds as his body parts float downstream.[1]

1. See *Metamorphoses* 11.1–66.

The central chapters of the present book aim to discuss certain fundamental Machauldian themes in as integrated a manner as currently possible. In order to attempt this, however, it is pertinent first of all to sketch the historiography of Machaut's rediscovery in the modern period, with the intent of positioning his oeuvre within the frameworks of each discipline's historically contingent interpretations. From a high point of fame in the second half of the fourteenth century, Machaut's artistic stock declined gradually during the century following his death in 1377 (see chapter 6). By the time eighteenth-century antiquarians began to resurrect interest in his works, Machaut's name had been absent from the pantheon of French writers for nearly three hundred years. The varied ways in which Machaut's works have been rediscovered, the aspects of them that have been points of focus, and their shifting evaluation and critical treatment betray a number of agendas that belong more to the modern scholarly community than to Machaut himself. Charting these agendas can help strip away the sometimes partisan concerns of the different branches of the modern academy; if this cannot ultimately reveal a pristine, authentically medieval Machaut, it can at least help form a more rounded picture of a figure who is, in our terms, toweringly interdisciplinary.

Machaut's Verbal Texts: From History to Literature

On 25 June 1743 Jean Lebeuf, a priest and canon of Auxerre cathedral, who had serious historical interests, read an address to the Académie Royale des Inscriptions et Belles-Lettres in which he made the first modern mention of the two volumes of Machaut's works now known by the sigla **F-G**, which he had rediscovered around 1735 in the library of the Discalced (that is, Barefoot) Carmelites of the rue de Vaugirard in Paris.[2] This was followed in December 1746 by another paper giving a fuller consideration to this source and to Machaut's writings as a whole.[3] The rediscovered Machaut was at this stage principally of interest to antiquarians of a French nationalist bent, keen to mine his works for information about, and eyewitness accounts of, historical events. In the third and final volume of his study of the ecclesiastical and civic history of Paris, for example, Lebeuf excerpted two of Machaut's motet texts as representative of the Latin complaints written to bewail the state of

2. L'abbé [Jean] Lebeuf, "Mémoire sur la vie de Philippe de Mezières, Conseiller du roi Charles V, et chancelier du royaume de Chypre," *Mémoires de littérature, tirés des registres de l'Académie Royale des Inscriptions et Belles-Lettres* 17 (1751): 377–98; Lawrence Earp, *Guillaume de Machaut: A Guide to Research* (New York, 1995), 91; and John Haines, *Eight Centuries of Troubadours and Trouvères: The Changing Identity of Medieval Music* (Cambridge, 2004), 93.

3. L'abbé [Jean] Lebeuf, "Notice sommaire de deux volumes de poësies françoises et latines, conservés dans la bibliothèque des Carmes-Déchaux de Paris; Avec une indication du genre de musique qui s'y trouve," *Mémoires de littérature, tirés des registres de l'Académie Royale des Inscriptions et Belles-Lettres* 20 (1753): 377–98.

France at the time of the depredations of the "grans compaignies."[4] He also included sections from the one longer narrative work by Machaut that was disproportionately to attract interest in the early phase of his rediscovery, the late verse chronicle *La prise d'Alexandre* (The Taking of Alexandria), which tells of Pierre de Lusignan's crusade to Alexandria. Although Pierre was king of Cyprus, Cyprus in the fourteenth century was a French outpost and thus part of French history and of interest to French historians. A month after Lebeuf's groundbreaking account of F-G, Anne-Claude-Philippe de Tubières de Grimoard de Pestels de Lévy, the Count of Caylus, read a paper to the same Académie Royale in which he avowed that "the poet seemed to me more interesting from the moment that I was able to see him as a historian."[5] Although the *Prise* was not presented in a modern edition until 1877, it was one of the first of Machaut's works to receive that particular mark of scholarly interest. Even before then it was extensively excerpted in several publications, notably those of its eventual editor, Jacques Marie Joseph Louis de Mas Latrie.[6]

From the poetry beyond the *Prise*, only passages that recounted items of historical record merited notice from early commentators: in addition to the two motet texts associated with the brigandage of the "great companies," historians extracted the paean to John of Luxembourg as an ideally chivalrous knight from the *Confort d'ami* (Comfort for a Friend), along with the opening part of the *Jugement de roy de Navarre* (Judgment of the King of Navarre) for its ostensibly eyewitness account of the Black Death.[7] The interest of eighteenth- and nineteenth-century readers in historical events was joined by a particular concentration on the personal experience of those events by

4. The triplum of M23 (*Felix virgo mater*) and the motetus of M22 (*Plange, regni respublica!*) form supplementary notes to Lebeuf's edition of Christine de Pizan's *Life of Charles V*, bk. 2, chap. 6, which is contained in this volume; see L'abbé [Jean] Lebeuf, *Dissertations sur l'histoire ecclésiastique et civile de Paris, suivies de plusieurs éclaircissemens sur l'histoire de France*, 3 vols. (Paris, 1739-1743), 3:147 and 431-33.

5. Anne-Claude-Philippe de Tubières de Grimoard de Pestels de Lévy, Comte de Caylus, "Second mémoire sur les ouvrages de Guillaume de Machaut: Contenant l'histoire de la prise d'Alexandrie, et des principaux évènements de la vie de Pierre de Lusignan, roi de Chypre et de Jérusalem; tirée d'un poëme de cet ecrivain," *Mémoires de littérature, tirés des registres de l'Académie Royale des Inscriptions et Belles-Lettres* 20 (1753): 416, cited in Earp, *Guillaume de Machaut*, 195n14; the translation is mine. This work was rapidly reported in the *London Monthly Mercury; or, Foreign Literary Intelligencer* (November 1753): 517, together with mention of Lebeuf's "Mémoire sur la vie de Philippe de Mezières."

6. Excerpts appeared in [Jacques Marie Joseph] Louis de Mas Latrie, *Histoire de l'Île de Chypre sous le règne des princes de la maison de Lusignan* (Paris, 1852); and idem, "Guillaume de Machaut et *La Prise d'Alexandrie*," *Bibliothèque de l'École des Chartes* 37 (1876): 445-70. The first edition was Mas Latrie, ed., *La Prise d'Alexandrie ou chronique du roi Pierre Ier de Lusignan par Guillaume de Machaut* (Geneva, 1877). See Earp, *Guillaume de Machaut*, 233-34, item 5.17. Recent publications are Peter W. Edbury, ed., *Guillaume de Machaut, The Capture of Alexandria* (Aldershot, 2001); and R. Barton Palmer, ed., *Guillaume de Machaut: La Prise d'Alixandre (The Taking of Alexandria)* (New York, 2002).

7. See the comments and bibliography in Earp, *Guillaume de Machaut*, 219.

historical actors. Machaut's account of the plague thus seemed more interesting because his poem is spoken by a first-person narrator referred to several times in the course of the dit as "Guillaume de Machaut." And his account of King John of Luxembourg was similarly that of someone who had known the king intimately, in person, and was therefore taken to be reliable, true, and historical fact.

In the nineteenth century, historians' ongoing predilection for autobiographical history meant that Machaut remained an attractive figure, since his works project a first-person narrator who has rather a lot in common with what (albeit little) is known about the historical figure Guillaume de Machaut (see chapter 1). While eighteenth-century historians seem to have been interested in the extent of French royal influence and its role in international politics, nineteenth-century historians cared more for the great figures of French regions; much of Machaut's biography was first reconstructed by historians focusing their attention on Reims or Champagne.[8] As a famous indigene, Machaut had his biography and works plumbed for their more personal local interest. Focus correspondingly broadened to encompass the ostensibly autobiographical and Reims-based *Livre dou voir dit* (Book of the True Story), a long late narrative poem—arguably Machaut's greatest work—which recounts the aging poet Guillaume's mainly epistolary love affair with a young girl. Its more than nine thousand lines of narrative verse with inset lyrics are animated by a series of forty-six prose letters, purporting to reflect a real exchange between Guillaume and his "Toute Belle" (All-Beautiful); these letters contain references to verifiable and datable historical events in 1362–63.[9]

In 1849 Louis Hardouin Prosper Tarbé published a number of the letters from the *Voir dit* in a book that combined these with excerpts from other narrative poems, together with lyric texts from the *Loange des Dames* (Praise of Ladies) and music sections. Tarbé's initial purpose was to flesh out a more rounded history of the Champagne region in the Middle Ages, but in the course of exploring the morals and customs of the period, the volume added to the knowledge of Machaut's life and works, drawing further on the latter—particularly the *Voir dit*—as a way of amplifying the former. Tarbé accepted the then current identification of the *Voir dit*'s heroine, Toute Belle, with the sister of Charles of Navarre and future wife of Gaston Fébus, Agnes

8. For example, Pierre Varin, *Archives administratives a la ville de Reims: Collection de pièces inédites pouvant servir à la histoire des institutions dans l'intérieur de la cité* (Paris, 1843–1848); idem, *Archives législatives de la ville de Reims: Collection de pièces inédites pouvant servir à la histoire des institutions dans l'intérieur de la cité. Seconde partie: Statuts* (Paris, 1844). See also [Louis Hardouin] Prosper Tarbé, *Les oeuvres de Guillaume de Machault* (Reims, 1849), and the comments on Tarbé later in this chapter.

9. See the arguments in Daniel Leech-Wilkinson and R. Barton Palmer, eds., *Guillaume de Machaut: Le livre dou voir dit (The Book of the True Poem)* (New York, 1998), xxxiii–xxxv, the notes to the narrative (713–51), and the chronology (752–53).

of Navarre. In 1856 he duly published a volume of her poems, which mainly included those ascribed to Toute Belle in the *Voir dit,* but additionally contained feminine-voiced lyrics from the *Loange.*[10] A refutation of this identification followed in Paulin Paris's 1875 publication of the *Voir dit,* which continued to focus on the poem as a source of biographical and historical detail, arguing that its events fit those of the years 1362 to 1364.[11]

The scholars of the eighteenth and nineteenth centuries clearly read Machaut's works for what they could tell them about fourteenth-century French or Champenois history rather than for their evidence of fourteenth-century French literary culture, let alone for their intrinsic value as literature. As mentioned earlier, when introducing Machaut to the modern world, the Count of Caylus had noted that only as history was Machaut's poetry interesting; he calls the *Dit de la harpe* (Story of the Harp) a "morceau très-ennuyeux" (very boring piece), hardly inspiring his readers to investigate further.[12] Passages that became Machaut's best known on account of their historical interest were seen as exceptional: even in the early twentieth century, George Lyman Kittredge deemed the account of the plague at the opening of *Navarre* "far above Machaut's usual level."[13]

In modern editions before 1900, Machaut's narrative poetry in anything approaching complete editions was represented only by Las Matrie's *Prise* and Paris's *Voir dit,* the latter of which was far from complete despite its own claims.[14] Short extracts from *Harpe* and the *Dit dou lyon* (Story of the Lion) were included in a textbook volume used to exemplify the grammar and vocabulary of Old French, but these extracts served a purely linguistic purpose

10. [Louis Hardouin] Prosper Tarbé, *Poésies d'Agnès de Navarre-Champagne, dame de Foix* (Reims, 1856). This identification was published in Anne-Claude-Philippe de Tubières de Grimoard de Pestels de Lévy, Comte de Caylus, "Premier mémoire sur Guillaume de Machaut, poëte et musicien dans le XIVe siècle: Contenant des recherches sur sa vie, avec une notice de ses principaux ouvrages," *Mémoires de littérature, tirés des registres de l'Académie Royale des Inscriptions et Belles-Lettres* 20 (1753): 413–14.

11. Paulin Paris, ed., *Le livre du Voir-dit de Guillame de Machaut: où sont contées les amours de Messire Guillaume de Machaut & de Peronnelle dame d'Armentières, avec les lettres & les réponses, les ballades, lais & rondeaux du dit Guillaume & de ladite Peronnelle* (Paris, 1875). The refutation of the Count of Caylus's identification of Toute Belle is on xviii–xx; Paris's proposal runs to xxiii.

12. Caylus, "Premier mémoire," 413.

13. George Lyman Kittredge, "Guillaume de Machaut and the Book of the Duchess," *Proceedings of the Modern Language Association* 30 (1915): 4.

14. It silently omits nearly six hundred lines in over a hundred different places, including the entire story of Polyphemus and Galatea, which Machaut took verbatim from the *Ovide moralisé.* In so doing, the edition reflected then current attitudes toward Machaut and his text; for the historiographical value of these, see Jacqueline Cerquiglini-Toulet, "Le *Voir Dit* mis à nu par ses éditeurs, même: Étude de la réception d'un texte à travers ses éditions," in *Mittelalter-Rezeption: Zur Rezeptionsgeschichte der romanischen Literaturen des Mittelalters in der Neuzeit,* ed. Reinhold R. Grimm (Heidelberg, 1991), 337–80. Nevertheless, it remained the only modern edition until 1998.

and were not deemed to have literary merit.[15] Then in the first decades of the twentieth century, the gaps in the availability of Machaut's works in print were largely filled. Most important, nearly all of the major narrative poems that had not yet been published were edited for the Société des anciens textes français by Ernest Hoepffner in three volumes (1908, 1911, and 1921).[16] In addition, a full publication of Machaut's lyrics appeared in 1909, edited by the Russian philologist Vladimir Fedorovich Chichmaref [Shishmarev], although without their accompanying music.[17] In fact the music had been transcribed independently by Friedrich Ludwig between 1900 and 1903, but his complete edition did not start to appear in print until 1926, the last volume (of four) appearing only posthumously in 1954 (see the discussion later in this chapter).

By the end of the 1920s, virtually all the major works of Guillaume de Machaut were in print and ripe for literary and musicological evaluation and commentary. As an object of critical interest, however, Machaut did not initially fare very well, despite the new availability of his output. The appearance of his collected works in literary and philological publications seems only to have reflected an awareness of Machaut as a literary writer, part of a pantheon of Occitan and Old French poets among whose illustrious predecessors were the troubadours and trouvères. These earlier lyric writers, in particular the earlier troubadours, had begun to be edited in earnest in the nineteenth century and were viewed as having initiated an original vernacular expression of erotic love.[18] The reasons for this are largely historiographical: philologists of French vernacular literary culture tended to view the thirteenth century as a high point. For them, the compilation of the large anthologies of troubadour poetry and romances represented the zenith of interest in a vibrant vernacular tradition, which was merely imitated with increasing artificiality and weariness by fourteenth- and fifteenth-century epigones who oversaw the "waning of the Middle Ages."[19] As evidence of the far-reaching geographical and

15. See Karl Bartsch, *Chrestomathie de l'ancien français (VIIIe–XVe siècles): Accompagnée d'une grammaire et d'un glossaire* (Leipzig, 1880). Twelve editions of this standard textbook were published between 1866 and 1920, with a reprint in 1958. The eighth edition (1901) was corrected and revised by Adolf Horning and from the ninth edition onward by Leo Wiese.

16. The smaller dits were edited variously in 1943 *(Harpe)*, 1970 *(Lis et marguerite)*, and 1979 *(Marguerite, Rose, Lis et marguerite,* again). See listings in Earp, *Guillaume de Machaut,* 223, 231–32, 234–35.

17. *Владимир Федорович Шишмарев;* the stress here falls on the last syllable: ShishmaryOFF. Vladimir Feodorovich Chichmaref [Shishmarev], *Lirika i liriki pozdnego srednevekov'ia: Ocherki po istorii poezii Franzii i Provansa* (Paris, 1911), includes musical notation only to illustrate earlier monophonic Romance song forms; polyphonic notation was not then widely understood (see the discussion later in this chapter).

18. See Haines, *Eight Centuries of Troubadours and Trouvères,* 155–204 ("The Science of Translation"); and Margaret Louise Switten, introduction to *Music and Poetry in the Middle Ages: A Guide to Research on French and Occitan Song, 1100–1400* (New York, 1995).

19. The reception of Johan Huizinga, *The Waning of the Middle Ages: A Study of the Forms of Life, Thought and Art in France and the Netherlands in the XIVth and XVth Centuries,* trans.

temporal influence of the troubadours (and thus further testimony to their greatness), these epigones were worth collecting and editing, if not studying or appreciating in themselves.

To some degree the century itself presents its literary culture in just such a way. Jacqueline Cerquiglini-Toulet's book *The Color of Melancholy* examines a variety of late medieval pessimism as displayed in the literary field, which tended to see all texts as glosses on earlier texts: everything has already been said, and all that is left is to make glosses with the sadness of the gleaners returning to the harvested field to pick for single grains.[20] But we should no more believe this literary trope than any other. Treating it *as* a trope, as Cerquiglini-Toulet does, allows the evaluation of the literature of this period on its own terms. Positive evaluation of fourteenth-century literature lagged at least half a century behind its publication in modern editions but was similarly reliant on a shift in contemporary (that is, twentieth-century) aesthetics and scholarly fashions.

The ground for Machaut's rehabilitation as a literary figure, at least for his narrative poetry (on the lyrics, see the discussion later in this chapter), was arguably prepared by his palpable influence on Geoffrey Chaucer. Machaut was footnoted in connection with the English poet in at least two publications before the end of the eighteenth century.[21] While the level of interest increased greatly in the nineteenth and early twentieth centuries, as usual when a particular artist is rediscovered only in his or her capacity as the model of one better known and more highly regarded, the model was assessed detrimentally in comparison to the latter genius. Comparing the description of the little dog in Chaucer's *Book of the Duchess* (ll. 388ff.) with passages in *Behaingne* (ll. 46, 1204–15) and *Lyon* (ll. 325–49), Kittredge noted that most readers "will cheerfully agree that Chaucer was writing under the spell of both passages,

---

Frederik Jan Hopman (London, 1924), is reflective of, and further perpetuated, this attitude. See James McConica, *The Waning of the Middle Ages: An Essay in Historiography* (Toronto, 1995). The English translation of *Herfsttij* (autumn) in the original Dutch title as "waning" removed any ambiguity as to whether this was a time of ripeness or decay. For the influence of this attitude on musicology specifically, see Christopher Page, *Discarding Images: Reflections on Music and Culture in Medieval France* (Oxford, 1993), 140–88 ("Huizinga, *The Waning of the Middle Ages*, and the Chanson.")

20. Jacqueline Cerquiglini-Toulet, *The Color of Melancholy: The Uses of Books in the Four-teenth Century*, trans. Lydia G. Cochrane (Baltimore, 1997).

21. Thomas Tyrwhitt, ed., *The Canterbury Tales of Chaucer, to which are added, An Essay upon his Language and Versification; an Introductory Discourse; and Notes*, 4 vols. (London, 1775), 3:313 (note to 277, l. 14), mentions Machaut's *Lyon* as a source for Chaucer's lost *Boke of the Leon*, and 4:191 (note to "Alisandre" in l. 51 of the *Prologue to the Canterbury Tales*) makes a reference to Machaut's *Prise*; Thomas Wharton, *The History of English Poetry, from the Close of the Eleventh to the Commencement of the Eighteenth Century: to which are Prefixed, Two Dissertations*, 3 vols. (London, 1774–1781), note to 466, refers to Machaut's dit *Lis et mar-guerite* on an unnumbered page at the back of the volume.

and will at the same time admit the originality of the English poet."[22] Yet
the very fact of being a model for an unequivocally valued author eventually
worked in Machaut's favor for two reasons: first, it kept his name alive and
people interested in reading his works; and second, he evidently had the readership and tacit admiration of Chaucer, so unless Chaucer's taste was to be
doubted, Machaut must have had something to offer.[23] The diagnostic works
of Kittredge and John Livingston Lowes, in which Machaut's dry artificiality
was transformed by the realism of Chaucer's originality and genius, eventually gave way to the more neutrally comparative work of Arthur K. Moore
and James I. Wimsatt.[24] The constitution of artistic originality not in terms of
absolute, ex nihilo novelty but in terms of the transformation and betterment
of a known model was in itself a shift that undermined the historical narrative
of artistic "waning" from the troubadour apogee. Less emphasis on originality per se—and a shift of attention from authors to readers—helped Machaut
to be seen instead as maintaining a creative engagement with his own literary
heritage (courtly love topoi from the troubadours, combined with the narrative strategies of the *Roman de la Rose* and *Ovide moralisé*), while at the same
time striking his own coin from this material in a way that reflected changed
social circumstances, audience expectation, and reading practices.

William Calin's 1974 monograph devoted to Machaut's narrative dits aided
their entry into the modern canon of Middle French literary works by offering a detailed chapter on each of them.[25] In the early 1990s both Calin and

22. Kittredge, "Guillaume de Machaut and the Book of the Duchess," 7. On the ongoing influence of these views (and a critique of them), see Steven Davis, "Guillaume de Machaut, Chaucer's *Book of the Duchess,* and the Chaucer Tradition," *Chaucer Review* 36 (2002): 391–93.

23. A similar trajectory can be seen in the musicological field at a similar period with the composers Johann Sebastian Bach and Antonio Vivaldi. Vivaldi's stock rose throughout the twentieth
century because of Bach's transcriptions of his concertos, initially accepted as Bach's own work
and criticized when found to be Vivaldi's; they were subsequently reevaluated as good in their
own right. See Michael Talbot, "Antonio Vivaldi," in *Grove.*

24. See the historiographical comments in Helen Philips, "Fortune and the Lady: Machaut,
Chaucer and the Intertextual 'Dit,'" *Nottingham French Studies* 38 (1999): 120–22. Arthur K.
Moore, "Chaucer's Use of Lyric as an Ornament of Style," *Comparative Literature* 3 (1951):
32–46, credits Machaut with being superior to Froissart as a poet because his use of interpolated
lyric is more judicious. He nevertheless finds only the lay in *Remede* to be instrumental to the narrative and thinks even that too long: *Remede*'s complaint is "tedious" and "patently digressive"
(41), and the other lyrics prolong the scene unnecessarily. In Moore's view, Chaucer contrasts with
both Froissart and Machaut in making his use of interpolated lyric fit its narrative frame perfectly.
James I. Wimsatt, "The Apotheosis of Blanche in *The Book of the Duchess,*" *Journal of English
and Germanic Philology* (1967): 26–44, treats Machaut fairly neutrally and seriously but strives
to show how Chaucer goes beyond his model both in combining textbook *descriptiones* that he
takes from *Behaingne* and *Remede* to give a less "stereotypical" account, and in exploiting latent
Marian language in the descriptions of the beloved, whose possibilities are, according to Wimsatt,
not followed up by Machaut (see especially "The Apotheosis of Blanche," 29).

25. William Calin, *A Poet at the Fountain: Essays on the Narrative Verse of Guillaume de
Machaut* (Lexington, 1974).

Wimsatt further buttressed Machaut's status through powerful comparative studies of the French and English poetic traditions, effectively extending the long-established value accorded in English studies to Chaucer, Gower, and their English contemporaries to include their French models, influences, and contemporaries.[26] In this way the Chaucerian pinnacle was planed off so that, rather than being seen as lesser prototypes for the first flowering of great literature in recognizable English, fourteenth-century French writers—Machaut chief among them—began to loom larger in merit by virtue of their influence and pathbreaking originality, albeit an originality now somewhat differently constituted.

Once the hierarchical relation between Chaucer and his models had been thus dismantled, the well-established critical interest in Chaucer's creative play with the first-person narrator was turned back onto Machaut's own works, enabling a new appreciation of his narrative strategies. Kevin Brownlee's 1984 monograph focused on Machaut's narrative personae in the dits with particular attention paid to the two most substantial: the *Remede de Fortune* and the *Voir dit*. Focus on the *Voir dit* was nothing new (although a complete modern edition was, at this time, still lacking), but viewed through poststructuralist lenses, the poem was no longer the true story of Machaut's affair with a young girl (as it had been for nearly all nineteenth- and early-twentieth-century commentators from Tarbé onward), but a highly confected play with historical truth and personal authenticity as a commentary on the making of fiction and the meaning of art.[27]

The reconstitution of originality as the transformation and betterment of a known model eventually also allowed Machaut's lyric poetry to be appreciated in itself, rather than viewed as a formulaic restatement of sentiments expressed with greater authenticity and freshness by the troubadours a couple of centuries earlier, although as Earp comments, "appreciation of Machaut's lyrical poetry has been slower to develop than appreciation—or at least tolerance—of his narrative poetry."[28] The lyrics rarely contain historical or autobiographical information of the kind that at least generated interest in (if not quite appreciation of) the dits in the eighteenth and nineteenth centuries. Although some lyrics from the *Voir dit, Loange,* and music sections were published in the two volumes by Tarbé, the selection of these is in itself suggestive of the kinds of interest that lyrics held in the nineteenth century. In the earlier

26. William Calin, *The French Tradition and the Literature of Medieval England* (Toronto, 1994); James I. Wimsatt, *Chaucer and His French Contemporaries: Natural Music in the Fourteenth Century* (Toronto, 1991).

27. An important early exception to this belief in the truth of the *Voir dit* is Georg Hanf, "Über Guillaume de Machauts *Voir Dit,*" *Zeitschrift für romanische Philologie* 22 (1898): 145–96, which argues that the poem was fictional. On the issue of the truth of the *Voir dit*, see the extensive list of references in Earp, *Guillaume de Machaut,* 228, under "autobiography," and also Cerquiglini-Toulet, "Le Voir Dit mis à nu par ses éditeurs, même."

28. Earp, *Guillaume de Machaut,* 256.

publication, aside from the poems that were included because they are part of the *Voir dit,* poems with anagrams or gnomic statements or in rondeau form were favored disproportionately above the balade, even though the balade is more representative of Machaut's work in lyric forms.[29] Among the relatively few balades chosen for inclusion were those ones atypically political, like *Donnez, signeurs* (B26), which beseeches an audience of lords to exercise largesse, or personal, like *Dou memoire* (Lo253), which bemoans the speaker's affliction with gout.[30] Tarbé's later publication, which prints Toute Belle's lyrics from the *Voir dit* augmented with feminine-voiced lyrics from the *Loange* and music sections, better represents the diversity and proportions of Machaut's lyric output, although this is because the rationale for collection is unrelated to the content or forms of the poems in question, but merely reflects their use of the feminine voice and Tarbé's historical interest in their presumed author, Agnes of Navarre.[31]

Even once the lyrics had been properly edited in 1909 by Chichmaref, more serious consideration was slow in coming. Tarbé's books continued to be the main source for some writers, up to and including Barbara Tuchmann's 1978 blockbuster, *A Distant Mirror: The Calamitous 14th Century.*[32] The first edition of Gustav Gröber's volume *Grundriss der romanischen Philologie* in 1902 made use of Tarbé for its discussion of lyrics, as well as of the editions of *Prise* and *Voir dit* by Mas Latrie and Paris, respectively.[33] By contrast, Stefan Hofer's 1933 revision and expansion of this volume drew on the publications of Hoepffner and Chichmaref, which had appeared in the interim. Its discussion of the lyrics focuses on their themes and is atypically

---

29. Tarbé, *Les oeuvres de Guillaume de Machault,* prints eighteen rondeaux and sixteen balades, of which thirteen rondeaux and twelve balades are not from the *Voir dit.* This rather even representation of these two forms compares to Machaut's "lifetime total" of 246 balades and 105 rondeaux, a ratio of rather more than two to one; see Earp, *Guillaume de Machaut,* 241–42. No virelays, lays, complaints, or chansons royals are given.

30. This is a generalization rather than categorically true. More typical, amorous balades are represented by the inclusion of *Se vos regars, douce dame, n'estoit* (Lo9, on the lady's look), *Je ne sui pas de tel valour* (Lo11), *Trop est crueus li maus de jalousie* (Lo51, on jealousy), *Las! amours me soloit estre* (Lo52), *On ne puet riens savoir si proprement* (Lo192, against ready belief in gossip), *Amis, je t'aporte nouvelle* (Lo212, feminine voice), *Onques mes cuer ne senti* (Lo218), and *Riches d'amour* (B5), although of these Lo11 and Lo52 have two-line refrains, a relative rarity in Machaut's work.

31. Tarbé, *Poésies d'Agnès de Navarre-Champagne,* gives examples of the complaint, chanson royal, and lay as well as the three *formes fixes.* The balade predominates (with thirteen examples), followed by the rondeau and then the virelay. This suggests that Machaut's use of the feminine voice is generally in proportion across at least those three *formes fixes.*

32. See Barbara Wertheim Tuchman, *A Distant Mirror: The Calamitous 14th Century* (New York, 1978), 209, for a mention of the *Voir dit* that relies on Tarbé, *Les oeuvres de Guillaume de Machault.*

33. See Gustav Gröber, ed., *Grundriss der romanischen Philologie,* 2 vols. (Strasbourg, 1902), 1:1042–47.

informative and largely free from negative value judgments.[34] Machaut's use of a more personal tone is also praised by Hofer, and is mentioned approvingly in a Dutch dissertation from 1936, which compares Machaut's works with those of Christine de Pizan.[35] Although for Hofer, Machaut's preoccupation with formal features such as rhyme, wordplay, and allegory are deemed sometimes excessive and lacking any relation to the content of the poetry, his innovations in these areas make him second to none as a wordsmith and place him at the head of a new school, retrospectively called the "second rhetoric."[36]

Nevertheless, to most writers in the first fifty years after Machaut's lyrics were fully edited, the more typical poetry of refined loving that dominates his lyrics seemed an unnecessary and—to then contemporary gender sensitivities—rather emasculated fiction, which produced inauthentic sentiment bound up in fairly mechanical verse. In the section of a 1921 history of French literature from its origins to Ronsard covering lyric from 1328 to 1437, the section author, Alfred Jeanroy, finds in Machaut's lyrics "banality, prolixity, and platitude" of a kind never before seen in such abundance: "These deficiencies abound in the two enormous volumes where the innumerable balades, rondeaux, lais, chansons royals, and motets are laid out, from which it would be hard to extract twenty lines worth citing."[37] In Bartlett Whiting's view, Machaut simply lacked the skill to write balades that avoided "a satiety bordering on nausea," producing instead "artificial puling melancholy and histrionic love-sick whining[,]...tiresome adulation and namby-pamby praise."[38] Jeanroy scolds Machaut for a lack of originality; Whiting chides his lack of masculinity. The scant interest in the courtly love content of these poems was

34. Stefan Hofer, ed., *Geschichte der mittelfranzösischen Literatur*, 2nd ed., 2 vols. *Vers- und Prosadichtung des 14. Jahrhunderts, Drama des 14. und 15. Jahrhunderts* (Berlin, 1933), 1:14–29.

35. Ibid., 27. Christine's personal revelations are judged to go beyond those of Machaut in Johanna Catharina Schilperoort, *Guillaume de Machaut et Christine de Pisan: (Étude comparative)* (The Hague, [1936]), 130. Earp, *Guillaume de Machaut*, 256, notes that this study contains a similarly dispassionate discussion of the lyrics' themes at 19–47. As a comparative study it is remarkably free of negative value judgments and frankly considers Machaut a master of the art of poetry.

36. This designation is drawn from the title of two fifteenth-century poetic treatises and applied by extension to several others from a similar period in M. E. Langlois, ed., *Recueil d'Arts de séconde rhétorique* (Paris, 1902).

37. Alfred Jeanroy, "La littérature de langue française des origines à Ronsard," in *Histoire des lettres: Premier volume, Des origines à Ronsard,* ed. Joseph Bédier, Alfred Jeanroy, and François Joseph Picavet (Paris, 1921), 465: "On comprend que les poésies écloses dans cette atmosphère artificielle soient d'une insigne faiblesse. Jamais la banalité, la prolixité, la platitude n'ont sévi plus cruellement qu'alors. Ces défauts s'étalent dans les deux énormes volumes où s'alignent á perte de vue les innombrables ballades, rondeaux, lais, chansons royales et motets de Guillaume de Machaut, dont on aurait peine à extraire vingt vers valant d'être cités."

38. Bartlett J. Whiting, "Froissart as Poet," *Mediaeval Studies* 8 (1946): 209–10, cited in Earp, *Guillaume de Machaut*, 256.

not aided by their highly stylized formal aspects. Neither Jeanroy nor Whiting can stomach the conventionality of this poetry's diction, content, and forms; in this they were at one with the vast majority of commentators before the twin influences of the formalism of Belgian poet and Romanist Robert Guiette and Daniel Poirion's 1965 book *Le poète et le prince*.[39]

At the opposite pole to Jeanroy's lament that Machaut's standardization of the so-called *formes fixes* contributed to further sterilizing a kind of poetry already much impoverished is the rarer treatment of his formal techniques as innovative.[40] Among the few critics who managed to display sensitivity to formal features in themselves is Guiette, who tackled Jeanroy's criticisms head-on. Guiette points out that it would be strange for poets to continue writing the same songs for a century and a half and refer to the genre in reverential terms if it was truly as bad as all that. Earlier critics had seemed surprised that Machaut was clearly so well regarded in his own day.[41] Guiette, however, is prepared to accept the late medieval interest in these poems as indicative of an aesthetic that prized form over content (without properly being able to separate the two) and the laying out of formal skill above the promotion of personal passion. For the appreciation of such work, the audience was highly attuned to the stylistic play of the poet rather than focusing on either emotional authenticity or originality of content.[42]

In retrospect these two critical tendencies with regard to Machaut's lyric—Jeanroy/Whiting versus Guiette—represent the twin aesthetics of romanticism and modernism in the first half of the twentieth century.[43] Romantic focus on original material and emotional expression noted only the repetitiveness of courtly love topoi. Modernism saw instead a valuable play with formal elements whose meaningful manipulation was enabled rather than precluded by the context of conventional constraints. Guiette's 1946 lecture "D'une poésie formelle en France au Moyen Âge" (On Formalist Poetry in Medieval France) was published in part in 1949 but seems to have exerted significant influence

39. Daniel Poirion, *Le poète et le prince: L'évolution du lyrisme courtois de Guillaume de Machaut à Charles d'Orléans* (Grenoble, 1965). Guiette's influence seems to have followed Robert Guiette, *Questions de littérature* (Ghent, 1960), although the essays in it had been delivered and published in the 1940s; on Guiette, see further discussion later in this chapter.

40. Jeanroy, "La littérature de langue française," 465–66.

41. Switten, *Music and Poetry in the Middle Ages*, 45, 47, notes the similarly surprised responses of Paulin Paris in the "Notice" to his edition of the *Voir dit* and Petit de Julleville in Louis Petit de Julleville, ed., *Histoire de la langue et de la littérature française des origines à 1900*, 8 vols. (Paris, 1896–1899).

42. Robert Guiette, "D'une poésie formelle en France au Moyen Âge," *Revue des sciences humaines* (1949): 61–64.

43. Guiette is included in the list of scholars who "sought a kind of *proof using the Middle Ages* of conceptions that were really theirs," in Michel Zink, "La poésie comme récit," in *Cultural Performances in Medieval France: Essays in Honor of Nancy Freeman Regalado*, ed. Eglal Doss-Quinby, Roberta L. Krueger, and E. Jane Burns (Woodbridge, 2007), 4.

only after its fuller publication in 1960, 1972, and 1978.[44] The influence of music (not medieval music but modernist music) on Guiette's view of medieval poetry as principally formal structure rather than meaningful semantic content has been insufficiently noted and will be examined further in the discussion of interdisciplinary study of Machaut's songs.

Guiette has been identified as having been the stimulus to a "series of largely independent but strikingly convergent studies" appearing in the late 1950s and early 1960s in which "the traditional, somewhat fruitless search for 'sincerity,' thematic originality, and realistic observation was replaced by the quest for meaningful patterns, significant formal structures which in themselves were to reveal and realize the aesthetic intentions of the trouvère, troubadour, or later medieval court poet."[45] His most direct influence is on Roger Dragonetti and, especially, Paul Zumthor, for whom the expression "I love" in medieval lyric simply means "I sing"; the content is an excuse for the form.[46] But perhaps his most important influence for Machaut's lyrics among mid-twentieth-century writings was on Daniel Poirion's study *Le poète et le prince*, which focuses on understanding how changing patterns of patronage affected courtly poetry. Within this framework Poirion offers a story of the evolution of its forms, style, and language in the period from Machaut to Charles d'Orléans which not only is free of derogation but also sets up a critical approach for ongoing appreciation.[47]

As mentioned, in the late 1970s and 1980s the rehabilitation of lyric was aided by the new appreciation of Machaut's narrative poetry; ultimately both

---

44. The original essay, Guiette, "D'une poésie formelle en France au Moyen Âge," was reprinted in his faculty's celebratory volume, Guiette, *Questions de littérature*, 9–18, with two supplementary notes on 19–23. Further reprints are contained in Robert Guiette, *D'une poésie formelle en France au Moyen Âge* (Paris, 1972) (which gathers various papers given between 1930 and 1940, along with this conference paper, which it details as having originally been given in February 1946 at the Institut des Hautes Études in Brussels and then, on 13 March 1947, at the Faculté des lettres at the University of Lille). See also Robert Guiette, *Robert Guiette: Forme et senefiance*, ed. Jean Dufournet, Marcel de Grève, and Herman Braet (Geneva, 1978), 16–24.

45. A. R. Press, review of *D'une poésie formelle en France au Moyen Âge* by Robert Guiette, *Modern Language Review* 70 (1975): 872.

46. Paul Zumthor, *Essai de poétique mediévale* (Paris, 1972); and see the comments in Zink, "La poésie comme récit," 6, and Zink's preface in Paul Zumthor, *Essai de poétique mediévale, novelle édition: Avec une préface de Michel Zink et un texte inédit de Paul Zumthor* (Paris, 2000). See also Dragonetti's essay in the *Festschrift* for Guiette, Roger Dragonetti, "'La poésie...ceste musique naturele': Essai d'exégèse d'un passage de L'*Art de Dictier* d'Eustache Deschamps," in *Fin du moyen âge et renaissance: Mélanges de philosophie française offerts à Robert Guiette*, ed. Henri Pirenne (Antwerp, 1961), 49–64.

47. Many of the reviews of Poirion's book comment on his overturning of then prevailing orthodoxies concerning the decline or decadence of poetry in this period; see, for example, the reviews of its dedicatee, Pierre Le Gentil (*Romania* 88 [1967]: 548–57), or Robert Guiette (*Revue belge de philologie et d'histoire* 46 [1968]: 533–35), or Pierre Jodogne (*Studi francesi* 10 [1966]: 296–99). An account of the interaction between interest in medieval lyric and specific shifts in critical modes of enquiry in the 1970s and 1980s can be found in Switten, *Music and Poetry in the Middle Ages*, 133–35.

Machaut's lyrics and narratives proved open to the new emphasis on his play with narrative personae, especially in the work of Kevin Brownlee and Jacqueline Cerquiglini (later Cerquiglini-Toulet).[48] Machaut's lyrics began to be viewed as reflective of a new interaction between narrative and lyric modes. On the one hand, lyrics were read as having been organized into sequences with narrative potential: the proto-narrative clusters of poems that Poirion identified in the *Loange,* for example, suggested it was not a miscellaneous lyric collection but a subtly organized one that formed a model for later writers of lyric cycles.[49] On the other hand, his narratives had intercalated lyrics that, rather than being chosen to fit the narrative—as had been the case with thirteenth-century uses of earlier lyrics and refrains by other composers in such instances—actually form a pre-extant core around which the narrative is built, as most obviously in the *Remede* and *Voir dit.*[50] In both narrative and lyric, Machaut's narrativization of the lyric was read to fit with his overall interest in textuality, bookmaking, and scribal organization: both the duplication of lyrics as a form of cueing and the building of narratives around them are embryonically representative of Machaut's attitude toward the organization of the book as a whole.

Poirion's work has led to a general acceptance of the useful, instructive, entertaining, and thought-provoking function of Machaut's poetry for his medieval audiences (whether readers or listeners). This realization has stimulated a new appreciation of Machaut's use of both interpolated lyrics and mythical or biblical exempla, which commentators before the mid-twentieth century almost universally thought excessive, boring, unnecessarily digressive, and a way of spinning out the story for a poet who lacked original material or inspiration.[51] The sources for exempla had been noted in the early twentieth

48. See Kevin Brownlee, *Poetic Identity in Guillaume de Machaut* (Madison, 1984); and Jacqueline Cerquiglini, *"Un engin si soutil": Guillaume de Machaut et l'écriture au XIVe siècle* (Geneva, 1985); more recently, see Didier Lechat, *"Dire par fiction": Métamorphoses du Je chez Guillaume de Machaut, Jean Froissart et Christine de Pizan* (Paris, 2005); Sarah Kay, *The Place of Thought: The Complexity of One in Late Medieval French Didactic Poetry* (Philadelphia, 2007); and Helen J. Swift, "The Poetic I," in *A Companion to Guillaume de Machaut: An Interdisciplinary Approach to the Master,* ed. Deborah McGrady and Jennifer Bain (Leiden, forthcoming).

49. On the proto-narrative *Loange* materials, see the identification of poems based on the same theme in Poirion, *Le poète et le prince,* 204; Nigel Wilkins, ed., *Guillaume de Machaut: La louange des dames* (Edinburgh, 1972), 14–17; and links between the *Loange* and the *Voir dit* in Cerquiglini, *"Un engin si soutil,"* 34–39. Later examples include the *Cent balades* of Jean le Seneschal and those by Christine de Pizan, Gower, and Charles d'Orleans; see Earp, *Guillaume de Machaut,* 199.

50. See Cerquiglini, *"Un engin si soutil,"* 23–49 (chap. 1).

51. See Moore, "Chaucer's Use of Lyric," 32, 39. The omission of the entire Polyphemus and Galatea episode from Paris's edition has been mentioned in note 14. The renewed interest in the refraction of classical tales through late medieval lenses has placed the second half of the *Voir dit* more securely in critical view. See, for example, Jacqueline Cerquiglini-Toulet, "Polyphème ou l'antre de la voix dans le *Voir dit* de Guillaume de Machaut," in *"L'hostellerie de pensée": Études*

century, when interest concentrated on the fact of their borrowing rather then their function, finding most to derive from the French moralized version of Ovid's *Metamorphoses,* the *Ovide moralisé.*[52] Nevertheless, the more recent willingness to set aside what pleases contemporary readers and credit instead what seems to have pleased audiences in the past has led critics to a renewed interest in these "digressions," which are now seen as rhetorically forceful stories.[53] They also tap into postmodern awareness of the intertextuality of all texts—medieval texts almost by definition.[54]

In summary, therefore, the engagement with Machaut's verbal texts in the period since his modern rediscovery has seen the replacement of Machaut the sometime historical chronicler and prolix third-rate versifier with Machaut the arch-reflector of a new culture of textuality based on a play with forms, narrative, and first-person personae.[55] These polarized Machauts have influenced and been influenced by—not always in chronological synch—both the understanding of Machaut's musical text and the engagement with his physical texts: the illuminations in his books, and the books themselves. I first treat these two disciplinary strands in isolation before looking at the interaction of modern disciplines in the ongoing construction of the modern Machaut.

Machaut's Music: From Opaque Trace to Transparent Harmony

Scholarly engagement with Machaut's music lagged somewhat behind the interest in his verbal texts, although the two disciplines share some basic contours in their critical trajectory. A teleology inherited from the eighteenth-century

---

sur l'art littéraire au Moyen Age offertes à Daniel Poirion, ed. Michel Zink et al. (Paris, 1995), 105–18; and Renate Blumenfeld-Kosinski, *Reading Myth: Classical Mythology and Its Interpretations in Medieval French* (Stanford, 1997).

52. Kevin Brownlee, "Literary Intertextualities in 14th-Century French Song," in *Musik als Text: Bericht über den Internationalen Kongreß der Gesellschaft für Musikforschung, Freiburg im Breisgau 1993,* ed. Hermann Danuser and Tobias Plebuch (Kassel, 1998), vol. 1, 295, suggests that "in terms of literary critical history, the key distinction would thus be between the 'source study' in which the presence of text 1 in text 2 is simply described; and intertextual analysis in which the *function* of this presence is the primary concern."

53. See especially Blumenfeld-Kosinski, *Reading Myth;* and Kay, *The Place of Thought.*

54. See Brownlee, "Literary Intertextualities in 14th-Century French Song." These *exempla* point elsewhere and carry more meaning with them than they appear to have within themselves per se. They can comment on a situation, lend ambiguity, allow subtle criticism, and offer advice; see the comments on the story of "How the Crow Turned Black" in *Voir dit* in chapter 5; see also Earp, *Guillaume de Machaut,* 200.

55. See also Sylvia Huot, *From Song to Book: The Poetics of Writing in Old French Lyric and Lyrical Narrative Poetry* (Ithaca, 1987); Douglas Kelly, *Medieval Imagination: Rhetoric and the Poetry of Courtly Love* (Madison, 1978); Nicolette Zeeman, "The Lover-Poet and Love as the Most Pleasing 'Matere' in Medieval French Love Poetry," *Modern Language Review* 83 (1988): 141–82.

antiquarian and literary interest in courtly love caused Machaut's musical works to be viewed initially from a perspective similar to that for the lyric texts, in which the monophonic songs of the trouvères represented the high point of the folkloric simplicity of a naïve and pastoral French Middle Ages. In such a context Machaut was a musical and lyric epigone. This interpretation was complemented increasingly through the nineteenth century by a contrary perspective from the nascent discipline of "musical archaeology," or musicology, which conducted a quest for the origins of the crowning glory of Western music history—tonal counterpoint—as seen in its key historical monuments (in the case of the Middle Ages, settings of the Mass ordinary). The historical goal of musicology was not the courtly song of the High Middle Ages but the masterworks of German music from Bach to Beethoven (or Brahms). In contrast to literary studies, whose focus tended to be on earlier courtly love lyrics, musicology saw Machaut as a very primitive forerunner rather than a Johnny-come-lately. Neither historical perspective provided a good fit. Moreover, the musical substance of Machaut's works posed far greater technical challenges than that of the lyrics. The sheer difficulty of reading the notation of the sources at first delayed any assessment of the music and then compounded negative prejudices about such a primitive period in music history, resulting in unaccommodating judgments that persisted until the twentieth century.

Eighteenth-century French music scholars took particular interest in the trouvères rather than the troubadours, largely because of those musicians' unalloyed Frenchness.[56] In the Enlightenment period songs were often published in editions that paraphrased their texts according to the principles of *copie réduite*. Where musical notation was given, it was heavily pastiched in versions with added piano accompaniment, metrical framework, and accidentals that defined the melody in anachronistic terms of major or minor keys.[57] In short, this music was reimagined in a manner that stressed simplicity, naïveté, and a romantic pastoralism that appealed to a largely noble, urban readership at the dawn of the industrial revolution.[58] Machaut's music was not treated to such editions, in part because he did not feature in the chief manuscripts of trouvère song, but also because the emphasis of antiquarians was on the originators of a French song tradition; as a later emulator, Machaut had no such importance within their historical narrative.[59]

---

56. Only one notated troubadour song was published in the eighteenth century, and that was in England rather than France. See Haines, *Eight Centuries of Troubadours and Trouvères*, 89–154 (chap. 3, "Enlightened Readers").

57. For a description of this practice in Saint-Palaye's edition of *Aucassin et Nicolette*, see ibid., 94–95.

58. Ibid., 125–41.

59. The composers who formed a particular focus were thus Thibaut de Champagne and the Châtelain de Coucy. See also ibid., 104–36 passim. Annette Kreutziger-Herr, however, in *Ein Traum vom Mittelalter: Die Wiederentdeckung mittelalterlicher Musik in der Neuzeit* (Cologne,

Jean-Baptiste-Bonaventure de Roquefort-Flaméricourt's 1815 book on the state of French poetry in the twelfth and thirteenth centuries presents an excellent summary of what the preceding century of antiquarianism had gleaned and construed regarding French medieval song.[60] Referring the reader to editions by Burney and Laborde, he comments that the melodies of the troubadour king of Navarre (that is, Thibaut de Navarre) are such agreeable and facile songs that one regrets that they were ever forgotten, and he reports a number of modern opera composers who have made use of them as a means of rejuvenating their own style and forms.[61] Roquefort-Flaméricourt then cites the list of musical instruments in Machaut's *Remede* as part of his discussion of the instruments that were developed in the Middle Ages. Despite acknowledging that this passage has been cited before (notably by Christian Kalkbrenner in 1802, discussed later in this chapter), Roquefort-Flaméricourt argues that it has not been satisfactorily explained, either because literary commentators are not really musicians, or because musicians do not read Old French literature. His discussion of all the instruments mentioned is much more ample than the footnote explanations given in Kalkbrenner, and integrates evidence from Machaut's own *Dit de la harpe* into the discussion of the harp.[62] The most influential aspect of Roquefort-Flaméricourt's book for music, however, was the fact that he heralded Adam de la Halle's *Jeu de Robin et de Marion* as the "oldest *opéra-comique* in existence."[63] Musicians from François-Joseph Fétis onward followed Roquefort's lead to extol the virtues of Adam de la Halle, whose *Jeu* served as one of the key "sources of Frenchness" throughout the nineteenth century.[64] According to Katharine Ellis, the reception of Adam's play "presents, in microcosm, the conflict in French musical historiography between learnedness and spontaneity, and between artifice and naturalness, especially when it came to defining the key qualities of a national music."[65] Its melodies were deemed either to have created folksong or, by later writers

---

2003), 127–28, notes a much later arrangement of *Douce dame jolie* (V4) as a strophic song with piano accompaniment in a collection by Jean Baptiste Weckerlin from 1857.

60. Jean-Baptiste Bonaventure de Roquefort-Flaméricourt, *De l'état de la poésie françoise dans les xiie et xiiie siècles* (Paris, 1815).

61. Ibid., 103–4. See also Haines, *Eight Centuries of Troubadours and Trouvères*, 130–40, on Grétry and others.

62. Roquefort-Flaméricourt, *De l'état de la poésie françoise*, 105–31; the mention of the *Harpe* starts on 113. Both these sections had earlier been briefly discussed in Christian Kalkbrenner, *Histoire de la musique* (Paris, 1802), 103–6.

63. See Katharine Ellis, *Interpreting the Musical Past: Early Music in Nineteenth-Century France* (New York, 2005), 165; and Daniel Leech-Wilkinson, *The Modern Invention of Medieval Music: Scholarship, Ideology, Performance* (Cambridge, 2002), 17, both citing *Revue musicale* spécimen (February 1827): 9.

64. Ellis, *Interpreting the Musical Past*, 164–70.

65. Ibid., 166. Ellis diagnoses a rift in the approach to Adam and later medieval music in general following the reception of the *Jeu*: Fétis differentiated the positively marked naïveté of its melodies from the artificial counterpoint of Adam's polyphony; in this he was followed by Bottée

reversing cause and effect, to reflect folksongs that preexisted their deployment in the *Jeu*.[66]

Machaut did not write any music dramas. Although a diplomatic transcription of one of his monophonic songs was published in a supplement to Kalkbrenner's *Histoire de la musique* in 1802, in line with the general disregard of his lyric verse at this time, his monophonic music was paid scant attention.[67] Kalkbrenner's supplement, however, also provided a transcription that would generate the beginnings of lasting interest in Machaut as a composer. As the musical antiquarianism of the eighteenth century mutated into the more self-consciously scientific discipline of musicology in the nineteenth, it was to a kind of music which set him apart both from the trouvères and from Adam de la Halle that its practitioners turned: his polyphonic setting of the Mass ordinary. In the early decades of musicology the cyclic Mass began to occupy a position of prominence in the history of music—a place parallel in many ways to that of the symphony, as the designation of its setting of the separate ordinary items as "movements" suggests. Machaut's Mass now appeared at the forefront of interest in his musical works precisely because it appeared to be the earliest Mass cycle written by a single known composer and was in four parts (a standard texture for the nineteenth-century and the richest for the fourteenth). It was also believed to have been written for the coronation of Charles V in 1364, so was both datable and of historical and French national interest.[68]

This attention did not necessarily benefit Machaut in the critical assessment of his Mass, although—initially at least—this was because of inadequate understanding of the notation. Its modern transcription history opens with a number of abortive attempts and false starts. There are several eighteenth-century references to the presence of musical notation in the Machaut manuscripts discovered in the library of the Discalced Carmelites in Paris.[69] It was still possible, however, for a general history of music in 1801 to claim that

---

de Toulmon's extension of negative artificiality to Adam's chansons, leaving only the *Jeu* as a pure naturalistic national artwork.

66. Ibid., 168–69.

67. The *Remede*'s chanson royal *Joie, plaisance* (RF3) is given as table 4, figure 4, in Kalkbrenner, *Histoire de la musique*, supplement, with figure 5 offering a transcription into modern notation with an eight-to-one reduction in note values (that is, with semibreves transcribed as eighth notes).

68. This suggestion is made tentatively in a library catalogue of 1769; see Earp, *Guillaume de Machaut*, 43–44, and my discussion in chapter 6.

69. Caylus, "Premier mémoire." The full black figures in the musical notation are noted in Charles Burney, *A General History of Music, From the Earliest Ages to the Present Period to which is Prefixed a Dissertation on the Music of the Ancients*, vol. 2 (London, 1776–1789), 195; and Jean-Jacques Rousseau, *The Complete Dictionary of Music, Consisting of a Copious Explanation of All Words Necessary to a True Knowledge and Understanding of Music*, trans. William Waring (London, [1779]), 322.

not a note of the earliest composers of polyphony in France had survived.[70]
Moreover, the author of this book, Johann Sebastian Bach's biographer Johann Nikolaus Forkel, was referring not to anyone as early as Guillaume de
Machaut but only to the early-fifteenth-century composers Gilles Binchois
and Guillaume Du Fay. That he was mistaken in this assertion was confirmed
the following year when Kalkbrenner published a diplomatic facsimile of the
opening of Machaut's Gloria in his *Histoire de la musique*.[71] Kalkbrenner
explains that he chose this part—the section "Et in terra pax" to "Laudamus
te"—because the prevalence of equal note values makes it easier to get a sense
of the sonorities.[72] Having offered a transcription of the monophonic chanson
royal from the *Remede* in his table 4, figure 5, he balks at any transcription
into modern note values of Machaut's polyphony. His ideas of harmonic propriety probably led him to doubt the validity of any tentative transcription
that he might have started.

Before 1810 an adjunct professor at the Paris Conservatoire, François-Louis
Perne, used a number of music theory sources to aid him in preparing a table
of note values and a transcription of the Mass.[73] These tables betray, however,
a misunderstanding of two fundamental principles of notation in this period:
imperfection and alteration. These are principles governing the contextual interpretation of note lengths and simply do not exist in the modern system, in
which a note's graphic shape fixes its relative length with respect to all other
notes in a piece. Perne had imagined that a similarly modern, unit-based system for rhythmic notation was in play, and his tables show him insisting on a
one-to-one equivalence between medieval note shapes and modern note values. He had finished his transcription of the Mass by the time he gave a lecture
on it in 1814, illustrated by facsimiles from manuscript **A**, in which he noted
that the harmony of the Machaut Mass offered "no charm to a practiced ear.

70. Rudolf Bockholdt, "Französische und niederländische Musik des 14. und 15. Jahrhunderts," in *Musikalische Edition im Wandel des historischen Bewusstseins*, ed. Thrasybulos Georgos Georgiades (Kassel, 1971), 149, citing J. N. Forkel, *Allgemeine Geschichte der Musik*, 2
vols. (Leipzig, 1788–1801), 2:515 (originally published in 1801; repr. Graz, 1967). "Von den
allerältesten Praktikern, nehmlich von Wilhelm Dufay und Binchois, die nach Tinctoris Nachricht
den Contrapunkt zuerst in Frankreich ausgeübt haben sollen, ist nach aller Wahrscheinlichkeit
keine einzige Note mehr vorhanden." See also Earp, *Guillaume de Machaut*, 277; Lawrence Earp,
"Machaut's Music in the Early Nineteenth Century: The Work of Perne, Bottée de Toulmon,
and Fétis," in *Guillaume de Machaut: 1300–2000. Actes du Colloque de la Sorbonne 28–29
septembre 2000*, ed. Jacqueline Cerquiglini-Toulet and Nigel Wilkins (Paris, 2002), 9–40; and
Kreutziger-Herr, *Ein Traum vom Mittelalter*, 122–29.
71. Kalkbrenner, *Histoire de la musique*, table 5, fig. 1.
72. Ibid., 107.
73. Earp, "Machaut's Music," 14–15. Perne also attempted to transcribe Machaut's *David
Hocket*. He relied on Anonymous VII (*F-Pn*, lat. 6286) and the *Ars* of Franco (then critically mis-
dated) in Gerbert's edition as well as Lambertus's *Tractatus* (*F-Pn* 11266) and the Berkeley anonymous, all borrowed in manuscript versions from their owners at the time. See also Kreutziger-Herr,
Ein Traum vom Mittelalter, 125.

Its effect is hard and savage." He termed it a "bizarre assemblage" and a monstrosity, but excused it as nonetheless quite an achievement for the time in which it was written.[74]

Recovering Machaut's music meant being able to represent its notation in modern notation by a process that has only recently been accepted as more akin to translation than is usually imagined, even by those engaged in it.[75] Although medieval French notation looks similar to modern notation—it has notes of different graphic types showing different durations, placed on a five-line stave, which gives the key to their pitches—the similarities are fundamentally deceptive, since the norms of pitch and rhythm operate under radically different principles. Although Kalkbrenner's facsimile was reprinted several times, its notation of musical sounds was not convincingly "unscrambled" for decades. The misinterpretation of the notation compounded the assessment of Machaut's tonal (harmonic) practice as at best "scholastic" if not downright primitive, something that fit the then current teleological history of polyphonic art music, which was seen as having achieved a high point of harmonic perfection only in the modern period (from Bach onward). Kalkbrenner's preface lays out this perspective succinctly:

> Among the arts and sciences that have flourished in the eighteenth century, music is distinguished by the rapidity of its progress: it has reached a degree of perfection unknown to the people of antiquity. From the chaos of rules and principles has finally emerged a system whose clarity and precision facilitate the instruction of musicians. The scientific part of this art has been purged of antique dogmas and errors, and the artificial or mechanical part carried to a degree beyond which it would seem impossible to ascend.
>
> It must be remarked, however, that the civilized nations of Europe did not show the same ardor for progress in this art; one alone has constantly directed

---

74. Earp, *Guillaume de Machaut*, 278, citing from Paris, Institut de France, MS 931, 97. Soon after this lecture, in 1815, Perne proposed a collaboration with Roquefort-Flaméricourt on Machaut's life and works, but they were unable to secure funding for a long enough book, and the project foundered as the conservatoire closed in 1815–16 on account of political unrest. Much later, in retirement in 1830, Perne provided musical transcriptions for twenty-three songs of the Chatelain de Coucy with texts edited by the young Francisque Michel (Francisque Michel, ed., *Chansons du Châtelain de Coucy* [Paris, 1830], 141–95). The songs are rhythmicized and provided with piano accompaniment. The pair announced publication of Machaut's Mass in a two-volume edition of Machaut's poetry for the following year, but the July Revolution intervened, and the project never materialized. See also Haines, *Eight Centuries of Troubadours and Trouvères*, 161–62.

75. Bockholdt, "Französische und niederländische Musik," 155, for example, comments that Ludwig's edition of Machaut is an exercise in transliteration and merely exchanges one notation for another in the same way that a different alphabet or font does without affecting the pronunciation. This view is soundly critiqued in Margaret Bent, "Editing Early Music: The Dilemma of Translation," *Early Music* 22 (1994): 373–92.

to this goal all the efforts of its genius in disengaging all the chains of prejudice and superstition: that is the German nation.[76]

From a perspective so marked by evolutionary and nationalist thinking, Machaut's music, even correctly transcribed, was inclined to incomprehension; with mis-transcriptions to boot, it was doomed to derision.

In the first edition of his influential history of music in 1834, the head of the War Department in Vienna, Rafael Georg Kiesewetter, published the same excerpt of Machaut's Mass together with a second version of a transcription he had first attempted in a publication of 1831.[77] His book organized its historical account into a serious of musical "epochs," each headed by a number of central figures and leading to the true beginnings of polyphony with Dufay, who Kiesewetter believed had worked from the 1380s on. Machaut's Mass he scorned as "the work of a presuming dilettante, who, being an adept at versification, and having a superficial degree of knowledge in regard to most things, was bold enough to try his skill in a musical composition" in a period when French theory had progressed beyond its musical products.[78] When he published an extract from *Dous viaire* (R1) among other monophonic songs by Machaut in his history of the origins of opera, he appended Cicero's tag "O tempora, o mores!" to its parallel fifths and sevenths.[79]

When the retired Kiesewetter revised his history, he began to remove many of the judgments he had formerly made, including that about Machaut's dilettantism. Instead he noted that while Machaut was "beloved as a poet and as an inventor [*Erfinder*] of very well-crafted [*sehr artiger*] song melodies, he was also known as a bold [*kühner*] but not correct contrapuntist."[80] This change

---

76. Kalkbrenner, *Histoire de la musique*, iii–iv.

77. Rafael Georg Kiesewetter, *Geschichte der europaeisch-Abendlaendischen oder unsrer heutigen Musik: Darstellung ihres ursprunges, ihres Wachsthumes und ihres stufenweisen Entwickelung; von dem ersten Jahrhundert des Christenthums bis auf unsre Zeit*, 1st German ed. (Leipzig, 1834); this was translated into English as Rafael Georg Kiesewetter, *History of the Modern Music of Western Europe, from the First Century of the Christian Era to the Present Day, with an Appendix, Explanatory of the Theory of the Ancient Greek Music*, trans. Robert Müller, 1st English ed. (London, 1848), appearing after the second German edition had already been published in 1846. The English translation, however, is of the first edition, although it incorporates a few changes made by Kiesewetter specifically for it and includes some correspondence from him in its appendices. The changes mainly relate to English music, which has a slightly expanded role in the English translation. For the earlier publication of Kiesewetter's Mass transcription, see the musical supplement to Rafael Georg Kiesewetter, "Fünfter artikel: Die Noten-Tablatur oder Partitur der alten Contrapunctisten," *Allgemeine Musikalische Zeitung* 33 (1831): 366–76.

78. Kiesewetter, *History of the Modern Music of Western Europe*, 101.

79. Rafael Georg Kiesewetter, *Schicksale und Beschaffenheit des weltlichen Gesanges vom frühen Mittelalter bis zu der Erfindung des dramatischen Styles und den Anfängen der Oper* (Leipzig, 1841); see also Leech-Wilkinson, *The Modern Invention of Medieval Music*, 18–19, 159–61.

80. Rafael Georg Kiesewetter, *Geschichte der europaeisch-Abendlaendischen oder unsrer heutigen Musik: Darstellung ihres ursprunges, ihres Wachsthumes und ihres stufenweisen Entwickelung; von dem ersten Jahrhundert des Christenthums bis auf unsre Zeit*, 2nd rev. and

reflects the rise in Machaut's nineteenth-century stock, possibly betraying some influence from the studies of Auguste Bottée de Toulmon, librarian of the Conservatoire from 1831 to 1848, who had also made a transcription of the Mass in 1836, although this seems not to have been published.[81] But the damage was done as far as incipient musicology was concerned: when Kiesewetter's nephew August Wilhelm Ambros came to write his multivolume music history, his first volume on the music of antiquity (1862) was followed in 1864 by one titled *Die ersten Zeiten der neuen christlichen Welt und Kunst: Die Entwickelung des mehrstimmigen Gesanges* (The First Period of the New Christian World and Art: The Development of Polyphonic Song). Two subsequent volumes covering the Renaissance, divided at the figure of Palestrina, took their cue from Kiesewetter in situating the musical Renaissance in the period *after* Machaut, largely because Ambros too was unacquainted with the music of the fourteenth century.[82] Jessie Ann Owens speculates that "perhaps if Ambros had been aware of fourteenth-century music, particularly Italian music, when he published the third volume of his history in 1868, he might have set the beginnings not in the mid-fifteenth century, but rather a century earlier, with music's sister arts."[83] But ignorant of Machaut's textual links to Petrarch and Dante, not understanding his self-consciousness as a writer, and not knowing musical works by him or by his Italian counterparts, Ambros was unable to do other than follow his uncle's lead.[84]

Ambros's influence on the historiography of music lasted well into the twentieth century, not least because his periodization was in turn followed, at least initially, by Hugo Riemann; the first volume of his 1904–5 *Handbook of Music History* also confined Machaut to the dark backward and abysm of time that the Middle Ages then represented. Riemann gives far more space to the theorist Vitry and notes only Machaut's dreadful parallel progressions,

---

expanded ed. (Leipzig, 1846), 41. See also Leech-Wilkinson, *The Modern Invention of Medieval Music*, 159–61.

81. Leech-Wilkinson, *The Modern Invention of Medieval Music*, 160, hypothesizes that the amelioration of Machaut's position resulted from ever-improving transcriptions; Earp, "Machaut's Music," 20–23, reports that Bottée de Toulmon's 1836 transcription was more accurate, but notes that even Bottée de Toulmon's few published studies do not seem to have exercised a wide influence. In 1846 Kiesewetter still thought Machaut an incorrect contrapuntist, but credited him with artistic merit (as "bold"); this might suggest that an increase in the perception of his overall importance as an artist was more of a factor.

82. See Andrew Kirkman, "The Invention of the Cyclic Mass," *Journal of the American Musicological Society* 54 (2001): 1–47; Andrew Kirkman, "'Under Such Heavy Chains': The Discovery and Evaluation of Late Medieval Music before Ambros," *Nineteenth-Century Music* 24 (2000): 89–112; and Jessie Ann Owens, "Music Historiography and the Definition of 'Renaissance,'" *Notes* 47 (1990): 305–30, on the importance of Netherlandish composers to the originally posited "late" Renaissance in music.

83. Owens, "Music Historiography," 328.

84. See ibid., 327–29.

archaisms, and other "shortcomings" ("die Mängel").[85] Riemann's initial two-part volume *Altertum und Mittelalter (bis 1450),* published in 1904 and 1905, overlapped in press with important work by Friedrich Ludwig and Johannes Wolf, who between them finally brought the music of the fourteenth century to the musicological community in modern transcriptions that allowed its importance to begin to be appreciated.[86] Although Riemann mentions Wolf's transcriptions in the second part of volume 1, he was already stuck with the overall volume title *Antiquity and the Middle Ages (to 1450),* which replicates Ambros's dating. By 1907, when the third and final part of the second volume of the *Handbuch* appeared, Riemann had more fully absorbed Wolf's and Ludwig's scholarship. In a foreword to the final part, Riemann regrets that he could not now incorporate a redated inception of the musical Renaissance in the *Handbuch.*[87] His later (and far less influential) *Kleines Handbuch der Musikgeschichte* (Concise Handbook of Music History), published in 1908, duly places the end of the Middle Ages around 1300, effectively making Machaut a creature of the "early Renaissance."[88] Nevertheless, Machaut's music is still barely mentioned, while Philippe de Vitry's ascribed theoretical writings continue to occupy a prominent position in the new periodization.

By 1900, only a few fragments of Machaut's music had yet been printed, and these were often reprints of earlier extracts from the same very restricted selection from his musical works, serving only to place them at the primitive beginnings of both the cyclic Mass and contrapuntal writing. This limited availability stymied early appreciation of Machaut's music as music, leaving its main positive functions within musicological narratives as a document of the new notational style of the so-called French *ars nova,* and evidence of the rise of the Urtext-producing composer figure. The earliest near-complete edition of the Mass appeared in the service of the first of these contexts—as part of Johannes Wolf's 1904 history of mensural notation.[89] Wolf's work was influential almost immediately on standard history books and continued to

---

85. Hugo Riemann, *Handbuch der Musikgeschichte,* 5 vols. (Leipzig, 1904–1913), 1.2:336–341. The two parts of volume 1 are titled *Die Musik des Mittelalters (bis 1450).*

86. Johannes Wolf, "Florenz in der Musikgeschichte des 14. Jahrhunderts" (doctoral thesis, University of Berlin, 1902), extracts of which had appeared in a journal the previous year; see Owens, "Music Historiography," 327n79. See also Friedrich Ludwig, "Die mehrstimmige Musik des 14. Jahrhunderts," *Sammelbände der Internationalen Musikgesellschaft* 4 (1902): 16–69.

87. Owens, "Music Historiography," 328.

88. Hugo Riemann, *Kleines Handbuch der Musikgeschichte mit Periodisierung nach Stilprinzipien und Formen* (Leipzig, 1908).

89. Johannes Wolf, *Geschichte der Mensural-Notation von 1250–1460: Nach den theoretischen und praktischen Quellen,* 3 vols. (Leipzig, 1904). See Friedrich Ludwig, review of *Geschichte der Mensuralnotation von 1250–1460* by Johannes Wolf, *Sammelbände der Internationalen Musikgesellschaft* 6 (1904): 597–641.

exert this influence even after it was superseded, with respect to Machaut at least, by the work of its most detailed reviewer, Friedrich Ludwig.[90]

In the first quarter of the twentieth century, Ludwig radically enlarged the availability of modern transcriptions of Machaut's works, preparing the way for a more sympathetic appreciation of their musical aspect. Ludwig transcribed not only from what we now call the Machaut manuscripts but also from many other books of medieval polyphony and had, in his day, an unrivaled knowledge of the original sources and notation of the medieval polyphonic repertoire. From 1900 to 1903 Ludwig made transcriptions from the manuscript F-G, which he collated first with A and later, in 1910, with Vg, an earlier source that was subsequently unavailable to scholars for many years, thereby making his work with it even more valuable.[91] In 1904 his transcriptions of Machaut's works, together with those from other fourteenth-century manuscripts, allowed him to publish the first thorough overview of music from this period, including a discussion of Machaut's works in the context of contemporary liturgical music, motets, and songs.[92] In 1911 he provided editions to accompany the facsimiles of the lyric items in the *Remede de Fortune* for Ernst Hoepffner's edition of this dit in the second volume of his three-volume edition of Machaut's narrative poems for the Société des anciens textes français.[93] Between 1926 and 1929 three of Ludwig's own four-volume edition of Machaut's complete musical works were published.[94] The second volume contains an extensive introduction to the sources and their music. When Ludwig died in 1930, his student Heinrich Besseler completed the fourth volume, which contains Machaut's lays and Mass, the latter of which Ludwig had transcribed originally in November 1903.[95] This volume, however, finally appeared only in 1954, as Allied bombing had destroyed the original plates in 1943.[96] The Mass's fame so far superseded that of Machaut's other works that, impatient of its posthumous appearance

---

90. Wolf's work is the basis for the edition and discussion of *S'amours ne fait* (B1) and *Ma fin* (R14) in the influential textbook Riemann, *Handbuch der Musikgeschichte*, 2.1: 336–41. See my earlier discussion and also the comments in Earp, *Guillaume de Machaut*, 279.

91. This source (*olim* Marquis de Vogüe, and then New York, Wildenstein, no shelf mark) is in the collection of James E. and Elizabeth J. Ferrell, Kansas City, Missouri, and on loan (from ca. 2004) to Corpus Christi College, Cambridge.

92. Ludwig, "Die mehrstimmige Musik," 21 (Mass); 25–26, 29–30 (motets); 33–41 (songs).

93. Ernest Hoepffner, *Oeuvres de Guillaume de Machaut*, 3 vols. (Paris, 1908–1922), 2:405–13, and a separately paginated supplement of transcriptions with selected facsimiles, 25, 27. In the secondhand copy of this volume that I acquired in 2007, the pages of music were completely uncut, suggesting that the original owner was not interested in, or did not have the skills to read, the music. One suspects that this was a widespread phenomenon.

94. Friedrich Ludwig, ed., *Guillaume de Machaut: Musikalische Werke* (Leipzig, 1926–1954).

95. According to a manuscript in the Ludwig Nachlass; see Earp, *Guillaume de Machaut*, 280.

96. See ibid., 280 and n. 18.

in Ludwig's edition, several other scholars had already transcribed it in the interim.[97]

For the first time, Ludwig's edition made the complete musical works of Machaut available, and a marked increase in both performances and scholarly studies followed. As with the dits, the distribution of interest was uneven, although the earliest outcome was some relative decline of interest in the Mass in favor of the polyphonic songs and motets. Indeed, in his 1950 review of the three editions of the Mass published in 1948 and 1949, Willi Apel was able to characterize it as an early work, perhaps Machaut's earliest, whose "basic idiom...is one of compact and massive harmonies, of granitic construction, of summary condensation, while his motets and ballades are marvels of melodic fluidity, of delicate delineation, of refined looseness."[98] This view was far from universal, however, because Machaut's Mass itself gained a new yardstick for evaluation: in the context of twentieth-century musical modernism—especially in the middle decades of the century—the elements that had been perceived in the nineteenth century as contrapuntally crude were newly appreciated. In a 1950 review article on the same three editions treated by Apel, for example, Otto Gombosi considers it the "reviewer's duty and pleasure" to comment extensively on the "masterpiece."[99] Modernism had brought about what Arnold Schoenberg—despite claiming heritage from, and continuity with, the works of the nineteenth century—called the "emancipation of the dissonance," a move away from the rules of functional tonal harmony which had governed musical composition in the West since the development of the equally tempered scale in the first half of the eighteenth century.[100] The usefulness of this in appreciating Machaut's pre-tonal music was aided by the

97. Performances in the 1920s and 1930s may have been based on Ludwig's unpublished transcription; various incomplete publications followed in the late 1930s; see Kreutziger-Herr, *Ein Traum vom Mittelalter,* 241–43. It was twice published complete in 1948: Jacques Chailley, ed., *Guillaume de Machaut (1300–1377): Messe Nostre Dame dite du Sacre de Charles V (1364) à 4 voix égales* (Paris, 1948); and Armand Machabey, ed., *Messe Notre-Dame à quatre voix de Guillaume de Machault (130?-1377) transcrite en notation moderne* (Liège, 1948). The following year saw Guillaume De Van, ed., *Guglielmi de Mascaudio: Opera I, La Messe de Nostre Dame* (Rome, 1949). These three are compared and reviewed in Otto Gombosi, "Machaut's *Messe de Nostre-Dame,*" *Musical Quarterly* 36 (1950): 204–24. A further edition, based on that of De Van, appeared in 1953: Hanns Hübsch, ed., *Guillaume de Machault: La Messe de Nostre Dame* (Heidelberg, 1953).

98. Willi Apel, review of *Guillaume de Machaut (1300–1377): Messe Nostre Dame dite du Sacre de Charles V (1364) à 4 voix égales,* edited by Jacques Chailley, *Speculum* 26 (1951): 189–90.

99. Gombosi, "Machaut's *Messe,*" 208; such comments occupy the remaining pages of his article.

100. For the development of this scheme, see Harold S. Powers, "From Psalmody to Tonality," in *Tonal Structures in Early Music,* ed. Cristle Collins Judd, vol. 1 (New York, 1998), 275–340; for its demise, see Carl Dahlhaus, "Harmony, §3: Historical Development, (iv) Early 20th Century," in *Grove.* The phrase is from composer and theorist Arnold Schoenberg's *Harmonielehre* (1911).

budding discipline of ethnomusicology, which increasingly demonstrated to composers, performers, and listeners that Western tonality was not a given but a cultural construct.[101] Ethnomusicological evidence from outside the West and the changed practice within Western music were both symptoms of a new cultural relativism, which had the happy adjunct of treating the past as another country, thereby lessening the normative force of negative value judgments about Machaut's harmonic practice.

Pupils and followers of Schoenberg also manifested a compositional interest in numerical structure, which they applied first to sequences of pitches and then to rhythms in a manner that made Machaut's so-called isorhythmic motets and similarly structured sections of the Mass—in which the lowest voice exhibits sequences of both pitches and rhythms—seem to be on the cutting edge.[102] In 1948 George Perle wrote:

> It is not simply a coincidence that Schoenberg's twelve-tone technique and the isorhythmic motet of the *Ars Nova* period should be described in interchangeable terms. When the eternal categories of diatonic tonality began to be suspected of some historical limitations, when men began to wonder whether the tonal cadence wasn't really a man-made convention and neither given by God together with the moral law nor yet an attribute of nature and a physical law, only then a new horizon appeared that enlarged our view not only of what lay ahead but also of what lay behind us.
>
> In order to understand and to justify, if only historically, the integrative devices that Arnold Schoenberg makes use of, we cannot do better than to compare them with those that served the purposes of Guillaume de Machaut.[103]

Several important composers working in the first half of the twentieth century cited Machaut as an influence on their creative thinking with respect to the pre-compositional organization of parameters of pitch and rhythm: Pierre

---

101. See, for example, the universalist approach of Jacques Handschin, which Anna Maria Busse Berger, *Medieval Music and the Art of Memory* (Berkeley, 2005), 36, suggests might have resulted from his studies with the ethnomusicologist Erich Moritz von Hornbostel. Handschin's pupil Hans Oesch drew specific parallels between the fourteenth-century *ars nova* and the new music of the twentieth century. See Herman Sabbé, "Techniques médiévales en musique contemporaine: Histoire de la musique et sens culturel," *Revue belge de Musicologie / Belgisch Tijdschrift voor Muziekwetenschap* 34–35 (1980–81): 220; and Hans Oesch, "Die Ars Nova des XX. Jahrhunderts," *Melos* 34 (1967): 385–88.

102. See Sabbé, "Techniques médiévales en musique contemporaine," 226–28 and 232; and Andres Briner, "Guillaume de Machaut 1958/59 oder Strawinskys 'Movements for Piano and Orchestra,'" *Melos* 27 (1960): 184–86. This contrasts with the use composers made of Machaut's works as melodic material in the nineteenth century; see the comments on Joseph Gabriel Rheinberger's use of *J'aim la flour* (L2) in his organ sonata op. 193 of 1891 in Kreutziger-Herr, *Ein Traum vom Mittelalter*, 128–29.

103. George Perle, "Integrative Devices in the Music of Machaut," *Musical Quarterly* 34 (1948): 169.

Boulez and the Belgian serialist Karel Goeyvaerts encountered Machaut's music when studying with Olivier Messiaen in Paris in the late 1940s.[104]

Some scholars, while not implicitly linking medieval isorhythmic and twentieth-century serialist techniques, drew parallels between the *ars nova* of the fourteenth century and the radical change and renewal of musical material in the twentieth.[105] Machaut's further influence on Stockhausen and Stravinsky has been noted by scholars, while his wider influence on less well-known figures such as Eric Chisholm or Günther Bialas has been little studied.[106] Some of the conduits of influence were from composer to composer, whether teacher to pupil or peer to peer, but some influence seem to have filtered through the broader musicological community; the overlap between performances, musicologists, and composers makes a substantial overview of the medieval musical influence on modernism as a whole a scholarly desideratum.[107]

A large number of later-twentieth-century composers have written arrangements, responses to, or recomposed versions of pieces by Machaut.[108] These include imaginative orchestrations and arrangements of the *Hoquetus David*,[109] pop versions of motets and chansons,[110] citation of themes for

104. Mark Delaere, "Karel Goeyvaerts: A Belgian Pioneer of Serial, Electronic and Minimal Music," *Tempo: A Quarterly Review of Modern Music* 195 (1996): 2–3, reports that Goeyvaerts began his studies in 1947. See also Earp, *Guillaume de Machaut*, 281–82; Martin Zenck, "Karel Goeyvaerts und Guillaume de Machaut: Zum mittelalterlichen Konstruktivismus in der seriellen Musik der fünziger Jahre," *Die Musikforschung* 43 (1990): 336–51; Herman Sabbé, *Het muzikale serialisme als techniek en als denkmethode: een onderzoek naar de logische en historische samenhang van de onderscheiden toepassingen van het seriërend beginsel in de muziek van de periode 1950–1975* (Ghent, 1977); Sabbé, "Techniques médiévales en musique contemporaine."

105. See Sabbé, "Techniques médiévales en musique contemporaine"; and Oesch, "Die Ars Nova."

106. On Stockhausen and Machaut, see Giuliano d'Angiolini, "Le son du sens: Machaut, Stockhausen. La Ballade 34 et le Chant des Adolescents," *Analyse musicale* 9 (1987): 43–51; on Stravinsky and Machaut, see Briner, "Guillaume de Machaut 1958/59"; and Horst Weber, "Zu Strawinskys Machaut-Rezeption," in *Alte Musik als ästhetische Gegenwart: Bach, Händel, Schütz; Bericht über den Internationalen Musikwissenschaftlichen Kongress, Stuttgart 1985*, ed. Dietrich Berke and Dorothee Hanemann, vol. 2 (Kassel, 1987), 317–24. See Caroline Mears and James May, "Erik Chisholm," and Erik Levi, "Günther Bialas," both in *Grove*. The former entry notes that Chisholm's opera *The Canterbury Tales* "used a free modification of Schoenberg's 12-note technique and ingeniously incorporated Ars Nova devices and adaptations of 14th-century tunes."

107. A short overview of "Guillaume de Machaut in der Legitimationsstrategie der Avantgarde" is given in Kreutziger-Herr, *Ein Traum vom Mittelalter*, 244–50.

108. See the preliminary listing given in Earp, *Guillaume de Machaut*, 69–72. This does not include, for example, works by György Kurtág inspired by Machaut, whose music he probably knew under the auspices of Benjamin Rajeczky and László Dobszay's Schola Hungarica (Rachel Beckles Willson, personal communication; see also her "György Kurtág," in *Grove*).

109. Earp, *Guillaume de Machaut*, 69–72, lists among others a two-piano version by David Bedford, an elaborate orchestration by Harrison Birtwistle, and an arrangement for tuned percussion by Simon Holt.

110. Ibid., 70, cites Eve Beglarian's *Machaut in the Machine Age* (1986; rev. 1990).

their symbolic value (as in Luciano Berio's use of *Ma fin* [R14]),[111] basing variations on fragments of his musical material, setting his texts anew,[112] and making more general use of his material as a self-conscious homage to the composer.[113] Some of the modern works based on Machauldian material are little more than elaborate orchestrations and arrangements, a radically modernized kind of performance practice that aims to capture the originals' presumed spirit of novelty.

As for the rediscovered Machaut of musical modernism, the invocation of his name and the use of the term *ars nova* were principally a way of claiming older historical authority for the radical program of modernist works by undermining the claims to universality and transcendence that had been promulgated for Western music of the immediately preceding tradition. In calling French radio's official new music ensemble Ars Nova in 1963, its founder Marius Constant—someone rather opposed to the serialism of the 1950s and 1960s—was extending this authority beyond the use of specific compositional techniques.[114] Similarly, Stockhausen was viewed as having shared Machaut's allegedly mystical attitude toward text because he similarly sets it in a manner incomprehensible to the ears in his polytextual pieces.[115] While this might represent a verifiable aspect of Machaut's twentieth-century reception history, it arguably misrepresents Machaut's purpose, which, far from recommending incomprehension as a goal, uses it to prompt and then reward the later visual contemplation of texts as manifestations of *concordia discors*.[116] Just as earlier generations had dismissed Machaut's works as crude, modernist composers saw in him a conveniently inspirational "other" who allowed them to reject the lingering ghost of expressive romanticism and focus on structure. And this occurred in just the period when Robert Guiette—influenced in turn by the idea of medieval poetry as song and modernist ideas of music—was similarly rejecting a romantic focus on the content of Machaut's lyrics in favor of formalist interest in structure.

The link between cutting-edge modernity and music whose performance traditions had been interrupted and had to be reconstituted imaginatively

111. In *A-Ronne* (1974; rev. 1974–75); see Earp, *Guillaume de Machaut*, 70. On Machaut's rondeau, see my discussion in chapter 6.

112. Earp, *Guillaume de Machaut*, 70, lists Violeta Dionescu's *Amont* (1985), which sets *Tant com je seray* (VD59).

113. Earp, *Guillaume de Machaut*, 69–72, lists Siegfried Thiele's *Hommage* (1979). To this could be added Günther Bialas's "Chanson variée nach Guillaume de Machaut for Cembalo, Klavier." Bialas also wrote an opera based on the medieval "chante-fable" *Aucassin et Nicolette.* See Levi, "Günther Bialas."

114. See Caroline Rae, "Marius Constant," in *Grove.*

115. See D'Angiolini, "Le son du sens."

116. See the discussion of *De triste cuer / Quant vrais amans / Certes je di* (B29) in chapter 3; and also Elizabeth Eva Leach, "Music and Verbal Meaning: Machaut's Polytextual Songs," *Speculum* 85 (2010): 567–91, whose HTML version has accompanying sound files.

has been widely acknowledged since Richard Taruskin's compelling analysis of "historically informed" performance as essentially modern(ist) performance.[117] This was particularly the case with music as old as Machaut's, for which very little hard historical evidence about performance practice exists. The making of this old music anew in performance was influential in proposing and enshrining a thoroughly modern musical Machaut whose appreciation among listeners (including scholars and composers) grew rapidly. The persuasive and influential role played by performance (and, later, recordings) in the appreciation and study of early music generally has been the subject of several recent studies. Katharine Ellis reports performances of adaptations of Machaut melodies as part of the choral society of the Prince de la Moskova.[118] This society was ultramontane in orientation, ignoring the French *grand motet* traditions to focus instead on the revival of Italian and Franco-Flemish music (within which remit Machaut vaguely fell). But Machaut's music was far from mainstream in the context of the performance of early music in the nineteenth century; and the problems in interpreting the notation of the polyphony (in tandem with distaste for its implied sounds, whether correctly or incorrectly transcribed) meant that the earliest public performances of Machaut's polyphonic works occurred only after the publication of the diplomatic facsimile and transcription of the Mass by Wolf in 1904.[119]

As the twentieth century progressed, the availability first of Ludwig's edition and then of another complete new edition that soon followed in the 1950s made his music more accessible to performers than ever before.[120] Though prepared on grounds less philologically sound than Ludwig's, Leo Schrade's presentation of Machaut's complete works was more readable to the modern musician and has arguably had greater influence on performance (including perpetrating the incorrect double repeat of virelay refrains between verses, heard on recordings from the 1960s and 1970s).[121] Performances and

---

117. See the classic formulation of this idea in Richard Taruskin, "The Pastness of the Present and the Presence of the Past," in *Authenticity and Early Music,* ed. Nicholas Kenyon (Oxford, 1988), 137–210. See also John Butt, *Playing with History: The Historical Approach to Musical Performance* (Cambridge, 2002).

118. Ellis, *Interpreting the Musical Past,* 32. Bottée de Toulmon seems most likely to have provided the transcriptions, given his role as the society's historical adviser.

119. Earp, *Guillaume de Machaut,* 279 and n. 16.

120. Leo Schrade, ed., *The Works of Guillaume de Machaut,* 2 vols. (Les Remparts, Monaco, 1956); Leo Schrade, ed., *The Works of Guillaume de Machaut: Commentary Notes to Volumes II and III* (Les Remparts, Monaco, 1956).

121. See, for example, the performance of *Douce dame jolie* (V4) on *The Art of Courtly Love: Guillaume de Machaut, Gilles Binchois, Guillaume Dufay* by David Munrow and the Early Music Consort of London, Virgin Veritas VED 5 61284 2 PM 617 (originally EMI, 1973; Virgin Classics re-release 1996), disc 1, track 12; or *Dame a vous* (RF6) on *Guillaume de Machaut: Chansons I* by Thomas Binkley and the Studio der frühen Musik (mit Chor) EMI 5 65625 2 3 (rec. 1971; original release 1972; CD re-release 1996), track 7.

sound recordings of performances increased exponentially in the run-up to Machaut's sexcentennial anniversary year in 1977.

The symbiotic relationship between modern performances and scholarly claims about medieval performance practices has been neatly chronicled by Daniel Leech-Wilkinson.[122] The earliest performances used instruments to double the voices at first merely because the music was deemed too difficult to sing unaccompanied (and, solely on the presumption that singers in late Victorian England couldn't be worse than their medieval counterparts, that it would have been too difficult to sing without instruments in the Middle Ages too).[123] The approximate tuning and wide vibrato of early-twentieth-century singing styles meant that the constantly crossing parts of medieval songs—including those of Machaut—sounded rather unpalatable and harmonically confusing without instrumental anchorage. Because the music was imagined by modernists as abstract and structural rather than emotionally expressive, until the mid-twentieth century it was deemed more suited to instrumental or mixed performance. But in the latter part of the twentieth century, once the early music movement had taken much of the swoop and vibrato out of vocal practice, the same goal (projection of an abstract harmonic structure) was even better achieved with all-vocal performance. Despite the change in performance practice, the interpretation of the underlying fact about the music that performance ought to project—that its raison d'être was the presentation of modernist, non-expressive structural harmony—remained constant; only the means to this end underwent a volte-face.[124]

Musicological engagement with Machaut's musical materials specifically in terms of their sounds—actual or imagined (that is, in terms of performance, performance practice, and analysis)—has focused on trying to understand the basic language of his musical style now that the teleological framing of classical functional tonality has been discarded. There are some areas of contention in these pursuits, which derive from the problematic relation of the musical trace to the musical work—that is, from the interpretation of the notation. Musicologists differ in their opinion of how tightly related notation and performance were for Machaut: on the face of it, the carefully prepared notation and luxurious manuscripts suggest something approaching an author-centered work concept, something that is more readily associated with musical practice after 1800;[125] yet the cultural context of what Zumthor has termed *mouvance* affects song even more than dit, since a song has even more scribes,

---

122. Leech-Wilkinson, *The Modern Invention of Medieval Music.*

123. Ibid., 24–25.

124. See ibid., 88–156 (chap. 2, "The Re-invention of the *A cappella* Hypothesis").

125. See Lydia Goehr, *The Imaginary Museum of Musical Works: An Essay in the Philosophy of Music* (Oxford, 1992); see also the essays in Michael Talbot, ed., *The Musical Work: Reality or Invention?* (Liverpool, 2000), especially Reinhard Strohm, "Looking Back at Ourselves: The Problem with the Musical Work-Concept," 128–52.

reciters, and singers, and individuals transmitting it can fill a complex mixture of these three roles.[126] Moreover, medieval musical notation is underprescriptive when considered in modern terms, so that scholars have not been able to agree whether it broadly signals a single sonic product (at least in so far as any two performances of, say, a Beethoven symphony are a "single" product), or whether it leaves certain choices open to the performer to realize within certain parameters (much as a figured bass is "realized" at the keyboard in baroque music). This lack of agreement about highly technical matters has unfortunately hindered the uptake of musicological insights by scholars in other disciplines. It is one of the goals of my book to rectify this. To some extent that will mean writing about the music as I understand it, while noting where this understanding is contentious and recognizing that it is undoubtedly in its turn historically contingent.

Suffice it to say here that the musicological study of Machaut in the second half of the twentieth century has generally jettisoned negative value judgments and stressed the artistry of Machaut's music and his control of its elements, and has sought to understand his compositional processes and reconstruct any musical assumptions that might be latent in the works or their notation. In addition it has tried to understand his musical language and its fashioning. In particular, given the type of music that makes up the bulk of his work, musicologists have become increasingly interested in the complex interaction of music and text. While musical and textual interaction is a key meeting point for Machaut as a modern scholarly subject who is at least potentially bi-disciplinary, the relative disciplinary separation of French literary studies and musicological enquiry has tended to miss the opportunities to combine the two, with blame attached to both sides at different points in the story.

Machaut's Songs: Words and Music Together

Partly because of its later start, partly because of the regulatory force of the tonal practice of the nineteenth century, musicological engagement with Machaut's works initially ran behind literary studies in terms of its critical evaluation of the works on their own terms. But scholars who engaged with Machaut's musical works tended to ignore their texts, which they viewed, in accord with scholars who had commented on the lyrics through the nineteenth century and culminating in the work of Jeanroy, as largely conventional. Musicologists also accepted that sensitivity to the meaning of a verbal text (that is, the origins of the dominant romantic aesthetic of text setting as seen, for example, in the German *Lied*) began in the Renaissance, which, because of

---

126. See Zumthor, *Essai de poétique médiévale*, 71–73; and Paul Zumthor, *La lettre et la voix: De la "littérature" médiévale* (Paris, 1987), 160–68.

Ambros's reliance on Kiesewetter and the relative ignorance of the fourteenth century when the standard textbooks on music history were compiled, began only in the fifteenth century for music.

The emergence of "post-tonal" music in the first part of the twentieth century opened a route for the appreciation of "pre-tonal" music insofar as it brought into question the naturalness of the triad, the system of tonality that was founded on it, and of the teleological music-theoretical narratives that had elevated tonal music. In addition, after the period of highly technologized warfare that lasted from 1914 into the mid-century and beyond, although both possibilities remained open, the dominant strain of medievalism shifted from viewing the period as one of primitive barbarism to one of premodern pastoral utopia.[127] But the amelioration of romantic aesthetics, while good for the appreciation of Machaut's musical substance, reinforced, if anything, the neglect of its music-text relations, since it supported the received idea that Machaut's songs had a largely arbitrary (at best numerical or formal) approach to text setting, rather than responding "romantically" to a text's emotional or verbal content.[128] All that changed in this regard was that rather than being a cause for accusations of barbarism and hypotheses that the texts were in fact never sung, as had been the case earlier with Schering, the "tearings-apart and choppings-up" of the poetry became a neutral or positive feature, indicative of interest in sound rather than sense.[129]

Given Robert Guiette's role in effecting a new appreciation of Machaut's lyric poems, the importance of musical scholarship in this regard deserves greater credit than it has typically received. Arguably the beginnings of appreciation for the lyrics *came* from the application of a musical analogy in which

127. The influence of the First World War on medievalism is detailed in Stefan Goebel, *The Great War and Medieval Memory: War, Remembrance and Medievalism in Britain and Germany, 1914–1940* (Cambridge, 2007). The view of what have commonly been regarded as two discrete world wars as episodes in a single period has been advanced persuasively in Tony Judt, *Postwar: A History of Europe since 1945* (London, 2005). On the varied uses of the Middle Ages in the twentieth century, see Umberto Eco, "Dreaming of the Middle Ages," in *Travels in Hyperreality: Essays*, trans. William Weaver (London, 1986), especially "Ten Little Middle Ages," 68–72.

128. Exceptions to this are Gilbert Reaney, "Guillaume de Machaut: Lyric Poet," *Music and Letters* 39 (1958): 38–51; and Willi Apel, "French, Italian and Latin Poems in 14th-Century Music," *Journal of the Plainsong & Mediaeval Music Society* 1 (1978): 39–56, which consider the poetic themes in the musical lyrics. Criticism of text setting per se, however, permeates the scholarship, much repeating the sentiments of Alfred Einstein, in "The Conflict of Word and Tone," *Musical Quarterly* 40 (1954): 341, that "Machault provided music for conventional poetry—impersonal love poems, as it were; thus, being restricted to poetic structure, the musician served an aristocratic ideal. Basically, there has been no change in the relationship of musician and poet, of minstrel and troubadour, except that the composer's task has grown in artistry and complexity, that his *scientia* is greater. Subjective expression not only remains forbidden, it is not possible at all."

129. On Schering's view that the text setting is so barbarous that the sources must be presenting organ music never intended for singing, see Leech-Wilkinson, *The Modern Invention of Medieval Music*, 44–47 (quotation at 45).

the poetry was treated as a kind of non-semantic music. Guiette's 1949 article uses music critic Boris de Schloezer's pronouncements on the relation of form and content in music as a means of stressing the unified multimedia song product.[130] De Schloezer, a prominent Russian émigré living permanently in Paris from the period following the 1918 October Revolution, was the first to apply the term "neoclassicism" to Stravinsky's music.[131] His books, on the mystic composer Scriabin, the existential philosophy of Kierkegaard, and Bach, show his taste for a modernist stripping-away of "all merely personal 'emotions, feelings, desires, aspirations'" and his embrace of a "universalist" position, "constructed in determined opposition to the German universalism of psychological profundity."[132] This move represents a general cultural trend, located especially in Paris in this period, but for Guiette it is expressly mediated through music because (instrumental) music could be nonverbally meaningful on the basis of form from which its content could not reasonably be separated. In this respect he followed the Hanslickian aesthetic line of viewing music as "sounding forms" and deriding those who experienced it instead as the sonic equivalent of a warm bath.[133]

Guiette's formal approach to Machaut's poetry—deriving from modernist musical aesthetics—was echoed by those scholars who saw the expression of the fact of its own performance and its representation of number as the key to the meaning of Machaut's music.[134] Guiette did not treat song as a musico-poetic whole but rather remarked the fact of its musicalization, excused his lack of expertise in this field, and then went on to understand the verbal text itself as, by analogy, a kind of music. This has the virtue of appearing to be an authentically medieval understanding, along the lines of the "musique naturele" described by Machaut's younger contemporary and probable protégé Eustache Deschamps. Yet rather than understanding the natural music of the verbal text as half the story (as Guiette did), later literary scholars conveniently took Deschamps's olive branch of "musique naturele" as a way of seeing music as an optional (and meaningless) add-on.[135]

130. Guiette, "D'une poésie formelle en France au Moyen Âge," 66, citing "Boris de Schloezer, *Mesures* (1937)." I have been unable to locate this latter source.

131. Scott Messing, "Polemic as History: The Case of Neoclassicism," *Journal of Musicology* 9 (1991): 490.

132. See Richard Taruskin, "Nationalism. §14: Musical Geopolitics," in *Grove*.

133. Eduard Hanslick, *On the Musically Beautiful: A Contribution towards the Revision of the Aesthetics of Music*, trans. Geoffrey Payzant (Indianapolis, 1986), 58, 59. On the permeation of this line of thought into music analysis in the early twentieth century, see Lee A. Rothfarb, "Hermeneutics and Energetics: Analytical Alternatives in the Early 1900s," *Journal of Music Theory* 36 (1992): 43–68.

134. See, for example, John Stevens, *Words and Music in the Middle Ages: Song, Narrative, Dance and Drama, 1050–1350* (Cambridge, 1986), 13–47.

135. Dragonetti, "La poésie...," argues that Deschamps is propounding a transcendent view of poetry. The reply to this article in Kenneth Varty, "Deschamps' *Art de dictier*," *French Studies* 19 (1965): 164–68, suggests instead that rather than driving music and poetry apart, Deschamps

Literary scholars typically downplayed or denied the importance of music within Machaut's output as a whole, commenting on how relatively few of his poems are set, and how even these are just as meaningful if they are only read. The cue for this comes from the embarrassment that nineteenth-century scholars—influenced by the then current judgments of Machaut's music—felt about his musical skills compared to his literary facility.[136] This continued into the twentieth century because of the rather recherché disciplinary skills needed to deal with this musical repertory, in which even very few musicologists were (or indeed are) sufficiently trained. Deschamps's seeming personal closeness to Machaut helped further a division between music and text even though, on the one hand, the interpretation of Deschamps's two kinds of music has been overdetermined, and on the other, there is no logical guarantee that the far more specialized lyric poet Deschamps espoused the same aesthetics as the highly versatile composer-poet Machaut.[137] Literary scholars were not wholly culpable in this: musical studies typically based their readings on assumptions about fourteenth-century lyric that were passé in literary scholarship, especially once Poirion's 1965 book had functioned as a successful apologia. Even when the rhetoric of the poems was noted, the music was often deemed unreflective of it.[138] Musicology's questions tended instead to be narrowly focused on issues of musical form and style, which seemed to have little relevance to literary scholarship; literary scholarship in turn unreflectively conceived music's ontology and social function in twentieth-century terms and remained fearful of its technical aspects.

While musicologists (enslaved to modernism's new neoclassical formalism) were busy ignoring or denying the affective nature of Machaut's music and engaging in formalist analysis, general music appreciation and music in popular culture (that is, the popular aesthetics for understanding both popular and

---

is joining them more tightly together with the idea that poetry is itself a kind of music. Both commentators focus on composition, whereas the treatise seems to me to refer more to performance; see Elizabeth Eva Leach, *Sung Birds: Music, Nature, and Poetry in the Later Middle Ages* (Ithaca, 2007), 57–61.

136. Paris, ed., *Le livre du Voir-dit*, xxxv, cited in Earp, *Guillaume de Machaut*, 279n15.

137. On Deschamps, see Jean-Patrice Boudet and Hélène Millet, eds., *Eustache Deschamps en son temps* (Paris, 1997); Deborah M. Sinnreich-Levi, ed., *Eustache Deschamps French Courtier Poet: His Work and His World* (New York, 1998).

138. For example, having noted the finely balanced oppositional rhetoric in the text of the opening two couplets of *Riches d'amour* (B5), Marie-Danielle Audbourg-Popin, "'Riches d'amour et mendians d'amie...': La rhétorique de Machaut," *Revue de musicologie* 72 (1986): 98, notes that "musically, the intentions of the text are not really perceptible: the two sequences that constitute the first phrase (lines 1 and 3) outline the same contour and present a certain analogy in the distribution of the cadential melismas [as the second; lines 2 and 4], in some way gluing together the opposing terms ('riches'/'mendians'). At best the second sequence seems redundant." Compare the word painting suggested for these same two phrases in Elizabeth Eva Leach, "Death of a Lover and the Birth of the Polyphonic Balade: Machaut's Notated Balades 1–5," *Journal of Musicology* 19 (2002): 493–96.

classical musics) were still basically romantic. Some literary scholars imagined that the unaffecting conventionality of Machaut's lyric poetry would have been given an affective coating by its musical performance.[139] This drew rebuttals from those who wanted to value the lyrics as verbal text in their own terms, and who in the process rejected music's ability to supply meaning and denied the ontological uniqueness of the musico-poetic whole that is song.

Douglas Kelly, whose book *Medieval Imagination* was significant in forming the contemporary understanding of the function of Machaut's courtly poetics in the mental life of its medieval audience, typically draws on his own personal and distinctly modern appreciation of music to reject the affective importance of the sung component of Machaut's works because he cannot believe that anyone has ever been swayed by words just because they are sung.[140] He also has some more historically grounded reasons: poets stress the importance of the words, lots of sources have no music, and an authority like Dante does not mention music. Sources, however, often lack notation but arguably do not lack music: lyrics are frequently "notated" by their texts alone, as they are in modern hymn books; it does not mean that they were not sung.[141] And Dante is talking about oral performance, and the rather different earlier situation in Italy is barely relevant to Machaut anyway.[142] In conclusion Kelly claims that "music is therefore not essential to the enjoyment or appreciation of thought and sentiment in the poetry of the Second Rhetoric, nor is it ancillary to the art of poetry. Rather it is a parallel and independently valid art."[143] For him, a particular part of the proof of music's irrelevance to the poetry is the way that it obscures the words, especially in polyphonic pieces where more than one text is sung simultaneously. Kelly comments that "the combination of religious, courtly, and scabrous verse in some of these compositions would hardly be conducive to sustain *sentement* or serious attention to content."[144] He seems to be thinking more specifically of thirteenth-century motets here, but the same applies to Machaut's motets and those few of his songs that set

139. A view ascribed to Northrop Frye in Kelly, *Medieval Imagination,* xiii.

140. Ibid. Singing a factual untruth might not make one believe it, but there would be little point to the many political uses of music, from political motets and balades, through ceremonial music, opera, to mass songs and national anthems, not to mention the anxious political censorship of music in many periods, if Kelly's statement were broadly accurate.

141. The classic case of this is the "chansonnier" in Oxford, Bodleian library, MS Douce 308; see Mary Atchison, *The Chansonnier of Oxford Bodleian MS Douce 308: Essays and Complete Edition of Texts* (Aldershot, 2005), 2; and the comments in my review in *Music & Letters* 87 (2006): 416–20.

142. See Margaret Bent, "Songs without Music in Dante's *De vulgari eloquentia: Cantio* and Related Terms," in *"Et facciam dolçi canti": Studi in onore di Agostino Ziino in occasione del suo 65o compleanno,* ed. Bianca Maria Antolini, Teresa M. Gialdroni, and Annunziato Pugliese, vol. 1 (Lucca, 2004), 161–81.

143. Kelly, *Medieval Imagination,* 11.

144. Ibid., 254.

different texts simultaneously.[145] One such piece, *De triste / Quant / Certes* (B29), forms a central part of chapter 3, where I attempt to show on the contrary that *only* the musical setting can cause the texts to be understood in the way that these pieces require; a nonmusicalized successive reading of the texts would miss much of the point.

Our current experience of songs and singing, whether expert, amateur, or entirely uninformed and passive, is almost entirely misleading when it comes to appreciating the singing of late medieval lyric. In the twentieth century, the rise of recorded sound led to the generalization of so-called acousmatic listening, that is, listening to sound whose ultimate originating agent is hidden from the listener (in this case, by being absent).[146] As a corollary, the pervasive presence of recorded popular music in the everyday soundscape fostered an emphasis on music's immediate aural comprehensibility. While the modernist avant-garde defined itself against such an emphasis,[147] its assertion of a musical ontology based squarely on music as (organized) sound showed that it shared with popular musical culture the acceptance of the new acousmatic norm. In terms of listening practice, this "new aurality" reduced the emphasis on music as both a textual object and an object of mental contemplation, such that it now tends to be considered instead as an object of immediate bodily experience.[148]

145. Machaut's motets have been treated extensively for their conveyance of textual meanings in Jacques Boogaart, "'O Series Summe Rata': De Motetten van Guillaume de Machaut. De Ordening van het Corpus en de Samenhang van Tekst en Muziek" (Ph.D. thesis, University of Utrecht, 2001); and Anne Walters Robertson, *Guillaume de Machaut and Reims: Context and Meaning in His Musical Works* (Cambridge, 2002). See the fuller discussion in chapter 6.

146. The term was appropriated from an obsolete usage by Pierre Schafer (see Frank J. Malina and Pierre Schaeffer, "A Conversation on Concrete Music and Kinetic Art," *Leonardo* 5 [1972]: 255–56) and has since become widely used in film studies; see Michel Chion, *Audio-Vision: Sound on Screen* (New York, 1994). At the time of writing the *OED* lists only the obsolete usage, but this entry dates from the nineteenth century; there are plans to include the new usage when it is next updated (email communication).

147. For a typically mid-twentieth-century modernist reaction against music's immediate aural comprehensibility, see the essay by the composer Milton Babbitt, "Who Cares If You Listen?," in *Contemporary Composers on Contemporary Music*, ed. Elliott Schwartz, Barney Childs, and James Fox (New York, 1998), 243–50, which was originally published in *High Fidelity* in 1958.

148. For a scholarly philosophical formulation of this now populist view, see Vladimir Jankélévitch, *Music and the Ineffable*, trans. Carolyn Abbate (Princeton, 2003). This work, originally published in 1961, has apparent roots in the mystical and Platonic focus of French and Russian Symbolism similar to those animating Boris de Schloezer's work, yet is exercising renewed power on contemporary Anglo-American musicology through its recent translation, and through Carolyn Abbate, "Music—Drastic or Gnostic?," *Critical Inquiry* 30 (2004): 505–36. In drawing attention to the "new aurality" of twentieth-century musical appreciation, I would not wish to deny either that modern music can have a significant mental component or that medieval music has a significant somatic and experiential dimension. Nevertheless, it should be understood as potentially detrimental to medieval music's scholarly reception, especially outside musicology. See Leach, "Music and Verbal Meaning," and my discussion in chapter 3.

The influence of the musicological Machaut on the literary Machaut and vice versa is complex and varied—and often confusing. Kiesewetter commented on Machaut's presumption at composing when he was really just a poet, a judgment Paulin Paris adopted to excuse Machaut's dabbling in music and extol instead his poetic skill. But for a literary scholar who found Machaut's lyrics boring, it was just as easy to imagine, as Jeanroy did, that conversely his importance must lie in the other field, that is, that he was really a musical creator.[149] It seems clear today that he is a central figure in both music and literature, and that not only should these not be separated, but also there is significant importance in the inseparable place of each in the book: Machaut the court secretary is bookmaker, poet, and composer. His epistemic trajectory is not just "from song to book" but also from book to song: he makes poetry writerly and makes writing lyric and sonic.[150] The book is at once a visual paratextual performance and a real script for sonic performance. In being no single thing, the work of Machaut shows the complex situation of courtly culture in a period whose products are neither for a once-only use nor wholly present in any single manifestation. This perspective is informed by the newest disciplinary Machaut of them all: the Machaut of the Book.

Machaut's Books: Pictures and Paratext

Until the interdisciplinary study of Sylvia Huot in 1987, very few literary scholars engaged with Machaut's works in their manuscript context after the publication of editions of the verbal texts.[151] Because of the issues surrounding the interpretation of the notation, musicologists, by contrast, were frequently forced back to the sources themselves, which they found remarkably luxurious compared to the contemporaneous musical sources for the music of other composers. Nevertheless, there are remarkably few illuminations in the music section of the Machaut manuscripts (as opposed to the rather generously illuminated narrative poems), and so it did not perhaps strike manuscript-oriented musicologists as strange that there was not a body of art-historical work on

149. Jeanroy, "La littérature de langue française," 465: "C'est surtout dans le domaine musical qu'il paraît avoir été créateur." Jeanroy admits that it is too early to pronounce definitely on this point; his speculation comes from Coussemaker, a suitably proximate source in 1896 (when Jeanroy thanks him for his patient help with Alfred Jeanroy, "Les chansons," in *Histoire de la langue et de la littérature française des origines à 1900*, ed. Louis Petit de Julleville, vol.1 [Paris, 1896], 390–400), but significantly out of date by 1921, given the publications of Ludwig and Wolf (see the discussion earlier in this chapter).

150. See the complementary perspectives of Huot, *From Song to Book*, and Ardis Butterfield, *Poetry and Music in Medieval France: From Jean Renart to Guillaume de Machaut* (Cambridge, 2002).

151. See comments in Keith Busby, *Codex and Context: Reading Old French Verse Narrative in Manuscript*, 2 vols. (Amsterdam, 2002), 1:1–3.

these sources of comparable size, weight, and venerability as could be found in literary studies and musicology. When art historians did turn to Machaut's books, though, their engagement with these multimedia objects was far more direct than that by scholars in disciplines—quintessentially literary studies, but to a lesser extent also musicology—whose objects could reasonably be mediated by modern editions. This in turn has led to art history being the discipline most frequently appropriated by scholars in other disciplines in an attempt to "interdisciplinarize" their home discipline's own Machaut.

The first art historian to dedicate significant attention to Machaut's books was François Avril, whose publications in the late 1970s contextualized their illuminations within the ateliers of fourteenth-century France, enabling the identification of certain artists if not by their given names then by names given to them on account of their work on other non-Machaut manuscripts.[152] These links gave further social context to the market for these books, and were suggestive of the relations between their patrons, audience, and author, even where the exact identity of the first two was not known. Art historians also proposed new datings for the main sources. Most spectacularly, Avril redated manuscript C—designated a fifteenth-century copy of an earlier source in its library catalogue and containing only half of Machaut's works—so that overnight it became the earliest of the collected sources. Because it was neither the most complete nor, according to its original misdating, one close in date to the composer, C had been largely sidelined in the making of the collected editions both of text and of music. Hoepffner's volumes of the dits preferred the readings of A, whose authorial index rubric bolsters its claims to have been compiled under Machaut's direct supervision, and F-G, which similarly was thought to preserve aspects of Machaut's own late redaction.[153] Ludwig made only an incipit catalogue of C; his edition of the music is based on transcriptions from F-G supplemented by a later stint with the earlier Vg, whose *Loange* ordering suggests that it lies "a bit outside the Machaut circle," but whose music readings are often very good (especially with regard to text underlay).[154]

An earlier text is not, however, necessarily a better one, and initially Avril's redating of C may have seemed of marginal interest on account of A's strong claims to authorial proximity. Earp, however, has shown for the music that Machaut rarely intervened at the level of individual readings within a song or

152. François Avril, "Les manuscrits enluminés de Guillaume de Machaut: Essai de chronologie," in *Guillaume de Machaut: Poète et Compositeur* (Reims, 1982), 117–33; idem, *Manuscript Painting at the Court of France: The Fourteenth Century (1320–1380)* (London, 1978); idem, "Un Chef-d'oeuvre de l'enluminure sous le règne de Jean le Bon: La Bible Moralisée manuscrit français 167 de la Bibliothèque Nationale," in *Monuments et mémoires de la Fondation Eugène Piot* (Paris, 1973), 91–125.

153. Hoepffner, *Oeuvres de Guillaume de Machaut*, 1:xliv–li.

154. Earp, *Guillaume de Machaut*, 244, 280.

dit in later redactions, when he was primarily concerned instead with overall ordering.[155] In their edition of *Behaingne* and *Remede,* Wimsatt and William W. Kibler found similarly that errors entering the transmission were not corrected in **A** and that, as the earliest source, **C** provided a better text.[156] This means that some of the readings of **C**—in the dits and music, and possibly also by extension in the *Loange*—are superior to those in later sources, although they do not appear in either of the collected musical or literary editions that were made before Avril's redating.

Art-historical evidence for dating thus has implications that should inform new editions (or the way the old ones are read), but its more important influence on the construction of the modern scholarly Machaut has been to emphasize his interdisciplinarity, since the pictures that illustrate his dits seem to be part of an authorial plan, especially in manuscripts **A** and **C**. Art history perforce deals directly with a far less mediated version of the primary source—the book—and is thus faced more unavoidably with the fundamentally multimedia nature of Machaut's works. In the wake of a rise of interest in the history of the book within literary studies, the insights of art history have been usefully combined in studies that have begun to construct an interdisciplinary Machaut, who, as both a book planner and an author, engages the gaze of his "audience" (who are also readers and viewers) as a means of creating a multiplicity of readings through the *mise-en-page* of illuminations and poetry, in combination with rubrication and other paratextual features.

Martha Wallen augmented her 1980 literary analysis of *Confort* by a reading of the miniatures in two of the sources (though unfortunately not in the source that carries the most developed program for this dit, **Vg**, which was then unavailable).[157] By showing some similarity with the iconography of manuscript images in versions of the *Ovide moralisé,* Wallen was able to elucidate a specifically visual frame of literary reference that would have been in play for the book's early readers and viewers. In the same way that Machaut's verbal texts draw on resonances from vernacular literature in their use of exempla, their miniatures cue similar external resemblances as well as having particular meanings generated from their specific place within Machaut's books.

---

155. See Lawrence Earp, "Scribal Practice, Manuscript Production, and the Transmission of Music in Late Medieval France: The Manuscripts of Guillaume de Machaut" (Ph.D. diss., Princeton University, 1983), passim; and idem, "Machaut's Role in the Production of His Works," *Journal of the American Musicological Society* 42 (1989): 461–503.

156. James I. Wimsatt, William W. Kibler, and Rebecca A. Baltzer, eds., *Guillaume de Machaut: Le Jugement du Roy de Behaigne and Remede de Fortune* (Athens, Ga., 1988), 8–26. E is placed in a secondary group, with **J** and **K** but still in the "early tradition" for the dit, despite its late date. There is, however, no watertight division between these groups (14), and E shows mixed sources for its musical items; see Margaret Bent, "The Machaut Manuscripts Vg, B and E," *Musica Disciplina* 37 (1983): 53–82.

157. Martha Wallen, "Biblical and Mythological Typology in Machaut's *Confort d'Ami,*" *Res Publica Litterarum* 3 (1980): 191–206. She uses manuscripts **A** and **F**.

Sylvia Huot's *From Song to Book* includes two chapters on Machaut in the context of a wide-ranging study of the role of vernacular books in the later Middle Ages. Like Wallen, Huot is primarily a literary scholar (she teaches French at the University of Cambridge), but in her analyses the physical trace is an important and meaningful constituent of literary meaning. In addition she views literary meaning less as an immanent (textual) fact and more as the result of a plethora of interactions and processes entertained between author, scribe, illuminator, reader, and audience (some of whom might be one and the same). Huot uses the program of miniatures in Machaut's *Remede* to show the difference between the importance of this work in **C** and its less central appearance in the later manuscript **A**.[158] Her analysis of the lays in **C** is similarly penetrating, although here, as in her analysis of *Harpe*'s illuminations in **A**, the performative nature of the book that she elucidates is the visually performative nature of the page rather than actual sounding musical (or spoken) performance from it.[159] More recently Deborah McGrady has used Machaut's books as a case study to investigate the ways in which readers are instructed and controlled through the mediation of the manuscripts' illuminations and *mise-en-page,* and the way in which such readers reciprocally shape these modes of mediation.[160]

In a 2005 doctoral dissertation on the illuminations of the Machaut manuscript, the art historian Domenic Leo creatively combines the approach of Huot with the art-historical work of Avril, the bibliographical work of Earp, and the literary study of Brownlee.[161] Leo explores the artists of the manuscripts, looking at their involvement in other manuscripts, and thereby situating the Machaut sources within a broader cultural realm of royal book production. Central to the meanings of the program of illuminations in his analysis is the projection of Machaut's authorial persona and the visual establishment of what Huot calls a "writerly poetics" of authorship.[162] Leo's study of the role of manuscript **A**'s *Prologue* illuminations in this regard are considered further in chapter 3.

Art history as a discipline can thus be credited with some of the movement toward interdisciplinary study of Machaut, since the materials that art history relies on—the manuscripts themselves—are not just composed of pictures. In addition, the pictures, while adding their own narrative layer, chiefly construct meaning by their interaction with the other parts of the page and the book as a whole. But the focus on the visual, in tandem with the literary focus on the

---

158. Huot, *From Song to Book,* 249–59, cf. 275–80.

159. Ibid., 260–72; on *Harpe,* see 286–93.

160. Deborah McGrady, *Controlling Readers: Guillaume de Machaut and His Late Medieval Audience* (Toronto, 2006).

161. Domenic Leo, "Authorial Presence in the Illuminated Machaut Manuscripts" (Ph.D. diss., New York University, 2005).

162. Huot, *From Song to Book,* 2.

writerly, has tended to obscure the sounds of the codex, as cued in its use of musical notation, texts referencing music, or, as in the *Voir dit,* paratextual rubrics that signal the presence of musical setting elsewhere in the codex for some of the lyric items. The treatment of notation as a kind of picture that tells a sonic rather than a visual story, and that cues mental aural (rather than mental visual) association, is still rather rare.[163]

My Machaut: Machaut's Oeuvre

There is much to be learned even from this brief consideration of the historiographies of the various disciplinary Machauts. Distilling each of these monodisciplinary Machauts and then chronicling their interaction has revealed some common themes and some warnings from history. In several respects, this is a highly propitious time to study this poet-composer: his complete works exist in modern editions, his manuscripts can be viewed on microfilm, his music is widely recorded in a variety of different styles, and there is now a critical mass of scholarly commentary on him which provides a context for understanding, reaction, questions, and future work. Like that of the preceding two centuries, our perspective on Machaut is informed to a large degree by our own concerns. This is, however, not always to the detriment of the material: in the nineteenth century, very few writers had much good to say about Machaut's poetry or music; today the negative aspects of the assessment of Machaut's works have largely evaporated from scholarly discourse. Given that no contemporary evidence suggests that Machaut's work was anything other than highly regarded by his contemporaries, this change at least seems to approach a more historically sympathetic understanding (although that statement will allow our successors to note that twenty-first-century scholars desired to show historical sympathy, probably concluding that this was because they worked from a relativistic base foreign to that of their nineteenth-century forebears).

Studies of the historiography of medieval studies—of medievalism—typically depend on the truism that there is no unmediated medieval material but merely an unending set of interpretations of its reception: in short, we have only our own self-constructed Middle Ages. Of course there is no longer any "real historical Machaut," because that human individual has been dead for over six hundred years, but then there never *was* a single Machaut, given that a person is not a monolithic self but an ever-changing series of discrete, crystallized selves hanging like jewels on life's spatiotemporal thread. There is also a difference—at least in that critically unfashionable but legally significant category of intention—between scholarly and popular constructions of the Middle Ages, as any scholar who has tried to make TV or radio programs

---

163. See, however, ibid., 54–79, 246–70; and McGrady, *Controlling Readers,* 127–45.

can attest. Popular medievalism, like train-spotting, angling, or other planks of popular culture in which I have extremely limited personal interest, has its place in human society and is studied in the academy by humanities scholars. The scholarly Machaut is no less of our own time than the popular Machaut, but is nevertheless rather different, because his construction is marked by the concerns of scholars and is a professional (rather than leisure) pursuit. Wanting to know what Machaut meant for his own contemporary audience—like trying to reconstruct medieval performance practices—is a modern scholarly avocation; it cannot help but be filtered through the state of modern scholarly judgments, assumptions, knowledge, and interests. By acknowledging the historical contingency of the scholarly Machaut's construction, scholars today are able to reflect self-consciously upon their own roles and adjust their sense of certainty accordingly.

Awareness of the history of Machaut scholarship is important because it makes possible a quick, if provisional, differentiation between those things about Machaut that are subject to change (and thus dependent on temporally and personally contingent perspectives) and those things that seem—at least so far—to have remained the same (and thus might provide irreducible traces of Machaut's period and works). Chief among the former are the value judgments and ideas about which part of his varied output is most essential or excellent. Chief among the latter are aspects such as the existence of collected-works manuscripts containing a generically varied output. Machaut the multimedia artist is more of a historical fact than a fiction of medievalism. If anything, scholarship from earlier periods is easier to interrogate for its agendas because it bore its distaste more proudly. Ours lie less in what is said than in what is unsaid, less in what is studied than in what is ignored.

Understanding what Machaut's contemporaries saw in him requires that any present-day distaste for elements of his works that seem odd, boring, or even offensive be placed on hold. Modernity has aided this endeavor, as has so-called postmodernism, since its accompanying cultural relativism proposes appreciation "in their own terms" of past products (although reconstructing those terms is another matter). But postmodernity brings its own agendas because of its focus on the crisis of epistemology and concomitant emphasis on the popular and the personal.[164] These factors have arguably elevated the *Voir dit*'s crisis of the constructed (meta)fictional self above all Machaut's other

---

164. Musicology's engagement with the postmodern has largely led to the abandonment of the study of the Middle Ages, except in so far as "medievalist" sounds and ideas are part of the popular present. See, for example, the essays in Annette Kreutziger-Herr and Dorothea Redepennig, eds., *Mittelalter-Sehnsucht? Texte des interdisziplinären Symposions zur musikalischen Mittelalterrezeption an der Universität Heidelberg, April 1998*, vol. 2 (Kiel, 2000); and Leech-Wilkinson's farewell to medieval scholarship, which subsumes it into a radically "presentist" study of Machaut's music as contemporary sound (Daniel Leech-Wilkinson, "*Rose, lis* Revisited," in *Machaut's Music: New Interpretations*, ed. Elizabeth Eva Leach [Woodbridge, 2003], 249–62).

works, since it problematizes personal authenticity.[165] But Machaut's other works are didactic, religious, and appreciative of hierarchy based on bloodlines, and the liberal Western academy tends to re-form its most prized subjects in its own democratic soft-left image. On the basis of scant biographical information, even recent scholars have done their best to imagine a demotic Machaut emerging from non-noble stock and working his way up in a medieval proto-meritocracy (court administration), engaging en route with aspects of popular piety.[166] Uncomfortable but unavoidable evidence—for instance the servility of poets in the fourteenth century to their patrons—has sometimes been treated as somewhat distasteful by modern commentators, who anachronistically expect art to be rather oppositional, socially progressive, and detached from thoughts of self-advancement. Condemning Christine de Pizan's references to Philip of Burgundy as flattering and sycophantic, for example, the historian Richard Vaughan goes on to say of Eustache Deschamps that while he "was by no means averse to currying favour at court by writing for or flattering the princes[,]...he was much less servile."[167] The post-Poirion acceptance of the important role of the patron in late medieval poetry has permeated slowly, if more quickly in literary studies than among historians and musicologists. Douglas Kelly has tackled the usual dismissal of dedications as mere flattery with an analysis of the patron in various roles and ultimately as a genius for whom the poet is a scribe.[168] Nonetheless, Machaut's glorifying chronicle (*Prise*) and his exemplar-rich consolation poem (*Confort*), arguably the two most geared to please their patrons, remain two of his least discussed.[169]

Other aspects of Machaut's social and political life and views are even more unpalatable to modern liberal readers. Not only was he no peasant commoner opposing the feudal hierarchy, but also he was an anti-Semite of a variety typical for Christians in this period. In the much-quoted opening of *Navarre*, he attributes the plague to the evil Jews' poisoning of the wells.[170] Elsewhere

---

165. After a century in which the inadequacy of Paris's edition was lamented, the *Voir dit* was published in two different editions, with translations into English and modern French in 1998 and 1999, respectively. The poem then became a set text for the "programme de l'Agrégation de lettres modernes" in 2002, prompting the publication of numerous guides to it for French university students.

166. See the comments in chapter 1.

167. Richard Vaughan, *Philip the Bold: The Formation of the Burgundian State*, new ed. (Woodbridge, 2002), 98. He patronizingly excuses Christine by noting that "to be fair to Christine, this fawning concealed the desperate enterprise of a woman who had been left, at the age of twenty-five, a penniless widow with three children: she wrote to live."

168. Douglas Kelly, "The Genius of the Patron: The Prince, the Poet, and Fourteenth-Century Invention," in *Chaucer's French Contemporaries: The Poetry/Poetics of Self and Tradition*, ed. R. Barton Palmer (New York, 1999), 1–27.

169. See the references in Earp, *Guillaume de Machaut*, 218–20, 233–34. The relative paucity of literary work on the *Prise* is particularly noticeable.

170. *Navarre*, ll. 181–228. This view was commonly held from 1348 on, and replicates the rationale for the expulsion of Jews from France in 1322, when they were implicated in

he berates them for theological errors and specifically for the foolish failure to recognize that Christ is the Messiah whose birth is foretold in their own scripture.[171]

My interest in Machaut comes first from my training as a musicologist, but my work is designed explicitly to produce a more than musicological Machaut. The rationale for the present book rests on two strongly held convictions: first, that Machaut's musical output is the most daunting ingredient of his work for modern scholarship to deal with (so I intend to deal with him from there outward), and second, that music is more central to his works than modern scholarship has (conveniently or disingenuously) assumed or claimed. On the latter point, the exposition in chapter 3 of the importance of music in manuscript A—from the opening *Prologue* to the very end of the book—will say more. On the former point I call as witness the fact that the most thorough documentation of Machaut's life, works, and writing on them has been compiled by a musicologist, Lawrence Earp, to universal acclaim.[172] There are practical scholarly explanations for this. The technical training for literary studies is similar to that for all humanities disciplines and involves core humanities skills of reading, assimilating, critiquing, and writing. The specifically technical aspects of Middle French poetry are relatively few compared to the specifically technical aspects of its music and notation, and while I cannot pretend to have mastered them, I can consult experts who can reply in a shared scholarly language, which is more than many musicologists—especially of a more analytical kind—can do when asked by literary scholars. The sheer difficulty of talking in language about a language-like but fundamentally nonlinguistic art

---

the so-called Leper's plot as suppliers of the poison that the lepers were then alleged to have used in wells at the behest of the prince of Granada; see Sophia Menache, "Faith, Myth, and Politics: The Stereotype of the Jews and Their Expulsion from England and France," *Jewish Quarterly Review,* n.s. 75 (1985): 369–70. Many Jews confessed to poisoning wells after 1348 under torture, and some were executed. The desire of Jews to murder Christians is also integral to Chaucer's *Prioress's Tale;* see the reading in Bruce W. Holsinger, *Music, Body, and Desire in Medieval Culture: Hildegard of Bingen to Chaucer* (Stanford, 2001), 259–92 (chap. 6, "Musical Violence and the Pedagogical Body: The Prioress's Tale and the Ideologies of 'Song'").

171. *Lay de Nostre Dame* (L15/10), stanza 8, ll. 1–2. This stanza notes that although the Jews now live in error, they had many signs of the Virgin Birth, such as the rod ("verge") of Moses turning into a snake and the sprouting of the dry tree seen by Aaron.

172. Daniel Leech-Wilkinson, "A Guide to Machaut," review of *Guillaume de Machaut: A Guide to Research* by Lawrence Earp, *Early Music History* 25 (1997): 137: "an astonishing book, perhaps the most significant publication on Machaut since his music and poetry was first edited early this century." Marielle Popin, review of *Guillaume de Machaut: A Guide to Research* by Lawrence Earp, *Revue de musicologie* 82 (1996): 368–70, and Jean Harden, review of *Guillaume de Machaut: A Guide to Research* by Lawrence Earp, *Notes* 53, 2nd ser. (1997): 785–87, call it indispensable. Laurence de Looze, review of *Guillaume de Machaut: A Guide to Research* by Lawrence Earp, *Speculum* 73 (July 1998): 844, and Peter Meredith, review of *Guillaume de Machaut: A Guide to Research* by Lawrence Earp and *The Tale of the Alerion* by Guillaume de Machaut, ed. Minnette Gaudet and Constance B. Hieatt, *Modern Language Review* 92 (1997): 967–69, also praise it wholeheartedly.

form is one of musicology's truisms. Whether it is a failing of musicology not to be able to translate its insights into language or of literary studies not to be able to learn the techniques of music analysis is hard to decide. I have at different times thought both. Art-historical studies similarly rely on literary models for their scholarly practices, and the advantage is that while I might not be in a position to write my own art-historical commentary, the representation of this by art historians is accessible to non–art historians, since very little of it is expressed in technical language.

In the chapters that follow I integrate musical readings and music's readings of lyrics into thematic discussions of Machaut's work in the round. This is not designed as a comprehensive treatment of every work—there is simply too much Machaut for that—but is rather a treatment of the central themes of his work as a whole that takes into account performance, musical notation, the book, *mise-en-page,* illuminations, and social function. In chapter 3 the approaches of Poirion and Cerquiglini-Toulet will be combined with that of Sylvia Huot and extended to a consideration of Machaut's complete oeuvre—not in terms comprehensive of all his works, but as a "super-work," a book of booklets that is explicitly organized by its author with a productive role for paratextual features and even for the seemingly careless duplication of lyrics.[173]

The lyrics set to music are much more than a specialist section relegated to the back of the codex as being of limited, specialist appeal. Very often songs serve as keys to the longer works, epitomizing or summarizing their central themes. In effect the music section is a florilegium, a distillation of doctrine used didactically as a sonic aide-memoire. Music was fundamental to religious schooling throughout this period, and it seems no surprise that it was found equally useful by court-based clerics charged with the ethical education and entertainment of their patron and his or her courtly *familia.*

With Machaut's musical works not making it into the Renaissance canon of music, earlier musicological commentators assumed that they lacked the kind of sensitive relationship with their verbal texts seen as a defining feature of the Renaissance. More recently musicologists have, in contrast, become excited both about "word painting" and about the projection of metrical and verse structures in Machaut's music. It seems clear that for Machaut the musicalization of a text was not merely a matter of replicating its "sounding number," but that it gave him an opportunity to control something that is not controlled

---

173. I have gone further than this in the chapters that follow to take as axiomatic that duplication between the *Loange* and other sections of the works cues readers to connect different parts of the book for a multifaceted and textually "polyphonic" series of lyrico-narrative voices and a kaleidoscopic take on a revised, Christianized, and highly idealized courtly doctrine. See also the arguments for this approach in Leach, "Death of a Lover"; and my "Singing More about Singing Less: Machaut's *Pour ce que tous* (B12)," in *Machaut's Music: New Interpretations,* ed. Elizabeth Eva Leach (Woodbridge, 2003), 111–24.

through the letter notation of verbal text: temporal delivery. In addition, the polyphonic setting of text allows that passage of time to be marked qualitatively as dissonance, or consonance, as stable or unstable sonority, so that the temporal flow is not just presented but marked and commentated on, allowing the setting up, fulfillment, and frustration of expectation.[174] In short, the potential relations between music and text are both multifarious and powerful. Once the ease of imprinting text and melody in memory is added to this mix, music becomes very important to a literature of ethical and didactic import.

At the back of my mind are the questions to which we cannot know the answer except by induction from the works: When, why, and for whom were Machaut's works performed and read? What did they mean to their audience, how did Machaut interact with them, and how did he integrate his life as an artist into his job at court? The evidence that at least one other near contemporary almoner may have been the author of a narrative poem with lyric and musical insertions suggests that the creative and professional aspects of Machaut's life might have been better integrated than is commonly thought. Janet F. van den Meulen has proposed that the author of *Le dit de la panthere d'amours*, whose name must be unscrambled from an anagram, is not the Nicole de Margival whose name is only otherwise known from a single copy of *Li trois mors et li trois vis* but Nicole de Gavrelle, almoner and chaplain at the court of Holland-Hainaut.[175] If so, this figure—author of a first-person but allegorical and didactic dit with interpolated lyrics by himself and by an older authority, Adam de la Halle—provides a clear precedent for the figure of Guillaume de Machaut, although Machaut's interest in preserving his own work, and thus making sure that we know exactly how much he wrote, still sets him apart.

My Machaut is a fascinating, intellectual, layered, and complex figure who cannot be contained in any single book except his own. Faced with the alternative of copying out manuscript **A**, the present book seeks instead to provide a commentary, if inevitably an introductory and partial one. What is new here

---

174. Two issues that have to do with the interpretation of the notational trace surface in regard to these types of readings. First, the exact alignment of text and music is at issue because this affects aspects of delivery. This is easy to diagnose in more syllabic genres (virelays, lays, motets) but harder in more melismatic ones (balades, rondeaux). See Lawrence Earp, "Declamatory Dissonance in Machaut," in *Citation and Authority in Medieval and Renaissance Music: Learning from the Learned*, ed. Suzannah Clark and Elizabeth Eva Leach (Woodbridge, 2005), 102–22. Second are issues that some writers call harmony but others designate as counterpoint, and the correct interpretations of the notation's underprescription of the semitones that animate it. See the essays in Margaret Bent, *Counterpoint, Composition, and Musica Ficta* (London, 2002); and, for an opposing view, Thomas Brothers, *Chromatic Beauty in the Late Medieval Chanson: An Interpretation of Manuscript Accidentals* (Cambridge, 1997).

175. Janet F. van der Meulen, "De panter en de aalmoezenier: Dichtkunst rond het Hollands-Henegouwse hof," in *Een zoet akkoord: Middeleeuwse lyriek in de Lage Landen*, ed. Frank Willaert (Amsterdam, 1992), 93–108, 343–48.

is the attempt (and it can only ever be that) to gather up Machaut's scattered texts from their different modern disciplines so that their constituent threads can be woven back into their greater textual whole.

More than most literary scholars (excepting those like Huot, Butterfield, and McGrady), I am keen to engage with Machaut's works in their manuscript copies (or at least on microfilm), to appreciate their "notation" (literary and musical) and layout. This is because the greater distance between medieval and modern musical notations (despite many similarities of appearance) convinces me that musical editions are too highly mediated to bear sole use. This view is central to Margaret Bent's 1994 article, which argues for viewing editions as wholesale translations rather than transcriptions or transliterations.[176] It has its text-based parallel in musicologist Leech-Wilkinson's approach to the presentation of his joint edition and translation of the *Voir dit* with R. Barton Palmer, which eschews all diacritics and includes manuscript capitals and images;[177] Palmer has since replicated aspects of this approach in his edition of the *Prise*.[178] The need to return to the manuscripts has also been expounded as a vital approach to medieval French texts by Keith Busby (2002), and other "diplomatically edited" texts have subsequently appeared, despite objections that this is a lazy editorial approach that eschews that which ought truly to be critical about the critical edition.[179] In the light of this divergence of views, and in pursuit of ready usability and readability, where texts are quoted here, I mostly make use of existing editions, noting features of the manuscript originals where appropriate. Despite my own preferences, where I edit from a source myself, on clear advice from the anonymous literary readers of the current book in manuscript, I deploy principles that have traditionally been standard in French studies regarding the use of diacritics, punctuation, capitalization, and so on.

Engagement with Machaut's book by art historians and then literary scholars willing to draw on their insights led the way to the more rounded multidisciplinary Machaut I want to present here. Bent's imprecation to engage with the original notation—or at least to be aware of the ways in which modern editions mediate (and obscure) its meanings—meant much the same: start with the medieval object and try to read outward to its contexts. Earp, a student of Bent's, did just that in his thesis on the Machaut manuscripts, an "old-fashioned" bibliographic enquiry which gives his much broader subsequent overview of the entire field of Machaut studies virtually impregnable

176. Bent, "Editing Early Music."

177. Leech-Wilkinson and Palmer, *Le livre dou voir dit.*

178. Palmer, *Machaut: Prise.*

179. Busby, *Codex and Context.* For the contrary view, see Peter F. Dembowski, "What Is Critical in Critical Editions? The Case of Bilingual Editions," in *"De sens rassis": Essays in Honor of Rupert T. Pickens,* ed. Keith Busby, Bernard Guidot, and Logan E. Whale (Amsterdam, 2005), 169–81, specifically rejecting Leech-Wilkinson's editorial presentation of the *Voir dit.*

foundations.[180] As Lawrence de Looze commented reviewing the latter in 1998: "For over a decade students of Guillaume de Machaut have been well aware that the person who knows the Machaut manuscripts best is the musicologist Lawrence Earp. With the publication of *Guillaume de Machaut: A Guide to Research* it becomes evident that Earp knows virtually everything about Machaut and his legacy."[181] My multidisciplinary Machaut therefore starts for me with musicological training and the manuscript material, because that is where it is most urgently visible that multidisciplinarity is required, but extends to the now separate fields of literature and history. And where better to start than at the very beginning of his works, the opening statement about poetic creation that the aging Machaut himself designed for the reader to confront: the Index and *Prologue* of what we now alphabetaphilically call manuscript **A**.

180. Earp, "Scribal Practice."

181. De Looze, review of *Guillaume de Machaut: A Guide to Research* by Lawrence Earp, 844.

3

Creation

Machaut Making

Toward the end of his life, in the early 1370s, Guillaume de Machaut decided to collect his complete works together into an organized book, which we know as manuscript **A**. This was not the first time he had overseen the compilation of his entire oeuvre, but that oeuvre had grown further since the copying of manuscript **C** in the mid-century, and Machaut seems to have felt that his enlarged summa needed the addition of a couple of framing devices.[1] For this purpose he composed two new items: the first, indicative of his scribal prowess, was an index (see figure 3.1); the second, the so-called *Prologue,* was a statement of a musical poetics that would stand as a key to his entire output, specifically discussing the role of emotional authenticity—*sentement*—in the creation of musical lyrics (see figures 3.2 and 3.3).[2] These framing devices make a good starting point from which to consider Machaut's entire works in their full multimedia manuscript *mise-en-page* glory. Both offer powerful interpretive tools for the reader, presenting an authorial persona whose poetics is at once musical and scribal, courtly and clerical, and addresses the two

1. On Machaut's supervision of manuscripts **C** and **A**, see Lawrence Earp, "Machaut's Role in the Production of his Works," *Journal of the American Musicological Society* 42 (1989): 463–72, 480–88; and Sylvia Huot, *From Song to Book: The Poetics of Writing in Old French Lyric and Lyrical Narrative Poetry* (Ithaca, 1987), 246–49, 274–75.

2. I use the title *Prologue* even though it is probably not authorial and occurs only in the posthumous manuscript E, which omits the narrative section (see Lawrence Earp, *Guillaume de Machaut: A Guide to Research* [New York, 1995], 203). E exhibits a thoroughgoing lack of interest in Machaut's authorial ordering intentions (the musical items are radically reordered within their genre sections, for instance) and a rather different scribal agenda, which nonetheless offers an important document of Machaut's posthumous reception; see chapter 6.

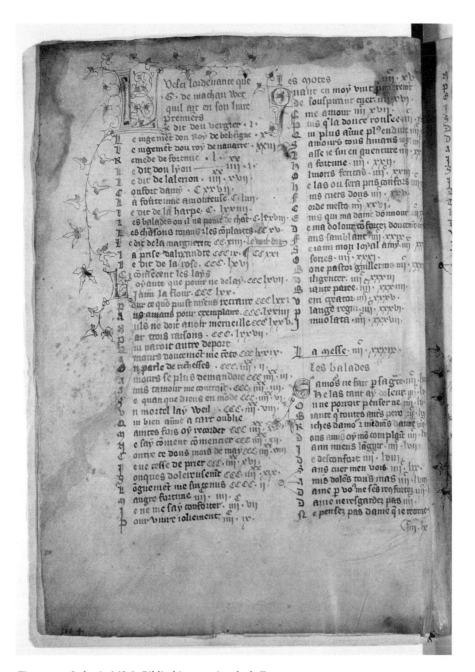

Figure 3.1. Index in MS **A**. Bibliothèque nationale de France.

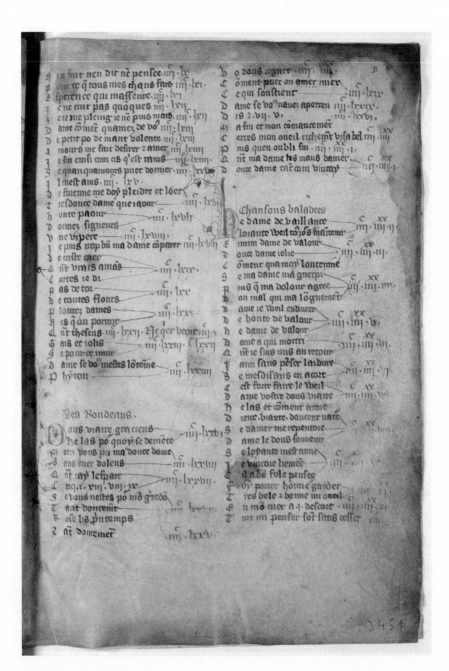

Figure 3.1. (*Continued*)

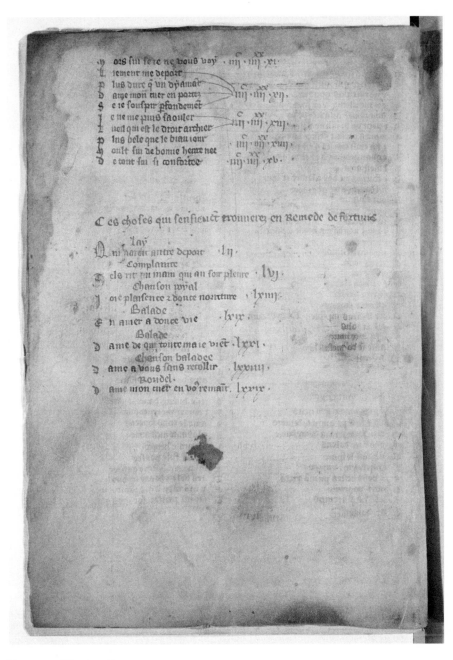

Figure 3.1. (*Continued*)

teachable senses: hearing and sight. Both items point to the unified nature of his entire output and underline clear imprecations to readers found throughout his works that the parts will be enriched by a consideration of the whole.

Machaut's Index

Of these two important innovations in manuscript **A**, the index, which starts with the red-inked statement "here is the order that G. de Machau[t] wants his book to have," has been noted by literary scholars who have adumbrated its role in the projection of a scribal poetics of ordering focused on Machaut's own name.[3] Musicologists interested in order, chronology, and the competing claims of variant musical readings between the sources of Machaut's works have also focused on the index. Lawrence Earp's study of this source has allowed him to reveal the extent and limitations of **A**'s authority in terms of its ordering, its reflection of chronology, and the accuracy of its texts.[4] It is,

3. F. Av: "Vesci lordenance que G. de Machau wet quil ait en son livre." See especially Laurence de Looze, *Pseudo-autobiography in the Fourteenth Century: Juan Ruiz, Guillaume de Machaut, Jean Froissart, and Geoffrey Chaucer* (Gainesville, 1997), 66–69; and also Kevin Brownlee, *Poetic Identity in Guillaume de Machaut* (Madison, 1984), especially 16–21; Huot, *From Song to Book*, 274–75; Ardis Butterfield, "Articulating the Author: Gower and the French Vernacular Codex," *Yearbook of English Studies* 33 (2003): 90–92; and Deborah McGrady, *Controlling Readers: Guillaume de Machaut and His Late Medieval Audience* (Toronto, 2006), especially chap. 3.

4. The ordering seems incontrovertibly authorial, even if scribal exigencies prevented its full implementation. The relationship of order to chronology is deeply problematic, however. Hoepffner's compelling arguments for the steady growth of the individual parts of the collection over time led early commentators to accept order as chronology for the music, even at the level of individual items within genre sections, but more recent arguments point out that although groups of songs occurring only in later sources are probably earlier, the manuscripts incontrovertibly provide only a date before which their contents must have been written, not a date after which things not included were composed. See, for example, Gilbert Reaney, "A Chronology of the Ballades, Rondeaux and Virelais Set to Music by Guillaume de Machaut," *Musica Disciplina* (1952): 33–38; Ursula Günther, "Chronologie und Stil der Kompositionen Guillaume de Machauts," *Acta Musicologica* 35 (1963): 96–114; Gilbert Reaney, "Towards a Chronology of Machaut's Musical Works," *Musica Disciplina* 21 (1967): 87–96; and Ursula Günther, "Problems of Dating in *ars nova* and *ars subtillior*," in *L'Ars Nova Italiana del Trecento IV* (Certaldo, 1978), 289–301. For the motets, twenty out of twenty-three of which occur in the earliest source in an order that remains relatively stable, Anne Walters Robertson notes that internal chronology cannot be determined because the ordering is thematic (Anne Walters Robertson, *Guillaume de Machaut and Reims: Context and Meaning in his Musical Works* [Cambridge, 2002], 185). For other less stable and continuously growing genre sections, order seems similarly thematic and appears particularly to thematize and represent chronology as an element of its pseudo-narrative nature, rather than presenting a true chronology (see Wulf Arlt, "*Helas! Tant ay dolour et peine*: Machaut's Ballade Nr. 2 und ihre Stellung innerhalb der Werkgruppe," in *Trent'anni di ricerche musicologiche: Studi in onore di F. Alberto Gallo,* ed. Patrizia dalla Vecchia and Donatella Restani [Rome, 1996], 99–114; and the arguments of Elizabeth Eva Leach, "Death of a Lover and the Birth of the Polyphonic Balade: Machaut's Notated Balades 1–5," *Journal of Musicology* 19 [2002]: 461–502, especially 496–97). Earp's findings about the quality of the musical items coincide with those of James I. Wimsatt, William W. Kibler, and Rebecca A. Baltzer, eds., *Guillaume de Machaut: Le*

significantly, a prescriptive index, with the discrepancies between it and the actual ordering providing a powerful tool for Earp's investigations into the copying history of the manuscript.[5]

Visually striking is the particular space given to the indexing of musical items, which are listed individually despite being relatively short, usually one side of a folio. While the dits are also listed individually, these occupy many folios and are far fewer in number than the musical items. The entire *Loange* is signaled en masse as "Les balades ou il na point de chant, Les chansons roiaus et les complaintes" (the balades which have no music, the chansons royals, and the complaints). Like the *Loange,* the musical items are a collection of single lyrics in the *formes fixes,* but they are not—as they might have been—listed collectively as "Les balade ou y a chant," (the balades which *have* music) or some such formulation, but instead are signaled individually, by incipit. The index is thus especially helpful to the reader in finding songs and, as is required by rubrics in the *Voir dit* (see the discussion later in this chapter), where necessary bringing them to bear on other parts of the manuscript.

The *Prologue*

That the index does not list the *Prologue* reflects the *Prologue*'s paratextual status, making it effectively part of the index itself.[6] The *Prologue,* like the index, appears to have been written especially for manuscript **A**. It similarly constructs a global authorial persona by presenting the poet and his ordered book, although it does so through allegorical poetry and illuminations rather than through a scribe-like rubrical mandate.[7] Jacqueline Cerquiglini-Toulet points out that Machaut's efforts mark a change from twelfth- and thirteenth-century prologues, which typically provide a purely scribal *accessus ad auctores* (explaining in genealogical fashion a book's provenance and how the author came to write it), to the later kinds of proud authorial prologues that set out a plan for the work that follows and introduce its themes.[8] A scribal-authorial hybrid, Machaut's *Prologue* introduces a book made of many items but emphasizes their authorial and thematic unity and the relation of the parts to the whole project of the manuscript book.[9]

Jugement du Roy de Behaingne and Remede de Fortune (Athens, Ga., 1988), 11–16, in broadly rejecting the extension of **A**'s authority from ordering to individual readings; see Earp, "Machaut's Role," 476, 486.

5. See Lawrence Earp, "Scribal Practice, Manuscript Production, and the Transmission of Music in Late Medieval France: The Manuscripts of Guillaume de Machaut" (Ph.D. diss., Princeton University, 1983); and idem, "Machaut's Role."

6. *OED* lists as an obsolete meaning of *index* "5a. A table of contents prefixed to a book, a brief list or summary of the matters treated in it, an argument; also, a preface, prologue."

7. Brownlee, *Poetic Identity,* 16–20.

8. Jacqueline Cerquiglini, *"Un engin si soutil": Guillaume de Machaut et l'écriture au XIVe siècle* (Geneva, 1985), 15.

9. See also Huot, *From Song to Book,* 232–38; Butterfield, "Articulating the Author," 90–92.

A theme central to Machaut's *Prologue,* even though the *Prologue* itself does not use musical notation, is the importance of music both in the book that follows and in living with joy. In particular, it argues not just that music is emotionally affecting (a standard claim) but that the creation of musical poetry requires a certain kind of emotional input from the creator in order to succeed. This stipulation extends the topos of requiring emotional authenticity from poetic to musical composition, reflecting Machaut's interest in music's ability to carry meaning as well as to inspire emotion.

The *Prologue* is a short but effective summa of Machaut's multimedia artistry. It opens with four balades, each preceded by an extensive rubric explaining the circumstances of its composition and introducing its speaker. The first pair of balades presents a conversation between Nature and Guillaume de Machaut, the second between Love and Machaut; both are illustrated (see figures 3.2 and 3.3, respectively).[10] The two allegorical personages visit the poet in turn and present him with their three children: *Sens,*[11] Rhetoric, and Music from Nature; Sweet Thought, Pleasure, and Hope from Love. The *Prologue* expounds on the projected use of these allegorical offspring in the practice of authorship, and in its last section—184 lines of narrative poetry in the rhyming octosyllabic couplets typical of most of Machaut's other dits—especially on the relationship between music and joy.[12] The explicit of the *Prologue* functions to introduce the manuscript's first proper narrative dit by locking its title into its rhyme: "Et pour ce vueil, sans plus targier, / Commencier *le Dit dou Vergier*" (And so I wish, without more ado, to start the *Story of the Orchard*).[13] Although it was added later, the *Prologue* thereby integrates itself seamlessly into one of Machaut's earliest poems, explicitly (authorially) and implicitly (scribally) binding the book's various contents into one authorial whole.

Despite its striking originality and multimedia presentation, the *Prologue* is not completely without precedent. The lesser-known Hainuyer poet Jehan de le Mote, who had a poetic spat with Philippe de Vitry and whose lyrics Machaut quotes in a number of his own, has a similar "prologue" at the start

10. The foliation here is modern and was added "when the appended bifolium was bound incorrectly, hence the inverted folio order for the miniatures." See Domenic Leo, "Authorial Presence in the Illuminated Machaut Manuscripts" (Ph.D. diss., New York University, 2005), 220n476 and Appendix 4; and Earp, *Guillaume de Machaut,* 87–89. In general the *Prologue* seems to have caused some difficulty with the organization of the gatherings; see Earp, *Guillaume de Machaut,* 205.

11. This term is problematic to translate and will not be translated here; see my discussion later in this chapter.

12. Divergence from the norm of octosyllabic couplets occurs in only a few of the shorter dits (*Harpe* has decasyllables, *Vezci les biens* has hexasyllables, the *Dit de la marguerite* has sixteen-line stanzas) and in *Behaingne,* which has heterometric quatrains in a concatenated rhyme pattern. See Earp, *Guillaume de Machaut,* chap. 5 (189–235), for further details.

13. *Prologue,* in Ernest Hoepffner, *Oeuvres de Guillaume de Machaut,* 3 vols. (Paris, 1908–1922), 1:12, ll. 183–84. (Except where otherwise noted, translations are mine.)

Figure 3.2. *Prologue* in **A**, f. Er. Bibliothèque nationale de France. Machaut receives the children of Nature.

of his eulogizing poem *Li regret Guillaume* (1339).[14] Jehan's poem operates by having a minimal narrative frame (a dream) that enables its subject to be "imaged" (figured forth) in thirty lyrics using the repetitive technique of *frequentatio* as a way of representing the bounteousness of Nature's own creation.[15] It laments the death of William I, Count of Hainaut, father of Queen Philippa of England (wife of Edward III). Like some oneiric peeping Tom, the narrator views thirty female personifications through a chink in a wall. Each in turn laments the dead count, but none is herself independently described or strongly individuated. Instead they are like the weepers on ceremonial tombs that became popular at this period, expressing lineage or adherence of other kinds (here, the attendance of virtues at the count's court).[16] In the ninety-six-line opening, before the narrative proper begins, Jehan de le Mote prays first to Nature for *Sens, Souvenir* (mental image), and *Mesure* (Moderation), with which to order his work.[17] He then prays to God, the Virgin, the archangel (that is, Gabriel), and the Trinity.[18] In Machaut's *Prologue, Sens* is the firstborn of the children of Nature, and the issue of ordering is also central: in replying to Nature, Guillaume de Machaut puns on the two senses of "order" to affirm that "drois est, quant vous m'ordenez / A faire diz amoureux ordenez" (it is right, because you have ordered me, to make love poems that are ordered).[19] Jehan de le Mote's invocation of the Christian God, the Virgin Mary, and the Angel of the Annunciation is paralleled in the latent Annunciation imagery of Machaut's presentation of Love in the second *Prologue* miniature and pair of balades, with both poets comparing poetry inspired by Nature to the production of a more literally salvific offspring by the Virgin Mary.[20]

14. On Jehan as a model for Machaut, see James I. Wimsatt, *Chaucer and His French Contemporaries: Natural Music in the Fourteenth Century* (Toronto, 1991), 55–58. All three poets are mentioned together in Gilles li Muisis's *Meditations;* see [Joseph-Marie-Bruno-Constantin, Baron] Kervyn de Lettenhove, ed., *Poésies de Gilles li Muisis*, vol. 1 (Louvain, 1882), 88–89, ll. 324–39. This poem itself has a lengthy opening incipit rubric (see Kervyn, *Poésies de Gilles li Muisis*, 79), which gives its title, names the author, who has "thought, ordered, and had written" [*a penset, ordenet et fait escrire*] the work, and gives Easter 1350 as the starting date for its composition.

15. Wimsatt, *Chaucer and His French Contemporaries*, 308–9n53; Douglas Kelly, *Medieval Imagination: Rhetoric and the Poetry of Courtly Love* (Madison, 1978), 29–53, especially 42.

16. On weepers, see *Les pleurants dans l'art du Moyen Age en Europe* ([Dijon], 1971); and Paul Binski, *Medieval Death: Ritual and Representation* (London, 1996), 104. Binski notes that "weepers" are often not depicted mourning; Anne McGee Morganstern, *Gothic Tombs of Kinship in France, the Low Countries, and England* (University Park, Pa., 2000), 3–4, differentiates between true weepers on ceremonial (usually royal) tombs, which depict the moment of the funeral, and the more genealogical focus of "kinship tombs," whose figures are not usually shown in funerary garb but rather are wearing clothing indicative of social status. See also my discussion in chapter 6.

17. [Jean] Aug[uste Ulrich] Scheler, ed., *Jehan de la Mote: Li Regret Guillaume, Comte de Hainaut. Poème inédit du XIVe siècle* (Louvain, 1882), 2, ll. 25–34.

18. Ibid., 3, ll. 49–66.

19. *Prologue* 2.5–6. See Cerquiglini, *"Un engin si soutil,"* 15–21.

20. For more on this iconographical interpretation of Love's presentation of his children to Machaut, see the discussion later in this chapter.

Figure 3.3. *Prologue* in **A**, f. Dr. Bibliothèque nationale de France. Machaut receives the children of Love.

From Jehan de le Mote's poem, which we know Machaut knew well, Machaut learned how to make "lyric content predominate and to feature lyric insertions in a slight narrative."[21] Machaut, typically, goes far beyond his models. His exploitation of three paratextual elements—rubrics, pictures, and music—makes his *Prologue* far more powerful than anything that precedes it. The extensive rubrics that herald the large illuminations are the mouthpiece of the scribal Machaut speaking as the voice of the book itself—usually, as here, in red ink. They are so detailed that they have been thought to be Machaut's own instructions to the illuminator.[22] In their copied context, however, they draw on an earlier precedent in the *Roman de la Rose* in which rubrication helps to define the separate sections of the text, and names the speakers of dialogue passages.[23] The pictures they introduce were painted by the Master of the Bible of Jean de Sy, an artist whose works include a number of French royal manuscripts.[24] Machaut is shown twice—once in each picture being visited by the two families of four allegorical figures, who are shown giving him the subject matter and practical skills for his works.

From the earliest modern edition of the *Prologue* it was pointed out that its mixture of lyric and narrative is a "run-through of the whole oeuvre of the poet."[25] This is not just a matter of lyric and narrative, however. The *Prologue* offers the viewer a snapshot of Machaut's completeness as an artist in containing lyric poetry, illuminations, and narrative, as well as pointing to the scribal activities of ordering, rubrication, and page turning. And music, too, is present

21. Wimsatt, *Chaucer and His French Contemporaries,* 57. Machaut cites lines from two of the lyrics in *Li regret Guillaume* in his own balades set to music, *On ne porroit* (B3) and *Biaute* (B4). Even citation in the opposite direction (which seems less likely) would, given the contemporaneity of the two men, still show their awareness of each other's work. See Leach, "Death of a Lover," 488–89 and 488n49, where "Isabelle of Hainault" should read *Philippa* of Hainaut.

22. Earp, *Guillaume de Machaut,* 205. On the later influence of Machaut's use of a scribal rubric to announce authorship, see Butterfield, "Articulating the Author."

23. Huot, *From Song to Book,* 250. Huot cites Brownlee's observation that in the later manuscripts of Machaut's *Remede* (A and F) the rubric "l'amant" appears only after the narrator has been educated by Hope. See Brownlee, *Poetic Identity,* 230n19. In C this designation appears in the rubric that precedes the complaint, which is at a point before Hope appears. See also chapter 4, note 85.

24. See François Avril, *Manuscript Painting at the Court of France: The Fourteenth Century (1320–1380)* (London, 1978), 28 and 96–103 (plates 29–32). Avril distinguishes the Sy Master from a number of hands in the so-called Boquetaux Master group; see Stephen Perkinson, *The Likeness of the King: A Prehistory of Portraiture in Late-Medieval France* (Chicago, 2009), 218–19; Peter Burkhart, "Eine wiederentdeckte Bible historiale aus der königlichen Bibliothek im Louvre: Stuttgart, WLB cod Bibl. 2.6," *Scriptorium* 53 (1999): 192–95; Carra Ferguson O'Meara, *Monarchy and Consent: The Coronation Book of Charles V of France, British Library MS Cotton Tiberius B. VIII* (London, 2001), 270; and Margaret Manion, "The Princely Patron and the Liturgy: Mass Texts in the *Grandes heures* of Philip the Bold," in *The Cambridge Illuminations: The Conference Papers,* ed. Stella Panatotova (London, 2007), 197n31.

25. Hoepffner, *Oeuvres de Guillaume de Machaut,* liv: "Ce *Prologue* est comme un raccourci de toute l'oeuvre du poète, tant dans la forme que dans le fond." Translation from Brownlee, *Poetic Identity,* 16.

here, despite the absence of musical notation from this part of the book. First of all, the presence of lyric is itself musical and performative: the implication that Nature, Love, and Machaut are in oral dialogue is grounded in the fact of their speech being pictured as *forme fixe* lyrics. Second, Music is one of the three children presented to Machaut by Nature and is thus depicted allegorically and visually, linking picture and music. Most important, the ensuing narrative mentions eight lyric genres in which the author promises to compose, and treats at some length the correct relation between artistic subjectivity and musical composition.[26] This narrative section is part of manuscript **A** proper; the opening four balades of the *Prologue* in this, its earliest instantiation, occupy folios that were added later.[27]

The paired portraits that open the *Prologue* in **A** appear on consecutive rectos, not facing across an opening. The reader must turn the page to see the second illustration. Yet the striking mirror imagery of the two portraits, and the fact that they articulate a number of meaningful binary oppositions germane to the whole of Machaut's output, pair them incontestably. As well as presenting the poet and introducing his iconographic, narrative, lyric, and musical work, the very opening of Machaut's book thereby teaches its readers one more practical skill: page turning. Turning pages and preserving mental links between objects in different parts of the unified whole that follows the *Prologue* will be of vital importance in reading Machaut's works. As Domenic Leo attests: "Before embarking on the grandest of journeys, through the poet's lifetime work, the artist/iconographer asks the viewer to leap back and forth within the *Prologue*—from image to image, and image to text—then within Machaut's *oeuvres complètes*. The more the viewer is familiar with Machaut's works and Machaut as a personality, the richer the associations in the *Prologue* images become."[28]

The refrain of the opening balade, voiced by Nature, introduces the three children in the order *Sens*, Rhetoric, and Music, which is the order in which they are discussed in the three stanzas of the balade as a whole. The picture, which has a commanding al fresco Machaut standing casually aside from his chair to receive the three children whom the crowned figure of Nature

---

26. *Prologue* 5.11–16; and see note 53 in this chapter.

27. See Earp, *Guillaume de Machaut*, 87–89, and note 10 in this chapter. Leo, "Authorial Presence," 244–48, has advanced a hypothetical historical scenario for this addition in which a royal patron chose to "upgrade" the dying Machaut's final overseen book of complete works by commissioning miniatures from a painter that were far better than those found throughout the rest of the manuscript, and a painter, moreover, who had illuminated Machaut manuscripts before. In this reading the author portrait is appreciative—a loving commemoration of a dying (or recently dead) poet. Support for this reading is lent by the fact of other commemorations in music (see my discussion in chapter 6). The irregularities of the gathering structure for the *Prologue* and the fact that it is not in **A**'s index suggest it was new at the point when this manuscript was finished. The current binding of the images reverses their proper order as specified in the rubrics. See Earp, "Scribal Practice," 85, 344.

28. Leo, "Authorial Presence," 219.

is introducing to him, has the allegories in the same order once the lineup is read from right to left because its goal, Machaut, is himself positioned on the right (figure 3.2).[29] At the front of the line is *Sens,* depicted as a capped and caped theologian, with a physiognomy whose level of detail approaches modern ideas of portraiture in showing "lifelike" attributes.[30] The wimpled female religious who accompany him are more standardized depictions. All three figures are heavily garbed in draped robes, which they pick up with their hands as they approach Machaut.[31] Their baggy religious clothing provides an observable contrast to the tight-fitting, secular apparel of the children of Love. Over the page, Guillaume de Machaut, now indoors, seated, and on the left of the image, is ostensibly startled by the entrance of the winged figure of Love and his three children (figure 3.3). Again the children form a line in which two standardized female figures are headed by an individuated male figure—Sweet Thought—whose buttocks, palpable through his tight-fitting hose, starkly differentiate him from the religious figures in the first miniature.

These two portraits articulate various dualities mirrored around a Machaut "hinge," contrasting sacred, chaste old age, with secular, reproductive youth, and complementing clerical subjects in a natural outdoor setting with aristocratic rulers indoors.[32] The religious and intellectual community of Machaut's clerkly peers, traveling from afar to see him in the opening picture, represents his "natural" gifts, needed in the practice ("la pratique") of poetry.[33] The "matere" ([subject] matter) of Love comes instead from his social superiors, the secular world of the court—aristocrats in whose service he is to deploy those gifts, making poems that will bring them joy.[34] The narrative's implied chronology— perhaps itself a form of the (pseudo-)autobiography so prevalent in Machaut's

---

29. On the subversion of more usual donation illustrations at the head of contemporary literary manuscripts, in which the author figure kneels, see Deborah McGrady, "Guillaume de Machaut," in *The Cambridge Companion to Medieval French Literature,* ed. Simon Gaunt and Sarah Kay (Cambridge, 2008), 116, 121, and my discussion later in this chapter.

30. See Perkinson, *The Likeness of the King,* 218–27. The reference to a real-life individual is strongly argued by Leo, "Authorial Presence," 229–30, who does not, however, venture an identification. Though writing about Bonneürté's possible representation of Bonne of Luxembourg in *Navarre* rather than *Sens* in the *Prologue,* Earp, in *Guillaume de Machaut,* 25n94, not only notes that "references to allegorical characters may mask references to specific personages," but also cites Raymond Cazelles's similar identification of the personification *Sens* in Gace de la Buigne's *Roman des Deduis* (Raymond Cazelles, *Société politique, noblesse et couronne sous Jean le Bon et Charles V* [Geneva, 1982], 402–14, especially 403) with Guillaume de Melun, archbishop of Sens. A good case could be made for identifying *Sens* in Machaut's *Prologue* also with Guillaume de Melun.

31. Leo, "Authorial Presence," 228–230; Perkinson, *The Likeness of the King,* 221–25.

32. Leo, "Authorial Presence," 228–29.

33. *Prologue* 1.7.

34. *Prologue* 3.8. The pairing of practice and matter in statements about the inspiration for the composition of poetry is similar to that of *sens* and matter in Machaut's *Harpe,* which is in turn based on this pairing in the prologue to Chrétien de Troyes's *Chevalier de la charrete;* see Huot, *From Song to Book,* 292.

works—implies that Machaut was first instructed by the Church and then took his gifts into the world of the court; it also sources his poetry jointly in engagement with the natural world (via his natural gifts) and in books.[35] In the courtly setting he appears in the guise of the comical "cowardly lover," familiar from the narrator of *Navarre* and the *Voir dit,* another Guillaume de Machaut alter ego.

Nonetheless, as Leo stresses, the composition of the pictures upsets an easy duality between religious and aristocratic worlds, since the winged figure of Love also resembles the archangel Gabriel in contemporary depictions of the Annunciation to the Virgin.[36] Viewed in this way, Machaut becomes a Marian figure, humble and lowly, startled, but ultimately about to engender something consoling for the whole of humanity. His book is in place of an infant—specifically, in place of the Christ child. The image inverts the more traditional author portraits found in other contemporary books, especially translations commissioned by Charles V and other members of the French royal house, in which the author comes to the enthroned king or patron and, often kneeling, presents his book.[37] In effect the image inverts social, natural, and religious order to establish the reign of the artist.[38] This analysis is supported by the visual resonance between the figures of Love here and in the *Roman de la Rose* in Pierpont Morgan manuscript M. 132, which is "reminiscent of" the work of the Master of the Bible of Jean de Sy, from a period roughly contemporary with manuscript **A**.[39] In the *Rose* illumination, Love is shown vesting Nature's priest, Genius (see figure 3.4). Machaut's Genius-like role within the *Prologue* has been independently advanced by Sylvia Huot on the basis of literary parallels.[40] Genius, the last poet in the *Rose,* posits a concordance between the natural and the divine, arguing that sexual fulfillment is akin to spiritual salvation. At the midpoint of the *Rose,* where the authors of the conjoined text are named, Jean de Meun's birth is presided over by Nature (in the form of the goddess Lucina), but he receives poetic inspiration from, and is crowned by, Love.

35. Leo, "Authorial Presence," 236; Perkinson, *The Likeness of the King,* 224–25.

36. Annunciation imagery also forms a point of reference for Deborah McGrady ("Guillaume de Machaut," 116–18). Leo points out ("Authorial Presence," 240) that the pair of portraits could also be drawing on the Annunciation to the shepherds and the Adoration of the Magi. But both those events would equally imply Christmastide and the birth of something wondrous, so the parallel between the birth of Christ and the "birth" of Machaut's work remains.

37. Leo, "Authorial Presence," 232.

38. Ibid., 221–22; and Françoise Ferrand, "Doux Penser, Plaisance et Espérance chez Guillaume de Machaut et Charles d'Orléans: Un nouvel art d'aimer," in *Plaist vos oïr bone cançon vallant? Mélanges de langue et de littérature médiévales offerts à François Suard,* ed. Dominique Boutet et al., vol. 1 (Villeneuve d'Ascq, 1999), 241–50.

39. See the information in the online catalogue, http://corsair.morganlibrary.org/msdescr/ BBM0132.htm, 1 (pdf download). Leo, "Authorial Presence," 6, proposes a date around 1380. The image may have been painted by another member of the Boquetaux Master group.

40. Sylvia Huot, "Reliving the *Roman de la Rose*: Allegory and Irony in Machaut's *Voir Dit,*" in *Chaucer's French Contemporaries: The Poetry/Poetics of Self and Tradition,* ed. R. Barton Palmer (New York, 1999), 60–64.

Sought out by Nature and Love, Machaut cuts a Genius-like figure not least because writing is centrally important to both Jean de Meun's Genius and Jean de Meun's own model—the *De planctu Naturae* (The Complaint of Nature) of Alan of Lille. As the reader views each *Prologue* miniature, the enormous bulk of Machaut's complete writings lie fatly under its recto folio. In *Rose* the ever-changing world is inscribed in Genius's book, and Nature asks him to tell Love the rules of the book of Nature. The parallels between natural and artistic creation—between sexual reproduction and writing—are explored by Machaut, *Rose,* and *Rose*'s model, *De planctu Naturae.* In *De planctu Naturae,* the active masculine hammer stamps its image on the new life it makes on top of the passive feminine anvil; in *Rose,* the phallus as a pen writes on the tablets that are women's bodies. Machaut, however, replaces procreation with poetic creation (the realization of natural creativity), offering a more literal response to Genius's recommendation: "greffez avez, pansez d'escrire" (you have pens, remember to write).[41] Writing in Machaut's book of Nature creates not new human life but other kinds of offspring: musical poems.[42]

The *Prologue* miniatures are the only works of the Sy Master in manuscript **A**.[43] The other miniatures in **A**, those in the originally foliated part of the book, are far less accomplished, even "provincial," and François Avril has speculated that they were done, with the rest of the book's contents, in Reims under Machaut's direct supervision.[44] Avril notes that they resemble the illuminations in a copy of a French translation of Boethius's *Consolation of Philosophy,* Montpellier, Bibliothèque de la Faculté de Medécine H. 43 (*F-MO H. 43*).[45] Although the editor of one Boethius translation (*Boece*) notes that the decoration on the smaller initials is reminiscent of the *style rémois,* this manuscript is generally thought to have been illuminated in Metz in the first third of the fourteenth century and was known to be in the possession of a Messine family in the sixteenth century.[46] This manuscript is a close match for the *style* of the *rest* of **A**, but one of its miniatures resembles aspects of the *composition* of the *Prologue* miniatures (see figure 3.5). In *F-MO H.*

41. Armand Strubel, ed., *Guillaume de Lorris et Jean de Meun: Le Roman de la Rose* (Paris, 1992), l. 19798, cited in Huot, "Reliving the *Roman de la Rose,*" 65.

42. Huot, "Reliving the *Roman de la Rose,*" 59–64; Jan M. Ziolkowski, *Alan of Lille's Grammar of Sex: The Meaning of Grammar to a Twelfth-Century Intellectual* (Cambridge, 1985), 27–30.

43. This artist also worked on **Vg**; see Earp, *Guillaume de Machaut,* 134, item 2.

44. François Avril, "Les manuscrits enluminés de Guillaume de Machaut: Essai de chronologie," in *Guillaume de Machaut: Poète et Compositeur* (Reims, 1982), 126–27.

45. Ibid., 126n28.

46. J. Keith Atkinson, ed., *Boeces, De Consolacion: Edition critique d'après le manuscrit Paris, Bibl. nationale, fr. 1096, avec Introduction, Variantes, Notes et Glossaires* (Tübingen, 1996), 8, compares the minor decoration to that in a missal from Reims (Bibliothèque municipale, MS 230), although his probable source (Jean Porcher, *L'enluminure française* [Paris, 1959], 49, fig. 54) cites a different example, a Bible from Reims (Bibl. mun. MS 39), reproducing f. 99. On the Messine provenance of *F-MO H. 43,* see Avril, "Les manuscrits enluminés de Guillaume de Machaut," 126n28; and Leo, "Authorial Presence," 240. See also chapter 5, note 58.

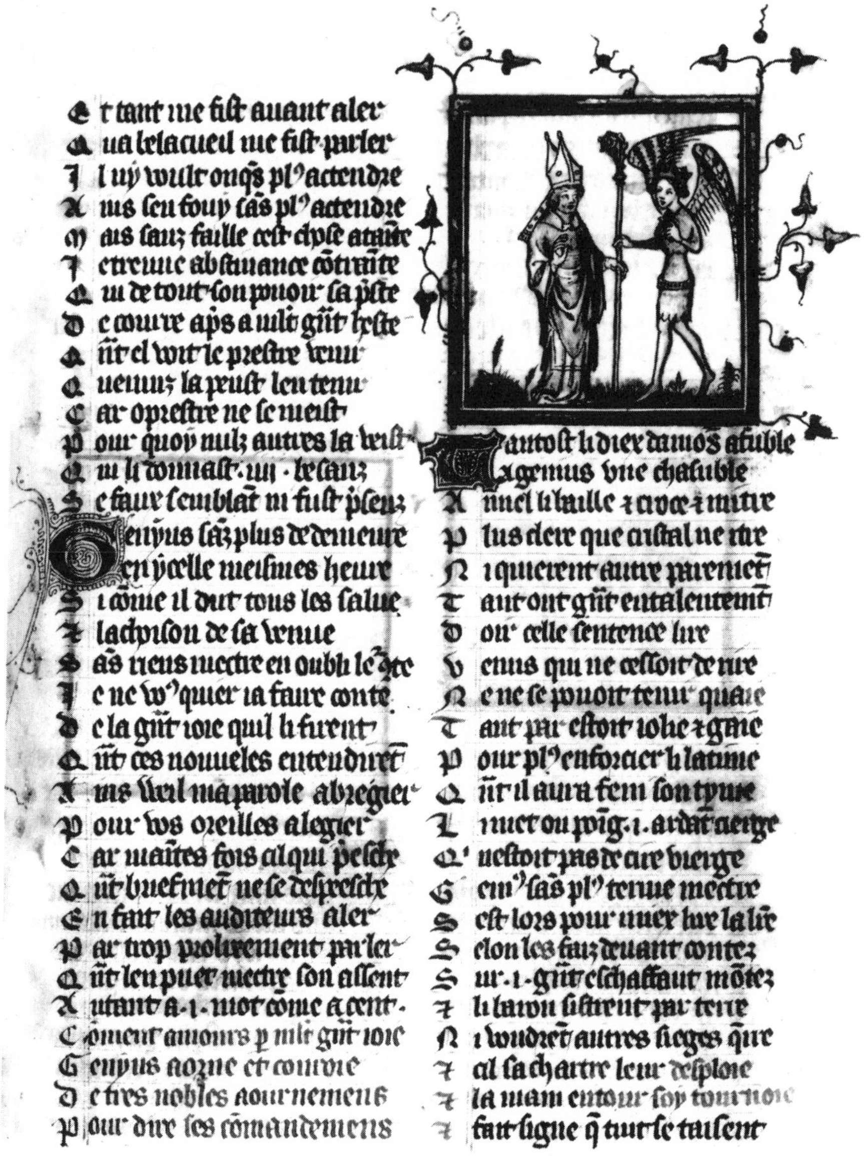

Figure 3.4. The god of Love vests Genius in New York, Morgan Library, MS M. 132, f. 138r.

43, Boethius is depicted lying down at the right of the image flanked by Philosophy (on the left) and the two figures she introduces (on the far right). J. Keith Atkinson states that these figures represent the liberal arts: Music with a notated book, and a figure Atkinson tentatively identifies as Rhetoric, which would fit with the text it accompanies—*Boece*, book 2, prose 1. Another

Figure 3.5. Philosophy introducing to the dreamer a crowned figure and Music, from book 2, prose 1, of *Boece,* in Montpellier, Bibliothèque de la Faculté de Medécine H. 43, f. 4v.

possible reading of this pair, suggested by the title of the image in the library's own online resource, is as a representation of the Church, with its liturgical rituals (the chalice) and music (the notated book). The crowned figure in the *Boece* depiction additionally has some visual resonance with the crowned personification of Nature in the *Prologue* miniature.[47] It is possible to hypothesize tentatively that if the same artist worked on this Boethius manuscript and on the rest of manuscript **A,** he or she perhaps originally drafted the *Prologue*'s images too, using models similar to those with which he or she was familiar in his or her work on the *Consolation;* these were perhaps then replaced by upgraded copies, taking compositional and visual details from the originals, but newly executed by the king's favorite artist, perhaps at the instigation of the king himself. An alternative scenario is merely that Machaut was familiar with the Montpellier source of the *Consolation* translation and bore it in mind when composing the *Prologue* and writing the rubrics for its miniatures.

47. The discussion of *F-MO* H. 43, f. 4v, in Leo, "Authorial Presence," 240, is erroneously illustrated in his plate 163 by a similar picture on f. 2r (seemingly taken from Porcher, *L'enluminure française,* 49, fig. 53). As Atkinson, *Boeces, De Consolacion,* 8, notes, f. 2r shows Plato and Socrates being introduced to the supine Boethius by Philosophy at the start of the third metrum of book 1. All images in this *Boeces* can be viewed via the library's website.

As a text, Boethius's *Consolation* offers clear parallels with Machaut's own literary project.[48] The *Consolation* is a prosimetrum; that is, it mixes sung lyrics with prose, and offers a moralization of secular ideas and an ethical way forward which is congruent with Christian ideals. Machaut's similarly generically mixed book also provides points of allegorical equivalence between the secular and the sacred forms of love. The opening images of the *Prologue* do exactly this with their diptych of sacred and then secular figures hinged on the central author figure, Machaut, especially in their retention of sacred resonances in the second, "courtly-secular" image. Leo has likened the "polyphonic" nature of the opening to a medieval motet, a form that typically at this period (and in the majority of the examples by Machaut contained within the book) mixes a sacred plainchant tenor with secular upper voices.[49] As noted earlier, the discourse of Genius in Jean de Meun's continuation of the *Rose* similarly (if problematically) juxtaposes spiritual and erotic registers.

As Leo's comparison between the *Prologue* miniatures and the polyphony of the motet emphasizes, music is especially well placed to bring sacred and secular registers into counterpoint and thus harmony. The narrative part of the *Prologue* cites music for the Mass and the songs of Orpheus, epitomizing sacred music and secular lyric: the book that follows contains both. The text describes singing in praise of the Virgin and of God's glory, but her place in the iconography is taken by Machaut. In the same way that the Virgin will intercede for sinners in heaven because she generates the son who will save

48. See Sylvia Huot, "Guillaume de Machaut and the Consolation of Poetry," *Modern Philology* 100 (2002): 169–95; Sarah Kay, "Touching Singularity: Consolations, Philosophy, and Poetry in the French *Dit*," in *The Erotics of Consolation: Desire and Distance in the Late Middle Ages*, ed. Catherine E. Léglu and Stephen J. Milner (Basingstoke, 2008), 21–38; and my discussion in chapter 4. Machaut's similarly consolatory *Confort* follows other French translations of Boethius's *Consolation* in Chantilly, Musée Condé, MS 485, and Bern, Burgerbibliothek, MS A 95, and **Pm** concludes with another copy of the *Boeces, De consolation*; see Earp, *Guillaume de Machaut*, 101–2, 107–8; Cerquiglini, "*Un engin si soutil*," 75 and 75n40; and Glynnis M. Cropp, "Les manuscrits du 'Livre de Boece de Consolacion,'" *Revue d'histoire des textes* 12–13 (1982–83): 263–68, 284–85.

49. Leo, "Authorial Presence," 240. On reading motets as sacred-secular allegories, see Sylvia Huot, *Allegorical Play in the Old French Motet: The Sacred and Profane in Thirteenth-Century Polyphony* (Stanford, 1997); and Suzannah Clark, "'S'en dirai chançonete': Hearing Text and Music in a Medieval Motet," *Plainsong and Medieval Music* 16 (2007): 31–59. On Machaut's motets read in this way, see Kevin Brownlee, "Machaut's Motet 15 and the *Roman de la Rose*: The Literary Context of *Amours qui a le pouoir / Faus samblant m'a deceü / Vidi Dominum*," *Early Music History* 10 (1991): 1–14; idem, "Polyphonie et intertextualité dans les motets 8 et 4 de Guillaume de Machaut," in "*L'hostellerie de pensée*": *Études sur l'art littéraire au Moyen Age offertes à Daniel Poirion*, ed. Michel Zink et al., trans. Anthony Allen (Paris, 1995), 97–104; Robertson, *Guillaume de Machaut and Reims*; Kevin Brownlee, "La polyphonie textuelle dans le Motet 7 de Machaut: Narcisse, la *Rose*, et la voix féminine," in *Guillaume de Machaut: 1300–2000*, ed. Jacqueline Cerquiglini-Toulet and Nigel Wilkins (Paris, 2002), 137–46; and Yossi Maurey, "A Courtly Lover and an Earthly Knight Turned Soldiers of Christ in Machaut's Motet 5," *Early Music History* 24 (2005): 169–211. See also chapter 6.

them, the sublunary virgin Guillaume de Machaut will generate (because he has already generated) his "son"—the huge book that the *Prologue*'s reader is holding—whose consoling and salvific function is practiced by reading, hearing, and contemplating the pages that follow.

The narrative section of the *Prologue*, which follows the images and their accompanying balades, involves a change in the ruling of the page and of scribal hand, suggesting that this part belonged to the original corpus. Of the 184 lines of the narrative section of the *Prologue*, over three-quarters (146) concern music. Their content is firmly about refined, secular loving, but for the reader who has viewed the preceding pages, their prefatory pair of images has already drawn the parallels between this and a more "spiritual and artistic experience: the chaste, mental birth of poetry and music."[50]

Music is central in mediating the varied aspects of lived experience: as Huot notes, "for Machaut, poetry and music are not only the interface between Eros and Nature, but also between Eros, Nature, and God," a triangular mediation that is also performed by Jean de Meun's Genius as he presides over the joining of soul and body.[51] Machaut's book, which contains many separate dits and lyrics within it but is intentionally unified into a single supersaturated whole by the *Prologue*, like Genius's sermon in *Rose*, links the erotic and the spiritual with a view to unification rather than comparison. At the end of the *Prologue*, Machaut prays to Nature, Love, and God. Huot notes that Machaut's vernacular poetry attempts to sanctify secular Love through its deployment of a polyvalent language able to express any one of the erotic, the divine, or the natural in terms of any other. Machaut's strongest means of effecting and expressing the harmonious unity of life's natural, divine, and erotic aspects, however, is through specifically *musical* poetry, because music has very strong claims to harmonic relations that go beyond that to which mere language—which is problematically implicated in Venus's misuse of Nature's procreative forge in Alan of Lille's *De planctu Naturae*—can aspire. This is not to say that music was not also perceived as problematic in its relation to desire, but rather the practice of a hopeful and joyful music fixed in written notation provides assurance that it is the divinity of Orpheus—a type for Christ—that permeates Machaut's work, while his more equivocal resonances are deliberately disregarded.[52]

In the light of Machaut's literalization of procreation in terms of artistic creation, it is no surprise that Nature and Love bring him their own offspring,

---

50. Leo, "Authorial Presence," 244.

51. Huot, "Reliving the *Roman de la Rose*," 64. God and Nature collaborate in this creation, which resembles the creation of the perfect man in Alan of Lille's *Anticlaudianus;* see Alan of Lille, *Anticlaudianus or the Good and Perfect Man,* trans. James J. Sheridan (Toronto, 1987).

52. In the *Prologue* he is mentioned only as a type for Christ; on his homoerotic connotations, see Bruce W. Holsinger, *Music, Body, and Desire in Medieval Culture: Hildegard of Bingen to Chaucer* (Stanford, 2001), 295–343 (chap. 7, "Orpheus in Parts"), especially 321–26, which treats Machaut's *Harpe.*

which are nouns-personified-as-children, designed to assist the birth of his poems-as-children. All six children and their parents are mentioned again in the narrative section of the *Prologue,* which establishes a theory of poetic creativity based on the need for joy. Machaut thanks Nature and Love and promises to put all his understanding (*entendement*) and feeling (*sentement*), heart, body, power, and whatever he has into composing "dits and little songs…double hockets, pleasing lays, motets, rondeaux, and virelays (that are called 'danced songs'), complaints, [and] grafted balades."[53] All of these genres are to be found in the book that follows.[54] Machaut writes that spending time composing songs causes happiness, gaiety, and joy because no one intent on such things quarrels, or argues, or thinks of immorality, hate, foolishness, or scandal. Composition requires concentration on its own process and thus precludes other thoughts.[55]

Car quant je sui en ce penser,
Je ne porroie a riens penser
Fors que seulement au propos
Dont faire dit ou chant propos;
Et s'a autre chose pensoie,
Toute mon ouevre defferoie.

For when I am so minded [as to write poetry], I wouldn't be able to think about anything except this sole purpose of making the proposed dit or song; and if I were to think of something else, I would completely undo all my work.[56]

Even if he is composing about a sad matter ("s'on fait de triste matiere" [5.43]) the manner of composing it should be joyful, because a heart full of sorrow will never compose or sing well ("car ja bien ne fera / Ne gaiement ne chantera / Li cuers qui est pleins de tristece" (ll. 45–47).

The idea that music causes joy when it is heard has a long pedigree stretching back to antiquity, but the idea that the composer should be composing

---

53. Hoepffner, *Oeuvres de Guillaume de Machaut,* 1:6, 5.11–16: "chansonettes / Pleinnes d'honneur et d'amourettes, / Doubles hoquès et plaisans lais, / Motès, rondiaus et virelais / Qu'on claimme chansons baladées, / Complaintes, balades entées."

54. The expression "grafted balade" might serve to denote balades with a refrain as opposed to chansons royals, or with a borrowed refrain as opposed to one that is newly composed. On "enté," see Ardis Butterfield, "*Enté*: A Survey and Re-assessment of the Term in Thirteenth- and Fourteenth-Century Music and Poetry," *Early Music History* 22 (2003): 94.

55. *Prologue* 5.31–35. Around 1300, the Parisian music theorist Johannes de Grocheio acted as an apologist for various types of secular music using much the same argument; see Christopher Page, "Johannes Grocheio on Secular Music: A Corrected Text and a New Translation," *Plainsong and Medieval Music* 2 (1993): 24–27; and Elizabeth Eva Leach, *Sung Birds: Music, Nature, and Poetry in the Later Middle Ages* (Ithaca, 2007), 207–8.

56. *Prologue* 5.37–42.

from his own joy seems to be Machaut's own stipulation.[57] He simply cannot agree ("Ne je ne m'y puis accorder" [l. 55]) with those who say that composing from a sad heart is better—the verb "acorder" here implying a lack of specifically musical concord with this view.[58] He maintains instead that when visual memory (*souvenir*) brings the image of the lady to mind, only if the love is happy can it produce the joy required for song composition.[59] Machaut effectively extends to music the ideal of composing verse authentically according to one's "sentement," a powerful concept that ranged in reference from the personally experienced feelings of the speaker, through the idea of feeling in general, to more cognitive, intellectual, and semantic resonances that are closer to its etymological root in *sens*.[60]

Machaut's view in the *Prologue* is clear, and its position there makes it authoritative. But at various points in the works contained in his book the composition of sorrowful songs appears to be sanctioned in the same terms, as being "selonc mon sentement" (according to my *sentement*). In each instance, for the sad poet to compose a joyful song would be to "contrefaire," to make it against oneself; composition from sorrow rather than joy is thus explained as obeying the higher poetic law of emotional authenticity as a guarantee of truth. Near the beginning of the *Remede de Fortune,* for example, the young, timid lover-protagonist relates how he writes in many different musical genres according to his fluctuating *sentement* because "he who does not compose according to his *sentement,* falsifies his work and his song."[61] Similar statements are made by both lover and lady in the *Voir dit,* especially in *Plourez, dames* (B32), but in all cases the lovers are unreliable authorities, despite their seeming truth to their feelings, as is betrayed both within the narratives of these particular dits and also, by the time of manuscript **A**, because they make these claims in the context of a book whose reader is authoritatively directed at the book's outset to the correct understanding of this particular issue.[62]

57. A discussion of the views of Plato and Aristotle can be found in Mary B. Schoen-Nazzaro, "Plato and Aristotle on the Ends of Music," *Laval Theologique et Philosophique* 34 (1978): 261–73. See also Aristotle, *Politics* 8.5–6; *Nicomachean Ethics* 3.10; Boethius, *De musica* 1.1; Augustine, *Confessions* 10.50.

58. *Prologue* 5.52–55.

59. *Prologue* 5.56–84.

60. See Nicolette Zeeman, "The Lover-Poet and Love as the Most Pleasing 'Matere' in Medieval French Love Poetry," *Modern Language Review* 83 (1988): 820–42; and Ardis Butterfield, "Lyric and Elegy in *The Book of the Duchess,*" *Medium Aevum* 60 (1991): 43–50.

61. *Remede,* ll. 401–8: "Et pour ce que n'estoie mie / Tousdis en un point, m'estudie / Mis en faire chansons et lays, / Baladez, rondeaus, virelays, / Et chans, selonc mon sentement, / Amoureus et non autrement; / Car qui de sentement ne fait, / Son oeuvre et son chant contrefait." See chapter 4.

62. The entire phrase occurs in *Voir dit,* 110, letter 8, which will be considered further later on in this chapter. In addition, toward the end of the poem, as both lovers come under the sway of Fortune, Toute Belle composes an angry and sorrowful virelay "de mon sentement" (ibid., 586, letter 43).

The presence of seeming doctrinal contradiction in Machaut's works is enabled by the proliferation of individual items, while the reader's working out of the proper concord from such discord is aided by the projection of an underlying unity in the book as a physical (and thus doctrinal) whole. Machaut's overarching poetic persona is didactic and authoritative, while the various speakers of the "je" in his poems are often unsure of themselves and frequently comically ill-suited to their roles as lovers. The incorporation of dialogue, and the multiplicity of voices that Cerquiglini-Toulet has adduced as one of his characteristic innovations, makes Machaut's book resemble the plurality and profusion of life itself, which, like the book, is nevertheless subject to a unifying view, whose proper understanding requires mental work of an intellectual and emotional kind.

The most interesting instance of the claim that the *Prologue* categorically contradicts—that music should properly be composed out of sorrow when one is sad—occurs in a sequence of three lyric texts copied only in the context of their musical setting in the music section of Machaut's book. Because this discussion of the correct role of *sentement* in musical composition itself occurs in a musical piece, it is worth special attention. This song exemplifies the exceptional power of music, in Machaut's hands at least, to instruct the emotional self through contemplation prompted by the teachable senses, vision and hearing.

Composing and Counterfeiting: *De triste cuer / Quant / Certes*

Most of Machaut's balades set to music present a single three-stanza text (with the same music for each stanza) voicing a first person who might be a sententious clerk or an emotionally engaged lover, whether happy or sorrowful. Uniquely among Machaut's musical balades, *De triste cuer / Quant vrais amans / Certes, je di* (B29) sets three different balade texts, built on the same versification and rhyme types and sharing the same refrain, which speaks of sorrowful sadness and weeping tears of blood (texts and translations are given in figure 3.7; the musical setting is reproduced in example 3.1).[63] The second of these three texts virtually repeats what the narrative section of the *Prologue* prescribes, urging that composition be done only from joy because sorrow

---

63. Polytextuality is normal only in motets: all of Machaut's twenty-three motets are polytextual. Two other notated balades carry more than one balade text: *Quant Theseus / Ne quier* (B34) has two simultaneous texts and two untexted accompanying parts; *Sans cuer / Amis / Dame* (B17) has three different balade texts sharing a similar (but not identical) refrain, but musically is a canonic *chace* in which the three voices have the same music sung at slightly different times in the manner of a round. This manner of dramatizing male-female dialogue occurs in other fourteenth-century songs. In addition, *Je ne cesse (Le Lay de la Fonteinne)* (L16/11) and *S'onques dolereusement (Le Lay de Confort)* (L17) have stanzas that are canonic *chaces*, but each voice sings the same text.

Example 3.1. Triple balade *De triste cuer / Quant vrais amans / Certes, je di* (B29), with text of first stanza underlaid.

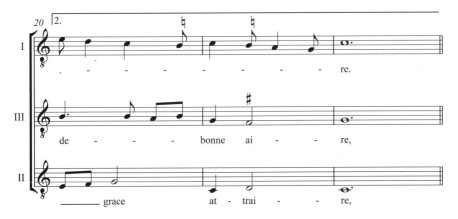

Example 3.1. (*Continued*)

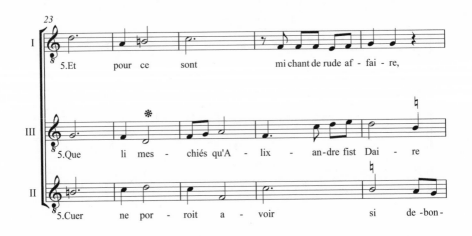

❋ Reading from **E** *(E in **VgBA**;*
    erased in **G**)

Example 3.1. (*Continued*)

Example 3.1. (*Continued*)

produces bad work, but the other two disagree in different ways. Because in their musical setting they would all be sung simultaneously—like a three-way conversation with everyone speaking at once—their arguments are designed to be taken conceptually in parallel. These are texts made to be heard. That their verbal discord (with their simultaneous sung declamation obfuscating each text's semantic immediacy) is presented in musical concord suggests the possibility for non-immediate (that is, reflective, studied) understanding and, ultimately, rational judgment.

Polytextuality in music has a specific effect, which seems at a first listening to militate against semantics in favor of the pleasures of pure sound.[64] The effect of three people "speaking" (in song) at once, however, is not chaotic in musical terms but highly ordered and organized, both rhythmically and harmonically.[65] And interested listeners would have had ready recourse to nonmusical versions of the texts—spoken, written, and remembered. The notation of the counter-point (that is, the placing of the notes in the different voices temporally against one another so that they harmonize with one another) locks the declamation of the texts into a temporal framework in a manner not possible without it. As this technique will be unfamiliar to most readers of poetry, a useful starting point is the three poems as they appear both in modern editions of the verbal texts

64. See comments on Kelly, *Medieval Imagination,* 254, in chapter 2; see also Christopher Page, "Around the Performance of a Thirteenth-Century Motet," *Early Music* 28 (2000): 343–57, for evidence that purely sonic pleasures are also present and meaningful.

65. More familiar to modern audiences, the operatic ensemble forms a partial point of comparison, since it usually involves a number of protagonists verbalizing private thoughts simultaneously. The comparison is not quite exact, however: the voices of an operatic ensemble are typically more differentiated in range than those in a medieval song, and they often both enter in a staggered manner and frequently sing a single textual phrase over and over, thereby making overall aural comprehension far more possible.

Figure 3.6. *De triste cuer / Quant vrais amans / Certes, je di* (B29), in manuscript **Vg**. Guillaume de Machaut: the Ferrell-Vogüé MS, f. 311v–312r. On loan to the Parker Library, Corpus Christi, Cambridge. Reproduced by kind permission of Elizabeth J. and James E. Ferrell. Digital imaging by DIAMM (www.diamm.ac.uk).

Q uardans delus momdnit (eaꝛ tenet : (on triſte cuer en douleur eꞇ en haꞷe : pourꝛe ne faiꞇ pas ſi
toltement : com alz qui toiꞇ eꞇ en voie repaꞷre : eꞇ ſe en li pꝛent ſoꝛuenirs ſon repaꞷre : qnt il ꝥ vienꞇ
tl le faiꞇ ſanz demeure ⁊ Tꝛiſte dol'· eꞇ č.

Qui ꝯl ymagine eꞇ penſe au grief tourment : ꝗ ſa dame li faiꞇ ſentiꝛ eꞇ traiꞛe : pour li ſeruir eꞇ a
mer loꝑaumeꞇ : helas dolens cꞁ a pouꝛe ſalaiꞛe : mieꞩ li vaurroiꞇ ſa vie vſer au quaiꞛe : qui en tel
ſeruice ou cuers eꞇ corps demeure ⁊ Tꝛiſte dolent eꞇ č.

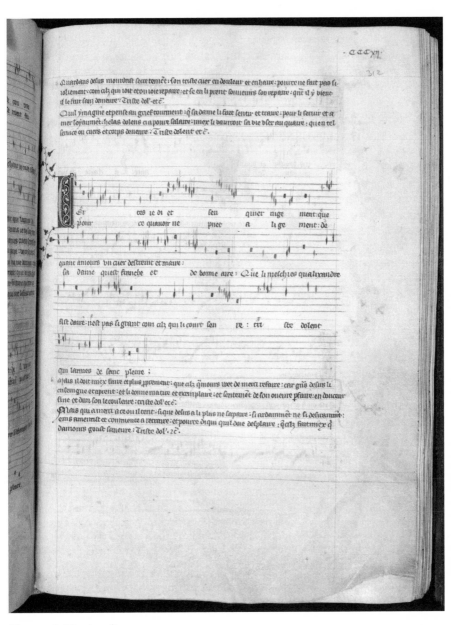

Eꞇ ces ꞁe di eꞇ ſen quier nige menꞇ : que
pour ce quauoir ne pneꞇ a li ge menꞇ : dꞷ
quanꞇ amours vn cuer deſtrenꞇ eꞇ maiꞛe :
ſa dame quieſt franche eꞇ de bonne aiꞛe : Que li melchies qualixandꞛe
fiſt dame neſt pas li granꞇ com alz qui li court ſen ꞛe : tꞷi lte dolent
qui larmes ꝺ ſanc pleuꞛe :

a) Ais il doiꞇ mieꞩ fruꞷre eꞇ plus pꝛuemenꞇ : que alz ꝗmours voeꞇ ꝺ merci refraiꞛe : car gꝛꝰ deſuꞛs li
en ſem que eꞇ aꝑrenꞇ : eꞇ li donne maniꞛe eꞇ exanplaiꞛe : eꞇ ſentemet ꝺ ſon onenꝛe pſaire : en doucenꝛ
fine eꞇ dun ſon ſecoulenꝛe : en fſte dol' eꞇ č.

P l ais qui a merci a ce ou il tenꞇ : ſi que deſuꞛs a li plus ne ſapaiꞛe : ſi ardammeꞇ ne ſi deſiramnꞇ :
em s amenriſt eꞇ conmence a reꞇraiꞛe : eꞇ pource diqui qui li doie delplaiꞛe : ꝗ alz fautmieꞩ ꝗ
damours gouꞇ ſeaneuꝛe ⁊ Tꝛiſte dol'· 2 č.

Figure 3.6. (*Continued*)

and on the manuscript page, that is, in sequence (see figure 3.6). Once they have been considered as sequential written or spoken texts, the additional meanings brought about by the music's pitting them against one another will be considered further (modern transcriptions and translations are given as figure 3.7).

The manuscript presentation of these three poems (and this single song) is shown in figure 3.6. The first poem is *De triste cuer*. The speaker—both poet-composer and lover—talks about making songs: "to compose [*faire*] joyously from a sad heart—in my opinion this is a contrary thing; but he who composes [*fait*] from joyous feelings, I say that he must compose [*faire*] more joyously." He goes on to explain that this is why his songs are all rather crude ("de rude affaire"), because they are made out of a heart blacker than a berry, which weeps tears of blood.[66] The crudeness of his song in turn means that he is blamed and reproved, because he does not know how to "counterfeit" his works ("mon ouevre contrefaire"). He humbly begs those who are blaming him to keep quiet because he cannot do otherwise. Instead he blames Fortune, who won't let him love anything more than himself and allows him only to please those who have a similarly sorrowing spirit.

"Contrefaire" is often translated as "counterfeit" or "feign," but it carries many senses, not all of them quite so negative. As Stephen Perkinson has shown, in the fourteenth century it generally referred to the copying of the outer appearance of a thing (rather than its inner essence).[67] While this might mean that the thing thus copied has the capacity to deceive, its fourteenth-century uses are closer to the idea of mimicking or mirroring than to the modern concept of duplicitous counterfeiting. In contracts (written in French) for the making of tomb images for the English king Richard II (1395), for example, the images were to "contrefaire" the king and queen.[68] This is a kind of portrayal, a representation, which is meant to be as close to the original as possible but is nonetheless at the second degree. In music the use of the prefix *contra* (Latin), *contre* (French), or *counter* (English) frequently implies not the faking of something but rather that something's counterpart, something

---

66. Loss of blood in medieval physiology means losing that which makes one sanguine or happy: to weep blood is to increase sorrow. An antiphon for the Tuesday or Wednesday of Holy Week draws on a similar idea in a disputed verse from Luke 22:44, in which Christ sweats tears of blood during the agony in the garden of Gethsemane. In Dante's *Inferno* 13.43–45, the suicides in the second circle of hell are transformed into trees that weep blood.

67. See Stephen Perkinson, "Portraits and Counterfeits: Villard de Honnecourt and Thirteenth-Century Theories of Representation," in *Excavating the Medieval Image: Manuscripts, Artists, Audiences; Essays in Honor of Sandra Hindman*, ed. Nina A. Rowe and David S. Areford (Aldershot, 2004), 13–36; idem, "Rethinking the Origins of Portraiture," *Gesta* 46 (2008): 135–57; and idem, *The Likeness of the King*, 135–88. On the significant use of this term in the refrain of another polytextual balade, see Elizabeth Eva Leach, "Nature's Forge and Mechanical Production: Writing, Reading, and Performing Song," in *Rhetoric beyond Words: Delight and Persuasion in the Arts of the Middle Ages*, ed. Mary Carruthers (Cambridge, 2010), 72–95.

68. Binski, *Medieval Death*, 103.

I [i.e., cantus]
De triste cuer faire joyeusement,
Il m'est avis que c'est chose contraire;
Mais cilz qui fait de joieus sentement,
Je di qu'il doit plus joieusement faire.
Et pour ce sont mi chant de rude affaire,
Qu'il sont tuit fait d'un cuer plus noir que meure,
Triste, dolent, qui larmes de sanc pleure.

To compose joyously from a sad heart—in my opinion this is a contrary thing; but he who composes from joyous feelings, I say that he must compose more joyously. Because of this all my songs are a crude affair, because they are all composed by a heart blacker than a berry, *sad, sorrowing, and weeping tears of blood.*

S'en suis repris et blasmés durement.
Mais je ne sçay mon ouevre contrefaire,
Eins moustre ce que mes cuers scet et sent;
Et les meschiés dont j'ay plus d'une paire—
Voire de cent!—si pert à mon viaire
Qu'ay l'esperit, où ma vie demeure,
Triste, dolent, qui larmes de sanc pleure.

So I am harshly reproved and blamed for it. But I do not know how to make my work contrary [to my heart], and so I show what my heart knows and feels; and the misfortunes of which I have more than a couple—truly a hundred!—appear in my face so that, where my life remains, I have a *sad, sorrowing* spirit, *weeping tears of blood.*

Et pour ce à tous suppli tres humblement
Que de mes chans blasmer se vueillent taire,
Car je ne sçay ne puis faire autrement
Pour Fortune qui tent à ce deffaire
Qu'aim miex que moy; n'elle ne me laist plaire
Qu'à ciaulz qui ont l'esperit à toute heure
Triste, dolent, qui larmes de sanc pleure.

And because of this I beg everyone very humbly that they please stop blaming me for my songs, because I do not know how to do them any other way on account of Fortune, who is trying to unmake that which I love more than myself; nor does she allow me to please anyone except those who always have a spirit *sad, sorrowing, and weeping tears of blood.*

II [i.e., tenor]
Quant vrais amans aimme amoureusement,
De si vray cuer qu'il ne saroit meffaire,
Et sa dame a tel cuer que nullement
N'en puet merci, douceur ne grace attraire,
Cuer ne porroit avoir si debonnaire
Que la liqueur dou sien à l'ueil ne queure,
Triste, dolent, qui larmes de sanc pleure.

When a true lover loves lovingly from such a true heart that he would not know how to misbehave, and his lady has such a heart that he can in no way attract from it *merci*, grace, or sweetness, he could not have a heart so debonair that the liquid from his heart would not seek a way out though his *sad, sorrowing* eye, *weeping tears of blood.*

Qu'Ardans Desirs mourdrist secretement
Son triste cuer en douleur et en haire;
Pour ce ne fait pas si joliement
Com cilz qui joit et ou joie repaire;
Et s'en li prent Souvenirs son repaire,
Quant il y vient, il le fait sanz demeure
Triste, dolent, qui larmes de sanc pleure.

Burning Desire secretly murders his sad heart in sorrow and in hatred; because of this he does not compose as merrily as he who rejoices where joy resides; and if Souvenir resides in him, when [Souvenir] comes there, [that man] without delay composes [in a manner] *sad, sorrowing, and weeping tears of blood.*

Qu'il ymagine et pense au grief tourment
Que sa dame li fait sentir et traire
Pour li servir et amer loyaument.
Helas! dolens, ci a povre salaire;
Miex li vaurroit sa vie user au Quaire
Qu'en tel service, où cuers et corps deveure
Triste, dolent, qui larmes de sanc pleure.

That he imagines and thinks of the deep torment that his lady makes him feel and bear in order to serve her and love her loyally. Alas, sorrowing, he has poor recompense; he would rather spend his life on a Crusade than in such service, which devours heart and body, *sad, sorrowing, weeping tears of blood.*

Figure 3.7. B29 texts and translations; I (cantus): *De triste cuer;* II (tenor): *Quant vrais amans;* III (contratenor): *Certes, je di.*

III [i.e., contratenor]
Certes, je di et s'en quier jugement,
Que, quant Amours un cuer destreint et maire,
Pour ce qu'avoir ne puet aligement
De sa dame qu'est franche et de bonne aire,
Que li meschiés qu'Alixandre fist Daire
N'est pas si grant com cilz qui li court seure,
Triste, dolent, qui larmes de sanc pleure.

Surely, I say (and seek the judgment of it) that
when Love destroys and mars a heart because
it cannot have relief from its lady, who is noble
and debonair, that the mischief that Alexander
did to Darius is not so great as that which he
runs after, *sad, sorrowing, and weeping tears of
blood.*

Mais il doit miex faire et plus proprement
Que cilz qu'Amours vuet de merci refaire,
Car grans Desirs li enseigne et aprent
Et li donne matire et exemplaire
Et sentement de son ouevre parfaire,
En douceur fine et d'un son le couleure,
Triste, dolent, qui larmes de sanc pleure.

But he might do better and more properly
than he whom Love wishes to remake through
merci, for great Desire teaches and instructs him
and gives him material and example and feeling
with which to perfect his work in fine sweetness
and color it with *sad, sorrowing* sound, *weeping
tears of blood.*

Mais [cilz] qui a merci, a ce où il tent,
Si que Desirs à li plus ne s'apaire
Si ardemment ne si desiramment,
Eins amenrist et commence à retraire.
Et pour ce di, qui qu'il doie desplaire,
Que cilz fait miex qui d'Amours goust saveure
Triste, dolent, qui larmes de sanc pleure.

But he who has *merci* has that which he is
attempting [to get], with the result that Desire
no longer appears to him so ardently nor so
fervently, but rather diminishes and begins to retreat. And because of this I say, whoever it might
displease, that he fares better who tastes the *sad,
sorrowing* tang of love, *weeping tears of blood.*

Figure 3.7. (*Continued*)

different but which resembles, enriches, and glosses, and with which it will
harmonize. This is the sense of the voice part "contratenor" as it relates to
the tenor. The contratenor is not a specific voice type (it is usually in the same
pitch range as the tenor part and would thus be sung by a singer with the
same vocal range or voice type), but instead a description of contrapuntal
function.[69] It is also the sense of the prefix in "counterpoint" (*contrapunctus*)
as a musical technique in which a note in one voice is placed against (that is,
simultaneously *and* in harmony with) a note in another. The sorrowing lover
of *De triste cuer* cannot make *joyful* musical poetry against—that is, simultaneously *and* in harmony with—his love situation because such joy would not
portray it accurately.

The second poem, *Quant vrais amans*, has a rather different kind of narrator. His voice is detached and clerkly as he ruminates on the fate of a true
lover who loves truly ("vrais amans aimme amoureusement"). Such a man,
he opines, when faced with an immovable lady, cannot, however noble he is,
prevent his heart's liquid issuing through his eyes. The mental image ("Souvenirs") of the lady comes to him and makes him compose without delay,
but, because he imagines the torment that his lady makes him feel, he does
so weeping tears of blood. Desire murders his heart in sorrow and hatred,

69. See Margaret Bent, "Naming of Parts: Notes on the Contratenor, c. 1350–1450," in *"Uno
gentile et subtile ingenio": Studies in Renaissance Music in Honour of Bonnie J. Blackburn*, ed.
Gioia Filocamo, M. Jennifer Bloxam, and Leofranc Holford-Stevens (Turnhout, 2009), 1–12.

and thus he cannot compose as well ("si joliement") as someone living in joy. Sorrow is a spur to composition, but it does not produce compositions of the same quality as those prompted by joy. The true lover imagined by the sententious voice here is in the same situation as the sad man described in the *Prologue*, who mentally pictures "the great beauty [and] the refined sweetness of the woman who does not care for him."[70] In the *Prologue* that man is unable to compose anything from his mournful material, and has only desire and the knowledge (literally the "povre espoir": poor hope) that his sorrow will grow.[71] The clerkly voice of *Quant vrais amans* comments that such a man would rather spend his life on a Crusade than endure the hardship of such a lady's service, which devours the sad, sorrowing heart and body by making him weep tears of blood.[72]

The final poem, *Certes, je di*, offers matching but opposite clerkly deliberation on the same set of issues. This speaker asserts his clerkly authority through an opening historical comparison: the mischief Alexander the Great did Darius is not as great at that which Love does to the man whose heart is destroyed by not having relief from his lady. And yet, he continues, there are advantages to such sorrow: such a man creates better and more properly ("miex faire et plus proprement") than the one whom Love wants to "remake" ("refaire") by granting him *merci*. *Merci* fully granted is "souffisance," and this would cause the ardency of desire to diminish and start to recede ("amenrist et commence à retraire"). Desire gives the man whose heart is destroyed the matter, exemplar, and *sentement* ("matire et exemplaire / Et sentement") with which to perfect his work in fine sweetness, and colored with sorrow and tears of blood.[73] This forces the speaker to conclude that the one who does best in love is the one who tastes the sad sorrowing tears of blood ("cilz fait mielx qui d'Amours goust saveure / Triste, doulent, qui larmes de sanc pleure" [3.3.5–7]).

The first speaker is the sorrowing lover, whose songs reflect his sorrow; the second speaker maintains that such a man writes worse songs than a lover experiencing joy, while the third speaker conversely asserts that he writes better songs. The individuality of the three speakers is emphasized by the fact that their one piece of shared text, the refrain, starts at different times in each voice (see example 3.1, mm. 33, 34, and 36), a practice different from that observed in Machaut's other non-canonic polytextual balade *Quant Theseus / Ne quier* (B34), where the voices declaim the shared refrain text together.[74] In sequence

---

70. *Prologue* 5.68–69.

71. *Prologue* 5.77–84.

72. The literal sense is to spend one's life in Cairo ("Quaire"), but this was a stopping point on the Crusades and here operates metonymically.

73. In the *Prologue* "matere et exemplaire" is given to Machaut not by Desire but by Love, in the shape of his three children. And Nature, it should be noted, had already given him not *sentement* but *Sens*.

74. On B34, see Elizabeth Eva Leach, "Machaut's Balades with Four Voices," *Plainsong and Medieval Music* 10 (2001): 63, ex. 5; and idem, "Machaut's Peer, Thomas Paien," *Plainsong and Medieval Music* 18 (2009): 107–8.

the texts lay out a problem, the preferred solution, and then the contrary solution, resembling in form the juxtaposition of contradictory authoritative statements found in medieval *quaestiones*.[75] The solution and refutation of the objections must be supplied by the audience through the joint study of reading and listening.

On the page in this sequence the three balades of B29 make an interesting set of views, but their value is significantly inflected—and their correct solution encouraged—by the arrangement of the poems into a musical whole. This is something that is not visible on the page: the musical parts are copied separately, so that the poems and their individual melodies appear in the sequence described and are not presented together visually in any kind of musical score.[76] Nevertheless, the musical structure that results in performance inflects the value of the voices in this sequence. (It should be noted that in the modern edition, the voices are arranged with *De triste cuer* at the top, *Certes, je di* in the middle, and *Quant vrais amans* on the lowest staff. This reflects the usual layout for modern scores, in which the voices are arranged according to their pitch content—lowest voice at the bottom, highest at the top. In this regard, the modern edition's interest in giving a single viewer oversight of the contrapuntal whole inadvertently removes a layer of information that is visually present in the medieval presentation.)

The first-copied poem, the sorrowing lover trying to write with emotional faithfulness, has the melody of the uppermost voice, and the highest range (*D-f*), and occupies the usual position of the cantus voice at the major section end cadences of the two parts of the balade—the closed cadence of the A section after the second time through (example 3.1, m. 22), and the end of the refrain section, that is, the very end of the piece (example 3.1, m. 41). The cantus voice in normal, single-texted balades is the voice that alone carries the words of the first-person speaker, usually, as here, a lover. In this regard, then, B29 conforms to a norm. What is unusual here is the texting of the other two parts, which are usually untexted in Machaut's balades, merely carrying labels denoting their contrapuntal functions: tenor and contratenor. The voice copied second, *Quant vrais amans*, which considers desire as the murderer of artistic creativity, occupies the traditional copying placement of the tenor part in three-part music; it is also functionally the tenor part, having the lowest and narrowest range (*C-d*), taking the lowest pitches at all major cadences, and governing the counterpoint (see example 3.1, mm. 22 and 41). In range, the third-copied voice, *Certes, je di*, lies between the other two, going

75. See John Marenbon, *Later Medieval Philosophy (1150–1350): An Introduction* (London, 1987), 10–14, 19, and especially the five-part model in table 2 (28–33); see also Anthony Kenny and Jan Pinborg, "Medieval Philosophical Literature," in *The Cambridge History of Later Medieval Philosophy: From the Rediscovery of Aristotle to the Disintegration of Scholasticism, 1100–1600,* ed. Norman Kretzmann, Anthony Kenny, and Jan Pinborg (Cambridge, 1982), 30–33.

76. Score format was not in regular use for songs in this period.

lower than the cantus but higher than the tenor (*C-e*). This voice is the least important to the contrapuntal structure (that is, least vital to the harmony), the most possible to excise (singing just the other two voices, which actually agree with each other that sorrow produces bad music, would make musical sense), and thus in terms of argument the last in merit.

The tenor alone makes regular (that is, rule-governed) counterpoint with the other two voices, each of which has a musically functional relation only to the tenor.[77] Copied between the other two parts, the tenor effectively mediates between them in musical (as in visual) terms; it is central and controlling. Poetically its clerkly speaker offers a commentary on the situation of the cantus voice and a refutation of his clerkly counterpart in the contratenor. For the tenor, Desire is the enemy of poetry; for the contratenor it is the progenitor of it. They are literally tenor and *contra*tenor. Thesis and antithesis are here synthesized into a harmonious whole as a joint advisory accompaniment to the lover who is suffering; the music thus provides the "body" of the *quaestio,* the author's own view that will aid the production of a solution.[78] This harmony is mirrored in a musical hierarchy reflecting the rational hierarchy of these views, in which that of the tenor is most fundamental.

The opinions of the tenor and of the contratenor offer a different emphasis in regard to lyric creation. *Certes, je di* propounds a poetics, familiar from troubadour and trouvère song, in which the authenticity of the lover's desire creates poetry that reflects his personal emotions, whatever they be. *Quant vrais amans* is Machaut's poetics as outlined in the *Prologue,* in which joy both creates music and is its result: music's proper function is to provide joy to its audience. The twin desiderata of music's joyfulness and the poet's authentic expression come into conflict because the latter does not allow for the authentic representation of a lover's sorrow: sad songs displease an audience in need of music's joy, and yet a singer cannot guarantee the truth of his lyric if it does not accord with his own personal *sentement*. Or can he? Cerquiglini-Toulet has contrasted the "new lyricism" of the fourteenth century with that of the thirteenth by identifying a shift in the manner of guaranteeing lyric truth parallel to an underlying change "from song to script." Bound closely with musical performance, thirteenth-century lyric was given its truth by being the direct communication of the singing body of the performer. As prosopopoeia, it allows its emotional truth to be sung, inhabited, and thus attested by a live presence. In the fourteenth century, however, the written lyric became orphaned from its singing body, and the projection of authentic *sentement* became the

---

77. On the diagnosis of contrapuntal function in Machaut's music, see Elizabeth Eva Leach, "Counterpoint and Analysis in Fourteenth-Century Song," *Journal of Music Theory* 44 (2000): 45–79; idem, "Machaut's Balades with Four Voices."

78. See Marenbon, *Later Medieval Philosophy,* 28–30.

index of a new kind of truth anchored in writing.[79] The move from song to script is also one from singing to *sentement*. As the increase in written culture was prompted by a professionalization of the courtly poet, who was often employed as a high-ranking but essentially servile administrator, the problem of how to compose at once from *sentement* and on command for patrons or audiences thereby emerges as a new topos whose discussion in itself attests to the authenticity of *sentement*.[80] As an example, Cerquiglini-Toulet cites a rondeau by Christine de Pizan in which the poetic persona smiles through tears to "sing joyfully with a sad heart" (see figure 3.8). Christine's rondeau is clearly based on, and responds to, Machaut's *De triste cuer*. In Cerquiglini-Toulet's reading, the lyric of Christine (and by implication that of Machaut on which it is based) is not about a sorrowing lover unable to write joyful poetry, but about a professional poet writing on command for patrons in a creative culture that elevates *sentement*.

Cerquiglini-Toulet recognizes that Machaut cannot be entirely annexed to the new lyricism, which she views as being accompanied by a shift from the poetics of joy, which produces dance and song, to a poetics that emphasizes instead the pleasures of reading and sorrow. Machaut's *Prologue* clearly attributes ongoing value to the former. But Machaut is far more than a merely transitional figure between these two poetics. He actively attempts to bring the poetics of joy and hope into a written practice predicated on *sentement*. Although it might appear paradoxical given the new role of writing, music—especially polytextual music—is central to his efforts because it requires that writing and song be kept constantly in a mutually informing hermeneutic circle in the mind of the reading-listening reader. The eye and ear as representative of the two teachable senses are the doors to memory, in which knowledge can be stored and organized.[81]

Machaut's works, especially the lyrics, voice the thoughts of many lovers who try but fail to maintain hope, and his musical works contain a number of sorrowful songs. But the frame of the book as a whole, opening with the *Prologue*, offers a means to interpret the necessary vicissitudes of human experience—life in the sway of Fortune—even if one can be true to its demands only intermittently.[82] Machaut's works show the essential humanity of both failure and striving to succeed, of both joy and sorrow, and of the

---

79. Jacqueline Cerquiglini, "Le nouveau lyricisme (XIVe–XVe siècle)," in *Précis de littérature française du Moyen Âge*, ed. Daniel Poirion (Paris, 1983), 287.

80. Ibid., 285–86.

81. These senses of the "doors of memory" are illustrated most literally in Richard de Fournival's *Bestiaire d'amours*; see Elizabeth Sears, "Sensory Perception and Its Metaphors in the Time of Richard of Fournival," in *Medicine and the Five Senses*, ed. William F. Bynum and Roy Porter (Cambridge, 1993), 17–20. Hearing is typically considered more vital for learning than sight, but both senses are "teachable."

82. Machaut's book effectively performs the function previously fulfilled by its author, who may have been a live didactic presence at court, aiding his employers and patrons in their interpretation of his texts and the understanding of the existential issues arising from them.

Rondeau 11

De triste cuer chanter joyeusement
Et rire en dueil c'est chose fort a faire,
De son penser monstrer tout le contraire,
N'yssir doulz ris de doulent sentement.

Ainsi me fault faire communement,
Et me convient, pour celer mon affaire,
De triste cuer chanter joyeusement.
[Et rire en dueil c'est chose fort a faire.]

Car en mon cuer porte couvertement
Le dueil qui soit qui plus me puet desplaire,
Et si me fault, pour les gens faire taire,
Rire en plorant et trés amerement

De triste cuer chanter joyeusement
[Et rire en dueil c'est chose fort a faire,
De son penser monstrer tout le contraire,
N'yssir doulz ris de doulent sentement.]

It is hard to sing joyfully from a sad heart and
smile in grief, to show what is completely op-
posite to one's thoughts—a sweet smile doesn't
come from sorrowful sentement.

But that is what I usually have to do and
I have to—in order to conceal what's going on
with me—sing joyfully from a sad heart and
smile in grief; that's a hard thing to do.

For in my heart I covertly carry what sorrow
there is, which would displease me even more,
and in order to keep people quiet, I therefore
have to smile while crying very bitterly.

It is hard to sing joyfully from a sad heart and
smile in grief, to show what is completely op-
posite to one's thoughts—a sweet smile doesn't
come from sorrowful sentement.

Figure 3.8. Christine de Pizan, *De triste cuer* (Rondeau 11), from *Oeuvres poétiques de Christine de Pisan*, ed. Maurice Roy.

authenticity of both written *sentement* and performative truth. By bringing these into conflict, he is able to address and reject a life of Desire in favor of a life of Hope, which is the consoling solution he brings to both readers and listeners.

B29 guarantees truth by the difficulty with which the listener and reader combines, de-combines, and mentally recombines the competing voices whose musical harmony performs a rational hierarchy. For instance, the contratenor and cantus are not "in counterpoint," that is, they do not make regular harmony between them. This is evident at the textual level, since the assertion of the contratenor (*Certes, je di*) that Desire and sorrow improve the songs of the lover experiencing them is contradicted by the claim of the cantus (*De triste cuer*) that his audience is complaining about his. The music makes this lack of agreement manifest. If the voice whose desire is producing sad songs were to sing only with the singer who claims that this produces better songs, the result would "speak" for itself in sounding incomplete, inharmonious, cacophonous, and unpleasant, proving the point made by the poor lover in *De triste cuer* and the sage cleric in *Quant vrais amans*. The words of the functional cantus, *De triste cuer*, and those of the functional contratenor, *Certes, je di*, do not make musical sense without the fundamental notes (and view) of the functional tenor, *Quant vrais amans*.

One further feature of the musical setting offers a layer of meaning additional to that of the texts alone: the song's three voice parts give the distinct idea of being almost a patchwork of highly characteristic Machauldian melodic gestures. As a song about making songs, B29 sounds as though it is in fact all made up of other songs. In this regard as in others, it returns to a similar technique deployed in the only other notated balade on a similar theme—*Pour ce que tous* (B12)—a song whose singer complains of the complaints of the audience about the sorrowful nature of his songs.[83] In this song, as more usually in Machaut's balades, there is only one texted voice (together with one untexted accompanying part, which may or may not have been sung). The singer of B12 again justifies this sorrow as being true to a "sentement" that is authentically sorrowful because of the lady's lack of reciprocation, making B29 and B12 the only two of Machaut's short musical lyrics to use this term.[84] In B29 the musical quotations are snippets from Machaut's own songs—short, characteristic, but nonspecific rhythmic-motivic figure that can be found in a host of other Machaut works with the same mensural organization (that is, which share B29's time signature). In B12 the citation involves an identifiable line of text and music from the opening of another composer's balade.[85] In B12 the text and music are cited specifically and prominently in the refrain, one of the prime locations of citational practice in this repertoire. In B29, although the musical references are more allusive and scattered throughout the song, the refrain itself represents a close verbal citation. And while B12's citation comprises both text and music from another composer, in B29 the text-only citation is self-citation, since a close version of the refrain of B29's three texts appears in letter 8 of the *Voir dit*.[86]

Establishing a direction of citation between B29 and the *Voir dit* is not possible from the manuscript evidence, and to attempt to do so would probably also miss the point. The *Voir dit*'s focus on truth acts as a filter for the other texts in Machaut's book, providing a conduit for their intertextual relations,

83. See Elizabeth Eva Leach, "Singing More about Singing Less: Machaut's *Pour ce que tous* (B12)," in *Machaut's Music: New Interpretations,* ed. Elizabeth Eva Leach (Woodbridge, 2003), 111–24; and Anne Stone, "Music Writing and Poetic Voice in Machaut: Some Remarks on B12 and B14," ibid., 128–35.

84. In pieces set to music, the word *sentement* occurs elsewhere only in the context of the two consoling lays *S'onques (Le Lay de Confort)* (L17/12) and *Pour ce que plus (Un lay de Consolation)* (L23/17), and in two motet triplum texts, *Quant en moy* (M1) and *Maugré mon cuer* (M14). Among unnotated lyrics, it appears only in two unnotated lays, *Amours, se plus (Le Paradis d'Amours)* (L9) and *Maintes fois* (L13), the prayer to Venus in the *Voir dit,* and seven items from the *Loange.*

85. Eglal Doss-Quinby, Samuel N. Rosenberg, and Elizabeth Aubrey, eds., *The Old French Ballette: Oxford, Bodleian Library, MS Douce 308* (Geneva, 2006), 70–71 (nos. 22 and 73). Contrary to the view expressed in Leach, "Singing More about Singing Less," 111, I now think it likely that Machaut took this refrain from the anonymous balette rather than from its occurrence in Denis le Grant's *chace Se je chant* (although I would uphold that Machaut probably also knew this earlier citational usage); see David Maw, "Machaut and the 'Critical' Phase of Medieval Polyphony," review of *Essays on Music and Poetry in the Late Middle Ages* by Marie Louise Göllner and *Machaut's Music: New Interpretations,* ed. Elizabeth Eva Leach, *Music and Letters* 87 (2006): 290–91.

86. *Voir dit,* 108–10 (even pages).

whether these be established by *mise-en-page* adjacency, overall sequential order, shared text, or a combination of these. The reading possibilities allowed by the establishment of a "complete works" book in the *Prologue* permit a reader to trace the relation of love and lyric creation through their mutual relation to *sentement* throughout Machaut's entire output. The poems of B29, for instance, share poetic topoi and lexes not only with balades that precede it in the music section—B25–28, the first four balades in the order that do not occur in the earliest manuscript, C—but also with the poems that in turn surround some of those same neighboring musical balades in their unnotated appearance in the *Loange des dames*.[87] The wholeness of Machaut's book, and the way in which its internal system of doctrinal cross-referencing is underpinned by its musical items, is exemplified by this wider web of connections, whose ramifications will be traced in the last parts of this chapter. First, these "technologies of the book" deserve a little further elucidation.

Technologies of the Book: Citation, Adjacency, *Mise-en-page,* Duplication

At the time of the compilation of the *Voir dit,* Machaut had already collected his works together at least once, and this multimedia work seems deliberately designed to be part of a larger whole rather than a stand-alone dit.[88] The reader of the *Voir dit* (who intermittently takes on, as reader, the role of the lady for whom the book is expressly being written) is specifically supposed to look elsewhere to supplement her or his reading with the musical sounds of the songs and the discussions of themes in other dits to which the protagonist Guillaume refers.[89]

In the introductory section of the *Voir dit,* Machaut names the poem he is about to write and situates this "True Poem" with respect to the authentic feelings—the *sentement*—of the author:

> Le voir dit veil ie quon appelle
> Ce traitie que ie fait pour elle
> Pour ce que ia ni mentiray

---

87. Lo200–205, of which Lo201 = B25, Lo203 = B28 and Lo204 = B27; see further discussion later in this chapter.

88. Evidence of widespread circulation as single items within mixed collections is strong only for the early poem *Behaingne,* which is the only Machaut work in eight of its nineteen sources (see Wimsatt, Kibler, and Baltzer, *Machaut: Behaigne and Remede,* 11). This situation pertains for only one of the eleven sources for *Remede,* one of the eleven for *Lyon,* and one of the ten for *Harpe.* Three of twelve sources for *Confort* show circulation outside Machaut's manuscripts, but two of these represent little more than excerpts; see ibid., 40; Earp, *Guillaume de Machaut,* 215, 223, 218; and also note 48 in this chapter.

89. *Fonteinne* is cited in four places, sometimes by its alternative title, *Morpheus: Voir dit,* 74 (letter 4), 124 (letter 10), 400 (letter 31), and 558 (l. 8198).

Des autres choses vous diray
Se diligemment les querez
Sans faillir vous trouverez
Aveques les choses notees
Et es balades non chantees

The True Poem is what I want people to call this treatise that I am making for her, because in it I shall not lie. As for the other things [i.e., other than the *Voir dit* poem itself but written for Toute Belle in the course of it], I tell you that if you seek them diligently, without fail you will find them with the notated things [i.e., in the music section] and among the ballades not sung [i.e., in the *Loange*].[90]

Like the *Prologue* to the whole manuscript, this prologue to the *Voir dit* asks its readers to make connections, not just within "ce traité" of the *Voir dit* but in the entire "livre" detailed in the index rubric. It specifies the two other important sections—the music section and the *Loange*—that contain lyric items. Sending the reader to the music section is necessary, given the copying of the *Voir dit* in its two principal sources, **A** and **F**, in which the songs are copied without musical notation, but with their musical setting cued by rubrics (typically, "y a chant"); these lyrics can then indeed be found set to music in the music section.[91] But why might Machaut wish to alert the reader to the *Loange* when the lyric texts shared between it and the *Voir dit* are copied in full in the context of the *Voir dit* itself? The *Loange* and music sections are the two parts of Machaut's book that have the greatest amount of duplication between them; the *Voir dit* imprecation suggests that the duplication of a lyric functioned as a kind of cross-reference, directing its readers' attention toward another *mise-en-page,* and in turn toward another context involving new links made by adjacency.[92] Certainly order and adjacency are, as the index

90. *Voir dit,* 32, ll. 518–29.
91. In manuscript E, however, the relevant music is copied with the relevant lyric texts directly into the *Voir dit,* as it usually is in those sources for the *Remede* that are notated; see McGrady, *Controlling Readers,* 127–45. E displays several other editorial decisions which suggest that its editors were expecting their readers to respond not to citation and cross-reference cued by duplication, but only more locally to ordering and *mise-en-page.* The editors of E clearly had their own rationale for its reordering both on the small scale within the music section (a feature that would merit sympathetic scholarly enquiry) and on the large scale, as treated by McGrady, who claims that it uniquely places music back at the heart of the book. From my comments in this chapter it will be apparent that I view music to be at the "heart" (albeit not the codicological center) of Machaut's enterprise. I do not share McGrady's belief that the terminal position of the music section in several sources is a matter of "relegating the music to a final section in the manuscript"; see McGrady, *Controlling Readers,* 132–34.
92. Cerquiglini, "Le nouveau lyricisme," 283, views Machaut as a turning point in the rupture between music and poetry because his manuscripts keep these two parts of his output separate. I would argue, however, that the sheer practical considerations of music copying lead to music being mostly confined to the last section of the source. The music in *Remede* and the insertion of

rubric attests, of importance to Machaut. Placing *Navarre* immediately after *Behaingne*, which it is purportedly written to correct, forms a physical diptych of opposing judgments on the question posed in both. Sequential order in general, and the visual juxtaposition of *mise-en-page* in the case of shorter lyric items in particular, are ways in which disparate materials can be presented to the reader so that they are read in conjunction with one another. The complement to adjacency, which can visually link highly differentiated items, is citation, which can verbally cue a link between items hundreds of folios apart.[93] Duplication of an entire lyric—an extreme form of citation—thus provides a verbal bridge between two different visual contexts.

Machaut was over fifty by the time he first collected his works into manuscript C, and it seems likely that only after this point did he start to conceptualize them into a whole output, at once plural and "polyphonic" (in the metaphorical literary sense, but also in the literal musical sense), as well as unified and harmonious (also in both senses).[94] Adjacency—placing longer items in order and short lyrics in visual proximity on the same opening—was a scribal technique that allowed Machaut to link items, perhaps in fairly long chains, that may be meaningfully read in tandem. Adjacency may represent Machaut's scribal strategy in his earliest phase of writing, during which his lyric works possibly circulated on small (now lost) bifolios or rotuli and his dits in single-dit fascicle manuscripts. Once he started to assemble a larger book entirely dedicated to his own works, however, he had more scope, more room, and more scribal power with which to make connections.[95]

In much the same way the reader is referred by title to *Fonteinne* in the *Voir dit* (or the *Remede* in *Confort*), the reader is also asked to go to the music section not just for the melody of certain lyrics, but because in that ordered section the lyric has its own context lent by *mise-en-page*, which can add further to the appreciation of its doctrinal content. And many of these lyrics are also present in yet another proto-narrative context lent by their duplication in the *Loange*. In short, in each place where a duplicated lyric occurs, it

---

Qui bien aimme (Le Lay de plour) (L22/16) after *Navarre* in some sources disrupt the separation further; the role of cross-reference provided by duplication between the music section, *Loange*, and the *Voir dit* suggests strongly that the integrated centrality of musical poetry argued in the *Prologue* was a reality for Machaut.

93. The homogenous surface of Machaut's lyric poetry hides a surprising degree of variety, especially with respect to aspects such as rhyme combination (often unique for any given combination of three rhymes), seemingly common phrases (rarely are more than two successive words shared between any two lyrics), and lexical items (some words are undeniably common, but many poems deploy markedly unusual vocabulary). In such a context, shared refrains and/or incipit lines plus shared rhyme types are significant factors.

94. On the idea that the motets at least had been conceived as a cycle before this date, see chapter 6.

95. On Machaut's ironic awareness of the size and variety of his own output, see the comments on the narrator figure in *Navarre*, ll. 881–914, in Huot, *From Song to Book*, 248–49.

partakes of a different order and takes its position within a different, often proto-narrative context. Focusing the discussion through the duplicated lyric, these contexts may be read against one another for a fuller perspective on the courtly situation in each individual case, creating greater complexity within the textual polyphony of Machaut's work as a whole.[96]

We know that such duplication was noticed by medieval users of these books. For example, the usual practice in the music section is to copy the second and third stanzas of balades as prose beneath the first stanza, which is overlaid with musical staves and notes. Because the first stanza's text is laid out to suit musical concerns, it is not visually clear where poetic lines begin and end. In **Vg** many of the underlaid texts have letters of the alphabet added at the start of each of the first stanza's poetic lines, either to facilitate the reader's understanding of their verse structure or perhaps to aid their possible copying as verse into text-only sources.[97] This can be seen in figure 3.6, where the underlaid text lines are lettered "a–g" and the prose residuum is labeled "h" above the staff to the left of the capital S of "Si." For many of the musical items whose lyrics are duplicated in the *Loange*, however, there is an X in the margin in their appearance in the notated ballades in **Vg**; some of these do not then have these superscript letters. While it is difficult to tell if the X dates from the medieval period or not, it could be that the scribe is indicating to the reader that these poems are to be found already laid out as verse in the *Loange*. If it is later, it at least attests to an awareness of the duplication of music items in the *Loange* at some point in the book's history. Moreover, a marginal note in a medieval hand alongside the incomplete copying of *Plourez, dames* in **Vg**'s *Loange* (where it is Lo229) shows that at least one medieval reader realized that the missing stanza could be found in the music section.[98]

The connections between the *Voir dit* and the other parts of Machaut's oeuvre go beyond the supply of melodies and other (proto-narrative) lyric contexts for its sung items and the explicit citation of other narrative items by title. The sharing of text, particularly refrain texts (the *forme-fixe* equivalent of a dit's title), between the *Voir dit* and a range of lyrics and narratives makes

96. The two posthumous manuscripts **F-G** and **E** attempt to remove duplication by pruning the *Loange*, though not consistently. This pruning nonetheless shows that later scribes were alert to duplication per se and thus were aware of the wholeness of Machaut's book. See also note 91.

97. There is some evidence of the use of music sources as exemplars for text-only copies. Earp has argued that **Pa** copies from **E**; see Earp, *Guillaume de Machaut*, 115–18. A comparison of errors and variants in their shared texts suggests that some of the Machaut lyrics in **I** are also copied from **E**.

98. See Leach, "Death of a Lover," 475n30. This is noted independently in Benjamin L. Albritton, "Citation and Allusion in the Lays of Guillaume de Machaut" (Ph.D. diss., University of Washington, 2009), 156, with an image from the source on 193.

other connections that flesh out a rounded "polyphonic" doctrinal picture.[99] Letter 8 of the *Voir dit*, for example, cites not just B29's refrain but also lines from the *Remede* on the same theme of how love and lyric composition relate to *sentement*. Reading B29 against the situation in the *Voir dit* illuminates both items and furthers B29's claims to being an ongoing object of contemplation as well as a joyful performative moment.

Making, Unmaking, Remaking: Lyric Practice and Loving Matter

Guillaume writes letter 8 in response to a report that Toute Belle, to whom he has been tardy in responding, has heard that he loves another. With dramatic irony, Guillaume avers that he feels more despairing than if he had suspected *her* of loving another, since his hope was founded on her *bonté* (goodness) and *loyauté* (loyalty), that is, on his belief in her belief in him. Now that he has heard that she doubts him, he has lost hope and comfort and is in such fear of losing her that his sad and sorrowing heart weeps tears of blood ("que mes tristes et dolens cuers pleure larmes de sanc").[100] He has become—verbatim— the sorrowing lover of *De triste cuer*. His letter goes on to deny the charge that he doubts her by citing as proof the claim that all his works in praise of her are composed directly from *sentement*:

> Car vous savez quil nest si iuste ne si vraie chose comme experience . Et vous poez assez savoir et veoir par experience que toutes mes choses ont este faites de vostre sentement . et pour vous especiaument de puis que vous menvoiastes . Celle qui onques ne vous vit . et qui vous aimme loiaument . car elles sont toutes de ceste matere . Et par ihesucrist ie ne fis onques puis riens qui ne fust pour vous . car ie ne say ne ne weil faire de sentement dautrui . fors seulement dou mien et dou vostre . Pour ce que *qui de sentement ne fait . son dit et son chant contrefait.*

For you know that there is no such right or true thing as experience. And you can well enough know and see by experience that all my works have been made of your *sentement* [i.e., from how I feel about you], and especially since you sent me "Celle qui onques ne vous vit / Et qui vous aimme loiaument" [VD1, i.e., the lady's rondeau from the beginning of the *Voir dit*], for they are all of this matter. And—by Jesus Christ—I have made nothing since then that was not for you, for I do not know how to compose other than from *sentement*, from mine and

---

99. *Nes qu'on porroit* (B33), for example, is denominated by its refrain when it is cited in the *Voir dit*. See Ardis Butterfield, "The Art of Repetition: Machaut's Ballade 33, *Nes qu'on porroit,*" *Early Music* 31 (2003): 347–60.

100. *Voir dit*, 110 (letter 8).

yours. This is why *whoever does not compose from sentement, counterfeits his dit and his song.*[101]

Guillaume then lists the works that he will stop composing should she continue to doubt him. He will no longer compose any "dis, loanges, ne chans, ne lais" (dits, *Loanges,* songs, or lays), this formulation encapsulating almost the entire contents of Guillaume de Machaut's book. To allay his fears, Toute Belle's response to this letter is to send her "image," the portrait of her that in Machaut's tale of Guillaume-Pygmalion will take on a life of its own and forge a closer relationship with the narrator than Toute Belle herself has.[102]

Letter 8 significantly links the authenticity of poetic *sentement,* its role in the creation of poetry, the subject of love, and the concomitant themes of desire, despair, and hope. The acute preoccupation with the sincerity topos in the light of the professionalization of the poet, which Cerquiglini-Toulet sees as characteristic of the "new lyricism" of the fourteenth century, is answered here by attesting to the truth of the lyrics in the narrative frame into which they are inset.[103] When this frame is itself pseudo-autobiographical in its high level of verisimilitude, it participates strongly in this trend. The close citation from the *Remede* (in italics in the translated passage), however, covertly instructs the reader as to how the present letter should be read because it cross-references the state of this lover to that of an earlier one. By so doing it assures the attentive reader of the doctrinal concord of two generically similar works (narrative poems with interpolated musical lyrics), despite their differences.

The *Remede de Fortune,* like the *Voir dit,* has a narrator who is an elderly poet, although this fact is easily forgotten because the dit proper depicts this same narrator's youth as he looks back on his own training in the arts of love and poetry. It opens with forty-four lines of a deeply didactic character, introducing the twelve things that one needs to learn something properly, before the narrator harks back to when he was in a state of innocence, governed by Youth.[104] All the subsequent events of the poem are thus distanced from the narrator's present mature and clerkly demeanor. When the *Remede*'s youthful lover-protagonist states that "Car qui de sentement ne fait, / Son oeuvre et son chant contrefait," he can be read as exhibiting the emotional instability of untutored youth.[105] At this point in the dit he has not yet been instructed and comforted by the central figure of the poem—the "Remedy" of the title—

---

101. Ibid. (emphasis added). The words in italics are close to those in *Remede,* ll. 401–8; see note 61.

102. See Huot, "Reliving the *Roman de la Rose,*" 55. Although in the iconography of A the image is a painted wooden panel, in F it is shown as a statue, connecting it more closely to the Pygmalion tale. See Cerquiglini, "*Un engin si soutil,*" 203–14, especially 205, and chapter 6.

103. Cerquiglini, "Le nouveau lyricisme," 285–91; and idem, "*Un engin si soutil,*" 159–200.

104. *Remede,* ll. 45–47.

105. *Remede,* ll. 401–8; see note 61.

Hope (*Esperance*). Belief in *sentement*-based composition is thus the mark of a lover early in his experience of love, who does not yet understand the self-sufficient and stable joy that comes from love mediated through Hope, but knows instead only the instability of love under the sway of Fortune. Although Guillaume in *Voir dit* is an old man in the present time of the dit, through sharing the thoughts of *Remede*'s youthful lover-protagonist, he too is, by implication, immature in this regard. In fact, he does not learn nearly as much in the course of the *Voir dit* as the lover-protagonist of *Remede* in the course of that dit, partly because the later poem reverses the order in which Fortune and Hope appeared in the earlier one. The final section of the *Voir dit* is dominated by the figure of Fortune, to which both Guillaume and Toute Belle are ultimately assimilated.[106] In *Remede*, Fortune is the subject of the lover's complaint at the point just before Hope appears to provide her remedy for Fortune's ills. In *Voir dit* it is Hope who is forced to complain, because she thinks Guillaume has forgotten her. She accosts Guillaume on the road as he comes away from his final, highly eroticized meeting with Toute Belle. After this point, although it is relatively early in the dit, the lovers never meet again, and they become increasing Fortune-like in their emotional instability, fed by credulous belief in each other's changeableness. *Remede* and *Voir dit* are thus complementary counterparts, showing respectively the course of love for a lover who amends his reliance on *sentement* and defeats Fortune to become stable and hopeful, and a lover who consummates his desire and maintains his reliance on *sentement* but is trapped in Fortune's ever-turning wheel by the unverifiability of gossip.[107]

In the order of manuscript **A**'s authorial index, B29 is the fifth musical balade of a group of balades that are not present in the earlier collected works manuscript, **C**. As figure 3.9 shows, *Honte, paour* (B25) is the first of these new post-**C** balades in the music section, and significantly, it is also the first post-**C** balade in the unnotated *Loange*, where it is L0201. In both instances it links to the preceding (and probably older) balade by picking up on one of its rhymes as its own first rhyme type ("-aire").[108] In the sequence of the first twenty-four music balades (the number contained in **C**), this particular rhyme had been unique in *Tres douce dame* (B24), where it was the refrain rhyme. In the balades of the music section, the five poems that are set as B24, B25,

---

106. See chapter 4.

107. In this context it is significant that in the *Remede* it is the entire oeuvre that will be "contrefait," whereas in the *Voir dit* it is just the dit. By the time of the *Voir dit*—with manuscript **A**—there *is* an oeuvre, but one belonging to Machaut the poet of the *Prologue* rather than Guillaume the narrator of the *Voir dit*.

108. As L0201, B25 uses rhymes from L0200 as its first two rhyme types, "-é" as well as "-aire." The "-aire" rhyme is much more frequent in the *Loange*, occurring in twenty-four balades in **C** and in an additional six that appear only in later sources. In addition, it occurs in six complaints, eleven lays, five motets, two virelays, three *Voir dit* lyrics, Love's balade in the *Prologue*, and the further complaint (RF2) from the *Remede*.

and B29 provide the only occurrences of this rhyme type in this part of the manuscript.[109] In the *Loange*, the "-aire" rhyme significantly also occurs in the balade that directly precedes B25 in its *Loange* incarnation as Lo201, *Aucuns parlent* (Lo200). This double linking of *Honte, paour* as B25 to B24, and as Lo201 to Lo200, bridges the gap in two different parts of the manuscript between the poems that first appear only in **A** and those that had already appeared in **C**, suggesting a deliberate move on Machaut's part to present a unified whole. While B29 and B25 are not adjacent in the music section, they are part of the sequence of new, "post-C" balades that occur before the collection of *Voir dit* balades starts in both the music section and the *Loange* (with *Plourez, dames,* which is B32, VD5, and Lo229).[110] Two of the three balades that lie between B25 and B29 in the music section—*Une vipere* (B27) and *Je puis trop* (B28)—occur in the *Loange* as Lo204 and Lo203 and thus in close proximity to B25 as it appears in the *Loange* (where it is Lo201).[111] The balades in these two sequences are thus already linked by duplication, which asks their reader also to read their associated (but not duplicated) items together. This linking of nonduplicated context is perhaps specifically invited, too, by the shared invocation of Alexander and Darius in the two unique balades from these two sequences, B29 (copied only in the music section) and Lo200 (copied only in the *Loange*). In Machaut's entire balade output, the mention of Alexander and Darius occurs only in these two items.[112]

Moreover, just as B29 is linked to *Voir dit,* letter 8, so too are the balades in the related *Loange* sequence, which culminates in a trio of rondeaux meditating repetitively on the death that will be caused to the lover if his lady loves another ("autre que my")—the explicit worry of Guillaume's letter 8.[113] The balades on either side of the *Loange* music duplicate, Lo201/B25, present lovers in a similar state, who have lost their hope in the lady. The lover of Lo202 opens declaring that he has lost comfort and hope ("Tant ay perdu confort et esperance"), has a pale face ("viaire pali") when he is not believed, and fears to lose his sweet beloved ("de perdre ay doubtance / Ma douce amour").

---

109. This rhyme is significantly a repository for the verb *faire* and its compounds, which are so central to B29.

110. The similarity of the musical figuration in B26, B27, and B28 to that in the minor prolation balades of the *Voir dit* (*Plourez, dames* [B32], *Nes qu'on* [B33], and *Se pour ce muir* [B36]) has been noted in Daniel Leech-Wilkinson, "*Le Voir Dit* and *La Messe de Notre Dame*: Aspects of Genre and Style in Late Works of Machaut," *Plainsong and Medieval Music* 2 (1993): 59n38.

111. B28/Lo203 is Machaut's Pygmalion balade; the *Voir dit*'s letter 8 prompts the sending of the image/statue of Toute Belle that turns Guillaume into a Pygmalion figure, as mentioned earlier.

112. Among his other lyrics, the comparison is used in only one other place (the late *Malgré Fortune [Le Lay de plour]* [L19/14]), although this comparison is used elsewhere by Machaut in narrative contexts.

113. *Quant je vous voy autre que my amer* (Lo206), *Se par amours n'amiés autrui ne moy* (Lo207), and *Pour Dieu, dame, n'amez autre que my* (Lo208).

LOANGE

End of MS C	Lo2oo	Aucuns parlent de .x. plaies d'Egipte	-ite	**-aire**	-é	-oie	ro'a ro'b ro'a ro'b roc roc 7c roc ro'd ro'd ro'D	**Alexander/Darius**
MS A continues	Lo2o1=B25	Honte, paour, doubtance de meffaire	-arde	**-aire**	-é	-er	ro'a rob ro'a rob 7c roc ro'd ro'D	AoAcBR
	Lo2o2	Tant ay perdu confort et esperance	-ance	-oir	-i		ro'a rob ro'a rob rob roc roC	
	Lo2o3 =B28	Je puis trop bien ma dame comparer	-er	-ion	-oit	-ont	roa rob roa rob roc roc rod roD	
	Lo2o4 =B27	En cuer ma dame une vipere maint	-aint	-eille	-ort	-art	roa ro'b roa roc roc rod roD	

MUSIC SECTION

End of MS C	B24	Tres douce dame que	-our	**-aire**	-er	-é	8a 8b | 8a 8b | 8b 8'c | 8'C |	AoAcBR
MS A continues	B25 =Lo2o1	Honte, paour	**-aire**	-er	-arde		ro'a rob | ro'a rob | 7c roc ro'd | ro'D |	AoAcBR
	B26	Donnez, signeurs	-ains	-ue	-ort	-oit	roa rob | roa rob | rob 8'C | 8'C |	AoAcBC
	B27 =Lo2o4	Une vipere	-aint	-eille	-art		roa ro'b | roa ro'b | roc roc rod | roD |	AoAcBR
	B28 =Lo2o3	Je puis trop	-er	-ion	-oit	-ont	roa rob | roa rob | roc roc rod | roD |	AoAcBR
Alexander/ Darius	B29	De triste/Quant/ Certes	-ent	**-aire**	-oure		roa ro'b | roa ro'b | ro'b ro'c ro'C |	AoAcB

Figure 3.9. Initial tranche of post-MS-C balades appearing in MS A's *Loange* and music sections, showing shared rhymes and interrelationships between the "older" and "newer" parts of each section.

In Lo200, as in letter 8, the lover talks of forces that have the power to "unmake" him. In Lo200, as in the "Contratenor" of B29 (*Certes, je di*), the mischief that Alexander did Darius fades into insignificance in comparison to the grief that the lady gives the lover ("Some speak of the ten plagues of Egypt and of the ills that Alexander did to Darius, but in truth these are but little things compared to that which my lady makes me bear").[114]

The play with compounds of *faire* links Lo200 to B29 and to letter 8 of the *Voir dit*. In the "Cantus" of B29 (*De triste cuer*), lines 3.4–5, the sorrowing lover complains that Fortune tries to unmake ("deffaire") that which he loves more than himself, and the "Contratenor" (*Certes, je di*), lines 2.1–2, asserts that the man who weeps tears of blood will compose better ("miex faire") than someone who wants *merci* in love to "remake" ("refaire") him. The lady's power over the lover of Lo200 is absolute: he comments, "you've made me, so you can unmake me ("fait m'avez, si me poez deffaire"). In letter 8 of the *Voir dit*, Guillaume worries that he will not be able to create lyrics again "because as quickly as you [Toute Belle] have made [*fait*] me, you can unmake [*deffaire*] me."[115] At the end of the dit, Guillaume will compare his lady much more directly to Fortune, but through this intertextual reference Toute Belle is already taking on that unflattering role.[116] Guillaume's worry is caused because he has heard that she doubts his sincerity. If she believes what she's heard and changes her own affections in response, he will lose hope and start to despair. She has "made" him; in fact, she has made him start making things—the "dis, loanges, ne chans, ne lais" that he fears will stop if he loses her to her belief in false gossip.

The lover at the start of *Remede* and the one described in *Certes, je di* are both convinced that *sentement* is all-important, that following and expressing one's true feelings, even if these are negative, is the way to create poetry. But their respective frames suggest that this is an immature attitude, likely to result in capitulation to Fortune, writing bad songs, and audience displeasure.[117] The inversion of this frame in the *Voir dit* and the parallel reactions of an adolescent woman and an old man project old age as a second immaturity in these matters.

114. "Aucuns parlent de.x. plaies d'Egipte / Et des meschies qu'Alixandres fist Daire / Mais vraiement, c'est chose petite / Contre ce que ma dame me fait traire."

115. *Voir dit*, 110.

116. See chapter 5.

117. Arguably the correct behavior is advised in the duplicated balade *Honte paour* (B25/Lo201) and its music section pair *Donnez, signeurs* (B26), which together form a diptych on the theme of largesse, the quality of which Alexander the Great is the traditional paragon. The noble man should be generous in giving (B26), but the lady who would keep good her honor should be generous only in refusals. For their medieval readers, the connections between items in Machaut's works could prompt lengthy engagement with such important existential matters. See Elizabeth Eva Leach, "Guillaume de Machaut, Royal Almoner: *Honte, paour* (B25) and *Donnez, signeurs* (B26) in Context," *Early Music* 38 (2010): 21–42.

Singing Less, Writing More?

Machaut's highly self-conscious book project seems to epitomize the textualization of vernacular court culture that has been seen as one of the defining features of the fourteenth century. As a trained scribe Machaut was an aficionado of the technologies of the codex. The images in the *Prologue* draw attention to the necessity of page turning, and the author whom it presents magisterially in a double portrait additionally wields an index, rubrics, and control over *mise-en-page* (including further illuminations). Using duplication, rubrics, and the citation of titles, the book capitalizes on—and combines—both the power of visual adjacency to bring disparate objects into dialogue, and the facility of an ordered sequence of items to gather narrative force. As a poet, Machaut fosters further interconnections by repeating words, rhymes, and longer phrases from works by others and himself, and by engendering broader thematic and topological links. Self-citation is manifest in various ways: through references in one dit to the title of another, through refrain citation, and through the entire duplication of a lyric text in a variety of generic contexts in different parts of the same manuscript book.

All of these features seem to relate to visual performance, so what space exists for music's sounding performance in the new textual culture of this period? In Machaut's hands, quite a large one. For the first time in history the notational system was developed enough to notate music almost as well as letters notate verbal text. (Neither notation system is precise about timbre, tempo, exact pitch, or other significant aspects of *pronunciatio*.)[118] Machaut used notation to its utmost; his books set the standard for new layout norms appropriate to his new kinds of polyphonic musical works.[119] Notational developments thereby allowed music to participate in textual culture. Machaut's notation spatializes the temporal and makes the sonic visual, which enables it to inhabit a new kind of "performance" space, and also to use all the technologies of the book enjoyed by poetry. On the one hand, the musicality of song is textualized and silenced. On the other hand, because it is recorded in this way, music becomes a kind of literature, takes on the ontological status of a work, and, like the verbal poetic texts it performs, is thereby able to be (re)enacted sonically so as to (re)temporalize the spatial and (re)sound the visual. The combined address to the two teachable senses makes Machaut's didacticism meet ear and eye, giving him unprecedented all-round sway over teaching, learning, listening, hearing, reading, and seeing. His works are both more effective because they are more versatile and longer-lasting because they are more varied—in kind and genre, as in type of delivery. The utmost courtly

118. See also the points in Leach, *Sung Birds*, 108–74 (chap. 3, "Birds Sung").

119. On the earlier precedent for the exploitation of what she terms "song space," see Emma Dillon, *Medieval Music-Making and the "Roman de Fauvel"* (Cambridge, 2002), 216–82 (chap. 6, "The Poetic Use of Song Text").

danger of *oisiveté* can be evaded by occupying time with a properly noble "leisured pursuit" (music), engagement with which in turn sends the listener back
to being a reader; at each stage, the need for active contemplation promotes
the effectiveness of the didactic project.

As a musician, Machaut can connect texts by having them "performed"
simultaneously—in actual sounding performances and/or in visual performances across an opening where the musical aspect both obscures and is the
key to unlocking the (literally) polyphonic discourse. Performance is an additional way of ordering text, which functions as a sonic analogue to visual
adjacency in that it can force an audience to read two otherwise unconnected
or seemingly disparate texts against each other. Having notated songs in his
book acts as a cue for listening rather than reading, and leads from book to
song and then back to the book in an endless hermeneutic circle. Not least
because musical performance is social and requires organization, the act of
following up this debate from book to song to book occupies time and mental
space, which aids in the very process of sublimating desire that the doctrine
presented recommends. In the *Prologue* Machaut's apologia for the composer
of vernacular love poetry claims that it absorbs the attention so thoroughly as
to prevent bad thoughts and ill actions; by implication, the audience too will
be so absorbed in the process of understanding their experience of music and
poetry that they will also be distracted, only to conclude, when the lesson of
these cultural products has been absorbed, that this social need for appropriate distraction is exactly what they have been taught.

In Machaut's cultural universe, then, music serves as the ultimate form of
consolation—an extension of the power of lyric itself into a temporal, sonic,
and harmonic existence. The *Prologue*'s clear injunction to compose from joy,
because music must make those who hear it rejoice, sing, and dance, prompts
questions as to what one does when one is unhappy, and why there are so
many sorrowful lovers who voice songs and lyrics. But Machaut claims that
even sad matter can be composed with joy, and that the measure of this is the
joy of the audience; sad song is of reduced value, and the audience typically
complains. As I have shown, the constraints of this situation in themselves
became part of the authenticity topos addressed by Machaut, who again ne-
gotiates the duality of his professional world in accommodating both Nature
(poetry born of *sentement*) and Love (his audience's demanded topic) in a poetics of joy. The complaint that love's joys are no longer inspiring the poet is a
way of generating poetry when *sentement* is deemed its only sincere generator.
In effect the confession of non-inspiration or lack of love becomes a sincerity topos all its own, driven by the new explicitness about the need for lyric
performance to inspire joy in the audience.[120] But the understanding of this

---

120. Zeeman, "The Lover-Poet," cites songs by Bernart de Ventadorn, Gace Brulé, and
Thibaut de Champagne and notes the contrast between personal experience and *sentement* in
Kelly, *Medieval Imagination*, 252–53.

topos requires engagement with more than the single lyrics in which it functions. In the codex as a whole—in Machaut's poetic works as a whole—these claims of the authenticity of sorrow are always met with lessons in consolation that typically use music as a consolatory vehicle.

The lyric first person of *Pour ce que tous* (B12) is a lover whose lady's displeasure at his love has caused him pain and sorrow. Because his songs inevitably reflect his suffering (because he is an "authentic" poet-lover), they attract the criticism of his auditors, who presumably require music to inspire joy. In the refrain the poet asks this audience not to blame him, therefore, "Se je chant mains que ne sueil" (if I sing less than I used to). As mentioned earlier, this text is itself a quotation from the incipit of another song, whose melody was the subject of at least one other ironic treatment by a contemporary of Machaut's, the composer-bishop Denis le Grant.[121] Ironies pervade all levels of the musical setting of B12: the refrain expressing the lover's stated intention to sing less not only presents the singer singing *another* song but also has the largest note values in the song and constitutes a ninth line when Machaut's simplex music balade stanzas usually have only seven or eight.[122] As occurs frequently in his narrative *dits,* Machaut succeeds as a poet in the act of failing as a lover; comically, his complaint, a genre traditionally detailing the sorrows of love, becomes a song complaining of the complaints of the audience about just such songs.

The solution to the audience's complaints, as Machaut's wider works attest, is the poet's joy, which, because he must fail as a lover (since he is a non-noble professional poet), must be sustained by sublimation, that is, by Hope. With scribal acumen the poet Guillaume de Machaut places after B12 a balade whose opening word offers the obvious solution to enable the singing (and, in the context of the book, the copying of the music section) to continue: *Esperance* (B13).[123] The presentation of Machaut's courtly doctrine in his book is neither straightforward nor linear but is, as the *Prologue* strongly implies, unified. Where contradictions seems to obtain, the reader's engagement must resolve them; like the biblical text, for which such hermeneutics were more fully developed, Machaut has created a book to live by, one that treats the important issues of life: Love, Hope, Fortune, and death.

121. See comments in Leach, *Sung Birds,* 222–29. Before its composer was known, Denis le Grant's *chace* was already edited as no. 290 in Willi Apel, ed., *French Secular Compositions of the Fourteenth Century,* 3 vols. (Rome, 1970–1972), 3:162–68, or no. 60 in the more readily available Richard H. Hoppin, ed., *Anthology of Medieval Music* (New York, 1978), 127–33. See also note 85 in this chapter.

122. *Pour ce que tous* (B12) is in fact the only nine-line balade that Machaut set to music, and the only non-duplex balade set to music in his entire output not to have either seven or eight lines.

123. On this song, see Elizabeth Eva Leach, "Love, Hope, and the Nature of *Merci* in Machaut's Musical Balades *Esperance* (B13) and *Je ne cuit pas* (B14)," *French Forum* 28 (2003): 2–3; and Leach, "Singing More about Singing Less."

4

Hope

Loving

For his readers and listeners, Machaut's poetry and music fulfilled a genuine social need: it consoled.[1] It might be thought that medieval aristocrats had little need for consolation, given their position at the top of a sharply tapered social and economic hierarchy. Their means and status, however, allowed access to, and time for, leisured pursuits, together with a degree of freedom that brought with it the possibility of dangerous engagements, especially sexual and affective ones. In a situation in which affective ties and sexual identities were regulated by feudal, familial, and religious constraints, it was important—for the individual and the community as a whole—that the more potentially destabilizing (that is, sexual) aspects of "idealized affect" (that is, love) be confined to mental and cultural life rather than manifesting themselves in sexual behavior played out for real in household rooms, forest clearings, caves, or fields. The varied but unified contents of Machaut's book teach his audience not merely how to live and love, but how to live *with* love and the

---

1. From the time of Douglas Kelly's influential study of the *imaginatio* of medieval poetry (which he identified as a metaphorical mode used to point to the ineffable reality lying beyond the reach of the senses by means of stories that can reveal historical, scientific, and moral truths), it has been broadly accepted that Machaut's particular contribution to this tradition was to combine the dialogue-based poetry of the *Roman de la Rose* with moralized kinds of text found in hunting manuals, bestiaries, and other didactic literature, so as to develop mental images—through fiction—that provided hope and consolation for medieval aristocrats. See Douglas Kelly, *Medieval Imagination: Rhetoric and the Poetry of Courtly Love* (Madison, 1978), 28–29; Sylvia Huot, "Guillaume de Machaut and the Consolation of Poetry," *Modern Philology* 100 (2002): 169–95; and Helen Philips, "Fortune and the Lady: Machaut, Chaucer and the Intertextual 'Dit,'" *Nottingham French Studies* 38 (1999): 120–36.

suffering it could potentially cause in the specific context of the aristocratic court. The central figure in his consolatory poetics is *Esperance*—Hope.

"Hope, who reassures me": *Esperance*

One of the most compact statements of the power of Hope to be found in Machaut's works occurs in a balade that appears only in the music section of his works: *Esperance* (B13).[2] The balades preceding B13 in the music section culminate in *Pour ce que tous* (B12), whose self-conscious singer threatens to stop composing and singing songs, asserting repeatedly, "Je chant mains que ne sueil" (I sing less than I used to).[3] In what I have argued is the proto-narrative context of the music balades, B13 cures and cancels the despair of B12 with the introduction of the figure that forms its opening word: "Esperance" (Hope). The situation with respect to the lady remains unchanged: the lady of B13 similarly has not reciprocated, but the presence of Hope reconfigures the sorrow of B12 as joy and enables the composition and singing of balades (as well as the copying and reading of them) to continue. The discrete snapshots provided by the adjacent pair of balades B12 and B13 match the mental state of the lover before and after his instruction in Hope's joyful approach to song composition as elaborated with narrative continuity—but also mirrored in interpolated lyric snapshots—in the *Remede de Fortune*.[4]

B13 reconfigures B12 verbally as well as psychologically, exemplifying the effect of emotional orientation on composition. It immediately takes up the refrain rhyme of B12, "-ueil," which in B12 had been a new rhyme in the context of the music balades. As the chief means of diversity and individuality within lyrics, rhymes are reused in adjacent balades as a significant form of linking. The link is aurally reinforced by B13's placement of "-ueil" as its b-rhyme in a rhyme royal verse form (ababbcC), meaning there are three such rhymes in each stanza, each emphasized cadentially in the musical setting (see example 4.1, box a).

B13 shares three of these "-ueil" rhymes words with B12, through which it rewrites the despair of B12 in the light of Hope (see figure 4.1). What remains constant between the two poems is the external circumstances: the lady's "welcome" (*acueil*) is pleasing and beautiful in B13, sweet in B12. What changes is the internal response. In B12, the lover's heart must "live in such torment"

---

2. A useful recording with two singers can be found on *Le Jugement du Roi de Navarre; Machaut: Ballades, motets, virelais et textes dits*, Ensemble Gilles Binchois, directed by Dominique Vellard (recorded 1994, CD issue 1998 as Cantus 9626), track 13. The song is actually fourteenth in the later authorial order of A, which places *Sans cuer / Amis / Dame* (B17) (a dialogue *chace* discussing the role of the exchange of hearts at parting) ninth.

3. See chapter 3.

4. See the discussion later in this chapter.

Example 4.1. *Esperance* (B13): a. "-ueil" b-rhyme emphasized by cadences at the *ouvert* and *clos*, and in the B section; b. unison *d* at the end of the first full musical phrase (mid–poetic line 2); c. opening and final cadences.

B13

1.1 Esperance qui m'asseüre,
    Joie sans per, vie a mon vueil,
1.3 Dous penser, sade nourriture,
    Tres bon eür, plaisant **accueil**,
1.5 Et maint autre grant bien **recueil**,
    Quant Amours m'a tant enrichi,
1.7 Que j'aim dame, s'aten merci.

2.1 Et se ceste atente m'est dure,
    En desirant pas ne m'en **dueil**,
2.3 Car le gré de ma dame pure,
    Et d'Amours tousjours faire vueil,
2.5 Et sa guerredon sans pareil,
    Ce m'est vis, puis qu'il est einsi,
2.7 Que j'aim dame, s'aten mercy.

3.1 Car Souvenirs en moy figure
    Sa fine biauté sans orgueil,
3.3 Sa bonté, sa noble figure,
    Son gent mainteing, son bel **accueil**,
3.5 Et comment si dous riant oueil
    Par leur atrait m'ont mené si,
3.7 Que j'aim dame, s'aten mercy.

8'a 8b 8'a 8b 8b 8c 8C

Hope, who reassures me, Joy without
equal, a life according to my wishes, Sweet
Thought, sweet sustenance, great happiness,
pleasing welcome, and many other very
good things do I receive because Love has
so enriched me *that I love a lady and await*
merci.
And although this waiting is hard for me, in
desiring her I do not torment myself, for I
want always to do the will of my pure lady
and of Love, and so there will be reward
without equal, I think, since my situation is
such *that I love a lady and await* merci.
For memory depicts within me her fine
beauty without pride, her goodness, her
noble figure, her genteel countenance, her
fair welcome, and the way in which her
sweet laughing eyes have led me by their
attraction so *that I love a lady and await*
merci.

B12

1.1 Pour ce que tous mes chans fais
    De dolereus sentement,
1.3 Et pour ce que ne chant mais,
    Repris sui de meinte gent;
1.5 Mais qui vraiement saroit
    Ce que mes las cuers reçoit
1.7 Pour ma dame au **dous acueil**
    Jamais ne me blasmeroit
1.9 Se je chant meins que ne sueil.

2.1 Car pour amer onques mais
    Si tres douleureusement,
2.3 Ne fu nuls amis detrais
    Com je sui; car vraiement
2.5 Langue raconter a droit,
    Ne cuers penser ne pourroit
2.7 La dolour que je **recueil;**
    Pour ce m'est vis que j'ay droit
2.9 Se je chant meins que ne sueil.

3.1 Mais endurer ce grief fais
    Me fait ma dame plaisant,
3.3 Quant ne puis n'en dis n'en fais
    Plaire a son viaire gent;
3.5 Ce tient mon cuer si estroit,
    Qu'assez miex partir vaudroit
3.7 En .ij. que vivre en tel **dueil**,
    Dont nulz blasmer ne me doit
3.9 Se je chant meins que ne sueil

7a 7b 7a 7b 7c 7c 7d 7c 7D

Because I make all my songs of sorrowful sentiment, and because I don't sing any
longer, I have been reproached by many people. But were there someone who truly knew
what my weary heart receives because of my
lady with her sweet welcome, he would never
blame me *if I sing less than I used to.*
For no lover was ever so sorrowfully slan-
dered as I am for being in love; for truly, no
tongue could ever properly tell and no heart
could ever imagine the sorrow that I receive.
Therefore I think that I am in the right *if I
sing less than I used to.*
But my pleasant lady makes me endure this
grievous burden because I cannot, either in
word or in deed, please her noble face. This
puts my heart in such straits that it would
better break in two than live in such torment.
Therefore no one must speak ill of me *if I
sing less than I used to.*

Figure 4.1. Texts and translations of *Esperance* (B13) and *Pour ce que tous* (B12), showing
shared rhyme words (text based on MS C).

("vivre en tel *dueil*") that no heart, he says, could ever imagine "the sorrow that I receive" ("La dolour que je *recueil*"). In B13, by contrast, the lover lists Hope, joy, sweet thought, and sustenance among "many other good things I receive" ("maint autre grant bien *recueil*"), such that, although the wait may be hard, "in desiring her I do *not* torment myself" ("en desirant pas ne m'en *dueil*"; emphasis added) These text segments emphasizing Hope's reconfiguration of despair as joy all fall prominently within the musical structure of B13 at either the *ouvert* cadence or the *clos* cadence. They receive further musical emphasis because, in a striking departure from Machaut's own normal practice, the two main musical phrases of B13's A section carry unequal amounts of text. In Machaut's balades, the two musical phrases of the A section are usually coterminous with its two poetic lines. In B13, though, the first musical phrase (mm. 1–5) carries both line 1 and the first four syllables of line 2. Its end is marked rhythmically by cantus rests and the tenor's solo linking figure (second half of m. 5), and tonally by a (mensurally weak) progression back to the opening's unison *d* (example 4.1, box b). The second, shorter musical phrase (mm. 6–8) carries the final four syllables of line 2, resulting in a four-breve-unit melisma, terminated by cadences that set the "-ueil" rhyme words. The coordination of text and music suggested by the sources is supported by musical logic: unison sonorities start all lines except 5 and 7 (which both start with tenths using the pitch classes A and F).[5]

As often but not always in Machaut, the *clos* and *ouvert* cadences of B13 provide a tonal hierarchy for (respectively) primary and secondary goals throughout the piece. The first cadence to G/d (start of m. 2) emphasizes the emblematic opening word, "Esperance," and prefigures the *clos* and final cadences of the piece. The next, resolving to a/e from the second to the third tenor notes within measure 2, prefigures the *ouvert* sonority. The remainder of the balade—sections B and R—sets each of every stanza's three remaining poetic lines more normatively to its own separate musical phrase. The whole of line 5 (mm. 10–12) promulgates the expectation of its eventual resolution to the G/g octave. Line 6 (mm. 13–15) is similar to the setting of line 2 (ending a/e), rounding off each of the two main sections A and B with similar material.[6] The refrain that follows summarizes the situation of the lover ("I love a lady and await her *merci*") and cadences to the same sonority that

5. Unison sonorities at the opening or closing of phrases in Machaut's balades are relatively unusual. While a unison might be thought to stand for the special completion and unity achievable by the desiring subject if his relation to the object is one overseen by Hope, in the earlier music balades unisons seem, on the contrary, to be associated with texts that mention refusal, silence, lack, and emptiness. While on one level the unison is the ultimate perfect consonance, on another it is no harmony at all, being instead an identity. Interpreted like this, the opening phrase progresses hopefully from the nonharmony of the isolated subject (a single tone) to the consonant harmony of two separate independent tones.

6. The parallel between the second phrases of the A and B sections is most visible in the readings of G; see Wulf Arlt, "Aspekte der Chronologie und des Stilwandels im französischen Lied des

forms the tonal goal at the opening and very end of the A section in each stanza.

In relation to his lady, the lover of *Esperance* (B13) is little better off than the unhappy lovers who dominate most of the music balades that precede B13 in the collected works manuscripts. The lady's beauty has attracted him, and he awaits her *merci*. But the presence of Hope verbally at the beginning of the song makes all the difference to the lover's emotional experience of his situation. Unlike the generally suffering lovers who pervade the first twelve music balades, the lover of B13 is reassured by Hope and does not torment himself with desire, even if the waiting is hard, since he has hope of reward without equal. Enriched by Love, he awaits Love's grace and the lady's *merci*. Kevin Brownlee has commented that "the *dame* is not synonymous with her *merci*."[7] In fact Machaut's music forges instead an aural connection between "merci," the final word of the refrain and thereby of the whole song, and the very opening word, "Esperance," by virtue of their very similar music (example 4.1, box c).[8] As the tenor of the refrain is slightly offset rhythmically compared to its presentation at the opening of the piece, the potential for a metrically emphasized directed progression is avoided until the end: the listener, like the lover, must wait for the *merci* of the final cadence.

Like B12 and *De triste cuer / Quant vrais amans / Certes, je di* (B29), discussed in chapter 3, B13 occurs only in the music section. As with B29, the context of B13 in the music section—in this case its "sister balade," *Je ne cuit pas* (B14), discussed in the final part of the present chapter—links it to the *Loange*. As with B12, however, the most significant connection of B13 to Machaut's wider works is achieved through its thematic content. It arguably presents a gnomic,

14. Jahrhunderts," in *Aktuelle Fragen der musikbezogenen Mittelalterforschung: Texte zu einem Basler Kolloquium des Jahres 1975* (Winterthur, 1982), 246–47.

7. Kevin Brownlee, "Literary Intertextualities in the *Esperance* Series: Machaut's *Esperance qui m'asseüre*, the Anonymous Rondeau *En attendant d'avoir*, Senleches *En attendant esperance conforte*," in *Musik als Text: Bericht über den Internationalen Kongreß der Gesellschaft für Musikforschung, Freiburg im Breisgau 1993*, ed. Hermann Danuser and Tobias Plebuch (Kassel, 1998), vol. 1, 311.

8. The refrain text is sung to this music in all three stanzas; the initial cadence has six different texts (two per stanza). Nevertheless, the initial cadence sets four key concepts in the poem, notably *Esperance* and Sweet Thought in the first stanza as well as "bonté" (goodness) and *Souvenir*. The slow-moving, near-syllabic refrain line summarizes the main tonal action of the balade with an initial resolution to G/g (m. 15), a displaced one to a/e (at m. 16), and a final cadence to G/d (m. 17). Its text quotes the final line of the three-line refrain of *Pour mon temps* (rondeau 26) in Oxford, Bodleian library, MS Douce 308 (full text published in Gaston Raynaud, ed., *Recueil de motets français des XIIe et XIIIe siècles*, 2 vols. [Paris, 1881–1883], 2:32–33; Mary Atchison, *The Chansonnier of Oxford Bodleian MS Douce 308: Essays and Complete Edition of Texts* [Aldershot, 2005], 565; and Nico H. J. van den Boogaard, *Rondeaux et Refrains du XIIe siècle au début du XIVe* [Paris, 1969], 74, rondeau no. 139, refrain no. 1511). As Douce 308 is an unnotated chansonnier, it is not possible to ascertain whether the refrain represents a musical as well as textual quotation, although this seems likely. Its longer note values, retrospectively revealing its key role in the harmonic generation of the song, resemble the refrain in B12, a song known to be quoting text and music together.

emblematic, cogent, and harmonious statement of the most important tenet of Machaut's courtly doctrine. Given that it lasts under six minutes and could be sung by two people—or even by a single vocalist playing his or her own instrument—its performance at court could have been easily achieved, permitting it to serve a much-repeated didactic purpose, simultaneously consoling, edifying, and enjoyable. Its thematic content would have cued the listener's memory to the many other places in Machaut's works where the importance of Hope is more thoroughly developed, notably—and most didactically—in the *Remede de Fortune.*

Fortune's Remedy

As numerous recent commentators have discussed, consolation in Machaut's works is achieved through the elevation of the personified figure of Hope as a sublimation of Desire, which works through an ongoing memorialization of the lady and her good qualities.[9] Desire, because it prompts mental fixation on the incompleteness of the subject who lacks the love object—it "unmakes him"—leads to endless suffering and (at least metaphorical or symbolic) "death." Hope, fed by the memorial image (*Souvenir*) and Sweet Thoughts, can nourish the lover in the sweet pasture of Love, bringing a self-sufficiency that makes refined loving socially workable.[10] Bringing about any act of reciprocation is not in the lover's control, rendering him powerless and subject to the arbitrary turns of Fortune's wheel. Moreover, as the last section of this chapter will show further, that which would satisfy Desire—Desire's *souffisance*—would be a form of *merci* whose enactment might imperil the honor of the lady. That which would satisfy Hope, however, is the mental picture of the lady and the goodness she represents. The potential state of waiting for *merci* is itself *souffisance* and in the lover's own mental control; hence the musical linking of the opening word "Esperance" and the final word "merci" seen in B13. Provided he is governed by Hope rather than Desire, the lover is completed by his own mental effort, ensuring his ongoing loyalty and the maintenance of the lady's honor.

9. Kelly, *Medieval Imagination,* 122, notes that Machaut's "love is in fact a sublimation. Machaut's attempt to effect such a sublimation is historically significant and intellectually original." Huot, "Guillaume de Machaut and the Consolation of Poetry," 172, notes that "Desire, with its emphasis on the isolation and deprivation of the poetic subject, leads to the breakdown of social bonds, to miscommunication, shame, and despair. Hope, on the other hand, with its emphasis on plenitude and fulfillment, allows for social interaction and cohesion, serenity, and the stylized public performance of courtly values." See also Jody Enders, "Music, Delivery, and the Rhetoric of Memory in Guillaume de Machaut's Remède de Fortune," *Proceedings of the Modern Language Association* 107 (1992): 450–64; and Alexandre Leupin, "The Powerlessness of Writing: Guillaume de Machaut, the Gorgon, and *Ordenance,*" *Yale French Studies* 70 (1986): 127–49.

10. On sweetness, see Mary Carruthers, "Sweetness," *Speculum* 81 (2006): 999–1013.

The most direct statement of this courtly doctrine can be gleaned from one of Machaut's most explicitly didactic dits—the *Remede de Fortune*. As at once an art of love and an art of musical poetry, and thereby strongly suggestive of the links between these two arts, this dit contains interpolated musical lyrics that serve to generate and resolve the surrounding narrative. The basic plot is outlined in figure 4.2, which also notes the position of the musical interpolations.[11] Though framed by a prologue and an epilogue, the main action of the dit occupies nearly three and a half thousand of the poem's 4,298 lines. The three main episodes show the lover at court before and after a central section in which he is instructed by the allegorical figure of Hope in the park at Hesdin.[12]

The opening prologue presents the voice of a clerkly narrator, pronouncing authoritatively on the subject of learning, which he maintains is best done when one is young (ll. 1–44). In a swift lyricization of this clerkly didacticism, the narrator then proceeds to the first episode of the dit proper, in which he will begin the story of his own instruction in love when he was in the youthful state of innocence.[13] In the first episode the lover extols the virtues of his lady, whose natural gifts are so great that Nature inclines his heart to her (ll. 45–60) and Love instructs him to love, obey, serve, and honor her above everything that God has made (ll. 87–106). Relating only to his lady and to Love, the inexperienced lover relies on them to teach him about both love and poetry. The lady's beauty introduces him to Desire and Hope: "Love increases and prompts Desire," which is for the *merci* of Love, whereas "joy brings Hope," (ll. 315–16).[14] This relation between Hope and Desire quickly proves unstable, since Desire's ability to feed off and thus emphasize the lack of the lady works against joy, whose absence brings not hope but despair. The lover is weakened by the merest glance from the lady, which causes him to "grow pale and flush, to shake, tremble, and shudder" (ll. 375–76).[15] He is driven to make poetry for her in secret, relating how he writes in many different musical

---

11. One lyric item is not notated, the prayer to love, *Amours, je te lo et graci;* see Lawrence Earp, *Guillaume de Machaut: A Guide to Research* (New York, 1995), 212. It appears between the lover's last poem in the garden (the balade *Dame, de qui* [RF5]) and the first back at court, and provides a retransitional palinode to the *déploration* of Fortune in the complaint by being an "imploration" of Love; see Daniel Poirion, *Le poète et le prince: L'évolution du lyrisme courtois de Guillaume de Machaut à Charles d'Orléans* (Grenoble, 1965), 417.

12. The importance of Hesdin as a locus for marvelous—even magical—happenings was well attested in the fifteenth century, when it was famed for its automata. Birgit Franke, "Gesellschaftsspiele mit Automaten: 'Merveilles' in Hesdin," *Marburger Jahrbuch für Künstwissenschaft* 24 (1997): 135–58, suggests that the existence of such mechanical marvels reaches back much further, citing the *Remede*'s mention of "engins" and "estranges choses" (*Remede*, ll. 813–14).

13. See Kevin Brownlee, *Poetic Identity in Guillaume de Machaut* (Madison, 1984), 37–63.

14. Translation from James I. Wimsatt, William W. Kibler, and Rebecca A. Baltzer, eds., *Guillaume de Machaut: Le Jugement du Roy de Behaigne and Remede de Fortune* (Athens, Ga., 1988), 184.

15. Trans. ibid., 188.

Le Remede de Fortune
(Fortune's Remedy, or The Cure for Bad Luck)

PROLOGUE (ll. 1–44)
Clerkly-didactic voice of the narrator in a present significantly after the events of his own youthful love apprenticeship, details of which he will now relate

I (ll. 45–782): AT COURT (lover and lady; lover's failure)
    1. (ll. 45–134) transition: presentation of the narrator as courtly lover in the first person
    2. (ll. 135–66) Love as a teacher
    3. (ll. 167–356) the lady as a teacher
    4. (ll. 357–681) the young lover's service to his lady: secret composition of poems for her (ll. 357–430) including:
        • his <u>lay</u> (ll. 431–680), *Qui n'aroit autre deport* (RF1)
    5. (ll. 681–782) the lady discovers the lay; the lover flees in despair

II (ll. 783–3044): THE PARK OF HESDIN (lover and Hope; lover instructed by Hope)
    1. (ll. 783–1480) the lover enters the park (ll. 783–904) and bewails his state to Fortune in:
        • his <u>complaint</u> (ll. 905–1480), *Tels rit au main qui au soir pleure* (RF2)
    2. (ll. 1481–2125) Hope's arrival as a mysterious figure; her defense and justification of Love argued in part in:
        • her <u>chanson royal</u> (ll. 1985–2032), *Joie, plaisance et douce norriture* (RF3)
    3. (ll. 2126–2347) after the lover asks her, Hope reveals her identity
    4. (ll. 2348–2892) Hope explains the nature of Fortune; before departing she sings:
        • her <u>baladelle</u> [= <u>duplex balade</u>] (ll. 2857–2892), *En amer a douce vie* (RF4)
    5. (ll. 2920–3044) the lover, now happy, leaves the park after singing:
        • his <u>balade</u> (ll. 3013–36), *Dame, de qui toute ma joie vient* (RF5)

III (ll. 3045–4258): BACK AT COURT (lover, lady, and Hope; the lover's "success")
    1. (ll. 3045–3348) sight of the lady's chateau paralyzes the lover with fear; Hope returns to support him; the lover performs an unnotated <u>Prière</u>, *Amours, je te lo et graci* (ll. 3205–3348) addressed to Hope and Love
    2. (ll. 3349–3516) at an outdoor courtly festivity, with dancing and singing, the lover sings to the lady:
        • his <u>chanson baladée</u> [virelay] (ll. 3451–96), *Dame, a vous sans retollir* (RF6)
    3. (ll. 3517–3872) at the lady's chateau the lover declares his love and the lady accepts it
    4. (ll. 3873–4116) dinner at the lady's chateau; they exchange rings in the presence of Hope; the lover sings:
        • his <u>rondelet</u> [rondeau] (ll. 4109–16), *Dame, mon cuer en vous remaint* (RF7)
    5. (ll. 4117–4258) after a brief absence, the lover finds that his lady treats him with indifference; his desperate complaint results in a series of (somewhat ambiguous) reassurances on her part

EPILOGUE (ll. 4259–4300)

Figure 4.2. Synopsis of *Remede,* showing position of lyrics.

genres according to his fluctuating *sentement* because "he who does not compose according to his *sentement* falsifies his work and his song."[16]

The problematic issue of how to uphold the emotional truth of composing from *sentement* and yet compose joyful songs when one is miserable was discussed in chapter 3. *Remede* upholds the view outlined there that the good of joy is so supreme that the composing lover must make his emotions joyful rather than his songs sorrowful. (The *Prologue*, moreover, suggests that the act of composition itself will assist in this by distracting the lover.) The lover of *Remede*, like the lovers of *De triste cuer* (the cantus voice of B29) and B12, is wrongly sacrificing the requirement for joy and modifying his songs. The poem will teach him—and his audience—how instead to modify their mental state.

At this point the lover-protagonist of *Remede* sings directly to the courtly audience of the dit, treating them to the first interpolated lyric of the poem, the lay *Qui n'aroit* (RF1). The lover's heart causes him to delight in composing and singing in the lady's honor, but he is not singing directly to her. Instead the audience reads or overhears this lay as an example of one of the compositions resulting from his fluctuating *sentement*. Here he claims it results from happiness, which gives birth to song because he has Sweet Thought, *Souvenir*, Loyalty, and Hope enclosed in his heart. This lay, like the other lyric items in the dit, is exemplary as a musico-poetic item, as well as offering insight into the mental state of the dit's protagonist while undercutting his claims to self-knowledge.

Lays—more properly referred to as lyric lays to distinguish them from the unrelated narrative form in isometric couplets—are often thought of as the foremost form of this period. Deschamps introduces the lay as "a long item, difficult to make and invent."[17] Except in the very earliest of the collected manuscripts (that is, in all those later than C), Machaut placed the lays at the head of the notated part of the manuscript, mirroring the premier placement of this form in the *Remede*.[18] In C their importance is indicated instead by the fact that they alone of the music outside the *Remede* merit a series of illuminations that add "an important theatrical dimension to the written text" by picturing the voices of the individual lays.[19] Musically, the lay comes closest of all forms at this period to being through-composed, in contrast to the strophic forms with refrains used in the balade, rondeau, and virelay. With the exception of the

16. Trans. ibid.; *Remede*, ll. 407–8: "Car qui de sentement ne fait, / Son oeuvre et son chant contrefait." See also chapter 3 and notes 31 and 144 in this chapter.

17. "Une chose longue et malaisiee a faire et trouver"; see Deborah M. Sinnreich-Levi, ed., *Eustache Deschamps' L'Art de dictier* (East Lansing, 1994), 94, ll. 570–71; see also her introduction, 46–52.

18. See David Fallows, "Guillaume de Machaut and the Lai: A New Source," *Early Music* 5 (1977): 477–83. A fuller bibliography can be found in Earp, *Guillaume de Machaut*, 286–87.

19. On these, see Sylvia Huot, *From Song to Book: The Poetics of Writing in Old French Lyric and Lyrical Narrative Poetry* (Ithaca, 1987), 260–72.

final stanza, which has the same melody as the opening one (usually at a different pitch), each of a lay's twelve stanzas has its own versification, rhymes, and music.[20] The poetry and music of each stanza are subdivided into two identical "versicles," with each half of the stanza sung to the same music, mostly with a tonally "open" cadence for the ending of the first half and a tonally "closed" cadence for the ending of the second. The manuscript presentation copies these two halves of each stanza's text under each other, beneath the music that will serve double duty. Deschamps describes the complete lay as effectively having twenty-four stanzas ("couples") on account of this subdivision.[21]

In many of the stanzas of Machaut's lays these two halves are themselves musically subdivided so that there are effectively four versicles with basically the same melody, differing only in that the odd versicles have a tonally "open" ending and the even ones a tonally "closed" cadence. David Fallows has described this "quadrupled versicle" structure as making each stanza of the lay into an almost self-contained four-stanza song, so that the entire lay becomes virtually a twelve-song cycle.[22] This prevalent quadruple versicle structure certainly provides a greater number of perceptibly parallel sections for each stanza of the song and is usually reflected in the versification and rhymes, but the copying layout in the music section does not generally abbreviate the melodic repeats further than the basic bipartite division, keeping that fundamental unit clear.[23] The opening stanza of *Amours doucement* (L7/6), for example, has a typical quadrupled versicle structure. Figure 4.3 shows it as texted in MS Vg; examples 4.2a and 4.2b show the opening stanza first in a modern transcription that replicates the double versicle layout of the manuscript and second in the quadrupled versicle layout of one of the published modern editions.[24] The lay offers a composer—and a singer—a large canvas on which to develop melodic musical ideas unencumbered by the shortness and repetition

20. Twelve-stanza lays are standard in Machaut's works, but contemporary poets vary this. See Isabelle Bétemps, "Les *Lais de plour*: Guillaume de Machaut et Oton de Granson," in *Guillaume de Machaut: 1300–2000. Actes du Colloque de la Sorbonne 28–29 septembre 2000*, ed. Jacqueline Cerquiglini-Toulet and Nigel Wilkins (Paris, 2002), 103; and Sinnreich-Levi, *Eustache Deschamps' L'Art de dictier*, 52n53.

21. Sinnreich-Levi, *Eustache Deschamps' L'Art de dictier*, 96, l. 584. The translation makes a distinction between strophe and stanza (the subdivision), although the French text uses *couple* for both parts. I use "stanza" for the large unit and "versicle" for subdivisions of the stanza.

22. Fallows, "Guillaume de Machaut and the Lai," 482. In general (but not always), subdivision of the versification is reflected by repeats of melodic material, even leading to some stanzas with an AAB, ABB, or ABA versicle structure.

23. Ironically, given its centrality to the discussion here, the lay in *Remede* in C is one that does copy its stanzas' text four lines deep for those with quadrupled versicles (that is, for all except the first and last), making it akin to the text layout of the modern edition. The other manuscript copies of this same lay have the more normal double versicle layout.

24. My transcription in example 4.2a represents the smallest note value (the minim) in the original as an eighth note, as per the normal level of rhythmic "reduction" applied in transcriptions of music in this type of notation from this period. For many of the lays, however, the editors

of fixed forms on the one hand or the distractions of polyphony on the other. It thus makes the ideal vehicle for the single secretive lover to compose and sing to himself, "overheard" only by the dit's audience.

The lay starts promisingly: the lover declares that as long as he has Sweet Thought, *Souvenir,* and Hope (*Espoir*), he should not seek anything else but will rather be consoled by seeing, hearing, and remembering his lady's appearance and voice, which will protect him from death. The short lines of this opening stanza make its point clearly and certainly, as if the lover is trying to aspire to sententious clerkly statements about his own love experience.[25] The second stanza criticizes anyone who doesn't think such goods are enough when they can mend a wounded heart and exile sadness, bringing joy merely through remembrance.

Stanzas 3 and 4 praise Sweet Thought and the sight of the lady. In stanza 5 (example 4.3) the lover states that any grief he receives from Desire is soothed by her look and Fair Welcome, which nourishes his heart with pleasure and enriches him so that his current state suffices. Desire's griefs are pictured musically in the leap between the end of the first line of poetry and the start of the next, which outlines an augmented interval, *G-c♯*. Not only is this a strikingly ungainly—even pained—effect, but also the sharpened note begs for resolution to *d,* which is achieved only locally, with the rest of the phrase heading instead back down to *a* for the end of the line, and to *G* at the end of the stanza. In the mid-century, the music theorist Johannes Boen commented that semitones that were foreign to the regular gamut were panted after by men bored with the usual placement of the notes.[26] Although the forward-leading force of these notes was felt more readily in polyphonic contexts in which they form part of the tension-resolution protocol of what modern theorists have termed the "directed progression," there is some evidence that their power extended to monophony.[27] In the second of the four versicles in this stanza, the leap links the line "le grief qui de Desir ist" with "si me plaist et abelist."

(like Schrade here in example 4.2b) apply a further level of reduction, representing the minim with a sixteenth note.

25. This stanza and the final one, which repeats its melody a fifth higher, are the only ones in this lay to be in the more expansive double versicle form, making a musically more spacious prologue and epilogue to the whole.

26. Elizabeth Eva Leach, "Gendering the Semitone, Sexing the Leading Tone: Fourteenth-Century Music Theory and the Directed Progression," *Music Theory Spectrum* 28 (2006): 12, citing Wolf Frobenius, *Johannes Boens Musica und seine Konsonanzlehre* (Stuttgart, 1971), 63, trans. Leofranc Holford-Strevens: "It must be noted more subtly that modern usage admits the said letters in *claves* [i.e., pitches] outside the nature of the manual monochord only for consonances or the wantonness of the song itself [*lasciviam ipsius cantus*]—for men did not formerly pant after so many wantonnesses [*lasciviis*] in the practical performance of a song as they do now." On the significance of this figure to the pains of Desire, see also William Calin and Lawrence Earp, "The Lai in *Remede de Fortune,*" *Ars Lyrica* 11 (2000): 39–75.

27. See Jennifer Bain, "Tonal Structure and the Melodic Role of Chromatic Inflections in the Music of Machaut," *Plainsong and Medieval Music* 14 (2005): 59–88; and the comments on the

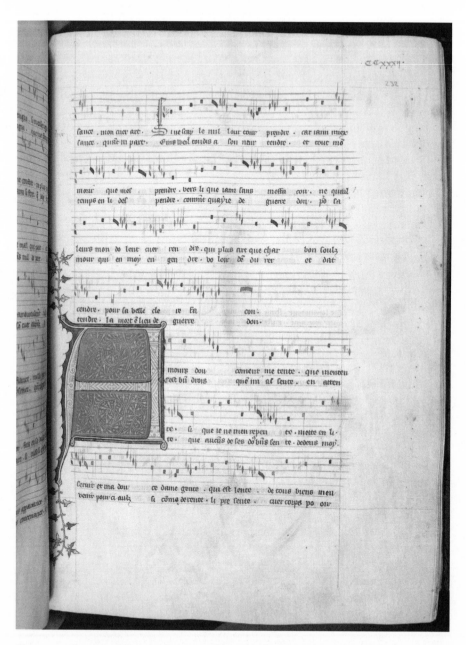

Figure 4.3. Opening of *Amours doucement* (L7/6), in Guillaume de Machaut: the Ferrell-Vogüé MS, f. 232r–232v. On loan to the Parker Library, Corpus Christi, Cambridge. Reproduced by kind permission of Elizabeth J. and James E. Ferrell. Digital imaging by DIAMM (www.diamm. ac.uk).

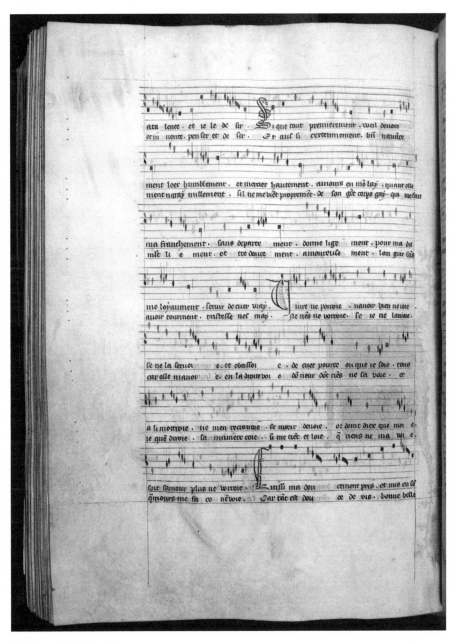

Figure 4.3. (*Continued*)

Example 4.2. *Amours doucement* (L7/6), opening stanza: a. transcription representing double versicle layout of the manuscripts; b. Schrade edition, showing quadrupled versicle structure. Reproduced by permission of Éditions de l'Oiseau-Lyre.

The contextual meaning of the entire stanza makes it clear that it is the lady's "sweet laughing eye" (from stanza 5, l. 3; *Remede*, l. 517) that "so pleases me," but the music's chopping up of the stanza gives a local meaning within the versicle in which the "grief that issues from Desire / so pleases me."[28] The "discort" of this line is even more evident to the ear because of a mismatch

---

setting up of expectation in Elizabeth Eva Leach, "Counterpoint and Analysis in Fourteenth-Century Song," *Journal of Music Theory* 44 (2000): 62–63 (discussion of ex. 9).

28. This stanza has some significant shared lexes and expressions with *Plaisant dame* (Lo165), which is discussed later in this chapter.

between the musical "rhyme" and the poetic rhymes.[29] In most quadruple versicle lay stanzas, all four versicles have the same rhyme types. Even in cases where the second half of the stanza has different (usually mirrored) rhymes from the first half, the second versicle always repeats the rhymes of the first, and those of the fourth repeat those of the third—*except here*. This means that here the same music has different rhymes, the musical "rhyme" has no poetic rhyme, and the audible mismatch pictures the discomfort of the singer.

Stanza 6 opens with an exception ("Fors tant"), which reveals that the lady is unaware of the lover's feelings for her because he deems himself too unworthy to reveal them. His love's steadfastness and his commitment to concealing it are restated in the next two stanzas, the second of which (stanza 8) is strikingly merry musically: its short musical phrases setting the short lines with the feminine rhyme "-elle" just seem to sing "she, she, she, she and only she" (example 4.4). In stanza 9 the lover turns to Love, who made him love the lady but now refuses to reveal his love to her, causing him to sigh. The music's quadrupled versicle setting contains rests of the shortest durational value used in the piece, which make the second and third lines of each versicle enter after the briefest of pauses. This manner of figuring the sighing with which the lover is venting the ardor in his heart—by having the singer deliver a short intake of breath—can be found in other pieces by Machaut and his contemporaries.[30] After the burning increases with his sighs, the very next two stanzas show a lover who is, as he claimed in the passage before the lay, "not always in one mood," and whose compositions reflect this fluctuating *sentement*.[31] The length and complexity of the lay have allowed this fluctuation to take place inside a single musico-poetic piece. In stanza 10 the lover vows to live joyfully and happily. If Hope (E*spoir*) does not lie, he claims, his suffering will be rewarded a hundred times over. Typically, Desire assails the lover again in stanza 11, which exploits violent imagery of battles and the piercing of the lover's body by the amorous dart, which "frequently slice[s] my heart / secretly with its shaft and point."[32] Once more the lover claims that the

---

29. On the generic link between the lay and the discort, see Pierre Bec, *Le lyrique française au moyen âge (xiie–xiiie siècles): Contributions à une typologie des genres poétiques médiévales, études et textes*, 2 vols. (Paris, 1977–78), 1:199–208.

30. Machaut himself uses this "sigh motif" in combination with images of fire in *Tous corps / De souspirant / Suspiro* (M2); see the remarks in Anne Walters Robertson, *Guillaume de Machaut and Reims: Context and Meaning in His Musical Works* (Cambridge, 2002), 113–15. Vitry uses it in his motet *Douce / Garison / Neuma;* see Elizabeth Eva Leach, *Sung Birds: Music, Nature, and Poetry in the Later Middle Ages* (Ithaca, 2007), 229–32.

31. *Remede*, ll. 401–6: "Et pour ce que n'estoie mie / Tousdis en un point, m'estudie / Mis en faire chansons et lays, / Baladez, rondeaus, virelays, / Et chans, selonc mon sentement, / Amoureus et non autrement." See notes 16 and 144. See also the emphasis on the lay's discord in Calin and Earp, "The Lai in *Remede de Fortune*," 48, which notes that the seeming process of psychological growth depicted by the lover during the course of the lay is in fact a "series of circles." The subject is here still trapped in Fortune's wheel by Desire, despite his efforts to reason his way out of it.

32. *Remede*, ll. 639–52.

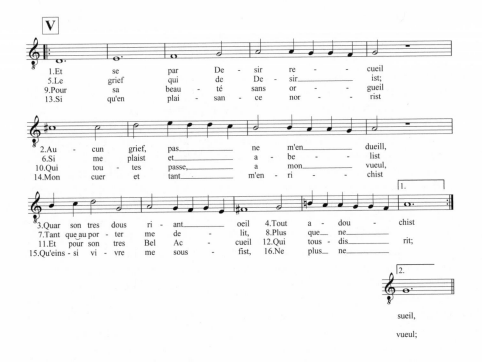

And if from Desire I receive
Any grief, I will not complain about it,
Because her very sweet laughing eye
Sweetens all
The grief that issues from Desire;
It so pleases me and gladdens
[Me] so much that I delight in bearing it
More than I am used to,

On account of her beauty without pride,
Which surpasses all others, in my view,
And on account of her very Fair Welcome,
Which always smiles,
So that it nourishes with pleasure
My heart and so enriches me,
That it suffices me to live like this,
Nor do I want more.

Example 4.3. *Qui n'aroit* (RF1), stanza 5 music (with translation of the text).

Sweet Look (*Dous Regart*) of the lady heals him, but the slicing entry of Desire's dart also dissects the musical structure so that this stanza is significantly more cut up (see example 4.5): the closed part of the odd versicles in the basic quadruple versicle section is a little longer than the open ending in such a way that it seems as though another "-aille" line has been spliced into the structure and unbalanced it. The remorseless repetition of the rhyme type "-aille" on repeated notes not only allows for frequent compounds on "taille" (cutting) but also even sounds like a cry of pain; the other rhyme, "-art," suggests the ongoing burning of the lover in the fire of Desire.

The final stanza brings the lay full circle, at least musically, since it has, like all Machaut's notated lays, the same melody as the first stanza, notated, as in the majority of Machaut's notated lays, at a pitch level a perfect fifth higher than at the opening.[33] The lover restates his resolve to serve, and think of, his lady, but now we know that he needs this to comfort him because he is assailed by a burning desire ("ardant desir") that causes him to grow pale and wan and makes his heart tremble and quake. Despite the lay's initial good intentions, the lover's clear expectation that comfort will come directly from the lady and her Sweet Look is shown to be unrealistic, especially when the fact of the lover's love is concealed.

After he has performed the lay for us, the audience, the narrative recounts how the lady chances upon the lay. Before he had performed it safely to his latter-day audience, he had mused that were she to find one of his songs, he would be pleased because she would then realize how much he loves her. But when this happens, it prompts his distressed flight from her, from court, and into the park at Hesdin.

At the outset of the second episode of the *Remede*, the lover makes his distress very clear to himself and the dit's listeners as he sits alone in the park at Hesdin making and performing a complaint to Fortune. (This musical piece and its illumination are dealt with more thoroughly in chapter 5.) This is the point at which the twin models of Boethius and the *Roman de la Rose* collide. Like the lover in *Rose*, the lover in *Remede* has entered a garden space; like the narrator of the *Consolation of Philosophy*, he is singing the song of the Muses, the kind of poetry that aestheticizes pain and leads to self-absorption, prolonging only itself (as is evident from the length of the complaint!), and preventing the desiring subject from developing a new psychological frame of reference that will relieve his suffering and offer a path onward into a serene future.[34] The lover has already effectively claimed to be the victim of Desire in the lay, although there at least he attempted to combat desire, even if this attempt ultimately failed because of his overreliance on the lady. The "staging

---

33. Of twenty-five lays by Machaut (including the two present only in E), six have no music; six have no transposition in the final stanza; one is written down a perfect fourth, one up a perfect fourth, and all the rest (eleven) are written up a perfect fifth, as here.

34. Huot, "Guillaume de Machaut and the Consolation of Poetry," 169.

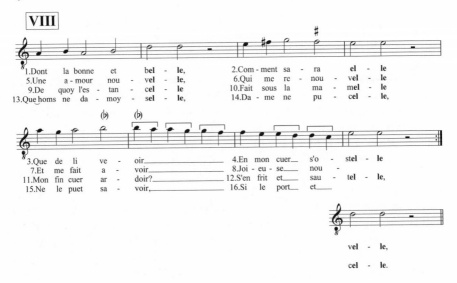

Example 4.4. *Qui n'aroit* (RF1), stanza 8 music, showing repetition of "-elle" rhymes in bold (with translation of the text).

The good and beautiful [lady],
How will she know
That from seeing her
In my heart is lodged
A new love,
Which renews me
And makes me have
Joyful news,

At which the spark
Makes, under my breast,
My refined heart burn?
It leaps and fries at it,
But in such a way that neither man nor woman,
[Neither] lady nor girl,
Might know it
Do I carry and conceal it.

of the self as victim" in the complaint is done overtly, bitterly, repetitiously, and lengthily as the lover performs his state of utter subjection to Fortune and her wheel in a song that goes round and round and round.[35]

35. This diagnosis of the complaint's repetitiveness is meant as a criticism not of Machaut's poetry but rather of the lover's absorption. See the more detailed comments in chapter 5.

Example 4.5. *Qui n'aroit* (RF1), stanza 11 music, showing aa'b structure and the "-aille" rhyme (with translation of the text).

For although Desire assails me   a
And makes many battles against me
And stabs me with the arrow of love,
Which often with shaft and tip   a'
Secretly cuts my heart,
Surely he works in vain
For her Sweet Look heals everything,   b

[It] feeds my heart with the victuals of love   a
And within it engraves
Her refined beauty with such an art
That there is no other that can move me;   a'
And it gives me love's goods
Until there is no joy that I lack
That I don't have from her, whom God keep.   b

Hope's appearance, like that of allegorical personages in prosimetra from Boethius's Philosophy to Alan of Lille's Nature, is mysterious; she is not at first recognized by the lover. Although he is in a dream-vision location (the garden), he is not a dreamer. (In this he resembles Boethius, who is in a location—his bed—where one literally dreams, but is not asleep.) In the Boethian model Philosophy teaches a new discourse—Christian philosophy (that is, theology)—allowing the narrator to conceptualize those things lying beyond mere earthly travails. Machaut's Hope instead posits courtly lyric as the medium for the constructive expression of the travails of Fortune, allowing the audience to resolve emotional tension in a highly un-Boethian way and experience joy and harmony through musical poetry.[36]

Machaut's *Prologue* argues that Nature's gifts would be wasted unless they were focused on joy and praise. Hope similarly shows the lover how to "develop a poetic discourse that will foster cheerful and optimistic sentiments and a serene disposition" in a way that reflects the links between love, desire, memory, and art in Machaut's works.[37] This conversion is made graphically in the musical content of Hope's teaching. The seven items set to music in the *Remede* are notated in two very different ways with respect to the set of graphic shapes used. Hope effects the transition from the older collection of note shapes (longs and breves with a few semibreves) to the newer collection (breves and semibreves with minims). Her first song, *Joie, plaisance* (RF3)—a chanson royal, a form akin to the trouvère *grand chant*—is, like the lover's lay and complaint, written mainly in longs and breves. Her second song, *En amer* (RF4), in one of the newer refrain dance forms, is a balade replete with the latest notational technology—the minim—the smallest note value that could at that time be written, whose speed is associated with youthful temperaments.[38] Hope's mastery of both notational styles, as well as of two registrally and historically differentiated poetic genres, allows her first to show the lover how he can reinterpret the kind of singing that he is already engaged in, and then how he can develop a new art and a new mental attitude toward joy in lyrics, music, and love.[39]

---

36. Huot, "Guillaume de Machaut and the Consolation of Poetry." See also Sarah Kay, "Touching Singularity: Consolations, Philosophy, and Poetry in the French *dit*," in *The Erotics of Consolation: Desire and Distance in the Late Middle Ages,* ed. Catherine E. Léglu and Stephen J. Milner (Basingstoke, 2008), 21–38. A similar suggestion, focused more tightly on *Navarre* and the symbolic use of harps and flutes, is made in Jacqueline Cerquiglini-Toulet, "Lyrisme de désir et lyrisme d'espérance dans la poésie de Guillaume de Machaut," in *Guillaume de Machaut: 1300–2000,* ed. Jacqueline Cerquiglini-Toulet and Nigel Wilkins (Paris, 2002), 41–51.

37. Huot, "Guillaume de Machaut and the Consolation of Poetry," 170.

38. See the comments on hocket involving short note values in Leach, *Sung Birds,* 185.

39. See Franco Alberto Gallo, *Trascrizione di Machaut: Remede de Fortune, Ecu Bleu, Remede d'Amour* (Ravenna, 1999); and the review of it by Lawrence Earp, *Speculum* 77 (2002): 1290–92.

In mid-fourteenth-century France, the surface movement of melody was generally notated by a mixture of semibreves and minims—the minim being the note shape with the briefest performed duration.[40] Depending on the prevailing mensuration (the medieval equivalent of a time signature, although it was rarely signaled explicitly in this period), two or three minims are worth a semibreve. In turn the semibreve is a part (not necessarily a half, sometimes a third) of a relatively long note, which is called (for historical reasons) a breve from the Latin *brevis* for "short."[41] The breve is usually transcribed into modern notation so as to occupy a whole measure. (The original notation does not have measures marked in it.)[42] The breve earned its now counterintuitive name because in the thirteenth century, when rhythmic differentiation was first shown graphically in a manner akin to that found in contemporary Western notation, two basic shapes were deployed: a long note (the long or "longa") and a short note (the breve or "brevis").[43] Both were square notes (familiar from chant notation and easy to make with the nibs of quill pens), differentiated by a downward pointing tail on the right to show the long. By the later thirteenth century, composers who desired greater levels of rhythmic differentiation additionally utilized a third shape drawn from chant notation—the half-turned square, that is, a rhombus—which was worth a part of a breve and was thus called a semibreve. Groups of semibreves could occupy the time of a breve, although they were not all the same length. In the early fourteenth century, the shortest of all—the "semibrevis minima"—was sometimes marked out of such larger groups of semibreves by the addition of an upward tail. As note durations were fixed only relatively (that is, there was no absolute length in terms of time for each shape), it seems unlikely that music, notated with increasing numbers of semibreves and minims, just became quicker and quicker, although the initially sparing use of minims might well have been reserved for rather fast notes. Instead, the levels of rhythmic differentiation that were available became greater, which meant that the shapes that had developed first came to represent a rather large number of these smaller notes and thus probably did signify greater durations than the same shapes

40. The French notational system was philosophically grounded in an Aristotelian unit-based system in which the smallest value was indivisible and larger ones built from it. Note values shorter than the minim were represented by using provisional (and theoretically unsanctioned) notations during the first two-thirds of the century. See Dorit Esther Tanay, *Noting Music, Marking Culture* (Holzerlingen, 1999); and Leach, *Sung Birds*, 135–41.

41. The fact that "semi" does not mean half is stressed in many medieval music theory writings, though more commonly with regard to the semitone; see Leach, "Gendering the Semitone," 1–3.

42. Whether that measure has a modern time signature of $\frac{9}{8}$, $\frac{6}{8}$, $\frac{3}{4}$, or $\frac{2}{4}$ depends on the specific combination (binary or ternary) of relationships between the levels of note durations in the original mensuration. For a full explanation, see "Notation, §III, 3: Polyphonic mensural notation, c1260–1500; (iii) French 14th-century notation," in *Grove*.

43. See "Notation, § III, 3: Polyphonic mensural notation, c1260–1500; (ii) Franconian notation," in *Grove*.

had previously. By the time Machaut was writing, the long was only really used for final notes of melodies and for organizing the tenors (and contratenors) of motets, a genre in which there was a far greater durational differentiation between the upper and lower parts than in songs, partly because of the centrality of large-scale rhythmic organization to the form.[44]

In the *Remede*, the first three items—the lover's lay, the complaint, and Hope's chanson royal—are notated predominantly in longs and breves. This fact is lost in modern transcription, since editors tend simply to reduce the modern notational level a further rung in order to compensate, thus removing a deliberate difference observable on the page in the original. (The difference can be seen by comparing Schrade's edition of *Amours doucement* [L7/6] in example 4.2b with my transcription in example 4.2a.) Of these forms, the complaint and chanson royal were set to music by Machaut only in the context of the *Remede*.[45] Although other examples by Machaut are found in the *Loange*, they never receive musical setting, and the chanson royal was not set at all by his contemporaries if the surviving sources can be deemed representative. All three types of poem have a longer history than the newer refrain forms that are set to music in the rest of the *Remede*, in the rest of Machaut's works, and in the works of his contemporaries. When added to the archaic "font" of the notation, the music of the *Remede* visibly suggests a temporal movement for the lover from a past of grief to a future of joy. Hope performs this transition between her two songs, but she has already begun the psychological transformation in her first song, the chanson royal, *Joie, plaisance* (RF3; example 4.6), whose first word is "joy."

Example 4.6 translates RF3 into modern notation applying the same level of reduction that is generally used for modern notations of Machaut's pieces, rather than the extra level that most editors apply in this case.[46] The song's antique gravity can be seen at once from the paucity of quick notes. Regardless of the pace at which the piece is sung, the *reader* is given the impression *visually* of an older piece. In a period when there was great respect for the past, especially in literature, this notation is to the tradition of the troubadours and trouvères what the *Remede de Fortune* is to Boethius's *Consolation:* something antique which lends authority but also appears strange and in need of translation and reinterpretation for contemporary (that is, fourteenth-century courtly) society.

44. On Machaut's notational levels, see David Maw, "'Trespasser mesure': Meter in Machaut's Polyphonic Songs," *Journal of Musicology* 21 (2004): 46–126.

45. *Ma chiere dame* (B40), copied among the balades in G and E, has no refrain but three stanzas and could be considered a chant royal. Nevertheless, its bipartite strophic form with mirrored rhymes shares some similarities with the *Remede*'s complaint, Toute Belle's complaint in *Voir dit*, two complaints by Froissart, and *J'ay tant* (triplum voice of M7), as well as the *Voir dit*'s prayer to Venus. **Pa**, however, labels it a "Demi lay."

46. Friedrich Ludwig, Leo Schrade, and Rebecca Baltzer (in the appendix to Wimsatt, Kibler, and Baltzer, *Machaut: Behaigne and Remede*) all reduce the values an extra level.

Example 4.6. *Joie, plaisance* (RF3) (with translation of the first stanza of the text).

Joy, pleasure, and sweet nourishment,
[And] a life of honor many take in love;

But there are many who have nothing but stabbing,
Sorrow, burning, tears, sadness, and bitterness.

They say this; but agree
I cannot, since in the suffering
Of Love there is no grievance,
For everything that comes from [Love]
Pleases the heart of a lover.

Structurally, in terms of its musical repeats, the chant royal is similar in
form to the "grand chant" of the trouvères and thus to the *ars nova* balade,
although unlike the latter, it has five stanzas and no textual refrain. Instead
it has an envoy—a partial stanza, in this case replicating the versification

of the poetic stanza's last three lines—a feature that is often present in the songs of the troubadour and trouvère repertoire but seems to reappear in the fourteenth-century balade only toward the end of the fourteenth century. It is almost never present in those set to music.[47] The chanson royal's relative brevity throws into relief and implicitly criticizes the excess of the lover's complaint with which it musically contrasts (see example 5.4). Hope's song is comfortably placed in a range of an octave and one note, with the small extension being the note below the final (F). The lover's complaint, by contrast, has its extended range in the upper register, over an octave above its final (G), with several phrases having sustained vocal exploration of this vocally taxing upper region. The complaint has far less melodic movement in general; its phrase ends are on sustained notes for both stressed and unstressed syllables of the pervasive feminine rhymes, save for the penultimate phase, which droops with a descending fifth. Hope's chanson royal by contrast opens in the middle of its range with a quick rising figure, and its first phrase explores the upper half of the melodic register, before the second phrase outlines the entire octave. The rest of the song explores the lower half of the range, with sensibly graduated stepwise motion, a stark contrast with the second half of the complaint, whose first two phrases lament painfully in the upper register, before the last phrase descends resignedly to the final.

Hope uses the fit between music and text to make a harmonious parallel that performatively underscores the contrast she makes poetically in the opening stanza: in the first performance of the A section, "many find joy, pleasure, and sweet nourishment, a life of honor in love [amer]"; in the second, "many find nothing but pricks, sorrow, ardor, tears, sadness, and bitterness [amer]." The rhyme word punningly parallels the two meanings of amer (both "love" and "bitterness"), but the musical whole parallels the two situations in their entirety by singing them to identical melodies. The B section offers Hope's judgment on these two situations, but we have already heard her bring them into a harmony, which was not simultaneous but successive, and thus requires the exercise of memory (something that will form one of her key teachings).[48] Note how the music chops up the delivery of the text: "They say this, but agree"—a pause—"I cannot, since in the suffering"—a pause—"of Love there is no grievance." Another pause is made in the couplet, whose change of rhyme type makes it function like the refrain section, although the words change each stanza: "Because all that comes from her"—small pause—"pleases the heart of a lover." With its long notes and short pauses, Hope's delivery is deeply rhetorical and didactic throughout each of the song's five strophes.

47. See the comments in Jacqueline Cerquiglini, "Le nouveau lyricisme (XIVe–XVe siècle)," in *Précis de littérature française du Moyen Âge,* ed. Daniel Poirion (Paris, 1983), 284.

48. On the importance of memory in Hope's teaching, see Enders, "Music, Delivery, and the Rhetoric of Memory."

In order to make the transition from these antique forms and notations to the new art that she will teach the lover, Hope then introduces herself and explains her function within the love relationship. The enemy is Desire, which makes the lady fatal, defines her as inaccessible and uncaring, and emphasizes the lover's lack of her. Hope provides completion using only the lover's own memory. As Jacqueline Cerquiglini-Toulet has pointed out, this memory—*Souvenir*—is not simply the recollection of past things but is also the imagining (in images) of anything that is not present outside the mind, whether past, geographically distant, or even just fictional.[49] Sylvia Huot has shown how Hope complements this kind of mental image by representing things that are yet to happen.[50] The impressive and high-quality illuminations in the copy of *Remede* in manuscript C are part of this imagistic didacticism, in which Hope functions as a teacher.[51] In two other copies of this poem, the opening image orients the reader to expect this level of didacticism by showing an image of teaching and learning: manuscript **Vg** has a woman holding the hand of a child while a cleric instructs; **A** has a child at the feet of a bearded, seated old man holding the traditional attribute of personifications of Grammatica—a switch.[52] Reading and listening to the art of poetry will train this kind of imaginative memory; allegorical personification is itself a standard kind of memory-related figuration.[53] Musical poetry will train it further: after Hope sings her exit aria—*En amer* (RF4), a duplex balade that the text terms a "baladelle"—the lover strives to memorize it.[54] As most music theorists of this period mention at the outset of their treatises, sounds perish if they are not committed to memory, which is why music is the ultimate product of the daughters of Jove and Memory (that is, of the Muses).[55] Machaut has rehabilitated the songs of the Muses—cast

49. Jacqueline Cerquiglini-Toulet, "Écrire le temps: Le lyricisme de la durée aux XIVe et XVe siècles," in *Le temps et la durée dans la littérature au Moyen Âge et à la Renaissance: Actes du colloque organisé par le Centre de Recherche sur la Littérature du Moyen Âge et de la Renaissance de l'Université de Reims (novembre 1984)*, ed. Yvonne Bellenger (Paris, 1986), 108–12.

50. Huot, "Guillaume de Machaut and the Consolation of Poetry," 174.

51. See Huot, *From Song to Book*, 249–59, 275–80; on the images in *Remede* as a projection of the author and his patron, see Domenic Leo, "Authorial Presence in the Illuminated Machaut Manuscripts" (Ph.D. diss., New York University, 2005), 89–136 (chap. 2).

52. See Leo, "Authorial Presence," 125–26.

53. See Enders, "Music, Delivery, and the Rhetoric of Memory"; and Mary Carruthers, *The Book of Memory: A Study of Memory in Medieval Culture* (Cambridge, 1991).

54. Enders, "Music, Delivery, and the Rhetoric of Memory," 454–55.

55. The source of this quotation is Isidore of Seville's *Etymologies* 3.15.2 (ed. W. M. Lindsay, *Isidori Hispalensis episcopi Etymologiarum sive originum libri XX*, 2 vols. [Oxford, 1911]), but by the fourteenth century it was a music-theoretical commonplace, cited by, for example, Johannes de Muris, Walter Odington, and John of Tewkesbury. The development of musical notation did not, as might be thought, make this observation redundant, because the *sounds* still perish; a subsequent performance from notation was not considered to bring the same sounds back again, but rather was thought to bring forth new ones. Music notation did not necessarily lessen the role of memory in singing; see Anna Maria Busse Berger, *Medieval Music and the Art of Memory* (Berkeley, 2005).

off as theatrical harlots by Philosophy in Boethius's *Consolation*—as central to the consolation of an audience that had to remain focused on the world because it was involved in its governance.[56] Desire's deleteriousness has not changed, but the recommended response is subtly different from that proposed by Boethius. His narrator is asked to turn his focus from the world—to look beyond to the truths that the soul knew before its contamination with the body. Machaut's audience is allowed instead to retain its focus on the lady, who functions pragmatically as a fetish, a substitution for the absolute good that can be constructed within one's own subjectivity. Similarly, the visible transformation from one notational "font" (longs, breves, and semibreves) to another (breves, semibreves, and minims) mirrors the interior transformation of the vision and understanding of the lover, especially since the change in the relative rhythmic organization of the performed sounds—like the change in the lover's circumstances—might be imperceptible.[57]

The lover's lay had shown him attempting to base joy on Sweet Thought and *Souvenir*; but he was unable to sustain his incorporation of the lady's goodness into his own mental picture because he lacked Hope.[58] The lover is a good student, immediately memorizing Hope's song.[59] After being instructed by Hope, he is able to sing a new song—new in its hopefulness, its notation, its refrain form, and its focused lyric terseness. He opens his balade *Dame, de qui* (RF5) by praising the lady and saying that the hope he has of seeing her gives him a hundred times more joy than he could deserve in a hundred thousand years. This doubly hyperbolic statement is emphasized by the musical setting, in which the words "cent mil ans" (a hundred thousand years) stand out from the texture as they are declaimed, since they form part of a clear cadence animated by melodic dissonances in the upper parts (marked X in example 4.7, box a).[60] This sweet hope (*Espoirs*) nourishes the lover and places within him all that he needs to comfort him and bring joy to his heart. Hope can do this even when he is far from her. Imagine, he remarks, what joy I will have when my hope of seeing her is realized. The phrase "within me" (*dedens moy*)

56. The centrality of the visual and aural memory of the lover is stressed in Huot, "Guillaume de Machaut and the Consolation of Poetry," 175–76, 179: "In his opposition of a poetics of desire with one of hope, Machaut presents a courtly, amorous recasting of the Boethian conflict between the songs of the Muses, focused on worldly desire and the associated feelings of deprivation, resentment, and alienation, and those of Philosophy, which release the soul from desire by reminding it that it already possesses spiritual wealth within itself" (179).

57. As stated earlier, music that includes minims does not necessarily sound faster than music that doesn't.

58. For example, at line 478; see Huot, "Guillaume de Machaut and the Consolation of Poetry," 175.

59. Enders, "Music, Delivery, and the Rhetoric of Memory," 455–56.

60. The recording *The Mirror of Narcissus: Songs by Guillaume de Machaut*, 7–8 April 1983, Gothic Voices directed by Christopher Page, Hyperion, track 1, makes this moment especially clear.

is used twice in the poem (l. 2.3, mm. 3–4, and l. 3.2, m. 7), both times with the first syllable of "dedens" being sung to a held note and the second syllable articulated by a large upwards leap (*a–e and G–e*, respectively). "Espoir" is also invoked twice, in the same metrical place in stanzas 2 and 3, just after the held note that forms a half-close at the end of the first musical phrase (syllable 2, m. 4). In the second part of each stanza, the music enjambs the short line 5 (the so-called *vers coupé*) by running the musical phrase that sets it on into the pre-caesural part of line 6 (that is, up to the fourth syllable of line 6). The enjambment makes sense rhetorically in each stanza—"Car le gracieus Espoir, / Douce dame," "N'il s'en part main ne soir, / Ainçoys me fait," and "Ma joye, si com j'espoir, / Ymaginer"—and also makes the declamation of the remainder of each stanza's sixth line very clear (see example 4.7).

The lover's balade proves that he is ready to be reintegrated into courtly society and thus presages the third episode of the dit, in which he leaves the park to visit the lady's castle. There, after a brief loss of confidence remedied by Hope's reappearance, he is able to display his new compositional, musical, and loving ability. This he does most graphically through the "danced song" (virelay) that he performs with the lady and her attendants (see figure 4.4). The illumination shows the narrator joining in the dance and unpicks the earlier iconography in which the narrator is cut off from the spaces inhabited by the lady.[61] The text of *Dame a vous* (RF6) reveals the lady's contradictory splendor: better than goodness itself, with grace that can heal, but with a beauty whose force destroys all others, she is "an almost arbitrary sign of transcendence and a means by which the lover constructs himself as either whole or lacking."[62] It is very apt that the lover chooses a virelay as his first effort at reintegration, since although it is a monophonic song form and thus could theoretically be performed by one musician singing alone, it is very specifically a social dance form, as the illumination that accompanies the musical notation makes clear. In this way the virelay exemplifies the efficacy of Hope's teaching, which has transformed the narrator from an excluded and isolated individual, sitting alone in an enclosed garden, to participatory and performing lover, dancing with his lady and others outdoors to a song whose text he has written and which he is singing.[63]

The role of music in the *Remede* thus rivals that of the lady in approaching a level of transcendence to which it is commonly thought to have first aspired in the nineteenth century.[64] Just as the lady is merely a means by which the

---

61. On this image, see Leo, "Authorial Presence," 127n269, which considers earlier readings of the image that saw the narrator as one of the figures not participating in the dance.

62. Huot, "Guillaume de Machaut and the Consolation of Poetry," 177.

63. See Leo, "Authorial Presence," 117–24; and Elizabeth Eva Leach, "Poet as Musician," in *A Companion to Guillaume de Machaut: An Interdisciplinary Approach to the Master*, ed. Deborah McGrady and Jennifer Bain (Leiden, forthcoming).

64. The emergence of a transcendent "work concept" as a regulative concept for music around 1800 has been argued by Lydia Goehr, *The Imaginary Museum of Musical Works: An Essay in the Philosophy of Music* (Oxford, 1992), although Reinhard Strohm, "Looking Back at Ourselves:

Example 4.7. *Dame de qui* (RF5) (four-part version with translation of text): a. cadence at "cent mil ans"; b. musical enjambment of ll. 5–6.

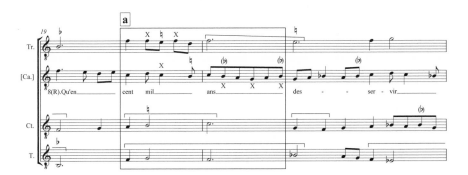

Example 4.7. (*Continued*)

Lady from whom all my joy comes,
I cannot love or cherish you too much
Nor praise you as much as is fitting
Nor serve, fear, honor, or obey you enough.
For the noble hope,
Sweet lady, that I have from seeing you
Makes me a hundred times more joy and goodness
Than in 100,000 years I could deserve.

This sweet hope keeps me alive
And nourishes me in loving desire
And within me puts all that which is necessary
In order to comfort my heart and make it rejoice.
It does not leave me morning or night,
But makes me sweetly receive
More of the sweet goods that Love grants to his own
Than in 100,000 years I could deserve.

And when Hope, who stays in my heart,
Makes such great joy come within me,
Then it happens, far from you, my lady,
That I might see your beauty, which I very much desire.
My joy, as I hope,
No one could imagine, think, or conceive,
For I have so much more of it
Than in 100,000 years I could deserve.

Example 4.7. (*Continued*)

Figure 4.4. Virelay miniature from MS C, f. 51r. Bibliothèque nationale de France.

lover can experience pain (via Fortune or Desire) or bliss (via Hope), music's semantic openness—its ability to provide a sonic vehicle for many things and take on meanings from text, context, and reception—makes it too a means of connecting with emotional states, depending on the mental state that the listener brings to it in the first place.[65] Not only does Machaut figure Desire and Hope with musical symbols, as Cerquiglini-Toulet has argued, but also the poetics of Hope is almost entirely animated by its interface with a music whose emotional content depends—like that of the love experience—on what the listener (lover) brings to it mentally, and whose temporal presence links a past and future image with hope of fulfillment. Moreover, musical notation forms just such an image: it sketches a past performance (whether sonic, memorial, or visual), and it forms a promise of a future one. Its realization is fleeting and can only be *held* in memory (whether aural or visual)—as a sonic *Souvenir,* which provides the Hope of eventual *merci* (another performance).

Dealing with Suffering and Death

In the *Remede* the inexperienced lover-protagonist is dealing with his own amorous timidity, principally a fear of rejection on the basis of his lack of worthiness. But Machaut's poetics of Hope is versatile enough to combat Fortune, Desire, and despair in other situations, including actual amorous rejection or betrayal, as well as absence caused either by geographical separation (a temporary "death" in a period before mass communications) or by death itself. Two of these kinds of situations are brought into direct comparison in Machaut's pair of *Jugement* poems. In the earlier *Jugement dou roy de Behaingne*—Machaut's most widely copied dit and probably the lengthy early work that established him as an important poet—the king (John of Bohemia), advised

---

The Problem with the Musical Work-Concept," in *The Musical Work: Reality or Invention?,* ed. Michael Talbot (Liverpool, 2000), 128–52, places it much earlier. I would argue that the elevation of art to a pseudo-religion in the romantic period was a means of masking the potential for trivialization that the removal of art from ethics (that is, the reduction of art—including music—to aesthetics) caused. See the comments on Martin Heidegger's "Origin of the Work of Art" in Julian Young, *Heidegger's Philosophy of Art* (Cambridge, 2001), 8–14.

65. Musicologists have generally eschewed discussions of the emotional content of medieval music, probably because its musical "language" lacks an unbroken tradition, and matters of emotional meaning are difficult to reconstruct with any degree of certainty. It seems possible, however, for one to claim that it is emotional without being able to pin down the details of the emotional language, since the affective nature of music is a commonplace in music theory and in literary mention of music throughout the period. Proposing affective interpretations effectively generates a field of possibility for the emotional aspect of the music, enabling claims to be countered and/ or refined by other scholars. Appreciation of Machaut's poetry has relied on a developing field of interpretations, reacting to and against one another. Musical interpretations similarly should (in my view) now move beyond an understanding of the grammar of this music's counterpoint to ideas about its rhetorical (persuasive and pathetic) force.

by a court of personified virtues, declares the knight whose lady has betrayed him for another to be experiencing worse pain than the lady whose beloved has died. In the *Jugement dou Roy de Navarre*—completed after the date of 1349 given in its opening prologue, but possibly begun some time before—the judge (Charles of Navarre), advised by Lady Goodness and a court of more and different personified virtues, overturns this decision, deciding instead in favor of the bereaved lady.[66]

Douglas Kelly has argued that the later palinode was demanded because Machaut's view of the role of Hope in love underwent a transition between the writing of these two dits, during the time of the composition of the *Remede*, which lays out his new poetics of Hope most overtly. The way in which the roughly contemporary *Navarre* then "corrects" the judgment of *Behaingne* ensures that its outcome accords with the *Remede*'s new poetics of Hope. In Kelly's view the earlier poem privileges a poetics of Desire: the counselors of the king of Bohemia are mainly those found in the *Roman de la Rose* and significantly include Desire, a character who is also in Love's retinue in the *Rose* and in Machaut's *Rose*-esque *Vergier*.[67] Love's counselors in *Behaingne* decide that the knight is unhappier than the lady because the sight of her, which incites desire, remains possible, since the knight's lady is still alive, whereas all vision of the lady's beloved is permanently erased by death, and so her suffering will ease.[68] In *Navarre,* Desire is no longer one of the king's counselors, whereas *Souffisance* is.[69] With Desire now newly negative and Hope's means to happiness based on *Souvenir*—that is, the remembered happy image of the beloved in the lover's own memory—the decision has to be reversed. *Souffisance* is that which can be enjoyed without the need for direct interaction: imagining, seeing, and hearing the lady. Sufficiency is effectively psychological and amorous *self*-sufficiency. Desire would ask for more, strapping the subject to the wheel of Fortune and an endless sense of lack—a metaphorical death.[70] In fact, now only real death can deprive the lover of Hope.

While it is possible that the shift Kelly perceives represents a temporal shift in Machaut's teaching and his espoused poetics, the continued inclusion of these early poems in the later collected works manuscripts—together with *Vergier,*

66. For a full discussion of the poem's date and possible patrons, see Earp, *Guillaume de Machaut,* 209–10.

67. With Desire the companions of the king are Bravery, Valor, Generosity, Wealth, Love, Beauty, Happiness, Thought, Will, Nobility, Sincerity, Honor, Courtesy, and Youth. In addition the chief counselor of the king is Reason. See *Behaingne,* ll. 1476–93.

68. *Behaingne,* ll. 1665–1784; see Kelly, *Medieval Imagination,* 138–39.

69. Kelly considers this a "replacement," but in fact there are only two "courtiers" in common between the two poems: Reason and Largesse. On the significant retention of Largesse, see Elizabeth Eva Leach, "Guillaume de Machaut, Royal Almoner: *Honte, paour* (B25) and *Donnez, signeurs* (B26) in Context," *Early Music* (2010): 21–42.

70. Kelly, *Medieval Imagination,* 134.

and the many short lyrics of pity, desire, and despair in the *Loange* and music sections—tells a slightly different story.[71] In particular, the way in which the end of the late *Prologue* locks *Vergier* (a dit little praised by modern commentators) into the head of the collection of dits would be a strange choice to make in the 1370s if its doctrine could not still be incorporated within a book containing post-*Remede* attitudes toward Hope. Kelly reads *Vergier* as suggesting that the working of Pity in the lady's heart at some time in the future is the only means of enduring the harshness of love, but this dit is more complex than has on occasion been imagined. In the dream-vision of Love and his court, there are six noble young men—Will (*Voloir*), (Sweet) Thought (*[Dous] Penser*), Sweet Pleasure (*Dous Plaisir*), Loyalty, Discretion (*Celer*), and Desire—and six noble young women: Grace, Pity, Hope (*Esperance*), *Souvenir*, Openheartedness (*Franchise*), and Self-Control (*Attemprance*).[72] The first three of the male attendants are seminal in starting the love relationship in tandem with the lady's own Sweet Look (*Dous Regars*). Most of the others are used to counter the six enemies who guard the joy that is Love's reward: Rebuff (*Dangier*), Trepidation (*Paour*), Shame (*Honte*), Hardheartedness (*Durté*), Cruelty (*Cruauté*), and Fear-of-Wrongdoing (*Doubtance de Mespresure/Meffaire*). Trepidation and Shame are tackled by two of the male courtiers—Loyalty and Discretion. The rest of the enemies are dealt with by the *damoiselles gentes*: Grace defends against Rebuff, Pity against Cruelty, Openheartedness against Hardheartedness, and Self-Control against Fear-of-Wrongdoing. The action that sets these enemies in motion, however, is the lover asking for *joie* from the lady, something he is prompted to do by the continued action not of an enemy but of the remaining *damoisiau* at Love's court: Desire. The two remaining women—Hope and *Souvenir*—serve not against enemies but against the power of Desire, one of their own court circle. *Souvenir* will remind the lover to make use of Sweet Thought to remember the beloved so that he will think of her so sweetly and with "si parfait sentement" that Hope will be born from the thought that *Souvenir* brings to mind.[73] "Esperance, la seure," will reassure him that such beauty must have Pity.[74] This is effectively the same role that these attributes have in Machaut's later works, although they assume greater importance as the other "courtiers" and "guardians" fade into the background. Unfortunately, warns Love, the success of Hope and *Souvenir* is eroded by the passage of time, and Desire will revive and prompt the lover to ask again for *joie,* thus setting in motion the six enemies that guard it.[75] Love's recommendation is to maintain loyalty and secrecy and wait for him (Love) to soften the lady's heart.

71. Ibid., 137.
72. *Vergier,* ll. 612–22.
73. *Vergier,* ll. 731–748, quotation from l. 738.
74. *Vergier,* ll. 749–68, quotation from l. 749.
75. *Vergier,* ll. 769–86, especially l. 774: "Ades Desirs en lui s'avive" (Desire once more springs back to life in him).

The lover, awakened by the dew brushed from the branches of the tree as Love flies off, sets forth on his way with good intentions, but the discussion of Desire has already suggested that Desire will, given sufficient time, return, spurring the lover to reveal his love to his lady and thus be attacked by the six unfriendly servants who are guarding her honor. Waiting increases both the likelihood of Love's being returned as long as it is not asked for, and also the desire that prompts the lover to ask for it. These opposed aspects of the effect of time are summarized in two proverbial maxims used by Machaut: "whoever loves well, forgets slowly" and "a long wait changes a lover's heart."[76] *Vergier* therefore sets up the basic situation that Machaut's works explore from different angles, showing the potential for the same external event (the passage of time) to have different personal consequences, depending on the mental attitude of the subject.

The relation of *Vergier* to the first part of the *Roman de la Rose* occupied earlier modern commentators, who typically saw Machaut's imitation as merely derivative or deficient.[77] As Kevin Brownlee stresses, however, *Vergier* serves an introductory role, outlining the principal characters at Love's court and their respective roles. Moreover, it playfully downplays the importance of "personal love experience," while "the value of the literary activity of the poète in the service of Amours has been both demonstrated and affirmed."[78] It is possible to view it as propadeutic, perhaps even a prototype prologue, which would explain the features usually thought to indicate a historically early date (its supposed technical inferiority, the absence of a personalized narrator, and its lack of authorial anagram).[79] As *Vergier* survives only in the Machaut manuscripts, the earliest source for it is—as with *Remede*—manuscript C, where it actually follows *Behaingne, Remede,* and *Alerion.* Its placement first of all the dits in later sources indicates only that Machaut wanted it to have this ordering, something he still wanted at the end of his life (especially in **A**, where he ties it into place by having its incipit as the *Prologue*'s explicit). The early placement of supposed "dits of Desire" (*Vergier* and *Behaingne*), while

76. On "Qui bien aimme a tart oublie," the incipit of the *Lay de Plour* (L22/16), see full references in Earp, *Guillaume de Machaut,* 366, and the discussion in this chapter, especially notes 95 and 96. "Longue demouree fait changier ami," which appears in the *Voir dit,* letter 30, where it is copied in large letters in **A**, is also the subject of *On dist souvent que longue demourée* (L014). See also note 96.

77. Ernest Hoepffner, *Oeuvres de Guillaume de Machaut,* 3 vols. (Paris, 1908–1922), 1:lv–lviii: "a real apprentice-piece, without originality" (lvii). William Calin, *A Poet at the Fountain: Essays on the Narrative Verse of Guillaume de Machaut* (Lexington, 1974), 23, speaks of its "failure." For a more positive reading, see Brownlee, *Poetic Identity,* 24–37. For further references, see Earp, *Guillaume de Machaut,* 206.

78. Brownlee, *Poetic Identity,* 36–37.

79. Hoepffner, *Oeuvres de Guillaume de Machaut,* 1:lvi–lvii. Hoepffner's assessment of the poem's technical inferiority is based on its far lower percentage of leonine and feminine rhymes compared with *Remede, Navarre,* and *Lyon* (see lvin1).

it *might* reflect a real chronological development, certainly proffers a fictional artistic and amorous "chronology"—an inter-dit one resembling that intra-dit one of the *Remede de Fortune* itself. *Remede*'s lover, miserably beset by Desire and making (in terms of notational font) *ars antiqua* music, is changed into a happy lover aided by Hope, making *ars nova* music, even though his exterior circumstances are unchanged.

Near the opening of *Navarre*, when Guillaume is berated for the alleged antifeminism of his earlier *jugement* poem, he shrugs it off with a casual (but proud) reference to the diversity of his writings.[80] He is not retracting them but inflecting them within a whole output, an entire life's work, a "super-dit," which is, like the Church Militant, diverse in unity to one ideal: Hopeful Love.[81] Rather than reflecting chronology, the ordering of Machaut's manuscripts takes the reader on a journey from the *Rose*-influenced introduction of Love's dramatis personae to a diptych on the same question, whose answer is "resolved" by the *Remede*'s clear didactic statement.[82] The poetic voice is on a similar journey, akin to that through life: the narrator of *Vergier* is an involved lover-protagonist; in *Behaingne* he is a clerical witness-participant, who in *Navarre* is specifically the poet Guillaume de Machaut; *Remede* ties these two time frames together in its clerical-didactic prologue, which situates the events of the first-person lover in the cleric's youthful past. The illusion of temporal development is very much part of the effect of the dits' later ordering in the collected manuscripts, but it should not necessarily be assumed, as it has so often been, that this can be readily equated with any actual chronology of writing.

The shift between *Navarre* and *Behaingne* is less a change of *jugement* than the opening up of a much broader discussion of what happens when love goes awry, and in particular the significance of gender difference in resolving responses to the sorrow this causes.[83] The pair of *jugement* poems presents the fullest possible rumination on the basic material, and between them they cover a number of arguments that could have formed the basis for lengthy,

---

80. *Navarre*, ll. 884–86: "J'ay bien de besongnes escriptes/Devers moy, de pluseurs manieres,/ De moult de diverses matieres, / Dont l'une l'autre ne ressamble" (Before me I've a good deal of things [I've] written, in many styles, about many diverse matters, no two of which are alike).

81. On the positive revalorization of diversity (from its negative position within classical rhetoric) under the Christian ideals of the universal Church and the doctrine of mixing in the incarnation, see Mary Carruthers. "*Varietas*: A Word of Many Colours," *Poetica: Zeitschrift für Sprach- und Literaturwissenschaft* 40 (2009): 33–54.

82. *Lyon*, which follows, then meditates on those unworthy in love, while *Alerion* presents such ladies available in an endless substitution using popular hawking metaphors (see the later discussion). The "professional" dits follow: *Confort, Fonteinne, Harpe*, and *Voir dit*.

83. See Huot, "Guillaume de Machaut and the Consolation of Poetry," 179–80. Calin, *A Poet at the Fountain*, 110–29, has even questioned whether the *jugement* is truly reversed at all (see especially 113–14).

wide-ranging, and ethically profitable discussion and cogitation by listening and reading courtiers. *Navarre* starts with the same situation as *Behaingne,* but its central issue is less the adjudication of quantities of sorrow and more the trial of Guillaume the poet on charges of slandering women in his works, something Love explicitly forbids him from doing in the *Prologue*.[84] In essence it is a meta-*jugement* in which the lady and knight are replaced by Goodness, and Guillaume, with the author, Machaut (differentiated from the protagonist "Guillaume" in the rubrication as "lacteur"), documenting everything and providing narrative continuity.[85]

The male lover of *Behaingne* correctly feels extreme sorrow because he has lost Hope; *Souvenir* is not working to foster Hope but rather brings despair, because he sees the lady with her new lover. Similarly the lady whose lover has died can despair because death removes all hope for responsive love in this life. Both knight and lady are haunted by *Souvenir* rather than helped by it, since the context of their loves has changed. Only the knight is challenged also by the real sight of the lady in the new context: he sees a concrete confirmation of the new context; the lady remembers an absence and feels the lack. The knight is like the lover of the *Prologue*, to whom *Souvenir* brings only "the great beauty [and] the refined sweetness of the woman who does not care for him."[86] As discussed in chapter 3, such a man is unable to compose from his despondency; he has only Desire and the poor hope ("povre espoir") that his sorrow will grow.[87] His poverty of Hope is a despair that silences poetry and song. The lady's sorrow might be deemed greater in the context of *Navarre*, but it is her plight that produces the poetic and musical offspring that Lady Goodness demands of Guillaume in recompense for his slandering of women. As copied in the earlier manuscripts, the debate-diptych of *Behaingne* and *Navarre* is sealed by the *Lay de Plour,* which represents the only completed one of the three poetic restitutions that Goodness demands of Guillaume at the end of the dit.[88]

Navarre's focus on the issue of gender suggests that men and women have different responses to the pain of suffering: men are apt to externalize it and distract themselves with chivalric exploits (or be driven to distraction by

---

84. *Prologue* 3.21–26. It could also be argued that the change of focus is a direct result of the difference in patrons between the two dits. But as the patron for *Navarre* may have been altered late in its composition, this is difficult to ascertain. See note 66.

85. As before *Navarre*, ll. 2561, 2693, 2925, 3393, 3725. In its dramatic use of rubrics, *Navarre* furthers the scribal techniques seen in *Remede*, which derive from the *Rose* (see Huot, *From Song to Book,* 250, and my discussion in chapter 3, note 23).

86. *Prologue* 5.68–69.

87. *Prologue* 5.77–84.

88. The incompletion of two-thirds of this threefold task perhaps supports Ursula Günther's idea that this dit was originally designed for Bonne, but that its completion was delayed by her death in 1349; see Ursula Günther, "Contribution de la musicologie à la biographie et à la chronologie de Guillaume de Machaut," in *Guillaume de Machaut: Poète et Compositeur* (Reims, 1982), 103, 106.

madness), whereas women internalize it and experience their suffering bodily (even to the point of death).[89] Madness represents a loss of humanity to the extent that it gives the madman immunity to human pain, and it thereby allows Desire to be blocked out with various animal desires (nutritional or aggressive).[90] Because the knight has the socially sanctioned possibility of externalizing his grief and distracting himself from pain, the allegorical virtues at the court of Navarre argue their way to adjudging the woman's suffering more grievous. But the actual outcome of the judgment becomes irrelevant: as the dits' diptych shows, after all, it can be successfully argued either way. The larger point is that all of this suffering can be commemorated and eternalized in musical poetry, which functions as the ultimate joyful *Souvenir* and can cope not only with unfaithfulness but with death as well. Sylvia Huot sees this as a more radical revision of Boethius than Machaut had presented in the *Remede*.[91] In effect, the ability of men to distract themselves, fictionalize themselves, and fashion themselves for public display (whether gaining fame or pity) is a useful sublimation of pain, but is available only to men. Moreover, in its aestheticization of suffering it is, like the songs of Boethius's Muses, theatrical and flauntingly selfish. Machaut's musical poetry offers—to men and women alike—a form of distraction that has all the potential for the sublimation of pain that can be found in chivalry, but it eschews both chivalry's gender exclusivity and its propensity for self-absorption.[92] In *Navarre*, therefore, Machaut ostensibly opposes bodily death (a female response to suffering) with symbolic death (a male one), but actually points out their underlying similarity, both being grounded in desire and expressed physically. Both are then contrasted with the "truly salvific symbolization of the self through poetic language."[93]

The proof of this salvation is the appending of a lyric lay to most manuscript sources of *Navarre*.[94] The *Lay de Plour, Qui bien aimme* (L22/16) offers a model of noble suffering and acts as a serious sonic and visual *Souvenir*. The incipit text serves as a motto for the whole act of remembrance since it echoes "one of the most widely cited refrains from either the thirteenth or fourteenth

89. Huot, "Guillaume de Machaut and the Consolation of Poetry," 179–80.

90. Ibid., 182, cites *Navarre*, ll. 2596–99, where a clerk of Montpellier, maddened by his lady's marriage, sleeps on a dung heap. See also Sylvia Huot, *Madness in Medieval French Literature: Identities Found and Lost* (Cambridge, 2003), 136–79 (chap. 4), especially 146.

91. Huot, "Guillaume de Machaut and the Consolation of Poetry," 181.

92. Ibid., 184; see also Ardis Butterfield, "Lyric and Elegy in *The Book of the Duchess*," *Medium Aevum* 60 (1991): 48.

93. Huot, "Guillaume de Machaut and the Consolation of Poetry," 193.

94. In A, however, the lay is moved back into the musical lay section—perhaps for copying reasons, perhaps to pair it with its original partner in C, the *Lay mortel* (see Huot, *From Song to Book*, 265–66). I would interpret this not as a rejection of its place as the denouement of *Navarre*, but as indicative of the heightened sense of the whole book that A promotes; see ibid., 275–80.

century," *Qui bien aimme a tart oublie* (Whoever loves well, forgets slowly).[95] Machaut himself used it in the *Remede, Voir dit* (several times), and a motet.[96] This piece of proverbial wisdom allows the singer to draw the audience into a sententious, communally agreed-upon act of remembering her beloved.[97]

Having stated the function of the music proverbially, the lay's opening image of the continued presence of painful memories is of a fire that never goes out. Desire stereotypically burns. Burning is the chief attribute of Desire as he is described in *Vergier,* and its fire drew intertextually on Dido's burning desire for Aeneas in book 4 of the *Aeneid,* which would have been familiar to all lettered members of medieval society and which is a story recounted in *Navarre.*[98] In *Navarre* the judging virtues had deemed the "ardant desir" of women—like Dido—to be to that of men as a real fire is to a picture of a fire; men's desire is mere representation of a reality that is feminine, personal, and somatic.[99] In the *Lay de plour,* like a fire that cannot be put out, the arrow of Love in the lady's heart cannot be pulled out; like Dido she is pierced in the heart and burning. But in the second and third stanzas this wooden shaft transmogrifies into a partially uprooted tree, and the element of fire is countered with water—the water of tears that nourish the tree, whose leaves thus continue to grow.[100] The music of these two stanzas (2 and 3) is related motivically, tonally, and structurally, showing them to be part of a single uni-

---

95. Friedrich Ludwig, ed., *Guillaume de Machaut: Musikalische Werke,* vol. 2 (Leipzig, 1926–1954), 34; van den Boogaard, *Rondeaux et Refrains,* 233, no. 1585. See also Ardis Butterfield, *Poetry and Music in Medieval France: From Jean Renart to Guillaume de Machaut* (Cambridge, 2002), 246–52, 335n49; Theodore Karp, "Borrowed Material in Trouvère Music," *Acta musicologica* 34 (1962): 100; and the references in note 96 in this chapter. See also Virginia Newes, "Machaut's *Lay de plour* in Context," in *Citation and Authority in Medieval and Renaissance Music: Learning from the Learned,* ed. Suzannah Clark and Elizabeth Eva Leach (Woodbridge, 2005), 123–38.

96. It appears in *Remede* (l. 4258) as the lover promises to remain true in life or death (that is, in the situation of either *Jugement*'s knight or its lady), and in *Voir dit,* 122 (letter 10), 394 (letter 30), and 506 (l. 7372), where it forms the antipode to the large "cry" of Guillaume: "Longue demouree fait changier ami." Machaut cites it again in *He! Mors / Fine* (M3), where it relates to death, not necessarily of the lady herself, but rather of the lover's love or feelings; see Jacques Boogaart, "Encompassing Past and Present: Quotations and Their Function in Machaut's Motets," *Early Music History* 20 (2001): 17–19; and idem, "Observations on Machaut's Motet *He! Mors / Fine Amour / Quare non sum mortuus* (M3)," in *Machaut's Music: New Interpretations,* ed. Elizabeth Eva Leach (Woodbridge, 2003), especially 18–19.

97. And this is regardless of whether the singer is an actual or prosopopoeic (fictional) woman.

98. *Vergier,* ll. 695–714; *Navarre,* ll. 2095–2132. And see Kevin Brownlee, "Fire, Desire, Duration, Death: Machaut's Motet 10," in Clark and Leach, *Citation and Authority in Medieval and Renaissance Musical Culture,* 79–93; and the comments in Leach, *Sung Birds,* 230–31. See also Huot, *Madness in Medieval French Literature,* 152.

99. *Navarre,* ll. 3200–3208; see Huot, "Guillaume de Machaut and the Consolation of Poetry," 183.

100. Ibid., 184–86. Boogaart, "Encompassing Past and Present," 20–21; and Bétemps, "Les *Lais de plour,*" 102–3, noted independently that this image is based on a chanson by Thibaut de

fied thought. Both stanzas are quadruple versicles, so the same music comes four times in each, with alternating open and closed cadences. These are to *a* and *G* respectively, as they had been in the opening stanza. In stanzas 4 and 5 the lady outlines the goodness of her dead beloved using melodies that seem to grow—like the tree—organically from one stanza to another, using similar melodic-motivic groups of notes. The declamatory rhythm of both mixes short-long and long-short groups, with the long of the short-long pattern often being subdivided into four equal notes, decorating a single text syllable. Overall, the musical and poetic sense is that after the introductory opening stanza, stanzas 2 through 5 hang together.

Then, in stanza 6, the music takes a decided change from the mixture of patterns of long and short notes (with four-minim groups substituting for the former) that have predominated, and presents instead a series of equal notes in a rising scalic pattern (example 4.8 gives stanzas 5 and 6 so that this change in rhythm and contour can be readily seen). This resolute musical repetition marks a similar resolve in the text, as the lady declares herself incapable and unwilling to undertake new love. *Souvenir,* mentioned toward the end of the stanza, will aid her in this, a theme she elaborates further in stanza 7. In the eighth to eleventh stanzas the lady alternately apostrophizes her lover—"dous amis" (stanzas 8 and 10)—and reflects on the parlous state of her own heart (stanzas 9 and 11).[101] The final stanza, like the lay of the *Remede,* presents the melody of the first notated a perfect fifth higher, transforming without actually changing (that is, transposing) its melody, making the final stanza higher, more elevated, more of a vocal stretch for the performer. The text ends similarly by transforming death into eternal life, invoking the Christian God ("Vray Dieu") to look on the lady and her beloved "with such a loving look, that in a book we might be alive."[102] Ostensibly the singing lady desires that she and her dead beloved be written into the eternal book of life, but the implication is that a much more immediate memorialization and eternalization is being achieved in the book of Machaut, the book that the reader or singer could be physically holding.[103] This "tree" (many medieval book bindings were made of wood) is certainly uprooted but continues to flower—with the

---

Champagne. Within *Navarre* itself, Charity uses the analogy of a tree that is grafted to describe marriage (see ll. 2463–68); and see Huot, *Madness in Medieval French Literature,* 148.

101. Stanza 8 resembles in poetic form, rhyme, and content the complaint voiced by the feminine *je* of *Dous amis* (B6), the first feminine-voiced song among the music balades.

102. L22/16, stanza 12, l. 16: "Qu'en livre soiens de vie." The lay ends with an unnotated "Amen" before the explicit in manuscript C, f. 189r. As "livre" and "livré" would be identical in the unaccented French script of this period, at least visually (that is, in the book), the text hopes that the lady and her lover might be brought back to life by both (Christian) deliverance and (oral/performative) delivery.

103. See Newes, "Machaut's *Lay de plour,*" 131; Huot, "Guillaume de Machaut and the Consolation of Poetry," 185.

Example 4.8. The *Lay de Plour, Qui bien aimme* (L22/16), stanzas 5–6 (with translation).

V

Also, it is seen clearly
That those hearts that loyally
And without folly
Love with a very refined love
Often think
That in something better and nobler
They are passing their time,
For Pleasure and her rigor
Teaches them this.

Now I know for certain
That my [lover] was undoubtedly
The true flower,
Of those that have more sweetness
—For everyone
Says it generally—
And the best,
For he had all worth
Entirely.

VI

And because none so good, better, nor more genteel
Exists, nor so handsome, nor so acquainted with honor,
—Judged correctly—
No one should
Marvel
If I do not wish, by the arrow of love
To be pricked anew by another love,
For I do not seek
To change this,
And I am right.

Since so firm and implanted in my heart is
My love for him that it can never be uprooted;
For my whole heart,
Which would know
No treachery,
Wants me to spur myself on though *Souvenir,*
So that I do not undertake or know another love,
Since to know another
Would do me
Harm.

Example 4.8. (*Continued*)

174

rhetoric of words and colors of pictures—nourished by the memory of the audience and/or performer. Machaut thus refutes Boethius's point that poetry prolongs desire and suffering with the idea that poetry instead prolongs the life of the person identified with suffering in "the sublimated, aestheticized image of the poetic subject."[104]

The beloved—in the *Lay de plour* a man, but more often a lady—thus becomes a fetish that embodies the absolute at both ends of a spectrum from death to life, from torment to bliss, and from Fortune to Goodness. For the loving subject to access the right end of that spectrum and avoid suffering, he has to change the lady from the tempting and taunting external object of desire into an internal object of contemplation in which she is "the fantasy of once and future wholeness and perfect love in which memory and hope become one."[105] Confirmation that this object of desire can be subject to eternal forms of substitution is given most clearly in Machaut's *Alerion,* which chronicles the narrator's relationship with four birds (ostensibly the avian variety, but symbolizing women), each of which in turn leaves him, provoking sorrow that is only short term because the narrator's hope allows new joy to reign.[106] A lover subject to Desire would cling to the object itself (as the man and woman in the two *Jugement* poems do) rather than clinging to the mental image (*Souvenir*) of the transcendent perfection to which the object gives them access and which it reflects. In this way contact with the absolute that the lady stands for can be "mediated through a potentially endless series of symbolic images," each image offering "consolation in its fantasy of possession and fulfillment."[107]

Music offers the perfect focus for this internal mental control over time. Hopeful loving avoids both the bodily death of feminine suffering (which focuses the mind on the past) and the symbolic masculine death (which focuses on present gratification) because it preserves the past while looking with Hope to a future. In performance arts like poetry and music, writing unites the past, present, and future. The notation of a song or a poem preserves a trace of past performance and also carries hope for future performance. By the mid-fourteenth century, however, changes in reading practices were beginning to threaten this equation, at least for poetry without musical notation. Although reading aloud was still the norm, there was the increased possibility of, and recourse to, silent reading.[108] Mental but silent "performance" removes

104. Huot, "Guillaume de Machaut and the Consolation of Poetry," 185.

105. Ibid., 192. See also Nicolette Zeeman, "The Gender of Song in Chaucer," *Studies in the Age of Chaucer* 29 (2007): 148, on the woman as the Lacanian "petit objet a," which stands for the object of desire.

106. Huot, "Guillaume de Machaut and the Consolation of Poetry," 194, notes that the reiteration of memory (which causes suffering) is replaced by "controlled amnesia."

107. Ibid., 194.

108. See Paul Saenger, *Space between Words: The Origins of Silent Reading* (Stanford, 1997).

both the future temporality of written literature and its ethical component—its social aspect. Conversely, sung poetry, especially that deploying poly-phonic music in a period for which the absence of scores makes it difficult (if not impossible) mentally to read a working multivoiced construction for the separately notated vocal parts, remains an unequivocal promise both of fu-ture performance—an embodiment of Hope—and of future social interaction. Huot says of Machaut's poetry that it "erase[s] the very distinction between past and future, memory and hope," but this is even truer of poetry with musi-cal notation, because such notation is not musical presence per se but is both present trace and present promise.[109] When a song deals directly—through its poetic text—with the pain of love, it acknowledges it and transforms it by displacement; it opens up a gap between the musical representation of suffer-ing and the suffering individual himself or herself, all the more so when the song is clearly a prosopopoeia, with a known gap between the male composer's identity, the feminine lyric persona, and the vocally performing person(s) (whether male or female).[110]

As the suffering that Machaut's musical poetry offers to displace is generic, it does not need to be exclusively amorous. In the *Remede* the comfort offered is indeed from the melancholic anxiety that results from loving; in the *Confort* the reader is instead offered comfort from his political woes; in *Navarre*, more global social suffering—heresies, plague, war, and civil unrest—are relieved; in *Fonteinne* the absent homeland is figured as an absent lady, in a reversal of the process in *Alerion*, in which the lady is figured as a series of raptors. In all these cases the one able to offer comfort and a means of actively sustaining internal serenity in the face of challenging (and often unchanging) external factors is none other than the poet, writing poetry.

Social Reasons for the New Centrality of Hope?

Esperance was the opening text not only of Machaut's balade 13 but also of one of the most widely copied fourteenth-century rondeaux, a piece that alludes musically to Hope's baladelle *En amer* (RF4) in the *Remede* and is itself cited in a large number of other pieces, *Esperance, qui en mon cuer s'embat*.[111] The word *Esperance* also saw a number of important broader

109. Huot, "Guillaume de Machaut and the Consolation of Poetry," 195.

110. "The gap that is opened between the suffering individual and the poetic [and, I would add, musical] representation of suffering grants some breathing space." Ibid.

111. Yolanda Plumley, "An 'Episode in the South'? Ars Subtilior and the Patronage of French Princes," *Early Music History* 22 (2003): 122n61; and idem, "Citation and Allusion in the Late Ars Nova: The Case of the *En Attendant* Songs," *Early Music History* 18 (1999): 287–363. See also Brownlee, "Literary Intertextualities in the *Esperance* Series"; Wulf Arlt, "Machaut, Sen-leches und der anonyme Liedsatz *Esperance qui en mon cuer s'embat*," in *Musik als Text: Bericht über den Internationalen Kongreß der Gesellschaft für Musikforschung, Freiburg im Breisgau*

cultural uses within fourteenth-century courtly society. It was used as a device or motto, taken, for example, by Louis of Bourbon after his return from captivity in England in 1366, and seems to have continued in use by the Percy family in England during the fifteenth century.[112] Such mottos could be used as rallying cries in battle, or more decoratively on courtly objects as a memento: some gilded spurs surviving from later in the century have "Esperance" engraved on them, and inventories record the embroidery of this word on clothing.[113] It seems clear that the role of Hope in court culture more broadly conceived was not negligible in this period and that courtiers found it attractive and efficacious.[114]

Courtly poetry probably helped courtiers understand and resolve pressing emotional problems and situations that must have arisen with frequency in a context of young men and women occupying proximate social spaces and meeting frequently. The hundreds of years during which "courtly love" poetry served in this capacity are a reflection of its social success. Although the central role for Hope in Machaut's version of the doctrine of *fine amours* seems to have been taken up in contemporary musical poetry, the synergies he established between its role in life, love, and art, especially the art of music, were innovations and do not appear to be ones taken up extensively by any of his contemporaries. As discussed earlier, whether he experienced a real change of view or merely a streamlining of the emphasis in the period between *Behaingne* and *Remede* is difficult to assess.[115] In discussing whether the important role of Hope in Machaut's work might have been prompted by historical reasons,

---

1993, ed. Hermann Danuser and Tobias Plebuch (Kassel, 1998), vol. 1, 300–310; and Susan Rankin, "Observations on Senleches' *En attendant esperance*," and Lorenz Welker, "Weitere Beobachtungen zu *Esperance*," in *Musik als Text*, Danuser and Plebuch, vol. 1, 314–18 and 319–21, respectively.

112. See Plumley, "Citation and Allusion," 346–51. See also the reference to this as the Percy family rallying cry in *Henry IV, Part 1*, 2.3.70 and 5.2.96, which probably derives from Raphael Holinshed's *Chronicles* (see Arthur Raleigh Humphreys, ed., *The First Part of King Henry IV* [London, 1960], Appendix 3, 175.

113. Stephen V. Grancsay, "A Pair of Spurs Bearing the Bourbon Motto," *Metropolitan Museum of Art Bulletin* 36 (1941): 171 (plate). See also Susan Crane, *The Performance of Self: Ritual, Clothing, and Identity during the Hundred Years War* (Philadelphia, 2002), 186n32, citing Linsa Monnas, "Fit for a King: Figured Silks Shown in the Wilton Diptych," in *The Regal Image of Richard II and the Wilton Diptych*, ed. Dillian Gordon, Linsa Monnas, and Caroline Elam (London, 1997), 165–77.

114. This refines Kelly's claim of Machaut's utter singularity in his focus on Hope. Once the musical lyrics, especially the popular and widely cited rondeau *Esperance*, are taken into account, the permeation of Hope, which, in the words of Galiot's rondeau, turns waiting into a pleasure ("En attendant d'amer la douce vie / Fait Doulz Espoir labour estre plaisance"), seems much more thoroughgoing.

115. The reasons affecting chronology are intractable: we simply do not know whether these poems circulated as stand-alone dits in copies that no longer survive. In a deeply intertextual culture, it seems doubtful that they would have been read that way even if they were copied independently. Each dit is therefore not a discrete statement on this topic but is inflected by Machaut's

scholars have considered in particular the role of patronage, with a focus on the putative original specific patron for *Remede, Navarre,* and manuscript C, Bonne of Luxembourg.[116] The seemingly wider role of hope in courtly society (whether or not personified as Hope) has been less well considered but is worth raising here. Might there have been particular reasons that increased the value of Hope in the context of court culture in this period? Did the use of a personification of Hope—a figure held in memory—allow entertainment to provide a practical ethical training of courtly minds for which there was a perceived need?

As one of the theological virtues, Hope (in Latin, *spes*) has clear Christian resonance. The lyric genre that places most emphasis on the role of Hope is the lay.[117] The lay, as I have mentioned, was the prestige poetic form—both difficult to write *and* difficult to learn for a reader or singer. As a mainly monophonic form, however, the lay could potentially have been taught to courtiers, even if they were unable to read musical notation.[118] The combination of technical accessibility (monophony) and vocal and verbal difficulty (large pitch range, complex motivic shapes over great length, and difficult and changing versification) would have made it an absorbing form for its audience, especially if they also had aspirations to perform it (whether through singing or reading aloud).[119] The only other subject to rival Hope in the lays is the Virgin Mary, a comparably perfect woman to be held in the mind for contemplation, who is sometimes known as "Nostre Dame de Bonne Esperance."[120]

In the context of a mid-century beset by plague, famine, a long war—and heretical popular responses to all of these things—the general need for spiritual succor and belief in a better future might well have been acute. Hope's ministry, however, clearly also had an erotic and courtly resonance that served a "profound human need" for aristocrats at court. Kelly sees Machaut's use of the figure of Hope as an extreme reaction to the vogue for erotic literature in the thirteenth and fourteenth centuries, which in Machaut became imaginatively sublimated.[121] Huot notes that in developing a cultural ideology that

works as a whole (and, in the earlier period, probably also by his personal didactic presence at court), as well as by related works by other authors.

116. See the references in Earp, *Guillaume de Machaut,* 25–26.

117. Kelly, *Medieval Imagination,* 148.

118. This form of learning is hinted at in both *Remede* and *Voir dit.*

119. Six of Machaut's lays are without musical notation in any source, and those with it also could have been simply recited on occasion, and are sometimes copied without notation in other sources. In the *Remede* the lover is commanded to read (*lire*) the lay to the lady, although we may surmise that he sings it for his readers at the earlier point in the dit where it is copied (with notation in most sources) as an example of his love poetry.

120. There is (and was) a large abbey dedicated to Our Lady of Good Hope in Estinnes (Hainaut).

121. Kelly, *Medieval Imagination,* 123, quotation xv.

had serious implications for personal identity, Machaut contributed to social stability.[122] But why was there a particular need for Hope in the northern French courts of the mid-fourteenth century?

Perhaps the all-too-real consequences of sexually satisfied desire were indelibly marked in Machaut's own mind. At an impressionably young age he would probably have been privy to the political, social, and individual consequences from the royal adultery scandal of 1314, which saw three princesses arrested and imprisoned, and eventually resulted in the annulment of the first marriage of Charles IV of France in 1322.[123] As the French king's second wife, Marie de Luxembourg, was the only sibling of King John of Bohemia, Machaut's earliest patron, discussions of this match (together with the indecorous events that had made it possible) might have occupied some of Machaut's earliest dealings with King John in his trusted inner-circle position. This adultery scandal coincided with the period of the trial of the Templars and fears for the extinction of the Capetian succession. The two of the three princesses who were found guilty had their heads shaved; their lovers were castrated and executed.[124]

A near reprise of this episode seems to have been enacted in a time closer to the composition of the *Remede*, even if perhaps too late to be a direct influence on it, and to a figure who appears to have been closer to Machaut. The chronicler Jean le Bel records rumors that Bonne of Luxembourg's death in 1349 was hastened, and the constable of France, Raoul d'Eu, summarily executed on his return to France from being held captive in England in 1350, because of their mutual love affair.[125] Jean le Bel repeatedly says that he does not know if these things are true, but gossip is just as damaging as the truth if one loves without Hope (as the *Voir dit* attests; see chapter 5).[126] Al-

122. Huot, "Guillaume de Machaut and the Consolation of Poetry," 195.

123. See Margaret Bent and Andrew Wathey, introduction to *Fauvel Studies: Allegory, Chronicle, Music, and Image in Paris, Bibliothèque Nationale de France, MS français 146*, ed. Margaret Bent and Andrew Wathey (Oxford, 1998), 10; and Elizabeth A. R. Brown, "*Rex ioians, ionnes, iolis*: Louis X, Philip V, and the *Livres de Fauvel*," ibid., 63–65. See also Elizabeth A. R. Brown, "Diplomacy, Adultery, and Domestic Politics at the Court of Philip the Fair: Queen Isabella's Mission to France in 1314," in *Documenting the Past: Essays in Medieval History Presented to George Peddy Cuttino*, ed. J. S. Hamilton and P. J. Bradley (Woodbridge, 1989), 53–83.

124. Madeline H. Caviness, "Patron or Matron? A Capetian Bride and a Vade Mecum for Her Marriage Bed," *Speculum* 68 (1993): 336, citing Armel Hugh Diverres, ed., *La chronique métrique attribuée à Geoffroy de Paris* (Strasbourg, 1956), 404–6, ll. 5868–6070; and Paul Lehugeur, *Histoire de Philippe le Long, roi de France (1316–1322)* (Paris, 1897), 16–18, 41, 168–69.

125. Jules Viard and Eugène Déprez, eds., *Chronique de Jean le Bel*, 2 vols. (Paris, 1904–5), 2:183, 198–200.

126. His doubts are twofold: he does not know if Bonne's death was hastened or not (ibid., 183: "Je ne sçay laquelle de ces II dames trespassa premierement; maiz moult de gens disoient que on avoit avancé la mort à madame Boine; je ne sçay pour quoy, ne ce fut vray ou non"); and he does not know if the reason for the execution of Raoul was that which was rumored (ibid., 200: "et ne sceut on pour quoy ce fut fait alors que les plus privés du roy, mais aucunes gens adevinoient que le roy avoit esté infourmé d'aucunes amours, lesquelles avoient esté ou debvoient estre

though he otherwise followed Jean le Bel closely in his chronicle for the same period, Froissart retracted this allegation. Bonne's husband, the future King John II, had far warmer relations with men than with women, especially with his boyhood companion and favorite, Charles de la Cerda of Spain, whom he made constable on his accession in 1350 and who was assassinated with the complicity of Charles of Navarre (who objected to his accession to the county of Angoulême) in 1354.[127]

The potential for claims and suspicions to result in very real hardship and misery for noblewomen (together with the lethal ire directed at male lovers of royal men and women) throughout the first half of the fourteenth century could have generated and nourished Machaut's decidedly moralizing and quietist approach to courtly love, in which eroticism is present but is ethically marked in a manner that requires active reading (reading, reflection, rereading) in order to complete the process of learning. Machaut's work thus serves a threefold purpose: to distract the reader's mind from real-life desires, to allow his or her vicarious (safe, literary, mental) enjoyment, and to instruct the reader in correct understanding and judgment.

The Hopeless Lover: Guillaume in the *Voir dit*

Hope remained a central figure in Machaut's work, and his earlier works continued to have relevance to his later ones, as is shown through self-citation. In *Confort,* Machaut refers Charles of Navarre, the protagonist whose political suffering he is seeking poetically to ameliorate, to the *Remede* and the "lay de bon espoir" for a more thorough exposition of how Sweet Thought is born of *Souvenir.*[128] The identity of the lay denoted here is disputed. The first editor of *Confort,* Ernest Hoepffner, suggested that this title refers to *S'onques* (*Le lay de confort*) (L17/12), whose feminine *je* addresses her lover in prison in the final stanza (seemingly apt with reference to Charles's own imprisonment).[129]

---

entre dame Bonne et le gentil connestable. Je ne sçay se oncques en fust rien à la verité, mais la maniere fu fait en fit pluseurs gens souspençonner").

127. Parallels have been drawn between this and the fate of Piers Gaveston, the favorite of Edward II of England, earlier in the century; see Raymond Cazelles, *Société politique, noblesse et couronne sous Jean le Bon et Charles V* (Geneva, 1982), 44–45. Leo, "Authorial Presence," 130–31, speculates that the "visual discourse of exclusion, melancholy, and isolation" (131) in the illuminations of lovers in C might reflect John's sadness—or even regret—after Bonne's death.

128. *Confort,* ll. 2248–49. The *Confort* then goes on to detail the importance of Hope in a number of exemplars, drawing mainly on classical sources but culminating in the example of King John of Bohemia.

129. Hoepffner, *Oeuvres de Guillaume de Machaut,* 3:249–50. The end of the lay reads: "Et vraiement, / s'en toy d'eus [Espoir] has fermement / l'impression, / tu vivras en ta prison / joieusement" (And truly, if thou hast the firm impression of Espoir in thee, thou shalt live in thy prison joyfully).

Two later sources call this piece the *Lay de confort*, which Hoepffner hypothesizes links it directly to *Confort*, despite Machaut's citation of it by another title within that dit.[130] Although he notes that *Qui n'aroit* (RF1/L19) is titled *Lay de Bon Espoir* in manuscripts **J** and **K**, the first music editor, Friedrich Ludwig, actually reaffirms Hoepffner's suggestion.[131] The *Remede* in these two sources is abbreviated, including the cutting of the lay's last six stanzas, so Ludwig argues that they are manuscripts without authority and that their title for the lay is therefore not authorial. Earp, however, disagrees: he thinks the lay of the *Remede* could indeed be the one that is referred to in the *Confort*.[132] A third candidate has been advanced by Douglas Kelly, who suggests that the dit refers to *Longuement* (*Le lay de Bonne Esperance* (L18/13), a lay that is interpolated into the *Voir dit*.[133] Given the general equivalence between *Espoir* and *Esperance* in Machaut's poetry, this last identification certainly seems possible. It would require the lay to have been written somewhat in advance of its inclusion in *Voir dit*, which probably postdates *Confort* by a few years, but it would not be the only lyric inclusion in *Voir dit* to have been composed earlier.[134]

While the chronology makes it unlikely that the *Confort* citations were intended when written to point to *Voir dit* as well as to *Remede* (that is, to the pair of dits with musical interpolations which together give the fullest exposition of Machaut's courtly doctrine from complementary perspectives), the fact that Machaut later chose to insert *Longuement* (*Le lay de Bonne Esperance*) (L18/13) into a broader narrative context would show even more clearly—if Kelly is right that this is the *Confort*'s "lay de bon espoir"—the ongoing importance of Hope in Machaut's later works.[135] Although it seems impossible

---

130. The title is in **G** and **E**, both posthumous, which might make this non-authorial (and thus incorrect), or might conversely represent the generally acknowledged reception of this lay as the one referred to in the *Confort*. It should be noted that "Espoir" is a rhyme word, which would have made a change to Machaut's text rather difficult. The only lay that includes the words "bon espoir" in its text is not L17/12 but rather the unnotated *Se quanque* (L11), titled *Le lay du mirouer amoureux* in **E** but otherwise without title.

131. Ludwig, *Guillaume de Machaut: Musikalische Werke*, 2:14*n1.

132. Earp, *Guillaume de Machaut*, 372.

133. Kelly, *Medieval Imagination*, 288n59.

134. Like several of the musical balades, the earliest surviving source for this lay is **Vg**, which does not include the *Voir dit*. Excepting the later redaction in **E**, *Voir dit* does not present the music of the lyrics in situ, making it far easier for Machaut to draw on a fund of pieces copied into the music section, to which he cues the reader through rubrics. *Sans cuer* (R4) is the earliest musical lyric included in *Voir dit*. It is first copied in the music section and *Loange* (Lo148) of **C**, predating the dit by at least a decade and probably several. A number of other lyrics in *Voir dit* are also in **C**'s *Loange*.

135. One of Hope's riding companions in *Voir dit* is Confort d'Ami, an unusual personification, perhaps included as a deliberate connection to the dit of this name, which—if Kelly is right—cites the very lay that Machaut will produce for Hope in the diegesis of the *Voir dit*.

to decide this question, a closer look at the *Voir dit*'s lay and the situation of forgetting Hope which prompts its composition will show how the points established in *Navarre* and *Remede* resonate in one of Machaut's last dits.

In the *Remede* the juvenile *amant*-narrator sits alone bewailing Fortune when Hope approaches him. In the later *Voir dit* (summarized in figure 4.5), Hope—similarly located in the middle episode of the dit—is forced instead to accost the now elderly Guillaume on the road on his way home from what will prove to have been his final encounter with Toute Belle. Hope accuses Guillaume of having forgotten her (ll. 4300–4461). In a replay of the penalty demanded of the poet Guillaume by Goodness in *Navarre*, Hope asks Guillaume to compose a lay, although this one is specifically in her (Hope's) honor, a "Lay d'Esperance."[136]

Guillaume, the elderly poet-lover-protagonist of *Voir dit*, has forgotten Hope in his inordinate focus on the lady: he is comically hopeless. In focusing on external reality—the lady—he is perfectly fine whenever things are going well, but even before he meets Toute Belle there is evidence (already seen in chapter 3's discussion of letter 8) of his liability to change. Like the young lover at the start of *Remede,* he expresses emotions that are not always stable; unlike the protagonist of *Remede,* he does not learn during the course of the dit but remains emotionally labile and both credulous of, and subject to, gossip—a liability that will result in his assimilation to the figure of Fortune at the end of the *Voir dit*.[137] As a lover Guillaume is hopeless and Hopeless, despite his protestations to the contrary. Like the lay of the *Remede,* that of the *Voir dit* (L18/13) shows that the singer is rationally aware of the importance of Hope but unable to incorporate theory into practice (he has *entendement* but not *sentement*). The difference from the *Remede* is that the lay in the *Voir dit* is composed *after* Hope has been and gone. The youthful lover of *Remede* learns, but the lover of *Voir dit* is too old a dog to be taught new tricks.

In *Voir dit,* Hope, riding with her companions Moderation (*Mesure*), Self-Control (*Attemprance*), Good Advice (*Bon Avis*), and Friend's Consolation (*Confort d'Ami*) accuses Guillaume of a "meffait" in not having written any special praise of her in his poem when she has comforted him, brought joy from afar, given delight and happiness, and turned sorrow into joy.[138] In particular she has allowed him to combat Shame (*Honte*) and Desire. Guillaume immediately admits that she is right; Good Advice suggests the "amande" (recompense) of a "rondel balade ou virelay," but Hope opts instead for the much more exacting penalty of a lay.[139]

The lay that is then copied (without notation in most sources) into the *Voir dit, Longuement me sui tenus (Le lay de Bonne Esperance)* (L18/13), had

136. *Voir dit,* l. 4414.
137. See chapter 5.
138. *Voir dit,* ll. 4338–83.
139. *Voir dit,* ll. 4408–17.

Le livre dou voir dit
(The Book of the True Story)

PROLOGUE (ll. 1–46)

I (ll. 47–4273): "Real" relationship
1. (ll. 47–614) Guillaume (G) receives letter 1 from Toute Belle (TB); replies with letter 2
2. (ll. 615–1716 and letter 10) G relapses into melancholy; epistolary relationship continues; G's doubts (letter 8) prompt TB to send her *ymage* (letter 9)
3. (ll. 1717–3098 and letter 14) MEETING 1 with novena as frame
4. (ll. 3099–3577) MEETING 2 in which G visits a patron
5. (ll. 3578–4273) MEETING 3 their pilgrimage

MIDPOINT SEQUENCE (ll. 4274–5260): Esperance
1. (ll. 4274–4461) G journeys home and is captured by Esperance
2. (ll. 4462–4717) *Lay d'Esperance* (L18/13)
3. (ll. 4718–31 and letter 21) G's letter to TB about the episode
4. (ll. 4732–39 and letter 22) TB's reply

II (ll. 5261–9050): "Fictional" relationship
1. (ll. 4740–5824) regular correspondence (interrupted by TB's silence); G doubts her love; DREAM 1 (ll. 5261–5806) *ymage* changes from blue to green dress; king's interpretation
2. (ll. 5825–6578 and letter 38) renewal of correspondence; lovers reconciled; joint work on book
3. (ll. 6579–7632) TB sends for G; dangerous roads (secretary; Circé; Polyphemus) and losengiers' slander (visiting lord) prevent G's visit
4. (ll. 7633–8493) the lovers estranged; DREAM 2 (ll. 7736–8183) *ymage* complains to G; recounts Ovidian exempla
5. (ll. 8494–9050) final reconciliation

EPILOGUE (ll. 9051–94)

Figure 4.5. Synopsis of *Voir dit.*

first appeared among the lays set to music in **Vg**.[140] It opens with the statement that the lover, empty of love, has not composed lays for a long time, but that henceforth he will write songs and virelays because he has surrendered to Love. His lady's sweet smiling look has captured him, having made two darts—one of Desire and one of Hope. Without Hope, the burning of Desire would have killed him. He meditates on the pain of love, his loyalty despite it, and the lady's qualities. He finds joy in seeing her, and "Hope makes me strong against Desire who bites me" ("Et lespoir qui me fait fort / Contre desir qui me mort").[141] He thus has no need to ask for anything from his lady (which

140. See Earp, *Guillaume de Machaut,* 337–38. The title *Le lay de Bonne Esperance* is given in the music sections of **A** and **G**, while **E**, which copies it with music within the *Voir dit,* gives the title *Le lay d'Esperance.*

141. *Voir dit,* ll. 4611–12 = L18/13, stanza 7, ll. 16–17.

she would not grant anyway because he is not worthy), and so he continues to serve her without suffering. The last three stanzas return to the theme of Hope, who corrects, masters, and softens Desire (stanza 10), is physician to the wound from Desire's arrow, and sustains the *je* as a true lover (stanza 12). The second half of stanza 11 presents a list of things Hope is to the lover:

Cest mes chastiaus cest mes ressors
Cest ce qui estaint mire
Cest lie avoirs cest le tresors
Dont on ne puet mesdire
Cest de ma vie li drois pors
Cest ma ioie a droit dire
Tous li argens et tous li ors
De france et de lempire
Ne vaut pas lun de ses confors
Ou desespoirs saire.[142]

She is my castle, she's my resort, she's the one who extinguishes my anger, she is the goods, she is the treasure that cannot be bad-mouthed, she is the real port in my life;[143] she is my joy, to tell it truly. All the silver and all the gold of France and of the empire is not worth one of her consolations when Despair prepares himself.

This lay's music as a whole is unusual in having long pauses between the lines of the poetry and thus a very choppy, short phrase structure. It is also unusual in having very few stanzas with the quadruple versicle structure that is common in Machaut's lays. Only stanzas 6 and 10 exhibit this, and they are both emphatic in other ways: stanza 6 is a statement of loyalty which has the rhymes "-er" (*amer*) and the feminine ending "-ée"; stanza 10 is praise of *Espoir*, with the rhyme "-ie" (*lie*) and the terminal rhyme "-oir" (*espoir*). As often, the repeated rhyme sounds—whose music is here repeated four times rather than two—are themselves suggestive of certain underlying themes and meanings within the lay.

The lay asserts that the lover does not wish to entertain even a thought that would harm his lady's reputation, let alone ask for anything. The pleasure he gains is specifically from seeing her, and there is no mention of other reward (*merci*) or (surprisingly) of the role of memory in Hopeful love. This lack of memory perhaps points to Guillaume's problem putting his understanding of Hope's value against Desire into practice: once he is gone from his lady

---

142. *Voir dit,* ll. 4692–701 = L18/13, stanza 11, ll. 11–20.

143. The singer refers indirectly to Hope's role in combating Fortune, who is often pictured as the wind that blows the subject about in his leaky oarless boat on life's hazardous seas. See the discussion of *Qui es / Ha! Fortune* (M8) in chapter 5; and also Hans Blumenberg, *Shipwreck with Spectator: Paradigm of a Metaphor for Existence,* trans. Steven Rendall (Cambridge, 1997).

(as he is for the rest of the poem), he cannot gain enough stability from his memory of her (even memorialized in her painted image and in his book), and so keeps doubting her. Immediately after the exchange of letters in which Guillaume sends Toute Belle the lay and she promises to learn it, the narrative recounts that the man who feels "lamoureus point . Nest mie toudis en un point"—exactly what the lover at the start of *Remede* claims about himself.[144] Guillaume goes on to announce that Desire has killed Sweet Thought, Hope, and himself, and sends the lady a scripture of a mono-rhymed versified letter on the rhyme "-our" (*amour*). Desire prompts literary excess as it did in *Remede* with the lover's excessively long complaint; in *Voir dit*, by contrast, Guillaume's excess results in forgetting, rather than having not yet learned, Hope's teachings.

Guillaume gets everything wrong and learns nothing. He understands but cannot employ the poetics of Hope because memory fails him; and he knows that *merci* should not compromise the honor of the lady, but he has met her naked in bed and written this meeting into a book. A lover's focus on Hope ought to allow the lady to avoid shame because it idealizes the love object and removes the need for external action to relieve suffering. (That is, without Hope, the lover needs erotic fulfillment, which brings shame; with Hope, the lover needs only his own mental focus on *Souvenir*.)[145] Again Hope is useful because if real external action were what was required, it would jeopardize either the lover's mental state or the lady's bodily honor. Honor can be maintained without killing the lover if the *merci* he is willing to accept is a sufficiency of seeing and hearing his lady, either for real or in recollected form in memory.[146]

In Middle French courtly lyric the word *merci* signifies a broad range of favors that the lady may grant her lover; its meaning overlaps with "pity," but it also carries the sense of remuneration, reward, or even salary—the payoff in the economy of noble love. Within Machaut's usage it has a specific resonance and range of meanings. By the time of Hope's lay in the *Voir dit*, *merci*

144. See notes 16 and 31, and Jacqueline Cerquiglini, *"Un engin si soutil": Guillaume de Machaut et l'écriture au XIVe siècle* (Geneva, 1985), 64–65, which has further examples from *Confort* and explores the equivalence between Desire, Fortune, and the fluctuating lover; on this see also my discussion in chapter 5.

145. The noble lover can be generous in terms of gifts, but the lady must be generous in refusals (a pairing of largesse elaborated in *Honte, paour* (B25) and *Donnez, signeurs* [B26] and in *Harpe*, ll. 207–20); see Leach, "Guillaume de Machaut, Royal Almoner."

146. Here, too, Guillaume has already failed in that he is unable to generate an image within his own mind but rather requires an external physical one. This portrait (which takes on a life of its own and is punished for her supposed offenses; see Sylvia Huot, "Reliving the *Roman de la Rose*: Allegory and Irony in Machaut's *Voir Dit*," in *Chaucer's French Contemporaries: The Poetry/Poetics of Self and Tradition*, ed. R. Barton Palmer [New York, 1999], 53–55) eventually causes him a great deal of doublethink about the truth of her love in the closing stages of the dit. See the discussion of the "story of how the crow turned black" and *Se pour ce muir* (B36) in chapter 5.

has been explicitly defined twice: once for Toute Belle in a letter, and later in the narrative just before the erotic climax of the dit. In letter 6 Guillaume writes, "*Merci* is nothing other than satisfaction [*souffisance*]."[147] But what is satisfaction? In the narrative preceding the Prayer to Venus, the rather premature erotic climax of the dit, Machaut addresses this issue. Here, Toute Belle and her *compaignette* Guillemette have forced the protesting (but essentially willing) Guillaume into Toute Belle's bed, where he lies rigid with trepidation, watching her sleep. As she wakens, she bids him embrace her, which he does, declaring:

> Sestoie com cils qui se baigne
> En flun de paradis terrestre
> Car de tout le bien qui puet estre
> Par honnour estoie assevis
> Et saouler a mon devis
> Sans plus pour la grant habundance
> Que iavoie de souffisance
> Car tout ce quelle me disoit
> Trop hautement me souffisoit
> Et tout le bien que je sentoie
> A goust de mercys savouroie
> Sans penser mal ne tricherie
> Car trop estoit de moy chierie
> Pour ce weil un po parler ci
> Quelle chose cest de merci.[148]

I was like one who bathes himself in the waters of an earthly paradise, for all of the goodness that could [ever] be was bestowed upon me through honor, and I was sated to my satisfaction without surfeit, because of the great abundance of sufficiency that I had. For everything that she had said to me had very highly sufficed me, and all the good that I had felt had savored of the taste of *merci* without ill thought or treachery for she was so dear to me. For this reason I wish to speak a little here of what thing *merci* is.

Having used the term "merci," Guillaume says a little about what it is by means of a short exemplum about two lovers. The first is loyal but often absent, serving his lady in deeds inspired by love, without asking anything from her. The second stays at court to joust, sing, dance, and *carole*, awaiting *merci* from an embrace or kiss which would be enough to satisfy him:

---

147. "Et merci nest autre chose que souffisance"; *Voir dit*, 94 (letter 6).
148. *Voir dit*, ll. 3814–26.

"It suffices that he might see her and enjoy himself beside her."[149] Guillaume draws a parallel between himself and the first lover, whose heart, like his, trembles when he sees his lady; but his claim for kinship with this first type of lover is undercut by his actions. He has stayed by his lady's side to the point of being in her very bed, has just embraced her, and has declared the sufficiency of his lady's embrace. It indeed sufficed to "see her and enjoy himself beside her." Moreover, the poem continues with Guillaume's own descriptions of himself engaging in several of the activities that his exemplum attributed to the second lover: he sings, dines, plays bowls, and remains at his lady's side in the garden, which he describes as prelapsarian (ll. 3865–3924). This "esbatement," repeatedly referred to as "honnourable," culminates in the arrival of Venus, whose dark cloud visually obscures the two lovers naked in bed long enough for Guillaume to compose a virelay celebrating the decapitation of Rebuff (*Dangier*) and dragging his carcass—unmourned by the singing of any Mass—to hell, while maintaining Toute Belle's honor.[150] In this aubade-like "chanson baladée" Guillaume still protests that "there [in the bed] honor, and the reputation of her comely, pretty body were well preserved, since never a base thought was engendered or born between me and her."[151] The rhyme words "engendree" (engendered) and "nee" (born) imply some form of procreation (although what is brought forth from this union is poetry); the next stanza of this same lyric makes implicit reference to the sexual act:

Souffissance menrichi
Et plaisance si
Quonques creature nee
Not le cuer si assevi
Ne mains de sousci
Ne joie si affinee
Car la deesse honnouree
Qui fait lassamblee
Damours. damie et dami
Coppa le chief de sespee
Qui est bien tempree
A dangier mon anemj.[152]

---

149. "Et ce que souffist que la voie / Et que dales li sesbanoie"; *Voir dit,* ll. 3859–60.

150. *Voir dit,* ll. 4134–93.

151. "La fu bien lonnour garder / Et la renommee / De son cointe corps ioli / Quonques villeinne pensee / Ne fu engendree / Ne nee entre moy et li." *Voir dit,* ll. 4146–51.

152. *Voir dit,* ll. 4158–69. Its reliance on Venus and phallic imagery (the sword as phallus and *Dangier*'s head as maidenhead) is reminiscent of the most explicit of the endings of the *Roman de la Rose,* in which the lover inserts his staff into an aperture. These were frequently illustrated; the cloud here alludes via Creation imagery to the getting of man but chastely obscures the deed.

Sufficiency and pleasure enriched me so that no creature born ever had a heart so fulfilled, nor less care, nor such refined joy; for the honorable goddess who brought together Love, lover, and beloved cut with her épée (which is well tempered) the head of Rebuff, my enemy.

Guillaume's reliability as a glossator of his own actions is here—as throughout the *Voir dit*—brought into question. His insistence on his honor, his own behavior, and his exemplum ill match the events he describes and thereby invite readers to make their own, opposite judgments. His lyrics betray the narrative: despite his protestations, the *merci* Guillaume receives is of exactly the kind that could jeopardize Toute Belle's good name, a name that will indeed increasingly be besmirched by the gossip of the succession of visitors to him in the last part of the poem.

The differences between the two lovers of Guillaume's exemplum are implied to characterize loving with and without Hope, respectively. The first, nobler lover serves loyally without asking for anything from the lady and is able to travel. His love is self-sufficient through the action of Hope, aided by *Souvenir* and Sweet Thought, which together can give the illusion of "seeing and hearing" the lady, even when the lover is physically parted from her. The second lover must stay at court to sing, dance, and *carole*—all of which Guillaume has effectively done simultaneously in composing the "chanson baladée" (danced song)—since a kiss or embrace is all that will suffice. The type of *merci* depicted at the erotic climax of the *Voir dit* is that which suffices when Hope is forgotten, a *merci* born of Desire, necessitating reciprocation from the lady, and which can ruin her honor and good name (as it goes on to do). By implication the *merci* that suffices for a lover *with* Hope is nobler, more sustainable, and less damaging. What such honorable *merci* entails is revealed in several places in Machaut's works, most notably in a feminine-voiced lyric found in the *Loange,* and in the music section, where it forms a pair with the balade with which this chapter opened: *Esperance* (B13).

Aural and Visual Satisfaction

Esperance (B13) foregrounds a lover for whom simply serving Love (and thereby his lady) in Hope is "souffisance." The song that follows it in the music section, *Je ne cuit pas* (B14), explores a further aspect of *merci* (see figure 4.6).

See Kevin Brownlee, "Pygmalion, Mimesis, and the Multiple Endings of the *Roman de la Rose*," *Yale French Studies* 95 (1999): 193–211; John V. Fleming, *The Roman de la Rose: A Study in Allegory and Iconography* (Princeton, 1969), figure 42; and my discussion in chapter 6. In Huot's analysis, however, the consummation is diverted into poetic creation so that Guillaume's sexual failure becomes Machaut's poetic success, especially a success in sacralizing the erotic; see Huot, "Reliving the *Roman de la Rose*."

Je ne cuit pas qu'onques à creature	1.1	I do not believe that Love has distributed
Amours partist ses biens si largement		her goods so generously to any creature
Comme à moy seule, et de sa grace pure;	1.3	as she does, out of her pure grace, to me
Nom pas qu'aie deservi nullement		alone—not that I have at all deserved the
Les douceurs qu'elle me fait,	1.5	sweetness that she bestows on me, for she
Car gari m'a de tous maulz et retrait,		has protected me from all ills, because she
Quant elle m'a donné, sans retollir,	1.7	has given without demur *my heart, my*
Mon cuer, m'amour et quanque je desir. R		*love, and everything that I desire.*

And because of this I am full of joy, light

Et pour ce sui pleinne d'envoyseüre	2.1	of heart, and I live most happily; and I always
Gaye de cuer et vif tres liement		give Love the dues which I owe her: that is, I
Et ren toudis à Amours la droiture	2.3	love loyally, faithfully, with all my heart and
Que je li doy: c'est amer loyaument		in all I do. In this love, no thought is left to
En foy, de cuer et de fait;	2.5	me that is not joyful for welcoming *my heart,*
Et ceste amour pensée ne me lait		*my love, and everything that I desire.*
Qui joieuse ne soit pour conjoïr	2.7	
Mon cuer, m'amour et quanque je desir. R		

So there is nothing on which I would fix

Si qu'il n'est riens où je mette ma cure	3.1	my attention except on loving and humbly
Fors en amer et loer humblement		praising Love, who feeds me with such pas-
Amours, qui me nourrist de tel pasture	3.3	ture as *merci* given sweetly from a loving
Com de mercy donnée doucement		and perfect heart; but the *merci* which thus
D'amoureus cuer et parfait;	3.5	renews me consists in simply seeing and
Mais la mercy qui einsi me refait,		hearing *my heart, my love, and everything*
C'est de veoir seulement et oïr	3.7	*that I desire.*
Mon cuer, m'amour et quanque je desir. R		

Figure 4.6. Text and translation of *Je ne cuit pas* (B14) (text based on C's music section).

In B14 the feminine-voiced *je* praises Love for bestowing her goods so generously. Although the lady of B14 claims already to enjoy *merci*, whereas B13's
lover merely awaits it, both receive the same kinds of riches from Love, partly
because the kind of *merci* enjoyed by the lady of B14 is the noble *souffissance*
of simply seeing and hearing "mon cuer, m'amour et quanque je desir" (my
heart, my love, and whatever I desire).

Although the lady tells of Love's gifts without mentioning a lover directly,
the refrain text can be seen as synonymous with her "amis," since he would
then be summed up as being the lady's heart, love, and everything that she
desires. A similar formulation is used to describe the dead lover of the lady
in *Behaingne*, where Machaut's advocacy of simply seeing and hearing the
lover as the honorable form of *merci*, especially for a feminine-voiced *je*, is
further confirmed by the occurrence of the phrase "veoir seulement et oïr,"
together with a close paraphrase of the refrain of B14:

Qu'en li estoit m'esperance et ma joie
Et mon plaisir,
Mon cuer, m'amour, mon penser, mon *desir*. [cf. B14, refrain: "*Mon cuer,*
                                      m'amour et quanque je *desir*"]

De tous les biens pooit mon cuer joïr.
Par *li veoir seulement et oïr*.[153] [cf. B14, l. 3.7: "C'est de *veoir
seulement et oïr*"]

In him were my hope and my joy and my pleasure, *my heart, my love*, my thoughts,
my desire; my heart could enjoy all goods *simply by seeing and hearing him.*

The grieving lady of *Behaingne* epitomizes noble loving, as does the *je* of
B14. But this appellation—my heart, love, and everything I desire—is also
how the rather less straightforwardly honorable Toute Belle addresses Guillaume at the opening of letter 18 of the *Voir dit*.[154] In this letter Toute Belle
affirms her love in the face of Guillaume's resurgent doubts and arranges the
final visit—the erotically charged "pilgrimage" already discussed. Guillaume
receives her letter while he is at Crécy and glosses it in a narrative that tells
how there is no horse so fine, no knight so brave, nor any woman so beautiful that bad behavior, cowardice, and loss of good name, respectively, would
not tarnish them. He praises "bonté" (goodness or virtue) over "biauté" (the
latter of which, in a couplet marked by a scribal "nota," is considered one
of Nature's lesser favors), and he vows never to cause a woman to lose her
honor. That the only honorable form of *merci* is the sweet look and fair welcome which the lover of B13 is reassured of obtaining by Hope, and which
the *je* of B14 receives simply in seeing and hearing her *amis*, seems borne
out by the narrative progress of the *Voir dit*, in which Toute Belle's "renom"
turns into the infamy of Fortune, to whom her erstwhile lover eventually
compares her.[155]

Within the *Loange, Je ne cuit pas* (B14), as *Je ne croy pas* (Lo175), forms
part of a group of twelve balades and a rondeau which Daniel Poirion identifies as being linked by the idea of "cuer" (Lo165–77).[156] Many of the
balades in this sequence treat the situation of lovers' parting, using the idea
either that the lover leaves his heart with his lady as a sustaining gift and
goes away "sans cuer," or that he himself is nourished by the image of the
lady inscribed in his heart by the action of *Souvenir* and Sweet Thought.[157]
The heart of the lover functions as "a record of personal memory" and

---

153. *Behaingne*, ll. 151–55 (emphasis added). Line 151 resembles line 3.9 of the chanson
royal *Onques mais nulz n'ama si folement* (Lo19). It should be noted that the mention of Hope
and Joy here echoes the pairing of these concepts in B13, as well as in the *Prologue;* see Arlt,
"Aspekte der Chronologie," 240.

154. *Voir dit*, ll. 3537–38.

155. See chapter 5, and Jacqueline Cerquiglini-Toulet, "*Fama* et les preux: Nom et renom à la fin
du Moyen Âge," *Médiévales* 24 (1993): 35–44. Toute Belle breaks all of the edicts laid down for the
keeping good of feminine honor in Machaut's balade *Honte, paour* (B25) and *Harpe*, ll. 207–20.

156. Poirion, *Le poète et le prince*, 521n45.

157. For a history of the heart as a wax tablet, see Eric Jager, *The Book of the Heart* (Chicago,
2000), 69–71 ("Making an Impression"). The heart of a youth is presented explicitly as a wax
tablet at the opening of the *Remede* (ll. 23–24).

is thus the place wherein these two personifications act.[158] Moreover, it is from the heart that Desire sucks out the blood, as is detailed in both *Remede* and (as was seen in chapter 3) *De triste / Quant vrais / Certes* (B29), in which the heart's blood loss removes the lover from a state of happy sanguinity.[159] When the lover is far from the lady, and thus can neither see nor hear her, Desire must be combated by Hope using Sweet Thought in conjunction with *Souvenir*. All three personifications, present in the final stanza of B13, explicitly sustain the lovers in the situation of absence central to the *Loange* sequence Lo165–78.[160]

Several adjacent lyrics in this sequence form pairs by sharing rhymes; others, not directly adjacent, share other significant text and/or rhymes.[161] B14/ Lo175's most obvious pair in the *Loange* is the following lyric, *Ne cuidies pas* (Lo176), whose incipit, "ne *cuidies* pas," directly challenges the lady's opening in the music section version of Lo175: "Je ne *cuit* pas."[162] Lo176 functions as Lo175's adjacent pair in the *Loange*, while additionally showing formal resemblances to the latter lyric's pair in the music section, notably because Lo176 makes use of B13's two most audible rhymes: "-i" and "-ueil." Lo176 uses B13's b-rhyme as *its* b-rhyme, has a feminized version of the same ("-eille") as its a-rhyme, and a feminized version of B13's "-i" ("merci") c-rhyme ("-ie") for *its* c-rhyme (see figure 4.7). In total the two lyrics share four rhyme words ("vueil," "accueil," "receuil," and "dueil"). These similarities of *practique* accompany Lo176's contrasting *matiere*, which delineates a poetics of Desire to complement B13's elaboration of Hope. Lo176 outlines the sorrow that leaving causes, describes the lady's peerless beauty, and identifies desire as the cause of sorrow—a sorrow against which the consolation of Hope in B13 would provide protection. The description of the lady in the second stanza of Lo176 in turn virtually paraphrases two parts of the *Remede*: the first, describing the lady, from a time when the lover is at the mercy of Desire, and the second, from the episode in the garden, describing Hope (see figure 4.8). As applied to Hope, this passage mirrors both the arrival of Philosophy in Boethius's *Consolation of Philosophy* and the effects of *Dous Regart* in the *Rose*, presenting Hope as "a fusion of Boethian and courtly models, offering not only philosophical but poetic consolation."[163]

158. Ibid., 70.

159. *Remede*, ll. 1923–28: "C'est Desir qui lappe et qui hume / Le sanc du cuer et la substance"; see Huot, "Guillaume de Machaut and the Consolation of Poetry," 173; and my discussion in chapter 3.

160. The connection between Hope and Sweet Thought is established in the *Roman de la Rose*, ll. 2613–64; see Armand Strubel, ed., *Guillaume de Lorris et Jean de Meun: Le Roman de la Rose* (Paris, 1992), 184–87.

161. For more detail, see Elizabeth Eva Leach, "Love, Hope, and the Nature of *Merci* in Machaut's Musical Balades *Esperance* (B13) and *Je ne cuit pas* (B14)," *French Forum* 28 (2003): 1–27.

162. In the *Loange* this lyric uses part of *croire*—"Je ne *croy* pas"—so that only the music section version confirms the *Loange* pairing.

163. Huot, "Guillaume de Machaut and the Consolation of Poetry," 172.

B13	Lo176

B13

1.1 Esperance qui m'asseüre,
    Joie sans per, vie a mon vueil,
1.3 Dous penser, sade nourriture,
    Tres bon eür, <u>plaisant **accueil,**</u>
1.5 Et maint <u>autre grant bien **recueil,**</u>
    Quant Amours m'a tant enrichi,
1.7 Que j'aim dame, s'aten merci.

2.1 Et se ceste atente m'est dure,
    <u>En **desirant** pas ne m'en **dueil,**</u>
2.3 Car le gré de ma dame pure,
    Et d'Amours tousjours faire vueil,
2.5 Et sa guerredon sans pareil,
    Ce m'est vis, puis qu'il est einsi,
2.7 Que j'aim dame, s'aten mercy.

3.1 Car <u>Souvenirs</u> en moy figure
    Sa fine biauté sans orgueil,
3.3 Sa bonté, sa noble figure,
    Son gent mainteing, <u>son bel **accueil,**</u>
3.5 Et comment si dous riant oueil
    Par leur atrait m'ont mené si,
3.7 Que j'aim dame, s'aten mercy.

8'a 8b 8'a 8b 8b 8c 8C
Hope, who reassures me, joy without
equal, a life according to my wishes, sweet
thought, sweet sustenance, great happiness,
<u>pleasing welcome,</u> and <u>many other very</u>
<u>good things do I receive</u> because Love has
so enriched me *that I love a lady and await*
merci.
And although this waiting is hard for me,
<u>in desiring her I do not torment myself,</u>
for I want always to do the will of my
pure lady and of Love, and so there will
be reward without equal, I think, since
my situation is such *that I love a lady and*
await merci.
For memory depicts within me her fine
beauty without pride, her goodness, her noble figure, her genteel countenance, her <u>fair</u>
<u>welcome,</u> and the way in which her sweet
laughing eyes have led me by their attraction so *that I love a lady and await* merci.

Lo176

Ne cuidiés pas que li cuers ne me dueille,
Tres douce dame, et que l'amoureus **dueil**
Moult durement ne m'assaille et accueille,
Quant je me part de <u>vostre bel **accueil,**</u>
Qu'au departir <u>si grant doleur **recueil**</u>
Qu'à vo dous vis dire "à Dieu" ne puis mie:
Tant me fait mal de vous la departie.

Car quant je voy vo biauté nonpareile
Et vo gent corps qui n'a point de pareil
Et vo fresche couleur qui à merveille
Coulourée est de blanc et de vermeil,
Resplendissant si com or en soleil,
Je n'ay vigour ne sens qui ne m'oublie:
Tant me fait mal de vous la departie

Adont <u>desir</u> asprement me traveille,
Art et bruist et [me] demainne à son **vueil,**
N'à riens qui soit il ne pense ne vueille
Fors au retour que tant desir et **vueil.**
Einsi partirs et **desirs** <u>dont me **dueil**</u>
Me font languir en paour de ma vie:
Tant me fait mal de vous la departie.

10'a 10b 10'a 10b 10b 10'c 10'C
Think not that my heart does not pain me,
very sweet lady, and that the pangs of love
don't very harshly accost and assail me when
I part from your beautiful welcome, since at
departure I receive such great sorrow that I
am completely unable to say "adieu" to your
sweet face, *so ill does your departure make me.*
For when I see your peerless beauty and your
noble body which has no peer, and your
fresh coloring, which is marvelously colored
with white and red, shining like gold in the
sun, I have no strength or idea that I do not
forget, *so ill does your departure make me.*
For then Desire sharply taxes me, burns, and
toasts me, and makes me await his pleasure
such that I might think or wish for nothing
except for the return that I so much desire
and wish for. Thus parting and desire, which
pain me, make me languish in fear of my life,
so ill does your departure make me.

Figure 4.7. Texts and translations of *Esperance* (B13) and *Ne cuidiés pas* (Lo176) (based on C and standard edition, respectively).

Ne cuidiés pas
(Lo176), stanza 2

Car quant je voy *vo biauté* nonpareile
Et *vo gent corps qui n'a point de pareil*
Et vo fresche coulour qui à *merveille*
Coulourée est *de blanc et de vermeil,*
Resplendissant si com or en soleil,
Je n'ay vigour ne sens qui ne m'oublie:
Tant me fait mal de vous la departie

For when I see your peerless beauty and your noble body which has no peer, and your fresh coloring which is marvelously colored with white and red, shining like gold in the sun, I have no strength or idea that I do not forget, *so ill does your departure make me.*

Remede, ll. 1257–67 (complaint, stanza 22)

Nonpourquant pas ne *merveil*—
Quant le regart de son douls oeil
Et son cler vis *blanc et vermeil*
Qui *resplendist*
De *biauté plus que or en solleil*
Et *son corps gent qui n'a pareil*
De doucour, de cointe appareil
Vers moy guenchist—
Se mes regars s'en esblouïst,
Se la parole m'en tarist,
Se ma vigour en amenrist.

Nevertheless I do not marvel when the look of her sweet eye and her bright face, white and red, which shines with beauty more than gold in the sun, and her noble body which has no peer in sweetness [or] in handsome clothing are turned toward me, although my look is blinded, my words are silenced, and my strength weakens.

Remede, ll. 1502–22

 Mes je vi seoir
Delez moy la plus belle dame
Qu'onques mes veisse, par m'ame,
Fors ma dame tant seulement.
Car tant estoit parfaitement
Belle, gent, et bien acesmee,
Que se Dieus de ses mains fourmee
L'eüst; s'estoit elle d'asfaire
Bel, bon, gent, doulz, et debonnaire.
Mes il ne me fu mie avis,
Quant je l'esgardai vis a vis,
Que ce fust creature humaine
De li, ne qu'elle fust mondeinne,
Dont j'avoie moult grant *merveille;*

Figure 4.8. The shining lady in *Ne cuidiés pas* (Lo176) and the complaint in *Remede,* ll. 1257–67, compared with Hope in *Remede,* ll. 1502–22.

Car *sa face blanche et vermeille*
Par juste compas faite a point
Si que mesfaçon n'i ot point,
Si clerement resplandissoit
Que sa clarté esclarcissoit
Les tenebres, la nuit obscure
De moy douloureuse aventure.

But I saw seated beside me the most beautiful lady that I ever saw, by my soul, excepting only my lady. For she [Hope] was so perfectly beautiful, noble, and well dressed as though God had formed her with his own hands; she was in her doings handsome, good, noble, sweet, and well bred, but it didn't seem to me at all, when I looked at her face-to-face, that she was a human creature nor that she was of this world, which made me marvel greatly; for her face, white and red, was made exactly in the right proportions so that it had not a jot of a mistake; she shone so brightly that her brightness illuminated the darkness, the obscure night of my sorrowful adventure.

Figure 4.8. (*Continued*)

The parallel between these passages shows how the lover may easily transfer his thoughts of love and loyalty to Hope when she is embodied as a lady with the same characteristics that his actual lady has, but without his lady's ability to initiate the burning of desire through a glance.

Virtually all of Machaut's central topics are elaborated in this *Loange* sequence and the music section pair to which it relates via the duplicated lyric *Je ne cuit/croy pas* (B14/Lo175). Lovers who have Hope survive parting because of the action of Sweet Thought and *Souvenir,* the mental picture of the beloved, which enables the lover to hope for honorable *merci* (that is, seeing and hearing the beloved) even when the beloved is far away. Hope removes the need for any real relationship with the lady: the lover's relationship is primarily with Hope herself. Hope protects the lover against Desire and the lady against the need to supply *merci* of a less honorable nature. This particular aspect is summarized in the last two balades of the *Loange* sequence, one of which is also duplicated in the music section.

Amours me fait (Lo177/B19) appears in the *Loange* sequence, two items after Lo175/B14. With the balade that follows it, *Helas! Desirs* (Lo178), it forms a summary of the sequence as a whole. B19/Lo177 is a complaint to Love; Lo178 apostrophizes Desire directly and intimately, concluding, "Certes, trop ay en toy [Desire] dur anemy" (I really have too hard an enemy in thee, Desire). The *Loange* group identified by Poirion can thus be extended to include *Helas! Desirs* (Lo178).

The two members of this extended *Loange* sequence (Lo165–78) that were set to music by Machaut—that is, *Je ne cuit/croy pas* (Lo175/B14) and *Amours me fait* (Lo177/B19)—effectively epitomize aspects of the overall topic here, offering honorable, hopeful female loving and a male lover assailed by desire, respectively. Although these two lyrics share only one rhyme, specifically musical features contribute more significantly to their relatedness. The two pieces are remarkably similar in their first twelve measures (see example 4.9).

They have the same mensuration, share much rhythmic-melodic material, and have measure-for-measure similarities of musical material: see especially measures 5 through 7, where B19's tenor resembles B14's cantus and vice versa (example 4.9, box a). Like B14's, B19's *ouvert* and *clos* cadences lack regular directed progressions in the cantus and tenor; moreover, B19's *ouvert* resembles B14's *clos*.

The opening word of B19 is "Amours"—Love makes the lover desire and love so that he is unable to hope or think. Both "desirer / Et amer" and "esperer / Ne penser" have the same music, aurally paralleling the cause of grief (desire) and its cure (hope). Musically, Love makes the singer "desire" too. The counterpoint setting the opening word, "Amours," forces the singer to perform a very unusual melodic interval at the outset of the piece, from G to c♯, offering a strange bisection of the overall G to g octave range of the first phrase (example 4.9b). This c♯ has contrapuntal "appetite," or "desire," for resolution to d. B19's lover endures such obduracy from his lady that he fears he will not last much longer, since desire makes his love burn so much that he forgets everything but her, and thus languishes without tasting joy, and will die if Love does not soon agree that he should have "it" without asking.[164]

The gift he might have without asking is ostensibly the first stanza's "joie"— the gift persistently requested, for example, by the lover of *Vergier*—but elision of the pronoun means that it is ambiguous in gender and could also refer to his lady, her *merci*, Love, Hope, or that which he desires. This last formulation parallels B14's refrain, which the opening of B19's B section musically resembles (cf. B19, m. 18, and B14, mm. 33–34, in example 4.10), in which Love *has* given the lady "mon cuer, m'amour et quanque je desir." In B14 this is seeing and hearing her lover—that is, honorable *merci*. In B19 the male lover voices a conceptual slippage of the desired object from the lady, to Love, to Hope, and to *merci*, the receipt of which (unlike the receipt of the lady herself) depends solely on the lover's own mental attitude.[165] Seeing and hearing is also what one does with poetry and music, which Machaut proposes as the ultimate surrogate for erotic desire and means of achieving a serene life. Hope thus embodies the solution to bad things that happen (or good things that don't happen): she is the *Remede de Fortune*. Her relation to the lady is to replace her as the sovereign perfection because she (unlike the lady and the lover) is not prey to Fortune. It is into Fortune's dark and shadowy light that we now step.

164. The obduracy—"durté"—of the lady is musically mirrored in the use of the note c♯, because the medieval equivalent of what we would term a sharp sign was borrowed from the sign for the "b-mi" or "hard b" (b-durum).

165. This song effectively lyricizes the situation just before that described in *Vergier*, ll. 769–86, when Desire renews his attack on the lover and causes him to ask for "joie." Significantly, B19 is one of the very few balades in the duplex balade form (that is, with a B section that, like the A section, repeats and has *ouvert* and *clos* cadences), strongly resembling in formal terms Hope's "baladelle," *En amer* (RF4).

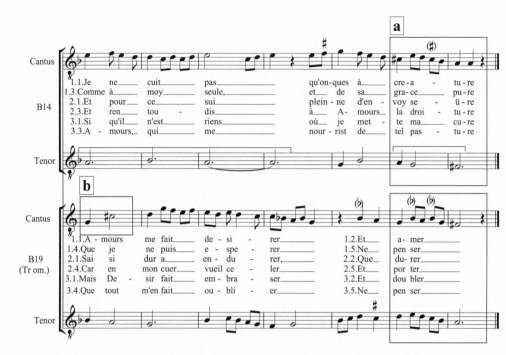

Example 4.9. *Je ne cuit pas* (B14) and *Amour m'a fait* (B19) compared: a. mm. 5–7, where B19's tenor resembles B14's cantus, and vice versa; b. unusual melodic interval for "Amours" at the outset of B19.

Example 4.10. Shared motive between opening of the refrain in *Je ne cuit pas* (B14) and *Amour m'a fait* (B19), m. 18.

5

Fortune

Suffering

Hope is central to Machaut's courtly doctrine, since it enables the lover to operate at a level of self-sufficiency whatever might be happening in the world outside his own imagination. Hope is presented as the "remede de Fortune," the remedy for mischance, the cure for ill luck. In Machaut's works Fortune is always a negative force, in whose power the desiring subject lies unless mental efforts in forging a primary relationship with Hope place him or her beyond it. Failure in the poetics of Hope results when the subject takes undue account of the fluctuating and varied external events that Fortune produces, and over which the subject has no control. In the extensive imagery associated with this pagan goddess, the subject then becomes trapped in Fortune's ever-turning wheel, or is blown about in the leaky boat of his or her own subjectivity on the tempestuous seas of life. An ever present danger is that the desiring subject will react to events and become changeable, unstable, and full of contradictions, starting to mirror the attributes of this negative goddess. When that desiring subject is female, such potential assimilation to Fortune is even clearer, prompting stereotypical misogyny from clerical voices in Machaut's texts, although the identification of these voices with Machaut's own is arguably undercut by narrative and other broader contexts.

Machaut's Fortune is modeled after the traditional representation of the goddess, drawing largely on the pagan version impersonated by Lady Philosophy in Boethius's *Consolation,* book 2. Following the imprecations of Hope in the *Remede,* this chapter seeks to understand the workings of Fortune through an examination of several of her multiple presentations in Machaut's music and poetry. First, a pair of notated balades will be shown to contain the kernel of knowledge about Fortune, first propounded didactically by a male cleric and then staged emotionally through the voicing of female grief. One of Machaut's more widely copied motets replicates this twofold presentation on the theme of Fortune using the motet genre's typical means of enacting simultaneous texts in a conceptual dialogue that demands contemplation. As well as being found in these lyric presentations, Fortune is a central figure in both the *Remede* and the *Voir dit,* represented iconographically and detailed at length in both poems. If Hope is the remedy for Fortune's depredations in the *Remede,* the *Voir dit* tells instead of Fortune's rule over the kingdom of tale-telling and gossip. Fortune's relation to slander on the one hand and fame on the other is shown by her real power in a courtly world of hearsay and written messages. Looking again at the two balades on the subject of Fortune in the music section, which are examined at the beginning of the chapter, reveals that they bookend a longer sequence of poems in the *Loange* which specifically connect Fortune with Evil Tongue. The problematic capacity of literature both to aid and to counter Fortune's power by telling tales of its own is discussed in the last part of this chapter.

Fortune Observed and Experienced

In chapter 4 the music section was shown to hold a complementary pair of adjacent balades that distilled the correct role of Hope in noble loving from male and female perspectives. Fortune's actions are similarly epitomized in a pair of music section balades, *Il m'est avis* (B22) and *De Fortune* (B23), which offer complementary perspectives on the power of Fortune, one voiced by a man and the other by a woman (see figure 5.1).[1] *Il m'est avis* (B22) is clerkly and sententious, a statement of an objective understanding (*entendement*) of Fortune's power. *De Fortune* (B23) is, by contrast, a dynamic personal testimony, whose anguished tone reflects its female speaker's firsthand emotional experience (*sentement*) of being subject to the goddess. Most of the manuscript sources duplicate these balades, both presenting them adjacently in the music section and also using them to bookend a short sequence of poetry in the unnotated *Loange* (as Lo188 and Lo195). The lyrics in the *Loange* sequence between Lo188 and Lo195 are interrelated formally by shared rhymes and key words, and thematically by their treatment of Fortune and rumor, or gossip, about infidelity (the *mesdisans*) from various different subject positions; but only these two lyrics from the *Loange* sequence also receive a musical setting.[2]

---

1. In the music section of manuscript C they occur separately in the disordered section that Ursula Günther has termed CII; see Lawrence Earp, *Guillaume de Machaut: A Guide to Research* (New York, 1995), 78. They are also separated in the musical balade section of manuscript E.

2. Manuscript G lacks the larger sequence from the *Loange* within which B22 and B23 normally occur. Manuscript E transmits the sequence but typically prunes the potential duplicates, B22 and B23, from the *Loange* as well as separating these lyrics in the notated section.

B21 (= Lo188)

1.1 Il m'est avis qu'il n'est dons de Nature,
1.2 Com bons qu'il soit, que nuls prise à ce jour,
1.3 Se la clarté tenebreuse et obscure
1.4 De Fortune ne li donne couleur;
1.5 Ja soit ce que seürté
1.6 Ne soit en li, amour ne loyauté.
1.7 Mais je ne voy homme amé ne chiery,
R Se Fortune ne le tient à amy.

2.1 Si bien ne sont fors vent et aventure,
2.2 Donné à faute, et tollut par irour;
2.3 On la doit croire où elle se parjure,
2.4 Car de mentir est sa plus grant honnour.
2.5 C'est.j. monstre envolepé
2.6 De boneür, plein de maleürté;
2.7 Car nuls n'a pris, tant ait de bien en li,
R Se Fortune ne le tient à amy.

3.1 Si me merveil comment Raisons endure
3.2 Si longuement à durer ceste errour,
3.3 Car les vertus sont à desconfiture
3.4 Par les vices qui regnent com signour.
3.5 Et qui vuet avoir le gré
3.6 De ceaus qui sont et estre en haut degré,
3.7 Il pert son temps et puet bien dire: "eimmy"
R Se Fortune ne le tient à amy.

B23 (= Lo195)

1.1 De Fortune me doy pleindre et loer,
1.2 Ce m'est avis, plus qu'autre creature;
1.3 Car quant premiers encommencay l'amer,
1.4 Mon cuer, m'amour, ma pensée, ma cure
1.5 Mist si bien à mon plaisir
1.6 Qu'à souhaidier peüsse je faillir,
1.7 N'en ce monde ne fust mie trouvée
R Dame qui fust si tres bien assenée.

2.1 Car je ne puis penser n'imaginer
2.2 Ne dedens moy trouver qu'onques Nature
2.3 De quanqu'on puet bel et bon*appeller
2.4 Peüst faire plus parfaite figure
2.5 De celui,**où mi desir
2.6 Sont et seront à tous jours sans partir;
2.7 Et pour ce croy qu'onques mais ne fut née
R Dame qui fust si tres bien assenée.

3.1 Lasse! or ne puis en ce point demourer,
3.2 Car Fortune qui onques n'est seüre
3.3 Sa roe vuet encontre moy tourner
3.4 Pour mon las cuer mettre à desconfiture.
3.5 Mais en foy, jusqu'au mourir
3.6 Mon dous amy vueil amer et chierir,
3.7 Qu'onques ne dut avoir fausse pensée
R Dame qui fust si tres bien assenée.

It is my opinion that there is no gift of Nature, however good it might be, that anyone would prize today if the shadowy and dark light of Fortune did not give it color, however much certainty, love, or loyalty might be in it. But I see no man loved or cherished, *if Fortune does not hold him to be a friend.*
Such goods are nothing but wind and chance, wrongly bestowed and withdrawn in anger; she [Fortune] should be believed when she perjures herself, for lying is her greatest honor. She is a monster, enveloped in happiness, but full of misery; for no one has any value, however much good is in him, *if Fortune does not hold him to be a friend.*
Thus I marvel at how Reason bears this error for so long, because the virtues are discomfited by the vices who rule as lords. And whoever wants to have the favor of those who are (or wants himself to be) of high degree is wasting his time and might as well say "ah me!" *if Fortune does not hold him to be a friend.*

Fortune I should blame and praise in my opinion more than any other creature; for when I first began to love him, I placed my heart, my love, my thoughts, and my care so completely at my pleasure that I could not have failed to wish that in this world there would not be found *a lady so well provided for.*
For I cannot think or imagine or find within myself that Nature would be able to fashion, from whatever is called handsome and good, a more perfect figure than him in whom my desires are and shall be forever, without leaving. And because of this I believe that *a lady so well provided for* was never born.
Alas! Now I cannot remain at this point because Fortune, in whom there is certainty, wants to turn her wheel against me in order to place my poor heart in discomfort. But in faith even unto death I wish to love and cherish my sweet friend, because *a lady so well provided for* ought never to have a false thought.

* bon et bel *Loange.*
** Comme est cils *Loange.*

Figure 5.1. Texts and translations of *Il m'est avis* (B22) and *De Fortune* (B23).

In the ordering of the balades in the music section, B22 and B23 are the first two that name Fortune. The clerkly *je* of *Il m'est avis* (B22) describes Fortune's public domain. As an individual lyric, it has been considered "rather flat" with "no real development throughout the poem"; the impersonal first-person presence serves "to generalize rather than to particularize" the poem, which is "a moral reflection on Fortune and the state of the world, entirely traditional."[3] Leonard W. Johnson argues that because of the conventionality and flatness of B22, its lyricism lies purely in the fact of its musical setting. I would argue both that the musicalization of this lyric contributes more and in more ways to its meaning than Johnson allows, and that it is not the fact of a musical setting that lifts it above the merely conventional. In the context of Machaut's ordered book, B22 transcends its seeming conventionality because its meanings are not restricted to its own boundaries as an individual lyric. Instead it informs, complements, and is informed by the notated balade that follows, B23. Together this pair forms a more complex lyric expression than either could articulate as an individual item.[4] The reader is alerted to the fact of their pairing by the introduction of a new topic in the notated balades, broached impressively by a four-voice work (the first in the balade section of the manuscript) which occupies an entire opening, while most songs fit on a single side of a folio.[5] This new topic continues to be explored in the following balade; the relationship between B22 and B23 is furthered by the sharing of significant words (especially rhyme words) and each other's incipit texts.[6]

The objectivity of the speaker in B22 is established by the opening phrase, "Il m'est avis" (in my opinion), and reinforced by his scholarly vocabulary (using the rhetorical term "color" as a verb) and the preponderance of verbs that are impersonal or have a generalized or personified subject.[7] The only first-person verb is in the penultimate line of the first stanza (l. 1.7), where the author introduces the refrain as his own objective and authoritative observation of the world: "I see no man loved or cherished, *if Fortune does not hold him to be a friend*" (ll. 1.7–8). Any gift of Nature, he claims, "however good it might be [*soit*]" (l. 1.2), is worthless until colored by Fortune's "dark light" (l. 1.3), one of her various paradoxical aspects: her cheery outside masks a

3. See Leonard W. Johnson, *Poets as Players: Theme and Variation in Late Medieval French Poetry* (Stanford, 1990), 41–54, where it is discussed first among five poems that exemplify Machaut's take on the theme of Fortune.

4. This statement holds true also for their connections with the broader *Loange* sequence that they demarcate. See my discussion later in this chapter.

5. See A, ff. 464v–465r. In the earliest source, C, B22 and B23 occur in the disordered second part (so-called CII) and show evidence of copying problems (B23 requires an impossible page turn; B22 has only the cantus entered on the staves and no space left for the triplum).

6. For more detail, see Elizabeth Eva Leach, "Fortune's Demesne: The Interrelation of Text and Music in Machaut's *Il mest avis* (B22), *De fortune* (B23), and Two Related Anonymous Balades," *Early Music History* 19 (2000): 47–79.

7. These include "nulz," "qui," "homme," "Fortune," "Raison," "les vertus," "les vices."

miserable interior (ll. 2.5–6), and lying is her greatest honor (l. 2.4). Her world is a topsy-turvy one in which the virtues are discomfited and the vices reign. The clerkly speaker shows his erudition in drawing on earlier descriptions of Fortune and her actions deriving from Philosophy's impersonation of her in book 2 of Boethius's *Consolation of Philosophy*.[8]

By contrast *De Fortune* (B23) is set in Fortune's internal, erotic, and private world; her actions affect the poem's first-person speaker, who is involved as a lover-protagonist. The speaker's gender is initially withheld: only the feminine agreement of the rhyme word just before the first refrain ("trouvée") reveals that she is the lady who is described in the refrain as "si tres bien assenée" ("so well provided for," or—as it might also be translated—"so very fortunate").[9] The opening line promises both blame and praise of Fortune, and in the first two stanzas the lady describes her love for a man who is the most perfect figure Nature could fashion out of whatever is called good or beautiful (ll. 2.1–4), as if praising Fortune.[10] The opening promise of blame, however, colors this praise with an expectation that is finally satisfied in the third stanza as the lady cries "alas" ("Lasse!"; l. 3.1). This bears out the clerkly advice of B22: any of Nature's gifts, however good it might be, will be colored by Fortune, and unless Fortune holds herself one's friend, the gift will have neither love nor loyalty in it (l. 1.6), and one might as well cry "ah me!" (l. 3.7).

The lady of B23 implies that she believes her lover to be unfaithful.[11] At the end of the poem, however, she berates herself for the unworthiness of this thought, vowing to continue loving and cherishing her sweet friend even unto death, because "a lady so well provided for ought never to have a false thought" (ll. 3.6–8). This provides another verbal link to B22, in which the authorial voice sees no man loved or cherished ("je ne voy homme *amé ne chiery*"; l. 1.7) unless Fortune holds him her "friend" (*amy*).[12] In B23 the lady will continue to love

8. See Howard Rollin Patch, "Fortuna in Old French Literature," *Smith College Studies in Modern Languages* 4 (1923): 1–45; idem, *The Goddess Fortuna in Mediaeval Literature* (Cambridge, 1927); Tony Hunt, "The Christianization of Fortune," *Nottingham French Studies* 38 (1999): 95–113.

9. The fact that the speaker's beloved is male is also hidden; the male direct object pronoun in line 1.3 is elided ("quant premiers encommancay l'amer") so as to appear effectively gender neutral.

10. The opening verbs are ambiguous: the phrase could mean "I must blame Fortune and praise [her]" but also "I must blame Fortune and yet be in her service."

11. Johnson comments that "we are not told exactly what her 'desconfiture' is, but one can only assume that it is some amorous *mis*fortune, perhaps her lover's absence" (Leonard W. Johnson, "'Nouviaus dis amoureux plaisans': Variation as Innovation in Guillaume de Machaut," in *Musique naturelle et musique artificielle: In memoriam Gustave Reese*, ed. Mary Beth Winn [Montreal, 1979], 45). That it is more than this is, I think, connoted by the relationship between the two texts, which implies a change (reported, if not real) in the man's love.

12. This was significantly the only *je* subject moment in the otherwise deeply impersonal B22, and although "homme" (man) is general in the context of B22, it is personalized through its connection with the *amis* of the lady in B23, whom she wishes to love and cherish. In B22 it is the holder of

and cherish her "friend." This parallel, together with the fact that B23's lady vacillates between thinking ill and good thoughts about her lover, surreptitiously posits an equation between her potential changeability and that of Fortune.[13]

Clerical Authority: *Il m'est avis*

As in other cases of duplication between the *Loange* and music sections, the musical setting adds layers of meaning to the texts that further enrich the presentation of the aspect of courtly doctrine outlined. Commentators often see musical form as merely subservient to verse form or, where it differs, as simply inept text-setting.[14] For example, Johnson comments only that B22's musical setting "underlines the structure of the strophe" by dividing it in two parts after line 4.[15] This is true as far as it goes, which is merely to describe the large-scale bipartite form of all balades. What Johnson fails to note is that the musical segmentation of the lines of text *within* those two large sections is actually rather unconventional, and allows the music to read the poem *against* its versification. The nature of this unconventionality resembles that seen in another of Machaut's notated lyrics, *De toutes flours* (B31), which is significantly also on the subject of Fortune, and where the musical setting serves the same subversive purpose, similarly executed: strong musical cadences are placed at the caesuras of all lines, while not all poetic line ends are similarly marked.[16]

B22 and B23 exemplify one of Machaut's most popular verse forms—three eight-line stanzas rhyming ababccdD, all decasyllables except for each fifth line (the so-called *vers coupé*), which has only seven syllables. In B22's A section, the rhyme words at the end of lines 1 and 3 occur musically mid-phrase, with short note values on an unstable imperfect sonority. The three musical phrases

Nature's gift who must be the *amis* of Fortune. In B23 it is the *amis* who is the gift. Since gift ("dons") is a masculine noun in B22, the gift is masculine; it therefore makes sense for B23's *je* to be a woman lamenting the spoiling of her gift (that is, her male lover) by Fortune's wheel-turning antics.

13. Such an assimilation to Fortune of inconstant lovers—swayed by hearsay—will be seen further in the discussion of the *Voir dit*.

14. See the discussion of the historiography of studies of text-setting in chapter 2.

15. See Johnson, "Nouviaus dis amoureux plaisans," 43. The musical A section with the *ouvert* cadence and its repeat with the *clos* cadence sets lines 1–4, and then a second musical section sets the rest of the text and the refrain.

16. Musical cadences are usually indicated by at least two of the following elements: a directed progression, a rest in the texted voice, or a held note in one or more voices. Johnson (ibid., 51–54) treats *De toutes flours* (B31) as the culmination of his discussion of Fortune in Machaut's lyrics, admirably bringing out its manifold poetic subtleties. Nevertheless, his diagnosis of the disparity between the conventionality of B22 and the subtlety of B31 is questionable when their similar musicalization is considered. See the discussion of B31 in Elizabeth Eva Leach, "Counterpoint as an Interpretative Tool: The Case of Guillaume de Machaut's *De toutes flours* (B31)," *Music Analysis* 19 (2000): 321–51. B31 further complements B22 and B23 by offering a third subject position, that of a male lover who sees his female beloved as the remaining "rose" in Fortune's garden. Fearful of Fortune's power to blast her, he nevertheless attests enduring loyalty in each stanza's refrain: "after her I will never seek another."

Section	musical phrase	suppressed **rhyme**	emphasized pseudo-rhyme	<u>**emphasized rhyme**</u>
A	1		Il m'est <u>avis</u>	
	2	qu'il n'est dons de **Nature,**	Com bons qu'il <u>soit</u>	
	3	que nuls prise à ce **jour,**		
A'	4 (=1)		Se la <u>clarté</u>	
	5 (=2)	tenebreuse et **obscure**	De <u>Fortune</u>	
	6 (=3')			ne li donne **coulour;**
B	7	Ja soit ce que **seürté**	Ne soit en <u>li,</u>	
	8	amour ne **loyauté**	Mais je ne <u>voy</u>	
	9			home amé ne **chiery**
R	10		Se <u>Fortune</u>	
	11			ne le tient à **amy.**

Figure 5.2. Musical emphasis of non-rhyme words and suppression of rhymes in *Il m'est avis* (B22) (rhyme words shown in **bold** and musically emphasized words <u>underlined</u>).

of the A section thus set, (1) the first four syllables, (2) the ten syllables from the caesura of line 1 to the caesura of line 2, and (3) the final six syllables of line 2. Although the *ouvert* cadence is a relatively long, held note (a breve), its sonority quality is imperfect, so that it does not provide a true point of musical rest. The rhyme words at the end of line 4 (respectively "coulour," "honnour," and "signour" at the *clos* cadence at the end of the A section in the three stanzas) are therefore the first in each stanza to coincide with a musically emphasized phrase-end cadence. In the B section, this plan of not matching musical phrases to poetic lines continues: the only poetic rhyme words to coincide with musical phrase-end cadences are those of lines 7 and 8, the end of musical sections B and R respectively. Figure 5.2 summarizes the first stanza as segmented by musical cadences.

In balade settings by Machaut and his contemporaries, rhyme words normally coincide with the ends of musical phrases. The offsetting of musical and poetic structures in B22 brings certain words to prominence by treating them as if they were rhyme words. Two of these words in B22's first stanza anticipate the poem's own later rhymes: the end of the first musical phrase in the second performance of the A section sets "clarté," which anticipates the c-rhyme; the end of the first phrase of the B section sets "li," which anticipates the d-rhyme.[17] Removing any musical security as to the structure of the poem in this way reflects the disruptive actions of Fortune herself. This deceptiveness is increased by the proportions of the A section (see example 5.1).

17. The anticipation of rhymes in the first stanza is also found in *De toutes flours* (B31). See Leach, "Counterpoint as an Interpretative Tool."

Example 5.1. *Il m'est avis* (B22) complete, with stanza 1 underlaid. a. caesura ll. 2 and 4 (midpoint of the A section); b. caesura of the refrain line.

The third phrase is as long (roughly so in the first performance of the A section, exactly in the second) as the preceding two phrases together, so that the expectation of a normal bipartite A section, setting two poetic lines in two poetic phrases, is deceptively met by the cadence in measure 15, which sounds like the end of the first poetic line (example 5.1, box a). It is here in the first stanza

Example 5.1. (*Continued*)

of B22 that the words "De Fortune" occur, both emphasizing Fortune's sovereign power and providing a link to the incipit text of B23.

The effects of the musical setting include such formal play with sounds and rhymes but also affect issues of meaning. The setting of the pre-caesural incipit

"Il m'est avis" to the opening musical phrase (mm. 1–9) emphasizes the clerkly nature of the balade that is to follow. Because every time Fortune is invoked her name is followed by a lyric caesura, the musical structure places "Fortune" first at the cadence at the midpoint of the second performance of the A section (the end of the second musical phrase, mm. 14–16; example 5.1, box a) in the first stanza, and subsequently in all stanzas at the first cadence in the refrain (mm. 44–45; example 5.1, box b).[18] The former has already been mentioned; the naming of Fortune in the refrain makes a musical rhyme with the *clos,* a feature usual for a final cadence, perpetrating a deceit which suggests that this cadence is the very end of the piece (when it isn't). In both places the cadence at "Fortune" is immediately followed by a melisma on the negative particle "ne," reiterating the final syllable of Fortune and linking her with the negativity that she represents. Obviously this feature is inherent even in a mere reading of the poetic text, but the musical setting brings it out particularly by using the ability of a melisma to prolong a text syllable temporally (mm. 45–48). In the musical setting, too, Fortune is far more prominent aurally in the first stanza than Nature, whose name forms the first rhyme word. On the page or read aloud, "Nature" is an emphasized rhyme word, a stopping point; but in the musical setting, caesural Fortune is contrapuntally emphasized, while Nature's a-rhyme is hidden away mid-phrase, set to an imperfect sonority, its status as a line end articulated only by the shortest possible rest after it. Fortune thus appears to be what she is not: a stable rhyme word. The music presents us with Fortune deceiving; she is not as stable as she seems or as she sounds.

The Lady Experiences (and Becomes) Fortune: *De Fortune*

The contrasting subject positions and poetic complementarity between B22 and B23 are reflected in their rather different musical settings. Without their poetic texts, it would be difficult to identify these balades as a specific pair: they are in contrasting vocal arrangements, have different tonal emphases, melodic contours, and ways of ornamenting and elaborating their basic directed progressions; they are in contrasting mensurations and allot different proportions to their major sections.[19] They share only those rhythmic figures

18. Johnson, "Nouviaus dis amoureux plaisans," 53, comments on the caesural placement of the word "Fortune" in B31, saying that "by its position, followed in each case...by a lyric caesura[,]...it becomes the epicenter of the poem." He does not note the similarly between B31 and B22 in this regard, having decided that B22 is irredeemably conventional. In fact both balades similarly reflect Fortune in their versificationally disruptive musical settings.

19. B22 has a relatively long A section (twenty-five breves with *ouvert,* thirty-one with *clos*) and very short B and R sections (eleven plus eleven breves). Each of the sections in the balade's second half is thus less than half as long as either of the performances of the A section. Its overall proportions in breves are fifty-six to twenty-two (that is, the first "half" of each stanza is over two and a half times as long as the second). In B23 the B and R sections together (twenty plus fifteen, totaling thirty-five breves) are longer than even the A section with its longer *clos* ending

that are pervasive in the work of Machaut and his contemporaries, especially variously contoured ornamental groups of four minims. Nevertheless, their poetic pairing on the one hand lends a certain emphasis to the sharing of these otherwise conventional and widespread features, and, on the other hand, enables their differences to be perceived (like those of the poems) as significant complementarities rather than mere dissimilarities.[20]

In B22 relatively conventional sentiments are set subversively and with great complexity: the placing of cadences disrupts the regular poetic verse structure. By contrast, the dynamic and shifting poetry of B23 is set to musical phrases that correspond to the lines of the poetic text (see example 5.2).[21] This generates the reverse form of disruption to that in B22, because the music responds as if the poetry were more line-bound. Musical breaks therefore occur at places where there is no corresponding syntactical or sense break in the poem, for example, at the end of line 4 in the first two stanzas. This is the place of the most major musical articulation—the end of section A—and has a cadence so terminal that it will eventually also serve for the very end of the song.[22] Although this might just seem sloppy—as if the music-text relations were based on an abstract ideal of number rather than any semantic projection—comparison to other Fortune pieces such as *Qui es / Ha! Fortune* (M8; discussed later in this chapter) in the context of the more ordinarily "semantic" setting of most other songs by Machaut suggests that this was a specific means of projecting Fortune's disruptive force to singers and listeners alike.

The opening melisma of *De Fortune* (B23) has a further element of musical disruption (example 5.2, box a). Its tenor line uncharacteristically sticks on a single pitch (G) and intersperses its repeated soundings of this pitch with rests. The upper voice moves in the intervals 5p–6i–5p–4d–3i–2d, the melody line being inflected by the tenor G into a fully varied sequence of sonorities—perfect (p), imperfect (i), perfect, dissonant (d), imperfect, dissonant. The stability of the G, like the fulcrum of a wheel, paradoxically makes the melody spun around it into a rotating sequence of harmonic qualities. Although the composite rhythm of all voices together is that of continuous minims (eighth notes

---

(twenty-nine breves). Its overall proportions in breves are fifty-three to thirty-five (the first half is only just over one and a half times as long as the second).

20. Even the conventional groups can then, however, become aurally suggestive. For example, the opening figure (musical notes 2–9) of the triplum in B22 sounds rather like the end of the first poetic line in the cantus (mm. 5–6: "plaindre et loer") of B23.

21. Only line 5 is not cadentially end-stopped, with a held imperfect sonority for its last syllable in measure 18 connecting it musically into the start of line 6 with a cadence to F/f in measure 19. This creates another twelve-breve phrase (mm. 17–21), which makes particular sense in the second stanza, when line 5 is enjambed.

22. B23 emphasizes caesural words only in lines 2 and 4, and this is done not by the clear held resolutions that set the caesuras in B22, but by a held imperfect sonority in the middle of the second musical phrase. In stanzas 1 and 3, the second line has at this point "Ce m'est avis" and "Car Fortune," respectively encapsulating the two incipits of B22 and B23.

Example 5.2. *De Fortune* (B23) complete, with stanza 1 underlaid. a. "wheel" motive;
b. unstable point of "durance."

in the transcription), the individual voices are syncopated from the second
measure—the triplum offset by a minim (eighth note) and the cantus by a semibreve (quarter note)—giving this seeming regularity a timbrally unbalanced
presentation. Musicologists have compared this odd configuration to the sound
either of a millwheel (by analogy with a similar use in a near-contemporary

Example 5.2. (*Continued*)

motet) or the irregular winding of a hurdy-gurdy, with the wheel in either case readily being identified with that of Fortune.[23] At this degree of historical

23. See Lorenz Welker, "Guillaume de Machaut, das romantische Lied und die Jungfrau Maria," in *Annäherungen: Festschrift für Jürg Stenzl zum 65. Geburtstag*, ed. Ulrich Mosch,

remove, musical hermeneutics at such a detailed level is tricky, but both readings seem possible, as does the alternative idea that the unusual tenor merely sets up the opening pain of the singer by picturing sighing through the intake of breath that rests allow.[24]

When the tenor tone changes, the held sonority on the sixth syllable ("doy"; m. 4; example 5.2, box b) is also striking and unusual. Aurally the imperfect sonority, held for such a long note, breaks up the flow of the line with a point of durational rest (a hold) that is, as a sonority type, unstable (an imperfect sonority), wanting to resolve to the very note (G) that had dominated the opening three measures (six breves) of the tenor. A better musical depiction of enduring instability would be hard to envisage. Visually, the use of a long—a square note with a downward-pointing stem on the right-hand side—in all voices at this point (m. 4; "doy") would have broken up the flow for contemporary singers expecting to see only shorter note values. This long marks something odd and throws up another deception: the long is a note shape usually reserved for the final note of a song, yet this is far from being the end.[25]

On Fortune's Tempestuous Seas: *Qui es promesses / Ha! Fortune / Et non est qui adjuvet*

If the geographical and temporal spread of the manuscripts that transmit them is any indication, laments and songs complaining about Fortune or otherwise associated with her seem to have been particularly popular throughout the Middle Ages. As well as being copied in the Machaut manuscripts, B22 survives in one other notated source, and B23—whose mention of Fortune in the incipit text may have provided a particular draw to scribes—is known from five other notated sources, a further text manuscript, and a printed text anthology.[26] B23 thus ranks among Machaut's most widely transmitted songs and is one of the most extensively copied songs of the century.[27] Given such

---

Matthias Schmidt, and Silvia Wälli (Saarbrücken, 2007), 70–87. Alan H. Nelson, "Mechanical Wheels of Fortune, 1100–1547," *Journal of the Warburg and Courtauld Institutes* 43 (1980): 227, notes that depictions of Fortune's wheel in the Middle Ages were modeled not on cartwheels but on those used as winches, as millwheels, or for spinning.

24. This said, the text lacks reference to burning, which is usually the accompanying topos in songs with sighs. See chapter 4, note 30.

25. For a similar argument about the visual force of longs in Machaut's songs, see the comments on the refrain of *Pour ce que tous* (B12) in Anne Stone, "Music Writing and Poetic Voice in Machaut: Some Remarks on B12 and B14," in *Machaut's Music: New Interpretations*, ed. Elizabeth Eva Leach (Woodbridge, 2003), 125–38. As tenors in motets are often organized at a far higher durational level than their upper parts, longs are found more frequently in motet upper voices than in those of songs in the *formes fixes*.

26. See Earp, *Guillaume de Machaut*, 328 (B22) and 309 (B23). For songs based on B22 and B23, see Leach, "Fortune's Demesne," 63–75. B23 received a Latin contrafact text, "Rubus ardens," in **Str**, and the printed copy in **Jp** adapts the lyric to make all lines the same length and the speaker a man.

27. It may have inspired the rondeau in **Vi**, no. 6, "De fortune plaindre me doy."

TRIPLUM

1. Qui es promesses de Fortune se fie,
2. Et es richesses de ses dons s'asseüre,
3. Ou cil qui croit qu'elle soit tant s'amie,
4. Que pour li soit en riens ferme ou seüre,
5. Il est trop folz, car elle est non seüre:
6. Sans foy, sans loy, sans droit, et sans mesure;
7. C'est fiens couvers de riche couverture,
8. Qui dehors luist et dedens est ordure,
9. Une ydole est de fausse pourtraiture,
10. Où nuls ne doit croire ne mettre cure.
11. Sa contenance en vertu pas ne dure,
12. Car c'est tous vens; ne riens qu'elle figure
13. Ne puet estre fors de fausse figure.
14. Et li siens sont toudis en aventure
15. De trebuchier, car par droite nature
16. La desloyal renoie parjure.
17. Fausse traitre, perverse et mere sure,
18. Oint et puis point de si mortel pointure,
19. Que ceaus qui sont fait de sa norriture
20. En traïson, met a desconfiture.

MOTETUS

1. Ha! Fortune, trop sui mis loing de port,
2. Quant en la mer m'as mis sans aviron,
3. En .i. batel, petit, plat, et sans bort,
4. Foible, pourri, sans voile et environ;
5. Sont tuit li vent contraire pour ma mort,
6. Si qu'il n'i a confort ne garison,
7. Mercy, n'espoir, ne deschaper ressort,
8. Ne riens de bien pour moy. Car sans raison
9. Je voy venir la mort amere a tort
10. Preste de moy mettre à destruction.
11. Mais celle mort reçoi je par ton sort,
12. Fausse fortune, et par ta traïson.

(Edition based on MS **C**).

TRANSLATION

Triplum: Whoever trusts in the promises of Fortune and is assured of the riches of her gifts or believes that she might be such a friend as to prove firm and sure in anything is a complete fool, because she is not secure: lacking faith, law, rectitude, and moderation, she is a fiend covered with a rich covering, who shines outside and inside is shit; she is an idol falsely represented in which no one should believe or place any care. Her countenance in virtue does not last, for it is all wind; nor can anything that she depicts be anything except a false depiction. And her people are always stumbling on their way, because, on account of her rightful nature, the disloyal one reneges and perjures herself. False traitor, perverse and bitter mother; she unctures and then punctures with such a fatal puncture that those who are made in treason by her nursing are placed in discomfort.

Motetus: Hey, Fortune! I have put too far from port, because thou hast cast me in the sea without oars in a little flat boat with no sides, weak, rotting, without a sail and surrounded by all the contrary winds that will cause my death if I do not have any comfort or cure, *merci*, hope, or resort to escape, nor [do I have] anything good. For without reason I see bitter death wrongfully coming near to me to destroy me. But this death I receive through thy caprice, false Fortune, and by thy treason.

Figure 5.3. Texts and translations of *Qui es / Ha! Fortune / Et non est* (M8).

TENOR
Et non est qui adiuuet

And there is none who might help.

Plainsong source: responsory for various
feasts in Passiontide and Lent

Circumdederunt me viri mendaces, sine
causa flagellis ceciderunt me: sed tu, Domine defensor, vindica me. V. *Quoniam tribu-
latio proxima est, et non est qui adiuvet.*

Lying men have surrounded me, without
cause they have struck me with whips: by
You, Lord my defender, avenge me. V. For
trouble is near, and there is no one to help.

Biblical source: Ps. 21

12. ne discesseris a me: *Quoniam tribula-
tio proxima est*: quoniam *non est qui
adiuvet.*

12. Do not depart from me. For tribulation
is near, since there is no one who may
help me.

13. *Circumdederunt me* vituli multi: tauri
pingues obsederunt me.

13. Many calves have surrounded me; fat
bulls have besieged me.

...

...

17. Quoniam *circumdederunt me* canes
multi: concilium malignantium obsedit
me. Foderunt manus meas et pedes
meos

17. For many dogs have surrounded me. The
council of the malicious has besieged me.
They have pierced my hands and feet.

(Literal translation from the Vulgate Latin by Ronald
L. Conte Jr. See www.sacredbible.org/studybible/OT-
21_Psalms.htm.)

Figure 5.3. (*Continued*)

a precedent, it is unsurprising that the only Machaut motet to evince wider
transmission outside the Machaut sources is the only one that also directly
addresses Fortune: *Qui es / Ha! Fortune* (M8).[28]

M8 has a number of similarities to the pair of motets B22 and B23; in effect it presents their sequential voices simultaneously. In the sequence of the
motets, it is the first to mention Fortune at any length and the only motet in
which Fortune is the clear subject of both upper voices (see figure 5.3 and
example 5.3).[29] It uses the same surface mensuration as B23, a striking duple
division of both semibreve and breve (albeit in M8 with the higher-level organization of a triple long, when B23 typically has irregular, but mainly duple,
modus organization).[30] It is also opens tonally on D (like B23), although

28. The motetus of *He! Mors / Fine* (M3) mentions Fortune in passing, and she is also mentioned in the motetus texts of *Helas! pour quoy virent / Corde* (M12) and *Maugré mon cuer / De
ma dolour* (M14). While none of these is addressed directly to the goddess, it has been suggested
that her tricks are implied in the details of the voice crossing in the last two; see Anna Zayaruznaya, "'She has a Wheel that Turns…': Crossed and Contradictory Voices in Machaut's Motets,"
Early Music History (2009): 185–240.

29. And see note 28.

30. The arguments for irregular modus organization in songs are made in David Maw, "'Trespasser mesure': Meter in Machaut's Polyphonic Songs," *Journal of Musicology* 21 (2004): 46–
126. In the modern edition this means that M8 effectively has measures of three half notes, with

its final cadence is on *F*, the goal of the opening part of B22. Like those balades, M8 is well represented (for Machaut's works) in wider fourteenth-century manuscript transmission, including (as with B23) the unusual attachment of Machaut's name to one copy (in this case a text-only source now in Stockholm).[31] With musical notation M8 occurs in **CaB** and **Iv**, and originally also in **Trém** (of which now only the index survives).[32] Literary evidence suggests that Chaucer knew at least the triplum text, since the knight's tirade against Fortune in *The Book of the Duchess* (ll. 618-51) uses several of its lines.[33] Furthermore, a technical aspect of its musical setting is cited in a manuscript of the so-called *ars nova* treatise (*F-Pn*, lat. 14741), copied in a book that formerly belonged to the abbey of St.-Victor in Paris.[34]

The triplum poem is akin to the description of Fortune in B22 and adopts a similar clerkly tone: "Whoever trusts in the promises of Fortune and is assured of the riches of her gifts or believes that she might be such a friend as to prove firm and sure in anything is a complete fool." Fortune's gifts ("dons") and

---

each of these divided into two quarter notes and each of those in turn being subject to a duple division into two eighth notes. This mensuration pairs it with *J'ay tant / Lasse!* (M7), the first motet in the ordered sequence to use this mensuration. This motet is discussed further in this chapter.

31. Earp, *Guillaume de Machaut*, 114, MS [46]; **St** dates from after 1477. The rubric introduces the triplum with "Tresble Guillaume de Marchant." Margaret Switten, "L'Oeuvre poético-musicale de Machaut: Paroles sans musique ou de la musique avant toute chose?," in *Guillaume de Machaut: 1300–2000. Actes du Colloque de la Sorbonne 28–29 septembre 2000*, ed. Jacqueline Cerquiglini-Toulet and Nigel Wilkins (Paris, 2002), 120, notes this source as an exception to the general rule that the texts of motets are not understandable without music. (They are omitted from the music section of the unnotated Machaut manuscript **M**; see listing in Earp, *Guillaume de Machaut*, 95, MS [10].) Although **St** is a late source, and **M**'s omission might well reflect the decision of its late-fourteenth- or early-fifteenth-century copyists rather than the situation in its exemplar, which comes from the 1360s, the texts of M8 exerted clear contemporary literary influence; see note 33. B23 is attributed to Machaut in **Ch**.

32. The *aa* given at the start of measure 19 in the motetus of the Machaut sources is corrected in other copies (variously to *g* or *bb*) because it is manifestly wrong. That **CaB** carries at least one better reading than that found in the Machaut sources is adduced by Earp as evidence that this motet enjoyed wider transmission at an early stage; see Lawrence Earp, "Machaut's Role in the Production of His Works," *Journal of the American Musicological Society* 42 (1989): 494–97. I would argue, however, that this is likely to be a subsequent emendation made by performer-scribes rather than reflecting an original reading. There is a clef change at this point in the motetus of **Vg**: my edition thus interprets the *aa* in the MSS as per the previous clef, giving an *f* (probably sung *f♯* in this case, with the triplum assuming temporary tenor function). This reading provides the same sonority for this note of the tenor's color as in the other two colores (something that is generally the case; cf. mm. 7 and 21).

33. Geoffrey Chaucer, "The Book of the Duchess," in *Chaucer's Dream Poetry*, ed. Helen Phillips and Nick Havely (London, 1997), 79, l. 626, "An ydole of fals portrayture," cites M8, Mo l. 9, "une ydole est de fausse pourtraiture"; l. 632, "Withoute feythe, lawe or mesure," cites Mo l. 6, "sans foy. sans loy. sans droit et sans mesure." *Remede* is the other main source for this passage; see also George Lyman Kittredge, "Guillaume de Machaut and the Book of the Duchess," *Proceedings of the Modern Language Association* 30 (1915): 1–24.

34. Earp, *Guillaume de Machaut*, 367.

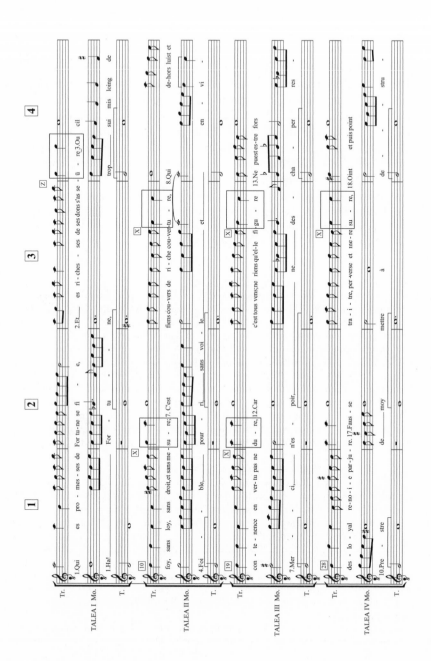

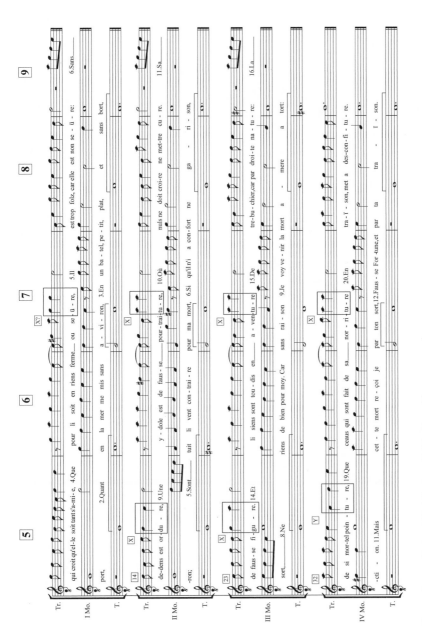

Example 5.3. *Qui es / Ha! Fortune* (M8) aligned by greater taleae.

friendship are shown to be insecure, lacking faith, law, rectitude, and moderation. As Kevin Brownlee notes, the opening general proposition (ll. 1–5) is
then given two proofs.[35] The first (ll. 6–13) is about the nature of Fortune: as
in B22 she is a rich covering hiding excremental filth within; she is an idol of
"false portraiture," because the inner essence that the verb "portraire" denotes
is false to her outer appearance; she is "wind."[36] The second proof concerns
her actions (ll. 14–20): disloyal and perjuring, one moment she anoints and the
next she stabs; she is a false, treacherous, bitter mother who discomfits those
she treacherously nurses.[37]

Just as the pair of balades B22 and B23 between them contrast clerkly
third-person sagacity with the emotional response of a first-person lover, so
too do the triplum (like B22) and motetus (like B23) of M8—but because it
is a motet, these voices are presented simultaneously rather than sequentially.
The motetus's opening exclamation, "Hey, Fortune," establishes it as a direct
address by a subject who has "put too far from port," and thanks to Fortune
is now adrift on a hostile sea in a shallow flat-bottomed skiff, without oar or
sail, and at the mercy of fatally opposing winds.[38] Fortune's false treachery
will lead to the death of this *je,* a wrongful death, described as a tort or legal wrong, confirming the triplum's summary of Fortune as lacking law and
rectitude.

The two upper voices are held together by the organization of a tenor with
the Latin text "Et non est qui adjuvet" (and there is none who might help),
which comes from a responsory proper to Passiontide, and draws ultimately on
a number of verses from a psalm that is read by Christians as prophetic of the
Crucifixion.[39] The idea of extreme suffering—described and experienced—in
the sway of Fortune takes place against the backdrop of the ultimate suffering unto death in Christian theology: the Crucifixion of Christ. The potential
theological and sacred resonances of this are explored further in chapter 6,

35. See Kevin Brownlee, "Polyphonie et intertextualité dans les motets 8 et 4 de Guillaume de
Machaut," in *"L'hostellerie de pensée": Études sur l'art littéraire au Moyen Age offertes à Daniel
Poirion,* ed. Michel Zink et al., trans. Anthony Allen (Paris, 1995), 99–102.

36. On "portraire" and "contrefaire," see chapter 3. See also Stephen Perkinson, "Portraits
and Counterfeits: Villard de Honnecourt and Thirteenth-Century Theories of Representation,"
in *Excavating the Medieval Image: Manuscripts, Artists, Audiences; Essays in Honor of Sandra
Hindman,* ed. Nina A. Rowe and David S. Areford (Aldershot, 2004), 13–36; Domenic Leo,
"Authorial Presence in the Illuminated Machaut Manuscripts" (Ph.D. diss., New York University,
2005), 214.

37. See Brownlee, "Polyphonie et intertextualité."

38. See Hans Blumenberg, *Shipwreck with Spectator: Paradigm of a Metaphor for Existence,*
trans. Steven Rendall (Cambridge, 1997), 1–2.

39. The exact liturgical designation and order varied locally and included Palm Sunday, Pas-
sion Sunday, and days in Holy Week; see http://publish.uwo.ca/~cantus/; and Alice V. Clark,
"Machaut Reading Machaut: Self-Borrowing and Reinterpretation in Motets 8 and 21," in
Citation and Authority in Medieval and Renaissance Music: Learning from the Learned, ed.
Suzannah Clark and Elizabeth Eva Leach (Woodbridge, 2005), 99n19.

but in terms of the description of Fortune in the triplum and of her effect on the suffering subject in the motetus, the idea of there being none to help encapsulates the hopelessness that allows Fortune's power to operate. Lack of hope is mirrored in the other kinds of lack that the upper-voice texts outline, epitomized in their multiple repetition of the word "sans" (without).[40] The full context of the responsory describes the subject being surrounded by liars: "lying men surround me and there is none to help."[41] This links Fortune to the theme of gossip, which will be explored shortly.

The setting of these texts in a motet allows further experience of Fortune's power for listener and singers alike. At a structural level the basic repeating rhythm of the tenor (the talea) comprises just four notes in the pattern breve, imperfect long, breve rest, imperfect long, perfect long. The repeating pitch sequence of the tenor (the color), however, has sixteen notes, so that each of its three presentations requires four repeats of the basic talea. This might be thought to make a greater talea of sixteen notes (potentially subdivisible into four more basic taleae), but very clear repeating rhythmic features in the two upper parts group these forty-eight notes *not* into three groups of sixteen but into four groups of twelve, giving four "greater taleae" each lasting nine triple-long measures (see example 5.3).[42]

The most immediately striking aspect of the surface sound of the piece is its flow of almost constant minims (transcribed as eighth notes), the near-perpetual motion of which can be heard as the continual instability of Fortune, or even more specifically as the turning of her wheel.[43] The only letup in this constant pattern is at the end of each of the greater taleae, when there is a cadence to a sustained breve (a long in the lower parts), and then the same "upbeat" figure of four minims descending from *aa* in the triplum (mm. 9, 18, and 27; m. 36 lacks the upbeat figure and has a sustained long in all parts as it is the end of the piece). The other aurally striking moment that confirms the presence of four greater taleae (rather than the three suggested by repetition of the tenor color) is the syncopation from the sixth to seventh long of each of them (mm. 6–7, 15–16, 24–25, 33–34), when both voices have a string of semibreves, but the triplum offsets its string by an initial minim rest. This syncopated passage also furthers the play between competing structural

40. Tr, l. 6, "Sans foy, sans loy sans droit et sans mesure"; Mo, l. 2, "sans aviron," l. 3 "sans bort," l. 4 "sans voile," l. 8 "sans raison."

41. "Lying men" represents a change from the source in Psalm 21, in which the first-person singer is surrounded by a number of animals, including bulls and dogs. See figure 5.4.

42. Example 5.3 gives the complete motet with the staves aligned by these greater talea. For a clear exposition of this, showing the tenor alone, see example XVII-3 in Richard H. Hoppin, *Medieval Music* (New York, 1978), 413.

43. Curiously Ludwig edits out some of this constant movement, giving the figure mimim-semibreve-minim (transcribed as eighth note–quarter note–eighth note) for four minims in cases when the second and third minims are at the same pitch, despite the agreement of all sources in measures 4, 14, and 23, and all except CaB in measure 11.

groupings of three and four since the upper-voice syncopation lasts for four breves against the perfect (triple) breve organization of the tenor.

As well as picturing instability and insecurity in its rhythm, the music provides deliberately unstable word-setting at key points.[44] The setting of the paroxytonic (feminine) "-ure" rhymes in the triplum is particularly striking in this regard: the regular instances (example 5.3, box X) using paired semibreves (stressed, unstressed) found at the start of measures 11 and 20, at the end of measures 12, 21, and 30, and in the middle of measures 14 and 23, and 7, 16, 25, and 34 throw into relief the shifted accent at measure 32, where the "pointure" of Fortune follows her "ointure" (box Y). The otherwise regular initial instance in measure 4 perpetrates a serious musical distortion of the verse structure by requiring the elision of the final unstressed "-e" at the end of line 2's "-ure" rhyme by the "Ou" at the start of line 3 (box Z).[45]

Counterpoint undermines another seemingly regular setting of the "-ure" rhyme in measure 7 when the lack of security in the gifts of Fortune being sung in the triplum is mirrored in the tenor's failure to provide contrapuntal security to that voice, with which it has parallel fifths; the tenor function shifts momentarily here into the motetus (box X?). I would argue that a similar removal of contrapuntal security occurs through the tenor rest and upper-voice dissonances in measure 17. The previous measure sets up an imperfect sonority $a/f\sharp$ between tenor and motetus (on "mort"), which eventually resolves to G/g in measure 17. But the motetus text in between these points says "si qu'il n'i a confort" (such that there is no comfort there), and the triplum for "Où nulz" steadfastly refuses to sing pitches that would take part in this progression ($c\sharp$ and d, for example, would be ideal), singing instead a held e at the end of measure 16 (dissonant with the contrapuntally important $f\sharp$ of the motetus, although the dissonance is reduced in actual sounding length by the motetus ornamentation to only the final minim) and then an accented f at the start of measure 17. Sources prepared outside Machaut's circle (E, Iv, and CaB) amend this latter note to g. Earp considers this a superior reading and possible evidence for an earlier, more accurate copy of this motet having entered the "peripheral" transmission. Even if he is wrong and the "peripheral sources" are *later* redactions of this motet, they would still be a sign that this dissonance was appreciated as so acerbic by near contemporaries that some scribes and/or singers thought it could not be right.[46] Regardless of the correct

---

44. See Lawrence Earp, "Declamatory Dissonance in Machaut," in Clark and Leach, *Citation and Authority in Medieval and Renaissance Music,* 114–16.

45. The only editorial alternative here would be to present measure 3 entirely syllabically, which would cause the unstressed final "-e" of the "-ure" rhyme syllable to fall on the stressed tone at the start of measure 4. Either "solution" preserves what seems to be an intended discomfort at precisely the point where the assured riches of Fortune's gifts are first mentioned.

46. Positing the common error of notes being out by a third and emending the two triplum notes to c (that is, $c\sharp$) and d would make the lack of "confort" signaled not by the triplum but by the tenor's

solution to these text-critical issues, the penultimate measure in the first two greater taleae is a moment of discomfort. Triplum figures at the end of measure 17 and the equivalent place in the first greater talea (m. 8) outline cadence formulas that are not supported by any actual directed progressions in the other parts; in tonal terms the first two large taleae tail off insecurely.

The simultaneity of the textual delivery allows for meaningful verbal collisions. For example, at the start of the second greater talea (m. 10), both voices sing "foi." Only with time do these similar syllables disaggregate to show that the triplum's "foi" (faith), something Fortune lacks, was actually heard against the first syllables of the motetus's "foible" (weak). The keywords "Fortune" and "traïson," which occur respectively near the start and end of both texts, can both be heard clearly in a piece whose rapid simultaneous text declamation elsewhere more usually offers aural confusion: "Fortune" is started together in both voices in measure 2, and "traïson," comes sequentially in first the triplum, then the motetus, in the penultimate measure (m. 35).

The text is so replete with invective that it is easy to read its dissonances as reflecting the anguished emotional soundworld of those in Fortune's power. For example, the bitterness of death is mentioned at the end of greater talea 3 in the prolonged series of dissonances of measure 26: seconds between the upper voices at the start of the measure when the tenor is silent, and then an accented ninth between tenor and triplum ("car"), a long fourth between tenor and motetus ("-mere"), soon compounded by sevenths—the second one accented—in the triplum ("droite"), and finally a cadence that is avoided by the use of *musica ficta* (F♯ in the tenor and c♯ in the triplum). Comparing measures 26–27 with measures 35–36 shows how a very similar cadential setup can be made to resolve successfully to F.

The theme of Fortune was popular in other fourteenth-century songs, and the idea of Fortune being contrary or perverse recurs in several of these, many of which seem to make reference to Machaut's Fortune settings. Among the hundred pieces in the non-Machaut manuscript that transmits the notated and ascribed version of Machaut's *De Fortune* (B23), the Chantilly codex (**Ch**), Fortune is mentioned in fourteen other texts (thirteen other songs), including in *Ma dame m'a congié douné* (Ch6), whose first and last lines are respectively the last and first lines of Machaut's *Se je me pleing* (B15), and in *Phiton, Phiton* (Ch18), whose opening cites the music of Machaut's *Phyton* (B38).[47]

---

supporting tone for the resolution being delayed by the rest at the start of measure 17, leaving an unsupported fourth sounding. No proposed emendation makes a textbook progression here, suggesting that whatever the text-critical situation, some disruption to the contrapuntal flow was intentional.

47. Fortune is also mentioned in both voices of Grimace's double balade *Se Zephirus / Se Jupiter* (Ch15), Franciscus's *Phiton, Phiton* (Ch18), Olivier's *Si con cy gist* (Ch41), Philippus's *De ma dolour* (Ch42) and *Il n'est nulz homs* (Ch56), Goscalch's *En nul estat* (Ch58), Solage's *Helas! Je voy* (Ch95), and Matheus de Sancto Johanne's *Fortune, faulce perverse* (Ch99). Fortune is also mentioned in the anonymous balades *Toute clarté m'est obscure* (Ch3), *Ma dame m'a congié*

The anonymous *Ha! Fortune* (Ch37) has the same terminal sonorities as Machaut's *De Fortune* (B23 = Ch78) at equivalent structural points, and additionally models the poetry of its opening line on that of the motetus of *Qui es / Ha! Fortune* (M8). Among fourteenth-century texts set to music, the phrase "Ha! Fortune" occurs only additionally in the anonymous **Ch** balade *Toute clarté m'est obscure* (Ch3), which also rails against Fortune.[48] Fortune was an extremely popular theme in this period, and Machaut's Fortune works rank among his most widely circulated. The evidence from the treatment of this theme in contemporary songs and poems is that he may also have established Fortune's lyric lexis and her musical soundworld. An examination of Fortune in his narrative works will show that they too exerted influence on contemporary poetry.

Complaining and Comparing: Fortune in the *Remede* and *Voir dit*

Machaut's two central interpolated dits place Hope center stage, although the attitude of the protagonist of each dit toward her differs. As that which necessitates Hope, Fortune is equally prominent and equally differentiated in treatment, given the differing outcomes of the two dits. In the *Remede*, Fortune appears in the first half of the dit, at the opening of the second episode, when the young narrator has run dismayed into the park of Hesdin and is sitting alone and lamenting his state (see the discussion in chapter 4 and figure 4.2). Hope appears in response to his complaint to Fortune, and Hope's instruction eliminates Fortune's power from the rest of the dit. The *Voir dit* reverses this: the discussion of Fortune comes at the very end of the poem, after Hope has been forgotten, has intervened to demand a lay, and has departed (see chapter 4 and figure 4.5). Both the narrator Guillaume and his beloved Toute Belle compare each other in turn to slightly different figures of Fortune. In both poems Fortune is depicted in the program of miniatures, but only in the *Remede* is she also addressed in song.

Blaming Fortune: The Complaint in the *Remede de Fortune*

Like Boethius's *Consolation,* the *Remede* shows the narrator as the prey of Fortune. The fundamental emotional instability at the opening of the story is reflected in his composition of musical poetry, which he creates according to his *sentement*. He is not always "en un point," that is, he is not a stable point—a *punctus*, a note, a mathematical and geometrical monad—but is

---

donné (Ch6), *Sans joie avoir* (Ch23), *Ha! Fortune* (Ch37), and *Adieu vous di* (Ch74), all of which have Fortune as "contraire."

48. In fact all three have the three-word string "Ha! Fortune trop."

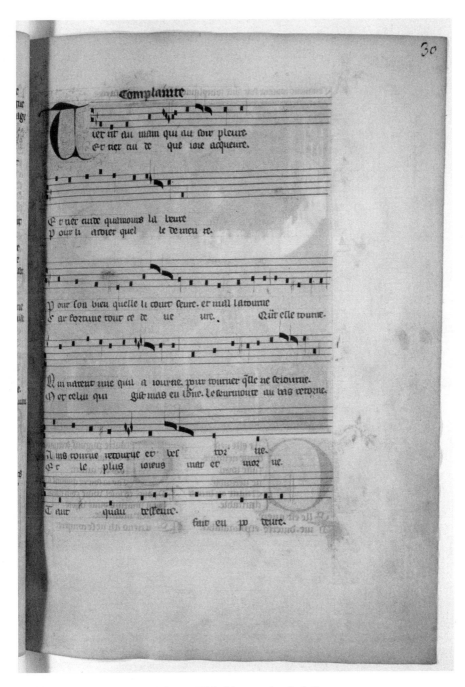

Figure 5.4. *Tels rit* (RF2) in MS C, 30r. Bibliothèque nationale de France.

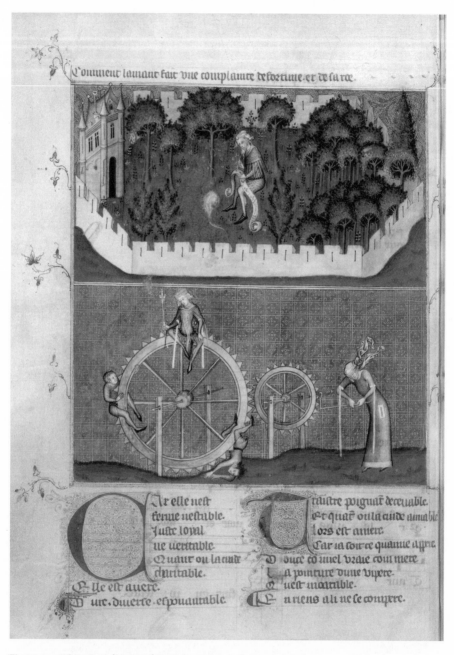

Figure 5.5. "Comment l'amant fait une complainte de Fortune et de sa roe" (How the lover makes a complaint about Fortune and her wheel): composing the complaint in MS C, 30v. Bibliothèque nationale de France.

in motion, like a wheel.[49] When he composes the lay *Qui n'aroit* (RF1), he is able to understand the importance of Hope, but when his lady is present and makes him perform it, he is discombobulated by the mismatch between his newly changed *sentement,* caused by his lady's presence, and that of the poem; he is thus unable to admit to the truth of his authorship. Fleeing the lady, he takes himself into the isolation of the park at Hesdin—a location famed in the fourteenth and fifteenth centuries as a large pleasure garden replete with magically self-moving machinery and mazes—and writes a long complaint.[50] Although Machaut wrote ten other complaints, the one in the *Remede* is the only one in the earliest source, and none of the later ones is set to music. The complaint is announced multiply: in the body of the poem, by a rubric (actually in blue ink), by the musical notation of its first stanza (30r; see figure 5.4), and in C—the earliest, most sumptuously illuminated copy of the poem—by a large miniature that takes up nearly a full page (30v; see figure 5.5).[51]

The narrator's growing despondency in the garden is marked by his taking back his earlier comment that a lover is always happy; now he sees that the contrary is the case with him (ll. 864–66). From his own experience he understands instead that the heart of a lover who loves strongly

> Or a joie, or a desconfort,
> Or rit, or pleure, or chante, or plaint,
> Or se delite en son complaint,
> Or tremble, or tressue, or a chaut,
> Or froit, et puis ne li chaut
> D'assaut qu'Amours li puisse faire;
> Or li plaist; or ne li puet plaire.[52]

Now has joy, now is discomfited, now laughs, now weeps, now sings, now laments, now takes delight in his lamentation, now trembles, now sweats, is now hot, now cold, and now cares no more what assault Love might make on it; is now pleased; now cannot be pleased.

---

49. *Remede,* ll. 401–8: "Et pour ce que n'estoie mie / Tousdis en un point, m'estudie / Mis en faire chansons et lays, / Baladez, rondeaus, virelays, / Et chans, selonc mon sentement, / Amoureus et non autrement." See chapters 3 and 4.

50. On the "marvels of Hesdin," see Birgit Franke, "Gesellschaftsspiele mit Automaten: 'Merveilles' in Hesdin," *Marburger Jahrbuch für Kunstwissenschaft* 24 (1997): 135–58.

51. In this source the complaint has four further illustrations (31v, 32v, 33v, 34v). All illuminations are reproduced in James I. Wimsatt, William W. Kibler, and Rebecca A. Baltzer, eds., *Guillaume de Machaut: Le Jugement du Roy de Behaigne and Remede de Fortune* (Athens, Ga., 1988), 452–68; and discussed further in Sylvia Huot, *From Song to Book: The Poetics of Writing in Old French Lyric and Lyrical Narrative Poetry* (Ithaca, 1987), 252–54.

52. *Remede,* ll. 876–82.

As will be seen more clearly in the exposition in *Voir dit*, this places the lover himself in perpetual motion between extremes that implicitly resemble those of Fortune herself. Still committed to composing from *sentement*, the lover decides to make a complaint:

> Et en ce penser ou j'estoie
> Je m'avisai que je feroie
> De Fortune et de mes dolours
> De mes pensers et de mes plours
> .I. dit qu'on appelle complainte,
> Ou il averoit rime mainte,
> Qui seroit de tristre matiere.
> Si commenchay en tel maniere:[53]
> *Complainte*

> And while I was thinking like this I decided that I would make of Fortune and my sorrows, of my thought and my tears, a dit that people call a complaint, where there would be lots of rhymes and which would treat this sad material. So I began in this way: *Complaint* [first stanza underlaid to the musical notation follows immediately on 30r].

Two things are worth noting here: first that he is *making* the complaint ("je feroie") and not explicitly performing it (which would require "diroie" or "chanteroie"), and second that he emphasizes the recognized generic appellation ("qu'on appelle complainte"), drawing attention to the number of rhymes. This lover-narrator is already loving as a means of generating poetry in which he has an authorial pride that will be even more palpable in the lover-narrator of the *Voir dit*. He emphasizes that he is making the complaint from his own sorrows, his thoughts and tears, and that it will be "de tristre matiere" (of sad matter). The scribe splits line 904, the last line of the poem before the complaint starts, into two halves to fill the right-hand column of folio 29v completely. The rubrication that follows—*Complainte*—then appears at the very top of the recto folio (30r), which is completely dedicated to the musical notation for the poem; the staves are copied more spaced out than they are for the other musical items in the poem in order that its six staves, setting sixteen lines of poetry, entirely fill out the page.[54]

Turning the page, we find a rubric (in blue ink) that describes the picture on 30v as "How the lover makes a complaint about Fortune and her wheel" (see figure 5.5).[55] The miniature takes up nearly the entire page and is divided horizontally into two halves. The top depicts the lover by a pool in the walled

---

53. *Remede*, ll. 897–904.
54. The six staves have one, one, two, two, one, and one lines of poetry on them, respectively.
55. "Comment l'amant fait une complainte de Fortune et de sa roe."

park of Hesdin, filled with green trees, grass, and flowers. He is fashionably dressed and sits with a pen and scroll, writing musical notes. Below, a vibrant orange background throws into relief the blindfolded figure of Lady Fortune indirectly turning her wheel by means of a crank on a second, adjacent wheel, whose cogged rim drives it. Both wheels are supported on double bearings. Atop the larger wheel sits a boy king, while two other children are respectively climbing up and falling down the wheel's sides.

The wheel of Fortune was a traditional image in the later Middle Ages, and there is evidence that by Machaut's period actual mechanical models were utilized in dramatic contexts.[56] Huot points out that juxtaposing the image of Fortune familiar from contemporary didactic iconography with that of the poet composing visually represents the fusion of lyrical and clerkly registers that is achieved by the complaint, especially in its first few stanzas.[57] The description of Fortune that is given in the complaint is also highly traditional, with the opening stanza seeming to draw on that of Boethius's *Consolation,* book 2, perhaps in the French translation contained in the same source that may have provided a model for the opening *Prologue* miniatures (see figure 5.6).[58]

There are ways, however, in which this image of Fortune and her wheel departs from the traditional iconography. The wheel "reveals particularly astonishing mechanical sophistication" that would give Fortune "a mechanical advantage of approximately 4:3."[59] The artist's fascination with technology perhaps here provides a response to the location, Hesdin, famed for its mechanical marvels. More important, the three human figures on the wheel, who represent (and are often labeled in other depictions) *regnabo, regno, regnavi* ("I shall reign," "I am reigning," "I have reigned"), are children.[60] Although the patron of manuscript C is not securely known, the quality of the illuminations and the identity of the artist associate it with other royal manuscripts of this period. The *Remede* is the most densely illuminated dit in this book and employs the best artist.[61] Although the dedicatee of the *Remede* is

56. "Dramatic" here includes within church spaces, paraliturgically; see Nelson, "Mechanical Wheels of Fortune."

57. Huot, *From Song to Book,* 252–54. See also Kevin Brownlee, *Poetic Identity in Guillaume de Machaut* (Madison, 1984), 43–46.

58. See the comments on *F-MO* H. 43 in chapter 3, note 47. This manuscript's particular Boethius translation is number 5 in the Thomas-Roques classification; see Glynnis M. Cropp, "The Medieval French Boethius," in *Boethius in the Middle Ages: Latin and Vernacular Traditions of the Consolatio Philosophiae,* ed. Maarten J. F. M. Hoenen and Lodi Nauta (Leiden, 1997), 249.

59. Nelson, "Mechanical Wheels of Fortune," 227.

60. These figures and designations go back to the earliest pictorial representations in the eleventh century and often contained a fourth figure under the wheel, labeled "non regno," or "sum sine regno"; see Hunt, "The Christianization of Fortune," 97n9. Rather than children, a more usual representation would have the four figures roughly aligned with the "four ages of man."

61. See François Avril, *Manuscript Painting at the Court of France: The Fourteenth Century (1320–1380)* (London, 1978), 76–77 (plate 19), 80–89 (plates 21–25); Earp, *Guillaume de Machaut,* 132–33.

Tels rit (RF2), stanza 1

1. Tieus **rit** au main qui au soir **pleure,**
2. Et tieus cuide qu'Amours labeure
3. Pour son bien, qu'**elle** li **court** seure
4. Et mal **l'atourne;**
5. Et tieus cuide que Joie acqueure
6. Pour li aidier, qu'elle demeure.
7. Car Fortune tout ce deveure,
8. **Quant elle tourne,**
9. Qui n'atent mie qu'il ajourne
10. Pour **tourner;** qu'elle ne sejourne,
11. Ains **tourne,** retourne, et bestourne,
12. Tant qu'au **desseure**
13. **Met** celui qui gist mas en l'ourne;
14. Le **seurmonté** au bas retorne,
15. Et le plus joieus mat et morne
16. **Fait en po d'eure.**

(from *Remede de Fortune,* ed. Wimsatt and Kibler, ll. 905–20)

He laughs in the morning, who in the evening weeps. And he believes that Love labors for his benefit when she surely jabs him and twists the knife; and he believes that Joy hurries to help him when she remains behind; because Fortune devours all this when she turns [her wheel]—she does not wait at all for day to come before she turns [it]; she does not rest, but turns, turns again, and inverts it so much that she puts to the top he who lies checkmated in the gutter; the uppermost one she returns to the bottom, and makes the most joyful checkmated and dejected in a small part of an hour.

Boeces, bk. 2, metrum i

1. **Quant** par orgueil **torne** sa main,
2. **Elle court** comme venz senz frain;
3. Les rois abat, povres mett haut,
4. Et de lour **plorer** ne lui chaut,
5. Mais **rit** quant les a fait **plourer:**
6. Ainsi joue pour soi **montrer.**
7. Merveilles **fait** quant **en une heure**
8. **Met** aucuns dessouz, puis **desseure.**

(ed. J. Keith Atkinson)

When her hand turns imperiously she flees like a wind without leadership; she strikes down kings, placing the poor on high, and cares nothing for their crying but laughs when she makes them cry. She plays like this to elevate herself. She does wonders when in [the space of] an hour she places someone underneath then uppermost.

Consolatio, bk. 2, metrum i

1. Haec cum superba verterit vices dextra
2. Et aestuantis more fertur Euripi,
3. Dudum tremendos saeva proterit reges
4. Humilemque victi sublevat fallax vultum
5. Non illa miseros audit aut curat fletus
6. Ultroque gemitus dura quos fecit ridet.
7. Sic illa ludit, sic suas probat vires
8. Magnumque suis demonstrat ostentum, si quis
9. Visatur una stratus ac felix hora.

(ed. and trans. S. J. Tester).

So with imperious hand she turns the wheel of change
This way and that like the ebb and flow of the tide,
And pitiless tramples down those once dread kings,
Raising the lowly face of the conquered—
Only to mock him in his turn;
Careless she neither hears nor heeds the cries
Of miserable men: she laughs
At the groans that she herself has mercilessly caused.
So she sports, so she proves her power,
Showing a mighty marvel to her subjects, when
The self-same hour
Sees a man first successful, then cast down.

Figure 5.6. Comparison of the opening stanza of *Tels rit* (RF2) with Boethius, *Consolation,* book 2, metrum i (in Latin and in a Middle French version).

unstated, recent scholarship has suggested that the book which gives it such a prominent place might have been destined for Bonne of Luxembourg, either commissioned by her or as a gift from her husband, John of Normandy (the future John II of France).[62] Perhaps the highly didactic *Remede* with its many high-quality illuminations might have served the particular purpose within the household of John and Bonne of schooling and entertaining the Valois princelings. The exact dating of *Remede* is unclear, but if its completion was interrupted by Bonne's death in 1349, as has been argued, her three oldest children—Charles, Louis, and John—would have been eleven, ten, and eight—approximately the same age as the three children on the wheel.[63] All three boys were destined to be important figures in the French royal house; their education would have been of the utmost importance. Machaut may well have been involved in this if he served Bonne in the period between the death of John of Luxembourg in 1346 and the start of his possible service with Charles of Navarre late in 1349, following Bonne's death in September of that year.[64] The bottom register of the complaint picture is presented as the product of the imagination of the poet-lover-narrator, who sits writing in the top half.[65] If the boys on the wheel are Bonne's, he imagines not his own subjection to Fortune in the dit but the subjection to Fortune of his patrons and their children—the readers (and possible owners) of his book.

The musical setting of the complaint allows the same single stanza of music to serve all thirty-six stanzas of the poem (the first stanza is given in example 5.4, its translation in figure 5.6). Like the lay, this piece is monophonic and written in the older style of rhythmic notation, predominantly using longs and breves.[66] Each stanza is formed of two musical sections, A and B, both of which are repeated with open and closed endings for their first and second performances (A°A^{c}B°B^c), rather like the form of a duplex balade but without a repeated verbal refrain. These two sections have extremely similar rhythmic

62. See the discussion and references in Earp, *Guillaume de Machaut*, 213; and Leo, "Authorial Presence," 130–36.

63. This idea was suggested to me by Domenic Leo (private communication), whose dissertation makes a convincing case for the importance of children more widely in the iconography of C (see Leo, "Authorial Presence," passim). Alternative datings for *Remede* of before 1342 or before 1357 have been posited; see Earp, *Guillaume de Machaut*, 213–14, for a synopsis of views. The reigning boy king even resembles later depictions of the blond, wavy-haired Charles as seen in his coronation book. See the plates in Carra Ferguson O'Meara, *Monarchy and Consent: The Coronation Book of Charles V of France, British Library MS Cotton Tiberius B. VIII* (London, 2001).

64. Bonne died on 3 or 11 September 1349; Charles d'Evreux became king of Navarre on 7 October that year, but was not crowned until the following May because of the level of plague in Pamplona. See Roger Bowers, "Guillaume de Machaut and His Canonry of Reims, 1338–1377," *Early Music History* 23 (2004): 12n32.

65. Huot, *From Song to Book*, 252.

66. It has four minims, two in each half of the setting, which serve an ornamental function and do not shift the basic "beat" of the song onto the more typical *ars nova* values of breves and semibreves.

Example 5.4. The first stanza of the complaint *Tels rit* (RF2) in modern notation (values quartered).

presentations, with movement mainly in groups of three equal breves; some of these breves are subdivided and some are held to double their usual length, but the overwhelming sense is of a measured progression of equal notes. The cadences of the second section are the same as the respective cadences in the first section (that is, both *ouvert* endings are the same, and both *clos* endings are the same). Given the paucity of marked variation and the high level of exact musical repetition within each stanza, a performance of all thirty-six stanzas would run to a level of repetition that would not have been considered a compositional good in a period that privileged variety.[67] Although the notation implies no particular tempo (and this is an aspect of performance about which we can only speculate), at a moderate modern tempo the whole song might last between forty minutes and an hour. No modern commercial recording is currently available—and for a very good reason: it would be extremely boring! The lover's subjection to Fortune may make him emotionally unstable, but, paradoxically, it makes him musically tedious. The song is deeply self-indulgent: the audience would blame the singer for subjecting them to such a thing.[68] The complaint seems intended to be ridiculous—musically a creative failure, despite its ingenious versification—which, like the lover's melancholy and emotional stability, is cured when Hope turns up and instructs him in the much more varied and compact *ars nova* song forms, complete with their joyful minims.[69]

We are not prepared to be bored because we expect our contemporary musical culture to provide entertainment and aesthetic pleasure, but the more ethically focused artistic culture of the Middle Ages would probably have allowed such a deliberately tedious performance—perhaps even found it darkly amusing—on account of its instructive purpose within a deeply didactic dit. The poetic tour de force represented by the versification would have provided a level of variety sufficient to distract from the musical repetition only to the extent that it could be withstood. With so many different words sung to the same music—both sections of the music will deliver seventy-two

67. See the comments on variety as a compositional good in Elizabeth Eva Leach, *Sung Birds: Music, Nature, and Poetry in the Later Middle Ages* (Ithaca, 2007), 160, which cites Nicole Oresme, an important scientist and translator at the court of Charles V. In his *Tractatus de configurationibus qualitatum et motuum*, bk. 2, chap. 22, Oresme discusses overfamiliarity as one of the "accidental" features that can make a melody seem uglier than it is in absolute terms; by contrast, novelty and unfamiliarity produce admiration and delight, causing sounds to seem more beautiful than they really are; see Marshall Clagett, ed., *Nicole Oresme and the Medieval Geometry of Qualities and Motions: A Treatise on the Uniformity and Difformity of Intensities known as Tractatus de configurationibus qualitatum et motuum* (Madison, 1968), 326–27. Machaut himself stresses the variety of his works, for example, in *Navarre*, ll. 884–95.

68. Medieval authorities acknowledged that most people like to hear their own singing, even if it sounds unpleasant to others. Augustine, *De musica* 1.4, notes that even irrational animals are charmed by their own voices.

69. See chapter 4.

different texts—any memorial music-text link would have been extremely weak, turning the pure melody, divorced from any textual association, into an earworm, an annoying reminder of the monotony of being trapped in Fortune's wheel.[70]

For Machaut, complaining and music do not go together, a feature that distinguishes him from earlier composers in the history of music. Some of the earliest notated music that exists in the West sets complaint or lament texts by classical writers, especially Virgil.[71] As noted earlier, complaints other than the one in the *Remede* are entirely absent from Machaut's earliest collected works manuscripts, although he included a small collection of unnotated works of this type in later sources. Manuscripts **A** and **G** collect them in a separate section.[72] In addition, all three of Machaut's dits with interpolated lyrics include complaints—one in *Remede,* one in *Fonteinne,* and three in *Voir dit*—but only that in the *Remede* is given a musical setting. The kind of setting it receives suggests that there is a mismatch between song and lament, confirming the need for joy in composition that the *Prologue* establishes most explicitly.[73]

Inveighing against Fortune, as is done in this complaint, is stagy and self-indulgent, much like the wallowing in sorrowful song enacted by the narrator at the start of Boethius's *Consolation.* Machaut can only unwrite Boethius with his own caveat in place: the problem for Machaut is not song itself but *sorrowful* song. As Huot points out, the lay is specifically performed by the narrator within the context of the *Remede,* but the complaint instead "serves rather to define the protagonist as a lover-writer and provides him with a literary voice, a language of text and image in which to formulate his experience."[74] The reader is presented not just with text and image but also—and in fact first of all in the sequence of the pages—with rubric and with music that is cast in a visually striking antiquated musical "font" of longs and breves.[75] Whether

---

70. The quadripartite form ($A^oA^cB^oB^c$) might even represent the four-segment wheel of Fortune.

71. See Jan M. Ziolkowski, "Women's Lament and the Neuming of the Classics," in *Music and Medieval Manuscripts: Palaeography and Performance; Essays Dedicated to Andrew Hughes,* ed. John Haines and Randall Rosenfield (Aldershot, 2004), 128, notes that of thirty-two classical speeches that are neumed, fourteen are voiced by women. All come from epics in dactylic hexameters: fifteen by Virgil (six in the feminine voice), six by Statius (four in the feminine voice), and seven by Lucan (two in the feminine voice). Dido's speeches are the most popular, with four distinct stretches of her words receiving neumations. The metra of Horace and Boethius were also set; see Silvia Wälli, *Melodien aus mittelalterlichen Horaz-Handschriften: Edition und Interpretation der Quellen* (Kassel, 2002); and Sam Barrett, ed., *Melodies for the De consolatione philosophiae of Boethius* (Kassel, forthcoming).

72. **Vg, B,** and **D** append the complaints to the *Loange,* as does **E,** although these manuscripts are not the closest to Machaut's authorial intention for his codex. See Earp, *Guillaume de Machaut,* 266, table 6.9 and 266–71, for full details.

73. See chapter 3.

74. Huot, *From Song to Book,* 254.

75. That is, music notated predominantly in longs and breves, rather than breves and semibreves. See chapter 4.

it was performed sonically as the poem was read, or whether the reader could simply imagine the performance from reading the notation or knowing the melody, matters less than the way in which the oversaturation of performative time is either sounded or pictured spatially in the ample spread of the musical staves, the pages of poetry, and their elaborate illuminations. This complaint serves to emphasize the insatiability of the kind of longing that the narrator experiences because he allows himself to be subject to the instability of external events.

The complaint is one of two kinds of lyric presentation that Fortune receives in the *Remede*. It is answered when Hope appears to offer a didactic explanation of Fortune that ought to enable the lover to understand his experience and combat it. *Remede*'s complaint and Hope's subsequent exposition, modeled on Boethius's opening metrum and Philosophy's book 2 impersonation of the goddess, together form a more expansive version of the same diptych— anguished experience and detached observation—found in the music section balades *De Fortune* (B23) and *Il m'est avis* (B22), or between the upper voices of *Qui es / Ha! Fortune* (M8). Once nourished on the three-course dit, the audience for *Remede*'s courtly and poetic didacticism could easily keep themselves full of good counsel by snacking on these tasty musical treats.

Comparing Fortunes: Different Models in the *Voir dit*

A comparison between Fortune and the courtly lady who is the object of love in Machaut's doctrine was implicit in the subtle shifting of the refrain's signified in B23. The changeability of the lover as he makes his complaint in *Remede* was described in terms of antitheses that subtextually made him, too, a type for Fortune. In addition, the lady in *Remede* "acts out the motif of changeability that dominates his image of Fortune: she first promises union of hearts with the narrator, later she seems cold."[76] The moral equivalence of male and female lovers, however, and their mutual assimilation to the figure of Fortune, is asserted most explicitly in the *Voir dit*: at their affair's dying ebb the narrator, Guillaume, compares his lady directly to Fortune, and is then himself compared to a different ("pagan") type of Fortune by a messenger who berates him for believing too readily everything he hears ("tout par legierement croire").[77] These two incidents are important enough to attract significant illuminations in all manuscripts that feature the *Voir dit*'s complete text, as well as in those that feature only this part of the poem.[78] The illuminations are particularly striking in manuscript **A**, where they overwrite (and "overpaint") the earlier visual and textual images of the lady and Guillaume

---

76. Helen Philips, "Fortune and the Lady: Machaut, Chaucer and the Intertextual 'Dit,'" *Nottingham French Studies* 38 (1999): 131.

77. *Voir dit*, ll. 8822, 8832, 8842, 8852, 8862.

78. The whole text is in **A**, **Pm**, **F**, and **E**; this part is in **J** and **K**; see Earp, *Guillaume de Machaut*, 223–31, and on the illuminations, 181–83.

with images of Fortune, emphasizing the moral aspect of the tale.[79] It has even been proposed that the cyclic narrative structure of the *Voir dit* forms a giant representation of Fortune's wheel.[80]

The Fortune episode is effectively the terminal one in the *Voir dit* and follows a long tailing-off of the relationship between Guillaume and Toute Belle, who have not met since Hope appeared to Guillaume on his way home from their third meeting.[81] Once he has doubly entombed the image of his lady in a coffer within a coffer, it appears to him in a dream. Guillaume decides to set it free, first because of the moral he draws from its story of "how the crow was turned black" (for telling an unpalatable truth to a lover; ll. 7792–8179, the dit's final exemplum), and second because it complains to him of its imprisonment (ll. 8180–8201). Guillaume agrees with Morpheus that messengers telling unpalatable truths are foolish (*fols*) because no lover, however devoted and loyal he is, can be perfect enough in his behavior to resist the anger and displeasure that will result (ll. 8202–33). Guillaume begins to curse Fortune and Love and turns to Titus Livius's description of Fortune (figure 5.7).

In the illumination of **A**, Fortune loops her arms around two of the four spokes of a large wheel to hold two of the four smaller wheels that are contained within it on each of the spokes.[82] The direct speech of the figure of Fortune recounted in the narrative verse (ll. 8286–87, 8290–91, 8294–95, 8300–8301, 8310–11) forms, in Latin, part of the picture, making a label for each of the five wheels.[83] Through the open fulcrum of the large wheel juts the *mons veneris* of Fortune herself, the folds of her dress suggestive of labia.[84] This emphasizes the dangerous draw of female sexuality—the usual lure that places the desiring subject in Fortune's power—and offers a visual Charybdis as a counterpart to the aural, siren-like Fortune whose song, according to the fourth article written in the circles, "deceives, falsifies, and lies." This fourth article fits Toute Belle, who is described as "la mieux chantans / Qui fust nee de puis.C. ans" ("the best at singing that was born in a hundred years";

---

79. See Catherine Attwood, "The Image in the Fountain: Fortune, Fiction and Femininity in the *Livre du Voir Dit* of Guillaume de Machaut," *Nottingham French Studies* 38 (1999): 137; and Jacqueline Cerquiglini, *"Un engin si soutil": Guillaume de Machaut et l'écriture au XIVe siècle* (Geneva, 1985), 150–52.

80. See Cerquiglini, *"Un engin si soutil,"* 56–63, especially the diagram on 57.

81. See chapter 4, figure 4.5.

82. Only the lower two wheels are correctly copied so that the spoke passes through them; the other two are seemingly placed entirely behind their spokes. Leo notes other instances where the artist clearly had difficulty executing the complex images that were demanded by this dit. See Domenic Leo, "The Program of Miniatures in Manuscript A," in *Guillaume de Machaut: Le livre dou voir dit (The Book of the True Poem)*, ed. Daniel Leech-Wilkinson and R. Barton Palmer (New York, 1998), xcii.

83. The equivalent illumination in **Pm** preserves **A**'s Latin inscriptions; **E** gives them in French. Manuscripts **J** and **K** have only three smaller wheels depicted. See Earp, *Guillaume de Machaut*, 181–82.

84. See Leo, "The Program of Miniatures," xciii.

Figure 5.7. "Comment Titus Livius descript lymage de fortune" (How Titus Livius describes the image of Fortune): Toute Belle as Fortune in the *Voir dit*, MS A, f. 297r. Bibliothèque nationale de France.

ll. 113–14) when she is originally introduced, and again as an accomplished singer in the response to this fourth article:

> Plus douce que vois de sereinne
> De toute melodie pleinne
> Est sa vois . car quant elle chante
> Mon cuer endort . mon corps enchante
> Einsi com fortune enchantoit
> Ses subies . quant elle chantoit
> Et les decevoit au fausset
> Pour ce que mauvaise et fausse est
> Ce tour ma fait ma dame gente.[85]

Sweeter than the voice of the siren, full of all melody is her [Toute Belle's] voice. For when she sings, my heart is put to sleep and my body is enchanted in the same way that Fortune enchants her subjects when she sings and deceives them with little falseness,[86] because she is bad and false; this is the turn my lady's done me.

Throughout the *Voir dit,* Guillaume has written songs for Toute Belle; in effect he authors her sirenic song. This serves to assimilate him to Toute Belle, who is, whether historically real or not, in the context of the *Voir dit* Guillaume's own creation, the image that Pygmalion has made.[87] Given Guillaume's similarity to Toute Belle and Toute Belle's assimilation to Fortune, Guillaume's assimilation to Fortune is already augured here.

After explaining how the five articles of Titus Livius's Fortune can be applied to Toute Belle, Guillaume concludes that his lady and Fortune could be good friends because they are both changeable, like a molting sparrow hawk. The narrator then goes on to elaborate this into a story about how a well-bred falcon can be trained and rewarded for its service with the heart of the bird it

85. *Voir dit,* ll. 8376–84.

86. R. Barton Palmer translates this as "deceiving them with her falsetto" (Leech-Wilkinson and Palmer, *Machaut: Le livre dou voir dit,* 573, l. 8382). The musical uses for "musica falsa," however, range from general performative malpractice (as in the idiosyncratic treatise of Elias Salomon; see Joseph Dyer, "A Thirteenth-Century Choirmaster: The *Scientia Artis Musicae* of Elias Salomon," *Musical Quarterly* 66 [1980]: 92) to technical uses (where it usually is synonymous with "musica ficta"; see "Musica ficta" in *Grove*). My translation leaves the exact referent open, but it is likely that the use of notes outside the regular gamut (musica ficta) is denoted here, since they are associated with femininity in other contexts. See Elizabeth Eva Leach, "'The Little Pipe Sings Sweetly While the Fowler Deceives the Bird': Sirens in the Later Middle Ages," *Music and Letters* 87 (2006): 187–211; and idem, "Gendering the Semitone, Sexing the Leading Tone: Fourteenth-Century Music Theory and the Directed Progression," *Music Theory Spectrum* 28 (2006): 1–21.

87. Attwood, "The Image in the Fountain," 139.

has killed for its master (ll. 8424–73).[88] This equation between women and hawks—famous to English-speaking scholarship because of its later uses, such as that in Shakespeare's *Taming of the Shrew*—is one that had already been made at length by Machaut in his earlier didactic *Dit de l'alerion,* which compares four different kinds of birds to different female beloveds.[89] The moral Guillaume draws from this story in *Voir dit* (ll. 8475–94) follows *Alerion* in casting the lady in the role of the wayward bird, but this makes little logical sense: Guillaume does not in fact recommend berating and starving a lady who will not see reason (and like the well-trained hawk return to its proper prey). Instead, he says one ought to cease crying and complaining, and thank her with head held high, saying, "If it's what pleases you, I strongly agree" (ll. 8489–91). This line of acid sarcasm is a tag from what was probably a well-known song; Machaut had used it earlier in the refrain of a virelay in which the lover responds to being cast off by his lady.[90] The lover ought to conclude that such a lady's love is worthless because she lacks loyalty. In this way the exemplum hints at a more triangular relationship, one that would better fit the context of the role of the court poet—a role that the *Voir dit* so thoroughly explores. The falcon hunts birds on behalf of his master, much as Machaut woos and praises ladies on behalf of his patrons. Like the falcon, if the poet starts to stray, he can be called back and redirected to the prey that is desired.[91] And like the falcon, the poet does not himself get the bird, which

88. Guillaume introduces this story as "an account recounted to a count" ("un conte/Que ioy conter a un conte"), who is his lord and great friend (ll. 8424–26), and who has placed all his *entente* in the delight of falconry (ll. 8427–28). Although falconry was almost universally practiced among the European nobility in this period, it seems possible that this refers to Jean II de Melun, the Comte de Tancarville, who is the judge of the debate between the hawkers and the huntsmen in Henri de Ferrières's *Livre des Deduis du Roy Modus* (see Leach, *Sung Birds,* 206–12; and Gunnar Tilander, ed., *Les livres du Roy Modus et de la Royne Ratio,* 2 vols. [Paris, 1932], 1:233–66 [section 118]) and might thus legitimately be described as the man who "en scet trop plus que homs / Et trop plus quautres si deduit" (knows more about it [hawking] than anyone else, and enjoys it more than others; *Voir dit,* ll. 8429–30).

89. Shakespeare, *The Taming of the Shrew* 4.1.182–205; on *Alerion,* see William Calin, *A Poet at the Fountain: Essays on the Narrative Verse of Guillaume de Machaut* (Lexington, 1974), 92–109 (chap. 5); Brownlee, *Poetic Identity,* 63–93.

90. *Se ma dame m'a guerpi* (V6) uses this line as an unchanging refrain in both the refrain proper and in the *tierce* section. The extra repetition it thus gains—its melody serving this text alone—draws attention to it, reinforcing the sarcasm. The refrain is found in the thirteenth-century motet *De mes amour / L'autrier / Defors Compiègne,* where it makes up the last line of the song tenor; see Jacques Boogaart, "Encompassing Past and Present: Quotations and Their Function in Machaut's Motets," *Early Music History* 20 (2001): 14. Boogaart does not mention the use of this refrain in V6, although he does mention *Douce dame, vous ociés à tort* (L073), which also uses this line as its refrain.

91. If the count whose story this is can be identified with Jean de Melun, Count of Tancarville, the judge of the two most widely disseminated hunting debate poems of this period, it is possible that this story refers also to Machaut's own seeming realignment (at least in terms of patronage) from the Navarrese party in the 1350s to the Valois in the 1360s.

is reserved for his master's degustation, but rather has its heart to sustain him and keep him from hunger. The poet addresses the lady on behalf of the patron but is nourished by the love of his audience, whose hearts are his.

Typically Guillaume fails to follow his own advice. Instead of breaking off with polite thanks, he sends a letter (letter 42) to his lady in which he does not recount all the gossip he has heard, but focuses only on the rumor that she is showing his work to everyone so that it seems a joke. He tells her he will no longer write anything that is private, is now affecting to love someone else, and is therefore no longer working on the *Voir dit*. He adds that he is sending her the new things he has already done and that she is welcome to show them to anyone she likes. He further emphasizes that he has taken great trouble over the composition of her poem (the *Voir dit*); even if *she* considers it a joke, there are not three people in the world for whom he would have undertaken it.

Toute Belle takes this letter very badly, dropping it from her hands, losing her color, collapsing into bed, and writing a virelay, which she sends to Guillaume with an accompanying letter (letter 43). She chides Guillaume for not coming to see her and then turns the accusations voiced by him in the narrative (but not expressed in his letter) explicitly back on him: he is changeable and not truthful ("vous esties variables et...vous ne tenies pas bien verite"). She denies she has done anything to cause him to become a figure of fun and asks that they forget anything that could make them angry with each other. She desires to see him and sends him a virelay "qui est fait de mon sentement" (that is made from my *sentement*). This virelay, *Cent mille fois esbahie* (VD62), expresses her misery and wish for the healing of death, an attitude typical of a lover who has lost hope because the beloved seems to have abandoned him or her. The virelay is only two stanzas long, which the narrator explains as a sign of how distressed—weary and afflicted, sad, sorrowing, and full of tears ("lasse et adolee / Triste dolente et esplouree")—the lady was when she wrote it.[92] Again, composition from *sentement* is shown to be hopeless, symbolic of lack (literally here, lacking a third stanza), and not to be recommended.

Toute Belle's letter also asks Guillaume to send her something of his (*des vostres*). She furthermore asks for the opening section of her book—which she has seen but already returned to Guillaume—to be sent back to her because she has not kept a copy. She adds that she has also seen a balade which has the (refrain) line "En lieu de bleu dame vous vestez vert" ("instead of blue, lady, you are wearing green," the refrain of *Se pour ce muir* [B36]), and denies that it can or should be applied to her, whose heart is enveloped in pure azure with the loyalty of her love for him. In the first section of the *Voir dit*, when Guillaume first met her, Toute Belle was indeed wearing a blue hood ("chaperon"; l. 2118), but it was, significantly, decorated with green parrots, arranged

92. *Voir dit*, ll. 8573–78.

in pairs looking away from each other, like the two-headed Fortune that constitutes the second of the large final images in the *Voir dit* (see figure 5.8).[93] The balade of which Toute Belle has heard rumors was in fact prompted by an image, that of Tout Belle herself, which had appeared in Guillaume's dream to turn its head away from him and to change its clothing from blue to green.[94]

The balade *Se pour ce muir* (B36/VD61) itself, the last musicalized item in the *Voir dit*, mentions Fortune in a phrase that is altered between the copy of this lyric in the *Loange* section (as Lo248) and its interpolation into the *Voir dit* (as VD61). In all the *Voir dit* copies, the terminal stanza's invective includes in its fifth line the cursing of Fortune and her false wheel-turning ("Et si maudi fortune et son faus tour"; *Voir dit*, l. 7681). In the *Loange*, this lyric does not censure Fortune but rather blames the lady's sweet look ("Le dous regart qui me mist en errour"; Lo248, l. 3.5).[95] The Fortune-specific line found in all copies of the *Voir dit* is also found in the text of this balade when it is copied as B36 in the music sections of three manuscripts, **G**, **A**, and **M**, even though the *Loange* copies in the same sources include the line relating to the lady's look.[96] It seems sensible to consider the *Loange* reading an earlier rendering, and to view the lyric as having been adapted at the time of the *Voir dit*'s composition specifically to bring Fortune into the picture. Manuscript **Vg**, which does not contain the *Voir dit*, transmits the *Loange* reading of this line in its music section copy as B36.[97] This implies strongly that the musical items of *Voir dit* (and possibly other musical pieces as well, especially those using *Loange* lyrics) were written after the versions in *Loange* but before the *Voir dit* itself was composed. When Machaut chose to include this particular song in the *Voir dit*, he probably changed line 3.5 for two reasons. The primary one was almost certainly to dovetail this balade with the pervasive presence of Fortune at the end of the dit. A secondary reason was perhaps to eradicate inconsistency: it was not Toute Belle's sweet look that put Guillaume in error, since in the first instance he did not see the lady. While such inconsistency might ordinarily be expected and even excused in such a long work, this is a dit purportedly "voir," and Guillaume's "grand desir" (great desire) to see Toute Belle was emphatically the inspiration for an earlier balade, a fact that

93. Attwood, "The Image in the Fountain," 141–42.

94. See ibid., 142–43; *Voir dit*, ll. 7633–94. The balade *Se pour ce muir* (B36/VD61/Lo248) forms ll. 7663–83.

95. Of manuscripts **Vg**, **B**, **D**, **J**, **A**, and **M**.

96. F-G excises this duplicated text from its *Loange*. **M** is copied without musical notation.

97. **B**, which is a direct copy of **Vg** and also lacks the *Voir dit*, transmits, like its exemplar, the *Loange* reading in the music section. **E** also has the *Loange* reading in the musical piece despite inserting B36 (along with all the other musical items) into the relevant place within the *Voir dit*; but evidence from the musical readings suggests that **E** was not copying from **B** in this case (see Margaret Bent, "The Machaut Manuscripts *Vg*, *B* and *E*," *Musica Disciplina* 37 [1983]: 78, table 2). **E** seems to have been copying (here as for about half of the music that is not copied from **B**) from an (even) earlier source.

Figure 5.8. "Comment li paien figuroient lymage de fortune" (How the pagans depicted the image of Fortune): Guillaume as Fortune in the *Voir dit*, MS A, f. 301v. Bibliothèque nationale de France.

might cause readers to remember that her sweet look was not what led Guillaume "en errour" (astray).[98]

The "new" line in VD61/B36 (as compared with Lo248) is, like everything about Fortune's description in the later Middle Ages, one that is itself cycled and recycled. It occurs earlier in the sequence of *Loange* poems as the opening of the summative final stanza (l. 3.1) of the balade *Je maudi l'eure et le temps et le jour* (Lo213, l. 3.1). There it similarly initiates the cursing of Fortune along the lines of troubadour *enveg.*[99] It also occurs as part of the complaint *Quant Ecuba vit la destruction* (Cp4), where again it comes first in a similar string of curses, although these encompass not—as in the other instances—the beloved, her traits, and the fact of having met her, but the place and day of the battle that caused the speaker (here personified feminine) to lose her "amis" into shackled captivity.[100]

The matter of B36 continues to rankle in the *Voir dit*. After Toute Belle's letter the narrative resumes. On a Monday, less than a fortnight after her correspondence, a logician-priest, a friend of Guillaume's who has previously acted as Toute Belle's confessor, comes to speak to Guillaume on her behalf (ll. 8591–95). He says that it would be a great sin if Toute Belle were to die from the torment she is experiencing from Guillaume's too ready belief in the rumors of her disloyalty (ll. 8596–8616). He hands Guillaume a letter, reportedly damp with her tears, affirming her faithfulness, which asks again for him to send his book and some of his other compositions (letter 44). The logician-priest reveals that the specific cause of the hurt is still the balade that the lady had referred to in her previous letter, *Se pour ce muir* (B36/VD61). The lady knows that her erstwhile lover has compared her to Fortune, so the logician-priest instead compares Guillaume himself to a differently drawn figure of Fortune, depicted for

98. This earlier balade is *Nes qu'on* (B33), whose refrain is "The great desire that I have to see you." On the genesis of this within the letters and narrative of the *Voir dit*, see Ardis Butterfield, "The Art of Repetition: Machaut's Ballade 33, *Nes qu'on porroit*," *Early Music* 31 (2003): 347–60.

99. Johnson, *Poets as Players*, 50. Fortune's "faus tour" is also cursed to her face in the address to Fortune that forms the final stanza of the highly popular music balade *De toutes flours* (B31), in which, if Fortune's false rotation dries out his Rose, the speaker will "never seek another after"; see Leach, "Counterpoint as an Interpretative Tool." L19/14 starts with the phrase "Malgre Fortune et son tour"—despite Fortune's vagaries the speaker will publish his complaint.

100. It has been suggested that Cp4 forms a prologue to *Fonteinne*, although it could fit the circumstances of numerous cases of exile and hostage in the 1350s and 1360s; see Earp, *Guillaume de Machaut*, 270; Françoise Ferrand, "Doux Penser, Plaisance et Espérance chez Guillaume de Machaut et Charles d'Orléans: Un nouvel art d'aimer," in *Plaist vos oïr bone cançon vallant? Mélanges de langue et de littérature médiévales offerts à François Suard*, ed. Dominique Boutet et al. (Villeneuve d'Ascq, 1999), 241–45. *Je maudi l'eure* (Lo213) is followed in the *Loange* by *Morray je dont sans avoir vostre amour* (Lo214), a poem that considers dying for love—exactly the thought that Lo248 itself (that is, *Pour ce muir* [B36]) opens with, but here joined to Lo213's refrain's idea of exile in a strange land. That Machaut's Hope-oriented doctrine was easily adaptable to situations of absence and exile in a period when nobles frequently served hostage terms may have been of great practical benefit.

the reader in the second large miniature in this section of the poem (figure 5.8). This is, according to the rubric, how the pagans depicted the image of Fortune. Here the wheel of Fortune is lifted so that the fulcrum frames the heart of the figure, not her pudenda. Instead of being monocephalic and crowned, this Fortune wears a demure skullcap on each of her two heads, which look in opposite directions and are explained in the text as representing joy and sorrow.[101] Instead of five wheels, there are five fountains, to which come five maidens who sing to appease the goddess.

Toute Belle's confessor accuses Guillaume of behaving like a woman in being so changeable, having two faces, and crying and laughing at will. The five maidens resemble the five messengers who have carried ill rumors of Toute Belle. These, he maintains, have sung more sweetly than sirens to appease Fortune. Guillaume has "too readily believed" all the negative rumors he has heard about Toute Belle; for each one of the rumors he enumerates, the confessor repeats the refrain "Et tout par legierement croire."[102] Fortune, worshipped as a sovereign goddess, gives comfort that is pain, luck that is mischance, and riches that are poverty. Everything is the opposite of how it appears. The priest begs Guillaume to reassert his faithful love and declares that Toute Belle will then forgive him. In letter 45 Guillaume duly does so, promising to finish her book and send it to her. In the narrative he sends an extra message with the priest—a long hyperbole saying that he loves her five hundred thousand times more than a great list of innumerable things (the number of drops of blood in all creatures, drops of water in the sea, birds in the sky, fibers in wool, and so on). The priest cuttingly responds that he would have to get up very early in order to be able to tell her all that, and leaves auspiciously on the first of May, the traditional date for a springtime renewal of love.[103]

---

101. This double-headed depiction resonates with the earlier description of the parrots on Toute Belle's hood, which are green on a hood of blue, and symbolize not only spoken eloquence and sweet song but also courtiers who are rather too eloquent to tell the truth. See Leach, *Sung Birds*, 250–51, 267–68; and Lee Patterson, "Court Politics and the Invention of Literature: The Case of Sir John Clanvowe," in *Culture and History, 1350–1600: Essays on English Communities, Identities, and Writing,* ed. David Aers (New York, 1992), 22–23. The parrots are not illustrated in any of the surviving copies of the poem, nor is the other bifurcated head image—the image of Semiramis with one tress done and one undone—although the latter seems to have been illuminated in a bas-de-page picture that survives only as a single scrap. See Donal Byrne, "A 14th-Century French Drawing in Berlin and the 'Livre du Voir-Dit' of Guillaume de Machaut," *Zeitschrift für Kunstgeschichte* 47 (1984): 70–81.

102. This is similar to the refrain of *On ne puet riens savoir si proprement* (Lo192), "De legier croire encontre son ami"; see the discussion earlier in this chapter and the *Voir dit,* ll. 8822, 8832, 8842, 8852, 8862. See also the extended discussion of both the "feminization of Machaut" as Fortune and the equation of Fortune with "fame" (i.e., both "woman" and "renown") in Cerquiglini, *"Un engin si soutil,"* 139–55.

103. Ironically spring is also a traditional time to wear green and affect new love; see Susan Crane, *The Performance of Self: Ritual, Clothing, and Identity during the Hundred Years War* (Philadelphia, 2002), 39–72 (chap. 2). See also Attwood, "The Image in the Fountain," 143.

The response from Toute Belle, letter 46—her last—notes that all is now pardoned and they will henceforth be able to live in perfect love, free from the rebuffs of Fortune ("hors des dangiers de fortune"). She is not sending his book back, however, because she is worried that it might become lost, and she wants several things changed, which she will tell him about when they next meet.[104] She sends him instead a rondeau using numbers to encode Machaut's name. This final lyric is followed by a narrative passage of virtuoso rhymes using words with the stem "-cord-," in which the lover describes the onset of harmony between himself and Toute Belle (ll. 9051–70), and then signs off (ll. 9071–94).

Throughout this concluding section of the *Voir dit*, a centripetal force draws both protagonists into the center of Fortune's wheel and into a fusion first with each other and then with the goddess herself. Fortune's femininity makes this an unsurprising assimilation for Toute Belle. The whirligig of Fortune is arguably prefigured by the very earliest description of her being apt to dance "oultre mesure," a phrase signifying excess and which perhaps also suggests turning in a round, like the main social dance of the Middle Ages, the *carole,* a version of which was probably danced to the fourteenth-century virelay.[105] Toute Belle's wish to assimilate herself to the figure of the poet is also signaled from her initial epistolary approach, asking for criticism of two of her own rondeaux (letter 1). Yet the assimilation of Guillaume to Fortune may at first seem more surprising. This only begins to make sense when one realizes that it is his failure as a lover, sealed in his forgetfulness of Hope, his espousal of *sentement,* and his resultant emotional instability, which enables Machaut's success as a poet. It is Machaut and Machaut's works—and not Guillaume and his—that successfully combat Fortune.

Fighting Fortune

The *Voir dit*'s pairing of two portrayals of Fortune—one purportedly from Titus Livius, the other that of the "pagans"—does not obscure Machaut's basic source for his picture of Fortune, which, like the vast majority of vernacular portrayals of this period, draws on the pagan goddess impersonated by Philosophy in the second prose of book 2 of the *Consolation*. Only the Fortunes found in *Fauvel* and Dante's *Divine Comedy* are sufficiently Christianized to incorporate the discussion in the later books of the *Consolation*, which link

---

104. She regrets that she does not have the two balades he wrote that he had sent (although these are not mentioned in the preceding letter) and is "fearful of their being shouted through [the] streets" before she has a chance to learn them. See *Voir dit*, letter 46.

105. *Voir dit*, ll. 115.

Fortune with divine providence in the context of a discussion of free will.[106] Because of this, as I have shown, Fortune is a predominantly negative force within Machaut's work.

While Hope is the key doctrinal figure in countering the ravages of Fortune, Hope requires constant upkeep through the action of *Souvenir*. This means that the instability of Fortune has one less negative, unintended consequence, an aspect that is brought particularly to the fore in *Navarre* and the *Voir dit*: she stimulates artistic creativity as a means of combating her.[107] In opposing oneself to Fortune's losses, Machaut suggests that one should use memory either to construct a durable picture of a living lady's goodness (as, for example, in *Remede*) or to enshrine the same for a dead beloved (as in *Navarre*). In both cases, memory is implicitly supported by visual storage—whether mental, as in the case of the Sweet Thought held in Memory, or physical, as in the case of writing or images.[108] The stability and truth of the visual and physical are contrasted with the instability and unreliability of the oral and aural. Machaut's work—poetic fiction but possessing truth-value and apt to console—is thereby differentiated from gossip, which is perhaps factually accurate but worthless or traumatic.

Enshrining truth in writing to counter Fortune's power involves both praising women's fidelity (writing "in praise of ladies," as Love urges Machaut to do in the *Prologue*) and proving the power of writing to act as a permanent record. *Navarre* does both, using music in its culminating lay to help remember the beloved "in a book."[109] Speaking as a woman, *Navarre*'s protagonist, Guillaume de Machaut, offers a poem that on the one hand memorializes the singing lady's dead lover, and on the other hand reassures male readers and listeners that women can be constant in their love for men. Similarly, the "true story" of Toute Belle and Guillaume, with its climactic double comparison to Fortune, actually creates a long and virtuoso literary artifact, a book that contains a large number of stories, further vernacular literary transformations of what are already *Metamorphoses,* and the full generic range of writing, from prose letters via narrative verse to lyrics in all the fixed forms. Amorous failure breeds literary success; the lady-as-Fortune in the *Voir dit* initially stimulates, then destabilizes but continues to inspire, the poetic ability of Guillaume. Thus poetry can either assure its audience of the stability of living love by praising ladies, or celebrate, memorialize, and enshrine in permanent "external memory" (that is, in letters) those who are, or will become, dead. Many of Machaut's later dits achieve the latter by comparing a living patron

106. Hunt, "The Christianization of Fortune," notes that several vernacular translations represent these later books in a somewhat attenuated form.

107. Attwood, "The Image in the Fountain," 140.

108. On the pictorial nature of memory, see Mary Carruthers and Jan M. Ziolkowski, eds., *The Medieval Craft of Memory: An Anthology of Texts and Poems* (Philadelphia, 2002), 11–13.

109. See chapter 4.

to a dead worthy: in *Confort,* for example, a living patron (King Charles of Navarre) is compared to a recently dead worthy and former employer (King John of Bohemia). In the process, Machaut's written record of an ongoing combat with Fortune—his entire manuscript book—provides a way of ensuring his own fame.

Both aspects of writing's riposte to Fortune involve dealing with detractors. In praising ladies, Machaut is forced explicitly to tackle men's fears about women. *Navarre* does this most clearly, with the character of Guillaume expressing standard misogynistic viewpoints; later in the chapter I discuss this further and also consider some of the lyric presentations of similarly negative depictions of women. In stressing the importance of the written representation of memory, Machaut emphasizes the dangers ascribed to nonliterate performances and to gossip. This is most evident in the *Voir dit,* both in the series of messengers who carry rumors of infidelity or disregard between the two lovers, and in the presence of various birds whose "songs" populate the stories near the end of the tale. Here, as throughout Machaut's works, the tension between written truth and oral rumor is explored as a way of discussing the ability of literature to commemorate, celebrate, and memorialize, preserving for posterity not just the "truth" but the name of the patron and poet. More than earlier vernacular writers, Machaut sought to link his name and person with his texts, not only celebrating patrons and dedicatees but also ensuring that his own fame would endure with theirs.

Praising Ladies

In the *Prologue,* having introduced his children in the first two stanzas of his balade, the god of Love insists in the final stanza that Machaut make only things that praise ladies:

> Mais garde bien, sur tout ne t'enhardi
> A faire chose ou il ait villenie,
> N'aucunement des dames ne mesdi;
> Mais en tous cas les loe et magnefie.
> Saches, se tu fais le contraire,
> Je te feray trés cruellment detraire.[110]

But take care above all that thou not embolden thyself to make anything in which there might be baseness, nor ever slander any ladies, but in all cases praise and magnify them. Know that if thou doest the opposite, I shall very cruelly make thee take it back.

---

110. *Prologue* 3.21–26.

At the end of his reply to this, Guillaume de Machaut claims that he will obey this imprecation:

Et des dames blasmer me garderay,
Ne, se Dieu plaist, ja n'en seray repris,
Mais honnourer et loer les vorray
A mon pooir, tant comme je vivray.[111]

And I will keep myself from blaming women, nor, if God pleases, shall I ever be reproved for this, but I intend to honor and praise them, *according to my powers, as long as I shall live.*

If Machaut's book seems to present lyrics and narrative passages that defy his own promise, this is as illusory as the seeming mismatch between the *Prologue*'s espousal of the joyful composing of songs and the inclusion of many sorrowful songs and composition from authentically sorrowful *sentement* in the pages that follow. The *Prologue* instructs the reader in the proper context for interpreting those aspects of the emotional and human world in Machaut's book that are meant to represent the negative side of his ethical doctrine, fit for active resistance and thoughtful rejection.

The character Guillaume in *Navarre* is the most urgent voice against women, and as Love threatens he will be in the *Prologue,* he is indeed forced in the end to "retraire," to take back his arguments, which derive in part from those used by Jean de Meun in the *Roman de la Rose.*[112] If Jean de Meun's or Guillaume's view of the absolute changeableness of women were true, Hope could not be sustained; belief in the goodness of women—at least in the abstract, as a guiding principle—is necessary to the poetics of Hope and the frustration of Fortune. The fear that women are unable to love as strongly and stably as men because they are too changeable is what especially torments the male lovers in *Navarre,* but Guillaume's assessment of women's instability is countered by examples presenting the female reaction to grief as more stable and real than that of men.[113] Men who are rejected in love are shown as being able to transform themselves through madness or chivalry: men, not women, are more truly mutable. Guillaume's misogyny is penalized when he is forced to write a lay in the feminine voice as a way of memorializing the lady and her dead beloved in a book. As well as providing the lady with a usefully absorbing (and diverting) expression of her own grief, the lay makes feminine suffering comprehensible to the male part of its audience and reassures them that

---

111. *Prologue* 4.27–30.

112. Douglas Kelly, *Medieval Imagination: Rhetoric and the Poetry of Courtly Love* (Madison, 1978), 142–43.

113. Sylvia Huot, "Guillaume de Machaut and the Consolation of Poetry," *Modern Philology* 100 (2002): 184.

women can sustain undying love. The lady reverses the normal direction of desire by seeing the man as the perfection that she obtains by incorporating him into herself.[114]

It is not only in *Qui bien aimme* (L22/16) that Machaut sings in the voice of a woman, nor are his feminine-voiced songs always the projection of such a reassuringly virtuous, constant woman.[115] Elsewhere Machaut envoices female subjects whose instability and questionable loyalty form potentially misogynistic constructs in which the *dame* becomes like Fortune. The case of Toute Belle has already been discussed: she is frequently undermined by the words put into her mouth in the *Voir dit*. The feminine voice of *De Fortune* (B23), too, has been discussed: in this song the lady seems to think her lover has been disloyal, but she is aware that such a false thought is itself disloyal. Her own change from happiness to discomfort, prompted by the change she has heard about in her lover, shows her belief in unsubstantiated gossip, her Hope-less reliance on exterior events, and her own potential similarity to the Fortune of whom she complains.

The implication of this song—and the broader context that it occupies in the *Loange*—is that women who believe in gossip become unstable like Fortune. The issue of gossip in this *Loange* sequence will be developed later in this chapter. For present purposes it is worth noting that a reading of B23 as a negative presentation of women en masse is complicated by Lorenz Welker's recent suggestion that the tenor is based on the melody of part of the *Salve Regina*, a Marian antiphon.[116] The two questions raised by this identification are whether this evocation is in fact "there," and if so, what it means. The latter question is somewhat easier that the former: the juxtaposition of Marian and secular love lyrics is common in the thirteenth and fourteenth centuries, and music displaying such juxtaposition has been subject to analogical interpretations by Sylvia Huot, Anne Walters Robertson, Suzannah Clark,

---

114. Ibid., 186. Kay reads *Navarre* as being more centrally concerned with interaction between Guillaume and abstractions personified as women but ultimately internal to the poet. In her reading, *Navarre*'s ending resituates sexual difference entirely within the internal world of the poet, rather than offering a consoling picture of gender opposition found in the earlier dits, and the lady of the lay is a fictional construct of the character Guillaume de Machaut. See Sarah Kay, *The Place of Thought: The Complexity of One in Late Medieval French Didactic Poetry* (Philadelphia, 2007), 115–18.

115. Among the *forme fixe* refrain songs set to music are five feminine-voiced balade texts (*Dous amis* [B6], the second voice of the triple balade *Sans cuer m'en / Amis / Dame* [B17], *De petit po* [B18], *De Fortune* [B23], and *Honte, paour* [B25]), three virelays (*Se d'amer* [V20], *Moult sui* [V37/31], and *De tout sui* [V38/32]), and one rondeau (*Puis qu'en oubli* [R18]). The ladies of B6 and R18 lament, and that of B23 suspects, a male lover's lack of loyalty; the lady of V20 imagines how terrible it would be to repent of loving her very loyal friend, given how virtuous and devoted he is.

116. See Welker, "Guillaume de Machaut, das romantische Lied und die Jungfrau Maria."

and David Rothenberg, as chapter 6 will explore further.[117] But whether this tenor really *is* a quotation, one meant to be understood as such—if not from listening then from singing or even from reading and instruction—is harder to assess. If such a reading is possible, the song does not simply present a mild misogyny but compares two feminine exemplars and, by extension, two Fortunes: a woman subject to a predetermined fate in the shape of Fortune, and a woman subject to a Christianized Fortune as divine intervention—the Virgin Mary. The issue is further compounded by the identification of a similar Marian plainsong—the final verse of *Alma redemptoris mater*—in another of the century's most widely circulated songs, Machaut's *De petit po* (B18).[118] This, too, is a feminine-voiced song and virtually a mirror image of the situation in B23: in B23 the lady has believed gossip about her lover and starts to doubt him; in B18 the lady's lover has believed gossip about her disloyalty and has stopped loving her. The existence of both songs suggests that credulousness affects men and women alike but that change of love inspired by gossip alone is always wrong.

The lady of B18 starts in a clerkly, sententious fashion uttering a proverbial statement found in works by the younger contemporary poets John Gower and Philippe de Mézières, where it refers to largesse. In these authors the received wisdom is that one with a little should give a little, give enough from a lot, and from nothing give good will.[119] At the last minute, however, the narrator of B18 subverts the thought from the idea of giving to the idea of taking: "De petit po, de niant volenté / De moult assés doit *penre*" (From a little a little, from nothing good will, from much enough, ought one to *take*;

117. Suzannah Clark, "'S'en dirai chançonete': Hearing Text and Music in a Medieval Motet," *Plainsong and Medieval Music* 16 (2007): 31–59; Sylvia Huot, *Allegorical Play in the Old French Motet: The Sacred and Profane in Thirteenth-Century Polyphony* (Stanford, 1997); Anne Walters Robertson, *Guillaume de Machaut and Reims: Context and Meaning in His Musical Works* (Cambridge, 2002); David J. Rothenberg, "The Marian Symbolism of Spring, ca. 1200–ca. 1500: Two Case Studies," *Journal of the American Musicological Society* 59 (2006): 319–98.

118. Welker, "Guillaume de Machaut, das romantische Lied und die Jungfrau Maria." Welker points out that the tenor rhythmicizes this in a way similar to that found at the opening of the upper parts in the motet *Rex Karole, Johannis genite / Leticie, pacis, concordie / [Virgo prius ac posterius]*. The upper parts of this motet paraphrase its tenor chant, which comes from the final strophe of the *Alma Redemptoris Mater*.

119. See ibid., 81n31,which cites James Woodrow Hassell, *Middle French Proverbs, Sentences, and Proverbial Phrases* (Toronto, 1982), 198, no. P139. The proverb appears in Philippe de Mézières, *Le songe du vieil pélerin*, bk. 2, l. 358: "Selon le proverbe qui dit: De pou, pou, et de nyent, bonne voulenté" (according to the proverb which says from a little [give] little, and from nothing [give] good will); and John Gower, *Mirour de l'omme*, ll. 15817–18 "Du petit poy serra donné, / Du nient l'en dorra volenté" (From little, a little should be given; from nothing, good will should be given). Gower's usage refers to the third daughter of Generosity, Almsgiving. Given that Machaut's earliest known employment was as a royal almoner, such concerns would at one time have been uppermost among his duties; see chapter 1, and Elizabeth Eva Leach, "Guillaume de Machaut, Royal Almoner: *Honte, paour* (B25) and *Donnez, signeurs* (B26) in Context," *Early Music* 38 (2010): 21–42.

B18, ll. 1–2). At this point the music reflects the unexpected turn with one of its own: an upward leap of a seventh in the cantus to introduce e^b, a pitch that shifts the tonal feel of the piece from a C-based "ut-tonality" (with $E^{\natural}$ and cadences to C achieved through the use of $b^{\natural}$), to a D-based "mi-tonality" (with cadences to D achieved through the use of E^b), which represents the secondary emphasis in the song (boxed in example 5.5).[120]

The opening clerkly register is additionally disrupted by the revelation that the speaker is in fact not a cleric but an emotionally involved female lover-protagonist, as she complains, "Lasse! dolente."[121] This makes the singing voice here an uneasy hybrid, swinging between the opening clerical register and feminine lament. The lady's lament is prompted because her lover has not taken only the little that he was offered and consoled himself with proverbial wisdom, but has instead left her, suspecting that her coldness is the fruit not of honorable loving but of lack of interest.[122] In the second stanza of B18, the lady reveals that her lover has abandoned her because he has believed the "mesdisans," who have told him that she has stopped loving him. The third stanza contrasts this with her own disbelief of those who have spoken basely of him to her. The refrain falls back once more on proverbial wisdom: "No one loved who hates for so little."[123] By implication she accuses her lover of never having loved her, so her earlier positive comments about his goodness, honor, and understanding ring somewhat hollow.

The proverbial statement used in B18's refrain appears in the middle of an earlier motet text by Machaut's illustrious Champenois forerunner Adam de la Halle, but with the gender of the protagonists reversed. A male lover, whose lady's belief in gossip about him has caused her to reject him, dreams of the hour when he will be able to see her and defend himself from the rumors: "Very dear beloved," he says "have pity on me, for God's sake have *merci*— no one loved who hated for so little."[124] B18's female *je* and Adam's male *je*

---

120. For a more basic exposition of this musical analysis, see Elizabeth Eva Leach, "Form, Counterpoint, and Meaning in a Fourteenth-Century French Courtly Song," in *Analytical and Cross-Cultural Studies in World Music* (New York, forthcoming).

121. See also example 1 in Welker, "Guillaume de Machaut, das romantische Lied und die Jungfrau Maria," 78.

122. The relation between largesse and honor is highly gendered in Machaut's courtly doctrine. For women in private amorous contexts, keeping good one's honor involves being "large en refus"; for men in public political contexts, giving freely of gifts, land, and money represents honorable largesse. The paired advice balades *Honte, paour* (B25) and *Donnez, signeurs* (B26) contrast these kinds of largesse most thoroughly. See Leach, "Guillaume de Machaut, Royal Almoner."

123. "Onques n'ama qui pour si pou haÿ."

124. He ends his text with another refrain bidding the gatekeeper to let him pass. The entire text forms the motetus of a three-part motet. A lady who is also keen to find a way to go to her lover voices the triplum: she initially says she will send her belt in her place, but it retains the scent of her beloved and she cannot do without it. Instead she sends her song to go to him because she cannot, informing him that he should come to her at nightfall and will hear her song when the time is right for him to take his pleasure. As this motet's texts are full of "grafted refrains,"

Example 5.5. *De petit po* (B18: A section).

are in identical situations, and both fall back on the same piece of proverbial wisdom, suggesting (as in the *Voir dit*'s more negative treatment) that the universality of Fortune's power renders her demesne one of equality between men and women. This is furthered by the unstable staging of gender in B18's text: this feminine-voiced poem is a skin-deep "contrefait" of a woman with the further deceptive interior of a cleric; like Fortune she is an "idol of false portraiture," not quite what she seems. The rather clerical practices of proverbial enunciation may be even more closely authenticated to Machaut as author if his refrain alludes overtly to Adam's motet, which is itself full of cited material. Even if the proverb hails from an independent source, the opening and closing tone of the song undermines the central feminine lament in B18, perhaps thereby emphasizing the point the lady herself makes—that one should not believe everything one hears.

The patently skin-deep adoption of the feminine voice is also a feature of the motet that precedes and is paired with the Fortune motet discussed earlier, *J'ay tant / Lasse!* (M7). M7 has two upper voices that are both those of women, ostensibly of the same woman (texts and translations are given in figure 5.9).[125] Having chronicled the instability in love of both herself and her erstwhile lover, the very end of the motetus text (l. 18) breaks out of its feminine lament to declare with stereotypical clerical antifeminism that "Telle est des femmes la nature" (this is the nature of women), transforming the seeming personal testimony of the motetus voice into a demonstration of a general principle concerning the variability of women.

The uppermost voice, the triplum, carries a direct narration of courtly love at the center of which is a change, in fact a complete mirrored reversal of status between the lady and her lover. The first sixteen lines lay out the situation: having refused her lover when he loved her and she didn't love him, she now loves him, but he has moved on to another beloved (ll. 1–16). The lady begs her audience to learn from her example and not to refuse men. The singer of the middle voice, the motetus, more succinctly outlines the same story: she did not care for her sweet friend until it was too late; now she loves him and he hates her. She compares herself specifically to Narcissus—the man who rejected the love of Echo in favor of self-love. In effect, as Kevin Brownlee argues, the lady of both voices has started as Narcissus (rejecting her Echo) only to become Echo, the rejected lady; in doing so she has switched sex.[126]

---

the one that forms Machaut's refrain in B18 might simply be another (albeit one that has not been considered as such by modern refrain commentators); if this is so, Machaut may conceivably have known it from a third source. See Ardis Butterfield, "*Enté*: A Survey and Re-assessment of the Term in Thirteenth- and Fourteenth-Century Music and Poetry," *Early Music History* 22 (2003): 89–90.

125. Translation from Kevin Brownlee, "La polyphonie textuelle dans le Motet 7 de Machaut: Narcisse, la *Rose*, et la voix féminine," in Cerquiglini-Toulet and Wilkins, *Guillaume de Machaut*, 137–46; and text based on manuscript C.

126. Brownlee, "La polyphonie textuelle," 141–42.

TRIPLUM

1. J'ay tant mon cuer et mon orgueil creü,
2. Et tenu chier ce qui m'a deceü,
3. Et en vilté ce qui m'amoit eü
4. Que j'ay falli
5. Aus tres dous biens dont Amours pourveü,
6. A par Pitié maint cuer despourveü,
7. Et de la tres grant joie repeü,
8. Dont je langui.
9. Lasse! einsi m'a mes felons cuers trahi,
10. Car onques jour vers mon loyal ami,
11. Qui me servoit et amoit plus que li,
12. N'os cuer meü
13. Que de m'amour li feïsse l'ottri;
14. Or sai je bien qu'il aimme autre que mi,
15. Qui liement en ottriant merci
16. L'a reçeü.
17. Si le m'estuet chierement comparer,
18. Car je l'aim tant c'on ne puet plus amer;
19. Mais c'est trop tart: je ne puis recouvrer
20. La soie amour.
21. Et s'ay paour, se je li vueil rouver,
22. Qu'il ne me deingne oïr ne escouter
23. Pour mon orgueil, qui trop m'a fait fier
24. En ma folour.
25. Et se je li vueil celer ma dolour,
26. Desirs, espris d'amoureuse chalour,
27. Destraint mon corps et mon cuer en errour
28. Met de finer.
29. S'aim miex que je li die ma langour
30. Qu'einsi morir, sans avoir la savour
31. De la joie qu'est parfaite douçour
32. A savourer;
33. Et dou dire ne me doit nul blasmer,
34. Qu'Amours, Besoins et Desirs d'achever
35. Font trespasser mesure et sens outrer.

TRANSLATION

[Exposition]
I have believed too much in my heart and my pride, and held dear that which has deceived me, and [held] vile that which has loved me, so that I have lost the very sweet goods that Love has purveyed by means of Pity to many unfurnished hearts and filled them with the very great joy for which I languish. (ll .1–8)
Alas! Thus my felonious heart has betrayed me, for every day toward my loyal friend who served and loved me more than himself I did not move my heart so that it might have made him the grant of my love. Now I know well that he loves another than me, who happily in granting him *merci* has received him. (ll. 9–16)
[Development]
So I must dearly compare myself to him, for I love him so much that no one could love more. But it is too late; I cannot recover his love. (ll. 17–20)
And I fear that if I ask it of him he will deign neither to hear nor to listen to me because of my pride, which made me so arrogant in my folly. (ll. 21–24)
And if I wish to conceal my sorrow from him, Desire burning with the heat of love makes my body and my heart err, placing them at an end. (ll. 25–28)
[Conclusion]
So I would rather tell him [of] my languor than die in this way, without having the taste of the joy that is perfect sweetness to taste. And for speaking [of this] none should blame me, whom Love, Need, and Desire of fulfillment make trespass measure and exceed sense. (ll. 29–35)

MOTETUS

1. Lasse! je sui en aventure
2. De morir de mort einsi dure
3. Com li biaus Narcysus mori,
4. Qui son cuer tant enorguilli,
5. Pour ce qu'il avoit biauté pure
6. Seur toute humeinne creature,
7. Qu'onques entendre le depri
8. Ne deingna d'Equo, qui pour li
9. Reçut mort amere et obscure.
10. Mais Bonne Amour d'amour seüre
11. Fist qu'il ama et encheri
12. Son ombre, et li pria mercy,

TRANSLATION

Alas! I am going to die a death as hard as the beautiful Narcissus died, whose heart was so proud of his having such perfect beauty—above that of all humankind—that he did not deign to hear the plea of Echo, who on his account received a dark and bitter death. (ll. 1–9)
But Good Love made him love and cherish his shadow with a steadfast love and beg it for *merci* so that in praying he died of burning. (ll. 10–13)
Alas! I too fear such a death because of my sweet friend, of whom, when he loved me from the

Figure 5.9. Texts and translations of *J'ay tant / Lasse! / Ego moriar* (M7).

13. Tant qu'en priant mori d'ardure.
14. Lasse! et je crien morir einsi,
15. Car onques de mon dous amy
16. Quant il m'amoit de cuer n'os cure;
17. Or l'aim et il me het, ay mi!
18. Telle est des femmes la nature

heart, I never had a care; now I love him and he hates me—Oh me! (ll. 14–17)

Such is the nature of women. (l. 18)

TENOR
Ego moriar pro te

TRANSLATION
I might die for thee.

Tenor Source: Historia of Kings, itself deriving from 2 Samuel 18:33

Rex autem David cooperto capite incendens lugebat filium, dicens: Absalon fili mi, fili mi Absalon, quid mihi det ut <u>ego morior pro te</u>, fili mi Absalon?

King David, greatly moved, mourned his son with his head covered, saying: my son Absalom, Absalom by son! Would God that <u>I might die for thee</u>, my son Absalom!

Figure 5.9. (*Continued*)

Meanwhile her erstwhile lover, too, has been unstable in his affections: having been her Echo, he is now mirroring her own reversal in becoming Narcissus and rejecting her. The precedent for reversing the gender of Narcissus in this way is already present in the authorial moralization of the story of Narcissus in the *Roman de la Rose*. As a negative example, *Rose* holds up Narcissus, whom ladies should not emulate if they do not want to kill their lovers.[127]

M7's tenor plainsong fragment is taken from the *Historia* of kings, specifically from the lament of King David for the death of his son Absalom, found in 2 Samuel 18:33. This fragment meditates on the topos of a change of heart being too late to prevent death.[128] In wishing to die *instead* of Absalom, David is deeply anti-narcissistic, forming a type for Christ, who does eventually die for his beloved (his children, his church). He is also akin to Mary, who, in various musical laments popular in this period, is also depicted wishing that she too could have died for her son. Although each lady in the two upper voices thinks that it is too late to retrieve the situation, the only voice in which this is true is the tenor, where death and not a change of living love has intervened. In this respect the motet presents a gender inversion of the situation in the two *jugement* poems: in the upper voices a woman's lover has changed to love another, and in the tenor a man's beloved has died. In this way the sense of rupture produced by the clerical pronouncement at the end of the motetus

127. *Rose*, ll. 1504–7.
128. The apparent reversal in the source text—the words "Absalon fili mi, fili mi Absalon"—is in terms of word order rather than sense. The grief of the speaker names his son at both ends of the opening utterance as a rhetorical gesture; the sense is unchanged.

is healed. If changeability is "the nature of women," then why has only David's changeability caused death, whereas the woman's change has hurt only herself? The male lover has also changed: after being rejected, he has simply moved on to love another. Once more the lady is changeable, but so too is the man. Machaut's appropriation of masculine clerkly antifeminism, gilded but not hidden by the ostensibly feminine voice, is itself undermined by the equation of masculine and feminine behavior, both in this motet and throughout his other works.

The removal of gender opposition in this fashion in M7 turns gender difference into something that operates not between men and women but rather within a single individual. Sarah Kay's book on French didactic poetry includes an interesting chapter on *Navarre,* which she sees as representing a change in Machaut's thinking about sexual difference in terms that can be marshaled to illuminate the present discussion.[129] Kay's book draws on the debate in medieval epistemology over universals, which by the fourteenth century had inflected a basic opposition between realism and nominalism with a new interest in the subjective psychology that was replacing an older Platonic epistemology. Although this debate might sound rather abstract, it should be possible to see how an interest in the psychological (that is, emotional and intellectual) experience of human subjects is central to Machaut's poetry. Kay views Machaut's poetry as constantly worrying away at how one might arrive at knowledge when knowledge relies on universal concepts—relayed in symbolic language—and yet our experience of reality contains only individual, singular, and particular instances that are often irreducible and inexpressible. In Kay's analysis of *Navarre,* sexual difference is shown to interfere with thinking in universal terms because "universality is blocked not just by the differences in particular experiences of happiness but also by the partiality that results from sexual difference."[130] Love, like misogyny, is "snagged on the thorn of sexual difference and positively exults in misery."[131]

In the original *Jugement* poem, *Behaingne,* the pain of the knight and the grief of the lady are presented oppositionally: they are neither the same, nor mirror images of each other, but rather different kinds of loss. As Kay notes, they exemplify the Lacanian lack of "sexual relation," because there is no common obstacle for men and women to overcome. In other early dits, Machaut epitomizes this lack of sexual relation by representing the gendered Other not as another human but as a member of an entirely different species—a lion for the lady's beloved in *Lyon* and avian raptors for the lady in *Alerion,* for example. Thus, Kay argues, the pain of love, like misogyny itself, reifies sexual difference by making women categorically different from (and inferior

129. Kay, *The Place of Thought,* 95–122 ("Universality on Trial in Machaut's *Jugement* Poems").

130. Ibid., 115.

131. Ibid.

to) men. Using Judith Butler's concepts of citation and performativity, Kay notes that the *Jugement* poems stress the way in which both parties "constitute their identity as 'male' or 'female' by repeatedly re-enacting their loss of their loved one before the judge."[132] The pain of love thus comes to define heterosexuality.

But Kay reads *Navarre* not as acquiescing in this lack of relation but rather as participating in a wariness of abstracting universal categories from individual identity—part of her book's broader thesis about the "complexity of one."[133] The individual suffering lover in *Navarre* is shown not to be something from which a universal is abstracted, but rather to be someone excluded from the universal. Kay detects a different treatment of gender and sexual difference in *Navarre* from that presented in the earlier dits, which she reads as consoling for this difference by presenting nonrelation and gender opposition. By contrast, in *Navarre*, gender difference is "humorously acknowledged," but this dit ultimately "opposes not a man and a woman, but Guillaume and a series of personified abstractions" that can be seen as internal to Guillaume himself.[134] In suggesting that sexual difference "lies as much within as between individuals," Kay reads *Navarre* as challenging universal categories like gender to suggest instead that knowledge might not only be undermined and subverted by the "incalculable private element" of the singular, which cannot be expressed through language, but also constitute it.[135]

It is certainly possible to see the double assimilation of Toute Belle and Guillaume to Fortune in *Voir dit* in these terms, and I would argue that the melding of feminine lament with clerkly sententiousness in both M7 and B18 also problematizes that universal category of gender which inscribes the lack of sexual relation, and which *Navarre* (in Kay's reading) suggests is central to both love and misogyny. Perhaps in the light of the androgynous polytextuality of M7, the hidden polytextuality of B23 and B18—if that is what the allusive tenors produce—can be understood as a means of attributing the implied negative authorial assessment of their first-person singers not to their gender but to the mechanism that drives their actions: gossip. If B18 and B23 present women whose love has been wounded by hearsay against a tenor that alludes to the woman whose love is unimpeachable (the Virgin Mary), the audience would have at once a negative and the most positive exemplar. Moreover, the women in the cantus lines are grounded, stabilized, and brought into harmony not by the content of their individual verbal lines but by the nonverbal content of a song in praise of the Virgin. Perhaps, if they can be read in this way,

132. Ibid., 116.
133. See ibid., xi and 1–18, for an outline of her critical orientation.
134. Ibid., 117.
135. Ibid., 118.

these songs suggest that ignoring words and focusing on music will defray the power of gossip and promote the power of concord.[136]

Resisting Gossip

The textual polyphony of Machaut's motet, possibly also of some of his balades, and certainly the twofold resolutions of the same problem in the two *jugement* dits with regard to the broad topic of Fortune, provided medieval courtiers with material for discussion, consideration, and much thought. While despite its feminine voice the "controlling gender" of the motetus of *J'ay tant / Lasse!* (M7) is masculine in its typical clerical antifeminism, the motet as a whole, like *Navarre*, undermines this stance.[137] The disjunction between the proverbial voice and the feminine voice makes the false nature of the projection of a woman patent, and therefore proves that clerical constructions of the feminine are also Fortune: a surface covering a different interior. By implication, real women are not like this; it is only by repute that women are assimilated to Fortune. The true conduit of Fortune is not femininity itself but the combination of ill repute (*mesdit* or gossip), the means of spreading it (those who speak ill, the *mesdisans* or gossips), and the overready belief ("tout par legierement croire") in such talk by credulous loving subjects. The full plainsong context for the tenor of *Qui es / Ha! Fortune* (M8) suggests this strongly: the subject is surrounded by liars and there is none to help. The liars turn Fortune's wheel as, wheel-like, they encircle the subject ("Circumdederunt me viri mendaces"), and their utterances form her winds, their tongues are whips. Only trust in the help of a supreme good who is not physically present (because there is no one to help) will rescue the subject, whether this is Hope (embodying the mental picture of the lady's supreme goodness) or God.

Change in the lover's attitude toward the lady can be effected by rumors of change in the lady's attitude toward the lover. Because the narrator hears tales of Toute Belle's mocking of him, he starts to believe that she has changed toward him, and thus he changes toward her. As with the woman who is the narrator of B23, the one who first suspects disloyalty is in fact the first to be disloyal, because loyalty is not an action but a thought. Believing that Fortune has turned her wheel against one is the thought that makes one subject to Fortune in the first place.

---

136. The use of song in *Remede* seems to imply that this might be the case. See Sarah Kay, "Touching Singularity: Consolations, Philosophy, and Poetry in the French *dit*," in *The Erotics of Consolation: Desire and Distance in the Late Middle Ages,* ed. Catherine E. Léglu and Stephen J. Milner (Basingstoke, 2008), 21–38; and Elizabeth Eva Leach, "Poet as Musician," in *A Companion to Guillaume de Machaut: An Interdisciplinary Approach to the Master,* ed. Deborah McGrady and Jennifer Bain (Leiden, forthcoming).

137. Kevin Brownlee notes that the definitive and controlling gender in both is masculine, despite the superficial feminine voice of the motetus. Brownlee, "La polyphonie textuelle," 144.

The group of poems that comes between the two music balades on Fortune, B22 and B23, in their *Loange* incarnations (Lo188 and Lo195) treats
the theme of Fortune from a number of viewpoints that expressly link it to the
issues of gossip and rumor. In addition, one of these poems, *Il n'est dolour,
desconfort ne tristece* (Lo194), is interpolated into the *Voir dit* (as VD48) in
the section just before Toute Belle is compared to Fortune. As a result of the
Loange sequence and its interfaces with the notated balades and the *Voir dit*,
Fortune becomes paradigmatic of the false woman. If a woman either believes the gossip about her lover (thus changing her view of him), or is herself
unfaithful (changing her love), she is as unfaithful as Fortune. In blaming
Fortune, the complaining lover is, for Machaut, effectively berating himself or
herself, just as the lady of B23 does in the penultimate line of the poem, for
having false thoughts, for being inconstant. The sensible solution, it seems, is
to continue in loyalty so as to rise above the blame that accrues to those who
are inconstant.[138]

The lyric that follows B22/Lo188 is the rondeau *Helas! pour ce que
Fortune m'est dure* (Lo189), in which the refrain laments "Alas! Because
Fortune is hard to me, the one that I love so much cares nothing for me," and
cites the seeming friendship of those who are in fact "hateful enemies."[139]
This lyricizes a situation in which Fortune's harshness turns a friend into an
enemy, behaving as the narrator of Lo188/B22 warns she will. Like Fortune
herself, friends are the opposite of what they appear to be, although the lyric
does not specifically feminize this duplicity, and does not even gender the
speaker. The plurality of the friends ("maint") even suggests that Fortune's
actions are perhaps here being described in a more political than amorous
sphere.

The prevalence of gossip is castigated specifically in the next lyric of the
sequence, *Langue poignant, aspre, amere et agüe* (Lo190), in which a male
lover vents his anger on "Tongue," a synecdochal personification, which enables him to depersonalize his invective. The next two poems in the sequence
exemplify the correct course of action in this respect: loyalty regardless of the
rumors one may hear. *La grant doucour de vostre biauté fine* (Lo191) is spoken by a man who suffers nobly, is of good cheer, and pledges loyalty, come
what may. *On ne puet riens savoir si proprement* (Lo192) is spoken by a man
who counsels that one ought not to believe false reports too readily, and notes
especially that his lady should not credit those circulating about him. This
lyric opens with a clear relative valuation of hearing and seeing:

On ne puet riens savoir si proprement
D'oïr dire comme on fait dou veoir;

---

138. This, it should be noted, is the basic advice to the lover at the end of *Vergier*.
139. "Helas! pour ce que Fortune m'est dure, / Ce que plus aim n'a mais cure de my," (Lo189,
ll. 1–2); "haïneus anemy" (l. 6).

Mais ce qu'on tient et voit tout clerement
Doit ou croire sans nulle doute avoir.
Et qui legierement croit,
Souvent sa pais et sa joie en descroit,
Car maint meschié sont venu et norri
De legier croire encontre son ami.

One cannot know as properly from hearing something said as from seeing it done, but that which one holds and sees completely clearly must be believed without having any doubt about it. But the one who believes too readily often destroys peace of mind and joy, because much mischief comes and is nurtured *by too ready belief against one's lover.*

The refrain text here is extremely close to that which Toute Belle's confessor cites five times against Guillaume in *Voir dit* when he is making exactly the same error. In the *Loange* poem, however, the second stanza reveals that the speaker is a man, who serves, cherishes, and humbly praises his lady. The gendering of amorous instability and overready belief in gossip is the reverse in the *Voir dit,* implying once again that men and women are, in the sway of Fortune, interchangeable. The actions of Fortune are less the result of problems associated with a specific gender, and more a problem related to the impermanence of words heard (gossip) over the permanence of seeing: writing, *Voir dit* implies, guarantees truth.

In the last two lyrics in the *Loange* sequence before B23/Lo195, the references to B22 and B23 increase, both through the lyricization of similar situations and through shared lexis. *Il ne m'est pas tant dou mal que j'endure* (Lo193) is very similar in terms of rhyme words and diction to both B22 and B23. It is spoken by a man who says he is downcast and discomfited ("Mise au dessous et à desconfiture"; l. 1.3) because "in a woman, full of great beauty, dwells treason and all falseness; she has no faith, law, reason, right, or moderation." He effectively describes both her effect on him and her attributes in terms that make her resemble Fortune.[140] He makes this accusation, he says, "because I know well that she has fallen in love with another."[141] By implication, this lover is as ill-advised as the lady of the lover in the preceding poem if he thinks he knows something without seeing it done. The man who slanders ladies in this way is condemned out of his own mouth (or, at least, out of the mouth of the poem next door).

---

140. "Car en dame, pleinne de grant biauté, / Meint traïson et toute fausseté, / Foy, loy, raison, droit n'i a ne mesure" (Lo193, ll. 1.4–6). Compare the description of Fortune in the triplum of *Qui es / Ha! Fortune* (M8), l. 6, "Sans foy, sans loy, sans droit et sans mesure"; combined with the idea that she has a beautiful outside but is false within, deriving from Boethius but mentioned in *Il m'est avis* (B22), *Remede,* and M8.

141. "Car je say bien qu'elle a autre enamé" (Lo193, l. 2.4).

Il n'est dolour, desconfors ne tristece (Lo194) is spoken by a woman suffering because she is far from her handsome, sweet, loyal lover, to whom she
pledges loyalty and promises that she will put aside all other men. Significantly this poem is interpolated into the *Voir dit* (VD48) as one authored by
Toute Belle just after the midpoint sequence, in response to Guillaume's excessively grieving and desirous verse letter (letter 23). In her responding letter, which accompanies the sending of *Il n'est dolour* (VD48/Lo194), Toute
Belle explains her surprise at Guillaume's "plains" and "clamours," and bids
him sustain himself in joy. She sends him the balade to attest to her own sorrow at their geographical separation and her ongoing loyalty nevertheless. In
the context of the *Loange* sequence of which it is also (and originally) part,
however, this lyric forms a narrative prelude to *De Fortune* (Lo195/B23), in
which another (the "same") feminine voice begins to doubt her lover. The
narrator of Lo195 is implicitly assimilated to Fortune by her own doubts;
Toute Belle will soon be compared much more explicitly. By its proximity in
the *Loange* to *De Fortune* (Lo195/B23), Toute Belle's *Il n'est dolour* (Lo194/
VD48) casts the all-pervasive, dark, and shadowy light of Fortune into the
Voir dit.

In the *Voir dit*, credulousness of oral reporting leads inexorably to the
dual Fortune comparisons at the end. After Guillaume has locked the image
of Toute Belle in two sealed coffers, it appears to him sighing and weeping
(ll. 7738–91). It accuses him of believing "trop legierement" (too readily)
that his lady has found other interests. It tells Guillaume that even were this
the case, it would be unfair to force it, the image, to suffer just because the
love affair between Guillaume and Toute Belle is over. And anyway, it goes
on, there is no truer lover than Toute Belle (l. 7774); he, Guillaume, should
confront her with his fears because "there's no good judge who doesn't listen
to both parties" (ll. 7780–81, marked with a marginal "nota" in A), which
makes it reprehensible that he is going to condemn her on the basis of three
or four reports that are "lies and falsehoods / More venomous than serpents
/ and contrived by slanderers."[142] In illustration of this, the image tells the
story of how the crow turned black, a tale that Machaut takes from the *Ovide
moralisé.*

Like many accounts in the *Metamorphoses*, this one has another tale em-
bedded within it, and both stories are relevant to the situation at hand.[143]
Guillaume has imprisoned the image because he thinks Toute Belle loves another, and both stories relate to the propriety of reporting the truth of a matter to the person who ought to know but will be hurt by it. The white crow
serves Phoebus, the god of poetry and music, who loves the bird more than
his harp and his bow. One day the crow sees Phoebus's beloved, Coronis,

---

142. "Mansonges et frivoles / Plus que serpens envenimees / Et de mesdisans controuvees";
Voir dit, ll. 7785–87.

143. *Metamorphoses* 2.531–632.

taking "nature's delight" in a young man whom she loves even more than Phoebus loves his white crow (ll. 7820–22). On the way to tell Phoebus, the crow is stopped by the raven, who seeks to dissuade him by relating his own story. In manuscript **A**, the raven's introduction is full of lines carrying marginal "nota" markings, which visually highlight particularly memorable sentences: "Not all truth is good to tell" (l. 7852), "Things often go wrong when you speak the truth" (ll. 7864–66), and "He nobly leaves off his folly who is chastened by the example of another" (ll. 7878–79). These are the phrases that the readers of the *Voir dit* should carry with them, recalling how the crow ignores them and was punished; perhaps every time they see or hear a black, unmelodious crow, this story's "notae" should be brought to mind.

The raven's story is of his own service in the house of Pallas when Vulcan was pursuing her. In frustration at her evasion, Vulcan fathers a motherless child by spilling his semen on the ground. Pallas brings this child up as her own but hides it in a coffer because she wishes the unnatural child's deformity to be kept secret. Three Cypriot sisters, who guard the chest from prying eyes, eventually fall prey to their own curiosity and open it to reveal the child's double shape and serpent feet.[144] For reporting the sisters' misdemeanor to Pallas, the raven is banished and replaced by the owl, a "vile incestuous creature." The raven concludes her tale with yet another proverb: "The goat that scratches a lot makes a lot of trouble."[145]

The crow chooses to ignore this advice and returns to Phoebus, who is playing his harp. The crow, swanlike, sings his own (symbolic) death in telling what he's seen. Phoebus drops his harp, takes up his bow, and shoots his beloved Coronis with an arrow. As she dies, she reveals that she is pregnant by him, at which news Phoebus curses all birds, especially the crow, and removes the child, Aesculapius, from her womb. As he banishes the crow, Phoebus turns its feathers—and those of its species in perpetuity—black, and deprives him of his song, condemning him to nothing but "janglerie."[146] The

---

144. The description may hint at conjoined twins with sirenomelia, the congenital deformity known as "mermaid syndrome." In the Latin original the snake and the male child are two separate contents of the osier box rather than a double form (although the father of the three Cypriot sisters, Cecrops, is thus described, as is the centaur Chiron, who looks after Coronis's posthumous child); see Ovid, *Metamorphoses* 2.531–632. See Cerquiglini, *"Un engin si soutil,"* 152–55, for the relation of this doubleness to poetry.

145. This proverbial line is also the refrain of *J'ay maintes fois oÿ conter,* the fifth balade set to music in the Cyprus manuscript, **Tu**, and of a pastourelle *Decha brimeu sur un ridel* (Pa14) in **Pa** f. 7a, an unnotated source that nonetheless contains many texts that were set to music.

146. On the even starker punishment in Chaucer's version of this story in *The Manciple's Tale,* see Nicolette Zeeman, "The Gender of Song in Chaucer," *Studies in the Age of Chaucer* 29 (2007): 177–78. On the crow as the epitome of *vox confusa,* see Leach, *Sung Birds,* 34–37.

two singers of this tale—a bird and a harp-playing god—both fare badly.[147] The first is a fool for telling those "de bonne affaire" news that will enrage them; the second is a self-deceiving woman killer.

The reports of the raven and crow are not untrue, they are just unwelcome; by contrast the writing of fiction is most welcome, even if it is not true. Toute Belle wants the book of her and Guillaume's love to be written and, at the end, refuses to send his manuscript back to him because she wants to change things in the text. The constant play between change and permanence, between instability and fixity, between Fortune and Fame is mapped onto a dichotomy between orality and textuality in which music and musical poetry can be both. It might be thought that the impermanence of gossip is gendered feminine as opposed to the masculine permanence of written fame. But the raven is female, the crow male; both "jangle." And in equating Toute Belle and the narrator by assimilating them first to each other and then to Fortune, Machaut shows the effeminacy of the writer figure, the virility of Toute Belle, and the androgyny of Fortune. The equation of male and female perspectives and the resulting radical disruption of gender categories serve to generate poetry.

Writing Fame

The complete denigration of song that might seem to form part of the story of "How the Crow Turned Black" does not tally with the elevated place that Machaut ascribes to music in his poetics (especially in the *Prologue*) and in his own book. But the referent in the *Voir dit*'s story of the crow is not song per se but oral culture, epitomized in birdsong and in instrumental music, neither of which is fully literate music making.[148] Similarly, poetry would commonly have been read aloud, even in conjunction with the presence of a book, but the important aspect of valorization is the possibility and fact of writing. The importance of writing is implicit in the depiction of the dangers of hearsay, belief in which can cause the assimilation of the hearer to the figure of Fortune, concomitantly feminizing him or her. Typically the image of Toute Belle comments that the child, Aesculapius, went on to great renown in his ability to restore the dead to life "si com ie le truis en mon livre" (as I find in my book; l. 8105): books preserve renown, they restore the dead to life; oral tittle-tattle—whether the "janglerie" of a crow, or the harp of Phoebus—leads only to foolishness.

---

147. Phoebus, the god of music and poetry, self-deceivingly believes that Coronis might be innocent, blaming the crow for making him kill the best woman in the world. See Zeeman, "The Gender of Song," 177–78.

148. See Leach, *Sung Birds*, 165–69.

As Cerquiglini-Toulet has emphasized, the stories of the raven and the crow are both tales of children engendered from unreciprocated desire without mothers, which thereby represent poetic creation.[149] This is clearest in the raven's tale, since Vulcan has the attributes of a poet and works a forge, often a locus symbolic of poetic (and musical) creation.[150] And in both cases, motherless engendering creates a new object that is extraordinary: it has a marvelous double form (the child of Vulcan), or the ability to bring the dead back to life (Aesculapius). Both characteristics could describe poetry, too, which can also bring the dead back to life and operate on multiple formal and semantic levels. Cerquiglini-Toulet concludes that for Machaut this understanding of poetic creation solved its potential narcissism; poetry is still born of desire for the other, it just no longer matters whether this is reciprocated never (as with Pallas) or no longer (as with Coronis). And like the nonmusical song of raven and crow, Narcissus functions as a negative exemplum in Machaut's work.

In placing *J'ay tant / Lasse!* (M7) before *Qui es / Ha! Fortune* (M8), Machaut put several watery poems on the subject of women's changeability in close proximity: M8, which specifically addresses Fortune as well as anatomizing her, depicts a subject adrift at sea; M7 has changeable human women, alludes to the fountain of Narcissus and has a tenor that references the tears of David for Absalom.[151] As well as femininity, singing, and turning or dancing—aspects of Fortune emphasized in the first image of Titus Livius's Fortune—Fortune is also like a spring or fountain, as is emphasized by the second *Voir dit* image of Fortune with the five fountains. Water and moisture are part of the feminine complexion in medieval physiology, but the fountain has some important literary precedents in the *Rose,* and in Ovid's *Metamorphoses,* book 5. This background text of Ovid, which will surface again in chapter 6 in relation to the idea of the song competition, has a fountain that symbolizes how an essentially oral transmission route, which personified Fame as a bird, with plumage of eyes and ears and mouths, flying around the world and spreading the word, was replaced by the Ovidian story of Pegasus's hoofprint causing a fountain of poetic inspiration to spring from the Muses' mountain. While both the Muses and Pegasus retain the rapidity of wings from the bird personification, Cerquiglini-Toulet interprets this shift in the representation of Fame as reflective of increased textualization: the vocal aesthetic of the bird's chatter has become the impress of the hoof, an aesthetic of writing. In short,

---

149. Cerquiglini, *"Un engin si soutil,"* 152–55.

150. See Elizabeth Eva Leach, "Nature's Forge and Mechanical Production: Writing, Reading, and Performing Song," in *Rhetoric beyond Words: Delight and Persuasion in the Arts of the Middle Ages,* ed. Mary Carruthers (Cambridge, 2010), 72–95.

151. Robertson, *Guillaume de Machaut and Reims,* 128–51 (chap. 5), reads M7–9 as a triptych on sin, which is explored in senses that are in turn amorous (M7), ethical (M8), and biblical (*Fons / O livoris* [M9]).

"La plume de l'oiseau est devenue plume du poète" (the feather of the bird has become the poet's quill pen).[152]

The ability of the fixity of writing to combat Fortune's instability is one of Machaut's constant themes, especially in the dits that name the narrator as Guillaume, or Guillaume de Machaut. In *Navarre*, Guillaume de Machaut is forced to write a lay in which the feminine first person wishes her and her beloved to be memorialized in a book, that is, in writing. Guillaume claims to have written the *Voir dit* at the bidding of Toute Belle, who eventually refuses to return the manuscript to him because she wishes to make some changes to it. That *Voir dit* tells of its own inspiration, commissioning, and writing—including logically paradoxical statements about not being able to work on it and no longer having the manuscript of it—makes it a teasing representation of reality, an insolubly involuted puzzle. The appearance of the portrait of Guillaume de Machaut at the head of his book in the illuminated *Prologue* serves as a stand-in for a role that must ordinarily and formerly have been taken by the real, living Guillaume de Machaut as he placed his own works in their correct didactic context while reading them aloud at court. That he enshrines himself in writing and pictures shows a recognition of his own death and the wish to self-memorialize. Machaut offers genealogies of musicians in both *Voir dit* and the *Harpe,* of which, by implication, he is the most recent member. Cerquiglini-Toulet lists the making of such genealogies as one of three ways to inscribe renown (the other two being comparison with worthy figures, and electing the person as a "tenth" worthy). Such a genealogy, based not on human engendering but on the production of artistic works, can be seen in the prestigious line of musical inventors in the *Voir dit,* which Machaut has voiced by the king in Guillaume's earlier dream.[153]

Chaucer most explicitly turns the story of how the crow turned black into a story of the silencing of a court poet, but this is not how Machaut uses the tale. Machaut's version instead emphasizes the motherless birth of that which provides the content of the birds' songs—something marvelously double in form and able to bring the dead to life. Court poets provided their masters with ennobling and consoling images of themselves, and also celebrated and memorialized them as patrons and past patrons. Machaut's identification of himself and his patrons in his longer narrative poems is a marked feature of his works. Two poems call the narrator Guillaume de Machaut (*Navarre* and *Prologue*); one calls him Guillaume (*Voir dit*); *Navarre* and *Behaingne* name their patrons or dedicatees because they are characters within the poem; the *Prise* does this but additionally links Machaut's name with that of Pierre de Lusignan by an anagram, one of eight poems to use this trick, the others

---

152. Jacqueline Cerquiglini-Toulet, "*Fama* et les preux: Nom et renom à la fin du Moyen Âge," *Médiévales* 24 (1993): 44.

153. Ibid., 38.

being *Behaingne, Remede, Lyon* (not solved), *Confort* (which also includes Charles of Navarre), *Fonteinne* (which also includes John, Duke of Berry and Auvergne), *Harpe* (not solved), and the *Voir dit. Alerion* has Machaut's name encoded in numbers in a manner found in several lyrics, notably those in the *Voir dit.*[154] Machaut's effectiveness in ensuring his own posterity is attested by the publication of books—like the present one—on him and his works, centuries after his death. Although, as chapter 2 suggests, Machaut's fame was not continuous, his name did outlive him for some time before rediscovery was made necessary by its temporary oblivion. It is to the theme of death in his works, to the fact of his own death, and to his immediate afterlife that this particular narrative now turns.

154. Leo, "Authorial Presence," 96–100.

6

Death

Remembering Machaut

"Ah, noble heart, must I die because I love you more than I really love myself?" asks the lover at the opening of Machaut's balade *Hé! gentils cuers* (L037), answering his own question immediately in the affirmative. But dying in this way—for the lady and for love—will, he claims in later stanzas, be a sweet death that will cause him to be held in honor by all the world. The refrain of this balade ("since I shall die for you and for love [*pour vous et pour amer morrai*]") is similar to the refrain of one of Machaut's balade texts that appears only among those set to music, *Biauté qui* (B4).[1] Each stanza of B4 enumerates a list of those things that have brought the lover to the point of dying for love, which include the fact that his lady's peerless beauty is estranged from him, that her fine sweetness is bitter to his taste, that her praiseworthy body and simple face hide a hard heart and a look fit to kill a lover, and that her joyful appearance masks a dismaying response. All these things, wails the first-person lover, "have brought me to the point where I will die for love [*pour amer morray*]." In later stanzas the list of this fatal beauty's vicious virtues includes a fair welcome that revenges itself on him, a hope that estranges him from joy, poor succor, burning desire, sad thoughts and sighing heart, harshness, disdain, rebuff, and refusal. In short, his eyes in combination with her beautiful indifference to him will be responsible for this lover's imminent death.

---

1. "Puis que pour vous et pour amer morrai" is the refrain of *Hé! gentils cuers* (L037); cf. the refrain of *Biauté qui* (B4), in which the various things listed in each stanza "M'ont a ce mis que pour amer morray."

In both these balades, as usual in Machaut's works, the death of a lover in
the sphere of refined loving is a symbolic one, always belonging to the near
future, a rhetorical reflection of being incapacitated rather than a genuine
threat to cease existing. Machaut's first-person lyrics are full of men threaten-
ing to die for their ladies, but real death features far less frequently in his works.
When it does, the point at issue seems to be effective commemoration—the
proper response of the living. John of Luxembourg is commemorated through
praise in both *Confort* and *Prise,* the latter of which also remembers (though
less wholly favorably) Pierre de Lusignan.[2] But because both mourning and
hopeful love require the exercise of *souvenir* to sustain a mental image of the
absent beloved, it is no surprise that unfulfilled lovers tend to echo the rhetoric
of mourning as a means of articulating a desire for *merci.* In the two *Jugement*
poems, however, the reality of the death of the lady's lover is contrasted with
the symbolic, even hyperbolic "death" of the rejected knight, despite the similarity of imaginative response (grief, mourning, the desire for consolation).[3]
But Machaut's poetry variously counters both the typically masculine and
feminine responses to loss (symbolic and real death) by proposing instead a
consoling role for poetry, which can alternatively (or simultaneously) commemorate loss and eternalize love in a manner that avoids either (male) madness or (female) death.[4]

The refrain *Biauté qui* (B4), for example, whose *je* claims to have been
brought to the point of imminent death by the lady's neglect, is significantly
shared with a balade found in Jehan de le Mote's *Li regret Guillaume* (1339).
Jean's narrative poem has already been discussed in chapter 3 as offering a potential model for Machaut's later *Prologue,* but the links between Machaut's
work and *Regret* are more extensive: several of Machaut's lyrics share entire
lines of poetry with the lyrics interpolated within Jean's poem. *Regret* laments
the real death of a historical figure, Guillaume I, Count of Hainaut (d. 1337),
and thus makes an interesting point of comparison with Machaut's more usual
suffering lovers, killed by their lady's glances. The speaker of the poem with
which Machaut's B4 shares its refrain, *La grascieuse et souffissans jouvente,* is
the allegorical character Good Manners (*Manière*), whose former "lodging"
(*hierbegie*) Count Guillaume—her "dear son," Tristan to her Isolde—has been
bitten by death.[5] Her sighs, thoughts, and sorrowful dismay "have brought

2. *Confort,* ll. 2923–3086, 3203–12, 3421–32; *Prise,* ll. 779–92, 831–38.

3. Helen J. Swift, "*Tamainte consolation / Me fist lymagination*: A Poetics of Mourning and
Imagination in Late Medieval *dits,*" in *The Erotics of Consolation: Desire and Distance in the
Late Middle Ages,* ed. Catherine E. Léglu and Stephen J. Milner (Basingstoke, 2008), 142.

4. Sylvia Huot, "Guillaume de Machaut and the Consolation of Poetry," *Modern Philology*
100 (2002): 181.

5. For the Tristan and Isolde comparison, see [Jean] Aug[uste] Ulrich Scheler, ed., *Jehan de la
Mote: Li Regret Guillaume, Comte de Hainaut. Poème inédit du XIVe siècle* (Louvain, 1882), ll.
1956–2016. The balade occupies ll. 2044–61.

me to the point where I will die for love [*pour amer morai*]."[6] The real death of Guillaume I, Count of Hainaut, is paralleled by the threatened (symbolic) death of Good Manners, and she is herself a personified abstraction, like a weeper on a contemporary funerary monument or ceremonial tomb rather than a real woman, staging a poetic death to commemorate the real death of another.[7] Jean's deliberately excessive presentation of thirty such personifications stages grief as a stylized and commemorative public "monument."[8] Poetry can safely perform one kind of death as a consoling reaction to another, so that the poetic enactment of a grieving speaker's "death" can revivify in memory the truly dead.

Machaut's Deaths: Threatened and Actual

Machaut's works do not just enact the symbolic lyrical deaths of male courtly lovers whose personae are clearly distinct from their author. Of a piece with his pseudo-autobiographical self-presentation, Machaut presents a more personal fear of death in some of his narrative works, especially those that date from the latter part of his life. The character named several times later in *Navarre* as Guillaume de Machaut flees the death brought by the Great Mortality at the start of the dit, locking himself in his house while the epidemic rages. Guillaume de Machaut's fear of death at the outset of this poem is partly reflected in the rhetoric of the poetic penalty the *jugement* extracts from him at its end: the composition of a lady's commemoration of her dead lover.[9] At the opening of the *Voir dit*, too, the aging Guillaume reflects on a recent serious illness, which he reexperiences in the narrative as a more symbolic "love death" in the context of his early contact with Toute Belle. The first song set to music that he sends her is his "testament," *Plourez, dames* (B32), about which he tells two rather different stories.

Guillaume's Testament

In the *Voir dit*, the narrator thematizes Toute Belle's quasi-divine power to inspire creativity and life. The messenger who brings her initial letter (letter 1) notes that it was prompted by reports that Guillaume had been grievously ill for a winter and most of the summer.[10] His reply (letter 2) says he has been

---

6. "Li souspir que pour men cier fil trai,...li penser c'à vous ai,...mi dolereus esmai / M'ont à çou mis que pour amer morai"; see ibid., ll. 2048–49, 2054–55, 2060–61.

7. On weepers, see the comments in chapter 3, especially the references in note 16.

8. See Ardis Butterfield, "Lyric and Elegy in *The Book of the Duchess,*" *Medium Aevum* 60 (1991): 39–40.

9. On *Qui bien aimme (Le Lay de plour)* (L22/16), see chapters 4 and 5.

10. *Voir dit*, ll. 144–45.

"deaf, ignorant, mute, and weak [*impotens*]" but that she has worked a miracle to give him strength to hear and speak.[11] After saying that he has newly written a balade on the joy she has given him, which he intends to set to music soon, he adds that he is also sending her an already musicalized balade "about the pitiable state that I have been in."[12] The description of this balade—which is here represented as having been written *before* Toute Belle initiated contact with Guillaume and brought him joy—identifies this song unequivocally as *Plourez, dames* (B32): Guillaume's letter says that in it "I beg ladies to dress in black out of love for me," which is the fifth line of B32's first stanza (for text and translation, see figure 6.1). This poem effectively serves as Guillaume's own *déploration,* urging ladies in general to weep and wear black for him because he will die if they and God do not take care of him (see example 6.1).

According to the dating followed by Leech-Wilkinson, B32 was written during a long illness that lasted from the winter of 1361–62 until July of the latter year.[13] The status of the *Voir dit,* however, as factual fiction or fictional fact makes it hard to say with certainty that "Machaut himself claims that he thought he would die."[14] The character Guillaume, not the historical person Machaut, makes this claim, and he undermines its truth-value in that he makes conflicting assertions about the reason for writing the balade. Having represented it in letter 2 as having already been written during the illness *before* Toute Belle's initial approach, Guillaume then attributes its composition to a relapse he thought would be fatal, and which occurs *after* the writing and presentation of letter 2 within the poem but before the messenger—to whom Machaut has painstakingly taught the music—is able to deliver it.[15] Too ill to travel to Toute Belle himself, with his own secretary abroad, Guillaume suffers through the winter with a melancholic malady that he thinks signals his end.[16] This relapse, he says, generated his "testament," which he then sends with a valet whom he finds.[17] It is only at this point in his tale that the texts of both B32 and the other balade mentioned in letter 2 (*Amours, ma dame* [Lo227/ VD6]) are copied as lyric texts inserted within the *Voir dit.*[18] This confusion

11. *Voir dit,* 34 (letter 2): "Car ie estoie . assourdis . arrudis . muz . et impotens."

12. *Voir dit,* 36: "Je vous envoie aussi une balade de mon piteus estat qui a este."

13. Daniel Leech-Wilkinson and R. Barton Palmer, eds., *Guillaume de Machaut: Le livre dou voir dit (The Book of the True Poem)* (New York, 1998), 713, note to ll. 144–45.

14. Jennifer Bain, "Balades 32 and 33 and the 'res dalamangne,'" in *Machaut's Music: New Interpretations,* ed. Elizabeth Eva Leach (Woodbridge, 2003), 205.

15. See *Voir dit,* 34–37 (letter 2) and ll. 640–96 (the relapse and text of B32). The description of teaching the music to the messenger is at ll. 601–9.

16. *Voir dit,* ll. 625–64. His secretary is "en un lontein pais" (in a far-off land; l. 633).

17. *Voir dit,* ll. 665–72.

18. In Leech-Wilkinson and Palmer, *Le livre dou voir dit,* 715, the note to ll. 607–8 says that Lo227/VD6 has a metrical structure so close to that of B32 "that performance to the same music would present few problems." The text of Lo227/VD6 claims that Love, my lady, Fortune, and my eyes, together with the lady's beauty, have made the *je* love her, but Fortune will destroy him because his lady is far away. Although Leech-Wilkinson and Palmer read letter 2 to imply that it

1.1	Plourés, dames, plourés vostre servant,	Weep ladies, weep for your servant [i.e., me],
1.2	Qui ay toudis mis mon cuer et m'entente,	who has always placed my heart and my inten-
1.3	Corps et desir et penser en servant	tions, body and desire and thought, in serving
1.4	L'onneur de vous, que Diex gart et	your honor, which God guard and augment.
	augmente.	Wear black for me, for I have a tainted heart
1.5	Vestés vous de noir pour mi,	and a pale visage, and so see only death in
1.6	Car j'ay cuer teint et viaire pali,	my future *unless God and you take me into*
1.7	Et si me voy de mort en aventure	*your care.*
R	Se Diex et vous ne me prenés en cure.	My heart I leave to you and place in your com-

Weep ladies, weep for your servant [i.e., me], who has always placed my heart and my intentions, body and desire and thought, in serving your honor, which God guard and augment. Wear black for me, for I have a tainted heart and a pale visage, and so see only death in my future *unless God and you take me into your care.*

2.1 Mon cuer vous lay et met en vo[1] commant
2.2 Et l'ame à Dieu[2] devotement presente,
2.3 Et voit où doit aler le remennant:
2.4 La char aus vers, car c'est leur droite rente;
2.5 Et l'avoir soit departi[3]
2.6 Aus povres gens. Helas! en ce parti,
2.7 En lit[4] de mort sui à desconfiture,
R Se Diex [et vous ne me prenés en cure.]

My heart I leave to you and place in your command, and my soul I present devotedly to God, and I see where the rest must go: the flesh to the worms, for it is their proper due, and my assets to be given away to poor people. Alas! I shall be discomfited in this parting on a deathbed *unless God and you take me into your care.*

3.1 Mais certeins sui qu'en vous de bien a tant
3.2 Que dou peril, où je sui sans attente,
3.3 Me getterés, se de cuer en plourant
3.4 Pries à Dieu qu'à moy garir s'assente.
3.5 Et pour ce je vous depri
3.6 Qu'à Dieu vueilliez faire pour moy depri,
3.7 Ou paier creing le treü de Nature,
R Se Diex et vous [ne me prenés en cure.]
Based on **Vg** music section, f. 313v

But I am certain that there is enough goodness in you that, without delay, you will cast me from the peril that I am in, if from your hearts, weeping, you pray to God that he assent to cure me. So I implore you that you might wish to implore God for me, or I fear I will pay the debt to Nature *unless God and you take me into your care.*

Notes
1. **Vg** *son.*
2. **Vg** *et lame a dieu et lame a dieu.*
3. **Vg** *departis.*
4. **Vg** *li.*

Figure 6.1. Text and translation of *Plourez, dames* (B32).

has fueled questions about the truth of the *Voir dit* and the carefulness of its copying, but it serves the purpose of showing the polyvalence of a single lyric, which will serve equally well to portray fear of actual death and fear of death caused by rejection in love.[19] A further fear—especially in the context of the

was this lyric rather than B32 that was specially written for Toute Belle on the grounds that it is "more personal" (715, note to l. 669), the balade makes reference to having seen the lady (which Guillaume hasn't yet), and it seems likely to be just as much a retrospectively appropriated ready-made as B32.

19. Patrick Little, "Three Ballades in Machaut's *Livre du Voir-Dit,*" *Studies in Music* 14 (1980): 51–55, notes the problems of the poem's placement and interrogates whether this is intentional, concluding that carelessness, dishonesty, and apathy are all characteristics of the authorial persona that might conveniently cover up a little laziness on the part of the author. I, too, consider the obviousness of the fact that B32 is not (as Guillaume claims) specifically written for Toute Belle to be part of Machaut's authorial construction of Guillaume as a pathetically self-deceiving and unreliable narrator.

Example 6.1. *Plourez, dames* (B32) music (complete).

2

Example 6.1. (*Continued*)

Example 6.1. (*Continued*)

Voir dit—is also hinted at: the fear of artistic death caused by the loss of the audience's love.

B32 is about sorrow and joy, life and death, singing and weeping. It is also about posterity for the poet, and thus especially apt to open the musical account within the *Voir dit*. As the first item in the *Voir dit* to receive a musical setting, the song is a suitably more complex whole than the text alone. The chief way in which the musical setting here ostensibly undercuts the verbal text (but in fact, as I shall argue, potentially reinforces its message) is that the music to this very sad *déploration* seems rather merry. Clearly the identification of the emotional content of the music of a song apart from its words is problematic at this historical remove. A perception of joy, even levity, in the music here partly depends on how the song is performed, on the articulation of the melody (especially in melismatic passages), and especially on the tempo at which it is taken. This dependence on performance can be strikingly illustrated by comparing two recordings of the song, both made in 1996.[20] Consideration of these specific recordings not only draws attention to how much poetic meaning might have depended on performative aspects but also emphasizes the status and role of recordings in the modern construction of Guillaume de Machaut.[21] The first recording, by the Oxford Camerata directed by Jeremy Summerly, is an all-vocal performance lasting nearly nine minutes; the second, by the Czech ensemble Ars Cameralis, has a female singer accompanied by two different kinds of instruments and lasts under five minutes.[22] Both recordings present all three stanzas of the balade, but the Czech group takes the piece at nearly twice the speed of the English ensemble, performing the stanzas in four minutes, fifty-three seconds, as opposed to eight minutes, fifty-five seconds. Such a huge discrepancy, which would be hard to imagine in recordings of later repertory, is indicative of the problems and uncertainties involved in presenting Machaut's music to the modern audience: it is possible to turn virtually any piece of music into a dirge through slow performance, or into something lighthearted or potentially ridiculous through fast rendition. Which is more correct in this case?

Certainly most musicological commentators, where they have talked at all of the music's contribution to the meaning of the song, have taken their cue from the text.[23] For example, Jennifer Bain, influenced by the comments of Sarah Fuller, views the musical setting as accentuating "Machaut's [sic] hopelessness and tenuous hold on life...through the many inflected, imperfect sonority cadences which create tension throughout the song."[24] The "extreme" use of what Bain and Fuller call "imperfect sonority cadences"—and which I would describe instead as held imperfect sonorities—certainly gives a sense of ex-

20. They therefore postdate the annotated discography in Lawrence Earp, *Guillaume de Machaut: A Guide to Research* (New York, 1995), 414, which gives details of earlier recordings.

21. On this, see Daniel Leech-Wilkinson, *The Modern Invention of Medieval Music: Scholarship, Ideology, Performance* (Cambridge, 2002), 132–47 and 157–214 (chap. 3, "Hearing Medieval Harmonies").

22. Oxford Camerata, *Guillaume de Machaut: La Messe de Nostre Dame / Songs from Le Voir Dit*, 1996, Naxos, 8.553833, track 7; Ars Cameralis, *Guillaume de Machaut: Chansons*, 1996, MK, 0027–2 931, track 14. Oxford Camerata (dir. Jeremy Summerly) presents the song sung by Caroline Trevor, Robert Rice, and Matthew Brook. Ars Cameralis (dir. Lukáš Matoušek) records the song with the melody sung by Zuzana Matoušková, the contratenor played on portative organ (by Hanuš Bartoň), and the tenor played on fiddle (by Jiří Richter).

23. Gilbert Reaney, "Guillaume de Machaut: Lyric Poet," *Music and Letters* 39 (1958): 42, cites B32 as one of two poems that form an exception to the general, unfeelingly conventional amorous subject matter of Machaut's poetry. B32, comments Reaney, may well be sincere since "Machaut [i.e., Guillaume] writes to Péronne [i.e., Toute Belle] that 'Plourés dames' is 'une balade de mon piteus etat qui a esté.'" This and its departure from the usual topics of love doctrine seemed, to mid-twentieth-century readers at least, to offer proof of sincerity.

24. Bain, "Balades 32 and 33," 205; see Sarah Fuller, "Tendencies and Resolutions: The Directed Progression in *Ars Nova* music," *Journal of Music Theory* 36 (1992): 248.

pectancy and tension, but then this song is an imprecation; it is designed to produce a reaction (pity and tears) and thereby prompt action (prayer) from the ladies who hear it. As an aspect of this piece of rhetoric's *pronunciatio,* the musical setting might be expected to further this end. Indeed, the most straightforward cadence comes—like that of *De Fortune* (B23)—at the caesura of the refrain line "Se Diex et vous" (m. 41), here stressing the power not, as in B23, of Fortune but of the audience of ladies (and God, whom they are asked to petition) in saving the singer from death.

Neither of the recorded performances I have mentioned seems entirely satisfactory. The slow performance of the Oxford Camerata sounds weary and lugubrious, but the all-vocal texture makes the full imperfect sonorities too solid and sustained to project a subject weakened by illness in any convincing way. The slow tempo detracts from the forward thrust of the held imperfect sonorities, as do the performers' decisions to make (unmarked) pauses after them, when they should be pressing forward to resolution.[25] In short, this group phrases the music in ways that suggest a misunderstanding of tension and resolution in this repertoire that is common among singers trained in performing equally tempered triadic music, in which triads are points of rest and resolution rather than, as in Machaut, points of tension and forward motion.[26]

The Ars Cameralis performance, by contrast, has a high density of attack, provided by the use of a quicker tempo, in combination with a lightly articulated voice, an organ, and a bowed fiddle; but this combination has other disadvantages. In timbrally differentiating the three contrapuntal lines, this recording also misses out on the tension-building effect of the three-part sonorities—the same problem as in the Oxford group's performance, just with a different cause.[27] In both recordings the words are unclear: in the Czech performance this is the fault of the singer, whose vibrato further obscures her weak French diction; in the English performance, the slowness of the tempo makes the syllables occur too slowly to be appreciated as constituting words. Given the status of this song as an impassioned imprecation to the listening ladies, neither seems wholly effective in this case. Of the five earlier recordings listed by Earp, two are even slower, taking over three minutes to perform one

25. Like Fuller and Bain, it seems, the Oxford Camerata view these held chords as cadence points, although Leech-Wilkinson's analysis of the relationship between scholarship and recordings makes it a distinct possibility that scholarship formed this view from such performances rather than vice versa. See notes 21 and 24 and 27.

26. For clarification of this point, see Margaret Bent, "The Grammar of Early Music: Preconditions for Analysis," in *Tonal Structures in Early Music,* ed. Cristle Collins Judd (New York, 1998), 45–48, especially ex. 11.

27. The move from presenting this repertoire as timbrally heterogeneous lines (as Ars Cameralis do) to performing the parts as timbrally homogeneous (as in the all-vocal performance of the Oxford Camerata) has been seen as accompanying (even prompting) a shift in the view of Machaut's harmony; see Leech-Wilkinson, *The Modern Invention of Medieval Music,* passim, but especially chap. 3, 132–47 and 157–214.

stanza of the song, and none is as quick as that of Ars Cameralis's 1996 recording, not even an earlier recording by the same musicians.[28]

The most striking features of the musical setting are the long melismas that terminate each of the main sections of the balade (mm. 20–26 and 43–49). The prolonging of a single syllable of text by a long melodic passage shifts the aural focus onto pure sound rather than verbal sense. This is emphasized further because these particular melismas are animated by striking sequential-rhythmic patterns (boxed in example 6.1) that make much use of the smallest note value (the minim, transcribed in example 6.1 as an eighth note). Similar patterns are also found in other songs in the same mensuration, including in two of the three other balades with musical setting in *Voir dit*, *Nes qu'on* (B33), and *Se pour ce muir* (B36); they also occur in the balades *Donnez, signeurs* (B26) and *Je puis trop* (B28), which are not in *Voir dit* but occur in the tranche of twelve music-section balades that first appear in manuscript **Vg** (that is, they are not present in the earliest source, **C**), a group that includes all of *Voir dit*'s musicalized balades.[29] The character of these patterns at a fast tempo is rather jocund, even dancelike, since they have a short rest followed by turning figures terminating in descending short-long patterns. If performed slowly, these figures would sound enforcedly slow and could thereby picture Guillaume's illness. They already contrast, however, with the longer note values that set the more syllabic declamation of the earlier phrases in the song (for example, mm. 1–3 or 7–10), which suggests that they should not drag (because if they did, those longer note values would be extremely ponderous and fail to present the more syllabic text declamation that accompanies them in a way that would be aurally comprehensible). At a moderate to quick tempo the melismas would contrast markedly with the more sustained syllabic passages that precede them, enabling the music to picture both Guillaume's near-death pallor (which he explains in the longer note values of the syllabic parts) and the merriment of his music making (which is expressed in melismas replete with short notes and dance rhythms).

An ideal performance of this piece might convey the imprecatory character of the held imperfect sonorities, preserve forward momentum throughout,

28. The earliest (from 1940), by baritone Yves Tinayre, lasts three minutes, fifty-one seconds; that from 1974 by countertenor Joseph Sage lasts three minutes, sixteen seconds; and the earlier recording by Zuzana Matoušková and Lukáš Matoušek (from 1978) lasts two minutes and ten seconds for a single stanza; see Earp, *Guillaume de Machaut*, 414. All recordings listed by Earp mix voices and instruments.

29. This larger sequence of music balades that postdate **C** but predate **A** (B25–36) not only includes all of the musicalized balades that would eventually be inserted in the *Voir dit*, but also contains many resonances between that dit and the balades that are not inserted. The *je* of B28, for example, uses Pygmalion as a significant point of comparison: Pygmalion is an important intertextual figure for Guillaume in the *Voir dit*. See Sylvia Huot, "Reliving the *Roman de la Rose*: Allegory and Irony in Machaut's *Voir Dit*," in *Chaucer's French Contemporaries: The Poetry/Poetics of Self and Tradition*, ed. R. Barton Palmer (New York, 1999), 56–58. On links between B29 and *Voir dit*, see my discussion in chapter 3.

and remind the ladies of the joyful lightness of musical recreation, even as they hear words that threaten its permanent withdrawal. The musicalization of the song would then turn a straightforwardly pathetic lyric into a piece of emotional blackmail, in which the "servant" Guillaume urges his audience—the ladies of the court—to value him and his works or face the prospect of lacking the exact kind of entertainment that the musical balade itself presents. Given that songs exist both as texts to be read or heard and as musical songs to be listened to (and one need not imagine a set routine or order for these experiences, since reading could occur before, during, and/or after listening, and there might have been much repetition of these discrete experiences, which are ultimately mutually informing), the reading listener would have two warring mental conceptions of this lyric: as a pathetic poem and as a joyful song. In squaring the circle thus presented, the rational conclusion to be drawn would be to feel more deeply the loss—by death or alteration in patronage—of the singer, whether "Guillaume" or Machaut himself, since it would mean an end to the fount of such performance pieces.

Machaut's Will

It has been assumed by scholars that Guillaume de Machaut made some practical provisions for his own death and for that of his brother Jean, who predeceased him. A poetic inscription that once occupied a brass plaque in Reims cathedral seems to link a donation in support of a weekly Lady Mass with the names of both Machaut brothers, although the interpretation of this poem has been much debated. It is probable that Machaut made a will, although no copy has been found.[30] In the absence of direct evidence, scholars have typically used Machaut's works to illuminate the situation deduced from the plaque, with rather varied results. In particular, Machaut's composition of a single setting of the Mass seems out of kilter with his otherwise secular works, prompting suspicion that this might be related to provisions for his soul after death, resulting from increased religiosity in the face of his own mortality in old age. Machaut's personal views on religion and the relation between sacred and secular spheres in his works and life will be the subject of the next section of this chapter. The present section addresses the issue of Machaut's provision for his death and asks whether or not his Mass has anything to do with it.

Speculation on the issues of Machaut's will and the function of his Mass has been based largely on the inscription on a brass plaque that was formerly

---

30. The inscription on the plaque refers to "executores," which suggests that there was a will, although Bowers notes that in line with the 1327 statues for the cathedral chapter, this could be a local usage referring to "those persons who were appointed by the chapter to wind up just those affairs of a deceased residentiary that directly concerned the cathedral (e.g. outstanding balances of stipend, the vacation of his house)"; Roger Bowers, "Guillaume de Machaut and His Canonry of Reims, 1338–1377," *Early Music History* 23 (2004): 33n82.

affixed to a pier in the nave of Reims cathedral.[31] Although the original was lost—probably during the late eighteenth century—it was transcribed independently by two early-eighteenth-century antiquarians, Charles Regnault and Canon Jean Herman Weyen, who produced texts so similar as to suggest that the original was clearly legible.[32] A recent translation by Roger Bowers offers the most nuanced reading of this Latin poem:

1. guillermus de machaudio	suusque Johannes frater	2
3. sunt in loco concordio	iuncti sicut ad os crater.	4
5. Horum aniversarium	est iuxta petitorium	6
7. oratio de defunctis	diebus sabbathi cunctis	8
9. pro animabus eorum	amicorumque suorum	10
11. dicetur a sacerdote	celebraturo devote	12
13. ad roellam in altari	missam quae debet cantari.	14
15. pro quorum oratione	cum pia devotione	16
17. ad eorum memoriam	percepimus pecuniam	18
19. trecentorum florenorum	nuncupatorum francorum	20
21. suis exequtoribus	pro emendis reddituris	22
23. ad dicte misse crementum	reddituum et fomentum	24
25. in eadem presentium	solerter venientium.	26
27. hos fratres salvet dominus	qui tollit omne facinus.	28

Guillaume de Machaut and Jean his brother have been joined in a place of harmony, as bowl to mouth. The memorial of these men is as according to legal deposition—for the souls of them and of their friends a prayer for the dead shall be recited on every Saturday by the priest who is about to celebrate devoutly that mass at the altar by the *Roella* which is required to be sung.

On the behalf of the [memorial-]prayer of these men, we, with pious devotion to their memory, have collected for their executors a fund of three hundred of the florins called francs, for the purchase of rents for the increase of the revenues of the aforesaid mass and for the sustenance of those present and attending upon it with their skills. May the Lord who takes away all sin redeem these brothers.[33]

This inscription—one of the most discussed of all Machaut-related texts—is not, although it has sometimes been so called, an epitaph, since it does not carry the death dates of the brothers.[34] Nor is it a marker for their burial

31. The position is described fully with a diagram, ibid., 26–27.

32. Regnault's manuscript collection "Recueil choisi des épitaphes anciennes et modernes" is in the municipal library in Reims (MS 1941); the transcription is on 94. Jean Herman Weyen's transcription is also there as MS 1773, f. 488v, no. 178. See Armand Machabey, "Le manuscrit Weyen et Guillaume de Machaut," *Romania* 76 (1955): 247–53.

33. Text and translation from Bowers, "Guillaume de Machaut," 25–26.

34. Anne Walters Robertson, "The Mass of Guillaume de Machaut in the Cathedral of Reims," in *Plainsong in the Age of Polyphony*, ed. Thomas Forrest Kelly (Cambridge, 1992),

site: as Bowers points out, it mentions that the brothers are buried together but does not indicate where.[35] Machabey, Leech-Wilkinson, and Robertson have interpreted the second stanza as an indication that the Machaut brothers themselves made the cash endowment for the weekly celebration of the "mass at the altar by the *Roella*," something Bowers states that it "certainly does not record."[36] In Bowers's reading, its Latin legalese points instead to a court case that preceded the institution of the plaque: the word "petitorium" in line 6 is not, as in earlier readings, the petition of the brothers themselves, but a written legal document indicating the origin of the endowment in a legal case; the verb "percepimus" in the second stanza means not "we have received" but "we have collected," indicating that the poem's author and those who placed the plaque have themselves gathered the fund and rents whose sum it records.[37] Thus in Bowers's reading, the first stanza merely alludes to an original provision made by the brothers: a very short weekly prayer for the benefit of the dead, lasting around thirty seconds, which would have named them and their patrons.[38] This prayer would have been spoken by the celebrant before the weekly Lady Mass at the nave altar near the most holy site in the cathedral (a stone marking the place where Saint Nicasius had been martyred in 406).[39] By the time of Machaut's death, this Mass had been sung rather than spoken for several decades.[40]

The request for the provision of a pre-Mass prayer is a relatively small one and would not have required much money to implement. For this reason, Bowers doubts that this formed the main benefaction of the Machauts, which must remain unknown unless their actual wills are ever brought to light. Instead, he hypothesizes that the lawsuit for which the *petitorium* was drawn up arose as a means of ensuring the funding for this minor benefaction, which was perhaps thought too slight to have merited formal documentation, but which was known to be Machaut's personal wish. The *petitorium* would therefore have been a written statement of witnesses' recollections of Machaut's wishes in this regard. These witnesses would most likely be people

101n1; Earp, *Guillaume de Machaut*, 43–44, 49–51, 344; Anne Walters Robertson, *Guillaume de Machaut and Reims: Context and Meaning in His Musical Works* (Cambridge, 2002), 258–59, 269–72; Bowers, "Guillaume de Machaut," 25n67. The only true tomb epitaph for Machaut is—fittingly—a fictional one from 1457 in René d'Anjou's *Livre du Cuer d'Amours espris* (see the discussion later in this chapter).

35. Bowers, "Guillaume de Machaut," 28.

36. Machabey, "Le manuscrit Weyen," 69–70; Daniel Leech-Wilkinson, *Machaut's Mass: An Introduction* (Oxford, 1990), 10–13; Robertson, "The Mass of Guillaume de Machaut," 125–26, 131–32, 135; Robertson, *Guillaume de Machaut and Reims*, 269–72; Bowers, "Guillaume de Machaut," 29.

37. Bowers, "Guillaume de Machaut," 29–31.

38. Full text of the prayer is given ibid., 45.

39. Maps can be found ibid., 27, fig. 2.

40. Ibid., 45.

who saw Machaut regularly—probably fellow canons, especially those who were also residentiaries, retired, noblemen, or administrators in noble service. Given the situation outlined on the plaque, however, this *petitorium* seems not to have carried enough legal weight to win the case.

The second stanza shows the response to this negative legal outcome: the parties who organized (and perhaps attested) the failed *petitorium* resorted instead to passing the hat, which raised far more money—about ten times the amount—than was actually required to rectify the situation.[41] They then decided to use the excess to fund further the same Mass, and to commission a brass plaque to mark their beneficence in the place where its effects would be enacted weekly.[42] Their funding was directed not at the person celebrating Mass and reciting the brief prayer for the Machaut brothers and their patrons, but to others who would have been already present at the Mass, "attending upon it with their skills." The foundation of this Mass in 1341 lacks definition as to how the monies originally endowed were to be apportioned and offers indulgences for those participating freely in it, features which suggest that the skills mentioned were musical ones for which the foundation was originally underfunded.[43]

In trying to understand why Machaut wanted to pay for a prayer prefixed to this Mass in particular, Bowers reasons that Machaut already had a connection with it because he had already turned it from a sung *chant* Mass to a sung *polyphonic* Mass. According to this theory, before there was any thought of funding a prayer for his soul, Machaut had already written a polyphonic setting for the Mass ordinary that would have followed such a prayer. Bowers is not alone in viewing Machaut's Mass as being designed for the Lady Mass at the Roella, although other scholars, reading the inscription as the direct bequest of the brothers, are more apt to assume that Machaut's Mass was a specifically posthumous gift to the Saturday Lady Mass rather than, as Bowers implies, an earlier donation that was then posthumously continued through the ad hoc financial support of his colleagues.[44] Robertson points to the large amount of money (three hundred florins) mentioned in the inscription, which would have been too much for chant alone.[45] Bowers

---

41. Ibid., 35.

42. Ibid., 36.

43. Ibid., 37–39. One of the eighteenth-century transcribers, Canon Weyen, appended a note suggesting that the Machaut brothers themselves founded this sung Mass, a point accepted by Leech-Wilkinson, *Machaut's Mass,* 11, but not by Bowers or Robertson.

44. Robertson, *Guillaume de Machaut and Reims,* 272, for example, suggests that the Mass was written in the mid-1360s when the Machauts probably drafted their wills, perhaps began to be sung after Jean de Machaut's death in 1372, but was certainly performed from 1377 on. She concludes that "for the first time, it seems, a composer specifically intended that his *Mass* outlive him, that it be sung not solely as a votive service to the Blessed Virgin, but also in 'pious devotion to [his] memory'"; Robertson, *Guillaume de Machaut and Reims,* 275.

45. Ibid., 270–72.

agrees that this amount would have yielded fair recompense for polyphonic singing.[46]

Earlier suggestions—starting with the eighteenth-century rediscovery of Machaut—that linked Machaut's polyphonic Mass setting to the coronation of Charles V in 1364 have been discounted by later scholars.[47] The sense has remained, however, that this extraordinary work, literally out of the ordinary in the context of Machaut's secular song-based output, must—like his other compositional oddity, the *David Hocket*—have been composed for a specific purpose, whether this was a one-off occasion or an ongoing use.[48] As early as 1955, Armand Machabey speculated that the Mass might be associated with the weekly Saturday service for the Virgin that had been celebrated at the Roella altar in Reims cathedral since 1341.[49] The Mass carries the title "Messe de Nostre Dame" in **Vg**, although **A**'s index calls it only "La Messe."[50] Nevertheless, not only was Marian devotion a hugely important part of any French court's religious life in this period, but also Machaut's artistic interest in Marian topics is well attested in his other works; and the cathedral of which he was a canon for over half his life was dedicated to the Virgin Mary.

If the writers of the inscription (probably some of Machaut's fellow canons or *amici* [patrons]) used the excess that resulted from the collection originally designed only to fund Machaut's unwritten wish for a short prayer at the start of the Mass to fund the singers, his colleagues' grander beneficence reflects a perception that the sung Lady Mass was of particular personal relevance to Machaut and perhaps also to his brother. The reason for this must be at once personal and well known, characteristics that would be fulfilled if the Lady Mass had regularly been sung during his lifetime to music composed by Machaut.[51]

Bowers makes this case, noting that the further endowment attested by the plaque would not have been necessary if the Machaut brothers had themselves left money to this foundation or given it during their own lives; their contribution was therefore not financial but personal in a nonprivate way. This, he explains, would be why Machaut's original wish was for a commemorative prayer to be recited before the entire Lady Mass itself, rather than before the prayer of consecration within it, as would have been more usual: a prayer

46. Bowers, "Guillaume de Machaut," 43.

47. A library catalogue of 1769 makes this suggestion; but see Earp, *Guillaume de Machaut,* 43–44. See also my discussion in chapter 2.

48. On the *David Hocket,* see Robertson, *Guillaume de Machaut and Reims,* 224–56 (chap. 8, "Machaut's *David Hocket* and the coronation of Charles V [1364]").

49. See the summary of the literature on this in Earp, *Guillaume de Machaut,* 344–46; also the discussion in Robertson, *Guillaume de Machaut and Reims,* 257–75; and Bowers, "Guillaume de Machaut," 33.

50. Earp, *Guillaume de Machaut,* 344.

51. Bowers, "Guillaume de Machaut," 42–43.

for mercy on the souls of the Machauts and their patrons would have directly preceded the very first section of the Mass, the Kyrie, which would then have asked for the Lord's mercy in a polyphonic setting by one of the souls just commemorated.[52]

Bowers's thesis is highly plausible. Another possible reason, however, for the Machauts' interest in this Lady Mass that could be both private and well known can be mooted—a reason that does not at all exclude Machaut's having composed the polyphonic setting of the ordinary for its celebration sometime after his arrival at Reims in the late 1350s. This reason is one that modern commentators, especially university academics in the postwar twentieth century, have been reluctant to contemplate: Machaut might have had a strong personal devotion to Mary and thus a marked religious interest in this particular foundation.[53] Having made compelling arguments for the use of Machaut's Mass in the Lady Mass at the Roella before and after his death, Bowers comments that "it is clear that in general Machaut's clerical status weighed but lightly upon him," seeing the composition of the Mass as a mere "bouquet," designed to mark the semiretired Machaut's more permanent arrival in the cathedral close.[54] It is possible to argue conversely, however, that for a composer with so little background in liturgical composition, the effort betrays not self-aggrandizement or merely fear for his own mortality but also a genuine devotion to the Virgin. The shifting understanding of Machaut's relationship with the sacred life of his day characteristically tells us more about modern scholarship's relation to religion than Machaut's.

The Christian Machaut

Some commentators have been struck by the apparent mismatch between the historical Machaut—canon of Reims, man of the cloth—and the output of Machaut the artist, which largely comprises secular courtly love poetry. Attempts to tie the life and works together have led scholars in two somewhat different directions: some have dismissed or at least downplayed the role of the Church and religion in Machaut's life; others, especially more recently,

---

52. Ibid., 44.

53. The founder of this service, Jean de Vienne (archbishop from 12 October 1334 to 14 June 1351), was perhaps also a colleague of Machaut's in his court capacity. He was *Maistre des requestes* for Philippe de Valois, a specialist diplomat in Spanish matters, and maintained good relations with Avignon. He employed Louis Thésard (a future Reims archbishop) as his vicar general, whose collation to a canonicate he oversaw. He also knew highborn aristocrats, whom he made canons, including Hugues de Chastillon (a later *Maistre des requestes*). Perhaps significantly, it was almost immediately after Jean de Vienne's death in 1351 that Machaut ran into trouble with the Reims chapter administration on account of his support of Hugues (see chapter 1); Pierre Desportes, *Diocèse de Reims* (Turnhout, 1998), 172–74.

54. Bowers, "Guillaume de Machaut," 46.

have read an assumed clericalism, spirituality, and religiosity back into the seemingly secular output. The motivation for these two orientations may emanate, at least in part, from the personal religious views of the scholars in question, although since scholars are rarely explicit about such matters, an analysis claiming this would rest on dangerously circular reasoning. Given the general trend in recent writing, however, it seems arguable that these two responses to the mismatch between Machaut's secular works and his religious life have been significantly inflected by larger shifts in attitudes toward religion within the scholarly West.

In broad terms, in the past century at least, the idea of a fundamentally secular Machaut tends to predate the reading of his secular works as presenting religious truths. For much of the twentieth century, academia espoused a secular, rationalist agenda that tended to privilege dissenting voices in the past, looking at ways in which hegemonic powers were resisted and opposed.[55] As the principal power of the Western Middle Ages, the Church could almost be "taken as read," with interest falling instead on cultural products, especially those that seemed to operate outside and/or in opposition to its sphere of influence. It seems as if scholars imagined the medieval Church much as they experienced the administrations of the modern nation-states they inhabited—as a fact of life whose rules one basically keeps, but for which one has no affection, in which one has little belief, and of which one is probably highly skeptical. The end of the twentieth century, however, saw a respiritualization of the everyday, given further impetus in the twenty-first century by the resurgence of the idea of wars of religion, especially post-9/11. The overt personal Christianity of several of the leaders of the fin-de-siècle Western world reintegrated the language of religious belief back into political life and, through the structures of the government funding of higher education in the UK at least, back into academia.[56]

Although both views (and their various admixtures) can be found at any chronological point in the modern study of Machaut, this shift from an almost complete rejection of Machaut's personal religious faith to a conviction that it permeates even his most erotic and amorous works can be seen as a general trend. It is therefore worth looking briefly at the ramifications of each end of this spectrum because of the way in which the overall orientation with respect to religion affects the interpretation of Machaut's works.

55. See the pertinent critique of these methods, drawing on Marxist readings, with respect to the public sphere in the eighteenth century in T. C. W. Blanning, *The Culture of Power and the Power of Culture: Old Regime Europe, 1660–1789* (Oxford, 2002), 7–14.

56. For instance, two of the main UK government funding bodies, the Arts and Humanities Research Council and the Economic and Social Research Council, contributed £12 million to fund "research of the highest quality on the interrelationships between religion and society" in their Religion and Society Research Programme, whose projects were to run from January 2007 to December 2012. As their website notes, "research is historical as well as contemporary in focus and many projects are investigating international contexts." See www.religionandsociety.org.uk.

On the view that dismisses religious preoccupation from Machaut's works, it is especially significant that Machaut was not ordained and spent most of his adult life in royal administrative service, that is, employed by temporal and secular powers rather than by the Church. It is noted that his works are predominantly love poems, with the musical works almost exclusively love poems, save for the token exception of a setting of the Mass ordinary.[57] In accounting for the presence of the Mass in Machaut's output, those who see Machaut as a secular artist find various ways to minimize the (to them) unpalatable idea that there may have been any personal religious conviction in its writing. The usual means for doing this is to provide an external rationale for its composition—whether this is the earlier explanation that it was written for the coronation of Charles V or Bowers's latter-day proposal that it was Machaut's "chapter-warming" present to his fellow canons when he retired to Reims. The former provides a convenient way of annexing even the Mass to a courtlier, public sphere; the latter makes it a mere personal expedient, even one that is more self-advertising than pious. Minimizing the religious nature of the Mass can readily be done by concentrating instead on its artistic nature, seeing its composition as a reflection of Machaut's seriousness as a composer. In this version of the story, Machaut's role in originating the cyclic Mass, with the unified coherence of its quasi-symphonic "movements," makes its composition a purely artistic decision.[58] The corollary of this emphasis on Machaut's public, artistic, and political life is that later centuries have been able to conceive of Machaut as a familiar figure, an essentially secular, educated man, writing love poetry and counterpoint, or—in more recent literary scholarship—as a professional poet, voicing open and multilayered texts through complex personae.[59]

The opposite and more recently ascendant view has instead sought out the spiritual and religious elements in Machaut's poetry. Despite serving a courtly constituency, runs this line of argument, Machaut was operating in the context of a Christian worldview; and the court is also a religious and spiritual space. On this view, the Mass setting is still significant artistically, but the motivation to expend such artistic effort points beyond mere artistry to a liturgical and personal-devotional meaning. Like the cathedral of whose chapter Machaut was a member for nearly four decades, the Mass setting seems to have been

57. See, for example, Bowers, "Guillaume de Machaut," 1–2.

58. See the discussion in Andrew Kirkman, "The Invention of the Cyclic Mass," *Journal of the American Musicological Society* 54 (2001): 1–47, especially 30–31.

59. Machaut's ability to function as a postmodern figure is particularly noticeable in late-twentieth-century critical appreciation of the indeterminacy and reader-centeredness of the *Voir dit*; see, for example, Robert S. Sturges, *Medieval Interpretation: Models of Reading in Literary Narrative, 1100–1500* (Carbondale, 1991), 100–124. As Sturges notes in his introduction (3), "the self-consciousness with which Derrida destabilizes texts is not the same thing as manuscript *mouvance*, though the terms in each of these comparisons do have obvious similarities"; see also ibid., 1–6.

dedicated to the Virgin Mary. Several of Machaut's lays are also explicitly addressed to Mary, and his courtly doctrine can be seen as implicitly Christian, offering moral recommendations in complete conformity with Christian teaching. To those espousing this view, Machaut's canonicate at Reims suggests his residence there and involvement in its day-to-day enactment of the liturgy.[60]

These two viewpoints illuminate Machaut's output in different ways, but both can be faulted on different grounds. The scholars in the first group make the mistake of seeing the courtly world, obsessed with erotic love, as entirely separate from religious love for the Christian God. As a phenomenon with Enlightenment roots, modern academic scholarship tends to assume that belief must be active and all-consuming to be real. The analogy with modern political institutions is again valid: a citizen of a mature democracy lives in a country organized at every level by the state and yet with the exception of "conviction politicians"—those with personal and overt political beliefs—most people just get on with their private life, on which the politico-legal superstructure impinges only at certain larger "life event" moments (typically birth, marriage, divorce, and death). Although the machinery of the state is large, its functionaries are mainly just doing a job, and many are apolitical. A cleric like Machaut can be viewed similarly as a kind of civil servant, using the Church to secure his income, and not a "conviction cleric." The problem with this view, however, is that belief in political ideals and belief in God are not equivalent in existential terms, and there is clear evidence that the court was a religious place, whose members had keen interests in devotional literature and moral education.[61]

The converse idea that Machaut was indeed a strongly religious person leads us to view his works as intrinsically pious. Because the expression of strong personal religious views (even in states with an established church) is deemed unusual in public or political life in the West, the assumption becomes that Machaut must have stood out from the crowd—as religious fundamentalists do in the West today—and should be treated as someone for whom such beliefs were irrationally adhered to and all-consuming.[62] This removes from Machaut's works their evident playfulness, humor, and latent (often comic) eroticism, making Machaut into a schoolmarmish moralist.[63]

---

60. This is the central thesis of Robertson, *Guillaume de Machaut and Reims.*

61. On the "extraordinary taste for instructive and devotional literature" of medieval readers, see David Chamberlain, ed., *New Readings of Late Medieval Love Poems* (Lanham, Md., 1993), 4; see also Malcolm Vale, *The Princely Court: Medieval Courts and Culture in North-West Europe, 1270–1380* (Oxford, 2001), 164–69.

62. The U.S., UK/Australasian, and European situations all differ somewhat, with overt religious expression being far more common among politicians and public figures in the United States. Robertson and Bowers, in this sense at least, seem to fit their national contexts perfectly.

63. Domenic Leo, for example, tends to see Machaut's moralizing and didactic aspects as precluding certain types of emphasis: he comments on another writer's reference to *Remede* as an

As the categories of secular and sacred are not medieval ones, moderated versions of both views of Machaut can perhaps be most helpfully combined, as they have been when the overly clean sacred-secular divide that modern scholars tend to project backwards in history has been problematized. The genre on which questions relating to Machaut's religious sentiment have focused in this regard is the motet, whose combination of a tenor part drawn from a segment of sacred plainsong, with upper voices carrying courtly French texts, seems to epitomize the problem that modern writers have with such genres. Despite more sensitive scholarly approaches to thirteenth-century motets, the treatment of Machaut's motets has tended to polarize scholars into those who see the motets as defined by the ludic dialogism of their courtly upper-voice texts and those who instead view their liturgically derived tenor plainchant as unlocking a spiritual master narrative.

Salvation in the Motets

The historical origins of the motet lie in the ornamentation of a plainsong melody within the medieval liturgy.[64] Melismatic sections of certain pieces of monophonic liturgical chants were made polyphonic through the addition of one or more other voice parts. Initially these added voices sang the same vowel that the plainsong melisma was itself prolonging, but eventually they received their own syllabic texts, sometimes poetically based on the original vowel, whose content usually glossed the liturgical situation of the chant as a whole. Eventually these polyphonic endings became detached from their longer chant context and were taken up as musical objects in their own right, receiving further textings of their upper voices—sometimes in the vernacular, and less obviously glossing the liturgical situation by treating erotic or satirical subjects. The late-thirteenth- and fourteenth-century motet's connection with the liturgy was attenuated or even, seemingly, lost.

The later medieval motet can appear as a puzzling genre once its texts are considered. For this reason early commentators tended to focus on the issue of musical structure and treat these kinds of works almost as abstract essays in measured polyphonic composition. Sylvia Huot's 1997 book on the thirteenth-century motet, however, turned attention not only to the often mixed upper-voice texts (which could be mixed linguistically by being in Latin and French,

---

"erotic education" that "Machaut would have most certainly downplayed any sexual reference"; see Domenic Leo, "Authorial Presence in the Illuminated Machaut Manuscripts" (Ph.D. diss., New York University, 2005), 124n124. For a reading of Machaut's didacticism that views it as *not* lacking complexity, eroticism, or humor, see Sarah Kay, *The Place of Thought: The Complexity of One in Late Medieval French Didactic Poetry* (Philadelphia, 2007), 95–122.

64. This discussion is a brief summary. For more detail, see Janet Knapp, "Polyphony at Notre Dame of Paris," in *The New Oxford History of Music: The Early Middle Ages to 1300*, ed. Richard Crocker and David Hiley (Oxford, 1990); and "Motet, I," in *Grove*.

as well as generically by juxtaposing pastourelles with Marian devotional poetry), but also to the seemingly arbitrary links between these texts and the few
words in the plainsong-derived tenor.[65] Viewing the tenor not (as musicologists had) merely as a convenient means of musical organization but as the cue
to a broader liturgical, biblical, and theological situation, Huot documents the
allegorical transformations of sacred and secular motifs in the upper voices to
view the motet as a virtuoso essay in analogical reading.[66]

Before Huot's work, relatively few motets by Machaut and his fourteenth-
century contemporaries had been read as indicative of any religious truth.[67]
The fact that Machaut's tenors use chant fragments different from those that
were used for whole families of (anonymous) motets in the thirteenth century
was thought indicative of the genre's complete remove from its liturgical origins.[68] Machaut's ostensibly free compositional choice of motet tenor sources
had merely completed the movement away from the liturgy that the addition of erotic and vernacular upper-voice texts to thirteenth-century motets
had started. With his older contemporary Philippe de Vitry, Machaut had, it
seemed, completed the transformation of the motet from its origins as a functional adornment to Christian worship into an expansive, sophisticated work
of musical art.

Musicologists initially gave attention to the progressively more complex
structural aspects of the fourteenth-century motet, looking at the organization of the repeating tenor pitches (the "color") and rhythms (the "talea")
and noting any reflection of these patterns in the notes of the upper voices.[69]
Even when they considered the text, it was understood in terms of its declamation, as part of another structural pattern of syllables, interacting with
those of the tenor's talea and color.[70] The stacking up of simultaneous texts
had received little musico-literary analysis until 1991, when Margaret Bent and
Kevin Brownlee published twinned studies of *Amour qui a / Faus Semblant*

---

65. See Sylvia Huot, *Allegorical Play in the Old French Motet: The Sacred and Profane in
Thirteenth-Century Polyphony* (Stanford, 1997).

66. Gerald R. Hoekstra, "The French Motet as Trope: Multiple Levels of Meaning in *Quant
florist la violete / El mois de mai / Et Gaudebit,*" *Speculum* 73 (1998): 32–57, which takes a similar approach, was in press when Huot's book appeared (see 33n7).

67. A notable exception to this is the analysis of Hans Heinrich Eggebrecht, "Machauts
Motette Nr. 9," *Archiv für Musikwissenschaft* 20 (1963): 281–93; and 25 (1968): 173–95, although Kurt Markstrom typically dismisses such a theological reading by commenting that "the
unusual nature of the texts and the secular cynicism of the age seem to suggest a topical interpretation"; Kurt Markstrom, "Machaut and the Wild Beast," *Acta Musicologica* 61 (1989): 19.

68. See the comments in Lawrence Earp, review of *Guillaume de Machaut and Reims: Context and Meaning in His Musical Works* by Anne Walters Robertson, *Journal of the American
Musicological Society* 57 (2004): 389.

69. See the detailed bibliographic listing in Earp, *Guillaume de Machaut*, 287.

70. The classic study is Georg Reichert, "Das Verhältnis zwischen musikalischer und textlicher Struktur in den Motetten Machauts," *Archiv fur Musikwissenschaft* 13 (1956): 197–216;
and see also the additional listings in Earp, *Guillaume de Machaut*, 285n32.

(M15), which Brownlee has since followed up with studies of several other of Machaut's motets.[71]

Brownlee's first point of intertextual resonance for Machaut's motet texts is usually the *Roman de la Rose*, clearly an important influence, but he also notes the centrality of Ovid, usually read by Machaut through the *Ovide moralisé*. Machaut's plainsong tenors—each a decontextualized verbal fragment making affective statements such as "most bitter," "I sigh," or "I languish for love"—are easily seen as analogically courtly in resonance, and the upper-voice texts are treated as relating to one another and to external literary sources.[72] Linking these lyrics to similar topics within narrative works was readily combined with the new emphasis on Machaut's attention to order and bookmaking: a decade after Bent and Brownlee's articles, a thesis by Jacques Boogaart and an article by Thomas Brown, drawing on the same kinds of approaches through vernacular literary sources, suggested (in different ways) that the first twenty motets form an organized set that tells a particular kind of courtly love story, and makes a balanced "super-work"—a song cycle, consisting of twenty individual works.[73]

Although all these commentators note the plainsong source of the tenor pitches, they tend to interpret the tenor in the context of the secular upper voices. This polarity was reversed by Anne Walters Robertson, who effectively combined the kinds of insights about sacred allegorical equivalence seen in Huot's work on the thirteenth-century motet with the focus on ordering seen in Boogaart and Brown.[74] Instead of secularizing the tenor fragments through

71. See Margaret Bent, "Deception, Exegesis and Sounding Number in Machaut's Motet 15," *Early Music History* 10 (1991): 15–27; and four essays by Kevin Brownlee: "Fire, Desire, Duration, Death: Machaut's Motet 10," in *Citation and Authority in Medieval and Renaissance Musical Culture: Learning from the Learned*, ed. Suzannah Clark and Elizabeth Eva Leach (Woodbridge, 2005), 79–93; "La polyphonie textuelle dans le Motet 7 de Machaut: Narcisse, la *Rose*, et la voix féminine," in *Guillaume de Machaut: 1300–2000*, ed. Jacqueline Cerquiglini-Toulet and Nigel Wilkins (Paris, 2002), 137–46; "Machaut's Motet 15 and the *Roman de la Rose*: The Literary Context of *Amours qui a le pouoir / Faus samblant m'a deceü / Vidi Dominum*," *Early Music History* 10 (1991): 1–14; and "Polyphonie et intertextualité dans les motets 8 et 4 de Guillaume de Machaut," in *"L'hostellerie de pensée": Études sur l'art littéraire au Moyen Age offertes à Daniel Poirion*, ed. Michel Zink et al., trans. Anthony Allen (Paris, 1995), 97–104. See also Margaret Bent, "Words and Music in Machaut's Motet 9," *Early Music* 31 (2003): 363–88.

72. These examples are from the tenors of *Quant en moy / Amour* (M1), *Tous corps / De* (M2), and *Maugré mon cuer / De ma dolour* (M14), respectively.

73. See Jacques Boogaart, "'O Series Summe Rata': De Motetten van Guillaume de Machaut. De Ordening van het Corpus en de Samenhang van Tekst en Muziek" (Ph.D. diss., University of Utrecht, 2001); and Thomas Brown, "Another Mirror of Lovers? Order, Structure and Allusion in Machaut's Motets," *Plainsong and Medieval Music* 10 (2001): 121–34.

74. Robertson, *Guillaume de Machaut and Reims*, 79–80, notes the influence of Huot (as does David J. Rothenberg, "The Marian Symbolism of Spring, ca. 1200–ca. 1500: Two Case Studies," *Journal of the American Musicological Society* 59 [2006]: 327) but actively disagrees with Boogaart and Brown (see Robertson, *Guillaume de Machaut and Reims*, 82, and the dismissive comment at 357n16).

the lens of the melodically and textually dominant upper voices, Robertson instead sacralizes the courtly upper-voice texts through the liturgical and mystical context of the contrapuntally fundamental tenor voice. The result is a song cycle of a rather different kind.

Robertson's 2002 book posits Machaut's domestic situation as a citizen of Reims and a canon of its cathedral as a context in which to understand his intellectual, artistic, and spiritual life.[75] She thus reads even the ostensibly courtly French-language texts of the motets' upper voices as reflective of a Christianity that is of a deeply layered, mystical nature, alien as much to the secular liberal culture of the modern university as to today's mainstream modern liberal Christianity.[76] Like Brownlee, she draws on texts external to the motets to understand their contents; like Brown and Boogaart, she posits an ordered sequence of motets in a proto-narrative sequence. Unlike these commentators, however, she uses points of reference that are predominantly sacred.

The central section of Robertson's book resituates the first seventeen of Machaut's motets within a spiritual narrative drawn from contemporary mystical and theological writings, specifically from Henry Suso's *Horologium Sapientiae* (*Wisdom's Watch upon the Hours*), a book of which there was a copy in Reims cathedral library.[77] As mentioned earlier, the plainsong sources of the tenors of Machaut's motets are not those commonly used in thirteenth-century motets but appear to have been freely chosen. Far from seeing this as a sign of the motet's movement away from its sacred origins, Robertson argues that Machaut's reasons for picking those particular musico-textual fragments can be found in their use as tags in Suso's work.[78] Their function as affective, meditative phrases keys a reader or listener into an exegesis which can be literal, allegorical, tropological, and typological, and which exemplifies a deep interpenetration of sacred and secular vocabularies. By viewing the motets' upper voices as this kind of commentary on the tenor, Robertson is able to

75. Robertson, who views Machaut as resident in Reims from the early 1340s at the latest, considers the holdings of the library at Reims cathedral significant in assessing potential sources for Machaut's motets and their proposed greater narrative. If Bowers is correct, however, Machaut's residency in Reims started well after the bulk of the motets were composed (since the first twenty were complete by the date of manuscript C). Neither interpretation precludes Machaut's using books in Reims if he was, as Robertson hypothesizes, educated there as a child (although there is no hard evidence for this). I see no need to limit Machaut's reading possibilities: given that he was in Bohemian royal service—possibly from his teens—he almost certainly had access to libraries far better stocked than that of Reims cathedral.

76. Robertson, *Guillaume de Machaut and Reims*, 84–96.

77. Ibid., 96–102. As Robertson notes (360n94), however, this copy is attested as being there only circa 1390 (that is, after Machaut's death). See Jacques Boogaart, review of *Guillaume de Machaut and Reims: Context and Meaning in His Musical Works* by Anne Walters Robertson, *Early Music* 33 (2004): 606.

78. Robertson notes that *Wisdom's Watch* includes every one of Machaut's motet tenor text fragments, either directly cited or implied; see Robertson, *Guillaume de Machaut and Reims*, 96 and the table on 98–99.

explain how something that seems unequivocally secular can stand allegorically for a spiritual journey in pursuit of sacred love, representing the Christian soul's twelve more or less standard steps on a spiritual journey to union
with the beloved—Jesus Christ.

This model, and the idea that the order is structural and meaningful, enables
the explanation of otherwise troublingly "low" secular texts such as *Lasse!
comment / Se j'aim* (M16), whose tenor is a secular song—"Pour quoy me bat
mes maris?"—in which a lady asks why her husband beats her when all she has
done wrong is lie naked with her lover.[79] Although not a text expounded per
se as the chant-derived tenor texts are by mystical writers, Robertson is able to
show that the idea of being beaten—and, in one example, specifically being a
beaten wife—is a stage that comes immediately before the full union with the
beloved at the journey's end.[80] Although such reasoning may amaze any modern reader unused to such analogical contortions, even if they are also acutely
aware of the otherness of medieval reading habits, Robertson's discussion of the
first seventeen motets as a narrative of the soul's mystical journey is strongly argued and offers a sustained attempt to read meaning into Machaut's significant
use of order. Her focus on the contemplative nature of motet texts sidelines
musicology's traditional taxonomizing of architectural musical structuring in
pieces whose simultaneously delivered texts cannot be appreciated semantically
in performance; her emphasis on the spiritual, devotional, and divine aspects
of love provides an important corrective to reading it as courtly eroticism; ultimately her seriousness about the seriousness of Machaut's message cuts deeply
against the idea that the motet is secular, courtly entertainment.

Responses to Robertson's thesis have been mixed, and once more offer a
commentary on modern scholarly attitudes toward religion rather than a pure
response to the interpretive power of her readings. To outline the range
of responses, it is necessary only to cite contrasting reviews by Earp and
Boogaart. Earp finds the results of her study "compelling because they con-
firm and complement a view of Machaut's artistic position revealed over the
last thirty years by the very different critical approach of literary scholars"
and because her "application of exegetical criticism is sanctioned by the external liturgical link of the tenor in most of the works she considers."[81] He notes
that the "analytical strategy of checking a tenor's association with biblical
sources and liturgical context... now has to be broadened to include both medieval commentaries on the Song of Songs... and Wisdom literature, of which
Suso's work is the most important."[82] Jacques Boogaart, by contrast, finds
Suso's *Horologium* an unlikely model and is not convinced "that Machaut

---

79. See ibid., 165–73; this case is singled out as exemplifying the weakness of her argument
in Boogaart's review of Robertson, 607.

80. Robertson, *Guillaume de Machaut and Reims,* 165–68.

81. Earp's review of Robertson, 393.

82. Ibid., 387.

meant his motets to be allegories of a one-sided Christian message," in part because "he did not have to disguise his religious themes, as is demonstrated by the *Lay de la Fonteinne* and *Lay de Nostre Dame.*" He concludes that "Machaut pictures himself as a rational and faithful man for whom love and religion were not hermetically separated worlds, and for whom the sacred stories could serve as edifying guides to human and courtly behaviour; but his ideas seem far removed from those of a passionate mystic like Suso."[83]

Although with one hand Robertson undoubtedly gives Machaut's motets new intertextual referents in Wisdom literature and commentaries on the Song of Songs, with the other hand she takes away, specifically focusing far less on the kinds of literary resonance with works such as *Rose* and *Ovide moralisé*, which had regularly been discussed as central to the texts of Machaut's motets by Brownlee and others.[84] Yet both these texts might have contributed to Robertson's thesis rather than detracted from it. In both these long and complex texts the interplay of religious and erotic varieties of love—and the way in which poetry can analogize them—is a central theme. The case with *Rose* is less straightforward and will be treated later on for its influence on *Voir dit;* but the role of the moralized Ovid in contextualizing motet upper voices can be seen to point exactly to the Christianization of a secular or non-Christian story: it is the *Metamorphoses* moralized after the fact, not an exposition of Christian doctrine illustrated by nice stories from the *Metamorphoses*. This is indicative of the status of the Christian religion for Machaut and his audience as their basic context, giving the essential existential facts. The same existential and moral issues, however, can equally be explored in non-Christian stories, which, even without an explicit action of *translatio studii,* can still be understood in Christian terms even if they were not constructed in them. I have argued, for example, that the first five balades in the music section form a sequence that in some ways intersects with and parallels the opening of the *Loange*.[85] From reading Robertson's work it becomes clear that this theme of the lover having to decide whether to languish with love unrevealed or declare his love and risk refusal is also found in the opening motets.[86] Might

---

83. Boogaart's review of Robertson, 604.

84. Robertson, *Guillaume de Machaut and Reims,* notes Machaut's inspiration by *Ovide moralisé* in general (17) and specifically (58) in *Bone pastor / Bone pastor* (M18); she notes *Rose* as a general source (109) and as a specific source (130) for *J'ay tant / Lasse!* (M7). Robertson also notes that Suso's *Horologium* has more surviving manuscript copies than *Rose,* although not so many as Boethius's *Consolation* (97). References to *Rose* and *Ovide moralisé* combined are vastly exceeded in Robertson's text by the number of references to Suso's work.

85. See Elizabeth Eva Leach, "Death of a Lover and the Birth of the Polyphonic Balade: Machaut's Notated Balades 1–5," *Journal of Musicology* 19 (2002): 461–502; and the comments on order in chapter 3.

86. This similarity is made closer, given that Robertson speculates that *Quant en moy / Amour* (M1) could have been fabricated retrospectively, something I have also argued for in *S'Amours ne fait* (B1); see ibid., 466–72.

it therefore be possible to view the balades as a spiritual journey by the same token? Such an argument is harder to sustain in the absence of plainsong-derived tenor cues, but might be made purely on the basis that these meanings are a feature not necessarily of the texts themselves but of readers and readings. If tropological and analogical reading can be shown to be the norm, then readers and listeners could have understood Machaut's *je* as a soul on a journey, regardless of whether they were hearing and reading the first motet or the first balade. And in both the series of balades and the series of motets (as well as more explicitly in the narrative dits), Machaut the poet-composer can readily be understood as succeeding in inverse proportion to the *je* lover's failure. These works are thus about related existential prerogatives: erotic love, religious love, and the practice of artistic creativity.

Sylvia Huot has more recently presented evidence that Machaut's motets might well have been read by his near contemporaries in the manner that Robertson suggests. She points out that only after singing a motet "sent from Reims" (a likely allusion to Machaut's work; see the discussion later in this chapter) does the narrator of Jehan Froissart's *Joli buisson de Jonece* (The Fair Bush of Youth) abandon his dream of success with his beloved and devote himself instead to the "one lady who is indeed eternally young, beautiful and virginal," that is, the Virgin Mary, celebrating her in a final lay.[87] *Joli buisson* represents a rewriting of Froissart's earlier *Espinette amoureuse,* which includes within it the deliberate contrasting of the imaginative processes of mourning loss in love and loss through death. Helen Swift has read *Joli buisson*'s rewriting of the earlier dit as a way of paralleling the processes of mourning and writing, to show that those who truly mourn "do not misuse their imagination and memory in pursuit of illusory comfort. They do not achieve consolation as relief from grief, because the process of mourning, whether literal or figurative, adhering repeatedly to a fixed mental image or recycling and transforming prior textual materials, is essentially incomplete."[88] Froissart's earlier dit is narrated by a persona with a skewed perception of consolation and memory so as to thematize the misuse of imagination to provide false comfort. When *Espinette* is recast in *Joli buisson,* the hearing of the "motet from Reims," and the poetic response of the narrator's final Marian lay, turns the focus so that imperfect earthly loves guide the narrator to perfect love of the Virgin. The potential role of Machaut's music in encouraging the rejection of the "bush of youth" in favor of the "burning bush" of Mary was, it seems, one of which at least some of Machaut's contemporaries were aware.[89] This would lend credence to the thrust of Robertson's interpretations, if not to her

---

87. Sylvia Huot, "Reading across Genres: Froissart's *Joli Buisson de Jonece* and Machaut's Motets," *French Studies* 57 (2003): 10. See further on this later in the chapter.

88. Swift, "*Tamainte consolation / Me fist lymagination,*" 159–60.

89. On Froissart's similar transformation of Machaut *S'onques (Le Lay de Confort)* (L17/12) in his lay *S'onques amoureusement,* see Benjamin L. Albritton, "Citation and Allusion in the Lays

predominant emphasis on mystical literature and biblical commentaries. Instead, Robertson's powerful case for reading Machaut's secular motet texts as affording contemplation of a religious kind that seems to have been always already present in Machaut's courtly world can be furthered by considering specifically his seemingly courtly, secular dits and their courtly, secular models.

Faith, Hope, and Analogous Kinds of Love

Machaut's other works can readily be understood in a Christian context, especially the *Remede de Fortune*. Given that Hope's efficacy "lies not in bodily contact but in private contemplation; not in communication with a particular individual but in communion with a sovereign perfection," she is at once a remedy for the vicissitudes of courtly love in the sphere of Fortune and, as a personification of the cardinal virtue *spes,* the expectation of the life to come that forms a Christian consolation for the miserable trials of this life.[90] Yet the exact workings of Hope and her relation to the *Remede*'s Boethian model have been appreciated in diverse ways, again largely dependent on the religious sympathies (scholarly, not necessarily personal, although these may be related) of particular commentators. Robertson, for example, says that the *Remede* introduces Hope so centrally as to make it consonant with the idea that happiness comes from God and is not found in this life. She therefore understands *Remede* to replicate Boethius's *Consolation*. Helen Philips claims, on the contrary, that *Remede*'s conclusion is the opposite: that, despite the facts, consolation *can* be found on earth in both loyalty and poetry, and that the latter promotes the former. This, Philips maintains, would not meet with the approval of Boethius, who has Philosophy banish the Muses of poetry at the very opening of his work.[91] Sarah Kay echoes this view in claiming that the French poets "systematically rewrote" the relation between the dreamer and Philosophy to make the consolation offered more consoling, physical, and embodied in the here and now.[92] The propensity for arguments based on the same material to generate diametrically opposed conclusions might hint that neither is exactly right: as I suggested in chapter 4, Machaut's purpose is neither complete agreement nor complete disagreement with Boethius; this incompleteness resonates with the incompleteness of the processes of grief and

---

of Guillaume de Machaut" (Ph.D. diss., University of Washington, 2009), chap. 5, "Machaut, Froissart, and Chaucer: Modeling Consolation."

90. Huot, "Guillaume de Machaut and the Consolation of Poetry," 195.

91. Helen Philips, "Fortune and the Lady: Machaut, Chaucer and the Intertextual 'Dit,'" *Nottingham French Studies* 38 (1999): 123. To be fair, she concludes more equivocally, stressing that sovereign good and virtue are beyond Fortune's power for Machaut as for Boethius, but for Machaut they can reside in erotic emotion and its literary expression. This is similar to the conclusion of Huot, "Guillaume de Machaut and the Consolation of Poetry."

92. Sarah Kay, "Touching Singularity: Consolations, Philosophy, and Poetry in the French *dit,*" in Léglu and Milner, *The Erotics of Consolation*, 21–38, especially the conclusion on 36.

consolation that Swift identifies in works by Machaut, Froissart, Martin Le Franc, and Alain Chartier.[93] Nonetheless, as *Remede*'s earliest editor pointed out a hundred years ago, Machaut remodels Boethius for more modern purposes: the interface between religious and secular vocabulary and ideas allows the adaptation of Boethius to a new social reality; in Kay's analysis, Machaut's reworking encapsulates the tension—typical of late medieval vernacular dits— between the unity of meaning that a didactic text wants to project and the *je* subject's awareness of the unique viewpoint of the first-person narrator (and, ultimately, the poet).[94]

Although the figure of Hope is most obviously liable to Christianizing readings, the *Voir dit* perhaps offers a more typical example of the capacity for Machaut's works to sustain them, even when the degree of sublimation to which Hope usually subjects the complex interlacing of the sacred and erotic is absent. Toute Belle, like Hope and beloved human ladies throughout Machaut's work, is described in terms applied elsewhere—in Machaut's own works and well beyond—to the Virgin Mary: she is the polestar, a miracle worker who cures, and a number of precious stones.[95] Even the framing of Guillaume's meeting with her—which he plans to take place before Pentecost as part of a pilgrimage—lexically sacralizes the chivalric in a way that draws on both the Song of Songs and the *Roman de la Rose*. The Mass that Guillaume and Toute Belle attend becomes their amorous tryst as they kiss "entre .ii. pilers" (between two pillars) during the Agnus.[96] In *Rose*, the final approach to the Rose is in order to worship at the beautiful, honorable sanctuary and penetrate the relics within: the *Rose* is also an erotic pilgrimage in which the pilgrim similarly kneels down "entre les .ij. biaus pilerez" (between the two beautiful little pillars), having been told by Nature's priest, Genius, that the Agnus Dei will lead the lovers in the "park of the merry field" (see figure 6.2).[97] In *Voir dit*, the image that Toute Belle sends Guillaume recalls the feminine image supported by the two pillars at which Venus fires her burning arrow in *Rose* (see figures 6.3 and 6.4), yet Guillaume vows to do it homage and adore it, lacing the comically idolatrous with covert eroticism.

In asking whether Machaut presents "erotic adventures with a spiritual significance, or spiritual and aesthetic adventures with an erotic significance," Huot reads his purpose as rather to prove language capable of mediating directly between the natural, the erotic, and the divine because it is able to

93. Swift, "*Tamainte consolation / Me fist lymagination.*"

94. Ernest Hoepffner, *Oeuvres de Guillaume de Machaut*, 3 vols. (Paris, 1908–1922), 2:xxiii–xxiv; Kay, *The Place of Thought*, 178–79; and idem, "Touching Singularity."

95. Huot, "Reliving the *Roman de la Rose*," 49; and compare the description of the lady and Hope in figure 4.8.

96. Ibid., 50. Huot even sees the parrots on Toute Belle's hood at first meeting as an echo of birds in the Garden of Delights of the *Rose*. See Huot, "Reliving the *Roman de la Rose*," 51–52.

97. *Rose*, ll. 21559, 19905.

Figure 6.2. The final approach to the Rose from the *Roman de la Rose* in MS 387, f. 147v. Biblioteca Histórica, Universitat de València.

express aspects of any one in terms of any other. The narrator, Guillaume, fails fully to grasp this; he experiences everything except what these things stand for: sex. The figure that Kevin Brownlee calls the "poète" (that is, the overarching author figure, Machaut, as distinct from the mere first-person protagonist, Guillaume) thereby shows the power of literary language just as Guillaume shows its limitations. In Huot's conclusion:

> Poetry cannot transform erotic love into divine Grace—cannot, to return to the language of the *Rose*, turn genitals into sacred relics, or relics into genitals, simply by a transfer of names. Machaut's ironic use of the *Rose* in the *Voir Dit* shows that he appreciated the comedy and the audacity of Jean's erotic allegory, his brilliant distortions of such authors as Boethius and Alain de Lille, his merciless lampooning of the pretensions of courtly diction. At the same time, the very success of such an enterprise, the real force of the literary parody, is bound up in the fact that, in a different sense, poetry *can* transform the erotic into the sacred, through the power of allegory. In the *Voir Dit,* as in the *Remede de Fortune* and the *Prologue,* Machaut affirms the potency of writing, of poetic discourse, to create a literary space for the interplay and mutual glossing of the many registers—sacred and erotic, chivalric and clerkly, mythic and historic—of language and experience.[98]

For literary language to be able to do this and to have its best effect through interior, personal communion with the text (even if this is in the direct context of having it read aloud in a group) was probably vital in dealing with the basic existential problems that beset members of Machaut's audience. In particular, the sexual continence of youths—in close physical proximity with one another in mixed-sex courts, but under huge pressure not to compromise the legitimacy of descent—would have been of paramount importance.[99] Literature and music served as a consolation that did more than merely occupy time and function as a distraction; that occupation also served to reinforce particular ethical codes that were certainly religious but practical and social as well, not least because religion was also both of those things.

Musical Fusion: Sacred-Secular

As Malcolm Vale has pointed out, court culture in the late Middle Ages seems paradoxically to cherish lavish display, cultural artifacts, and pleasure yet to revere austerity.[100] Purposeful rejection of extravagant display in response to the liturgical year was connected to the frequent appointment of mendicants or austere religious as royal confessors and chaplains. The asceticism of mendicancy was given meaning by the presence of material affluence, because by rejecting it for specific periods at court, one could give the making of vows or the observance of penitential periods of the church year extraordinary

---

98. Huot, "Reliving the *Roman de la Rose*," 66.
99. See chapter 4.
100. Vale, *The Princely Court,* 168–69.

Figure 6.3. The *ymage* that Toute Belle sends Guillaume in **A**, f. 235v. Bibliothèque nationale de France.

Figure 6.4. The avatar of the image, the feminine image supported by the two pillars at which Venus fires her burning arrow in *Rose*, as shown in MS 387, f. 145r. Biblioteca Histórica, Universitat de València.

truth-value.[101] In his initial job as court almoner Machaut would have been placed at the intersection of culture and religion at court: on the one hand, charitable giving was a spiritual duty of court magnates, which interfaced with the rhythms of the liturgical year; on the other hand, cultural artifacts were frequently commissioned as part of charitable giving—whether to serve as purses for monetary gifts or as gifts of charity in their own right (such as gifts of silverware, vestments, or furniture to religious institutions).[102]

Marian devotion in particular was an important feature of broader court culture in late medieval Europe. Several of Machaut's lays are overtly Marian, and it is perhaps unsurprising that the lays are the lyric genre in which, when they are not overtly Marian, the personified figure of Hope is most prominent.[103] When Mary is the theme, she effectively substitutes for Hope. The *Lay de Nostre Dame, Contre ce dous* (L15/10), for example, offers a conspectus of Mary's life and theological significance, and would have served its listeners as an item of contemplation, whose performance or hearing alone would have occupied at least half an hour. It opens (see example 6.2) with the spring topos—a motive

101. Ibid.

102. See Xavier de la Selle, *Le service des âmes à la cour: Confesseurs et aumôniers des rois de France du XIIIe au XVe siècle* (Paris, 1995). On the specific case of the almoner Nicole de Gavrelle, see Janet F. van der Meulen, "De panter en de aalmoezenier: Dichtkunst rond het Hollands-Henegouwse hof," in *Een zoet akkoord: Middeleeuwse lyriek in de Lage Landen*, ed. Frank Willaert (Amsterdam, 1992), 93–108, 343–48. An alms purse is pictured in Vale, *The Princely Court*, before 271 as plate 37; see also www.cottesimple.com/alms_purse/alms_purse_history. html; and Elizabeth Eva Leach, "Guillaume de Machaut, Royal Almoner: *Honte, paour* (B25) and *Donnez, signeurs* (B26) in Context," *Early Music* 38 (2010): 21–42.

103. "Esperance" or other forms of *espoir* occur in all but three of Machaut's lays. Two of these, *Contre ce dous (Le Lay de Nostre Dame)* (L15/10) and *Je ne cesse (Le Lay de la Fonteinne)* (L16/11), have Mary instead of Hope, leaving only *Aus amans* (L4), whose lover has neither Hope nor Mary but turns and re-turns on Fortune's wheel. See also Douglas Kelly, *Medieval Imagination: Rhetoric and the Poetry of Courtly Love* (Madison, 1978), 148.

that is shared by *fine amour* and Marian registers: "In harmony with this sweet month of May, in order to have a merrier heart (and a happier one), and for her to whom I am pledged, I wish to make a lay."[104] The speaker worries that he has too little "senz" to make the lay, and is unworthy of praising her. Then, placing his faith firmly in her, he announces his intention to begin. Effectively he already *has* begun, but in his opening stanza the lady's identity is not yet clear, despite her having suggestively elemental power over nature to brighten every-thing up and "illuminate us with the true sun."[105] Only in the second half of the second stanza is she unequivocally identified as the "Lady, Virgin and Mother," who can only be Saint Mary.[106] But in the manuscript, the title rubric had also announced the Marian nature of this song, as if to cancel the preceding, idolatrous *Ne say comment (Lay de l'Ymage)* (L14/9), with whose minim-rich musical notation B15/10 contrasts visibly. The *Lay de Nostre Dame* (L15/10) is notated in modus notation—that is, predominantly in longs and breves with semibreves. In terms of its "musical font" it visually resembles Hope's chanson royal in *Remede*, with similar figures in semibreves (quarter notes in the tran-scription in example 6.2; cf. example 4.6). The lays that precede and follow it are notated in the more normal tempus notation (mixing breves and semibreves with minims), making this lay stand out visually.[107]

One of Machaut's most telling works for this paradoxical courtly integra-tion of serious ethical contemplation and ludic, self-consciously artistic cre-ativity is the short rondeau *Ma fin* (R14). This poem presents the voice of the song itself, ostensibly instructing the singers in how to sing it, but actually describing its rather intricate musical construction, something further flagged by its notation (see figure 6.5 and example 6.3).[108] In the whole rondeau the same melody (A) is present simultaneously forward (Ap) and backward (Ar) in the cantus and tenor respectively, so that the end is its beginning and the beginning is its end, because the beginning and end of the melody are sung simultaneously at both the beginning and the end. At the same time, the

104. *Lay de Nostre Dame* 1.1–5: "Contre ce doulz mois de may / Pour avoir le cuer plus gay / Et plus joli / Et pour celle a qui m'ottri / Vueil faire un lay."

105. Ibid. 1.11–13: "Car c'est le ray / Qui embelli / Nous a tous et esclarci."

106. Ibid. 2.9: "Dame vierge et mere appellee."

107. As with *Joie, plaisance* (RF3), it seems doubtful whether the lack of minims in the nota-tion of B15/11 had any impact on the performance of the song. David Maw, "'Trespasser mesure': Meter in Machaut's Polyphonic Songs," *Journal of Musicology* 21 (2004): 50–51, points out that L15/10 and L14/9 share melodic figuration and style to the extent that modern commentators have been unable to assume other than that these notations sounded similar in performance and merely represent visual differences. His example 1 (52) demonstrates this by comparing passages in the two lays which have similar figuration written at the two different rhythmic levels. The opening of the third stanza of L15/10 also shares a motive with the opening of the refrain of *Il m'est avis* (B22), again notated at different rhythmic levels, in terms of note values, where it sets the word "Fortune."

108. See Craig Wright, *The Maze and the Warrior: Symbols in Architecture, Theology, and Music* (Cambridge, 2001), 111–15; a diagram (112) illustrates clearly the structure of the canon.

In harmony with this sweet month of May,
In order to have a merrier heart,
(And a happier one),
And for her to whom I am pledged,
I wish to make a lay.
But how I shall do it
Greatly concerns me,
Because I have in me too little sense
Of how to do it.

I am not worthy—this I know well—
To praise her, because she is the beam
That brightens
Us up from everything, and illuminates
Us with the true sun.
So I have my faith
So firmly in her,
And thus, ever to her honor,
Shall I begin.

Example 6.2. *Contre ce dous (Lay de Nostre Dame)* (L15/10), stanza 1 and translation.

contratenor voice presents another kind of retrograde melody (B)—it sings a melody that is half the length of the other two parts, presented twice—first forwards (Bp) and then backwards (Br). This means that at the midpoint of the rondeau refrain, the contratenor starts to "unsing" the pitches of its melody to that point. At the same point the cantus and tenor parts appear to "cross," because this is where the cantus and tenor start singing what is the equivalent of the other voice's part backwards from the point just reached. This double retrograde—a double palindrome—is visually signaled in the manuscript not by any sign of retrogression but by the inversion of text, as if upside down and back to front were equivalent.[109]

As well as an artful piece of pleasure—an impressive composition that has elements of play for singers, readers, and listeners alike—R14 is a seriously ethical statement on existence, forcing its singers and listeners to meditate both on their own bodily deaths (since they come from, and go to, dust) and on their own soul's salvation (since the beginning and end is Christ—the consonant music of the universe).[110] It replicates the experience of existence because the end and the beginning do not *sound* the same: the beginning has the beginning of the melody and contratenor forwards and the end of the melody backwards (in the tenor), whereas the end has the beginning of the melody and contratenor backwards and the melody's end forwards (in the tenor). Music played backwards does not present a perceptible identity with a forwards presentation to the listener, who hears a continuous forward progression; similarly, unless marked by dementia, life's "declining" years seem an ongoing personal development, not an unpicking of existence—at least not until the end has come. Perhaps signaling forward and retrograde motion by something notated upside down (inversion), which thereby equates temporal and spatial axes, even depicts the axes of a wheel, the wheel of Fortune and of life, whose course can only be borne through the maintenance of Christian Hope, mediated through the cognate female figure of Mary.

Given that Machaut was an inner-circle court functionary, a secretary, a cleric, and a writer, it is not surprising that his work addressed those existential questions that concerned his masters. To couch those questions in religious terms is a way of communicating their ethical import, which is not to suggest that this was just a convenience: the necessity for religion was, like the

109. See Anne Stone, "Music Writing and Poetic Voice in Machaut: Some Remarks on B12 and B14," in Leach, *Machaut's Music*, 136. NB: the labeling of the parts as cantus and tenor in a fully realized modern score is effectively arbitrary, since these both derive from a single, notated, texted melody.

110. For a more involved theological reading of this song as "an elegant reformulation of the semiotics of divinity," see Michael Eisenberg, "The Mirror of the Text: Reflections in *Ma fin est mon commencement*," in *Canons and Canonic Techniques, 14th–16th Centuries: Theory, Practice, and Reception History*, ed. Katelijne Schiltz and Bonnie J. Blackburn (Leuven, 2007), 83–110.

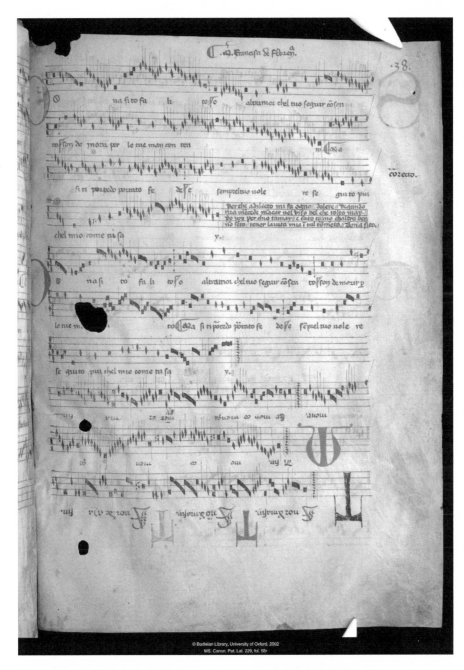

Figure 6.5. *Ma fin* (R14) in **PadA**. Reproduced by permission of the Bodleian Library, University of Oxford, MS Canon Pat. lat. 229, f. 56r. Digital imaging by DIAMM (www.diamm.ac.uk).

Example 6.3. *Ma fin* (R14) with a translation of the text.

necessity of a good marriage for courtiers, simply a given, a fact of life. But to explain one set of life facts in terms of another was useful, and to present this explanation as a musical diversion did not just sweeten the didactic pill but made it more efficacious and meaningful because it forestalled times of dangerous privacy with a social occupation of divine and cosmic resonance.

My end is my beginning
and my beginning my end.
And I really hold to this tenor—
My end is my beginning.
My third [part] sings three times only
In retrograde and is then at an end.
My end is my beginning
and my beginning my end.

Example 6.3. (*Continued*)

Machaut's Afterlife

Guillaume de Machaut, secretary, poet, and musician, was remembered for some time after his death in at least two of these capacities. A letter in the form of a Latin dream-vision by a secretary of the royal chancery, the "early humanist" Jean Lebègue, invokes him as the "eminent late rhetorician, Guillaume de Machaut."[111] Written around 1395, this letter was ostensibly a request for

---

111. "Eximium condam rethoricum Guillelmum de Mascaudio." See Earp, *Guillaume de Machaut*, 59; and Guy Ouy, "Le songe et les ambitions d'un jeune humaniste parisien vers 1395,"

the hand of its addressee's daughter in marriage, but it is replete with classical allusions. Machaut is the only postclassical and vernacular author mentioned, and it seems possible that Lebègue, who had clear interests in bookmaking, manuscript programs, order, and the compilation of indexes, viewed Machaut as a kindred spirit.[112] The eclectic mixture of classical and biblical references in Lebègue's letter echoes those that fill Machaut's dits, and the dreamer's wish that Morpheus might reveal his love to the young lady in a dream is identical with that of the lover in Machaut's *Fonteinne* (a dit repeatedly referred to in the *Voir dit* and in various manuscript rubrics as the *Book of Morpheus*).[113] The letter's valuation of virtue over the insecure gifts of Fortune accords with Machaut's own doctrine, and the allusions to Alan of Lille's *Complaint of Nature* also place Jean Lebègue firmly within the sphere of Machaut's ethical sympathies. Other uses of the term "rhetorician" for Machaut (discussed later in this chapter) make it possible that this term implies Lebègue's recognition of Machaut's musical as well as poetic talent, especially since Lebègue is reported to have participated in a performance of Adam de la Halle's *Jeu de Robin et Marion* in Angers in 1392.[114]

At Reims, of whose chapter Machaut was a member for nearly four decades, the prayer at the start of the Saturday Lady Mass—the one that seems to have represented his unwritten wish and prompted the failed *petitorium* and subsequent collection of the enormous sum of three hundred French florins—was associated with his name well into the fifteenth century. When the chantry and intercessory arrangements for a later canon of Reims, Jean le Verrier, were recorded in 1411, they comprised two Masses a year at one of the other altars in the cathedral, each including "the prayer for the dead...namely 'Inclina domine aurem tuam,' which has been accustomed to be said for Guillaume de Machaut, sometime canon of Reims, deceased, on Saturdays in the mass of the Blessed Mary celebrated at the Roella of the said church."[115] That Machaut's

---

in *Miscellanea di studi e richerche sul Quattrocento francese*, ed. F. Simone (Turin, 1967), 401. The letter is addressed to Pierre Lorfèvre, chancellor of Louis d'Orléans, regarding his daughter Catherine. It appears to have been unsuccessful as a marriage proposal.

112. See Donal Byrne, "An Early French Humanist and Sallust: Jean Lebègue and the Iconographical Programme for the *Catiline* and *Jurgurtha*," *Journal of the Warburg and Courtauld Institutes* 49 (1986), 41–65. As Lebègue was not born until 1368, any personal contact with Machaut would have been at an early, potentially formative age.

113. See Ouy, "Le songe et les ambitions d'un jeune humaniste," 400. *Fonteinne* is titled *Morpheus* in E and M, although in both cases the other title is also given; see Earp, *Guillaume de Machaut*, 220, and the references there in nn. 70, 72, and 73.

114. Ouy, "Le songe et les ambitions d'un jeune humaniste," 370, cites no source for this statement. In the letter Jean confesses that he cannot dance, sing, or play the harp sweetly (see ibid., 401), but this is part of a rhetorical trope bewailing his unworthiness rather than a frank admission of inability. The term "rethoricum" is echoed in the refrain of Deschamps's *déploration* balades and also in the anonymous *Art of the Second Rhetoric* treatise (see the discussion later in this chapter).

115. Bowers, "Guillaume de Machaut," 41–42.

desired memorial was a benchmark in this case might have been influenced by his status as a revered vernacular author, possibly one that Jean le Verrier, himself the author of a historical chronicle of the conquest of the Canaries, had sought to emulate.[116]

Machaut's posthumous fame as a poet is thus attested by the citation of his name in these and a number of other sources, both theoretical and literary, as well as by the continued copying of his works in the fifteenth century. Those wishing to minimize his posthumous musical influence as part of an apologia for literary studies' neglect of this aspect of Machaut's importance have claimed that his literary fame vastly exceeded his musical impact.[117] But if the historical length of his musical fame appears less than that of his literary fame, it is only because literary scholars have not counted citation and reference to Machaut both within the nonverbal content of songs and verbally in technical treatises on music. As the medium of literature is words, it is unsurprising that Machaut is emulated, cited, and named in words in other literary works; that he is not named as a composer in songs can be countered by asserting that the medium of song is also music: he is emulated, cited, and if not named then certainly "sung" in later musical works. And Machaut is certainly named in musical works—not songs, but works of music theory, a tradition of citing him as an authority akin to that found in fifteenth-century poetry treatises. Moreover, many unequivocally musical contexts in which Machaut's name is invoked, but which do not mention him specifically as a composer, so strongly imply this by their context that it might be wise to read other references to him as a poet as including music writing within the remit of that term when applied to Machaut.[118]

One posthumous mention of Machaut as a composer in a poem set to music has been widely discussed by literary and musical scholars alike, although it is too often seen as an exception that proves the rule to the received view of Machaut's annexation to unsung poetry in his posthumous reception history. Some scholars have gone so far as to claim that its musical setting—by the

116. See Richard Henry Major, ed., *The Canarian: or, Book of the Conquest and Conversion of the Canarians in the year 1402 by Messire Jean de Bethencourt, Kt, composed by Pierre Bontier and Jean Le Verrier* (London, 1872).

117. See, for example, the remarks in Jean-Claude Mühlethaler, "Un poète et son art face à la postérité: Lecture des deux ballades de Deschamps pour la mort de Machaut," *Studi Francesi* 33 (1989): 401–2. This view of Machaut slots into the "divorce" of music and poetry that Deschamps supposedly heralds, in which scenario Machaut is the last to combine both arts. Poetry and music are then radically separated in Machaut's posthumous reception as a supposed reflection of their separation in contemporary practice post-Deschamps. As usual, this skewed story is a product of modern, not medieval, disciplinary divisions; plenty of composers after Machaut were also poets.

118. For example, the listing of him with Vitry and Jehan de le Mote by Gilles li Muisis, and as a poet among a large number of musicians (both composers and singers, so far as these groups were distinct) in the triplum of the motet *Apollinis / Zodiacum / In omnem* (see the discussion later in this chapter).

otherwise unknown F. Andrieu—was not intended by the author of its poetry, Eustache Deschamps, and moreover obscures its message, while others merely cite this *déploration* of his death as (incorrectly) the only specific mention of him as a composer.[119] But the fact that he seems to have been the first musician whose death merited a composed musical lament attests directly to his fame as a poet-musician, a role that seems to have been encompassed by the designations "fayseur" (maker) and "rhetorique" (rhetorician).

Deploring Machaut's Death

The interest in his own posterity attested by Machaut in his life and works seems to be, in the short term at least, affirmed by the composition of the musical *déploration* that mourns his death. This song—a polytextual balade, generically akin to Machaut's own *Quant Theseus / Ne quier* (B34)—is the earliest polyphonic commemoration to have survived for one composer set to music by another. Its two poetic texts—balades sharing a refrain—are by Eustache Morel, more commonly known as Eustache Deschamps, and are known from several sources, but survive with music in only one, where the music is ascribed to "F. Andrieu," a figure unconfirmed elsewhere.[120]

Speculation about the personal relationship between Deschamps and Machaut has focused on a reference in the anonymous *Regles de la Seconde Rettorique* (Rules of the Second Rhetoric), which calls Deschamps "nepveux de maistre Guillaume de Machault" (nephew of Master Guillaume de Machaut).[121] Deschamps himself merely says, in the context of a comic poem that is addressed to the supposed heroine of the *Voir dit,* that Machaut "m'a nourry et fait maintes douçours" (nurtured me and did me many kindnesses).[122] Commentators have therefore variously considered Machaut and Deschamps blood relations, master and pupil, or master and secretary.[123] Deborah

---

119. See, for example, Robert Magnan, "Eustache Deschamps and His Double: Musique naturele and Musique artificiele," *Ars lyrica* 7 (1993): 47–64; and the references in Earp, *Guillaume de Machaut,* 386–87.

120. The identification of F. Andrieu with "Magister Franciscus," composer of a balade that cites Machaut's *Phyton* (B38), has been proposed. See Earp, *Guillaume de Machaut,* 386n95.

121. M. E. Langlois, ed., *Recueil d'Arts de séconde rhétorique* (Paris, 1902), 14. See also Earp, *Guillaume de Machaut,* 56, item 2.1.1c; and my discussion in this chapter of this treatise, which earlier also names Machaut.

122. Earp, *Guillaume de Machaut,* 57, item 2.1.1j. James I. Wimsatt, *Chaucer and His French Contemporaries: Natural Music in the Fourteenth Century* (Toronto, 1991), 248, translates "norry" as "educated"; Deborah McGrady, *Controlling Readers: Guillaume de Machaut and His Late Medieval Audience* (Toronto, 2006), 155, translates it as "nourished/raised." The sense that Machaut somehow mentored Deschamps and was kind to him is clear enough.

123. See Wimsatt, *Chaucer and His French Contemporaries,* 55–58, and the bibliography there. See also A[uguste Henry Edouard, le marquis de] Queux de Saint-Hilaire and Gaston Raynaud, eds., *Oeuvres complètes de Eustache Deschamps,* 11 vols. (Paris, 1878–1903), vol. 4, 37 (no. 578), 43 (no. 585), 270 (no. 772). The Machaut in Deschamps's scatological rondeaux—in

McGrady has stressed the way in which Deschamps not only helped establish but also manipulated Machaut's legacy as a way of defining his own identity and fame.[124] Deschamps is a very different kind of poet from Machaut; he wrote nearly exclusively lyrics, and these were far more frequently on courtly, satirical, subversive, obscene, or historical topics than on the amorous ones that dominate Machaut's output. Most significantly for the historiography of this period, Deschamps is also thought of as distinct from Machaut because he did not set his poetry to music and authored a treatise that specifically theorizes the "natural music" of spoken verse.[125] Seduced by the idea of natural music (which fits so well with the Guiette-inspired valorization of form and sonic content over literary content with which the modern(ist) rehabilitation of *forme-fixe* verse had begun), modern commentators have seen Deschamps as representing a break with Machaut's musico-poetic aesthetic.[126]

During Machaut's lifetime Deschamps had an attested role in the dissemination of Machaut's works. As he documents in a balade addressed to Machaut, he read from the *Voir dit* to the court of Louis de Mâle, Count of Flanders, at Bruges.[127] Deschamps opens his balade by asking Machaut to give thanks for

---

which first Deschamps, then Meliant, Enguerran, and "Machaut" complain about the farting of one Oudart (no. 578), and the farter then defends himself against Machaut's charges of farting and soiling the bed (no. 585)—is identified with the poet in McGrady, *Controlling Readers*, 272n6, who reads the rondeaux as evidence of "intimate familiarity." In the index to Deschamps's collected works (Queux de Saint-Hilaire and Raynaud, *Deschamps, Oeuvres complètes*, 10:208), this Machaut is listed as Robert de Machaut, mentioned with his brother Jean, equerry to the Count of Valois in 1384, in balade no. 772. The poet's name is spelled "Machault" in the index. Neither of the poems gives a full name, however, and neither writer gives further evidence for these varied attributions.

124. See McGrady, *Controlling Readers*, 152–69 (chap. 6, "Eustache Deschamps as Machaut's Reader: Staking Out Authority in the Master['s] Text"). Nevertheless, McGrady's characterization of Machaut as a poet of lyric heartfelt sentiment, who "could seduce his chosen lady" (157), and Deschamps as conversely cultivating failure in love both downplays Machaut's own thematization of failure and overstates his view of *sentement*. See my discussion in chapters 3 and 4.

125. See Deborah M. Sinnreich-Levi, ed., *Eustache Deschamps' L'Art de dictier* (East Lansing, 1994), 62–67, ll. 123–96.

126. See Roger Dragonetti, "'La poésie...ceste musique naturele': Essai d'exégèse d'un passage de L'*Art de Dictier* d'Eustache Deschamps," in *Fin du moyen âge et renaissance: Mélanges de philosophie française offerts à Robert Guiette*, ed. Henri Pirenne (Antwerp, 1961), 49–64; Kenneth Varty, "Deschamps' *Art de dictier*," *French Studies* 19 (1965): 164–68; Nigel Wilkins, "The Late Medieval French Lyric: With Music and Without," in *Musik und Text in der Mehrstimmigkeit des 14. und 15. Jahrhunderts: Vorträge des Gastsymposions in der Herzog August Bibliothek Wolfenbüttel*, ed. Ursula Günther and Ludwig Finscher (Kassel, 1984), 155–74; and, for a musicological reading that runs somewhat contrary to the received opinion, see Elizabeth Eva Leach, *Sung Birds: Music, Nature, and Poetry in the Later Middle Ages* (Ithaca, 2007), 57–61. I intend to treat the misunderstood subject of Deschamps's musicality elsewhere. On Guiette, see chapter 2.

127. Balade, *Treschiers sires* (Queux de Saint-Hilaire and Raynaud, *Deschamps, Oeuvres complètes*, 1:248–49, no. 127); see Earp, *Guillaume de Machaut*, 57, item 2.1.1e; and McGrady, *Controlling Readers*.

"the art of music and the merry *sentement* that Orpheus initiated in you," for which he is "highly honored," and he notes that all Machaut's works are well received in many foreign lands.[128] Machaut is the darling of the great lords, who take delight in all his "things."[129] Deschamps then tells how the count received and read the *Voir dit*.[130] In the balade's last stanza Deschamps also reports delivering letters on paper to the count from Machaut as well as "vo livre" (your [i.e., Machaut's] book), which the count dearly loves and from which he had Deschamps read before many knights.[131] Earp speculates that this reference to Machaut's book in the last stanza is to the *Voir dit* already mentioned in the first, since Deschamps's poem says he went first to the place where Fortune speaks about how she gives her goods to some and not others, a section of the *Voir dit* famous enough to be the only one contained in manuscripts **J** and **K**.[132]

Deschamps's two balade texts lamenting Machaut's death have many resonances with lyrics by Machaut, of which three stand out (see figure 6.6).[133] The first is their use of a rhyme very rare in lyric—"-ique"—placed prominently as the shared refrain rhyme.[134] This rhyme occurs prominently in Machaut's lyrics in the opening *Prologue* balade, *Je, Nature*, when Nature gives Machaut the "practique" in the form of her three children: *Sens*, Rhetoric, and Music. Here too it provides the refrain rhyme in the form of "Musique," the last of Nature's three children.[135]

The second resonance lies in the imprecations to weep ("plourés," l. 1.7, cantus 1) and dress in black ("vestés vous noir," l. 3.7, cantus 1), which are reminiscent of Machaut's setting of Guillaume's (i.e., Machaut's "own")

---

128. "Treschiers sires, vueilliez remercier / L'art de musique et le gay sentement / Que Orpheus fist en vous commencier, / Dont vous estes honouriez haultement: / Car tous voz faiz moult honourablement / Chascuns reçoit en maint pais estrange" (ll. 1.1–6). See also McGrady, *Controlling Readers*, 157–69.

129. "Les grans seigneurs, Guillaume, vous ont chier, / En voz choses prannent esbatement," (ll. 2.1–2). "Choses" is how Machaut designates his musical works in *Voir dit*, l. 524, and his complete works in *Voir dit*, letter 33.

130. "Monseigneur de Flandres.../ Qui par sa main reçut benignement / Vostre Voir Dit sellé dessur la range, / Lire le fist," ll.2.4–7.

131. "Je lui baillié voz lettres en papier / Et vo livre qu'il aime chierement; / Lire m'y fist; present maint chevalier," ll. 3.1–3.

132. Earp, *Guillaume de Machaut*, 57, item 2.1.1e.

133. See also Mühlethaler, "Un poète et son art."

134. This is the only example of the "-ique" rhyme in any fourteenth-century song that has survived with music, although it is the refrain rhyme of *Qui est de moy* (Pa17), a balade in the unnotated chansonnier **Pa**, which contains many song texts (especially those by Machaut). Elsewhere Deschamps uses it in his lexically related poem *O Socrates* (2:138–40, no. 285), where, tellingly, the word "musique" is not used), which celebrates Chaucer (where, tellingly, the word "musique" is not used). He also uses it in the balade *Force de corps* (3:182–84, no. 399), an "ubi sunt" poem, naming the nine worthies and listing other figures of renown, which mentions Orpheus's "douce musique."

135. This use, together with one in a stanza of the complaint in *Remede, Tels rit* (RF2), are the only occurrences of this rhyme in Machaut's lyrics.

Cantus 1	Cantus 2
1.1 Armes, amours, dames, chevalerie,	O flour des flours de toute melodie,
1.2 Clers, musicans et fayseurs en françoys,	Tres doulz maistres qui tant fuestes adrois,
1.3 Tous sosfistes, toute poëterie,	[O] Guillaume, mondains diex d'armonie,
1.4 Tous cheus qui ont melodieuses vois,	Apres vos fais, qui obtendra le choys
1.5 Ceus qui cantent en orgue aucunes foys,	Sur tous fayseurs? Certes, ne le congnoys.
1.6 Et qui ont chier le doulz art de musique,	Vo nom sera precieuse relique,
1.7 Demenés duel, plourés, car c'est bien drois,	Car l'en ploura en France [et] en Artois,
1.8 La mort Machaut, le noble rhetouryque.	La mort Machaut, le noble retorique.
2.1 Onques d'amours ne parla en follie,	Le fons Cirée et la fontayne Helie,
2.2 Ains a esté en tous ses dis courtois,	Dont vous estes le ruissel et le dois,
2.3 Aussi a molt pleü sa chanterie	Où poëtes mirent leur estudie,
2.4 Aus grans seigneurs, aus contes, aus bourgois.	Convient taire, dont je suy molt destrois.
2.5 He! Horpheüs, asses lamenter dois,	Las! c'est pour vous, qui mort gisiés tous frois,
2.6 Et regreter d'un regret autentique,	[Qu']ay un dolent depit, faillant replique,
2.7 Arethuse aussi, Alpheüs, tous trois,	Plourés, arpes et cors saracynois
2.8 La mort [Machaut, le noble rhetouryque.]	La mort Machaut [le noble retorique.]
3.1 Priés por li, si que nulls ne l'oublie	Rubebe, [leuths], viële et ciphonie,
3.2 Ce vous requiert le bayli de Valois,	Psalterion, tout instrumens courtois,
3.3 Car il n'en est au jour d'ui nul en vie	[Rothes], guisternes, fleustes et chelemie,
3.4 Tel com il fu, ne ne sera des moys.	Traversaynes et vous, nimphes de bois,
3.5 Complains sera de contes et [de] roys,	Timpane ossy, metés en euvre doys,
3.6 Jusqu'au lonc tamps pour sa bone practique.	Tous instrumens qui estes tout antiques
3.7 Vestés vous noir; plorés, tous Champenois,	Faites devoir; plourés, gentil Galoys
3.8 La mort [Machaut, le noble rhetouryque.]	La mort [Machaut le noble retorique.]

Arms, love, ladies, chivalry, clerks, musicians, and makers in French, all sophists, all poets, all those who sometimes play instruments and hold dear the art of music, lead the mourning, weep, because it is indeed right, for the death of Machaut, the noble rhetorician.

About love he wrote nothing foolish but was always courteous in his dits. His songs also greatly pleased great lords, counts, and townsfolk. Hey, Orpheus, you should lament enough and regret with a heartfelt regret, [and with] Arethusa and Alpheus—all three—for the death of Machaut, the noble rhetorician.

Pray for him so that no one forgets him; the bailli of Valois [i.e., Eustache Deschamps] requires this of you, for there is none living today such as he was, nor will his like be seen again for a long time. He will be lamented by counts and kings for a long time on account of his great skill. Wear black; weep, all Champenois, for the death of Machaut, the noble rhetorician.

O flower of the flower of all melody, very sweet master who was so adroit! O Guillaume, worldly god of harmony, after what you've made, who will become the choice of all the makers? I certainly don't know him! Your name will be a precious relic, for they weep in France and in Artois for the death of Machaut, the noble rhetorician.

The fount of Cirrha and the fountain of Helicon [the Hippocrene] of which you are the river and the conduit whence poets take their study must be silent, for which I am much distressed. Alas! It is for you, whom death has laid down all cold, that I have a sorrowing defiance, beggaring reply. Weep, harps and Saracen horns, for the death of Machaut, the noble rhetorician.

You must put to work, rebec, lute, fiddle, and symphony, psaltery, all courtly instruments, rotes, gitterns, flutes, and chalumeau, and you wood nymphs, drums too—all instruments which are completely venerable, do what you must; weep, gentle Gauls, for the death of Machaut, the noble rhetorician.

Figure 6.6. Texts and translations of Deschamps's *déploration* balades.

1.2 et fayseurs] faititres Des123

2.2 ses] ces

2.3 molt pleü] mols a pleut, Ch

2.4 Aus grans] As grans Ch

2.4 aus contes} a dames. Des

2.4 aus bourgois} aus l'ogus Ch

2.5 lamenter dois} lamenter te dois

2.6 d'un regret] d'un regart. Des123; d'un regi
et Ch

2.7 Arethuse aussi] Arethusa et. Des123;
Artheus aussi Ch

3.1 si que nul} siques nul Ch

3.1 l'oublie} s'oublier Ch

3.2 requiert] requier Ch

3.2 bayli} vayli Ch

3.3 il n'en est] ynest Ch

3.5 contes et de roys] princes et de roys
Des123; contes et roys Ch

3.6 Jusqu'au] Jusquo Ch

3.6 pour] per Ch

3.7 vous noir] vous de noir

1.1 toute] touto Ch

1.3 Guillaume] Guillame Ch

2.1 Ciree] Chierie Ch; Circé Des124

2.4 destrois] esbais Ch

2.5 Convient taire] comment caront Ch

2.5 mort] mont Ch

2.6 Qu'ay un] Ay mi

2.6 Qui de tous chans avez esté cantique.
Des124

2.7 arpes] arples Ch

2.8 Machaut] Mathant Ch

3.1 Rubebe, [leuths]] Plourés Rebele Ch

3.1 viele et] vielles. Des124

3.2 tout instrumens courtois] trestous instrumens coys. Des124

3.3 [Rothes], guisternes, fleustes et chelemie,]
Guisternes fleustes herpes et chelemie
Ch

3.3 fleustes et chelemie] flaustes chalemie.
Des124

3.4 Traversaynes et vous, nimphes de
bois] et traversaynes et vous imples
de vois Ch

3.5 euvre] or se Ch

3.6 Timpane ossy, metés en euvre doys] Et le
choro n'y ait nul qui replique. Des124

Figure 6.6. (*Continued*)

testament, *Plourez, dames* (B32; see figure 6.1).[136] The shared nature of these two poems—the fact that they are both *déplorations*—makes such resonance unsurprising, but the link with Machaut's own poem is likely to be deliberate, given Deschamps's level of engagement with Machaut's work in general. In the *Armes, amours* text, people in general ("on") in France and Artois are directed to weep, along with an enormous list of musical instruments, including listening singers ("vous amples de vois," l. 3.4, cantus 2). Instructing listeners to weep serves to remind the living consumers of this commemoration of their responsibilities to the dead, while here wittily making one singer refer to the other three in the very act of performing a highly Machauldian song. Weepers on tombs and funeral monuments of this period are constructions of group solidarity, often showing the dead figure as paterfamilias, with a

136. The standard version from the principal Deschamps collection (Paris, Bibliothèque nationale de France, MS français 840) has the correct number of syllables. The "de" in the Ch version (which thus reads "Vestés vous de noir") is hypermetrical but brings the line even closer to Machaut's wording in *Plourez, dames* (B32): "Vestés vous de noir pour my" (B32, entire l. 1.5).

new emphasis on descendants rather than ancestors.[137] Machaut's "family," as presented in the cantus I text, consists of three figures commanded to lament. The first of these is Orpheus, whose story Machaut had told in *Confort* and *Harpe*.[138] The other two figures—Alpheus and Arethusa—provide the third principal textual resonance between Deschamps's double balade texts and Machaut's own works.

Machaut is quite sparing with classical names in his lyric texts. Alpheus and Arethusa occur in one lyric—a late balade, *Je pren congié* (Lo223; see figure 6.7).[139] This *congié* initiates a series of similar leave-taking poems in the *Loange,* whose members exploit parallels between parting from the lady and departing from life, and precede the *Loange* copying of Machaut's own testament, *Plourez, dames* (B32), as Lo229.[140] Alpheus and Arethusa are used as quintessential weepers because in Ovid's version of their story in *Metamorphoses,* book 5, the Nereid Arethusa dissolves in her own tears to become a spring, in which watery form she is joined by her amorous pursuer, the hunter Alpheus, who becomes a river. As Lo223 relates, she was "changed into water."[141] In *Metamorphoses* their story is told by Ceres in the course of the song sung by Calliope, mother of Orpheus, in a song contest with the nine human daughters of Pierus and Euippe (the Pierides), an episode that provides an important back-story to Deschamps's commemoration.[142]

137. See Anne McGee Morganstern, *Gothic Tombs of Kinship in France, the Low Countries, and England* (University Park, 2000), 132. Paul Binski, *Medieval Death: Ritual and Representation* (London, 1996), 99, 103–5, uses the example of the tomb of another famous figure who died in 1377, Edward III, which shows his descendants. This image of musical progeny is highly prevalent in later composer elegies, as documented by Paula Higgins, "Musical 'Parents' and Their 'Progeny,'" in *Music in Renaissance Cities and Courts: Studies in Honor of Lewis Lockwood,* ed. Jessie Ann Owens and Anthony M. Cummings (Warren, Mich., 1997), 168–86. See also idem, "Musical Politics in Late Medieval Poitiers," in *Antoine Busnoys: Method, Meaning and Context in Late Medieval Music,* ed. Paula Higgins (Oxford, 1999), 155–74. Higgins comments that Deschamps's *déploration* lacks the specific imagery of patriarchy and descent; I would argue that this is implicit by analogy with the figures of weepers, which at this time shift from celebrating ancestry to providing solidarity and future lineage. See also my earlier discussion and chapter 3, note 16.

138. *Confort,* ll. 2277–2352, 2517–2644; and *Harpe,* ll. 31–76. A much more attenuated (and positive) version is given in *Prologue* 5.135–46, on which see Huot, "Reliving the *Roman de la Rose,*" 64; and idem, "Guillaume de Machaut and the Consolation of Poetry," 189–92.

139. See Earp, *Guillaume de Machaut,* 386–87. In **Ch,** "Arethuse" is, incorrectly, given as "Artheus," that is, Arthur. Given the references to Arthur in several other Chantilly texts (*Se Galaas* [Ch55], *Lorques Arthus* [Ch61], *Se July Cesar* [Ch66], and possibly also *En Albion* [Ch75]), this error is perhaps understandable.

140. This sequence is interesting for its parallels with, and echoes of, the music balades B31–34, a link established by the copying of *Plourez, dames* (B32 and Lo229) and *Nes qu'on porroit* (B33 and Lo232) in both places.

141. "Fist en iaue muer," l. 2.5.

142. Machaut inserts part of this section—the tale of Proserpina—into the middle of the tale of Orpheus in *Confort,* ll. 2353–2516.

Je pren congié à dames, à amours,	I take my leave from ladies, love, and all lov-
À tous amans, à l'amoureuse vie,	ers, [and] from the amorous life, and thus I
Et si renoy le bon temps, les bons jours	renounce the good times, the lovely days, and
Et tous les diex qu'onques eurent amie;	every god that was ever my friend. I do not
Ne plus ne vueil aourer	wish to adore Venus or Hope, nor live in sweet
Venus n'Espoir, ne vivre en doulz penser,	thought. Instead I wish to flee from and hate all
Eins vueil fuir et haïr toute joie,	joy *because I have lost her whom I loved more*
Quant j'ay perdu la riens que plus amoie.	*than anything.*
Si vueil user toute ma vie en plours	Thus I shall spend my life in weeping, and weep
Et tant plourer que m'arme soit noïe	so much that my soul will be drowned in my
En mon plourer et qu'avec mes dolours	weeping, and that with my sorrows my form
Ma fourme soit en larmes convertie.	might be converted into tears. A goddess of the
Une deesse de mer	sea, Arethusa, was made to change into water—
Aretusa fist en iaue muer	and [so was] Alpheus. I would wish to become
Et Alpheüs; tel devenir vorroie,	such a one *because I have lost her whom I loved*
Quant j'ay perdu la riens que plus amoie	*more than anything.*
Las! c'est honneur qui est en maintes cours	Alas! Honor is wrongfully dead in many courts
Mors à grant tort et Loyauté bannie,	and Loyalty banished and Truth, which used
Et Verité, qui estoit mes recours,	to be my recourse, is also dead and buried.
Y est aussi morte et ensevelie.	One ought indeed to weep [for] such death,
Doit on bien tel mort plourer.	one ought indeed to complain of it and regret
La doit on bien complaindre et regreter.	it. It would please me greatly if I were able to
Moult me plairoit, s'en plours fondre pouoie,	dissolve myself in weeping *because I have lost*
Quant j'ay perdu la riens que plus amoie.	*her whom I loved more than anything.*

Figure 6.7. *Je pren congié* (Lo223) text and translation.

Arriving at mount Helicon, Minerva, goddess of wisdom, addresses the Muses to explain why she has come: "The fame of a new spring has reached my ears, which broke out under the hard hoof of the winged horse of Medusa. This is the cause of my journey: I wished to see the marvellous thing."[143] Urania welcomes her and confirms that "the tale is true, and Pegasus did indeed produce our spring."[144] After Minerva has viewed and approved the Muses' domicile and had it explained to her that such a retreat keeps the virgins safe from the violent attentions of the likes of Pyreneus, the arrival of nine chattering magpies prompts one of the Muses to relate the story of the day the Pierides—the former human forms of these birds—challenged them to a song competition. The nine ill-advised girls sang of the primal battle between the gods and giants, adding insult to their original effrontery by ascribing undue honor to the giants. In reply, Calliope sang in praise of Ceres, telling the story of Proserpina, all of which is thereby retold to Minerva, and which

143. Ovid, *Metamorphoses* 5.256–59. Translation from Ovid, *Metamorphoses,* trans. Frank Justus Miller, 2 vols. (London, 1984), 3:256–57.
144. Ovid, *Metamorphoses* 5.262–63 (translation ibid., 3:262–63).

includes the story of how Arethusa became a spring.[145] The nymphs, judging the songs of the Pierides and Calliope, naturally adjudged Calliope the winner. The "hoarse garrulity" (*raucaque garrulitas*) of the girls' unmusical song was duly punished by their being transformed into magpies; the Muses thenceforth expropriated the Pierides' collective name.

The veiled reference to a song competition, which contextualizes the invocation of Arethusa and Alpheus in Deschamps's *déploration,* is apt for a poem so clearly modeled on textual and musical aspects of the sung poetry of the person whose death it mourns. Just as the poetic texts use aspects of Machaut's lyrics, so too does the musical setting use aspects of his songs. Machaut's Fortune balade, *De Fortune* (B23), has the same tonal emphases as the *déploration*'s musical setting; the two songs have similar tenor notes at key structural points.[146] Between them these two songs address the two main kinds of loss that desiring subjects can experience in the domain of Fortune: a lover's unfaithfulness in Machaut's B23, and a subject's death in the *déploration.* Machaut's own constant paralleling of these two kinds of loss and their relative grief—discussion of which opened this chapter—is accompanied by an emphasis on the important role of music and poetry in enabling them to be socially expressed, brought to mind, and consoled (if perforce incompletely).

Andrieu's *déploration* also appears to quote the tune from the second line of the balade *Dame qui fust,* an anonymous work based on Machaut's B23 and found in the Reina codex (example 6.4).[147] In the *déploration* this motive occurs in an aurally prominent moment of rare musical imitation between the two cantus voices. It sets texts inviting "those who hold dear the sweet art of music" to weep (cantus 1, l. 1.6) and declaring, "Your name will be a precious relic" (cantus 2, l. 1.6).[148] The former establishes the identity of the "weepers," asserting an interest in Machaut's memory by those who value music after him. As a relic is a physical remnant of a person, usually a saint, rather

145. There is a link between the two songs. The Pierides praise the giant Typhoeus for forcing the gods to hide in other forms. Calliope's song starts when the same giant is eventually tamed by having Sicily placed on top of him, where it is his spewing of flame and ash through Mount Etna that makes Pluto come above ground and expose himself to Cupid's arrow. This arrow makes him so enamored of Proserpina that he carries her back off below.

146. *De Fortune* (B23) is also coped in **Ch** (as Ch78).

147. The relationship between B23, *Dame qui fust,* and Fortune in Machaut's lyrics is explored further in Elizabeth Eva Leach, "Fortune's Demesne: the Interrelation of Text and Music in Machaut's *Il mest avis* (B22), *De fortune* (B23), and Two Related Anonymous Balades," *Early Music History* 19 (2000): 47–79.

148. Depending on their relative chronology, this could alternatively suggest that the composer of *Dame qui fust* is citing Andrieu's *déploration* as well as works by Machaut himself. Citation of melody carrying significant text is used in memorializing composers of the fifteenth century. See, for example, the link between Binchois and Pullois suggested for the text "ne vous peut mon cuer oublier" by David Fallows in "Binchois, Gilles de Bins, dit," in *Grove,* and explored further in Sean Gallagher, "After Burgundy: Rethinking Binchois's Years in Soignies," in *Binchois Studies,* ed. Andrew Kirkman and Dennis Slavin (Oxford, 2000), 39: 27–48.

Example 6.4. Shared motive between Deschamps's *déploration* balades set to music
by F. Andrieu, and Anon., *Dame qui fust.*

than a second-degree representation, like an effigy, the second text is a bold
counter to traditional Platonic thinking, implying that his name alone is the
essence of Machaut the Poet, rather than a mere representation. For a name to
be made physical, it must, as it is in the refrain of both balade texts here, be
inscribed on parchment—as indeed Machaut's often was.

Although there is only one copy set to music that survives, the texts exist in
two other manuscript sources. In a verse letter to a nun, moreover, Deschamps
says that he has enclosed "what I have made concerning master Guillaume de
Machaut," which Earp notes could refer to this double balade.[149] It might also
be the case that Jean Lebègue's reference to Machaut as a "rhetorician" was suggested by his knowledge of the refrain of Deschamps's double balade, although
Jean's apt description could equally have been arrived at independently.

Machaut as Musical Model and Authority

Aside from the clear testimony of Deschamps's *déploration*, Machaut is named
as a composer-poet in a number of other texts. Gilles li Muisis's *Meditations*

149. Both texts are copied in *F-Pn*, fr. 840, f. 28r–v, and *Armes, amours* is also in *I*, f. 16v;
see Earp, *Guillaume de Machaut*, 386–87. The reference that could be to these poems is in Queux
de Saint-Hilaire and Raynaud, *Deschamps, Oeuvres complètes*, 8:52–53, no. 1416, l. 45; see also
Earp, *Guillaume de Machaut*, 57, item 2.1.1h. It could, however, also refer to any of the other
balades by Deschamps that mention Machaut, listed in McGrady, *Controlling Readers*, 153–54.

(1350) links his name with those of Philippe de Vitry and Jehan de le Mote, and was clearly written when all three were still living.[150] Although it does not expressly treat him as a composer, sandwiching him between Vitry and the specific mention of Jehan de le Mote making "le lettre et le notte" suggests that all three were known as composer-poets.[151] This inference of his being a composer-poet from the company he keeps would also seem to be the case when Machaut's name is invoked in two motets that present lists of musicians. In *Apollinis eclipsatur / Zodiacum signis / In omnem* he is cited as "rejoicing in poetry," with no specific mention of musical composition. But his place in a list of twelve others (including Johannes de Muris, Philippe de Vitry, Denis le Grant, and Egidius de Murino) cited or otherwise known for being musicians implies strongly that it is *musical* poetry for which he is being praised.[152] In the related motet *Musicalis scientia / Sciencie laudabili*, Machaut is merely named in a list of the "beloved disciples of music," which also includes Johannes de Muris, Philippe de Vitry, Denis le Grant, Egidius de Murino, and others.[153]

In Johannes de Muris's treatise *Ars practica mensurabilis cantus* (commonly known as the *Libellus*), Machaut is the only named example of the "many composers" who use two related notational devices, both of which can indeed be seen in a number of his works.[154] This very widely copied

---

150. [Baron Joseph-Marie-Bruno-Constantin] Kervyn de Lettenhove, ed., *Poésies de Gilles li Muisis* (Louvain, 1882), 88, ll. 324–39.

151. No music attributed to Jehan de le Mote has survived, but so much anonymous music is transmitted—and so much has been lost—that there seems no reason to doubt this testimony that he was also a composer. Lyrics were ordinarily sung, but their musical setting could range from the highly literate and wrought music of a Machaut or a Vitry to simpler, more oral or semi-improvised settings, possibly monophonic. If Jehan de le Mote's music was in this latter tradition, it might well have circulated without specific musical notation, since the text alone could have cued a simple melody.

152. See text and translation in David Howlett, "*Apollinis eclipsatur*: Foundation of the 'Collegium musicorum,'" in Clark and Leach, *Citation and Authority in Medieval and Renaissance Musical Culture*, 153–54. Demarcations between writing theory, singing, and composition were less clearly drawn in this period than they are today. Most theorists wrote music; most composers were singers. Writing poetry as well may have been seen as a distinct or additional skill, hence Machaut's specific citation for it here.

153. See Frank L. Harrison, ed., *Musicorum Collegio: Fourteenth-Century Musicians' Motets* (Les Remparts, Monaco, 1986), nos. 2 and 5.

154. Christian Berktold, ed., *Ars practica mensurabilis cantus secundum Iohannem de Muris: Die Recensio maior des sogenannten "Libellus practice cantus mensurabilis"* (Munich, 1999), 103–4: "Et nota, quod quidam cantores, puta Gulielmus de Mascandio et multi alii, imperficiunt brevem perfectam minoris prolationis ab una sola minima, et brevem imperfectam maioris prolationis a duabus minimis simul sequentibus vel precedentibus" (It is to be noted that some singers, like Guillaume de Machaut and many others, imperfect the breve in minor prolation with a single minim, and the breve in imperfect time, major prolation with two minims together after or before it). This reading is that of version B of the treatise; version A has "nonnulli alii"; see ibid., 25. The second version of this notational feature is found, for example, near the opening of the tenor of *De petit po* (B18; see example 5.5, mm. 3–4) and near the opening of the contratenor of *Rose, lis* (R10). Machaut and Johannes de Muris may have known each other at the court of Navarre,

treatise was written during Machaut's lifetime, probably in the mid-fourteenth century, but it retained a high degree of currency in the fifteenth century and beyond. Considering the wide temporal and geographical distribution of the many sources for this treatise, Machaut's name would have been known as that of a literate composer among other musicians throughout the whole of western Europe well into the sixteenth century.[155] Treatises that cite Johannes de Muris's *Libellus* in the fifteenth century preserve the mention of Machaut's name, even in one case glossing it to attest that he was "a distinguished master in the art of music, in which art he composed many things."[156] In the 1430s the Italian theorist Ugolino of Orvieto provided a commentary on the *Libellus,* which suggests that the songs of Machaut, "elegantly composed with the sweetest harmonies and melodies, are still in use today."[157] Nevertheless, most of the later Italian commentators on Johannes de Muris, such as Ugolino and Franchino Gaffurio (in his *Practica musice* [1496]), consider this notational usage to be erroneous.[158]

Machaut's musical works themselves continued to be copied until the mid-fifteenth century. Although only two balades, both in the Chantilly manuscript, have his name correctly ascribed to them, the misattribution of several pieces to him in the now burned fifteenth-century Strasbourg source (**Str**) is good evidence that his name was still current as that of an important French

---

where Johannes's service preceded the putative service of Machaut; see Lawrence Gushee, "New Sources for the Biography of Johannes de Muris," *Journal of the American Musicological Society* 22 (1969): 26.

155. "Muris, Johannes de," in *Grove*, notes that the *Libellus* "is found mostly in 15th-century manuscripts of Italian origin (39 out of 47 are apparently Italian)." Other provenances include Germany, England, and France; see the full discussion of sources in the introduction to Berktold, *Ars practica mensurabilis cantus secundum Iohannem de Muris.*

156. This is from Prosdocimus de Beldemandis's *Expositiones* (ca. 1404), a manuscript treatise. See F. Alberto Gallo, ed., *Prosdocimus de Beldemandis, Opera: Expositiones tractatus pratice cantus mensurabilis magistri Johannis de Muris,* vol. 1 (Bologna, 1966), 84 (chap. 33); see also Earp, *Guillaume de Machaut,* 69, item 2.4.1d. "Gulielmus de Mastodio" (i.e., Guillaume de Machaut) is also cited in the anonymous late-fourteenth-century Italian treatise *Ars cantus mensurabilis mensurata per modos iuris* (see C. Matthew Balensuela, ed., *Ars cantus mensurabilis per modos iuris [The Art of Mensurable Song Measured by the Modes of Law]: A New Critical Text and Translation on Facing Pages,* vol. 10 [Linoln, 1994], 234–35, and comments 27–28); see also Earp, *Guillaume de Machaut,* 68, item 2.4.1c.

157. "Hic ponit auctor quorundam cantorum antiquorum opinionem, de quorum numero quidam Gulielmus de Mascandio nominatus per auctorem in littera fuit. Iste Gulielmus in musicis disciplinis fuit singularis et multa in ea arte optime composuit, cuius cantibus temporibus nostri usi sumus bene politeque compositis ac dulcissimis harmoniarum melodiis ornatis." Albert Seay, ed., *Ugolini Urbevetanis Declaratio musicae disciplinae* ([Rome], 1960), 144. See also Earp, *Guillaume de Machaut,* 69, item 2.4.1g; and Agostino Ziino, "Guillaume de Machaut: Fondateur d'École?," in *Scritti offerti a Gino Raya dalla Facoltà di magistero dell'Università di Messina,* ed. Antonio Mazzarino (Rome, 1982), 508–9.

158. See Earp, *Guillaume de Machaut,* 69, items 2.4.1g–h; Franchino Gaffurio, *Practica musice* (Milan, 1496), f. bbiiijr.

composer of the previous century.[159] It is highly likely that the knowledge of his authorship among singers and listeners was more widespread than the textual notation of it. Even text-only sources, a number of which were copied from sources with musical notation, can reflect knowledge of Machaut's musical prowess: that which attributes the triplum text of *Qui es / Ha! Fortune* (M8) to Machaut signals clearly that this was a musical piece by labeling the poem "tresble" (i.e., triplum part).[160]

A more problematic index of Machaut's afterlife is his influence on the composed musical pieces of the period following his death. Two problems make it particularly difficult to be categorical in this regard. The first is that the notion of "influence" is nebulous: although longer musical or textual citations in songs can be spotted readily, "Machauldian" style is diffuse as a concept (though time might make appreciation of individual styles in this period more nuanced in the future). The second is that the dating of songs in the fourteenth century is woefully inexact: manuscript collections are all significantly retrospective, making it impossible to date music other than by stylistic comparisons (which brings the issue back around to the first problem).[161] Particularly in a case where imitation or homage is intended, it would be possible for the imitative song to look contemporaneous in style with the song being imitated, without necessarily dating from the same period. What follows here, therefore, will briefly consider songs that cite Machaut's songs and seem to be in a similar style. Whether they represent Machaut's imitation of earlier works, are evidence of a contemporary song competition, or are posthumous homage to Machaut is currently impossible to say.

The anonymous balade *Dame qui fust* has already been mentioned in relation to the *déploration*. This song has the first and last lines of Machaut's poetry and music from *De Fortune* (B23) as its last and first lines respectively. Whichever way the borrowing operated, this inversion is a meaningfully emblematic thing to do to a song on Fortune, the great inverter—and perverter—of everything. *Dame qui fust* also has a different contratenor for these lines. A similar procedure can be seen operating between *Se je me pleing* (B15) and the

---

159. See Earp, *Guillaume de Machaut*, 64–65.

160. See ibid., 65 and 114 (MS no. 46 St). Manuscripts I and **Pa** are both also copied from notated song sources, as is **Ta**, although they contain no ascriptions to Machaut. See chapter 5, note 31.

161. The classic attempt at this kind of stylistic chronology is Willi Apel, ed., *French Secular Music of the Late Fourteenth Century* (Cambridge, 1950), 9–15. See the comments in Otto Gombosi, review of *French Secular Music of the Fourteenth Century* by Willi Apel, *Musical Quarterly* 36 (1950): 603–10; Glen Haydon, review of *French Secular Music of the Late Fourteenth Century* by Willi Apel, *Speculum* 26 (1951): 145–48; and the response in Willi Apel, ed., *French Secular Compositions of the Fourteenth Century*, 3 vols. (Rome, 1970–1972), 3:xxiv–xxvi. See also Ursula Günther, "Chronologie und Stil der Kompositionen Guillaume de Machauts," *Acta Musicologica* 35 (1963): 96–114.

anonymous balade *Ma dame m'a congié douné* (Ch6).[162] The tonal scheme
of this latter balade gives better evidence than is available for the earlier pair
that the anonymous piece is a later engagement with Machaut's rather than the
other way around. Because the first line of Machaut's song ends on the *ouvert*
sonority (*D/d*), *Ma dame m'a congié* alone of all surviving balades from this
period ends on a sonority that resembles that of its *ouvert* (*D/a/d*), rather than
the *clos* of its first part (*C/g/c*) and that of Machaut's balade's refrain (*C/g*).
It seems unlikely that this situation would have come about without being
caused by the act of borrowing being *from* Machaut's balade.

Both B23 and B15 seem to have influenced *Se je me plaing de Fortune*,
a balade by the Italian composer Matteo da Perugia. His piece is copied in
ModA, a source with which he himself was closely connected and which transmits a number of Machaut's works (without ascription, although this does not
mean that the manuscripts' scribes, readers, and singers did not know of his
authorship).[163] **ModA** includes a couple of other ways in which Machaut's
works were received and updated in the wider circulation outside his direct
control (and probably after his death), which can be cited as evidence of his
ongoing fame. The first is a setting by Anthonello da Caserta of a balade by
Machaut that Machaut himself placed only in his unnotated *Loange*. This
song, *Biauté parfaite* (Lo140), shows no evidence of musical citation from
Machaut's other works, and is in the style of the so-called *ars subtilior,* whose
"advanced" notational techniques, especially those relating to rhythm, are
considered the fascination of an essentially post-Machaut generation (ca.
1378–1417).[164] If this is correct, it would be noteworthy that Anthonello
selected a much older poem to set to cutting-edge music; on the one hand, the
text is included in manuscript **C**, so was certainly written before the middle of
the century, probably decades before Anthonello's setting of it. On the other
hand, this might lead us to question a further aspect of chronology of the fourteenth century, placing the *ars subtilior* during Machaut's lifetime.

The second indication of a reception response to Machaut as a composer in
ModA is the composing of alternative or additional voice parts to his pieces,
something that probably arose out of musicians' oral practices but has left
some notational traces. Two-part pieces have third parts added to them: this
has already been seen in *Ma dame m'a congié*, which, because it is in three
parts, is forced to add a brand-new contratenor to the sections it cites directly
from Machaut's two-part balade *Se je me pleing* (B15). In **ModA** the two-part

---

162. CMM 53/2, 75–76, no. 163; and PMFC 18, no. 6.

163. Matteo may have copied (or compiled) the manuscript. See Ian Rumbold, "The Compilation and Ownership of the 'St Emmeram' Codex (Munich, Bayerische Staatsbibliothek, Clm
14274)," *Early Music History* 2 (1982): 167. It contains *De petit po* (B18), *De toutes flours*
(B31), *Gais et jolis* (B35), and *Se vous n'estes* (R7).

164. CMM 53/1, no. 4. See Ursula Günther, "Das Ende der *ars nova*," *Die Musikforschung*
16 (1963): 105–20, which introduces the term and its dating; and Elizabeth Randell Upton, "The
Chantilly Codex (F-Ch 564): The Manuscript, Its Music, Its Scholarly Reception" (Ph.D. diss.,
University of North Carolina at Chapel Hill, 2001), especially chap. 3, which questions it.

rondeau *Se vous n'estes* (R7) has a new contratenor part copied on a separate folio, which differs from another contratenor that is added in a number of other sources.[165] Older three-part combinations of tenor, cantus, and triplum typically received a contratenor part that was designed to serve instead of the triplum. Again, this is seen in parts of *Dame qui fust,* which has a new third part—a contratenor—added in the sections otherwise directly quoted from Machaut's three-part version with triplum. *De Fortune* itself, however, received a contratenor in a number of other sources, which, like the contratenor that **ModA** transmits for *De petit po* (B18), is not compatible with Machaut's triplum.[166] The reverse sometimes occurred (which throws doubt on the chronology, although whether on the chronology of stylistic change or on the chronology of the composition of the extra voice parts is hard to assess), as when *De toutes flours* (B31), which is copied with cantus, tenor, and contratenor in the main Machaut sources, receives an additional triplum part in **E, PR,** and **Str.**[167] The possibilities for adapting a precomposed piece like this were very flexible: even some pieces that already had contratenors received further alternative contratenors in other sources, perhaps because they sometimes circulated in versions with just the two core parts of cantus and tenor, or perhaps because other singer-composers wished to adapt them.[168]

The reversal of opening and closing lines of text and music seems to have been a common way of shaping one musical piece based on another and perhaps grew out of the common inversion of the verbal texts of balades' incipit and/or refrain lines as a means of making new balades.[169] When a shorter section of Machaut's material is cited, it tends to be one or another of these prominent identifying sections. For example, Magister Franciscus's balade *Phiton* cites the first three measures of Machaut's *Phyton* (B38), and parts

---

165. Matteo was a composer of additional contratenors for a large number of pieces by other composers and may have partaken in a particularly Italian tradition in this regard. See "Matteo da Perugia" in *Grove;* and Signe Rotter-Broman, "Die Grenzen der dreistimmigen Tercento-Satztechnik: Zur Mehrfachüberlieferung von Ballaten und Madrigalen," *Die Musikforschung* 60 (2007): 2–12. R7 has empty staves for a triplum in C but is two-part except in E, where it receives the same contratenor found fragmentarily in **Gr** 3360. CaB transmits both this and a triplum, in addition to the two Machauldian parts.

166. On this "compendium" practice, see Elizabeth Eva Leach, "Machaut's Balades with Four Voices," *Plainsong and Medieval Music* 10 (2001): 47–79. B23 has an added contratenor in E and Ch; on the alternative added contratenor that it receives in **PR,** see the discussion later in this chapter.

167. See Earp, *Guillaume de Machaut,* 311–12.

168. For example, *De Fortune* (B23) has a contratenor in **PR** different from those in E and Ch; *Se vous n'estes* (R7) has a contratenor in **ModA** different from that in the other sources that add one; see ibid., 378.

169. On this practice, see Yolanda Plumley, "Intertextuality in the Fourteenth-Century Chanson," *Music and Letters* 84 (2003): 355–77; idem, "Playing the Citation Game in the Late 14th-Century Chanson," *Early Music* 31 (2003): 20–40; and Lorenz Welker, "*Soit tart tempre* und seine Familie," in *Musik als Text: Bericht über den Internationalen Kongreß der Gesellschaft für Musikforschung, Freiburg im Breisgau 1993,* ed. Hermann Danuser and Tobias Plebuch (Kassel, 1998), vol. 1, 322–34.

of the refrain section of Machaut's *Il m'est avis* (B22) are cited in the anonymous balade *Se je ne suy*.[170] A strange cross-genre borrowing is present in the anonymous balade *S'espoir n'esoit,* which cites the B section of Machaut's widely circulated rondeau *Se vous n'estes* (R7). But as the entire music of any rondeau *is* its refrain (and arguably the A section is the refrain "incipit" and the B section the refrain "refrain," as it were), this is akin to treating the source rondeau as if it were a balade and appropriating its "refrain."

The identification of more subtle allusions to Machaut would require its own separate study with the concomitant development of a rigorous methodology. When a song cites text from Machaut's songs without its accompanying music, this has rarely been treated as a citation. It seems significant, however, that these citations are nearly always from other songs, not from unnotated lyrics. In these cases the textual citation may be designed to hint at a more subtle musical allusion, as can be seen, for example, in the anonymous balade *En la maison,* whose opening B section line (l. 1.5) cites the text only of line 2.3 of Machaut's *Nes qu'on porroit* (B33), but whose pervasive melodic-rhythmic figures in major prolation are similar to those in B33, as well as the other two simple balades in the *Voir dit,* all of which were probably well known.[171]

For nearly all the Machaut songs that spawned citational counterparts, evidence exists that the originals were present in the broader circulation outside the Machaut manuscripts.[172] If the borrowing is *from* Machaut rather than *by* him, the fact that his more widely circulated songs—rather than random other ones by other composers—were selected for imitation may signal popular knowledge that these were indeed by him, an important and well-known composer, even if his name does not appear linked to them in written form on the parchment. The function of these citations (and their direction) requires further individual studies, although it seems clear that their use went beyond

170. For editions of *Phiton,* see CMM 1:54–55, no. 27, and PMFC 18:47–49, no. 18; for *Se je ne suy,* see CMM 2:96–97, no. 174. See also Christian Berger, "Die melodische Floksel im Leidsatz des 14. Jahrhunderts: Magister Franciscus' Ballade 'Phiton,'" in *Trasmissione e recezione delle forme di cultura musicale: Atti del XIV congresso della società internazionale di musicologia. Bologna, 27 agosto–1° settembre 1987, Ferrara–Parma, 30 agosto 1987,* ed. Angelo Pompilio, Donatella Restani, Lorenzo Bianconi, and Alberto F. Gallo, vol. 3 (Turin, 1987), 673–79; and Leach, "Fortune's Demesne."

171. In addition, line 1.2 of *En la maison* is similar to B33's line 2.1, and its refrain is very similar to that of Machaut's *Trop se peinne* (Lo164). The anonymous composer ostensibly elevates his own creativity by remaking things by Machaut, the great Daedalus of book, song, and music. See Elizabeth Eva Leach, "The Fourteenth Century," in *The Cambridge Companion to Medieval Music,* ed. Mark Everist (Cambridge, forthcoming); and Leach, *Sung Birds,* 119n17.

172. The main exceptions to this are *Phiton* (B38) and *Se je me pleing* (B15). Although it might just be chance that we lack the sources that would show their wider circulation, to assert conversely that any Machaut songs that are imitated must have circulated more widely quickly results in circularity. The presence of Machaut's works *within* the Machaut sources was already broad circulation of a kind, considering the likely social milieu of their owners.

mere homage so as to engage—as in the intertextual literary culture—in "reading," adaptation, and commentary.

Machaut as Literary Authority

Machaut's influence on contemporary and younger generations of poets has been more thoroughly studied than his influence in the musical sphere. Indeed, as chapter 2 outlined, it was his importance as a model for the recognized genius of Geoffrey Chaucer that led to his works being read with any attention at all in the modern period. Chaucer seems to have read Machaut's works extremely widely, including (as chapter 5 discussed), the texts of pieces that are only in the music section, such as *Qui es / Ha! Fortune* (M8). Wimsatt has even speculated that Chaucer must have had access to a complete works manuscript.[173]

Chaucer, however, never names Machaut, nor, despite his obvious influence on them, do Christine de Pizan or Jehan Froissart.[174] Froissart comes close in playful allusion in the *Joli buisson de Jonece* (discussed earlier), whose narrator sings a motet "sent from Reims," but his narrative verse has clear models in Machaut's dits, and his lyrics frequently cite those of Machaut.[175] Of those poets who were clearly influenced by him in the later fourteenth century, only Oton de Granson and Eustache Deschamps invoke Machaut's name.

Some of Deschamps's references to Machaut have been partly treated in this chapter, but they also include the linking of Machaut's name to that of Philippe de Vitry, both in the balade *Veulz tu la congnoissance* (no. 1474), as those poets "whom Music held dear," and the balade *He! gentils rois* (no. 872), which mentions them as both already dead, while praising their successor to whom it is addressed.[176] In addition to these, a pair of poems addressed to "Peronne" (the anagrammatical identity of Toute Belle) and a rondeau that parodies her first lyric in the *Voir dit* show an ongoing play with Machaut's legacy.[177] As well as making the comment that Machaut "nurtured him and

---

173. See Earp, *Guillaume de Machaut*, 55, citing James I. Wimsatt, *Chaucer and the French Love Poets: The Literary Background of the Book of the Duchess* (Chapel Hill, 1968), 86–87. See also Albritton, "Citation and Allusion in the Lays of Guillaume de Machaut," chap. 5.

174. See references in Earp, *Guillaume de Machaut*, 53–54 and 62–63, and item 2.3.2a, respectively.

175. Earp (ibid., 54) doubts that this really does refer to a motet, but Huot, "Reading across Genres," has made a persuasive argument to the contrary. Machaut's contribution to the texts of B34, *Ne quier veoir*, is clearly the model for Froissart's *Ne quier veoir* (Rae S. Baudouin, ed., *Jean Froissart: Ballades et rondeaux* [Geneva, 1978], no. 6); see Elizabeth Eva Leach, "Machaut's Peer, Thomas Paien," *Plainsong and Medieval Music* 18 (2009): 1–22. Other similarities between Froissart's and Machaut's lyrics are mentioned in Earp, *Guillaume de Machaut*, 54n6.

176. Earp, *Guillaume de Machaut*, 56, item 2.1.1b, and 58, item 2.1.1l. The addressee of the latter is unknown, although the editor (Queux de Saint-Hilaire and Raynaud, *Deschamps, Oeuvres complètes*, 5:53) suggests it is addressed to Deschamps by an anonymous writer and merely appended to Deschamps's works; see McGrady, *Controlling Readers*, 169.

177. Earp, *Guillaume de Machaut*, 57–558, items 2.1.1i, j, and k.

did him many kindnesses," Deschamps pairs himself with Machaut in a lay as twin writers of the deeds of lovers.[178]

The poet Oton de Granson names Machaut as an authority on Desire, and his works betray the influence of Machaut—both directly and through Chaucer, whom he knew personally.[179] The manuscripts that present Oton's works include many poems by Machaut that are not separately ascribed.[180]

Of those poets who do not name but clearly imitate Machaut, Froissart and Christine de Pizan stand out because they also imitated his production of ordered books in which they placed their entire works. The engagement with Machaut's works in those of Froissart—in terms of form, content, and material disposition—is so consistent and sustained that the lack of reference to him by name shows either that this was felt unnecessary or betrays a certain anxiety of influence.[181]

In the fifteenth century, Machaut's name is well represented in the works of other poets. This might reflect how those who had not known him personally considered him more of a distant authority and thus felt more obliged—or more able—to name him, gaining prestige from the association, as compared to his contemporaries, who engaged with his work in a more competitive, self-conscious, and emulative fashion. In Alain Chartier's *Debat de Reveille Matin,* for example, the lover invokes the authority of Machaut with that of Oton de Granson.[182] The two poets are held up as examples of how the love of one more socially elevated requires hard work on the part of the lover.[183] Michault Taillevent puns on the similarity of his and Machaut's names, and pairs Machaut with Jean de Meun as older and greater authorities: "If it's not as well composed as [Jean] de Meun or Machaut, take it gracefully: it's by Michault."[184] The author of the continuation of the *Rose* is also named with Machaut somewhat differently by Martin le Franc, who cites a number of composers and poets, and places Machaut with Alan of Lille on the morally favorable side of a double comparison between them and Mathiolet and Jean de Meun, respectively.[185]

---

178. Ibid., 56–7, item 2.1.1d; see Queux de Saint-Hilaire and Raynaud, *Deschamps, Oeuvres complètes,* vol. 2, no. 306.

179. See Earp, *Guillaume de Machaut,* 58–59, D.

180. For details, see ibid., 105–6.

181. See the arguments in Sylvia Huot, *From Song to Book: The Poetics of Writing in Old French Lyric and Lyrical Narrative Poetry* (Ithaca, 1987), especially 302–27 (chapter 10) on Froissart. See also McGrady, *Controlling Readers,* 170–89 (chap. 7, "'Nouveleté gaires me gist': Jean Froissart's Reinvention of the Author-Reader Relationship").

182. Earp, *Guillaume de Machaut,* 63, item 2.3.2b. See *Le Debat de Reveille Matin,* stanza 29, l. 231, in J. C. Laidlaw, ed., *The Poetical Works of Alain Chartier* (Cambridge, 1974), 314.

183. Laidlaw, *The Poetical Works of Alain Chartier,* 461 (note to l. 231); and the comments in Jacqueline Cerquiglini, *"Un engin si soutil": Guillaume de Machaut et l'écriture au XIVe siècle* (Geneva, 1985), 137–38.

184. Earp, *Guillaume de Machaut,* 63, item 2.3.2c.

185. Ibid., 63, item 2.3.2d.

Et Jehan de Meun le villain,
Qui en parlant courtoisement
N'a pas resemblé maistre Alain,
Failly et pecha grandement.
Mathiolet semblablement
Qui n'a pas ensuÿ Machault,
A mal dit du saint sacrement,
Mais de leur jengle ne me chault.[186]

And the base Jean de Meun, who did not resemble Master Alan [of Lille] in speaking courteously, failed and sinned greatly. Mathiolet similarly, who did not follow Machaut, spoke ill of the holy sacrament. But I do not care for their chatter!

Later in the poem the Champion refers to Machaut's *Behaingne* in a discussion of how a lover should remain loyal to a promise, disagreeing with the idea that the lady suffers less because she can no longer see her dead lover:

Je ne m'acorde au jugement
Machaut, car la dame pouoit
Son amy mort incessamment
plourer et daire le debvoit.
Sa douleur, dist il, mendre estoit
Car ce que cueur ne voit ne deult,
Mais tousjours l'esciver veoit
Ce qui ung cueur tourmenter seult.[187]

I do not agree with Machaut's *Jugement* [*Behaingne*], because the lady could have wept for her lover ceaselessly and should have done so. Her sorrow, he says, is the lesser, because that which her heart does not see does not grieve it; but it [her heart] sees [her lover] always fleeing away, which is wont to torment any heart.

The following stanza agrees instead with Cicero that things imagined, alive or dead, are as much ours as if we saw them for real.[188]

In his *Livre du Cuer d'Amours espris* (The Book of the Love-Smitten Heart [1457]) René d'Anjou, the son of one of Machaut's most avid readers, Yolande de Bar, names Machaut in second place among the six poets buried in the

---

186. Robert Deschaux, ed., *Martin le Franc: Le champion des dames,* 5 vols. (Paris, 1999), 2:112, stanza 1865, ll. 6913–20. Earp wrongly identifies this Alain as Chartier. The fourteenth-century *Livre de Matheolus,* by the author calling himself "Mathieu the Bigamist," is an overtly antifeminist text.

187. Ibid., 3:74–75, stanza 1593, ll. 12737–44.

188. On this poem as a response to *Behaingne,* see Swift, "*Tamainte consolation / Me fist lymagination.*"

cemetery of the Hospital of Love. As one of six tombs set aside from the others on account of their excellence, Machaut's is found immediately after that of Ovid but before Boccaccio, Jean de Meun, Petrarch, and Alain Chartier.[189] This order is clearly not chronological (although the most recently deceased is last and in a wooden coffin), but neither is it necessarily honorific, since Petrarch's tomb is listed as being bigger than all others save that of Ovid and, like Ovid's, garlanded with laurel.[190] Perhaps Machaut follows Ovid because his work is closest in content to that of the Philosopher of Love; certainly René would have been very familiar with Machaut's dits on account of the literary taste of his mother, who owned Machaut manuscripts. Each poet is introduced in prose by the author and then speaks in his own voice a verse epitaph from the tomb. Machaut is introduced by René as having a tomb "incised with well-notated chansons, virelays, sirventois, lays, and motets made and composed in various manners."[191] When the epitaph speaks, it names the tomb's owner in full as "Guilllaume de Machaut, born in Champagne and of very great renown."[192]

It is evident from the history of the lyric forms in the fifteenth century that Machaut's norms were highly influential, even if he did not originate any of them. Machaut's works were also cited in theoretical treatises from this period, starting with Eustache Deschamps's *Art de dictier* (1392). Without naming Machaut, Deschamps uses two of his rondeaux to illustrate the section in the treatise dealing with this form.[193] *Vo doulz regart* (R8) and *Certes mon oeuil* (R15) form the last two examples of a total of seven rondeaux, and significantly both appear in the music section of his works, although the latter is also found in late manuscripts of the *Loange* as Lo234. Moreover, the first rondeau inserted in the treatise—*Cilz qui onques* (no. 447)—is palpably modeled on *Celle qui unques* (VD1), the lyric that initiates Toute Belle's epistolary approach to Guillaume in the *Voir dit*.[194]

The anonymous and probably slightly later treatise *The Rules of the Second Rhetoric* goes beyond Deschamps to cite Machaut's name—not just, as

189. Earp, *Guillaume de Machaut, 64*, item 2.3.2e. See Stephanie Viereck Gibbs and Kathryn Karczewska, eds., *René of Anjou: The Book of the Love-Smitten Heart* (New York, 2001), sec. 209, 1.

190. Gibbs and Karczewska, *René of Anjou: The Book of the Love-Smitten Heart,* 177 (sec. 215, 1).

191. Ibid., 172 (my translation).

192. Cerquiglini, *"Un engin si soutil,"* 239–43, notes that a nineteenth-century misreading of "voix" for "voir" betrays the nineteenth-century reception of Machaut as a musician first of all, whereas, she claims, the fifteenth-century reception—at least in René's poem—is of him as primarily a poet. René does, however, list "chancons" (songs) among Machaut's works as well as "dits"; once more, the twentieth-century reception—at least among literary scholars—tends to downplay his status as a musician.

193. The rondeau section is Sinnreich-Levi, ed., *Eustache Deschamps' L'Art de dictier,* 88–95 (ll. 494–561). Sinnreich-Levi's note (ibid., 136n92) seems overly cautious in the light of the appearance of these poems in musical settings by Machaut.

194. See Earp, *Guillaume de Machaut,* 57, item 2.1.1i.

mentioned earlier, as Deschamps's uncle, but also in his own right in a list of poets from Master Guillaume de Saint Amour to "Master Jehan de Suzay."[195] Machaut follows directly behind Philippe de Vitry, who is noted as having "invented the manner of motets and balades, lays, and simple rondeaux and having invented in music the four prolations and red notes and the novelty of proportions."[196] Machaut himself is cited as the "grand retthorique"—a term that chimes both with the declaimed opening of the refrain of Deschamps's déploration balades and also with the designation given him by Jean Lebègue—and is praised for beginning all the new "tailles" (verse forms) and writing perfect lays.[197] Machaut's name is followed by that of (Jean) Brisebarre, who is cited as the author of Le livre de l'Escolle de foy and Le tresor de Nostre Dame, as well as of a serventois whose opening two lines are given and "many other good poems" (though he is today chiefly known for a continuation of the Alexander romance called Li Restor du paon, which was written ca. 1340).[198] Later, in the main body of the treatise, the verse form "de 3 et 1" is explained as being that found in Behaingne (cited by its opening line as "le Temps Pasquour"), as if this poem is commonly known (something suggested by Martin le Franc's reference to its content).[199] Although The Rules of the Second Rhetoric is a "rhetoric" treatise focused on poetry, its opening hall of fame includes a number of musicians, some of whom it cites specifically in connection with music (as with Philippe de Vitry and Jehan Vaillant) and some of whom it does not (as with Tapissier, Jehan Suzay, and Machaut himself).[200] Again, the context of the company that Machaut's name keeps seems to obviate the need to specify that he is also a composer. Cases where Machaut is not mentioned specifically as a musician, therefore, should not lead to the conclusion that he was not known as such at that period.

A tacit acknowledgment of Machaut's musical aspect might be contained in an even later treatise, Baudet Herenc's Doctrinal de la Seconde Rhetorique, which cites the opening stanzas of three of Machaut's lays in its section on this form. All three of those chosen are from among those set to music.[201]

---

195. The dating of circa 1411–1432 in Langlois, Recueil d'Arts de séconde rhétorique, xxviii, relies on a death date for Froissart (whom the treatise mentions in the past tense) of 1411. Earp, Guillaume de Machaut, 61n31, notes that this is now placed around 1404, but not that the terminus post quem would therefore pass to Deschamps (also mentioned in the past tense in the treatise and now thought to have outlived Froissart), giving a date of after 1406 or 1407. The date range ca. 1404–1432 given several times in Earp, Guillaume de Machaut, 62, should thus now be ca. 1406–1432.

196. Langlois, Recueil d'Arts de séconde rhétorique, 12.

197. Ibid., 12: "Après [Vitry] vint maistre Guillaume de Machault, le grant retthorique de nouvelle fourme, qui commencha toutes tailles nouvelles, et les parfais lays d'amours."

198. See Enid Donkin, ed., Jean Brisebarre: Li restor du paon (London, 1980).

199. See Langlois, Recueil d'Arts de séconde rhétorique, 33; and Earp, Guillaume de Machaut, 62, item 2.3.1c.

200. Langlois, Recueil d'Arts de séconde rhétorique, 11–14.

201. See ibid., 166–68; and Earp, Guillaume de Machaut, 62, item 2.3.1d. The lays cited are Par trois raisons (L6/5), Amours doucement (L7/6), and Qui bien aimme (L22/16).

Machaut's influence was undoubtedly helped by the turbulent historical situation into which his works were born, as well as his clear response to the needs of his readers. His many references to "estrange countrée" (foreign lands), to the separation of lovers for "longue durée" (a long time), and his elevation of Hope to the figure with which communion was sought allowed his readers and listeners to bear the anxiety of separation from loved ones, the uncertainty of loss through death—whether by disease, accident, or war—and the pain caused by inappropriate desires of all kinds. Musicians as court servants in a time of itinerant nobility traveled widely in this period; nobles in a time of war, diplomacy, and hostage taking were frequently far from home and loved ones. Professionally Machaut was not a musician but rather a court administrator, although he certainly traveled in that latter capacity. Many of those court servants who sang his songs or nobles who heard them would have traveled even more widely. When music traveled, it traveled with musicians, whether in written form or inscribed in memory; books also traveled with courtiers, some of whom probably also knew numerous poems by heart, especially, I would argue, if they knew them to listen to as songs.

Yolande of Bar—daughter of the Duke Robert whose "disruptive" presence is mentioned several times by Guillaume in *Voir dit,* and probably the original owner of **Vg**—offers much evidence of the circulation of books of Machaut's works throughout francophone courts in western Europe.[202] Wife of the king of Aragon, John I, Yolande not only borrowed books by Machaut from other nobles (on one occasion specifically so she could fix lacunae in her own copies), but also attracted letters from others who wished to borrow her own copies, lent these out, and even wrote to request them back.[203]

What this sketch of Machaut's immediate reception history shows is that, wonderful as they are, the Machaut manuscripts have not misrepresented or overrepresented his historical importance. As the first poet to be called "poète" in the French vernacular, Machaut is historically on a par with Dante, Petrarch, and Chaucer. As a musician he shared an international contemporary reputation with Philippe de Vitry. In light of the fact that Vitry partook of the literate tradition of music theory and that much of his influence on the musical tradition can be linked to this fact, Machaut is by far the more influential on other composers through the media of music and poetry.[204] Combining these two aspects sets him apart, even if it has given his latter-day

202. On Robert, Duke of Bar, see *Voir dit,* letters 33 and 35; and Earp, *Guillaume de Machaut,* 46, item 1.15.2a.

203. Earp, *Guillaume de Machaut,* 60, items 2.2.1a–f. Evidence of close acquaintance with Machaut's poetry in Aragon lasts well into the middle of the fifteenth century, when Ignatius Lopez de Mendoza, Marqués de Santillana, cites them in a letter to the constable of Portugal.

204. Admittedly we lack the balades that Vitry is said to have written; only one unnotated lyric in French has survived. See F. N. M. Diekstra, "The Poetic Exchange between Philippe de Vitry and Jean de le Mote," *Neophilologus* 70 (1986): 504–19; E. Pognon, "Ballades mythologiques de Jean de le Mote, Philippe de Vitri, Jean Campion," *Humanisme et Rénaissance* 5 (1938): 385–417.

reputation all sorts of problems on account of the modern academy's fractured disciplinarity.

Nonetheless, by the late fifteenth century, Machaut was named only to be condemned as a breaker of notational rules.[205] By the end of the sixteenth he was just "a trouvère who lived around 1300 and composed a book of his love life"; nothing explicitly connected the two.[206] Over a hundred years of obscurity would pass before the wheel would turn full circle and lead back from Machaut's medieval remembering to his modern dismembering (see chapter 2). It is to be hoped that this book has gone some way to "re-membering" another Orpheus.

205. Gaffurio, *Practica musice,* bbiiii, calls his practice "absurd"; see Earp, *Guillaume de Machaut,* 69, item 2.4.1h.

206. Antoine Du Verdier in his *Bibliotheque françois* (1585); see Earp, *Guillaume de Machaut,* 62.

Glossary

The aim here is to provide a quick gloss of the usage deployed in this book to enable the nonexpert to understand the salient features of the terms. For more detailed and historically nuanced explanations, the reader is referred to the *Grove Dictionary of Music and Musicians,* available online in most university and some public libraries. Open electronic resources can also be reliable; Wikipedia, for example, tends to take its definitions from *Grove.* (Small capitals indicate that a term is defined elsewhere in the glossary.)

⌁

ambitus The overall ambitus or range of a VOICE PART or song, expressed by the interval between the highest and lowest PITCHES sounded within it.

balade A musical form that has one or two main sections, either AB or ABR, depending on whether it sets the refrain in a separate section. The A section—typically setting text lines 1–2—is usually repeated for lines 3–4, but with OPEN and CLOSED endings respectively. See also DOUBLE BALADE and DUPLEX BALADE.

breve A rhythmic note value, written as a square shape without any descending or ascending stroke. In the thirteenth century this was a note of relatively short duration (hence the name, which is Latin for "short" or "brief"), but by Machaut's time it was usually subdivided into semibreves, which were in turn subdivided into MINIMS. (At each level the subdivision could be duple or triple depending on the MENSURATION.) In modern transcriptions, this value is usually equivalent to that of the entire MEASURE.

cadence, cadential formula A formal articulation within a musical phrase that usually has a closural function. It usually consists of two elements:

a TENSION SONORITY and a RESOLUTION SONORITY. These two are often connected by a DIRECTED PROGRESSION. The degree of closure achieved can depend on the mensural "strength" of the formula (i.e., whether the resolution falls on a strong beat), the length of the two elements, the tonality of the resolution, and the articulation of text. NB: Other writers use cadence as a virtual synonym for directed progression. This practice is eschewed here (despite its medieval precedents) so as to make a clear terminological distinction between formulae that are closural articulation and those tension-resolution progressions that have other functions.

cantus   The texted vocal line (VOICE PART) of a composition. Also, the name of the singer who would sing this part.

closed cadence, *clos* cadence   A kind of sectional termination that typically represents the second-time ending of a repeated section of a song. In tonal terms it often has the same level of finality as the end of the song.

color   A sequence of PITCHES, especially a repeated sequence in motets.

compound (interval)   An INTERVAL when one of its PITCHES is displaced by one or more octaves. For example, compounds of a third include a tenth, an eighteenth, and so on.

consonance   A SONORITY type with a degree of stability and a pleasing sound. Fourteenth-century consonances are divided into PERFECT CONSONANCES (unisons, fifths, octaves, and their COMPOUNDS) and IMPERFECT CONSONANCES (thirds, sixths, and their compounds). The former are more stable than the latter, which are considered "sweet."

contratenor   A specific vocal line (VOICE PART) of a composition, which in Machaut's work lies in range between the TENOR and the CANTUS.

counterpoint   For Machaut's music, this term designates what might, in later periods, be called harmony. In Machaut's work it is always fundamentally dyadic, that is, it relies on two pitches. DYADIC counterpoint thus refers to the analytically posited underlying two-part harmony animated by the rhythmicized surface of a given composition, regardless of the number of sounding parts. The analytically posited underlying counterpoint (sometime called "simple counterpoint") is deemed to be without rhythm and to include only CONSONANCES. The surface "harmony" (sometimes called "florid counterpoint" or "diminished counterpoint") has both rhythm and DISSONANCES. Where there are more than two parts, the underlying consonances can be seen as being formed from a number of simultaneously performed contrapuntal duets.[1]

directed progression   A term coined by Sarah Fuller to describe a PROGRESSION from a TENSION SONORITY to a RESOLUTION SONORITY.[2] Here is it used to describe exclusively a progression from an IMPERFECT to a perfect DYAD where one voice part moves by SEMITONE step.

dissonance   A SONORITY type with a degree of instability. Fourteenth-century dissonances are seconds, fourths, sevenths, and their COMPOUNDS.

double balade   A POLYTEXTUAL BALADE in which two balade texts are sung simultaneously in different voice parts. Typically, the balade texts will share a refrain.[3]

duplex balade   A BALADE form that has two parts, A and B, both of which have OPEN and CLOSED endings. In a duplex balade, the refrain line does not have its own musical section, but will share at least some of the music setting of an earlier line from the B section.

dyad   A SONORITY consisting of two pitches in two different voice parts (even when they are the same pitch).

equal temperament   The modern tuning system for the octave scale in which all the semitones are the same size. Earlier tunings had semitones of different sizes at different places in the octave, in order to accommodate the so-called Pythagorean comma—a small interval that represents the difference between a rationally tuned octave (in a string or pipe ratio of 1:2) and the addition of a rationally tuned fifth (2:3) and fourth (3:4). This acoustic feature effectively prevented the possibility of the complete cycle of major and minor keys until equal temperament was adopted so as to make all keys equally "in tune" (or out of tune, depending on one's perspective). The effect of the lack of equal temperament in medieval music is to make major thirds

---

1. For more detail, see Elizabeth Eva Leach, "Counterpoint and Analysis in Fourteenth-Century Song," *Journal of Music Theory* 44 (2000): 45–79; "Machaut's Balades with Four Voices," *Plainsong and Medieval Music* 10 (2001): 47–79; and "Form, Counterpoint, and Meaning in a Fourteenth-Century French Courtly Song," in *Analytical and Cross-cultural Studies in World Music* (New York, forthcoming).

2. See Sarah Fuller, "On Sonority in Fourteenth-Century Polyphony: Some Preliminary Reflections," *Journal of Music Theory* 30 (1986): 35–70. For my more specific usage, see Leach, "Counterpoint and Analysis."

3. See Elizabeth Eva Leach, "Music and Verbal Meaning: Machaut's Polytextual Songs," *Speculum* 85 (2010): 567–91.

and sixths slightly larger and minor thirds and sixths slightly smaller, in all cases making them sound less consonant.

figure   A musical motive, usually short, with a particular outline of PITCH and rhythm.

figured bass   In music of the seventeenth and early eighteenth centuries, the player of a keyboard part in an instrumental ensemble would not have his or her part fully written down but would be expected to realize it from a combination of the bass melody line and a series of figures that designate the harmony. Details of harmonic voice-leading and rhythm were essentially improvised (within fairly strict constraints).

final   The last pitch of a melody.

functional tonality   The way that harmonic motion was governed in Western art music from the eighteenth and nineteenth centuries, and which posits certain kinds of operative relationships between the PITCH CLASSES and their associated harmonization within a given key.

Guidonian gamut   The collection of PITCHES used in medieval music that is not affected by MUSICA FICTA. All pitches were named with an alphabetic letter and a syllable giving the interval context. This book designates PITCHES using only the letters plus, where necessary, a flat sign for the note "*b*-fa." The letters began with gamma as the lowest note (with the syllable "ut"; hence "gamut" from "gamma-ut") and then in two cycles of A–G, first majuscule and then minuscule. Notes higher than this had their lower-case letters doubled. The gamut is thus *Γ, A, B, C, D, E, F, G, a, b♭, b, c, d, e, f, g, aa.*

imperfect consonance, imperfect sonority   A DYAD with the INTERVAL of a third or a sixth, as well as COMPOUNDS of these intervals.

interval   The difference (or "distance") in PITCH between two pitches. The size of an interval can be expressed by counting the number of letters that would theoretically fill out the steps from one note to another. Thus, the interval between A and C is a third (A–B–C); the interval between F and C is a fifth (F–G–A–B–C).

ligature   A notational feature in which more than one pitch is expressed by a single graphic shape. These are more common in the untexted and slower-moving tenor and contratenor parts of fourteenth-century music.

long A rhythmic note value, written as a square shape with a descending stroke on the right. By Machaut's time it could usually be subdivided into BREVES, SEMIBREVES, and MINIMS, each level being capable of duple or triple subdivision depending on the MENSURATION. Longs are uncommon in Machaut's songs, except for the final notes of pieces, and generally occupy more than one bar in transcriptions. The exception to this is when the piece is organized throughout at the MODUS level, as typically in motets and in some songs (mainly lays).

major and minor keys The organizational modalities of the system of FUNCTIONAL TONALITY that came to dominate Western art music from the eighteenth century. Its thoroughgoing implementation relies on the use of EQUAL TEMPERAMENT.

measure (bar) An organizational metrical unit in modern musical notation in which the opening "beat" is stronger than the others. The number of beats in a measure can be duple or triple, and these beats can be subdivided into two or three, depending on the TIME SIGNATURE. In modern transcriptions, measures are divided by a vertical line running through the staves.

melisma, melismatic A melody or melodic segment of more than one pitch, which sets a single text syllable. A melisma effectively stretches a single verbal syllable temporally. Melismatic music has frequent melismas. Cf. SYLLABIC SETTING.

mensural stress For the purposes of discussion here, the mensural stress is deemed to lie at the beginning of the group of notes equivalent to the BREVE. In effect, this means that the first beat of each measure is deemed stronger than the other beats. This analytical premise is asserted here since its argumentation from first principles in fourteenth-century music is complex.[4]

mensuration Mensuration describes the way in which the different rhythmic note values are related to one another. Four basic mensurations are used in standard fourteenth-century French notation, and modern notation represents the length of the BREVE with a whole measure in the transcription. (There are no measures in the original notation.) If the breve is divided into three semibreves, which in turn are divided into three minims, this is perfect time, major PROLATION (and typically transcribed in $\frac{9}{8}$). If the breve is divided into three semibreves, which in turn are divided into two minims, this is perfect time, minor prolation (and typically transcribed in $\frac{3}{4}$). If the breve is divided into two semibreves, which in turn are divided into three minims, this is imperfect

4. See Leach, "Form, Counterpoint, and Meaning in a Fourteenth-Century French Courtly Song."

time, major prolation (and typically transcribed in $\frac{6}{8}$). If the breve is divided into two semibreves, which in turn are divided into two minims, this is imperfect time, minor prolation (and typically transcribed in $\frac{2}{4}$).

minim   A rhythmic NOTE VALUE, written as a diamond shape with an ascending stroke. In modern transcriptions this value is usually equivalent to an eighth note and is the smallest rhythmic value used by Machaut.

mode   1. Mode in its mensural usage refers to the quantity of BREVES equivalent to each LONG. Modus organization can be binary (minor) or ternary (major).
   2. Mode can refer to the tonal organization of a melody and is assessed on the basis of the FINAL and the position of the final in the overall AMBITUS. Mode was of practical benefit in the singing of ecclesiastical chant, since it enabled singers to use the right melodic formulae to effect seamless joins between different parts of the chant that were variable depending on the liturgical calendar. Some modern studies of medieval music apply mode to secular music, but this book does not.

modern notation   Standard modern notation "reduces" the note values by one-quarter for the four standard patterns of MENSURATION in this music. This is most obvious in the British terminology for note values, where the terms BREVE, SEMIBREVE, and MINIM are still in use (applying to the double whole note, whole note, and half note, respectively).[5] The fourteenth-century minim (i.e., half note) is represented by a modern eighth note, representing a quartering of the values. In pieces with MODUS organization, most modern editions apply an extra level of reduction to the original rhythmic values, so as to transcribe a semibreve (whole note) with a modern eighth note according to the idea that in such notations the "beat" shifts up a rhythmic level. In this book I have avoided this practice so as to make clearer some of the arguments concerning the "archaic font" of modus notation.

modus   Modus designates the relationship between the LONG and the BREVE. This is the highest level of rhythmic organization used in Machaut's music. see MODE 1.

monophony, monophonic   Monophony is music in which there is only one voice part. Monophonic music effectively has no harmony (or COUNTERPOINT), no accompanying part, and consists only of a single line of melody, which (in Machaut's music) carries the text. Cf. POLYPHONY.

---

5. As can be observed, the modern default relation between each level is binary.

musica ficta   The medieval definition of musica ficta is complex, referring to the singing of pitches outside the regular gamut. In modern transcription the term is used to apply to the adjustment by a SEMITONE of pitches by the application of sharps and flats. B♭ is, however, strictly speaking not musica ficta, since the pitch was available within the regular GAMUT.

neumes, neumed, neumation   A neume is a graphic shame that depicts one or more PITCHES. In the earliest notations neumes were added directly to texts without the use of any staff lines. Such texts are said to be "neumed."

notational level   The notational level of a piece is represented by the prevailing kinds of note values present. A piece in which the melodies have frequent MINIMS, organized in groups of SEMIBREVES, these in turn organized into BREVES, is notated at the level of tempus and prolation in semibreves. See also REDUCTION, MODUS, PROLATION, TEMPUS.

note values   Both fourteenth-century mensural and modern notations use differentiated graphic shapes to depict notes of different durations. These note values are related proportionately according to the medieval MENSURATION or modern TIME SIGNATURE.

offsetting, rhythmic offsetting   Rhythmic offsetting can describe the use of a different rhythm so as to realign slightly the two voice parts in a particular sequence of sonorities compared to a similar sequence found elsewhere. The use of rests to offset rhythmic patterns can result in SYNCOPATION.

open cadence; *ouvert* cadence   The open or *ouvert* cadence is a kind of sectional termination that typically represents the first-time ending of a repeated section of a song. In tonal terms it often represents a secondary level of focus, which may be juxtaposed with that of the *clos* cadence throughout the song.

perfect consonance, perfect sonority   INTERVALS of unisons, fifths, octaves, and their COMPOUNDS.

pitch   A specific tone (note), designated by a letter of the alphabet, which gives its position relative to other tones. There is no agreed absolute pitch standard in the Middle Ages, so the pitch *a* is not (as it would be today) a tone at a specific frequency, but it is higher in pitch than the note G. See GUIDONIAN GAMUT for the designation of pitches in this book.

pitch class   All tones designated by the same alphabetical letter, regardless of their octave register. Pitch classes are given in this book by capital letters in Roman type. (Specific pitches are given in italics, with capital and lower case representing different octave registers for the same pitch class.) See GUIDONIAN GAMUT.

polyphony, polyphonic   Polyphony is music that has more than one VOICE PART. Machaut's polyphonic music is in two, three, or four parts. Cf. MONOPHONY.

polytextual, polytextuality   A piece of music is polytextual when two or more voice parts perform different verbal texts simultaneously.

progression   Progression is a common way of designating a sequence of two or more SONORITIES that occur in immediate succession. See also DIRECTED PROGRESSION.

prolation   Prolation designates the relationship between the SEMIBREVE and the MINIM. This is the lowest level of rhythmic organization used in Machaut's music. A binary relationship (two minims to a semibreve) is termed minor prolation; a ternary relationship (three minims to a semibreve) is termed major prolation.

range   See AMBITUS.

reduction, rhythmic reduction   Modern transcriptions typically have their rhythms "reduced" in comparison to the NOTE VALUES of the medieval original. The standard reduction in editions of fourteenth-century music is to quarter the values (so a whole note is represented by a quarter note). See also MODERN NOTATION and MODUS.

regular gamut   See GUIDONIAN GAMUT.

resolution sonority   A perfect sonority that resolves the TENSION SONORITY of a DIRECTED PROGRESSION.

semibreve   A rhythmic NOTE VALUE, written as a rhombus.

semitone   The smallest interval in medieval music, being part (but not precisely half) of a tone. Modern semitones under EQUAL TEMPERA-MENT are exactly half a tone, but medieval semitones came in two slightly different sizes.[6]

simplex balade   A version of the BALADE form which has the musical form AAB or AABR, depending on whether the refrain text is in a discrete musical section or not. The repeated A section has first an OPEN and then a CLOSED

---

6. See Elizabeth Eva Leach, "Gendering the Semitone, Sexing the Leading Tone: Fourteenth-Century Music Theory and the Directed Progression," *Music Theory Spectrum* 28 (2006): 1–21.

ENDING. Unlike in the DUPLEX BALADE, the B section of the song is not repeated, although in the AABR form, one common option is for the B and R
section endings to replicate the open and closed CADENCES respectively.

sonority   A sonority is formed by the simultaneous sounding of more than
one voice part. The interval between the two voices can be described as
a CONSONANCE or DISSONANCE. A sonority whose interval is a unison is
formed by two or more voice parts singing the same PITCH simultaneously.

syllabic setting   A kind of text setting in which there is one melodic PITCH
for each syllable of the verbal text. This typically makes the delivery clear.
Cf. MELISMA.

syncopated, syncopation   This term is used in its modern sense to signal
when an element of rhythm delay or OFFSETTING is used so that an otherwise
MENSURALLY stressed "beat" lacks a strong PROGRESSION.

talea   The pattern of rhythms that are repeated in the tenor part of a motet.

tempus   Tempus (time) designates the relationship between the BREVE
and the SEMIBREVE. The tempus represents the beat. A ternary relationship
(three semibreves to a breve) is termed perfect time and has three "beats" in
the "measure" (bar) of a modern transcription. A binary relationship (two
semibreves to a breve) is termed imperfect time and has two "beats" in the
"measure" (bar) of a modern transcription.

tenor   The lowest vocal line (VOICE PART) of a composition. Also, the name
of the singer who would sing this part. In the present book, this does not
imply a specific voice type for this individual.

tension sonority   An IMPERFECT CONSONANCE, especially one that resolves
to PERFECT CONSONANCE in the DIRECTED PROGRESSION.

text-setting   Text-setting refers to the coordination of verbal text and
melody. The delivery can be SYLLABIC or MELISMATIC, or combine the two.

tierce   The tierce is the terminal section of a virelay stanza, in which new
verbal text is performed to the music of the refrain. This section occurs immediately before the repeat of the refrain in each stanza.

timbre, timbral differentiation   Timbre is used to describe the sonic quality
of a sound. For example, a glockenspiel and a violin might both play a note
of the same PITCH and duration, but they will not sound the same because
they are timbrally differentiated. Different singers' voices may have different

timbre, and timbre may also differ in separate parts of a single singer's over-all REGISTER.

time signature   A time signature is the modern equivalent of the MENSURAL organization of the rhythmic aspect of a piece. In modern scores it is usu-ally given explicitly by what appears as a fraction at the start of the score, although this practice is not followed in the transcriptions given here (just as most medieval manuscripts do not give explicit signs for their mensuration, although such signs existed in theory).

tonal   The adjective tonal is used without reference to the FUNCTIONAL TONALITY or MAJOR AND MINOR KEYS of later music and refers purely to the interrelation of the tones or PITCHES in a given piece. See also TONAL HIERARCHY.

tonal hierarchy   A hierarchy of PITCH CLASSES and SONORITIES with these pitch classes in the TENOR part that gives a sense of the degree of closure of certain PROGRESSIONS and can also lead to listener expectations of certain kinds of PROGRESSION. In general, the most important tone or sonority in a piece is that which occurs at the very end. Where this is identical to the CLOSED SONORITY, a secondary focus can be provided by the sonority of the OPEN CADENCE.

triad   A collection of three PITCHES or PITCH CLASSES, usually comprising a third and a fifth above the lowest pitch or pitch class.

triplum   The highest vocal line (voice part) of a composition.

voice part   The voice part of a song is a self-contained musical part, which, in polyphonic music, is combined with other voice parts. The use of "voice" is metaphorical and does not denote whether or not the given voice part is meant to be sung. The voice parts in Machaut's music are called CANTUS, TENOR, CONTRATENOR, and TRIPLUM.

Bibliography

Abbate, Carolyn. "Music—Drastic or Gnostic?" *Critical Inquiry* 30 (2004): 505–36.

Alan of Lille. *Anticlaudianus or the Good and Perfect Man.* Translated by James J. Sheridan. 1973. Toronto: Pontifical Institute of Mediaeval Studies, 1987.

Albritton, Benjamin L. "Citation and Allusion in the Lays of Guillaume de Machaut." Ph.D. thesis, University of Washington, 2009.

Apel, Willi. "French, Italian and Latin Poems in 14th-Century Music." *Journal of the Plainsong & Mediaeval Music Society* 1 (1978): 39–56.

——, ed. *French Secular Compositions of the Fourteenth Century.* 3 vols. Vol. 53 of Corpus Mensurabilis Musicae. Rome: American Institute of Musicology, 1970–1972.

——. Review of *Guillaume de Machaut (1300–1377): Messe Nostre Dame dite du Sacre de Charles V (1364) à 4 voix égales,* edited by Jacques Chailley. *Speculum* 26 (1951): 187–90.

——, ed. *French Secular Music of the Late Fourteenth Century.* Cambridge: Medieval Academy of America, 1950.

Arlt, Wulf. "Machaut, Senleches und der anonyme Liedsatz *Esperance qui en mon cuer s'embat.*" In *Musik als Text: Bericht über den Internationalen Kongreß der Gesellschaft für Musikforschung, Freiburg im Breisgau 1993,* edited by Hermann Danuser and Tobias Plebuch, vol. 1 of 2, 300–310. Kassel: Bärenreiter, 1998.

——. "*Helas! Tant ay dolour et peine:* Machaut's Ballade Nr. 2 und ihre Stellung innerhalb der Werkgruppe." In *Trent'anni di ricerche musicologiche: Studi in onore di F. Alberto Gallo,* edited by Patrizia dalla Vecchia and Donatella Restani, 99–114. Rome: Torre d'Orfeo, 1996.

——. "Aspekte der Chronologie und des Stilwandels im französischen Lied des 14. Jahrhunderts." In *Aktuelle Fragen der musikbezogenen Mittelalterforschung: Texte zu einem Basler Kolloquium des Jahres 1975,* 193–280. Winterthur: Amadeus, 1982.

Atchison, Mary. *The Chansonnier of Oxford Bodleian MS Douce 308: Essays and Complete Edition of Texts.* Aldershot: Ashgate, 2005.

Atkinson, J. Keith, ed. *Boeces, De Consolacion: Edition critique d'après le manuscrit Paris, Bibl. nationale, fr. 1096, avec Introduction, Variantes, Notes et Glossaires.* Tübingen: Max Niemeyer, 1996.

Attwood, Catherine. "The Image in the Fountain: Fortune, Fiction and Femininity in the *Livre du Voir Dit* of Guillaume de Machaut." *Nottingham French Studies* 38 (1999): 137–49.

Audbourg-Popin, Marie-Danielle. "'Riches d'amour et mendians d'amie...': La rhétorique de Machaut." *Revue de musicologie* 72 (1986): 97–104.

Avril, François. "Les manuscrits enluminés de Guillaume de Machaut: Essai de chronologie." In *Guillaume de Machaut: Poète et Compositeur,* 117–33. Reims: Klincksieck, 1982.

——. *Manuscript Painting at the Court of France: The Fourteenth Century (1320–1380).* London: Chatto and Windus, 1978.

——. "Un Chef-d'oeuvre de l'enluminure sous le règne de Jean le Bon: La Bible Moralisée manuscrit français 167 de la Bibliothèque Nationale." In *Monuments et mémoires de la Fondation Eugène Piot,* 91–125. Paris: Presses Universitaires de France, 1973.

Babbitt, Milton. "Who Cares If You Listen?" In *Contemporary Composers on Contemporary Music,* edited by Elliott Schwartz, Barney Childs, and James Fox, 243–50. New York: Da Capo Press, 1998.

Bain, Jennifer. "Tonal Structure and the Melodic Role of Chromatic Inflections in the Music of Machaut." *Plainsong and Medieval Music* 14 (2005): 59–88.

——. "Balades 32 and 33 and the 'res dalamangne.'" In *Machaut's Music: New Interpretations,* edited by Elizabeth Eva Leach, 205–19. Woodbridge: Boydell and Brewer, 2003.

Balensuela, C. Matthew, ed. *Ars cantus mensurabilis per modos iuris (The Art of Mensurable Song Measured by the Modes of Law): A New Critical Text and Translation on Facing Pages.* Lincoln: University of Nebraska Press, 1994.

Barrett, Sam, ed. *Melodies for the De consolatione philosophiae of Boethius.* Kassel: Bärenreiter, forthcoming.

Bartsch, Karl. *Chrestomathie de l'ancien français (VIIIe–XVe siècles): Accompagnée d'une grammaire et d'un glossaire.* Leipzig: Vogel, 1880.

Baudouin, Rae S., ed. *Jean Froissart: Ballades et rondeaux.* Geneva: Droz, 1978.

Bec, Pierre. *Le lyrique française au moyen âge (xiie–xiiie siècles): Contributions à une typologie des genres poétiques médiévales, études et textes.* 2 vols. Paris: A. and J. Picard, 1977–78.

Bent, Margaret. "Naming of Parts: Notes on the Contratenor, c. 1350–1450." In *"Uno gentile et subtile ingenio": Studies in Renaissance Music in Honour of Bonnie J. Blackburn,* edited by Gioia Filocamo, M. Jennifer Bloxam, and Leofranc Holford-Stevens, 1–12. Turnhout: Brepols, 2009.

——. "Songs without Music in Dante's *De vulgari eloquentia: Cantio* and Related Terms." In *"Et facciam dolçi canti": Studi in onore di Agostino Ziino in occasione del suo 650 compleanno,* edited by Bianca Maria Antolini, Teresa M. Gialdroni, and Annunziato Pugliese, 161–81. Lucca: LIM, 2004.

——. "Words and Music in Machaut's Motet 9." *Early Music* 31 (2003): 363–88.

——. *Counterpoint, Composition, and Musica Ficta.* London: Routledge, 2002.

——. "Fauvel and Marigny: Which Came First?" In *Fauvel Studies: Allegory, Chronicle, Music, and Image in Paris, Bibliothèque Nationale de France, MS français 146,* edited by Margaret Bent and Andrew Wathey, 35–52. Oxford: Oxford University Press, 1998.

——. "The Grammar of Early Music: Preconditions for Analysis." In *Tonal Structures in Early Music,* edited by Cristle Collins Judd, 15–59. New York: Garland, 1998.

——. "Editing Early Music: The Dilemma of Translation." *Early Music* 22 (1994): 373–92.

——. "Deception, Exegesis and Sounding Number in Machaut's Motet 15." *Early Music History* 10 (1991): 15–27.

———. "The Machaut Manuscripts *Vg, B* and *E.*" *Musica Disciplina* 37 (1983): 53–82.

Bent, Margaret, and Andrew Wathey. Introduction. In *Fauvel Studies: Allegory, Chronicle, Music, and Image in Paris, Bibliothèque Nationale de France, MS français 146,* edited by Margaret Bent and Andrew Wathey, 1–24. Oxford: Oxford University Press, 1998.

Berger, Christian. "Die melodische Floksel im Leidsatz des 14. Jahrhunderts: Magister Franciscus' Ballade 'Phiton.'" In *Trasmissione e recezione delle forme di cultura Vmusicale: Atti del XIV congresso della società internazionale di musicologia. Bologna, 27 agosto–1° settembre 1987, Ferrara–Parma, 30 agosto 1987,* vol. 3 of 3, 673–79. Turin: EDT, 1990.

Berktold, Christian, ed. *Ars practica mensurabilis cantus secundum Iohannem de Muris: Die Recensio maior des sogenannten "Libellus practice cantus mensurabilis."* Munich: C. H. Beck, 1999.

Bétemps, Isabelle. "Les *Lais de plour:* Guillaume de Machaut et Oton de Granson." In *Guillaume de Machaut: 1300–2000. Actes du Colloque de la Sorbonne 28–29 septembre 2000,* edited by Jacqueline Cerquiglini-Toulet and Nigel Wilkins, 95–106. Paris: Presses de l'Université de Paris–Sorbonne, 2002.

Binski, Paul. *Medieval Death: Ritual and Representation.* London: British Museum Press, 1996.

Blanning, T. C. W. *The Culture of Power and the Power of Culture: Old Regime Europe, 1660–1789.* Oxford: Oxford University Press, 2002.

Blumenberg, Hans. *Shipwreck with Spectator: Paradigm of a Metaphor for Existence.* Translated by Steven Rendall. Cambridge: MIT Press, 1997; orig. *Schiffbruch mit Zuschauer.*

Blumenfeld-Kosinski, Renate. *Reading Myth: Classical Mythology and Its Interpretations in Medieval French.* Stanford: Stanford University Press, 1997.

Bockholdt, Rudolf. "Französische und niederländische Musik des 14. und 15. Jahrhunderts." In *Musikalische Edition im Wandel des historischen Bewusstseins,* edited by Thrasybulos Georgos Georgiades, 149–73. Kassel: Bärenreiter, 1971.

Boogaard, Nico H. J. van den. *Rondeaux et Refrains du XIIe siècle au début du XIVe.* Paris: Klincksieck, 1969.

Boogaart, Jacques. Review of *Guillaume de Machaut and Reims: Context and Meaning in His Musical Works* by Anne Walters Robertson. *Early Music* 33 (2004): 605–9.

———. "Observations on Machaut's Motet *He! Mors /Fine Amour / Quare non sum mortuus* (M3)." In *Machaut's Music: New Interpretation,* edited by Elizabeth Eva Leach, 13–30. Woodbridge: Boydell and Brewer, 2003.

———. "Encompassing Past and Present: Quotations and Their Function in Machaut's Motets." *Early Music History* 20 (2001): 1–86.

———. "'O Series Summe Rata': De Motetten van Guillaume de Machaut. De Ordening van het Corpus en de Samenhang van Tekst en Muziek." Ph.D. dissertation, University of Utrecht, 2001.

Boudet, Jean-Patrice, and Hélène Millet, eds. *Eustache Deschamps en son temps.* Paris: Publications de la Sorbonne, 1997.

Bowers, Roger. "Guillaume de Machaut and His Canonry of Reims, 1338–1377." *Early Music History* 23 (2004): 1–48.

Brejon de Lavergnée, M.-É. "Note sur la maison de Guillaume de Machaut à Reims." In *Guillaume de Machaut, poète et compositeur,* 149–52. Paris: Klincksieck, 1982.

Briner, Andres. "Guillaume de Machaut 1958/59 oder Strawinskys 'Movements for Piano and Orchestra.'" *Melos* 27 (1960): 184–86.

Brothers, Thomas. *Chromatic Beauty in the Late Medieval Chanson: An Interpretation of Manuscript Accidentals.* Cambridge: Cambridge University Press, 1997.

Brown, Elizabeth A. R. "*Rex ioians, ionnes, iolis:* Louis X, Philip V, and the *Livres de Fauvel.*" In *Fauvel Studies: Allegory, Chronicle, Music, and Image in Paris, Bibliothèque Nationale de France, MS français 146,* edited by Margaret Bent and Andrew Wathey, 53–72. Oxford: Oxford University Press, 1998.

——. "Diplomacy, Adultery, and Domestic Politics at the Court of Philip the Fair: Queen Isabella's Mission to France in 1314." In *Documenting the Past: Essays in Medieval History Presented to George Peddy Cuttino,* edited by J. S. Hamilton and P. J. Bradley, 53–83. Woodbridge: Boydell, 1989.

Brown, Thomas. "Another Mirror of Lovers? Order, Structure and Allusion in Machaut's Motets." *Plainsong and Medieval Music* 10 (2001): 121–34.

Brownlee, Kevin. "Fire, Desire, Duration, Death: Machaut's Motet 10." In *Citation and Authority in Medieval and Renaissance Musical Culture: Learning from the Learned,* edited by Suzannah Clark and Elizabeth Eva Leach, 79–93. Woodbridge: Boydell and Brewer, 2005.

——. "La polyphonie textuelle dans le Motet 7 de Machaut: Narcisse, la *Rose,* et la voix féminine." In *Guillaume de Machaut: 1300–2000,* edited by Jacqueline Cerquiglini-Toulet and Nigel Wilkins, 137–46. Paris: Presses de l'Université de Paris–Sorbonne, 2002.

——. "Pygmalion, Mimesis, and the Multiple Endings of the *Roman de la Rose.*" *Yale French Studies* 95 (1999): 193–211.

——. "Literary Intertextualities in 14th-Century French Song: Machaut's *Esperance qui m'asseüre,* the Anonymous Rondeau *En attendant d'avoir,* Senleches *En attendant esperance conforte.*" In *Musik als Text: Bericht über den Internationalen Kongreß der Gesellschaft für Musikforschung, Freiburg im Breisgau 1993,* edited by Hermann Danuser and Tobias Plebuch, vol. 1, 295–99. Kassel: Bärenreiter, 1998.

——. "Polyphonie et intertextualité dans les motets 8 et 4 de Guillaume de Machaut." In *"L'hostellerie de pensée": Études sur l'art littéraire au Moyen Age offertes à Daniel Poirion,* edited by Michel Zink, Danielle Bohler, Eric Hicks, and Manuela Python; translated by Anthony Allen, 97–104. Paris: Presses de l'Université de Paris–Sorbonne, 1995.

——. "Machaut's Motet 15 and the *Roman de la Rose:* The Literary Context of *Amours qui a le pouoir / Faus samblant m'a deceü / Vidi Dominum.*" *Early Music History* 10 (1991): 1–14.

——. *Poetic Identity in Guillaume de Machaut.* Madison: University of Wisconsin Press, 1984.

Burkhart, Peter. "Eine wiederentdeckte Bible historiale aus der königlichen Bibliothek im Louvre: Stuttgart, WLB cod Bibl.2.6." *Scriptorium* 53 (1999): 187–99.

Burney, Charles. *A General History of Music, From the Earliest Ages to the Present Period. To which is Prefixed, A Dissertation on the Music of the Ancients.* 4 vols. London: T. Becket, J. Robson, and G. Robinson, 1776–1789.

Busby, Keith. *Codex and Context: Reading Old French Verse Narrative in Manuscript.* 2 vols. Amsterdam: Rodopi, 2002.

Busse Berger, Anna Maria. *Medieval Music and the Art of Memory.* Berkeley: University of California Press, 2005.

Butt, John. *Playing with History: The Historical Approach to Musical Performance.* Cambridge: Cambridge University Press, 2002.

Butterfield, Ardis. "The Art of Repetition: Machaut's Ballade 33, *Nes qu'on porroit.*" *Early Music* 31 (2003): 347–60.

——. "Articulating the Author: Gower and the French Vernacular Codex." *Yearbook of English Studies* 33. Medieval and Early Modern Miscellanies and Anthologies (2003): 80–96.

——. "*Enté:* A Survey and Re-assessment of the Term in Thirteenth- and Fourteenth-Century Music and Poetry." *Early Music History* 22 (2003): 67–101.

——. *Poetry and Music in Medieval France: From Jean Renart to Guillaume de Machaut.* Cambridge: Cambridge University Press, 2002.

——. "Lyric and Elegy in *The Book of the Duchess.*" *Medium Aevum* 60 (1991): 33–60.

Byrne, Donal. "An Early French Humanist and Sallust: Jean Lebègue and the Iconographical Programme for the *Catiline* and *Jurgurtha.*" *Journal of the Warburg and Courtauld Institutes* 49 (1986): 41–65.

——. "A 14th-Century French Drawing in Berlin and the 'Livre du Voir-Dit' of Guillaume de Machaut." *Zeitschrift für Kunstgeschichte* 47 (1984): 70–81.

Calin, William. *The French Tradition and the Literature of Medieval England.* Toronto: University of Toronto Press, 1994.

——. *A Poet at the Fountain: Essays on the Narrative Verse of Guillaume de Machaut.* Lexington: University Press of Kentucky, 1974.

Calin, William, and Lawrence Earp. "The Lai in *Remede de Fortune.*" *Ars Lyrica* 11 (2000): 39–75.

Carruthers, Mary. "*Varietas:* A Word of Many Colours." *Poetica: Zeitschrift für Sprach- und Literaturwissenschaft* 40 (2009): 33–54.

——. "Sweetness." *Speculum* 81 (2006): 999–1013.

——. *The Book of Memory: A Study of Memory in Medieval Culture.* Cambridge: Cambridge University Press, 1991.

Carruthers, Mary, and Jan M. Ziolkowski, eds. *The Medieval Craft of Memory: An Anthology of Texts and Poems.* Philadelphia: University of Pennsylvania Press, 2002.

Caviness, Madeline H. "Patron or Matron? A Capetian Bride and a Vade Mecum for Her Marriage Bed." *Speculum* 68 (1993): 333–62.

Caylus, [Anne-Claude-Philippe de Tubières de Grimoard de Pestels de Lévy, Comte de]. "Premier mémoire sur Guillaume de Machaut, poëte et musicien dans le XIVe siècle: Contenant des recherches sur sa vie, avec une notice de ses principaux ouvrages." *Mémoires de littérature, tirés des registres de l'Académie Royale des Inscriptions et Belles-Lettres* 20 (1753): 399–414.

——. "Second mémoire sur les ouvrages de Guillaume de Machaut: Contenant l'histoire de la prise d'Alexandrie, et des principaux évènements de la vie de Pierre de Lusignan, roi de Chypre et de Jérusalem; tirée d'un poëme de cet ecrivain." *Mémoires de littérature, tirés des registres de l'Académie Royale des Inscriptions et Belles-Lettres* 20 (1753): 415–39.

Cazelles, Raymond. *Société politique, noblesse et couronne sous Jean le Bon et Charles V.* Geneva: Droz, 1982.

Cerquiglini, Jacqueline. *"Un engin si soutil": Guillaume de Machaut et l'écriture au XIVe siècle.* Geneva: Slatkine, 1985.

——. "Le nouveau lyricisme (XIVe–XVe siècle)." In *Précis de littérature française du Moyen Âge,* edited by Daniel Poirion, 275–92. Paris: Presses Universitaires de France, 1983.

Cerquiglini-Toulet, Jacqueline. "Lyrisme de désir et lyrisme d'espérance dans la poésie de Guillaume de Machaut." In *Guillaume de Machaut: 1300–2000*, edited by Jacqueline Cerquiglini-Toulet and Nigel Wilkins, 41–51. Paris: Presses de l'Université de Paris–Sorbonne, 2002.

——. *The Color of Melancholy: The Uses of Books in the Fourteenth Century.* Translated by Lydia G. Cochrane. Baltimore: Johns Hopkins University Press, 1997; orig. *Couleur de la mélancholie.*

——. "Polyphème ou l'antre de la voix dans le *Voir dit* de Guillaume de Machaut." In *"L'hostellerie de pensée": Études sur l'art littéraire au Moyen Age offertes à Daniel Poirion,* edited by Michel Zink, Danielle Bohler, Eric Hicks, and Manuela Python, 105–18. Paris: Presses de l'Université de Paris–Sorbonne, 1995.

——. "*Fama* et les preux: Nom et renom à la fin du Moyen Âge." *Médiévales* 24 (1993): 35–44.

——. "Le *Voir Dit* mis à nu par ses éditeurs, même: Étude de la réception d'un texte à travers ses éditions." In *Mittelalter-Rezeption: Zur Rezeptionsgeschichte der romanischen Literaturen des Mittelalters in der Neuzeit,* edited by Reinhold R. Grimm, 337–80. Heidelberg: 1991.

——. "Écrire le temps: Le lyricisme de la durée aux XIVe et XVe siècles." In *Le temps et la durée dans la littérature au Moyen Âge et à la Renaissance: Actes du colloque organisé par le Centre de Recherche sur la Littérature du Moyen Âge et de la Renaissance de l'Université de Reims (novembre 1984),* edited by Yvonne Bellenger, 103–14. Paris: Nizet, 1986.

Chailley, Jacques. "Du cheval de Guillaume de Machaut à Charles II of Navarre." *Romania* 94 (1973): 251–58.

——, ed. *Guillaume de Machaut (1300–1377): Messe Nostre Dame dite du Sacre de Charles V (1364) à 4 voix égales.* La musique française au moyen-âge: Répertoire de la Psallette Notre-Dame. Paris: Rouart & Lerolle, 1948.

Chamberlain, David, ed. *New Readings of Late Medieval Love Poems.* Lanham, Md.: University Press of America, 1993.

Chaucer, Geoffrey. "The Book of the Duchess." In *Chaucer's Dream Poetry,* edited by Helen Phillips and Nick Havely, 219–80. London: Longman, 1997.

Chichmaref [Shishmarev], Vladimir Feodorovich. *Lirika i Liriki pozdniago srednevekovia: Ocherki po istorii poezii Franzii i Provansa.* Paris: Danzig, 1911.

Chion, Michel. *Audio-Vision: Sound on Screen.* New York: Columbia University Press, 1994.

Clagett, Marshall, ed. *Nicole Oresme and the Medieval Geometry of Qualities and Motions: A Treatise on the Uniformity and Difformity of Intensities Known as Tractatus de configurationibus qualitatum et motuum.* Madison: University of Wisconsin Press, 1968.

Clark, Alice V. "Machaut Reading Machaut: Self-borrowing and Reinterpretation in Motets 8 and 21." In *Citation and Authority in Medieval and Renaissance Music: Learning from the Learned,* edited by Suzannah Clark and Elizabeth Eva Leach, 94–101. Woodbridge: Boydell and Brewer, 2005.

Clark, Suzannah. "'S'en dirai chançonete': Hearing Text and Music in a Medieval Motet." *Plainsong and Medieval Music* 16 (2007): 31–59.

Crane, Susan. *The Performance of Self: Ritual, Clothing, and Identity during the Hundred Years War.* Philadelphia: University of Pennsylvania Press, 2002.

Courtenay, William J. "The Early Career of Nicole Oresme." *Isis* 91 (2000): 542–48.

Cropp, Glynnis M. "The Medieval French Boethius." In *Boethius in the Middle Ages: Latin and Vernacular Traditions of the Consolatio Philosophiae,* edited by Maarten J. F. M. Hoenen and Lodi Nauta, 243–65. Leiden: Brill, 1997.

——. "Les manuscrits du 'Livre de Boece de Consolacion.'" *Revue d'histoire des textes* 12–13 (1982–83): 263–352.

D'Angiolini, Giuliano. "Le son du sens: Machaut, Stockhausen. La Ballade 34 et le Chant des Adolescents." *Analyse musicale* 9 (1987): 43–51.

Davis, Steven. "Guillaume de Machaut, Chaucer's *Book of the Duchess,* and the Chaucer Tradition." *Chaucer Review* 36 (2002): 391–405.

Dearmer, Percy. *The Parson's Handbook.* 8th ed. London: H. Milford, 1913.

Delaere, Mark. "Karel Goeyvaerts: A Belgian Pioneer of Serial, Electronic and Minimal Music." *Tempo: A Quarterly Review of Modern Music* 195 (1996): 2–5.

De Looze, Laurence. Review of *Guillaume de Machaut: A Guide to Research* by Lawrence Earp. *Speculum* 73 (July 1998): 844.

——. *Pseudo-autobiography in the Fourteenth Century: Juan Ruiz, Guillaume de Machaut, Jean Froissart, and Geoffrey Chaucer.* Gainesville: University Press of Florida, 1997.

Dembowski, Peter F. "What Is Critical in Critical Editions? The Case of Bilingual Editions." In *"De sens rassis": Essays in Honor of Rupert T. Pickens,* edited by Keith Busby, Bernard Guidot, and Logan E. Whale, 169–81. Amsterdam: Rodopi, 2005.

Deschaux, Robert, ed. *Martin le Franc: Le champion des dames.* 5 vols. Paris: Honoré Champion, 1999.

Desportes, Pierre. *Diocèse de Reims.* Vol. 3 of *Fasti Ecclesiae Gallicanae: Répertoire prosopographique des évêques, dignitaires et chanoines des diocèses de France de 1200 à 1500.* Turnhout: Brepols, 1998.

——. *Reims et les Rémois aux XIIIe et XIVe siècles.* Paris: A. & J. Picard, 1979.

——. "Reims et les Rémois aux XIIIème et XIVème siècles." Doctoral thesis, University of Paris I, 1976.

De Van, Guillaume, ed. *Guglielmi de Mascaudio: Opera I, La Messe de Nostre Dame.* Vol. 2 of Corpus Mensurabilis Musicae. Rome: American Institute of Musicology, 1949.

Dibben, L. B. "Secretaries in the Thirteenth and Fourteenth Centuries." *English Historical Review* 25 (1910): 430–44.

Diekstra, F. N. M. "The Poetic Exchange between Philippe de Vitry and Jean de le Mote." *Neophilologus* 70 (1986): 504–19.

Dillon, Emma. *Medieval Music-Making and the "Roman de Fauvel."* Cambridge: Cambridge University Press, 2002.

Diverres, Armel Hugh, ed. *La chronique métrique attribuée à Geoffroy de Paris.* Strasbourg: Faculté des lettres de l'Université, 1956.

Donkin, Enid, ed. *Jean Brisebarre: Li restor du paon.* London: Modern Humanities Research Association, 1980.

Doss-Quinby, Eglal, Samuel N. Rosenberg, and Elizabeth Aubrey, eds. *The Old French Ballette: Oxford, Bodleian Library, MS Douce 308.* Geneva: Droz, 2006.

Dragonetti, Roger. "'La poésie … ceste musique naturele': Essai d'exégèse d'un passage de *L'Art de Dictier* d'Eustache Deschamps." In *Fin du moyen âge et renaissance: Mélanges de philosophie française offerts à Robert Guiette,* edited by Henri Pirenne, 49–64. Antwerp: Nederlandsche Boekhandel, 1961.

Dricot, Michel. "Note sur la formation de Guillaume de Machaut." In *Guillaume de Machaut: Poète et Compositeur,* 143–47. Reims: Klincksieck, 1982.

Du Chesne, André. *Histoire de la Maison de Chastillon sur Marne.* Paris: Sebastien Cramoisy, 1621.

Dyer, Joseph. "A Thirteenth-Century Choirmaster: The *Scientia Artis Musicae* of Elias Salomon." *Musical Quarterly* 66 (1980): 83–111.

Earp, Lawrence. "Declamatory Dissonance in Machaut." In *Citation and Authority in Medieval and Renaissance Music: Learning from the Learned,* edited by Suzannah Clark and Elizabeth Eva Leach, 102–22. Woodbridge: Boydell and Brewer, 2005.

——. Review of *Guillaume de Machaut and Reims: Context and Meaning in His Musical Works* by Anne Walters Robertson. *Journal of the American Musicological Society* 57 (2004): 384–93.

——. "Machaut's Music in the Early Nineteenth Century: The Work of Perne, Bottée de Toulmon, and Fétis." In *Guillaume de Machaut: 1300–2000. Actes du Colloque de la Sorbonne 28–29 septembre 2000,* edited by Jacqueline Cerquiglini-Toulet and Nigel Wilkins, 9–40. Paris: Presses de l'Université de Paris–Sorbonne, 2002.

——. Review of F. Alberto Gallo, *Trascrizione di Machaut: Remede de Fortune, Ecu Bleu, Remede d'Amour. Speculum* 77 (2002): 1290–92.

——. *Guillaume de Machaut: A Guide to Research.* New York: Garland, 1995.

——. "Machaut's Role in the Production of His Works." *Journal of the American Musicological Society* 42 (1989): 461–503.

——. "Scribal Practice, Manuscript Production, and the Transmission of Music in Late Medieval France: The Manuscripts of Guillaume de Machaut." Ph.D. dissertation, Princeton University, 1983.

Eco, Umberto. "Dreaming of the Middle Ages." In *Travels in Hyperreality: Essays,* translated by William Weaver, 61–72. London: Pan, 1986.

Edbury, Peter W., ed. *Guillaume de Machaut, The Capture of Alexandria.* Aldershot: Ashgate, 2001.

Eggebrecht, Hans Heinrich. "Machauts Motette Nr. 9." *Archiv für Musikwissenschaft* 20 (1963): 281–93; and 25 (1968): 173–95.

Einstein, Alfred. "The Conflict of Word and Tone." *Musical Quarterly* 40 (1954): 329–49.

Eisenberg, Michael. "The Mirror of the Text: Reflections in *Ma fin est mon commencement.*" In *Canons and Canonic Techniques, 14th–16th Centuries: Theory, Practice, and Reception History,* edited by Katelijne Schiltz and Bonnie J. Blackburn, 83–110. Leuven: Peeters, 2007.

Ellis, Katharine. *Interpreting the Musical Past: Early Music in Nineteenth-Century France.* New York: Oxford University Press, 2005.

Enders, Jody. "Music, Delivery, and the Rhetoric of Memory in Guillaume de Machaut's Remède de Fortune." *Proceedings of the Modern Language Association* 107 (1992): 450–64.

Fallows, David. "Guillaume de Machaut and the Lai: A New Source." *Early Music* 5 (1977): 477–83.

Ferrand, Françoise. "Doux Penser, Plaisance et Espérance chez Guillaume de Machaut et Charles d'Orléans: Un nouvel art d'aimer." In *Plaist vos oïr bone cançon vallant? Mélanges de langue et de littérature médiévales offerts à François Suard,* edited by Dominique Boutet, Marie-Madeleine Castellani, Françoise Ferrand, and Aimé Petit, vol. 1 of 2, 241–50. Villeneuve d'Ascq: Conseil Scientifique de l'Université Charles de Gaulle–Lille 3, 1999.

Fleming, John V. *The Roman de la Rose: A Study in Allegory and Iconography.* Princeton: Princeton University Press, 1969.

Forkel, J. N. *Allgemeine Geschichte der Musik.* 2 vols. Leipzig, 1788–1801.

Franke, Birgit. "Gesellschaftsspiele mit Automaten: 'Merveilles' in Hesdin." *Marburger Jahrbuch für Künstwissenschaft* 24, Kunst als Ästhetisches Ereignis (1997): 135–58.

Frobenius, Wolf. *Johannes Boens Musica und seine Konsonanzlehre.* Edited by Hans Heinrich Eggebrecht. Stuttgart: Musikwissenschaftliche Verlags-Gesellschaft, 1971.

Fuller, Sarah. "Tendencies and Resolutions: The Directed Progression in *Ars Nova* music." *Journal of Music Theory* 36 (1992): 229–57.

———. "On Sonority in Fourteenth-Century Polyphony: Some Preliminary Reflections." *Journal of Music Theory* 30 (1986): 35–70.

Gaffurio, Franchino. *Practica musice.* Milan: Johannes Petrus de Lomatio, 1496. Reprint, New York: Broude Bros., 1979.

Gallagher, Sean. "After Burgundy: Rethinking Binchois's Years in Soignies." In *Binchois Studies,* edited by Andrew Kirkman and Dennis Slavin, 27–48. Oxford: Oxford University Press, 2000.

Gallo, F. Alberto. *Trascrizione di Machaut: Remede de Fortune, Ecu Bleu, Remede d'Amour.* Ravenna: Longo, 1999.

———, ed. *Prosdocimus de Beldemandis, Opera: Expositiones tractatus pratice cantus mensurabilis magistri Johannis de Muris.* Bologna: Università degli Studi di Bologna, 1966.

Gibbs, Stephanie Viereck, and Kathryn Karczewska, eds. *René of Anjou: The Book of the Love-Smitten Heart.* New York: Routledge, 2001.

Goebel, Stefan. *The Great War and Medieval Memory: War, Remembrance and Medievalism in Britain and Germany, 1914–1940.* Cambridge: Cambridge University Press, 2007.

Goehr, Lydia. *The Imaginary Museum of Musical Works: An Essay in the Philosophy of Music.* Oxford: Clarendon Press, 1992.

Gombosi, Otto. "Machaut's *Messe de Nostre-Dame.*" *Musical Quarterly* 36 (1950): 204–24, errata 466.

———. Review of *French Secular Music of the Fourteenth Century* by Willi Apel. *Musical Quarterly* 36 (1950): 603–10.

Grancsay, Stephen V. "A Pair of Spurs Bearing the Bourbon Motto." *Metropolitan Museum of Art Bulletin* 36 (1941): 170–72.

Gröber, Gustav, ed. *Grundriss der romanischen Philologie.* Vol. 1 of 2. Strasbourg: Trübner, 1902.

Guiette, Robert. *D'une poésie formelle en France au Moyen Âge.* Paris: A.-G. Nizet, 1972.

———. *Questions de littérature.* Ghent: Rijksuniversiteit te Gent, faculteit der wijsbegeerte en letteren, 1960.

———. "D'une poésie formelle en France au Moyen Âge." *Revue des sciences humaines* (1949): 61–68.

———. *Robert Guiette: Forme et senefiance,* edited by Jean Dufournet, Marcel de Grève, and Herman Braet. Geneva: Droz, 1978.Günther, Ursula. "Contribution de la musicologie à la biographie et à la chronologie de Guillaume de Machaut." In *Guillaume de Machaut: Poète et Compositeur,* 95–115. Reims: Klincksieck, 1982.

———. "Problems of Dating in *ars nova* and *ars subtillior.*" In *L'Ars nova italiana del Trecento IV: atti del trentesimo congresso internazionale sul tema "La musica al tempo del Boccaccio e i suoi rapporti con la letteratura" (Siena–Certaldo 19–22 luglio 1975),* 289–301. Certaldo: Centro di studi sull' ars nova italiana del trecento, 1978.

——. "Chronologie und Stil der Kompositionen Guillaume de Machauts." *Acta Musicologica* 35 (1963): 96–114.

——. "Das Ende der *ars nova.*" *Die Musikforschung* 16 (1963): 105–20.

Gushee, Lawrence. "New Sources for the Biography of Johannes de Muris." *Journal of the American Musicological Society* 22 (1969): 3–26.

Haidu, Peter. *The Subject Medieval/Modern: Text and Governance in the Middle Ages.* Stanford: Stanford University Press, 2004.

Haines, John. *Eight Centuries of Troubadours and Trouvères: The Changing Identity of Medieval Music.* Cambridge: Cambridge University Press, 2004.

Hanf, Georg. "Über Guillaume de Machauts *Voir Dit.*" *Zeitschrift für romanische Philologie* 22 (1898): 145–96.

Hanslick, Eduard. *On the Musically Beautiful: A Contribution towards the Revision of the Aesthetics of Music.* Translated by Geoffrey Payzant. Indianapolis: Hackett, 1986.

Harden, Jean. Review of *Guillaume de Machaut: A Guide to Research* by Lawrence Earp. *Notes* 53, 2nd ser. (1997): 785–87.

Harrison, Frank L., ed. *Musicorum Collegio: Fourteenth-Century Musicians' Motets.* Les Remparts, Monaco: L'Oiseau-Lyre, 1986.

Hassell, James Woodrow. *Middle French Proverbs, Sentences, and Proverbial Phrases.* Toronto: Pontifical Institute of Mediaeval Studies, and Leiden: Brill, 1982.

Haydon, Glen. Review of *French Secular Music of the Late Fourteenth Century* by Willi Apel. *Speculum* 26 (1951): 145–48.

Higgins, Paula. "Musical Politics in Late Medieval Poitiers." In *Antoine Busnoys: Method, Meaning and Context in Late Medieval Music,* edited by Paula Higgins, 155–74. Oxford: Oxford University Press, 1999.

——. "Musical 'Parents' and Their 'Progeny.'" In *Music in Renaissance Cities and Courts: Studies in Honor of Lewis Lockwood,* edited by Jessie Ann Owens and Anthony M. Cummings, 168–86. Warren, Mich.: Harmonie Park Press, 1997.

Hoekstra, Gerald R. "The French Motet as Trope: Multiple Levels of Meaning in *Quant florist la violete / El mois de mai / Et Gaudebit.*" *Speculum* 73 (1998): 32–57.

Hoepffner, Ernest. *Oeuvres de Guillaume de Machaut.* 3 vols. Paris: Firmin-Didot, 1908–1922.

Hofer, Stefan, ed. *Geschichte der mittelfranzösischen Literatur.* Edited by Gustav Gröber. 2nd ed. 2 vols. Berlin: Walter de Gruyter & Co., 1933.

Holsinger, Bruce W. *Music, Body, and Desire in Medieval Culture: Hildegard of Bingen to Chaucer.* Stanford: Stanford University Press, 2001.

Hoppin, Richard H., ed. *Anthology of Medieval Music.* New York: Norton, 1978.

——. *Medieval Music.* Norton Introduction to Music History. New York: W. W. Norton & Company, 1978.

Howlett, David. "*Apollinis eclipsatur:* Foundation of the 'Collegium musicorum.'" In *Citation and Authority in Medieval and Renaissance Musical Culture: Learning from the Learned,* edited by Suzannah Clark and Elizabeth Eva Leach, 152–59. Woodbridge: Boydell, 2005.

Hübsch, Hanns, ed. *Guillaume de Machault: La Messe de Nostre Dame.* Heidelberg: Süddeutscher Musikverlag Willy Müller, 1953.

Huizinga, Johan. *The Waning of the Middle Ages: A Study of the Forms of Life, Thought and Art in France and the Netherlands in the XIVth and XVth Centuries.* Translated by Frederik Jan Hopman. London: E. Arnold, 1924; orig. Johan Huizinga, *Herfsttij der Middeleeuwen: studie over levens- en gedachtenvormen der veertiende en vijftiende eeuw in Frankrijk en de Nederlanden.* Haarlem: H. D. Tjeenk Willink, 1919.

Humphreys, Arthur Raleigh, ed. *The First Part of King Henry IV.* Arden Edition of the Works of William Shakespeare (Second Series). London: Routledge, 1960.

Hunt, Tony. "The Christianization of Fortune." *Nottingham French Studies* 38 (1999): 95–113.

Huot, Sylvia. *Madness in Medieval French Literature: Identities Found and Lost.* Cambridge: Cambridge University Press, 2003.

———. "Reading across Genres: Froissart's *Joli Buisson de Jonece* and Machaut's Motets." *French Studies* 57 (2003): 1–10.

———. "Guillaume de Machaut and the Consolation of Poetry." *Modern Philology* 100 (2002): 169–95.

———. "Reliving the *Roman de la Rose*: Allegory and Irony in Machaut's *Voir Dit.*" In *Chaucer's French Contemporaries: The Poetry/Poetics of Self and Tradition,* edited by R. Barton Palmer, 47–69. New York: AMS, 1999.

———. *Allegorical Play in the Old French Motet: The Sacred and Profane in Thirteenth-Century Polyphony.* Stanford: Stanford University Press, 1997.

———. "Voices and Instruments in Medieval French Secular Music: On the Use of Literary Evidence for Performance Practice." *Musica Disciplina* 43 (1989): 63–113.

———. *From Song to Book: The Poetics of Writing in Old French Lyric and Lyrical Narrative Poetry.* Ithaca: Cornell University Press, 1987.

Jager, Eric. *The Book of the Heart.* Chicago: University of Chicago Press, 2000.

Jankélévitch, Vladimir. *Music and the Ineffable.* Translated by Carolyn Abbate. Princeton: Princeton University Press, 2003; orig. *La musique et l'ineffable* (1961).

Jeanroy, Alfred. "La littérature de langue française des origines à Ronsard." In *Histoire des lettres: Premier volume, Des origines à Ronsard,* edited by Joseph Bédier, Alfred Jeanroy, and François Picavet, 237–576. Paris: Société de l'Histoire Nationale and Plon-Nourrit & Co., 1921.

———. "Les chansons." In *Histoire de la langue et de la littérature française des origines à 1900,* edited by Louis Petit de Julleville, vol. 1 of 8, 345–404. Paris: Armand Colin, 1896.

Johnson, Leonard W. *Poets as Players: Theme and Variation in Late Medieval French Poetry.* Stanford: Stanford University Press, 1990.

———. "'Nouviaus dis amoureux plaisans': Variation as Innovation in Guillaume de Machaut." In *Musique naturelle et musique artificielle: In memoriam Gustave Reese,* edited by Mary Beth Winn, 11–28. Montreal: Ceres, 1979.

Judt, Tony. *Postwar: A History of Europe since 1945.* London: Pimlico, 2005.

Julleville, Louis Petit de, ed. *Histoire de la langue et de la littérature française des origines à 1900.* 8 vols. Paris: Armand Colin, 1896-1899.

Kalkbrenner, Christian. *Histoire de la musique.* Paris: Amand Koenig, 1802.

Karp, Theodore. "Borrowed Material in Trouvère Music." *Acta musicologica* 34 (1962): 87–101.

Kay, Sarah. "Touching Singularity: Consolations, Philosophy, and Poetry in the French *Dit.*" In *The Erotics of Consolation: Desire and Distance in the Late Middle Ages,* edited by Catherine E. Léglu and Stephen J. Milner, 21–38. Basingstoke: Palgrave Macmillan, 2008.

———. *The Place of Thought: The Complexity of One in Late Medieval French Didactic Poetry.* Philadelphia: University of Pennsylvania Press, 2007.

Kelly, Douglas. "The Genius of the Patron: The Prince, the Poet and Fourteenth-Century Invention." In *Chaucer's French Contemporaries: The Poetry/Poetics of Self and Tradition*, edited by R. Barton Palmer, 1–27. New York: AMS, 1999.

——. *Medieval Imagination: Rhetoric and the Poetry of Courtly Love*. Madison: University of Wisconsin Press, 1978.

Kenny, Anthony, and Jan Pinborg. "Medieval Philosophical Literature." In *The Cambridge History of Later Medieval Philosophy: From the Rediscovery of Aristotle to the Disintegration of Scholasticism 1100–1600*, edited by Norman Kretzmann, Anthony Kenny, and Jan Pinborg, 11–42. Cambridge: Cambridge University Press, 1982.

Kervyn de Lettenhove [Joseph-Marie-Bruno-Constantin, Baron], ed. *Poésies de Gilles li Muisis*. Louvain: J. Lefever, 1882.

Kiesewetter, Rafael Georg. *History of the Modern Music of Western Europe, from the First Century of the Christian Era to the Present Day, with an Appendix, Explanatory of the Theory of the Ancient Greek Music*. Translated by Robert Müller. 1st English ed. London: T. C. Newby, 1848.

——. *Geschichte der europaeisch-Abendlaendischen oder unsrer heutigen Musik: Darstellung ihres ursprunges, ihres Wachsthumes und ihres stufenweisen Entwickelung; von dem ersten Jahrhundert des Christenthums bis auf unsre Zeit*. 2nd rev. and expanded ed. Leipzig: Breitkopf & Härtel, 1846.

——. *Schicksale und Beschaffenheit des weltlichen Gesanges vom frühen Mittelalter bis zu der Erfindung des dramatischen Styles und den Anfängen der Oper*. Leipzig: Breitkopf & Härtel, 1841.

——. *Geschichte der europaeisch-Abendlaendischen oder unsrer heutigen Musik: Darstellung ihres ursprunges, ihres Wachsthumes und ihres stufenweisen Entwickelung; von dem ersten Jahrhundert des Christenthums bis auf unsre Zeit*. 1st German ed. Leipzig: Breitkopf & Härtel, 1834.

——. "Fünfter artikel: Die Noten-Tablatur oder Partitur der alten Contrapunctisten." *Allgemeine Musikalische Zeitung* 33, no. 23 (8 June 1831): 366–76 and musical supplement.

Kirkman, Andrew. "The Invention of the Cyclic Mass." *Journal of the American Musicological Society* 54 (2001): 1–47.

——. "'Under Such Heavy Chains': The Discovery and Evaluation of Late Medieval Music before Ambros." *Nineteenth-Century Music* 24 (2000): 89–112.

Kittredge, George Lyman. "Guillaume de Machaut and the Book of the Duchess." *Proceedings of the Modern Language Association* 30 (1915): 1–24.

Knapp, Janet. "Polyphony at Notre Dame of Paris." In *The New Oxford History of Music: The Early Middle Ages to 1300*, edited by Richard Crocker and David Hiley, 557–635. Oxford: Oxford University Press, 1990.

Kreutziger-Herr, Annette. *Ein Traum vom Mittelalter: Die Wiederentdeckung mittelalterlicher Musik in der Neuzeit*. Cologne: Böhlau, 2003.

Kreutziger-Herr, Annette, and Dorothea Redepennig, eds. *Mittelalter-Sehnsucht? Texte des interdisziplinären Symposions zur musikalischen Mittelalterrezeption an der Universität Heidelberg, April 1998*. Kiel: Wissenschaftsverlag Vauk, 2000.

Laidlaw, J. C., ed. *The Poetical Works of Alain Chartier*. Cambridge: Cambridge University Press, 1974.

Langlois, M. E., ed. *Recueil d'Arts de séconde rhétorique*. Paris: Imprimerie Nationale, 1902.

La Selle, Xavier de. *Le service des âmes à la cour: Confesseurs et aumôniers des rois de France du XIIIe au XVe siècle.* Paris: École des chartes, 1995.

Leach, Elizabeth Eva. "The Fourteenth Century." In *The Cambridge Companion to Medieval Music,* edited by Mark Everist, 87–103. Cambridge: Cambridge University Press, forthcoming.

——."Poet as Musician." In *A Companion to Guillaume de Machaut: An Interdisciplinary Approach to the Master,* edited by Deborah McGrady and Jennifer Bain. Leiden: Brill, forthcoming.

——. "Form, Counterpoint, and Meaning in a Fourteenth-Century French Courtly Song." In *Analytical and Cross-cultural Studies in World Music.* New York: Oxford University Press, forthcoming.

——. "Guillaume de Machaut, Royal Almoner: *Honte, paour* (B25) and *Donnez, signeurs* (B26) in Context." *Early Music* 38 (2010): 21–42.

——. "Music and Verbal Meaning: Machaut's Polytextual Songs." *Speculum* 85 (2010): 567–91.

——. "Nature's Forge and Mechanical Production: Writing, Reading, and Performing Song." In *Rhetoric beyond Words: Delight and Persuasion in the Arts of the Middle Ages,* edited by Mary Carruthers, 72–95. Cambridge: Cambridge University Press, 2010.

——. "Machaut's Peer, Thomas Paien." *Plainsong and Medieval Music* 18 (2009): 1–22.

——. *Sung Birds: Music, Nature, and Poetry in the Later Middle Ages.* Ithaca: Cornell University Press, 2007.

——. "Gendering the Semitone, Sexing the Leading Tone: Fourteenth-Century Music Theory and the Directed Progression." *Music Theory Spectrum* 28 (2006): 1–21.

——. "'The Little Pipe Sings Sweetly While the Fowler Deceives the Bird': Sirens in the Later Middle Ages." *Music and Letters* 87 (2006): 187–211.

——. "Love, Hope, and the Nature of *Merci* in Machaut's Musical Balades *Esperance* (B13) and *Je ne cuit pas* (B14)." *French Forum* 28 (2003): 1–27.

——. "Singing More about Singing Less: Machaut's *Pour ce que tous* (B12)." In *Machaut's Music: New Interpretations,* edited by Elizabeth Eva Leach, 111–24. Woodbridge: Boydell and Brewer, 2003.

——. "Death of a Lover and the Birth of the Polyphonic Balade: Machaut's Notated Balades 1–5." *Journal of Musicology* 19 (2002): 461–502.

——. "Machaut's Balades with Four Voices." *Plainsong and Medieval Music* 10 (2001): 47–79.

——. "Counterpoint and Analysis in Fourteenth-Century Song." *Journal of Music Theory* 44 (2000): 45–79.

——. "Counterpoint as an Interpretative Tool: the Case of Guillaume de Machaut's *De toutes flours* (B31)." *Music Analysis* 19 (2000): 321–51.

——. "Fortune's Demesne: The Interrelation of Text and Music in Machaut's *Il mest avis* (B22), *De fortune* (B23), and Two Related Anonymous Balades." *Early Music History* 19 (2000): 47–79.

Lebeuf, L'abbé [Jean]. "Notice sommaire de deux volumes de poësies françoises et latines, conservés dans la bibliothèque des Carmes-Déchaux de Paris; Avec une indication du genre de musique qui s'y trouve." *Mémoires de littérature, tirés des registres de l'Académie Royale des Inscriptions et Belles-Lettres* 20 (1753): 377–98.

——. "Mémoire sur la vie de Philippe de Mezières, Conseiller du roi Charles V, et chancelier du royaume de Chypre." *Mémoires de littérature, tirés des registres de l'Académie Royale des Inscriptions et Belles-Lettres* 17 (1751): 491–514.

——. *Dissertations sur l'histoire ecclésiastique et civile de Paris, suivies de plusieurs éclaircissemens sur l'histoire de France.* 3 vols. Paris: Lambert & Durand, 1739–1743.

Lechat, Didier. *"Dire par fiction": Métamorphoses du Je chez Guillaume de Machaut, Jean Froissart et Christine de Pizan.* Paris: Champion, 2005.

Leech-Wilkinson, Daniel. *"Rose, lis* Revisited." In *Machaut's Music: New Interpretations,* edited by Elizabeth Eva Leach, 249–62. Woodbridge: Boydell and Brewer, 2003.

——. *The Modern Invention of Medieval Music: Scholarship, Ideology, Performance.* Cambridge: Cambridge University Press, 2002.

——. "A Guide to Machaut." Review of *Guillaume de Machaut: A Guide to Research* by Lawrence Earp. *Early Music History* 25 (1997): 137.

——. *"Le Voir Dit* and *La Messe de Notre Dame:* Aspects of Genre and Style in Late Works of Machaut." *Plainsong and Medieval Music* 2 (1993): 43–73.

——. *Machaut's Mass: An Introduction.* Oxford: Clarendon Press, 1990.

Leech-Wilkinson, Daniel, and R. Barton Palmer, eds. *Guillaume de Machaut: Le livre dou voir dit (The Book of the True Poem).* New York: Garland, 1998.

Lehugeur, Paul. *Histoire de Philippe le Long, roi de France (1316–1322).* Paris, 1897.

Leo, Domenic. "Authorial Presence in the Illuminated Machaut Manuscripts." Ph.D. dissertation, New York University, 2005.

——. "The Program of Miniatures in Manuscript **A**." In *Guillaume de Machaut: Le livre dou voir dit (The Book of the True Poem),* edited by Daniel Leech-Wilkinson and R. Barton Palmer, xci–xciii. New York: Garland, 1998.

Leupin, Alexandre. "The Powerlessness of Writing: Guillaume de Machaut, the Gorgon, and *Ordenance." Yale French Studies* 70, Images of Power: Medieval History/Discourse/Literature (1986): 127–49.

Lindsay, W. M., ed. *Isidori Hispalensis episcopi Etymologiarum sive originum libri XX.* 2 vols. Oxford: Clarendon Press, 1911.

Little, Patrick "Three Ballades in Machaut's *Livre du Voir-Dit." Studies in Music* 14 (1980): 45–60.

Ludwig, Friedrich, ed. *Guillaume de Machaut: Musikalische Werke,* 4 vols. Publikationen älterer Musik. Leipzig: Breitkopf & Härtel, 1926–1954.

——. Review of *Geschichte der Mensuralnotation von 1250–1460* by Johannes Wolf. *Sammelbände der Internationalen Musikgesellschaft* 6 (1904): 597–641.

——. "Die mehrstimmige Musik des 14. Jahrhunderts." *Sammelbände der Internationalen Musikgesellschaft* 4 (1902): 16–69.

Machabey, Armand. *Guillaume de Machault 130?–1377: La vie et l'oeuvre musical.* 2 vols. Bibliothèque d'études musicales. Paris: Richard-Masse, 1955.

——. "Le manuscrit Weyen et Guillaume de Machaut." *Romania* 76 (1955): 247–53.

——, ed. *Messe Notre-Dame à quatre voix de Guillaume de Machault (130?–1377) transcrite en notation moderne.* Liège: Aelberts, 1948.

Magnan, Robert. "Eustache Deschamps and His Double: Musique naturele and Musique artificiele." *Ars lyrica* 7 (1993): 47–64.

Major, Richard Henry, ed. *The Canarian: or, Book of the Conquest and Conversion of the Canarians in the year 1402 by Messire Jean de Bethencourt, Kt, composed by Pierre Bontier and Jean Le Verrier.* London: Hakluyt Society, 1872.

Malina, Frank J., and Pierre Schaeffer. "A Conversation on Concrete Music and Kinetic Art." *Leonardo* 5 (1972): 255–60.

Manion, Margaret. "The Princely Patron and the Liturgy: Mass Texts in the *Grandes heures* of Philip the Bold." In *The Cambridge Illuminations: The Conference Papers,* edited by Stella Panatotova, 193–203. London: Harvey Miller, 2007.

Marenbon, John. *Later Medieval Philosophy (1150–1350): An Introduction.* London: Routledge, 1987.

Markstrom, Kurt. "Machaut and the Wild Beast." *Acta Musicologica* 61 (1989): 12–39.

Mas Latrie, [Jacques Marie Joseph] Louis de., ed. *La Prise d'Alexandrie ou chronique du roi Pierre Ier de Lusignan par Guillaume de Machaut.* Geneva: J.-G. Flick, 1877.

——. "Guillaume de Machaut et *La Prise d'Alexandrie.*" *Bibliothèque de l'École des Chartes* 37 (1876): 445–70.

——. *Histoire de l'Île de Chypre sous le règne des princes de la maison de Lusignan.* Vol. 2. *Documents et mémoires servant de preuves à l'histoire de l'île de Chypre sous les Lusignans.* Part 1, *Documents.* Paris: Imprimerie Impériale, 1852.

Maurey, Yossi. "A Courtly Lover and an Earthly Knight Turned Soldiers of Christ in Machaut's Motet 5." *Early Music History* 24 (2005): 169–211.

Maw, David. "Machaut and the 'Critical' Phase of Medieval Polyphony." Review of *Essays on Music and Poetry in the Late Middle Ages* by Marie Louise Göllner, and *Machaut's Music: New Interpretations,* edited by Elizabeth Eva Leach. *Music and Letters* 87 (2006): 262–94.

——. "'Trespasser mesure': Meter in Machaut's Polyphonic Songs." *Journal of Musicology* 21 (2004): 46–126.

McConica, James. *The Waning of the Middle Ages: An Essay in Historiography.* Toronto: Pontifical Institute of Mediaeval Studies, 1995.

McGrady, Deborah. "Guillaume de Machaut." In *The Cambridge Companion to Medieval French Literature,* edited by Simon Gaunt and Sarah Kay, 109–22. Cambridge: Cambridge University Press, 2008.

——. *Controlling Readers: Guillaume de Machaut and His Late Medieval Audience.* Toronto: University of Toronto Press, 2006.

Menache, Sophia. "Faith, Myth, and Politics: The Stereotype of the Jews and Their Expulsion from England and France." *Jewish Quarterly Review,* n.s. 75 (1985): 351–74.

Meredith, Peter. Review of *Guillaume de Machaut: A Guide to Research* by Lawrence Earp, and *The Tale of the Alerion* by Guillaume de Machaut, edited by Minnette Gaudet and Constance B. Hieatt. *Modern Language Review* 92 (1997): 967–69.

Messing, Scott. "Polemic as History: The Case of Neoclassicism." *Journal of Musicology* 9 (1991): 481–97.

Meulen, Janet F. van der. "De panter en de aalmoezenier: Dichtkunst rond het Hollands-Henegouwse hof." In *Een zoet akkoord: Middeleeuwse lyriek in de Lage Landen,* edited by Frank Willaert, 93–108, 343–48. Amsterdam: Prometheus, 1992.

Michel, Francisque, ed. *Chansons du Châtelain de Coucy.* Paris: Crapelet, 1830.

Millet, Hélène. *Les chanoines du chapitre cathédral de Laon, 1272–1412.* Rome: École française de Rome, 1982.

Monnas, Linsa. "Fit for a King: Figures Silks Shown in the Wilton Diptych." In *The Regal Image of Richard II and the Wilton Diptych,* edited by Dillian Gordon, Linsa Monnas, and Caroline Elam, 165–77. London: Harvey Miller, 1997.

Moore, Arthur K. "Chaucer's Use of Lyric as an Ornament of Style." *Comparative Literature* 3 (1951): 32–46.

Morganstern, Anne McGee. *Gothic Tombs of Kinship in France, the Low Countries, and England*. University Park: Pennsylvania State University Press, 2000.

Mühlethaler, Jean-Claude. "Un poète et son art face à la postérité: Lecture des deux ballades de Deschamps pour la mort de Machaut." *Studi Francesi* 33 (1989): 387–410.

Nelson, Alan H. "Mechanical Wheels of Fortune, 1100–1547." *Journal of the Warburg and Courtauld Institutes* 43 (1980): 227–33.

Newes, Virginia. "Machaut's *Lay de plour* in Context." In *Citation and Authority in Medieval and Renaissance Music: Learning from the Learned*, edited by Suzannah Clark and Elizabeth Eva Leach, 123–38. Woodbridge: Boydell and Brewer, 2005.

O'Meara, Carra Ferguson. *Monarchy and Consent: The Coronation Book of Charles V of France, British Library MS Cotton Tiberius B. VIII*. London: Harvey Miller, 2001.

Oesch, Hans. "Die Ars Nova des XX. Jahrhunderts." *Melos* 34 (1967): 385–88.

Ouy, Guy. "Le songe et les ambitions d'un jeune humaniste parisien vers 1395." In *Miscellanea di studi e richerche sul Quattrocento francese*, edited by F. Simone, 357–407. Turin: Giappichelli, 1967.

Ovid. *Metamorphoses*. Translated by Frank Justus Miller. 2 vols. London: Heineman, 1984.

Owens, Jessie Ann. "Music Historiography and the Definition of 'Renaissance.'" *Notes* 47 (1990): 305–30.

Page, Christopher. "Around the Performance of a Thirteenth-Century Motet." *Early Music* 28 (2000): 343–57.

———. *Discarding Images: Reflections on Music and Culture in Medieval France*. Oxford: Oxford University Press, 1993.

———. "Johannes Grocheio on Secular Music: A Corrected Text and a New Translation." *Plainsong and Medieval Music* 2 (1993): 17–41.

Palmer, R. Barton, ed. *Guillaume de Machaut: La Prise d'Alixandre (The Taking of Alexandria)*. New York: Routledge, 2002.

Paris, Paulin, ed. *Le livre du Voir-dit de Guillame de Machaut: où sont contées les amours de Messire Guillaume de Machaut & de Peronnelle dame d'Armentières, avec les lettres & les réponses, les ballades, lais & rondeaux du dit Guillaume & de ladite Peronnelle*. Paris: Pour la Société des bibliophiles françois, 1875.

Patch, Howard Rollin. *The Goddess Fortuna in Mediaeval Literature*. Cambridge: Harvard University Press, 1927.

———. "Fortuna in Old French Literature." *Smith College Studies in Modern Languages* 4 (1923): 1–45.

Patterson, Lee. "Court Politics and the Invention of Literature: The Case of Sir John Clanvowe." In *Culture and History, 1350–1600: Essays on English Communities, Identities, and Writing*, edited by David Aers, 7–42. New York: Harvester Wheatsheaf, 1992.

Pellegrin, Elisabeth. *La bibliothèque des Visconti et des Sforza, ducs de Milan, au XVe siècle*. Paris: Centre National de Recherche Scientifique, 1955.

Perkinson, Stephen. *The Likeness of the King: A Prehistory of Portraiture in Late-Medieval France*. Chicago: University of Chicago Press, 2009.

———. "Rethinking the Origins of Portraiture." *Gesta* 46 (2008): 135–57.

——. "Portraits and Counterfeits: Villard de Honnecourt and Thirteenth-Century Theories of Representation." In *Excavating the Medieval Image: Manuscripts, Artists, Audiences; Essays in Honor of Sandra Hindman,* edited by Nina A. Rowe and David S. Areford, 13–36. Aldershot: Ashgate, 2004.

Perle, George. "Integrative Devices in the Music of Machaut." *Musical Quarterly* 34 (1948): 169–76.

Philips, Helen. "Fortune and the Lady: Machaut, Chaucer and the Intertextual 'Dit.'" *Nottingham French Studies* 38 (1999): 120–36.

Les pleurants dans l'art du Moyen Age en Europe. [Dijon]: Musée des beaux-arts de Dijon, 1971.

Plumley, Yolanda. "An 'Episode in the South'? Ars Subtilior and the Patronage of French Princes." *Early Music History* 22 (2003): 103–68.

——. "Intertextuality in the Fourteenth-Century Chanson." *Music and Letters* 84 (2003): 355–77.

——. "Playing the Citation Game in the Late 14th-Century Chanson." *Early Music* 31 (2003): 20–40.

——. "Citation and Allusion in the Late *Ars Nova:* The Case of the *En Attendant* Songs." *Early Music History* 18 (1999): 287–363.

Poe, Elizabeth W. "The *Vidas* and *Razos.*" In *A Handbook of the Troubadours,* edited by F. R. P. Akehurst and Judith M. Davis, 185–97. Berkeley: University of California Press, 1995.

Pognon, E. "Ballades mythologiques de Jean de le Mote, Philippe de Vitri, Jean Campion." *Humanisme et Rénaissance* 5 (1938): 385–417.

Poirion, Daniel. *Le poète et le prince: L'évolution du lyrisme courtois de Guillaume de Machaut à Charles d'Orléans.* Grenoble: Imprimerie Allier, 1965.

Popin, Marielle. Review of *Guillaume de Machaut: A Guide to Research* by Lawrence Earp. *Revue de musicologie* 82 (1996): 368–70.

Porcher, Jean. *L'enluminure française.* Paris: Arts et Mètiers graphiques, 1959.

Powers, Harold S. "From Psalmody to Tonality." In *Tonal Structures in Early Music,* edited by Cristle Collins Judd, 275–340. New York: Garland, 1998.

Press, A. R. Review of *D'une poésie formelle en France au Moyen Âge* by Robert Guiette. *Modern Language Review* 70 (1975): 872–73.

Queux de Saint-Hilaire, A[uguste Henry Edouard, marquis de], and Gaston Raynaud, eds. *Oeuvres complètes de Eustache Deschamps.* 11 vols. Paris: Firmin–Didot, 1878–1903.

Rankin, Susan. "Observations on Senleches' *En attendant esperance.*" In *Musik als Text: Bericht über den Internationalen Kongreß der Gesellschaft für Musikforschung, Freiburg im Breisgau 1993,* edited by Hermann Danuser and Tobias Plebuch, vol. 1 of 2, 314–18. Kassel: Bärenreiter, 1998.

Raynaud, Gaston, ed. *Recueil de motets français des XIIe et XIIIe siècles.* 2 vols. Paris: F. Vieweg, 1881–1883.

Reaney, Gilbert. *Guillaume de Machaut.* London: Oxford University Press, 1971.

——. "Towards a Chronology of Machaut's Musical Works." *Musica Disciplina* 21 (1967): 87–96.

——. "Guillaume de Machaut: Lyric Poet." *Music and Letters* 39 (1958): 38–51.

——. "A Chronology of the Ballades, Rondeaux and Virelais Set to Music by Guillaume de Machaut." *Musica Disciplina* (1952): 33–38.

Reichert, Georg. "Das Verhältnis zwischen musikalischer und textlicher Struktur in den Motetten Machauts." *Archiv fur Musikwissenschaft* 13 (1956): 197–216.

Riemann, Hugo. *Handbuch der Musikgeschichte.* 5 vols. Leipzig: Breitkopf & Härtel, 1904–1913.

——. *Kleines Handbuch der Musikgeschichte mit Periodisierung nach Stilprinzipien und Formen.* Leipzig: Breitkopf & Härtel, 1908.

Robertson, Anne Walters. *Guillaume de Machaut and Reims: Context and Meaning in His Musical Works.* Cambridge: Cambridge University Press, 2002.

——. "The Mass of Guillaume de Machaut in the Cathedral of Reims." In *Plainsong in the Age of Polyphony,* edited by Thomas Forrest Kelly, 100–139. Cambridge: Cambridge University Press, 1992.

Roquefort-Flaméricourt, Jean-Baptiste Bonaventure de. *De l'état de la poésie françoise dans les xiie et xiiie siècles.* Paris: Fournier, 1815.

Rothenberg, David J. "The Marian Symbolism of Spring, ca. 1200–ca. 1500: Two Case Studies." *Journal of the American Musicological Society* 59 (2006): 319–98.

Rothfarb, Lee A. "Hermeneutics and Energetics: Analytical Alternatives in the Early 1900s." *Journal of Music Theory* 36 (Spring 1992): 43–68.

Rotter-Broman, Signe. "Die Grenzen der dreistimmigen Tercento-Satztechnik: Zur Mehrfachüberlieferung von Ballaten und Madrigalen." *Die Musikforschung* 60 (2007): 2–12.

Rousseau, Jean-Jacques. *The Complete Dictionary of Music, Consisting of a Copious Explanation of All Words Necessary to a True Knowledge and Understanding of Music.* Translated by William Waring. London: Fielding and Walker, [1779]; orig. *Dictionnaire de musique.*

Roy, Maurice, ed. *Oeuvres poétiques de Christine de Pisan.* 3 vols. Société des anciens textes français. Paris: Firmin–Didot, 1886–1896.

Rumbold, Ian. "The Compilation and Ownership of the 'St Emmeram' Codex (Munich, Bayerische Staatsbibliothek, Clm 14274)." *Early Music History* 2 (1982): 161–235.

Sabbé, Herman. "Techniques médiévales en musique contemporaine: histoire de la musique et sens culturel." *Revue belge de Musicologie / Belgisch Tijdschrift voor Muziekwetenschap* 34–35 (1980–81): 220–33.

——. *Het muzikale serialisme als techniek en als denkmethode: een onderzoek naar de logische en historische samenhang van de onderscheiden toepassingen van het seriërend beginsel in de muziek van de periode 1950–1975.* Ghent: Rijksuniversiteit te Gent, 1977.

Saenger, Paul. *Space between Words: The Origins of Silent Reading.* Stanford: Stanford University Press, 1997.

Scheler, [Jean] Aug[uste Ulrich], ed. *Jehan de la Mote: Li Regret Guillaume, Comte de Hainaut. Poème inédit du XIVe siècle.* Louvain: J. Lefever, 1882.

Schilperoort, Johanna Catharina. *Guillaume de Machaut et Christine de Pisan: (Étude comparative).* The Hague: De Swart & Zoon, [1936].

Schoen-Nazzaro, Mary B. "Plato and Aristotle on the Ends of Music." *Laval Theologique et Philosophique* 34 (1978): 261–73.

Schrade, Leo, ed. *The Works of Guillaume de Machaut.* 2 vols. Polyphonic Music of the Fourteenth Century. Les Remparts, Monaco: L'Oiseau-Lyre, 1956.

——, ed. *The Works of Guillaume de Machaut: Commentary Notes to Volumes II and III.* Les Remparts, Monaco: L'Oiseau-Lyre, 1956.

Sears, Elizabeth. "Sensory Perception and Its Metaphors in the Time of Richard of Fournival." In *Medicine and the Five Senses,* edited by W. F. Bynum and R. Porter, 17–39. Cambridge: Cambridge University Press, 1993.

Seay, Albert, ed. *Ugolini Urbevetanis Declaratio musicae disciplinae.* Vol. 7 of Corpus scriptorum de musica. [Rome]: American Institute of Musicology, 1960.

Sinnreich-Levi, Deborah M., ed. *Eustache Deschamps French Courtier Poet: His Work and His World.* New York: AMS Press, 1998.

——, ed. *Eustache Deschamps' L'Art de dictier.* East Lansing, Mich.: Colleagues Press, 1994.

Stevens, John. *Words and Music in the Middle Ages: Song, Narrative, Dance and Drama, 1050–1350.* Cambridge: Cambridge University Press, 1986.

Stone, Anne. "Music Writing and Poetic Voice in Machaut: Some Remarks on B12 and B14." In *Machaut's Music: New Interpretations,* edited by Elizabeth Eva Leach, 125–38. Woodbridge: Boydell and Brewer, 2003.

Strohm, Reinhard. "Looking Back at Ourselves: The Problem with the Musical Work-Concept." In *The Musical Work: Reality or Invention?,* edited by Michael Talbot, 128–52. Liverpool: Liverpool University Press, 2000.

Strubel, Armand, ed. *Guillaume de Lorris et Jean de Meun: Le Roman de la Rose.* Paris: Librairie générale française, 1992.

Sturges, Robert S. *Medieval Interpretation: Models of Reading in Literary Narrative, 1100–1500.* Carbondale: Southern Illinois University Press, 1991.

Swift, Helen J. "The Poetic I." In *A Companion to Guillaume de Machaut: An Interdisciplinary Approach to the Master,* edited by Deborah McGrady and Jennifer Bain. Leiden: Brill, forthcoming.

——. *"Tamainte consolation / Me fist lymagination:* A Poetics of Mourning and Imagination in Late Medieval *dits."* In *The Erotics of Consolation: Desire and Distance in the Late Middle Ages,* edited by Catherine E. Léglu and Stephen J. Milner, 141–64. Basingstoke: Palgrave Macmillan, 2008.

Switten, Margaret. "L'Oeuvre poético-musicale de Machaut: Paroles sans musique ou de la musique avant toute chose?" In *Guillaume de Machaut: 1300–2000. Actes du Colloque de la Sorbonne 28–29 septembre 2000,* edited by Jacqueline Cerquiglini-Toulet and Nigel Wilkins, 119–35. Paris: Presses de l'Université de Paris–Sorbonne, 2002.

——. *Music and Poetry in the Middle Ages: A Guide to Research on French and Occitan Song, 1100–1400.* New York: Garland, 1995.

Talbot, Michael, ed. *The Musical Work: Reality or Invention?* Liverpool: Liverpool University Press, 2000.

Tanay, Dorit Esther. *Noting Music, Marking Culture.* Holzerlingen: Hänssler, 1999.

Tarbé, [Louis Hardouin] Prosper. *Poésies d'Agnès de Navarre-Champagne, dame de Foix.* Reims: Brissart-Binet, 1856.

——. *Les oeuvres de Guillaume de Machault.* Reims: Techener, 1849.

Taruskin, Richard. "The Pastness of the Present and the Presence of the Past." In *Authenticity and Early Music,* edited by Nicholas Kenyon, 137–210. Oxford: Oxford University Press, 1988.

Tilander, Gunnar, ed. *Les livres du Roy Modus et de la Royne Ratio.* 2 vols. Paris: Société des anciens textes français, 1932.

Tuchman, Barbara Wertheim. *A Distant Mirror: The Calamitous 14th Century.* New York: Knopf, 1978.

Tyrwhitt, Thomas, ed. *The Canterbury Tales of Chaucer, to which are added, An Essay upon his Language and Versification; an Introductory Discourse; and Notes.* 4 vols. London: T. Payne, 1775.

Upton, Elizabeth Randell. "The Chantilly Codex (F-Ch 564): The Manuscript, Its Music, Its Scholarly Reception." Ph.D. dissertation, University of North Carolina at Chapel Hill, 2001.

Vale, Malcolm. *The Princely Court: Medieval Courts and Culture in North-West Europe, 1270–1380.* Oxford: Oxford University Press, 2001.

Varin, Pierre. *Archives administratives a la ville de Reims: Collection de pièces inédites pouvant servir à la histoire des institutions dans l'intérieur de la cité.* Vol. 2/1–2 and 3 of Collection de documents inédits sur l'histoire de France. 1st ser. Histoire politique. Paris: Crapelet, 1843–1848.

———. *Archives législatives de la ville de Reims: Collection de pièces inédites pouvant servir à la histoire des institutions dans l'intérieur de la cité. Seconde partie: Statuts.* Vol. 1 of Collection de documents inédits sur l'histoire de France. 1st ser. Paris: Crapelet, 1844.

Varty, Kenneth. "Deschamps' *Art de dictier.*" *French Studies* 19 (1965): 164–68.

Vaughan, Richard. *Philip the Bold: The Formation of the Burgundian State.* New ed. Woodbridge: Boydell, 2002; orig. London: Longman, 1962.

Viard, Jules, and Eugène Déprez, eds. *Chronique de Jean le Bel.* Paris: Renouard, 1904–5.

Wallen, Martha. "Biblical and Mythological Typology in Machaut's *Confort d'Ami.*" *Res Publica Litterarum* 3 (1980): 191–206.

Wälli, Silvia. *Melodien aus mittelalterlichen Horaz-Handschriften: Edition und Interpretation der Quellen.* Kassel: Bärenreiter, 2002.

Wathey, Andrew. "Musicology, Archives, and Historiography." In *Musicology and Archival Research / Musicologie et Recherches en Archives / Musicologie en Archiefonderzoek,* edited by Barbara Haggh, Frank Daelemans, and André Vanrie, 3–26. Brussels: Algemeen Rijksarchief / Archives générales du Royaume, 1994.

Weber, Horst. "Zu Strawinskys Machaut-Rezeption." In *Alte Musik als ästhetische Gegenwart: Bach, Händel, Schütz: Bericht über den Internationalen Musikwissenschaftlichen Kongress, Stuttgart 1985,* edited by Dietrich Berke and Dorothee Hanemann, vol. 2 of 2, 317–24. Kassel: Gesellschaft für Musikforschung, 1987.

Welker, Lorenz. "Guillaume de Machaut, das romantische Lied und die Jungfrau Maria." In *Annäherungen: Festschrift für Jürg Stenzl zum 65. Geburtstag,* edited by Ulrich Mosch, Matthias Schmidt, and Silvia Wälli, 70–87. Saarbrücken: Pfau, 2007.

———. "*Soit tart tempre* und seine Familie." In *Musik als Text: Bericht über den Internationalen Kongreß der Gesellschaft für Musikforschung, Freiburg im Breisgau 1993,* edited by Hermann Danuser and Tobias Plebuch, vol. 1 of 2, 322–34. Kassel: Bärenreiter, 1998.

———. "Weitere Beobachtungen zu *Esperance.*" In *Musik als Text: Bericht über den Internationalen Kongreß der Gesellschaft für Musikforschung, Freiburg im Breisgau 1993,* edited by Hermann Danuser and Tobias Plebuch, vol.1 of 2, 319–21. Kassel: Bärenreiter, 1998.

Wharton, Thomas. *The History of English Poetry, from the Close of the Eleventh to the Commencement of the Eighteenth Century: to which are Prefixed, Two Dissertations.* 3 vols. London, 1774–1781.

Whiting, Bartlett J. "Froissart as Poet." *Mediaeval Studies* 8 (1946): 189–216.

Wilkins, Nigel. "The Late Medieval French Lyric: With Music and Without." In *Musik und Text in der Mehrstimmigkeit des 14. und 15. Jahrhunderts: Vorträge des Gastsymposions in der Herzog August Bibliothek Wolfenbüttel*, edited by Ursula Günther and Ludwig Finscher, 155–74. Kassel: Bärenreiter, 1984.

——. "A Pattern of Patronage: Machaut, Froissart and the Houses of Luxembourg and Bohemia in the Fourteenth Century." *French Studies* 37 (1983): 257–84.

——, ed. *Guillaume de Machaut: La louange des dames*. Edinburgh: Scottish Academic Press, 1972.

Wimsatt, James I. *Chaucer and His French Contemporaries: Natural Music in the Fourteenth Century*. Toronto: University of Toronto Press, 1991.

——. *Chaucer and the French Love Poets: The Literary Background of the Book of the Duchess*. Chapel Hill: University of North Carolina Press, 1968.

——. "The Apotheosis of Blanche in *The Book of the Duchess*." *Journal of English and Germanic Philology* (1967): 26–44.

Wimsatt, James I., William W. Kibler, and Rebecca A. Baltzer, eds. *Guillaume de Machaut: Le Jugement du Roy de Behaigne and Remede de Fortune*. Athens: University of Georgia Press, 1988.

Wolf, Johannes. *Geschichte der Mensural-Notation von 1250–1460: Nach den theoretischen und praktischen Quellen*. 3 vols. Leipzig: Breitkopf & Härtel, 1904.

——. "Florenz in der Musikgeschichte des 14. Jahrhunderts." Doctoral thesis, University of Berlin, 1902.

Wright, Craig. *The Maze and the Warrior: Symbols in Architecture, Theology, and Music*. Cambridge: Harvard University Press, 2001.

Young, Julian. *Heidegger's Philosophy of Art*. Cambridge: Cambridge University Press, 2001.

Zayaruznaya, Anna. "'She has a Wheel that Turns…': Crossed and Contradictory Voices in Machaut's Motets." *Early Music History* (2009): 185–240.

Zeeman, Nicolette. "The Gender of Song in Chaucer." *Studies in the Age of Chaucer* 29 (2007): 141–82.

——. "The Lover-Poet and Love as the Most Pleasing 'Matere' in Medieval French Love Poetry." *Modern Language Review* 83 (1988): 820–42.

Zenck, Martin. "Karel Goeyaerts und Guillaume de Machaut: Zum mittelalterlichen Konstruktivismus in der seriellen Musik der fünziger Jahre." *Die Musikforschung* 43 (1990): 336–51.

Ziino, Agostino. "Guillaume de Machaut: Fondateur d'École?" In *Scritti offerti a Gino Raya dalla Facoltà di magistero dell'Università di Messina*, edited by Antonio Mazzarino, 499–509. Rome: Herder, 1982.

Zink, Michel. "La poésie comme récit." In *Cultural Performances in Medieval France: Essays in Honor of Nancy Freeman Regalado*, edited by Eglal Doss-Quinby, Roberta L. Krueger, and E. Jane Burns, 3–13. Woodbridge: Boydell and Brewer, 2007.

——. "The Time of the Plague and the Order of Writing: Jean le Bel, Froissart, Machaut." *Yale French Studies* 80, Contexts: Style and Values in Medieval Art and Literature (1991): 269–80.

Ziolkowski, Jan M. "Women's Lament and the Neuming of the Classics." In *Music and Medieval Manuscripts: Palaeography and Performance: Essays Dedicated to Andrew Hughes*, edited by John Haines and Randall Rosenfield, 128–50. Aldershot: Ashgate, 2004.

——. *Alan of Lille's Grammar of Sex: The Meaning of Grammar to a Twelfth-Century Intellectual*. Cambridge: Medieval Academy of America, 1985.

Zumthor, Paul. *Essai de poétique médiévale, novelle édition: Avec une préface de Michel Zink et un texte inédit de Paul Zumthor*. Paris: Seuil, 2000.

——. *La lettre et la voix: De la "littérature" médiévale*. Paris: Seuil, 1987.

——. *Essai de poétique mediévale*. Paris: Seuil, 1972.

Index

Index of Machaut's Lyrics

Balades

Chanson royal

Complaints

Lays

Motets

Rondeaux

Virelays